# Social Psychology

## SHAPING IDENTITY, THOUGHT, AND CONDUCT

**Michael Kearl**
*Trinity University*

**Chad Gordon**
*Rice University*

**ALLYN AND BACON**
Boston  London  Toronto  Sydney  Tokyo  Singapore

Managing Editor: Susan Badger
Senior Editor: Karen Hanson
Editorial Assistant: Laura Lynch
Production Administrator: Deborah Brown
Editorial Production Service: Spectrum Publisher Services
Photo Researcher: Laurie Frankenthaler
Cover Administrator: Linda Dickinson
Manufacturing Buyer: Megan Cochran
Photo Credits: Page 4 © AP/Wide World Photos, Inc. Page 38 © AP/Wide World Photos, Inc. Page 64 © Reuters/Bettmann Newsphotos. Page 110 © Michael Dwyer/Stock, Boston, Inc. Page 168 © AP/Wide World Photos, Inc. Page 192 © AP/Wide World Photos, Inc. Page 213 © Dave Schaefer/The Picture Cube, Inc. Page 235 © Deborah Kahn Kalas/Stock, Boston, Inc. Page 285 © Spencer Grant/The Picture Cube, Inc. Page 329 © Frank Siteman/Stock, Boston, Inc. Page 343 © Akos Szilvasi/Stock, Boston, Inc. Page 383 © Ed Carlin/The Picture Cube, Inc. Page 404 © Christopher Johnson/Stock, Boston, Inc. Page 442 © UPI/Bettmann Newsphotos. Page 481 © Barbara Alper/Stock, Boston, Inc. Page 488 © UPI/Bettmann Newsphotos.

See Text Credits following the Index.

Copyright © 1992 by Allyn and Bacon
A Division of Simon & Schuster, Inc.
160 Gould Street
Needham Heights, Massachusetts 02194

**Library of Congress Cataloging-in-Publication Data**
Kearl, Michael C.
    Social psychology/Michael Kearl, Chad Gordon.
        p.   cm.
    Includes bibliographical references and index.
    1. Social psychology.   I. Gordon, Chad.   II. Title.
    HM251.K388 1992      302—dc20       92-33089

    ISBN 0-205-13268-5

Printed in the United States of America

10  9  8  7  6  5  4  3  2  1     96  95  94  93  92  91

# Contents

# Preface

There are numerous challenges in writing an introductory textbook in a relatively new field. Worship of the discipline is tempting in paying homage to early pioneers, but probably does not engage the reader in the logic and dynamics of current inquiry. Inclusion of a wide variety of topics is also appealing, but too much breadth sacrifices sustained focus and coherent treatment of important topics and themes. On the other hand, any depiction of coherency in a field like social psychology is largely artificial. Many researchers spend lifetimes studying and refining their insights on one or a few puzzle pieces, assuming that some harmonious whole exists. Alternatively, individual researchers may perceive that pieces from other puzzles are mixed in with their own and that chaos generally overcomes coherence.

Social psychology is dedicated to developing knowledge and comprehension about the interface between self and society. For several decades both psychologists and sociologists have attempted to stake out the boundaries of this field that resides in the "no man's land" between their respective disciplines. But psychologists have often ignored much of the sociological, just as sociologists have neglected much of the psychological. Both fields have frequently ignored cultural and historical influences as well as theorists and researchers from social science disciplines who have been making strong contributions to the development of social psychology. For instance,

- *History* provides rich context and detail concerning particular places and events in which persons have constructed lines of conduct that have affected others even centuries later—whether in ancient Africa, Mesopotamia, Greece, Israel, China, India, Europe, Peru, or Iran—or regarding any of the thousands of settings and actions that shape our world today.
- *Anthropology* contains a rich tradition of research and theory based on the interrelationship of language, culture, religion, social structure, material circumstances, and personality.
- *Linguistics, semiotics, literary criticism, and communications studies* have made great strides in showing the importance of all forms of interpretation of the meanings of oral, written, and visual communications, especially regarding the concepts of discourse, textual and semiotic analyses of the signs and symbols in every cultural form from ancient myth and ritual to contemporary music and television.

- *Gerontology* has provided numerous studies on the effects of retirement, hospitals, nursing homes, and role loss on the identities of older people.
- *Political Science* research has analyzed the nature and interrelationships among power, influence, leadership, decision-making, conflict, violence, revolution, war, loyalty and alienation, focusing on topics such as mobilization of support for various forms of government and connections to various national character patterns, and strategies of leadership and influence.
- *Economics* has demonstrated many ways in which the production and distribution of goods, services, income, and wealth and the differential structure of markets can affect the levels of status, happiness, and sense of justice or alienation of huge populations.

Such is the context that these two sociologists found themselves in when attempting to construct a more sociologically oriented social psychology. We wanted to write a book that would not be obsolete immediately (there are over 2,400 scholarly articles annually published in sociology alone). Nor did we want it to be confined to the traditional demarcations of the field (which typically have been established by psychologists). Our endeavor was to create a work that provided sample coverage of the classic theoretical works and important research investigations, while offering full scope for instructors to pursue their own distinctive interests. Most importantly, we wanted to put students in the role of social psychologists, giving them the conceptual and analytic tools with which to illuminate their own lives and to make connections on their own between wide-ranging subject matters they encounter in their academic careers. The result, we believe, is a unique and enjoyable approach that combines the strongest features of the institutional and symbolic interaction perspectives in social psychology.

To provide order where there was none, and a logic in which each chapter builds upon the preceding ones, this text begins with biological matters and progresses through cognitive, emotional, and symbolic templates to self-systems, interactive dynamics between selves, to the workings of groups, and finally to the influence of broad institutional forces.

*Part One* introduces the central theories and methods of the field as well as the basic tensions underlying the human condition. Featured are the tensions between the angel and the beast (that is, the dilemma between free will and determinism, between genetic constraints and cultural variabilities), and between the needs of self as opposed to the needs of society. Several themes are introduced that run throughout the book: the motivational roles of sexual urges and fear of death and morality, the nature of social control, and how social rhythms shape the meaningfulness of social existence.

*Part Two* discusses the major ways in which experiences and thoughts are socially patterned by integrating discoveries from cognitive psychologists, physiologists, linguists, and researchers in the rapidly growing area of emotions. Here we consider the ways in which attitudes, beliefs, and language determine what is perceived and remembered, and how feeling states such as anger and love are, in fact, social constructions. This section sets the stage for later chapters in which the strategy is to map the social sources of these subjective processes.

*Part Three* explores the complex set of ideas relating to self-systems as imputed centers of individual interpretation and socially constructed action. Selves are here viewed as systems of symbols, roles, needs and desires, self-conceptions, and self-representations to others. Taking advantage of our own work in adulthood socialization, social gerontology, and generational analyses, we consider the impacts of historical personality types, and how selves change in their trajectories toward death.

*Part Four* deals with selves negotiating social interaction and social realities in and through relationships and affiliations. Here we pursue such topics as presentations of self, interpersonal power and influence, the social psychology of social class and inequality, and how interpersonal bonds are created, maintained, and ended. The section concludes with presentations regarding the dynamics produced in social groups, and how social systems arise which often operate independently of their members' intentions and contrary to their desires.

*Part Five* considers the broadest social influences determining the thoughts, emotions, identities, relationships, and behaviors of individuals. Specifically, we develop the social psychologies of collective behavior, religion, work, and modernization. Though not typically covered in social psychology tests, we believe that topics such as religious conversion, worker alienation, leisure, consumerism, urban psychology, the drug epidemic, and the social psychological effects of mass media are prime illustrations of the interfaces between self and society.

Throughout the text we have included illustrations of new research directions informed by our conceptions of the field. Many of these illustrations draw upon the General Social Surveys conducted by the National Opinion Research Center—a resource available in many colleges and universities. These research examples are intended to kindle the sociological imaginations of students, inspiring them to create and test their own hypotheses. In pretesting the manuscript for this work, Kearl has used the NORC General Social Survey data in conjunction with MicroCase software. He found that with one hour of training in using this remarkably user-friendly computer program for PCs that freshmen and sophomores are ready to perform their own analyses of the NORC surveys. As a result, the classroom experience has shifted from a lecture format to empirically "playing" with the ideas of the text. Class-generated hypotheses can be instantly tested with clear visual displays of the results.

Enterprises such as this book are possible because of the contributions and sacrifices of many others. First we wish to thank our wives (Joan Kearl and Paddy Gordon) and the rest of our families for their support and toleration of so many evenings and weekends of absence and absent-mindedness. The manuscript's final polish owes much to Joan's proofreading skills. Thanks also go to several generations of students, whose questions and expectations forced us to constantly improve upon the manuscript. One Trinity University student in particular, E. Forrest Christian, was particularly helpful, and gave three months of his time to reviewing drafts and tracking down resources. Timetables were met only because Trinity University generously gave Kearl a semester of leave and because Rice University provided substantial research and administrative assistance. Karen Hanson, our editor at Allyn and Bacon, believed in this project right from the start and remained an unwavering source of support.

The manuscript benefited immensely from the critical reading and copy-editing performed by Carolyn Smith.

We hope that readers of this book will experience the interest, excitement and pleasure that we have found in learning about the meanings, complexities, and interconnections of self and society, and of the contributions to such understanding made by this sociological approach to social psychology.

# PART ONE

# Overview

How did talking apes become capable of putting men on the moon or desirous of designer label evening wear? Their closest relatives in the animal kingdom are unable to forge iron, create musical harmony, or even worry about such questions. What is the civilizing impulse of the creature we know as man? Such questions underlie this first section.

In Chapter 1 we define social psychology and its place in the social sciences. We will see that social psychology is a hybrid field whose problems often come from the humanities and whose strategies for answering them come from the sciences. This chapter reviews the central theories of social psychology and the methods by which they are tested.

Chapter 2 focuses on the fundamental duality of human nature—the fact that people are both biological creatures and symbolic beings who desire immortality, respect, and aesthetic pleasures. Here we consider some of the latest scientific findings on one of the oldest philosophical questions, namely, the degree to which human fate is a function of nature as opposed to nurture.

Chapter 3 explores the central tension characterizing the human condition—the tension between self and society. The chapter addresses the often incompatible needs of individuals and of societies and how they can be meshed. As illustrations, we will examine altruism (the motivation to help others) and instances of violence and suicide.

# The Field of Social Psychology

The end of a school term means final examinations and course grades. The experience of dying occasions "life reviews." The end of a life brings funerary eulogies and obituaries. The arts feature musical resolutions and television epilogues.

As the year 2000 approaches, the close of the current millennium inspires significant reflection. For some, the central motif is apocalyptic: The dissolution of the communist system means the end of history; mass production and mass consumption mean the end of craftsmanship; environmental pollution and massive population growth may mean the end of nature; urbanization and geographic mobility mean the end of community. Others see not the death of an old order but the birth of a new one populated by new kinds of people. All agree that we aren't what we used to be.

The twentieth century has featured some of the most extreme social changes ever experienced by our species. What used to take place over centuries now occurs within a single lifespan. New technologies and organizations have altered traditional social relationships, producing profound transformations in personal consciousness, behavior, and identity. The activities of these new selves beget further changes in the social orders of which they are a part. The analysis of such interdependencies and tensions between self and society is the central focus of social psychology.

## SOCIAL PSYCHOLOGY'S PLACE IN THE SOCIAL SCIENCES

Insights into the human condition are addressed by a profusion of disciplines: psychology, sociology, anthropology, history, economics, political science, philosophy, business administration, sociolinguistics, sociobiology, and human ecology. How does one distinguish among these various disciplines, let alone grasp social psychology's place within them?

And how does one distinguish between the social sciences and the humanities? Sociology, for instance, has been described as the bastard child of

New technologies have created fundamental changes in personal consciousness, identity, and behavior. Here in Times Square, flooded with symbols of the global community, events halfway around the globe are instantaneously reported and bring international repercussions.

the humanities, where it gets its subject matter, and of the natural sciences, where it gets its methods (Berger 1957).

**Social psychology** obviously has something to do with both sociological and psychological matters. But is it the sociology of psychological processes or the psychology of sociological matters? This distinction is not simply a play on words. At least two distinctive social psychologies have emerged (Saxton and Hall 1987; Stephan and Stephan, 1985). The psychological approach involves "the attempt to reduce social regularities to universal constants, rooted somehow in man as man" (Gerth and Mills 1964:xv). In other words, the individual is taken as the principal unit of analysis, and variations in behavior are seen to reside in personal differences in personality, temperament, and aptitude. An example is research investigating how certain personality types became attracted to the Nazi movement and committed unfathomable atrocities in its name. The sociological approach, in contrast, investigates how social dynamics shape identities, cognitions, and behaviors. Here the principal units of analysis are social contexts and their influence on thought and action. For instance, this approach considers how the mass media can instill conformity or how bureaucracies produce personality types oriented toward conformity rather than problem solving. The approach attempts to discover how we experience ourselves and others and to what degree (and by what processes) these ways of perceiving are structured by our social environment.

**TABLE 1.1   The Psychological and Sociological Traditions of Social Psychology**

| Psychological | Sociological |
|---|---|
| **Predictors of Behavior and Belief** | |
| (= internal dispositions and mental activities) | (= individual's location in society and roles played) |
| *Singular Influences* | |
| situations | historical context |
| personality traits | position in the social order |
| psychological maturation | gender |
| cognition and perception | age |
| drives, motivations, and | religion |
| their intensity | work |
| reinforcements | group membership |
| memory | ethnicity and race |
| emotional states | region |
| | media consumption |
| *Combined (or Interactive) Influences* | |
| person–situation interactions (e.g., the attraction of certain personality types to radical religious cults, how different individuals react to same) | interactions between stratification orders and institutional arenas (e.g., the interactions between gender stratification and age stratification in the work world) |
| **Predicted Actions and Beliefs** | |
| attraction | social participations (e.g., church |
| conformity | attendance, role in community) |
| aggression | political views |
| helping, prosocial behavior | family size, attitudes toward abortion |
| mental illness, health | rise of nationalism and ethnic identity movements |

As summarized in Table 1.1, these psychological and sociological traditions can be viewed as two sides of the same coin. Social psychology sensitizes its practitioners to the relationships between individuals and their social structure. For sociologically oriented social psychologists, this typically involves considering how individuals reside in society, whereas their psychological counterparts study how society resides within individuals.

## The Individual within Society

In a variety of ways, individuals are products of their social milieu. Such factors as birth order, peer groups, and social contexts are assumed to have a certain

## The Stanford Prison Experiment

To demonstrate the power of situations to shape human behavior, Philip Zimbardo and his associates created a mock prison in the basement of Stanford's psychology building. Subjects were selected from a screened sample of psychologically stable Stanford undergraduates. Nine of the subjects were awakened early one morning by the sound of sirens. After being frisked and handcuffed, they were taken to the police station for booking. From there they were taken blindfolded to the "prison," where six of them were randomly assigned the role of prisoners and three the role of guards. Both groups were issued role-appropriate apparel: The guards received uniforms and intimidating reflective dark glasses while the prisoners were given prison garb. To simulate the depersonalizing qualities of such institutions, the prisoners' hair was covered by nylon stockings and their names were replaced by numbers.

Over the next six days the power of the guards became arbitrary and wanton, and their activities resembled those employed by Nazi guards in World War II concentration camps. Supervised bathroom visits became a privilege. Sleep was interrupted. Attempts at rebellion were crushed. As prisoner unity declined, the solidarity between guards increased. Ultimately the prisoners lapsed into depression and apathy. In fact, so dangerous had their symptoms become that the experiment had to be terminated more than a week ahead of schedule:

> It was no longer apparent to most of the subjects . . . where reality ended and our roles began. The majority indeed became prisoners or guards, no longer able to clearly differentiate between role playing and self. . . . In less than a week the experience of imprisonment undid (temporarily) a lifetime of learning. . . . We were horrified because we saw some boys (guards) treat others as if they were despicable animals, taking pleasure in cruelty, while other boys (prisoners) became servile, dehumanized robots who thought only of escape, of their own individual survival and of their mounting hatred for the guards. (Zimbardo 1971:3)

predictive value of personality and behavior. From this perspective, each individual is a product of his or her particular culture as well as his or her position in the social order. One's culture (Chapter 2) and language (Chapter 5), familial background (Chapter 6), age-related roles (Chapter 7), gender, ethnicity, and social class (Chapter 10), religion (Chapter 14), and occupational experiences (Chapter 15) are all assumed to leave indelible stamps on one's self-concept, thoughts, and behaviors.

On a **macro level**, this concept is illustrated by the intersection of individual biographies with social history. Consider the rate at which charismatic leaders appear in a given society. One hypothesis deals with the relationship between economic cycles and the density of firstborns in a generation. Firstborns are hypothesized to have a higher achievement orientation, which may increase the likelihood of having charismatic powers. And as every economy goes through booms and busts, varying densities of this personality type may occur. During economic hard times, for instance, birthrates decline, producing small generations and more single-child families. During the 1950s only about one child in four was a firstborn, whereas in 1986 the figure was close to one in two (*Wall Street Journal* 1987). In sum, as birth order and the size of a generation affect one's opportunities in life, history, and personality become dynamically interrelated (Easterlin 1980).

On a more **micro level**, "society" can be conceived of as a set of stages on which individuals act out various scripts in their attempts to find recognition, attention, acceptance, and praise. Social scripts are determined in part by social context: A different self is called for in a supermarket than at a high school reunion or in a prison. They are also determined by one's perceived competencies: In normal situations, beggars are not supposed to act as kings, nor men as women, nor children as adults.

In sum, sociologically oriented social psychologists consider the ways in which social and historical forces create the models and stereotypes by which people judge themselves and others. Psychologically oriented social psychologists examine how these models and stereotypes interact with the subjective experiences of individuals. Each of these processes shapes the other. For instance, the meaning of "old age" in America is conditioned by the meaning of "youth," just as the meaning of "youth" is determined by the meaning of "old age." Any change in one leads to a change in the other.

## Society within the Individual

Social psychologists are alert not only to ways in which individuals reside within society but also to the processes by which society enters the individual. Here the focus is on such matters as "commonsense knowledge" and "you know" assertions, how the self-concept impressed upon the individual by society (e.g., "Act like a lady," "Don't forget your Jewish heritage") is internalized, and how cultural stereotypes filter our perceptions of others.

In the chapters to follow, we will explore how individuals' satisfactions and drives are conditioned by social and historical ageism, orientations to time and space, fatalism, the Protestant work ethic, national character structures, and the psychological consequences of the "closing" of the American West. We will examine the distinctive mentalities that emerge from participation in various institutional spheres, such as religiosity, worker alienation, and patriotism. Finally, we will examine the sociological consequences of these inner lives, noting how attitudes, emotions, commitment, sense of justice, and self-concept shape behavior.

## THEORIES AS EXPLANATIONS OF SOCIAL BEHAVIOR

Social psychology is a search, a *scientific search*, for explanations of human behavior. It is through **theory** that we describe, explain, and possibly even predict the social behaviors, thoughts, and feelings of individuals. Viewing social life through different theories, or sets of principles and hypotheses, is analogous to wearing assorted lenses: Each sensitizes the viewer to accentuate certain things while ignoring others.

The approaches of various disciplines to understanding the human condition lead to different kinds of questions. Are we puppets of our genes and/or our social environments, or do we truly have free will? Are our interactions with others best perceived as theatrical productions, in which each actor assumes a prescribed role and acts out its associated script, or might one's performances be more accurately described as improvisations?

Such metaphorical thinking is the first stage of any science. At a minimum, it lends an overarching perspective to what otherwise may be seen as random unrelated phenomena. (A good example is the comparison of the postwar baby boom to a "pig in a python," which points up the difficulty for a society that must "digest" such a large population cohort.) At a maximum, it provides an *operating model* of the phenomena to be studied. To claim, for example, that educational systems are feudal arrangements leads one to consider parallels between student–faculty and peasant–lord relationships, or how the various disciplinary fiefdoms are held together by the president–king.

In the abstract, science is nothing more than the exercise of **developed perception.** Its metaphors and theories direct our attention to particular phenomena and inform us about those we are to ignore. As Kenneth Burke observed, "A way of seeing is also a way of not seeing—a focus upon object A involves a neglect of object B" (1935:70).

Theories of both the natural and social sciences make generalizations about the phenomena they describe or predict. Each unique phenomenon is seen to be a variant of an *ideal type,* a theoretical abstraction that captures the optimal conditions for a particular event to occur. In social psychology, instead of predicting precisely how a given individual will behave, probabilities are computed for groups of individuals who share a set of common attributes. For instance, instead of projecting your own marital history, our predictions may take the following form: Married Anglo females, aged 20 to 24 and without children, are twice as likely to divorce as their counterparts who are ten years older and parents.

Unlike most natural sciences, which over time produce fewer competing hypotheses, the social sciences have generated an increasing multitude of metaphors and theories. To date the social sciences have no grand, unifying theory that conceptually integrates the different levels of social reality (e.g., sensory stimulation, language, or the dynamics of small groups or entire nation-states). As a result, social psychology remains influenced by several theoretical traditions derived from a number of disciplines. Each has carved out its own niche in the intellectual landscape, providing a distinctive way of looking at things and laying claim to its own realm of social and/or mental phenomena.

Theories themselves are statements that organize and specify relationships among a set of concepts. The relationship may be causal: Increases in religiosity, for instance, may produce increases in the likelihood of belief in life after death. The relationship may be logically deductive: If Jack likes Jill and Jill likes walking to the well, then Jack, too, will like walking to the well. As theories evolve, they tend to go from merely specifying an association (e.g., violence increases with temperature) to making increasingly refined predictions (e.g., between the temperatures of 75 and 90 degrees Fahrenheit, for each degree of increase, a city's aggravated-assault rate will rise by 2.4 percent).

## Knowledge Growth as a Function of Scientific Paradigms

In many ways, "scientific" knowledge of natural phenomena is thought to represent the epitome of human achievement. This kind of knowledge has grown rapidly in recent history. Is this growth a function of the social organization of knowledge, or is it an aspect of scientific knowledge itself? Thomas Kuhn (1970) believed it to be the latter.

According to Kuhn, the organization of scientific knowledge—the paradigm—itself gives rise to the perception of certain puzzles. The paradigm serves as a means of filling in gaps in a body of scientific knowledge or expanding it. However, a paradigm's "success" is not due to the extent of its approximation to truth. As Max Planck wrote around 1900: "A new scientific truth does not triumph by convincing its opponents and making them see the light, but rather because its opponents eventually die, and a new generation grows up that is familiar with it." Likewise Kuhn observed, "When, in the development of a natural science, an individual or group first produces a synthesis able to attract most of the next generation's practitioners, the older schools gradually disappear" (1970:18).

Inevitably anomalies appear in any given paradigm. If they continue to mount, if there are too many disconfirmations of what was predicted, a crisis is reached. Such "paradigm cracks" may lead to overthrow of a reigning paradigm and a shift in paradigms. Thus, from Kuhn's perspective knowledge growth does not occur in a straightforward, incremental, linear fashion. The emergence of a new paradigm is analogous to a political change, not always for the better, but with one side or model winning out because its advocates succeed in being more persuasive and outliving their opposition.

Social-psychological theories differ in their underlying assumptions about free will and the human condition. Do individuals really have conscious control over their actions, or are they the product of either internal factors like genes or situational factors such as temperature? In other words, theories vary in terms of where they place the **locus of control**.

Theories also vary in terms of the **bearing of consciousness**. Do we consider individuals' interpretative and reasoning abilities, their attempts to discover the meanings underlying what others say or do? Or do we see people merely responding to the cues of their environments—either doing things for which they are rewarded and avoiding doing those for which they are not, or simply doing what everyone else happens to be doing?

Another difference among social-psychological theories lies in the extent to which human impulses are seen as harnessed by social requirements. Are **human motivations** cumulatively shaped by experiences—particularly during one's formative years—or are they largely a function of one's immediate social setting? To understand why some husbands batter their wives, some theories focus on their relationships with their parents and their parents' relationship with each other. Others direct attention to repeated interaction sequences within their marriages, such as reinforcing cycles of brutality and intense reconciliations.

Finally, theories also vary in terms of the degree of their **formalism**. Their predictions may be derived from logical deduction or induction, from a mathematical equation, or from inferences made from unobservable phenomena.

The following sections present brief overviews of the different theoretical traditions normally employed by social psychologists. Observe the central metaphors underlying each tradition—they are, in effect, the templates of theorists. These metaphoric templates do not emerge out of thin air; they are the product of their times. Thus, not only does cultural evolution produce new selves but also new theories with which to understand those new selves.

## Psychoanalytic Theory

In *Civilization and its Discontents,* Sigmund Freud (1930[1961]) portrayed human social history as a long chronology of frustration, of individuals never being able to fully obtain the pleasures and happiness toward which they are propelled by their instincts. The human condition, according to this theory, features an "irremediable antagonism" between the demands of instinct and the restrictions of civilization. Civilization represents the renunciation of instinctual urges and the natural order. Any resurgence of those impulses becomes the source of cultural taboos.

Freud postulated the existence of three systems, existing in a check-and-balance relationship with each other that together determine the personality: id, ego and superego. The **id**, the beast within us and the site of the unconscious, knows of no other state but pleasure. The energy generated by its libido (desire for pleasure) flows throughout the personality structure. Although the other personality systems can refocus and redirect this energy, they cannot dissipate it.

The **ego** is the organized subdivision of the personality, the "executive" responsible for perception, learning, memory, and reasoning. Its primary function is to protect the individual against the external world. This requires that it gain control over the instinctive and unsocial demands of the id. Having no energy of its own, the ego resorts to trickery to borrow and harness the energies of the id through the process of **identification**. When the barriers between id and ego weaken, anxiety results and serves as a danger signal. To protect itself against such anxieties, the ego employs **defense mechanisms** such as repression, regression, projection, and sublimation.

Finally, the **superego** emerges out of the ego. It is the seat of morality. Parental punishments and rewards are injected into the superego, where the former become the voice of conscience and the latter become the sense of pride. As Riesman (1950[1961]:30fn10) observed, "Freud saw the superego as the internalized source of moral life-directions, built in the image of the awesome parents, and transferred thereafter to parent-surrogates such as God, the Leader, Fate."

Freud's ideas about the human being's unconscious and irrational nature and the inevitable tensions between self and society have left a deep imprint on social psychology. The scapegoating of the Jews by the Germans after their humiliating defeat in World War I, the narcissism of the so-called "me generation" of the 1970s, and psychobiographical analyses of major historical figures are applications of psychoanalytic ideas.

# Stimulus–Response Theory

In sharp contrast to psychoanalytic theories, stimulus–response theories hold that people act the way they do because of the rewards or punishments they have received for similar behaviors in the past. According to B. F. Skinner, because the mind (including memory and perception) cannot be directly observed and measured, it is unworthy of scientific study. Only observable stimuli can be shown to cause behavior. People's actions are viewed not as the products of free will but, rather, of the **reinforcements** (i.e., rewards and punishments) provided by their culture and environment.

Early researchers using this approach focused on two reinforcement systems: **Pavlovian** (or **classical**) and **instrumental** (or **operant**) **conditioning**. In his famous series of experiments, Ivan Pavlov used the salivation response in dogs to demonstrate how a previously neutral stimulus (a ringing bell) can be paired with a positive stimulus (food) so that eventually its occurrence can produce the response (salivation) that was previously associated only with the positive stimulus. Although Pavlov's experiment was limited to an involuntary response, some of his successors focused on the voluntary responses that serve social ends.

A variant of classical conditioning is "counterconditioning," which is used in desensitization therapy. This process begins with the laying out of an individual's hierarchy of fears. Starting with the fear that is least severe, the therapist works on extinguishing its associated anxieties and then moves on to address the next-greater fear. For example, acrophobics (people who fear heights) may first learn to feel comfortable when standing on a chair, then on a ladder, on the second story of a building, and so forth.

Operant conditioning entails the direct application of positive or negative reinforcers following a particular act—or no reinforcement at all. Positive reinforcements are what particular individuals find rewarding—being honored at an award banquet, receiving a high letter grade, improving one's Nintendo skills, being given a kiss and hug, or whatever. Animal trainers often use affective training, in which love is the reinforcer; teachers reinforce young students with gold stars. Negative reinforcement, such as spanking a child following an antisocial act, leads to behavior aimed at punishment avoidance: The reward is to avoid the punishment. This is the principle underlying so-called aversion therapies for smokers, problem drinkers, and others with problem behaviors.

The scheduling and payoffs of reinforcers can be either variable or fixed. The nature of the timing of reinforcers has a major effect on behaviors. The variable scheduling and payoffs of Las Vegas slot machines, for instance, produce an almost constant rate of response over time. The amount of time students study for a course is determined by whether or not exams are prescheduled or randomly administered (see Figure 1.1). Prescheduled tests produce a scalloped curve, with increasing amounts of study time occurring with the approach of an exam. Variable and unpredictable "pop tests" produce more constant rates of studying during the academic term.

***Applications of Stimulus–Response Theory.*** One variant of behaviorism is **social-learning theory**. For example, observing how young children imitate their parents with no apparent outside reinforcement, Miller and Dollard (1941)

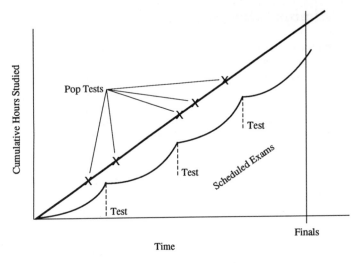

**FIGURE 1.1  Cumulative Hours Studied, by Whether Exams Are Scheduled or Unscheduled**

argued that imitation itself becomes rewarding and is generalized to many situations. Bandura and Walters (1963) employed the notion of vicarious reinforcement, or seeing and experiencing another person's positive reinforcements, to explain apparently novel behavior.

Another variant of behavorism is **social-exchange theory** (Homans 1958; Thibaut and Kelley 1959; Kelley and Thibaut 1978). According to this theory all social interaction is viewed in terms of economic transactions, with each actor weighing the potential rewards against the "costs" of interacting with others. This notion can be seen in maxims like "Every man has his price," "You scratch my back and I'll scratch yours," "Do as you would be done by," "You can't eat your cake and have it too," "No cross, no crown," "Fair exchange is no robbery," "To each his own," "*Noblesse oblige*," and "Whosoever hath, to him shall be given" (Homans, 1961:1).

Exchange theorists do not argue that individuals always seek to maximize their rewards, but they assume that people make calculated efforts to obtain some profit from their negotiations with others. Consider the case of a student who needs help with a homework assignment. Social norms specify that the student should approach his or her instructor for help, but the student fears that this would be seen as a sign of incompetence. The student therefore approaches another student who seems to know what's going on. From the perspective of the person seeking help, there's a debit in asking for help and a profit in getting the assignment done. From the perspective of the helper, the "debit" in the form of time spent assisting the classmate may be balanced by the "profit" of having another person acknowledge one's expertise.

The next realm of psychological theory is an outgrowth of efforts to restore the role of reasoning in explanations of human behavior. It challenges both the psychoanalytic thesis of uncontrollable impulses and the behavioral thesis that cognitions are irrelevant because they cannot be measured.

# Cognitive Theories

**Cognitive psychology** entails studying how the mind perceives, thinks, and remembers; how attention is directed; and how goals and plans influence behavior. It focuses on social sources of stimulation and incentives as well as on internal processes such as logical reasoning and memory. Human behavior is not viewed as a series of passive reactions. Instead, cognitive theories assume that humans are active and purposive, that people pursue goals and seek to improve themselves. From the standpoint of research, this entails focusing on how people define situations, their goals, and the meanings things and events hold for them.

**Cognitions** are an important element of cognitive theories. They encompass "any knowledge, opinion, or belief about the environment, about oneself, or about one's behavior" (Festinger 1957:3). Cognitions are a form of mental shorthand. They are structures composed of interdependent parts—attributes, categories, expectations, models, schematas, stereotypes—that aid in the perception and interpretation of a person's environment. According to cognitive theory, humans respond to the *meanings* of events in their environment— meanings that are provided through the interpretation of stimuli on the basis of previously acquired cognitions.

This theoretical orientation has occupied a prominent place in psychology in recent decades, a period that has also witnessed the advent and widespread use of computers. It is not surprising, therefore, that a key metaphor of cognitive theory is a systems, or input–output, approach to the explanation of information processing by humans (see Figure 1.2.).

***The Gestalt Tradition.*** Cognitive theories have been strongly influenced by gestalt-based principles of organization. In **gestalt psychology**, wholes are seen to be more than the sum of their parts; people are seen to be constantly seeking coherent impressions from the scattered experiences of their lives. Theorists of

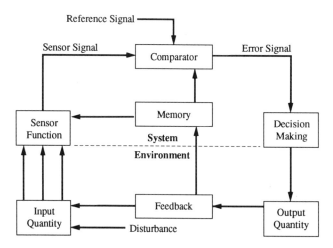

**FIGURE 1.2  A Systems Model of Information Processing**
Source: Kantor and Lehr (1976:13).

this tradition view humans as order-seeking creatures. This is illustrated by people's attempts to find order and meaning where, in fact, there is none. When, for instance, events occur in clusters and streaks (like the coincidence of airliner crashes or three hot summers in a row), people refuse to believe they are random and look for explanations. Observes Tversky: "Very often the search for explanation in human affairs is a rejection of randomness" (*New York Times,* 1988).

In formulations of this approach, much consideration has been given to the way context (background) interacts with attention; investigators have shown that what is "seen" or understood depends on where attention is focused. For example, in his studies of the visual perception of competing figure-ground themes (as in the black-and-white patterns in which one can see either a vase or two head silhouettes), Edgar Rubin discovered that one cannot see both themes simultaneously. Once the background has been established, the foreground is determined. Consider "dirt" as background, for instance. In her study of purification rituals, Mary Douglas elaborates:

> Dirt is essentially disorder. There is no such thing as absolute dirt: It exists in the eye of the beholder. . . . Dirt, then, is never a unique, isolated event. Where there is dirt there is system . . . we are left with the old definition of dirt as matter out of place . . . [which] implies two conditions: a set of ordered relations and a contravention of that order. (1966:48)

Ideas of gestalt were implicit in Solomon Asch's (1946) search for organizing principles in the process of impression formation. Asch presented groups of subjects with lists describing a fictitious person (Table 1.2), varying only the characteristics in boldface letters. He found considerable differences in the inferences subjects made (Table 1.2). For instance, whereas 91 percent of subjects who were given the stimulus word *warm* thought the person described was generous, only 8 percent of those given the world *cold* agreed. The inferred traits clearly were a function of some components being more central than others. And this centrality was a function not of the trait's intrinsic quality but of its relationship with others on the list.

Fritz Heider (1958) also applied gestalt-based ideas in his balance theory of social perception and interpersonal relations. Heider assumed that people have a strong tendency to maintain consonance (consistency) among the elements of their cognitive system and that any disequilibrium motivates change. To sell Wheaties, for instance, the company arranges for a highly respected individual, such as an Olympic gold medalist to endorse the product. If I like gymnast Mary Lou Retton and if she likes Wheaties, then I must like Wheaties to be consistent. If, however, I have tried the product and dislike it, I either change my attitude toward the gymnast or infer that she actually dislikes the product.

***Phenomenology.*** **Phenomenology** focuses solely on the *experiences* of individuals. It is concerned with the relationship between one's experience of others and others' experiences of oneself. Because such personal experiences are invisible to all but the experiencer, individuals seek to indicate how they experience others through their behavior. And what they understand about others' experiences is also indicated through their behavior. For example, rubbing of the nose may be inferred as indicating puzzlement, a yawn as

**TABLE 1.2   Asch's Demonstration of Gestalt in Impression Formation**

Stimulus Lists Presented

| intelligent | intelligent | intelligent | intelligent | intelligent |
|---|---|---|---|---|
| skillful | skillful | skillful | skillful | skillful |
| industrious | industrious | industrious | industrious | industrious |
| **warm** | **cold** | **polite** | **blunt** | |
| determined | determined | determined | determined | determined |
| practical | practical | practical | practical | practical |
| cautious | cautious | cautious | cautious | cautious |

Personality Inference Made from Stimulus Lists

Percentage of Subjects Agreeing

|  | Warm | Cold | Polite | Blunt | No key trait |
|---|---|---|---|---|---|
| generous | 91 | 8 | 56 | 58 | 55 |
| wise | 65 | 25 | 30 | 50 | 49 |
| happy | 90 | 34 | 75 | 65 | 71 |
| good-natured | 94 | 17 | 87 | 56 | 69 |
| reliable | 94 | 99 | 95 | 100 | 96 |
| important | 88 | 99 | 94 | 96 | 88 |

showing boredom, and an intent gaze with expanded pupils as a sign of interest.

In the **natural attitude**, the individual generally does not question that which is experienced. It is assumed that objects exist independently of the way in which they are perceived (Schutz 1973). But have we not all had experiences that cast doubt on this assumption? Optical illusions constantly surprise us; our initial impressions are incongruent with our later observations; and others frequently see things that we miss. Nevertheless, there is a coherence to our perceptions; discrete experiences are somehow transformed into a continuous stream of consciousness. Moreover, that consciousness is shared: I assume that everything that is meaningful to me is similarly meaningful to you, unless otherwise noted.

From the standpoint of phenomenology, the social "reality" that one experiences is strictly a social, not a biological, phenomenon. For instance, what we "see" is determined by where society directs our attention. Accordingly, phenomenologists begin their inquiries by treating all modalities of experience (dreaming, imagination, fantasy, reverie, memory) as initially equivalent. When one modality appears to take precedence—for example, when people treat "wide awake" reality as "more real" than dream reality, or are more willing to accept as "fact" what they view on television than what they read in a grocery store tabloid—attention is directed toward the social and cultural rules that specify one mode as superior to others. By controlling attention (e.g., in gestalt terms, what is foreground and what is background), societies control individuals' sense of order.

The radical bearing of phenomenology is that the social order is viewed not only as existing precariously but as having no existence whatsoever independent of the social members' communications. Interaction becomes possible because physical time and space are translated into the social time–space referents that are assumed to be commonsense knowledge. In fact, one possible conclusion from physicists' subatomic research is that there may be no actual substance to the material world, that our perceptions of physical reality are quite likely the direct result of how we have chosen to examine it.

***Applications of Cognitive Theory.*** Leon Festinger's theory of **cognitive dissonance** is an extension of Heider's balance model. However it considers only pairs of elements. Like unbalanced states, cognitive dissonance is a motivational state that arises whenever two cognitions are not logically consistent with each other.

Festinger hypothesized that people are motivated both to avoid situations that produce dissonance and to seek situations that are consonant with their existing cognitions, attitudes, and beliefs. Early studies showed that subjects who received the least external incentives for taking dissonant stands changed their attitudes the most in the direction of their stated views (e.g., as when students choose to argue in favor of a tuition hike). To reduce dissonance, individuals can resort to one of three strategies: selective exposure to information, changing behavior, or adding other cognitions to reduce the extent of the dissonance.

Let's say that two groups of individuals are asked to spend two hours circling each occurrence of the letter *e* in the Book of Genesis and counting the number of times it appears. Individuals in one group are thanked and paid fifty dollars, whereas those in the second group are also thanked but are given only five dollars. Members of the second group will be most likely to report having enjoyed the enterprise. Why? Because members of the first group know that being so richly rewarded means that the task must be drudgery, whereas those of the second group assume that being paid so little implies that the task must have been enjoyable.

Cialdini (1984) cites a story about the owner of a jewelry store in Arizona who was having difficulty selling turquoise jewelry even at the height of the tourist season. Before leaving on a buying trip, she told her head salesperson to place a sign on a display case saying "Everything in this case, price × 1/2." The salesperson misinterpreted the instructions and doubled the prices. When the owner returned, she found that all of the items had sold! Why? Because people assume that price equals quality and that you get what you pay for.

In testing dissonance theory, it has been found that people do not always avoid dissonance. Moreover, the predictions have been found to hold only when subjects feel that they are performing the dissonant behavior out of free choice. In addition, the predicted dissonant behavior generally occurs only when the task is performed publicly.

## Symbolic Interactionism

Like cognitive theories, **symbolic interactionism** seeks to understand the social world from the point of view of individual actors. But its focus is more dynamic and sociological. From this perspective, human society is conceived of as consisting of people who continually create and maintain social reality through their interactions. In the course of those interactions, people not only are directly influenced by others but also influence themselves. Moreover, individuals are seen as responding to the *meanings* of phenomena rather than to the phenomena themselves—hence the term *symbolic* interaction—and those meanings are understood to be socially created and perpetuated. It is our capacity to engage in symbolic interaction that enables us to negotiate, improvise, or redefine our roles (i.e., to step away from the social or cultural definition of those roles) without threatening the coherence of interaction in extended social networks.

How do we account for the fact that a vast number of individuals with different goals can interact in meaningful ways? The answer, in part, is a function of symbols.

To "normal" people, the social landscape appears ordered and structured. It is a symbolic landscape within which individuals orient their lives according to such abstractions as love, honor, economy, God, and pride. It is a landscape that we assume to be shared by others. This is referred to as the **problem of intersubjectivity**. To be able to share with another person one's emotions, sensations, visions, sounds, or whatever, one must be able to transform one's private, subjective reality into a public, objective reality. This is accomplished through language, which enables one to encapsulate something that is personally unique (e.g., feeling profound morning sickness and afternoon sleepiness) into something that is socially typical (e.g., "I am pregnant").

A related issue is referred to as the **problem of order**. Does a predictable, socially created world really exist "out there," or is it located within the consciousness of individuals? From this perspective, the successfully socialized individual is one for whom subjective reality is equivalent to objective reality. Order is a social accomplishment.

According to George Herbert Mead (1934[1962]), one of the originators of social psychology, the capacity of related subjective reality to objective reality becomes possible when individuals learn to internalize the perceptions of others. This occurs in three stages. In the preparatory stage, young children begin learning to put themselves in the position of others through imitation. Then, in the play stage, there is actual role playing: Children learn to place themselves in such roles as "mother" or "teacher." Still later, in the so-called game stage, children learn to take on a number of roles simultaneously. This leads to a *generalized* perception and the ability to transcend oneself.

For those who have witnessed groups of 4-, 6-, and 8-year-olds playing baseball, Mead's stages may be clearer. The youngest children have little conception of the game or of their place in it. Outfielders may view the action through the webbing of their mitts, if they're not focusing on the parking lot or cloud formations. With greater age, they may learn the difference between the responsibilities of the shortstop and those of the right fielder, but the role views of each have yet to merge into a totality. Finally they do, as the players eventually internalize all the role perspectives of the game and understand their interrelationships.

Two variants of symbolic interactionism are the **sociolinguistic theory**, and **labeling theory**. As Chapter 5 will show, the acquisition of language serves to educate the senses:

Our sensory awareness is conditioned and directed by our ideas. Thus we do not merely have sensations of light, sound, touch, etc., to which we respond, but these sensations are integrated into perceptions of objects of which we have ideas and know the names. This is shown, for example, by the fact that in children the naming of things is an indispensable part of the education of their senses; or again, by the fact that people who through some brain injury have forgotten the names of things become confused in their reaction to those things. (Ropers 1973:50)

In other words, "reality" is largely a function of language. And as can be seen in the biography of Helen Keller, not only does the acquisition of words give one an intellectual grasp of the world, but it also alters one's attitudes toward things and people and toward oneself. Language allowed Keller—who was deaf, blind, and mute—to converse about things she had never seen and sounds she had never heard.

According to labeling theory, labels can create a **self-fulfilling prophecy**. That is, people tend to become the labels that significant others affix to them. Part of the therapeutic strategy of Alcoholics Anonymous is getting problem drinkers to define themselves as alcoholics. Only with such a self-definition is one ready to begin assuming the role of ex-drinker.

## Role Theory

**Role theory** assumes that people behave according to the roles assigned to them, fulfilling the normative demands associated with their positions in social hierarchies. Taken to an extreme, this theory perceives people as no more than their roles:

For the sociologist, to be human is to be socialized. To be socialized is to be roles. To be human, therefore, is to be roles. (MacKay 1973:28)

An individual's role repertoire is determined by his or her status in some social system or hierarchy of interrelated statuses. These statuses often specify complementary patterns of rights and obligations. Statuses may be ascribed at birth, such as being female or black, or they may be achieved in the course of one's life, such as becoming a college graduate or a retiree.

Roles are the dynamic aspect of status. The status of being married, for instance, can include the roles of spouse, parent, and in-law. These roles are dynamically related: One cannot play the role of parent without someone playing the role of child; similarly, historical changes in the roles of females imply changes in the roles of males. And as we will see in later chapters, people are often judged on the basis of their role performances.

Role theorists consider such things as how people move through a series of age-graded roles, observing the embarrassment that is felt when one is not "on time" in such matters as finishing school or getting married. In studies of the stresses associated with the role sets of contemporary American women, focus has been directed to the role tensions and role conflicts experienced by women who try to cope with the contradictory demands arising out of the roles of mother and worker. Role theorists also study the tension between a person's "role self" and his or her "real self."

## Evaluating Theories

How do we determine whether one theory is "better" than another? First, and perhaps most important, a theory must be **falsifiable**: Good theories not only encourage and guide scientific research but produce **testable** assertions which are easily disconfirmed. By this criterion, the proposition that weak egos and strong superegos produce highly conforming people is inferior to one predicting greater time spent studying for students in a course with unannounced rather than scheduled examinations. Second, theories differ in predictive capacity, or **determinacy**. A theory that predicts a 2.5 percent increase in the suicide rate for each percentage point increase in a country's unemployment rate is clearly superior to one that predicts some unspecifiable change in the suicide rate.

The greater the range of phenomena described and predicted by a theory—that is, the greater its **scope**—the better it is. Ideally, a theory's concepts are **universal**, meaning that they apply to all situations regardless of their applicability; a theory might, for instance, apply only to second-generation Hispanic American males aged 18–25 living in the American Southwest. Some theories are highly explanatory and cover a very limited range of social phenomena; others explain limited aspects of a broad range of phenomena. To broaden their scope, some theories have become extremely complex, incorporating huge numbers of variables, whereas others are known for their simplicity, or *parsimony*.

Finally, good theories exhibit a higher degree of conformity with known facts and integrate known empirical findings within logically consistent frameworks (in academic terms, they have a greater **degree of formalization**). They also indicate gaps in existing knowledge.

*A "Perfect" Theory?*   When one considers the success of the *Voyager II* spacecraft—and, hence, of the theories predicting the gravitational tugs of stellar bodies, allowing for a twelve-year, 2-billion-mile voyage—the predictive value of social-scientific theories seems minimal. All of the theories just described are far from perfect and appear sadly lacking when compared with theories in the physical sciences, with their broad scope and high level of determinacy. But is there such a thing as a "perfect" theory? A "perfect" theory in social psychology would predict precisely who would do what, when, and where. Policy makers would be able to foresee, for instance, where and when racially motivated violence will break out, when political regimes will topple, and who will win presidential elections even before the parties nominate their candidates. Madison Avenue would know precisely what products will sell and how to package and advertise them to maximize profits. First-graders could be tested and future deviants identified and tracked.

But if such were the case, if social behavior could be predicted with the accuracy that is seen in the forecasting of tides and sunsets, what would be the status of free will? A "perfect" social-psychological theory would deny that individuals have any choice over how they will act.

In general, the search for *universals* in human behavior has turned up little. Instead, social psychologists have created a set of probabilistic statements concerning the likelihood of certain events.

# THE RELATIONSHIP BETWEEN THEORY AND RESEARCH

Theories without facts are useless. On the other hand, facts do not speak for themselves. Theories give order to that which is observed; without theory, facts have all of the coherency of an almanac and can be used for little more than playing *Trivial Pursuit*.

In gathering the facts that will support or disprove their theories, social scientists attempt to meet the same standards as researchers in the physical sciences, although their research often deals with matters that are more ephemeral and less conducive to measurement. According to Robert Merton (1957), those standards include the following:

**Universalism:** Whether they are looking at Lapp reindeer herders, Australian aborigines, Polish shipworkers, Indian chamars (the lowest rank of Hindu untouchables), or Haitian voodoo practitioners, social scientists seek to find what is common to all of them. Truth is understood to be objective and impersonal; the phenomena observed must truly exist "out there" as opposed to being a product of the imagination, dogmas, poor methodologies, or vested interests of the observer.

**Communism:** All substantive scientific findings belong to the entire scientific community not to one individual or group. Through scientific journals, professional meetings, and media accounts of scientific inquiries, knowledge is shared so that its claims can be independently verified and built upon by others. When secrecy is a motivation, such as when a person waits to copyright a procedure or withholds a breakthrough so that it can be used to gain a competitive advantage, the advance of knowledge is retarded.

**Disinterestedness:** The motives of individual scientists must be subordinated to the norm of scientific or objective detachment. (See "Research Ethics," page 30.) Specifically, findings must be "scientific" rather than ideological. In the social sciences inquiries should be **value-free**. It is not the business of researchers to determine whether certain phenomena are more moral than others or superior to others.

**Organized skepticism:** A basic working assumption in social psychology is that things are not as they seem. A smile may be a sign of appeasement or a note of deception; "help" given to another person may be a means of subordinating the other; a politician's disavowal of complicity in an illegal activity may be an admission of guilt. One needs to be skeptical not only about the phenomena being studied but also about the adequacy of the methods used to measure them and the theory underlying the research.

The "bottom line" of these scientific imperatives is the **minimization of error**. Error does not come just from incorrectly entering scores into a computer, having a preconceived bias or a vested interest in the results, or applying the wrong statistical analysis. The longer one's chain of inferences, the greater the likelihood of error.

As anthropologist Marvin Harris has observed: "Facts are always unreliable without theories that guide their collection and that distinguish between superficial and significant appearances" (1979:7). To illustrate how theories give order to facts, consider the research of political scientists and gerontologists addressing how individuals' political attitudes change with age. One theory is that as they grow older people become increasingly conservative in their political views. Suppose that in 1950 a national survey was conducted on this matter and that the results were as reported in the first column of Table 1.3. From these findings it might appear obvious that liberalness consistently decreases with age. But does this mean that age somehow alters one's political outlook?

To answer this question, measurements on the same individuals would have to be taken over time (this is known as a **longitudinal** research design). But when this is done a host of other temporal issues come into play and must be included in any theory that attempts to explain the phenomena under study.

First, consider each survey year (1950, 1960, 1970, and 1980) as resembling a snapshot, freezing numerous ongoing processes at a single point in time. In some years the general climate may be more conservative than in others; this **historical period effect** will influence the results of the survey. For instance, people were generally more liberal in 1980 than in 1950. If generalizations were made on the basis of the 1970 or 1980 survey, the correlation between age and political outlook might appear more curvilinear than it would if an earlier survey were used.

Second, people who were 35–44 years of age in 1950 may be distinctly different from those who were 35–44 years of age in 1980. This is known as a **cohort effect**. The first group, born between 1906 and 1915, entered adulthood during the Great Depression and found their work lives profoundly affected by World War II. The second group, born between 1936 and 1945, experienced the relative prosperity of the 1950s while they were adolescents.

Finally, people's outlook may indeed shift with age. This is called an **aging effect**. With increasing age, one's commitments to job, mortgage pay-

**TABLE 1.3** Hypothetical Percentages of Individuals of Different Age Groups Identifying Themselves as Politically "Liberal," by Year

|  |  | Survey Date | | | |
|---|---|---|---|---|---|
|  |  | *1950* | *1960* | *1970* | *1980* |
| Age | 35–44 | 60 | 60 | 65 | 60 |
|  | 45–54 | 50 | 60 | 70 | 65 |
|  | 55–64 | 45 | 50 | 60 | 75 |
|  | 65–74 | 40 | 45 | 50 | 60 |

**TABLE 1.4  Percent of Individuals of Different Cohorts Identifying Themselves as Politically "Liberal," by Age**

| Cohort | Age | | | |
|---|---|---|---|---|
| Birth Years | 35–44 | 45–54 | 55–64 | 65–74 |
| 1876–1885 | | | | 40 |
| 1886–1895 | | | 45 | 45 |
| 1896–1905 | | 50 | 50 | 50 |
| 1906–1915 | 60 | 60 | 60 | 60 |
| 1916–1925 | 60 | 70 | 75 | |
| 1926–1935 | 65 | 65 | | |
| 1936–1945 | 60 | | | |

ments, and dealings with growing children may cause one to become more conservative.

Rearranging the data by birth cohort rather than by year yields the results shown in Table 1.4. We find that, with the exception of only one cohort (those born between 1916 and 1925), political attitudes do not change with age. Of those born between 1906 and 1915, for instance, 60 percent identified themselves as being politically liberal during each of the four periods of their life course. The tendency of those born during and immediately after World War I to become increasingly liberal with age may have something to do with how their biographies intersected social history—specifically, the fact that their childhood occurred during the Great Depression.

In addition to guiding the analysis of data, theory is often built into the actual instruments of research. When, for instance, one looks at a thermometer to determine the temperature, one is not "seeing" coldness or warmth. Instead, one is viewing the height of a column of mercury, which is theoretically related to air temperature. In fact, our conception of temperature as a continuum is derived from our measurement of it.

## The Problems of Validity and Reliability

If one is to move from the realm of theory into the realm of research, theoretical concepts must be transformed into measurable variables. In addition, the methods used to measure variables must be both valid and reliable.

The scientific method requires, in part, that different observers agree as to how a phenomenon is to be gauged. For example, although we may agree in the existence of religiosity, how is this concept to be measured? Does one inquire how often an individual attends church, reads the Bible, and prays, or whether he or she believes that God directly intervenes in the affairs of humans? Might one use galvanic skin response to record physiological reactions when subjects hear such words as *Jesus, morality,* or *resurrection* and analyze the results? These are issues of **internal validity**, that is, whether one is really measuring the concept in question. Generally, the more macroscopic the concept (e.g., "cold war," "esprit de corp," nationalism), the less amenable to measurement it is and the more difficult it is to establish a valid means of measuring it.

Related to validity is the methodological problem of **reliability**. This term refers to the extent to which two evaluators, using the same instrument and measuring the same phenomenon, can agree on a value to be assigned to it. This is not as easy as it may seem. Consider the grading of rare coins. Dealers classify coins on a seventy-point scale; a rating of MS-70 (MS stands for "mint state") signifies nearly impossible perfection. Certainly dealers will be tempted to assign lower grades when buying and higher grades when selling their merchandise (Siconolfi 1986), making the reliability of their measurements doubtful. If there are problems reliably grading rare coins, consider the difficulties in measuring such social psychological concepts as religiosity, worker alienation, or sexism.

## Establishing Causality through Comparison

Most theories deal with causal relationships. But how does one "prove" that something *causes* something else? What does it mean, for instance, to say that television viewing causes aggressive behavior among children, that economic downturns produce nostalgia fads, or that birth order causes people to have certain personality traits? Are these phenomena analogous to one billiard ball striking another, causing it to move? David Hume argued that we experience only succession and frequency, not laws or necessity. It is we who attribute causality to events. Such causality is frequently attributed to time: "Time will heal," "Time brings decay." But time, in and of itself, "causes" nothing.

Over a century ago, philosopher John Stuart Mill (1806–1873) proposed two strategies for inferring causality through comparative inquiry. In his *method of agreement*, researchers consider events with the same outcome and locate antecedent similarities. In his *method of difference*, events leading to different outcomes are compared. The researcher matches all antecedents; those that differ are inferred to be possible causal agents.

Consider as an example the hypothesis that people who were abused as children become violently aggressive as adults. You note that a sizable percentage of serial killers and child abusers were indeed abused when they were children; they include such notorious individuals as cult leader Charles Manson and John Wayne Gacy, Jr., who was convicted of thirty-three sex-related murders. Does being a victim *cause* one to later become an aggressor? If all abusers were themselves victims as children and if all childhood victims grew up to become abusers, this hypothesis holds.

Pursuing the illustration further, let's say that you discover a sizable number of adults who, though they were victims of childhood persecution, become law-abiding citizens and loving, nonabusive parents. Being abused as a child now has become a *necessary but not a sufficient condition* for being an adult abuser. And if you also find some abusive parents who were not victimized when they were young, being abused as a child suddenly is neither necessary nor sufficient. In sum, the hypothesis must be continually modified to include a number of personality and social conditions, which are required for the victim-becomes-victimizer correlation to hold.

# Null Hypotheses and Negative Results

Theories are never proven. One reason for this is the organized skepticism mentioned earlier. In addition, there always exist an infinite number of alternative theories that can lead to the same conclusion. In fact, the way one goes about enhancing the status of a theory is by disproving as many alternative theories as possible. This is akin to the logic that Spock often employs on "Star Trek." When, for instance, the source of transmissions from Planet X is unknown, Spock says, "Captain, I suggest that if we don't know where the transmission is coming from, we first determine where it is not coming from."

To illustrate this logic, consider the results of the June 1990 "National Rolaids Heartburn Index" (Pisano 1990). Nearly two hundred American cities were rank-ordered in terms of per capita consumption of Rolaids. Following is a sampling of the cities with the greatest and least levels of heartburn (note the potential problem of internal validity):

| Rank | City | Rank | City |
|------|------|------|------|
| 1 | Eureka, California | 191 | Lubbock, Texas |
| 2 | San Francisco, California | 192 | St. Joseph, Missouri |
| 3 | Chico-Redding, California | 193 | Columbia, Missouri |
| 4 | Santa Barbara, California | 194 | Colorado Springs, Colorado |
| 5 | Sacramento, California | 195 | Ada, Oklahoma |
| 6 | Boise, Idaho | 196 | Fort Smith, Arkansas |
| 7 | Reno, Nevada | 197 | El Paso, Texas |

How would you explain the differences?

Among the possible hypotheses are the following:

—The richer the diet of a people in a city, the higher its heartburn rate.
—As people age, they are more likely to suffer from gastrointestinal problems; therefore, the higher the average age of a population, the higher its heartburn rate.
—Pregnant women are great consumers of antiheartburn substances. Thus, the greater a city's pregnancy rate, the higher its heartburn rate.
—Higher-status persons may eat more varied diets. The more varied the diet, the more likely one is to have heartburn. Thus, the greater the proportion of a city's population that is in the upper middle and upper classes, the higher its heartburn rate.
—Because so many of the top-ranked cities are in California, and because that state has the nation's largest Hispanic population, the heartburn rate may be a function of per capita Mexican food consumption.
—Because so many of the top-ranked cities are in California, and because there was increased earthquake activity between 1989 and 1990, the heartburn rate may be a function of seismic activity.

Observe how each of these hypotheses can be tested and falsified. For instance, if the Mexican food consumption hypothesis is true, why is it that El Paso is at the bottom of the list and no cities in Arizona or New Mexico appear among the top ten? (Such inconsistencies do not necessarily disprove the hypothesis. Tums, Rolaids' chief competitor, may have a more successful market in these cities.)

## Sampling

One potential source of error in any survey is the **sample** of the population that is considered. For the same reasons that one would not generalize findings from two southern religious colleges to represent the attitudes of all American college students toward premarital sex, the population to which a theory applies must be adequately represented in the group studied. **External validity** refers to the extent to which findings within the sample studied can be generalized to a broader population. In numerous social-psychological studies the subjects have been college undergraduates, producing results that were rarely replicated among other age groups and social classes. These studies are said to lack external validity.

A famous case in which sampling error diminished external validity is the telephone survey of American voters' presidential preferences conducted in 1936 by *Literary Digest* magazine. From the results it seemed obvious that the Republican candidate, Alf Landon, would win by a landslide. Yet Franklin D. Roosevelt scored one of the most decisive victories in American political history, winning every state except Vermont and Maine. What could have happened? Because the survey was conducted in an era without computers, using relatively primitive sampling techniques, is it possible that the telephone exchanges were not randomly selected? The answer is that over half a century ago telephones could be found only in the residences of the relatively affluent, who typically were Republicans. Even randomly selected telephone numbers would result in a sample that was predominantly Republican and planning to vote for Landon.

Even today telephone polling suffers from sampling biases. For example, women answer an estimated 70 percent of all telephone calls. A test poll conducted during the 1984 presidential elections found that Republicans were less likely to be at home than Democrats: When only people who were available on the first try were interviewed, Mondale was found to be trailing Reagan by only three percentage points; however, when as many as thirty attempts were made to reach those whose phone numbers were randomly selected, Reagan's lead increased to 13 percent (Budiansky and Levine 1988).

## METHODS USED IN SOCIAL-PSYCHOLOGICAL RESEARCH

The different theoretical traditions have spawned differing methodological strategies. To understand sexuality, for instance, psychoanalytic researchers may record the free associations inspired by inkblot tests, whereas behaviorists may tally sexual activities and role theorists may record individuals' use of Don Juan as a role model. However different these approaches seem, all are modifications of a single method: the classical experiment.

## The Classical Experiment

The only research method that can actually establish the existence of causal relationships is the classical experiment. If there is a causal relationship, there should be a statistical correlation between the **independent variable**, that which does the "causing," and the **dependent variable**, that which is changed as a result.

Consider how researchers would test the effectiveness of a new anticancer drug. First, subjects are randomly assigned to one of two groups: the **experimental group**, which receives the new drug, or the **control group**, which does not. Through randomization, extraneous variables—such as subjects' ages, life-styles, and extensiveness of cancer—are supposedly controlled. At time 1, then, the degree of cancer observed in the two groups should be equal $(0_1 - 0'_1 = 0)$. Then the experimental group receives the new agent while the control group receives a placebo, which is an inert substance resembling the agent given to the experimental group. Then the measurement of the extent of cancer is repeated; any difference between the two groups in cancer extensiveness $(0_2 - 0'_2)$ can be inferred to be due to the drug.

|                          | Experimental |         |        |
| ------------------------ | ------------ | ------- | ------ |
|                          | Time 1       | Effect  | Time 2 |
| experimental group       | $0_1$        | present | $0_2$  |
| control group            | $0'_1$       | absent  | $0'_2$ |

Randomize

Over time, a number of refinements have been made in this basic strategy. For instance, consider the temptation to fudge the data when the hypothesis being tested might bring the researcher a promotion or international recognition. Or consider what might happen if those being studied know whether they are in the experimental group or the control group. Knowing that one is receiving a possible cure, one might be more motivated to observe the prescribed regimen, and, having one's hopes rekindled, one might take better care of oneself in other aspects of one's life-style. To avoid such biases of human nature, a **double-blind** strategy is employed in which neither the subjects nor the researchers know who has been assigned to which group.

***The Hawthorne Effect.*** In the late 1920s and early 1930s, Elton Mayo lead a team of social scientists investigating the ways in which worker productivity could be increased. They observed female assemblers in a bank wiring room at the Hawthorne plant of Western Electric, recording how changes in lighting, number of coffee breaks, length of lunch hours, and means of payment influenced their productivity. Each time anything was done—for example, providing more light or lengthening breaks—productivity went up. However, when the changes were reversed and the original conditions were restored, productivity increased again! Was this result something that could be incorporated into management strategies? Hardly. The explanation was that the subjects enjoyed the attention they were receiving and went out of their way to please the researchers. This phenomenon became known as the **Hawthorne effect.**

## Field Observations

The experimental research design is a powerful method only if one knows precisely the independent variables that produce the changes in the dependent variables. Frequently—particularly in the social sciences—this is not the case. Instead, central processes are often recognized and conceptualized only by witnessing how they are expressed in everyday life. For example, to gain insight into the processes of normal interaction, some researchers have placed themselves in psychiatric wards and mental asylums to understand what happens when everyday norms are routinely breached.

Such phenomena as mob behavior and mass hallucinations are so dependent on the contextual features of real-life situations that it is probably impossible to replicate them adequately in an experimentally controlled setting. Moreover, as demonstrated by the Hawthorne effect, the experimental designs and observational strategies employed when studying human behavior can produce artificial results. When researchers go "into the field" and systematically report everything they see, there is no attempt to control the phenomena being studied. However, some investigators may choose to become part of the process they are studying—for example, by joining a commune or a religious cult so as to understand the mindset of the participants. Those who engage in such **participant observation** run the risk of becoming absorbed in the phenomenon being studied (this is called "going native") and becoming unable to detach themselves from the experience and report on it objectively.

## Interviews, Informants, and Questionnaires

One of the quickest and least expensive methods of studying large populations is simply to interview people regarding their values, outlooks, and activities and the motives behind their behaviors. Political pollsters have queried voters about their concerns for over half a century. Advances in survey sampling have enabled pollsters to come within three percentage points of, say, the proportion of adult Americans favoring a reduction in military spending, using a carefully constructed sample of only 1500 individuals. But the advantages of public surveys over most experiments in terms of external validity are counterbalanced by diminished internal validity. For instance, do prejudicial attitudes correlate with prejudicial behaviors?

Although individuals are normally flattered when others inquire about their views, questionnaires and interviews produce their own thorny set of methodological issues and problems. After President Kennedy's assassination, for instance, more individuals claimed to have voted for the popular president than had actually done so. Respondents may alter their answers according to

**TABLE 1.5 How Differences in Questionnaire Wording Lead to Differences in Results**

*The following are the results of nationwide surveys conducted in the late 1980s on the topics of abortion, gun control, and welfare spending. Observe the differences in the results based on how the questions were phrased.*

### Abortion

*Constitutional amendment "prohibiting abortions"?*

|  |  |
|---|---|
| for: | 29% |
| against: | 67% |

*Constitutional amendment "protecting the life of the unborn"?*

|  |  |
|---|---|
| for: | 50% |
| against: | 39% |

### Gun Control

*Waiting period and background check before guns can be sold?*

|  |  |
|---|---|
| for: | 91% |
| against: | 6% |

*National gun-registration program costing about 20% of all dollars now spent on crime control?*

|  |  |
|---|---|
| for: | 37% |
| against: | 61% |

### Welfare

*Are we spending too much, too little, or about the right amount on welfare?*

|  |  |
|---|---|
| too little: | 22% |

*Are we spending too much, too little, or about the right amount on assistance to the poor?*

|  |  |
|---|---|
| too little: | 61% |

Source: Survey by National Opinion Research Center, University of Chicago; reported by Budiansky and Levine 1988.

the sex or race of the interviewer, or because they are unwilling to reveal an unpopular opinion. Moreover, as can be seen in Table 1.5, the very wording of questions can produce highly discrepant results.

## Unobtrusive Measures

To get around the biases encountered when people know they are being studied, researchers have devised numerous unobtrusive or nonreactive observational strategies.

Suppose that you have been hired by a local art museum to ascertain which exhibits attract the most spectators. You could stand in each room, armed with a counter and a stop watch, and produce a detailed log showing how many people look at each exhibit and for how long. You could also hand out questionnaires to people as they leave the museum, perhaps including small pictures of the exhibits next to blank spaces in which visitors could record their enjoyment scores.

But these methods take time, and you are not sure that the expensive illustrated questionnaire can really be trusted. You suspect, for instance, that the painting of nude females is more popular among the male patrons than they are willing to admit. Sitting in the gallery near closing time, you look up to see the janitor waxing the floors and overhear him cursing as he scrubs the area in front of the nudes. Suddenly you realize that he has provided you with what is probably your best measure of visitor preferences: Where the floors are most scuffed and the ashtrays are fullest is probably where people spend the most time. You can obtain the information you need without counting or interviewing museum visitors.

## Archival Analysis

In the early evening, the national news features daily statistics, like the Dow Jones Industrial Averages, which are used to gauge the state of the economy. The *New York Times*'s list of best-selling books is often cited as a barometer of current cultural trends. The infant mortality and life expectancy rates are used to infer the quality of a country's medical system, level of pollution, and humanitarianism. Through content analyses of television programming and children's stories, researchers study stereotypical images of old age. Obituary analysis is used to track sexism over time. Bumper stickers are used to determine the degree of students' pride in their university.

The interpretation of these social indicators is akin to the early Greeks reading the entrails of animals for portents of critical events. It also involves the Sherlock Holmes methodology of carefully analyzing and organizing minute details to create a coherent model.

To illustrate this methodology, which is referred to as archival analysis, consider the case of UFO sightings in the Soviet Union in 1989. As the Soviet Union became embroiled in internal dissension, with *glasnost* triggering nationalist sentiments and critical reflections on the nation's past, reports trickled in from Voronezh that between nine- and twelve-foot-tall aliens with small heads had been seen landing in the city's park. In 1952, in the midst of the McCarthy era, numerous UFOs were reported (and even photographed) over the White House. Might there be some connection between moral upheaval and crises of legitimacy in a nation and sightings of UFOs?

Figure 1.3 plots the numbers of UFO stories reported in the *New York Times* and the *Reader's Periodical Guide* between 1947 and 1988. (Through 1958 the index category was "flying saucer"; after that year it was "UFO.") It is evident that there is a high correspondence between these two sources. In addition, the data follow a longitudinal pattern that is far from uniform, with peaks in the early 1950s, mid-1960s, and late 1970s. The peaks seem to correspond with acknowledged periods of moral uncertainty in the United States: McCarthyism in the early 1950s, the Vietnam War in the late 1960s, and the Watergate scandal in the 1970s.

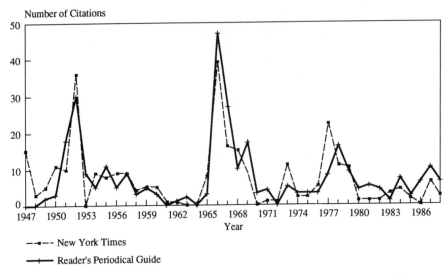

Number of Citations

--•-- New York Times

—+— Reader's Periodical Guide

**FIGURE 1.3   Number of "Flying Saucer" (1947–1958) and "UFO" (1958–1988) Articles in the Mass Media**

Why does moral doubt become symbolized in the form of alien spacecraft rather than, say, angels? Perhaps it is a legacy of Orson Welles's famous radio broadcast in the midst of the Depression and on the eve of World War II. Perhaps in an age when our culture's high priests come from science and technology, social and ethical uncertainty lead people to desire the intervention of a morally (and scientifically) superior force.

## RESEARCH ETHICS

Although scientists are supposedly trained to think rationally and to study evidence impartially, the truth is that they are human. They react a little differently when their intellectual or emotional worlds are threatened by new discoveries. Usually the more highly trained and highly committed a person is in any particular field, the less likely he or she is to be open-minded when faced with significant change. Thus, during the 1980s there were numerous stories of prominent scientists losing their objectivity, letting financial incentives dictate their research agendas, plagiarizing (i.e., publishing as their own the findings of their students), and even fudging or fabricating their results.

Even more important is the issue of the impact of research on the people being studied. What is knowledge worth? In 1988 the Environmental Protection Agency (EPA) was interested in the effects of phosgene, a gas that is widely used in the manufacture of plastics and pesticides. Available were the results of Nazi experiments on concentration camp prisoners, who had been unwillingly exposed to the gas in 1943 and 1944 in an effort to ascertain possible antidotes. Several of these human guinea pigs died. Was it ethical to use the

## The Structure of a Research Paper

The logic of social-scientific inquiry is perhaps best seen in the standard form in which findings are presented in a typical research paper. Following is a brief description of the structure of a research paper.

*Statement of the Problem.*  A problem may be timely (e.g., reasons for drug use among adolescents) or theoretically significant (e.g., when two theories lead to contradictory conclusions). This section of the paper states the problem and indicates the reasons for its significance.

*Review of the Literature.*  The cumulative nature of scientific knowledge is revealed when the researcher summarizes the findings of others on matters relevant to the present inquiry. In this section the research enterprise is placed in the context of theory and prior investigations. One may be replicating studies done by others, conducting new research to address inconsistencies found in other research, or revealing gaps in the research tradition.

*Methods.*  Here the researcher states precisely what he or she did to test the hypothesis. Enough information is given so that others may replicate the procedure. In 1989 the issue of replicability came to prominence amid claims by two Utah researchers that they had obtained fusion at room temperature. So far, no other researchers have replicated their findings.

In this section of the paper the theoretical concepts and hypotheses are transformed into measurable variables and statistical hypotheses and presented in a falsifiable form. Matters of both internal and external validity must be addressed. For instance, how appropriate is it to measure the concept of religiosity by counting the number of times a person goes to church each month, or to measure the concept of social class by coding the type of automobile a person drives?

*Findings.*  This section presents the specific findings that address the hypothesis being tested. These results may be presented in statistical forms such as contingency tables and regressions, or in graphs.

*Discussion.*  What is the status of the hypothesis, given the results? Again, hypotheses are never "proven." Even when data support the hypothesis, this does not mean that the hypothesis is correct, nor does it mean that the disconfirmed hypothesis is necessarily wrong. In addition to discussing these possibilities, one should also address those who may conduct similar inquiries. Given one's experiences, what new strategies might be employed? Is the question even worth pursuing further?

data? Some investigators thought it was—that perhaps some good could come out of the suffering inflicted. Others argued that using such information would give legitimacy to such experiments, possibly encouraging others to perform other unethical research. As matters turned out, the head of the EPA disallowed the use of the data (Shabecoff 1988).

Science becomes corrupted when it loses its accountability to the public.

# CONCLUSION

This chapter has presented an overview of social psychology and its place among the sciences focusing on the human condition. It has shown that in many ways social psychology's position is central, as it alone aspires to map the interfaces of mind, self, and society.

We view social psychology not as a separate discipline or as a subject matter monopolized by a single social science or any single theory. Rather, it examines the relationships between self and society from a number of vantage points and considers subjects ranging from how television shapes the morality of children to how language shapes subjective experiences. Social psychology is a style of consciousness that distrusts the normal assumption that things are as they seem, that alerts us to both the intended and unintended consequences of human behavior.

In the next two chapters we turn to the basic issues underlying all social-psychological inquiries. The first is the philosophical issue of free will and the question of to what extent humans are a product of their genes as opposed to their cultures. The second explores the old idea that "no man is an island," examining the interfaces between self and society.

# REFERENCES

Altman, Lawrence. 1986, April 29. Negative results: A positive viewpoint. *New York Times*, pp. 15, 18.

Asch, Solomon. 1946. Forming impressions of personality. *Journal of Abnormal and Social Psychology* 41:258–290.

Bandura, A., and R. H. Walters. 1963. *Social learning and personality development*. Fort Worth, TX: Holt, Rinehart and Winston.

Berger, Bennett M. 1957. Sociology and the intellectuals: An analysis of a stereotype. *Antioch Review* 17:257–289.

Berger, Peter. 1965. Toward a sociological understanding of psychoanalysis. *Social Research* 32 (1):26–41.

Berger, Seymour, and William Lambert. 1968. Stimulus–response theory in contemporary social psychology. In Gardner Lindzey and Elliot Aronson (eds.), *The handbook of social psychology, Volume One* (2nd ed.). Reading, MA: Addison-Wesley.

Biderman, Albert D. 1966. Social indicators and goals. In Raymond A. Bauer (ed.), *Social indicators*. Cambridge, MA: M.I.T. Press.

Budiansky, Stephen, and Art Levine. 1988, July 11. The numbers racket: How polls and statistics lie. *U.S. News & World Report*, pp. 44–47.

Burke, Kenneth. 1935. *Permanence and change*. New York: New Republic.

Cialdini, Robert B. 1984, February. The triggers of influence. *Psychology Today*, pp. 40–45.

Douglas, Mary. 1966. *Purity and danger: An analysis of concepts of pollution and taboo*. London: Routledge and Kegan Paul.

Easterlin, Richard. 1980. *Birth and fortune: The impact of numbers on personal welfare*. New York: Basic Books.

Festinger, Leon. 1957. *A theory of cognitive dissonance*. Evanston, IL: Row, Peterson.

Freud, Sigmund. 1930 [1961]. *Civilization and its discontents*. New York: Norton.

Gerth, Hans, and C. Wright Mills. 1953 [1964]. *Character and social structure: The psychology of social institutions*. New York: Harbinger/Harcourt.

Harris, Marvin. 1979. *Cultural materialism: The struggle for a science of culture*. New York: Random House.

Heider, Fritz. 1958. *The psychology of interpersonal relations*. New York: Wiley.

Homans, George. 1958. Social theory and exchange. *American Journal of Sociology* 63:597–606.

Homans, George. 1961. *Social behavior: Its elementary forms.* New York: Harcourt Brace and World.

Kantor, David, and William Lehr. 1976. *Inside the Family.* San Francisco: Jossey-Bass.

Kelley, H. H., and J. W. Thibaut. 1978. *Interpersonal relations: A theory of interdependence.* New York: Wiley Interscience.

Kuhn, Thomas. 1970 *The structure of scientific revolutions* (2nd ed.), vol. 2, no. 2, of *International encyclopedia of unified science.* Chicago: University of Chicago Press.

Lapham, Lewis. 1979, June. A juggernaut of words. *Harper's Magazine*, pp. 8–16.

MacKay, Robert. 1973. Conceptions of children and models of socialization. In Hans Peter Dreitzel (ed.), *Recent sociology no. 5: Childhood and socialization.* New York: Macmillan.

Mead, George Herbert. 1934 [1962]. *Mind, self and society: From the standpoint of a social behaviorist.* Chicago: University of Chicago Press.

Merton, Robert. 1957. Priorities in scientific discovery: A chapter in the sociology of science. *American Sociological Review* 22:635–659.

Miller, Neal, and John Dollard. 1941. *Social learning and imitation.* New Haven, CT: Yale University Press.

*New York Times.* 1988, April 19. "Hot hands" phenomenon: A myth? pp. 23, 25.

Pisano, Marina. 1990, June 15. Munchers' manna: S.A. emerges 149th in heartburn poll. *San Antonio Express-News*, p. 7A.

Riesman, David. 1950 [1961]. *The lonely crowd.* New Haven, CT: Yale University Press.

Ropers, Richard. 1973, Mead, Marx and social psychology. *Catalyst* 7 (*Winter*):42–61.

*San Francisco Chronicle.* 1974, April 4. The devil is gaining. p. 21.

Saxton, S. L., Jr., and P. M. Hall. 1987. Two social psychologies: New grounds for discussion. In N. K. Denzin (ed.), *Studies in symbolic interaction*, vol. 8. Greenwich, CT: JAI Press.

Schutz, Alfred. 1973. *Collected papers I: The problem of social reality.* The Hague: Martinus Nijhoff.

Shabecoff, Philip. 1988, 23 March. Head of E.P.A. bars Nazi data in study on gas. *New York Times*, pp. 1, 9.

Siconolfi, Michael. 1986, April 17. Dealer group seeks consensus in coin grading. *Wall Street Journal*, p. 27.

Stephan, Cookie, and Walter Stephan. 1985. *Two social psychologies: An integrative approach.* Homewood, IL: Dorsey Press.

Thibaut, J. W., and H. H. Kelley. 1959. *The social psychology of groups.* New York: Wiley.

*Wall Street Journal.* 1987, May 5. Birth rate hits a record low." p. 39.

Zimbardo, P. G. 1971, October 25. The psychological power and pathology of imprisonment. Statement prepared for the U.S. House of Representatives, Committee on the Judiciary, Subcommittee no. 3: Hearings on Prison Reform, San Francisco, CA.

# Nature Versus Nurture

In 1981 Christine English was conditionally discharged by a British court even though she had killed her lover with a car. One day earlier, a London barmaid was put on probation for threatening police with a knife, despite a long criminal record of violence. The successful defense for both women was irrationality and loss of control due to a disorder called premenstrual syndrome, or PMS. The barmaid's lawyer said that once a month his client is transformed "into a raging animal" (Brozan 1982). This defense did not, however, hold up in the United States for a mother accused of brutally assaulting her 4-year-old daughter.

Assuming for the sake of argument that the phenomenon of PMS is "real" for a portion of women in their childbearing years, how should society legally manage such cases of violence? If such deviance is uncontrollable and unintended—if, as research shows, it stems from involuntary physiological changes as opposed to psychological distress (Eckholm 1985)—are these victims of PMS liable to prosecution? And if women are pardoned for acts committed under the influence of hormonal changes—a variant of the insanity plea—what will become of the female status in society (particularly when men do not use hormonal excuses, such as excesses of testosterone, to justify violent behavior)?

A prominent theme in all inquiries into the human condition is the extent to which our fate is a function of free will or of forces beyond our control—whether **internal and biological** or **external and environmental.** Philosophical orientations toward this centuries-old question, which is known as the nature/nurture or free will/determinism controversy, oscillate from one extreme to the other. For instance, throughout history human fate has been portrayed as a kind of tapestry woven by invisible, potent, and uncontrollable forces. In the not-too-distant past, life was often assumed to be divinely preordained; nowadays scientific inquiries attempt to discover the extent to which gender roles, career choices, and criminal activity are the expressions of genetic predispositions. We vacillate, in other words, between "The Devil made me do it" and "It runs in the family."

Such philosophical trends often determine the political ideology of the times. The founders of the American nation, for instance, were split on the issue of nature versus nurture. One school, embodied by Thomas Jefferson (who was influenced by the philosophy of Locke), believed that man could achieve perfection through individual freedom. (At this time only men were considered; women were not yet perceived as capable of controlling their biological impulses.) On the basis of this assumption, Jefferson campaigned for a weak central government. On the other hand, there were those, such as Alexander Hamilton (influenced by the philosophy of Hobbes), who took a dimmer view of human nature, viewing humans as being motivated by dark, selfish impulses and therefore requiring a strong central government to control their actions.

If we take a pessimistic view of human nature and see true freedom (and, hence, the ability to control our own fates) as unattainable, then political curbs and/or religious controls are unavoidable if societies are to maintain order and civilization is to evolve. Nevertheless, even if one sees environmental rather than innate forces as determining personality and dictating the behavior of individuals, one must still set up "nature" as one's null hypothesis. As argued in Chapter 1, substantiation of an hypothesis requires disproving as many alternative hypotheses as possible. For instance, to argue that a gifted student's talents are derived from favorable environmental conditions, one must disprove the theory that his or her aptitudes are determined by genetic factors. Even if environment or nurture should be discovered as not playing a major role in shaping the human condition, the matter of free will remains: It is possible that the process of enculturation is so thorough that individuals, in their social roles, really have little choice as to how they behave.

## BIOLOGICALLY BASED THEORIES

People make numerous attributions about others solely on the basis of their appearance (see Chapter 4). They make inferences about other people's personality, intelligence, and moral worthiness—in other words, deductions about their **true identity**—from their beauty, size, race, eyes, age, and other characteristics. Examining data collected in the 1960s by the National Center for Health Statistics on 14,000 children between the ages of 6 and 17, Darrell Wilson and his associates (1986) found that tall children score somewhat higher on intelligence tests than their shorter classmates. The association remained even after controlling for such factors as socioeconomic status, birth order, family size, and rate of physical maturation. Wilson postulated that this correlation occurs because more is expected of taller children, who are often assumed to be older than they actually are. See Table 2.1 for importance of physical appearance.

The potency of such bodily attributions is perhaps most evident when considering the sad social fate of those who are born deformed or chronically disabled. John Merrick, the so-called "Elephant Man," was doomed to be a public spectacle because of his hideous appearance. Often an obvious physical handicap leads others to infer that a person's inner self is similarly flawed. For example, in studying the interactions of "normals" toward amputees, Kleck and his associates (1966) found their behaviors unnatural and uncomfortable. "Normals" maintained greater interpersonal distance when interacting with a wheelchair-bound confederate (disguised so as to appear to have a missing leg) than when interacting with the same confederate without the disability. Norms of eye contact and attention focus were also violated.

## TABLE 2.1  Bend Me, Shape Me

*So central is physical appearance to some individuals that they are willing to spend considerable money to surgically alter their bodies to conform to cultural ideals of good looks. Following is an inventory of some of the procedures to which Americans subject themselves.*

| Surgical Procedures and Fees | | Number of Procedures per Year | |
|---|---|---|---|
| | | *Men* | *Women* |
| Hair transplants | $250–4,000 | 2,650 | 140 |
| Forehead lift | $1,000–4,000 | 1,590 | 14,310 |
| Eyelid tuck | $1,000–4,000 | 15,244 | 69,446 |
| Nose reshaping | $1,500–6,000 | 20,558 | 61,672 |
| Ear repinning | $1,000–3,500 | 6,547 | 8,333 |
| Facelift | $2,000–10,000 | 6,693 | 60,237 |
| Facial liposuction | $500–4,000 | 2,349 | 23,751 |
| Breast enlargement | $1,800–4,000 | | 93,540 |
| Breast lift | $1,500–5,000 | | 17,160 |
| Tummy tuck | $2,000–6,000 | 2,264 | 30,076 |
| Abdominal liposuction | $750–4,000 | 2,146 | 21,704 |
| Buttock liposuction | $500–3,000 | 557 | 18,013 |
| Thigh liposuction | $750–4,000 | 924 | 29,886 |

Source: Data from American Society of Plastic and Reconstructive Surgeons, Inc. (U.S. News & World Report 1987).

Some people make personality assessments on the basis of less obvious biological indicators. For instance, when testing for AIDS, nicotine, alcohol, and illegal drugs, insurance companies and employers obtain blood and urine samples to determine not only an individual's state of health but his or her "social worthiness" and moral quality as well.

A second way in which the body determines social behavior is through its physiological functioning. In addition to the premenstrual syndrome mentioned at the beginning of the chapter, there are other biological equilibria with behavioral and cognitive implications. For instance, there are cycles of sleep and wakefulness. According to many accounts, the absence of sleep is the most devastating form of torture. Just as one is about to escape through slumber, interrogators enter the cells, turn on bright lights, and resume the interrogation.

A third way in which social psychology is linked to biology involves the extent to which the human being, a self-aware creature that employs symbols, attempts to transcend, hide, and control its "natural urges." We do not like to think of ourselves as animals—as creatures who must eat, defecate, and die. Thus, Americans are often repulsed by adults who drool or wet their beds or have uncontrollable sex drives or addictions. They expect that individuals will be able to control both their biological and symbolic selves in specified social settings.

French women accused of consorting with occupying Nazi soldiers were shorn of their hair and paraded through the streets of their liberated country. Involuntary alterations of the body-self are employed to bring shame and attention to stigmatized individuals.

All societies have rules of obscenity that normally (but not universally) involve the biological functions of copulation and excretion. However, the Trobrianders, a South Pacific people, surround eating with as much shame as they do excretion (Malinowski 1922). Cultural historians have recorded how the specific pruderies of a culture can shift over time. For instance, in the West there has been a shift in the acceptability of public nudity and the perceived seemliness of matters related to copulation and death. During the Middle Ages, according to Norbert Elias (1939), there was no segregation of the sexes in public bathhouses, and a widespread wedding custom was to have family and friends accompany the newlyweds to their wedding bed, where they would not only help them undress but also observe the consummation of the marriage. By the nineteenth century, sexuality had become a cultural taboo for the Victorians (even to the extent of using doilies to obscure the sexual suggestiveness of furniture legs). However, death was romanticized and the deathbed scene was a public event. One century later Western culture made every effort to hide the presence of death (Feifel 1959:xii), which had replaced sex as a cultural taboo (Gorer 1965).

Another way in which biology is related to social psychology has to be with the influence of cultural and social dynamics on physiological processes. Female menstrual cycles, for instance, seem to be sensitive to social processes. When women spend considerable time together—for example, in dormitories—their menstrual cycles tend to become synchronized (Preti et al. 1986). They may also differ in different historical eras. In the West, the average age at menarche has declined by three-fourths month per decade over the past two centuries. In the 1840s the average Norwegian girl began menstruating at 17; she now does so just after age 13. In 1900 the average age at which American girls began to menstruate was 14.3; in 1984 this figure had declined to 12.9.

Cultural dynamics can even determine the biological well-being of individuals, as anthropologist Wade Davis noted in his study of Haitian voodoo practices:

> For just as an individual's sickness may have a psychosomatic basis, it is possible for a society to generate physical ailments and conditions that have meaning only in the minds of its people. . . . An individual breaks a social or spiritual code, violates a taboo, or for one reason or another believes himself a victim of a putative society. Conditioned since childhood to expect disaster, he then acts out what amounts to a self-fulfilling prophecy. (1985:136)

In the extreme, such "disaster mindsets" can cause death; this has occurred when individuals have received the evil eye in Greece or a voodoo hex in Haiti. Such situations can generate extreme fear, leading to overstimulation of the sympathetic adrenal system; thus, a person can literally be "scared to death."

Though less exotic than voodoo curses, the social influences of modern life are no less lethal. For instance, cases of alcoholism, heart disease, suicide, and mental disorder increase during difficult economic times. Even beginning the work week can be lethal. A long-term study of nearly four thousand men conducted by the University of Manitoba found that thirty-eight had died of sudden heart attacks on Mondays, whereas only fifteen had died on Fridays. Monday was particularly dangerous for men with no history of heart disease: Averaging 8.2 heart attack deaths for Tuesday through Sunday, these men suffered nearly three times as many on the first day of the week (Rabkin et al. 1980).

Social relations can have a life-enhancing effect as well. Other things being equal, the life expectancy of married people is nearly three years longer than that of single people. Helsing and associates followed 1204 men and 2828 women who had been widowed between 1963 and 1974, matching them with married persons in terms of age, race, sex, education, cigarette smoking, age when first married, and even number of pets. They found that the mortality rate of widowers between the ages of 45 and 64 was over 60 percent higher than the rate for married men of the same age. For widowers less than 55 years old, the death rate for those who remarried was over 70 percent lower than the rate for those who did not (Helsing, Szklo, and Comstock 1981).

Phillips and Feldman (1973) discovered another way in which death is postponed for social reasons. Desiring to demonstrate the concept of equiprobability in a statistics course, Phillips had his students plot the month of death of over thirteen hundred famous deceased Americans, expecting that the results would indicate roughly 110 deaths per month. But such a pattern did not appear. Replotting the data in terms of the individuals' month of birth, they looked at monthly death rates before and after that month. A relationship between birthdays and time of death was detected, with lower than statistically

**TABLE 2.2** Mean Physical Aggression Scores of Siblings Exposed and Not Exposed to Progestin

|  | Males | Females |
|---|---|---|
| Exposed to progestin | 9.75 | 4.0 |
| Unexposed siblings | 4.88 | 2.5 |

Source: Hall 1986.

expected death rates in the month prior to the birth month (a "death dip") and a greater than statistically expected rate for the following month (a "death peak"). Phillips (1972) postulated that famous individuals manage their time of death in order to receive the public attention and expressions of respect that typically come on their birthdays.

In a number of ways, society has altered the biochemistry, physiology, and behavioral inclinations of its members. For instance, in 1981 there were reports of animal studies using synthetic hormones that had been taken by twelve million pregnant American women to prevent miscarriages. The studies found significantly more aggressive behavior among animals that had been exposed to these substances before birth than among animals that had not been exposed to them (CBS News 1981). In studying the aggressiveness of children who were prenatally exposed to synthetic progestin, a substance that has masculinizing effects, with siblings who were not, Reinisch found that such exposure had a powerful effect on whether a child expected to handle conflict through physical aggression or by other means (Hall 1986). Table 2.2 shows that males were twice as physically aggressive, and females 60 percent more aggressive, if they had been exposed to progestin.

## BIOLOGY AS A DETERMINANT OF BEHAVIOR

Can behavior or consciousness be reduced to biochemical factors? In other words, do humans truly have any control over their fates? What bearing does consciousness have on the course of social action? This is the basic riddle of **human nature.** For Kenneth Bock, the pressing question is not "why we have refused to accept ourselves as animals, but why we have insisted on doing so" (1980:33). On the other hand, Jon Franklin (1987) claims that human beings are "mechanisms, pure and simple, explainable without resort to the concept of the soul. . . . That is the central, cold, hard, emotionless truth of the revolution in molecular psychology. If we really desire the safety we seek, the safety from chemicals and radiation and war, then we must renounce the romantic, dualistic view of humanity."

There is a widely shared cultural reluctance to acknowledge a major biological role in determining human social destiny. In part, this hesitancy is derived from the values of activism, faith in science, personal control, and equal opportunity. To accept, for instance, the existence of a powerful genetic predisposition toward violent behavior is to admit society's inability to make life better. Our hesitancy also stems from unfortunate historical episodes in which "experts" linked body attributes with social worthiness, often using biological criteria to strip certain individuals of their civil rights. For example, Nazi claims of Aryan supremacy led to the extermination of Jews, gypsies, the retarded, and the deformed. They also led to the creation of *lebensborns*, the baby factories for producing the "superior race." In the 1970s, William Shockley, a Nobel Prize winner in physics, spoke of the genetic inferiority of blacks. And in 1986 Japanese Prime Minister Yasuhiro Nakasone remarked that the average American intellectual standard is lower than the average Japanese standard because of the large numbers of blacks and Hispanics in the U.S. population, in contrast to Japan's "racial homogeneity."

***The Genetic Connection.*** Scientific research conducted in the 1980s produced impressive evidence of genetic predispositions toward a wide range of illnesses. Defective genes were linked with manic-depressive disorder, heart disease, cystic fibrosis, Huntington's disease, polycystic kidney disease, Duchenne's muscular dystrophy, eye cancer (retinoblastoma), alcoholism, and Alzheimer's disease (Schmeck 1987).

Evidence of possible genetic factors shaping the direction of individuals' lifelong interests and behaviors also increased. For example, Alexander Graham Bell, who accidentally invented the telephone while working on ways to help the hearing impaired, came from a family that was preoccupied with matters of speech and sound. Both his mother and his wife were deaf. His paternal grandfather wrote a book on phonetics and developed a cure for stammering, which was taught by his father and uncle. The family of writer Eugene O'Neill was marked by a three-generation pattern of estrangement between father and children (McGoldrick and Gerson 1985). To detect such intergenerational legacies, psychologists employ **genograms** to map the proclivities of family members over time (Goleman 1986a). Such continuities, however, still may be due to environmental factors. Required is a research designed that controls for genetic predispositions while varying the socialization contexts.

***The Minnesota Twin Studies.*** The ideal methodological strategy for resolving the nature-nurture debate is to study identical twins raised in different households. One indication of our culture's sensitivity to genetic determinism is the fact that until 1980 no such studies had been conducted in the United States for forty years. Now, however, a team of psychologists, psychiatrists, and physicians at the University of Minnesota are looking at the life histories, medical histories, physiology, tastes, psychological inclinations, abilities, and intelligence of identical twins raised separately. Their findings, as shown in Table 2.3, indicate that about one-half of the measured personality diversity was found to be due to genetic factors and between 20 and 35 percent to be due to environmental factors. Other characteristics have been found to be less inheritable; they include aggressiveness and the ability to listen in the presence of competing noise.

***Sociobiology.*** Research by Jane Goodall and other behavioral biologists indicates that humans are not unique in their ability to make tools, use symbols, or create norms and culture. Several prerequisites of social groups are found in other species, including organization, specialized division of labor oriented toward a common goal, psychological unity, and elaborate communication systems. For example, termites build an elaborate caste system around the queen (monarch). And while the Egyptians portrayed important people as larger than average, among termites this occurs in reality: If the average termite were the

**TABLE 2.3  The Genetic Roots of Personality According to the Minnesota Study of Identical Twins Raised Separately**

*The degree to which eleven key traits of personality, as measured by the Multi-dimensional Personality Questionnaire, are estimated to be inherited is as follows:*

|  | Percent |
|---|---|
| **Harm Avoidance** | 55 |
| Shuns the excitement of risk and danger, prefers the safe route even if it is tedious. | |
| **Social Potency** | 54 |
| A person high on this trait is masterful, a forceful leader who likes to be the center of attention. | |
| **Stress Reaction** | 53 |
| Feels vulnerable and sensitive and is given to worries and easily upset. | |
| **Absorption** | 50 |
| Has vivid imagination readily captured by rich experience; relinquishes sense of reality. | |
| **Well-being** | 48 |
| Has a cheerful disposition, feels confident and optimistic. | |
| **Alienation** | 45 |
| Feels mistreated and used, that "the world is out to get me." | |
| **Traditionalism** | 45 |
| Follows rules and authority, endorses high moral standards and strict discipline. | |
| **Aggression** | 44 |
| Is physically aggressive and vindictive, has taste for violence and is "out to get the world." | |
| **Control** | 44 |
| Is cautious and plodding, rational and sensible, likes carefully planned events. | |
| **Social Closeness** | 40 |
| Prefers emotional intimacy and close ties, turns to others for comfort and help. | |
| **Achievement** | 39 |
| Works hard, strives for mastery and puts work and accomplishment ahead of other things. | |

Sources: Tellegen et al. 1988; Goleman 1986b.

size of a human, the queen would be the size of a jet plane. Like a human monarch, a termite queen is constantly tended to by workers. These workers must also tend to the feeding of the warriors, whose mandibles are so specialized for war that they cannot feed themselves. The queen is also the communications hub, exchanging information with other termites through salival secretions.

Given the apparent efficiency and rationality of termite social organization, one wonders about the extent to which humanity's social structures are similarly the product of genetic evolution. Could it be that culture is merely a symbolic veneer, while underlying innate drives are the "true" cause of human behavior? For instance, is war a consequence of the same ecological forces that underlie the territorial disputes of wolves when population pressures exceed food supplies? Perhaps human warriors fight not for such social abstractions as patriotism, loyalty, or moral righteousness but, rather, out of animalistic competition for mating opportunities and other benefits. Social-scientific research suggests that this is possible. For example, Napoleon Chagnon's study of the Yanomamo, a particularly belligerent South American people, found that men who had killed at least once (an estimated 44 percent of those age 25 and older) had more than twice the number of wives and children than those who had not killed. Some particularly successful warriors had as many as six wives (Chagnon 1988).

According to sociobiologists, the propensity to engage in such behaviors as cooperation, conflict, domination, and self-sacrifice are genetically encoded in a species through the forces of natural selection acting on its members. At the individual level, life's game is to ensure that as much of one's genetic code as possible is passed on to succeeding generations; this is accomplished by maximizing both one's own reproduction and that of one's genetic relatives. Over time, those traits enabling one creature to have more descendants than others eventually predominate in its species' gene pool. In the view of sociobiologists, therefore, altruism is actually genetic selfishness. One is more likely to act unselfishly for one's sister than for a distant cousin because one shares more genes with her than with a cousin.

From a sociobiological perspective, courtship rituals are derived from the differential energies invested by the two sexes in raising their young. When females contribute significantly more to this activity, they tend to be more coy and selective of their mates, who compete—through size, color, promiscuity, trickery, or strength—for breeding rights. When the male makes the greater investment of time and energy in raising the young, it is he who chooses among competing females. In sum, individual organisms may be perceived as " 'pawns' of their DNA molecules, competing for an arrangement of environmental resources that is favorable to their making more copies (or approximate copies) of themselves" (Ellis 1983).

## Social Implications of Genetic Determinism

Given the predictive possibilities of genetic factors, various agencies are tempted to use them in screening individuals for employment or other purposes. Thus, *Wall Street Journal* columnist Jerry Bishop claims that

> there is the specter of labeling and discrimination, by employers, by insurers, by the legal system and even by friends. A few years ago, when it was discovered that a higher-than-expected number of prisoners carried an extra sex chromosome, proposals were made to monitor children with the abnormality. The idea was

dropped after critics objected that such children might become tagged as potential criminals and that the label alone might cause them to be treated in a way that would turn them toward criminality. (1986)

In 1988 an expert committee of the National Research Council recommended that the United States embark on a $3 billion, fifteen-year project to describe and map the human genes, which may total as many as 100,000!

It is tempting to speculate on the possibility of genetic testing of first-graders. If talents could be identified, would it not be efficient for social systems to track their young members and funnel them into programs designed to maximize those talents? Of course, the potential deviants would be identified as well. As we will see, personality tests are already employed by personnel offices to identify possible thieves and laggards. With recombinant genetics, instead of simply testing to locate desirable and undesirable traits, society could actually design the types of individuals needed to fill the spectrum of social roles.

On the other hand, genetic testing would also raise a host of ethical issues. Children labeled ungifted, whether diagnosed correctly or not, could easily become the victims of self-fulfilling prophecies. As will be elaborated on in chapters to come, people typically act toward others on the bases of labels and stereotypes. In addition, there are matters of privacy and confidentiality, cornerstones of America's civil liberties. If court cases are already being waged over whether individuals' privacy rights extend to the contents of their trash bags, it is certain that any information concerning their DNA epitomizes the essence of personal private property.

## SOCIAL ECOLOGY AND ENVIRONMENTAL PSYCHOLOGY

So far we have considered models in which genetic codes and physiological processes determine human behavior and fate. In addition to these internal-deterministic characterizations of the human condition, there are also external-deterministic models. These **ethological** theories of human behavior employ insights derived from observation of the ways in which natural settings affect animal behaviors.

Social ecologists and environmental psychologists study how the objective physical world affects people's moods and behaviors. They note that more infants are born nine months after a hurricane than at other times; that instances of wife beating and suicide increased following the eruption of Mt. St. Helens; that menstrual cycles, sexual activity, and homicides may be interrelated (Lieber and Sherin 1972); and that suicides may correspond to full moons. Weather conditions have been found to be correlated with accident rates and visits to plant dispensaries (Muecher and Ungeheur 1961); hot temperatures with negative moods (Griffitt and Veitch 1971); and population density with mental illness, fertility, and juvenile delinquency (Galle, Gove, and McPherson (1972).

In the United States, considerable attention has been given to the effects of the frontier culture of the American West. In 1890, when the frontier was declared closed by the U.S. Census Bureau, people wondered about the implications of losing this huge social safety valve. The West had represented a second chance, a place where society's adventurers, nonconformists, and "losers" could retreat from the confines of civilization and begin a new life. However, leaving the protective confines of civilization has a cost: an increased possibility of premature death. Today the suicide and homicide rates of white adolescents between the ages of 15 and 24 are greatest in the West, particularly in the counties with the lowest population (Greenberg et al. 1987). A study of mortality data for remote parts of Utah found that residents lost 33.5 percent more working years from their lives owing to accidents, disease, suicide, and auto accidents than residents of urban areas.

Environmental factors include the characteristics of artificial interior spaces. For instance, the way rooms are lit has social consequences. Blood donors sit closer together and interact more when recovery rooms are lit with table lamps than when they are lit with direct overhead lighting (Meer 1985). Investigations of people who suffer from fall and winter depression, seasonal affective disorder, reveal that the pineal gland secretes more melatonin (a hormone linked to sensitivity to light) as the days grow shorter (Meer 1985).

In sum, humans are profoundly affected by their physical environment. One issue that arises in this connection is the extent to which we can use animals in their natural habitats as models for understanding human behavior.

## Nature as a Model for Understanding Human Behavior

A major feature of social evolution is the urbanization of human populations. In the United States, nearly 90 percent of the population lives in urban areas. Such areas are characterized by high population densities: In downtown Manhattan one can theoretically meet a quarter of a million people within a ten-minute walking radius from one's office. What are the social and psychological consequences of such crowding?

A classic experiment on the effects of crowding was conducted by Calhoun (1962), who created a colony of forty-eight rats living comfortably in four interconnected pens. By increasing the supply of food and water, Calhoun allowed his rat population to swell to eighty. This "urbanization" spawned a host of pathologies: Male aggressiveness increased, with dominant animals controlling various territories; there were instances of homosexual behavior and cannibalism; and females abandoned their young, three-quarters of whom died. To what extent can these findings be generalized to human populations? Does crowding underlie epidemics of homicide and child abuse and stories of urban bystanders refusing to intercede on behalf of people who are being victimized?

If crowding actually causes aggressiveness, then more violent crime should be found in areas with high population densities. It is true that major crimes are more than five times as likely to occur in big cities than in small ones, eight times as likely to occur in big cities than in the suburbs, and eleven times as likely to occur in big cities than in rural areas. But the largest cities are not necessarily the areas with the highest population densities. In fact, according to Freedman et al. (1975), when factors like income, education, and other life situations are equal, the relationship between population density and violent crime disappears.

Nevertheless, attempts to apply the ecological model to human affairs continue. Ecology (from the Greek word *oikos*, meaning "house, home, or place of residence") explores the relationships between organisms and their environments. The broad definition of environment includes predators, inter- and intraspecific competition, and various forms of cooperation both within and among species. Originating as a branch of biology, the field was stimulated by Charles Darwin's theory of evolution, which explains how life forms are modified by the forces of the environment, a process commonly referred to as **natural selection;** organisms that fail to adapt quickly enough risk extinction.

In its broadest application, ecology examines entire **ecosystems,** detailing the complex interdependencies between organisms and their environment. In part, ecologists describe these interrelationships in terms of *niches,* which is what animals do in their environments to survive, their "job." One or two rainy springs may dramatically modify a rabbit species niche, leading to an increase in their population size. This positively affects the niches of predatory animals, producing a somewhat lagged increase in the number of foxes. Owing to the habitat's limited carrying capacity for rabbits and the increasing numbers of foxes, rabbit populations decrease. As their niche contracts, fox populations follow.

Applying such ideas of ecological interdependency to economic relations between two ethnic groups, Barth (1969) noted that different groups may occupy clearly distinct niches and hence reduce the competition for resources. For instance, in the early twentieth century in the United States, the Chinese opened laundries, the Germans made beer, and the Italians grew fruits and made wine. Attempts to monopolize niches were sometimes challenged by the competition of new arrivals: Koreans entered the fruit trade; Greeks began making pizzas. When competition for resources occurs, ethnicities engage in political conflict. On the other hand, ethnic groups may provide important goods and services for each other, that is, occupy reciprocal and therefore different but interdependent niches.

To further illustrate how ecological ideas have been applied to social behavior, consider the notions of territoriality and boundary maintenance. To maximize reproductive success, individual creatures of a given species stake out a territory in which to harvest or hunt. The boundaries of these territories are guarded against intruders. To minimize the energy expended on boundary maintenance, dogs mark their territories and birds sing—conveying to others of their species that "this is mine" and "it's me" that's here.

How analogous are such human endeavors as preserving one's place at a library table with stacks of books to a dog marking off its territory? In one experiment, female confederates approached other females seated at library tables. The confederates were generally ignored when they sat several chairs away from the "victim," but if they sat down in adjoining seats, the "victim" displayed signs of discomfort. She would draw in her head or an arm, turn her shoulder or back to the intruder, or mark off her territory with coat, purse, or books (Sommer 1969).

Related to boundary maintenance activities are the distancing games played between subordinate and superior, between friends, or between urban strangers (between whom there is a minimum of body contact, eye contact, and expressivity [Lofland 1973]). These types of *nonverbal communication* will be described in more detail in Chapter 5.

# NATURE AND NURTURE: AN INTERACTIVE VIEW

The social and biological sciences no longer depict human nature as a product of only culture or only genes. Instead, they attempt to understand the complex interactions between the two. Culture and genes have evolved together: As genetically shaped cognitive properties have affected the evolution of culture, so culture has affected the evolution of the brain structure genes that determine cognition (Lumsden and Wilson 1985).

Relative to other primates, the enlarged size of the cranium makes it necessary for the human fetus to be born prematurely so that it can pass through the birth canal. Consequently, the infant is especially helpless and unformed at birth, bereft of any directed and specialized drives. As Berger and Luckmann observe: "Important organismic developments, which in the animal are completed in the mother's body, take place in the human infant after its separation from the womb. . . . The human organism is thus still developing biologically while already standing in a relationship to its environment" (1966:48).

One of the most extensive studies of the interrelations of genes and environment in shaping individuals' social fates was conducted in Sweden, which maintains detailed records of its citizens' medical, economic, and legal histories. Researchers examined the criminal records of adopted Swedish men and compared the legal histories of those born to law-abiding parents and those born to parents with a criminal record, relating both to the quality of their childhood home life. In Table 2.4 we see that among the adopted men born to individuals with a criminal record, 12 percent of those raised in the homes of skilled workers had been convicted of a crime, compared with forty percent of those who had been shuttled through several institutions and ended up in low-status homes (Bishop 1986).

We see in the first column that among the men raised in the homes of skilled workers, those born to parents with a criminal record were four times as likely to commit a crime than those born to law-abiding parents (12 percent versus 3 percent). For those raised in lower-status homes (column 2), this ratio increases to nearly sixfold (40 percent versus 7 percent). Among the men born to parents with a criminal record (the second row), those raised in the less

TABLE 2.4 Percentage of Men Convicted of Crime, by Criminal Status of Biological Parents and Quality of Home Life Wherein Raised

| Biological Parent | | Environment within Which Raised | | |
|---|---|---|---|---|
| | | Skilled Workers (HI) | Foster and Low-Status Homes (LO) | (LO/HI) |
| Law-abiding | (L) | 3% | 7% | 2.33 |
| Criminal record | (C) | 12% | 40% | 3.33 |
| (C/L) | | 4.00 | 5.71 | |

stable, low-status home environments (40 percent of whom were convicted criminals) were 3.33 times more likely to commit a crime than those who had been socialized in higher-status settings.

Pushing the analysis one step further, let's take ratios of these ratios. Dividing 5.71 by 4.00 gives us 1.43. What this means is that the odds that one will commit a crime if one is born to criminal parents as opposed to law-abiding ones increases 43 percent if one is raised in a lower-status environment than if one is raised in a higher-status one. Dividing 3.33 by 2.33 also gives us 1.43. Hence, the odds that one will commit a crime if one is raised in a poorer as opposed to richer situation increase 43 percent if one's parents had a criminal record as opposed to not having a criminal record.

The fact that both ratios of ratios are approximately equal is evidence that nature and nurture have roughly similar inputs in determining one's criminal fate. The influences of genes and social environment are so thoroughly interwoven that it is meaningless to specify the separate influence of each.

## Difference between Humans and Animals

What is it that distinguishes our species from all others? Recent research by Jane Goodall (1986) and other behavioral biologists indicates that humans are not unique in their ability to make tools, use symbols, or create norms and culture. For example, Seyfarth (1984) has observed African vervet monkeys making different alarms for different kinds of threats (e.g., different cries indicating the presence of a leopard as opposed to a snake); the monkeys thus are able to represent different objects with sound. But these sounds are only denotations of something tangible and concrete. Humans reside totally within symbolic universes in which ideas have reality. We are concept-making creatures who experience our environments through our concepts. Unlike any other animal, we have a natural ability to group objects or events together into categories and to give them abstract labels, which enables us to think about the world in highly efficient ways. These labels, or symbols, engender concepts that make possible the planning and coordination of collective action toward some future goal.

Another unique characteristic of humans has to do with time. Animals and young children live in the present while mature adults live simultaneously in the past, present, and future (Meerloo 1970). Observes Lindesmith et al. (1977:75) "The possession of language has enabled human beings to 'invent' time and space—past, present, and future. Humans have the capacity to respond to events that took place hundreds or even thousands of years ago, to predict or conceive future events, and to imagine objects and events that are remote in space or entirely nonexistent." In other words, only the behavior of humans is influenced by generations removed in space and time, to whom many of our activities and their products are directed.

Humans are also unique in their awareness of themselves as individuals. Although chimpanzees may recognize themselves in a mirror, what they recognize is a distinctive physical being and probably not a distinctive social being. Humans, on the other hand, recognize a symbolic identity defined in terms of ancestry, religion, politics, ethnicity, age, and social class.

Finally, only humans have a sense of morality. Our moral commitments to others often conflict with self-serving, hedonistic desires. Cultural values influence both our choices of goals and the way we proceed to accomplish them (Etzioni 1989).

In sum, unlike the rest of the animal kingdom, humans respond to an environment that is primarily man-made and symbolic in quality. Instead of being figures of the landscape, like antelopes on the African savanna, humans are shapers of their surroundings (Bronowski 1973:19), creating artificial milieus such as cities. Humans transform natural space and time into social space and time, around whose definitions they orient their behaviors (McHugh 1968). Thus, instead of being governed by the natural rhythms of the sun and seasons, our behaviors are governed by such artificial rhythms as work schedules, age norms, and store hours. These external influences are part of what is called *culture*. Cultural theorists, the "nurturists" on the nature–nurture continuum of behavioral explanations, argue that culture creates minds, selves, and emotions in a society just as reliably as DNA creates the various tissues of a living body.

## THE HUMAN CONDITION AS A CULTURAL PRODUCT

Although nature produces sophisticated social systems with highly specialized members, there are profound differences between human action and that of social insects. The activities of both are structured by the roles they occupy. But the roles of termites and ants are totally *ascribed*—that is, built into their biological being—and their role behaviors are dictated entirely by instinct. In contrast, human roles are derived from biological, psychological and sociological dynamics. People act on the basis of other people's expectations regarding their role performances.

Modern humans are nearly identical genetically to their cave-dwelling ancestors of 20,000 years ago. Human evolution occurs as a result of cultural rather than biological adaptation. The reason that arrows have been replaced by intercontinental missiles, the horse by a 747, and the beat of distant drums by telephones and television sets is that the human species is characterized by cultural evolution. This points up the importance of culture in explaining human behavior.

Culture (from the Latin *cultus*, meaning "worship") is the embodiment of the *man-made symbolic* environment that shapes and governs the human condition. It is a shared system of interrelated ideas about the nature of the world and rules about how people should think, feel, and behave within it. This system is the primary source "of solutions to unlearned problems, as well of learned problems and their solutions, all of which are acquired by members of a recognizable group and shared by them" (Ullman 1965:5). Over time the goals, values, norms, and orientations of any given cultural system coalesce into a general pattern. This pattern has internal consistency, so that a change in any one of its elements has consequences for all the others.

Culture involves such matters as music, food, humor, taboos, personality types, means of social control, and the statuses assigned to members of different age groups and genders. These ideas are encoded in public symbols such as literary texts, art, music, dance, drama, religious ritual, customs, mores, and laws. These systems emerge over time and are transmitted to succeeding generations through language. Through the process of *enculturation* the cultural system is learned by every child and forms a template for understanding the underlying conceptions of self, society, and human nature that guide behavior in that child's community. Cultures thus become "imprinted" in each new generation as metaphors and beliefs. An individual's culture appears so "natural" that it may lead to ethnocentrism, the belief that one's own culture is superior to all others.

The role of cultural templates will be better understood if we consider an example. In Western culture the formation of friendships is understood to result from two individuals randomly coming together, interacting, discovering commonalities, and finding that each enjoys the presence of the other. But an alternative cultural perspective claims that in each of a succession of lives one repeatedly encounters the same group of individuals, albeit in varying roles. For instance, a husband in one life may be a wife in another; this is the basis for attraction between individuals. How truly different are these two worldviews? Although from the first perspective randomness seems to account for how individuals first come together, the process is by no means accidental. Social-scientific research shows that such encounters can be conceptualized as a series of probabilistic instances. Consider the case of two people who meet and become friends in college: Here proximity leads to friendship, and this proximity itself is determined by social class and economic opportunities. Thus, from both cultural perspectives friendship can be perceived not as a product of happenstance but, rather, as something that is determined, whether it is a result of economic history and class dynamics or a relationship that persists through numerous reincarnations.

## Cultural Influences on Sensation and Attention

The mental worlds experience by humans depend on their social environment; perception is largely shaped by social factors. For example, for natives of New Guinea, "color classifications are so different that they see yellow, olive-green, blue-green, gray, and lavender as variations of one color" (cited in Lindesmith et al. 1977:185). Culture shapes not only our perceptions of color but also the way we experience space and time.

***Cultural Shaping of Space.*** Anthropologist Edward T. Hall (1969) uses the term **proxemics** to refer to people's use of space as an aspect of culture. One's culture dictates the appropriate social boundaries between oneself and others; these are translated into a set of rules governing spatial distance. For instance, we allow the intimate space surrounding our bodies to be invaded by lovers but maintain greater distance with work associates and still greater distance with strangers. These spatial zones for intimates, friends, and strangers vary considerably around the world, depending both on relations between people and on assumptions about where one's self resides relative to one's body. In northern European cultures "the person is synonymous with an individual inside a skin," whereas in the Middle East the person is located deep inside the body, where it "is protected from touch but not from words" (Hall 1969:157). The greater pushing and body contact found in public places in the Middle East occurs because inner selves are not interpreted as being violated, in contrast

## The Everyday Idiom of Witchcraft

The following is an account of a clash between two cultural mindsets, the Western rationality of anthropologist Evans-Pritchard and the magical logic of the Azande, a central African culture. As is seen, both thought systems are equally flexible and capable of explaining everyday events.

Unless the reader appreciates that witchcraft is quite a normal factor in the life of Azande, one to which almost any and every happening may be referred, he will entirely misunderstand their behavior towards it. To us witchcraft is something which haunted and disgusted our credulous forefathers. But the Zande expects to come across witchcraft at any time of the day or night. He would be just as surprised if he were not brought into daily contact with it as we would be if confronted by its appearance. To him there is nothing miraculous about it. It is expected that a man's hunting will be injured by witches, and he has at his disposal means of dealing with them. When misfortunes occur he does not become awestruck at the play of supernatural forces. He is not terrified at the presence of an occult enemy. He is, on the other hand, extremely annoyed. Someone, out of spite, has ruined his ground-nuts or spoilt his hunting or given his wife a chill, and surely this is cause for anger! He has done no one harm, so what right has anyone to interfere in his affairs? It is an impertinence, an insult, a dirty, offensive trick! It is the aggressiveness and not the eeriness of these actions which Azande emphasize when speaking of them, and it is anger and not awe which we observe in their response to them.

I found it strange at first to live among Azande and listen to naive explanations of misfortunes which, to our minds, have apparent causes, but after a while I learnt the idiom of their thought and applied notions of witchcraft as spontaneously as themselves in situations where the concept was relevant. A boy knocked his foot against a small stump of wood in the centre of a bush path, a frequent happening in Africa, and suffered pain and inconvenience in consequence. Owing to its position on his toe it was impossible to keep the cut free from dirt and it began to fester. He declared that witchcraft had made him knock his foot against the stump. I always argued with Azande and criticized their statements, and I did so on this occasion. I told the boy that he had knocked his foot against the stump of wood because he had been careless, and that witchcraft had not placed it in the path, for it had grown there naturally. He agreed that witchcraft had nothing to do with the stump of wood being in his path but added that he had kept his eyes open for stumps, as indeed every Zande does most carefully, and that if he had not been bewitched he would have seen the stump. As a conclusive argument for his view he remarked that all cuts do not take days to heal but, on the contrary, close quickly, for that is the nature of cuts. Why, then, had his sore festered and remained open if there were not witchcraft behind it?

Source: Evans-Pritchard 1937.

---

to what would occur, for example, if a stranger merely touched an Englishwoman's clothes.

Space also entails boundaries, territory, and matters of visual and acoustical privacy. These, too, are largely culturally prescribed. Whereas an American family might feel cramped in a 1200-square-foot apartment, a family in Hong

Kong might rent out some of that area. American families place their furniture around the edges of a room; the Japanese gather furniture in the middle. For Germans, bedroom privacy requires thick walls and doors; the Japanese are satisfied with onionskin partitions.

***Cultural Shaping of Time.*** For the vast majority of human history, cultures have imposed social time systems on the rhythms of the natural order. It is culture that dictates the cadences of social existence (Hallowell 1955). These cultural rhythms are echoed in biology. For instance, on top of such biological clocks as physiological maturity or cycles of sleep, social systems have placed age-graded role expectations and cycles of work time, prime time, and sleep. Condon and Sander (1974) showed that within a few days infants flex their limbs and move their heads in rhythms matching the speech of people around them.

Cultures differ in their general orientation toward the future or past and in whether they understand time as flowing cyclically or linearly. Although nearly all languages allow their speakers to discriminate among past, present, and future time, the precision with which they do so varies considerably. Hall observed that in many Mediterranean Arab cultures there are only three sets of time: no time at all, now (which is of varying duration), and forever (too long). Similarly, the Hopi Indians have no tenses indicating past, present, or future events, but they do indicate an event's duration. Whorf (1956) concluded that the Hopi do not think of time as a series of discrete instants. For them, events are not unique but are cumulative through time.

***Cultural Determination of Sensory Priorities.*** Members of different cultures interpret sensory data differently and combine them in different ways. Arabs, for instance, rely more on smell and touch than Americans do (Hall 1969:3). It has been argued that because of their Puritan heritage, many Americans have an underdeveloped sense of touch.

The significance of dreams also varies from one culture to another. Although they spend one-third of their lives in sleep and, on average, dream for one and one-half hours every night, most contemporary Americans attribute little significance to their dreams and generally forget them. Yet in many cultures dreams are seen as a source of enlightenment. In fact, for the Senoi, a jungle people of the Malay Peninsula, dream reality is more "real" than wide-awake reality. The Senoi are trained to remember their dreams. Each morning they gather to discuss their sleep visions, assisted by *halaks* who act as dream psychologists (Rheingold 1988:131–135).

In sum, it is culture that gives order and meaning to the numerous experiences of everyday life. Basically sharing the same templates for deciphering reality, a number of social scientists believe that a shared character structure emerges in each society. Fromm (1963), for instance, viewed this "social character" arising from those responses best suited for individuals' survival and success given their culture's distinctive social requirements.

## Ritual and Culture

Cultures routinely employ ritual ceremonies to reaffirm their beliefs and values. Although people tend to think of a ritual as an unthinking routine that one performs either out of habit or on traditional occasions, ritual actually involves much more. Victor Turner defined ritual as "prescribed formal behavior for occasions not given over to technological routine, having reference to beliefs in invisible beings or powers" (1982:29). These invisible powers, often viewed as sacred, are the transcendent forces that bind social groups together.

Rituals communicate collective understandings, the cultural schemas that give order to chaos and meaning to meaninglessness through condensed symbolism (Douglas (1973). They provide "not only models of what [people] believe, but also models for the believing of it" (Geertz 1973:114). Through ritual, individuals are moved outside of mundane reality; the ordinary becomes infused with greater meaning:

> In its repetition and order, ritual imitates the rhythmic imperatives of the biological and physical universe, thus suggesting a link with the perpetual processes of the cosmos. It thereby implies permanence and legitimacy of what are actually evanescent cultural constructs. (Moore and Myerhoff 1977:8)

Ritual goes beyond merely acknowledging and categorizing (Harman 1987). Rituals also bring change, "almost always accompany[ing] transitions from one situation or state to another" (van Gennep 1904 [1960]:13). It is through ritual that personally unique events are transformed into socially typical occasions and crisis situations are addressed with socially constructed recipes for coping. As Benford and Kurtz note:

> Rituals provide solutions to problems on a number of levels. They relieve social and psychological tensions by focusing attention on ritual details rather than uncontrollable aspects of a crisis situation . . . ; they link those detailed activities to broader world views, and provide participants with a series of rationalizations which enable them to escape the angst associated with the crisis. . . . What is to be done, said, and thought are ritually defined and those caught in the crisis are reassured that their fundamental world view somehow answers the questions raised by the situation. By following socially approved rituals for such situations, the individual can avoid social faux pas and at the same time be assured that his or her own identity is secure. (1984)

## SEXUAL URGES AND FEAR OF DEATH

Two biological processes figure prominently in explanations of what ultimately motivates human behavior: sexual urges and fear of death. Although they are viewed as polar opposites on the continuum of empirically verifiable theories, both psychoanalytic and sociobiological theories have focused on the centrality of sex and death. Much to the chagrin of many of his contemporaries, Sigmund Freud argued that the sex drive is one of the most basic and powerful of human motivations. A century later, the modern notion that humanity has evolved beyond bestial impulses, and that people control their own fates, was shaken by the sociobiological argument that culture may be a veneer obscuring the drives of selfish genes seeking replication and immortality.

## Females Are Segregated in Mexico City Subway

Mexico City women have so much trouble fending off sexually aggressive men that they are provided with their own segregated subway cars so they won't be jammed in with members of the opposite sex.

During peak hours on the most popular line, transit officials stand at the entrance marked "Women and Children."

If a man tries to pass through, he is told by transit guards to use the other entrance. Once on the platform, a glass wall separates men from women. And inside women's cars, not a single man is in sight.

Source: *San Antonio Express-News* 1990.

As we will see throughout this book, cultures have harnessed sex drives and fear of death in a myriad of ways to establish and maintain control over the actions of individuals. Religions, for instance, have created fears and hopes about an afterlife (e.g., heaven and hell, resurrection or reincarnation) as a means of keeping their members "in line." During World War II troop morale was heightened by sexual stimuli such as poster girls and the Hollywood stars featured in movies and on tours of overseas posts. As Bob Hope once quipped, "Boys, this is what you are fighting for."

Perhaps nowhere can we find a clearer example of the difficulties posed by the human being's dual nature as beast and angel than in the tensions surrounding sexuality. When a woman claims that a man "only wants me for my body," she illustrates that dual nature: She is saying that she views herself as considerably more than mere flesh. Feminists argue that women's "higher" self is only perfunctorily acknowledged by men in male-dominated societies, and that men's sexual motives are always lurking.

The history of sexuality features the tension between biological spontaneity and culturally prescribed restraint (Gay 1983). Some believe that the ability to bridle sexual urges is correlated with biological and social evolution. Arguing that Asians are the most intelligent and hardworking race, Rushton claims they are also more sexually restrained than other races (a quality that is determined from reported frequency of intercourse, sexual fantasies, and other factors [Wheeler 1989]). Conversely, several eighteenth-century European philosophers argued that the supposed inferiority of American Indians was due to their lack of sexual passion, which, in turn, led to weaker family attractions (Boorstin 1989:117).

Every great civilization has contributed distinctive ideas concerning the nature of sexuality and its relationship to religious, philosophical, economic, political, legal, family and educational systems. These include definitions of the "proper" role of sexuality in the lives of various categories of people (i.e., men vs. women, marrieds vs. singles vs. widowed, teenagers vs. young adults vs. older individuals). The potency of these definitions in determining sexual behaviors and experiences is evidence of their central role in contemporary cultural heritages.

Mortality also plays a central role in human cultures. As far as we know, humans are unique in the animal kingdom in their awareness of their own inevitable demise. Our species has a peculiar need to believe that the universe is characterized by purpose and design. This belief is threatened by the prospect of death, particularly as the same fate awaits both the virtuous and the wicked.

Perhaps the most basic accomplishment of any cultural system is its capacity to shield its members from doubt about the meaningfulness of life. This is achieved in at least two ways. First, culture identifies *causes* so that the society's members need not worry about what life means or reflect on the terrors of death. Second, culture offers some *promise of immortality*, whether it depicts death as a transition rather than an end or, at a minimum, promises that one's earthly existence will never be forgotten.

The flip side of the ability of culture to protect its members against the terrors of extinction is the power gained by threatening them with death. The potency of this mechanism of social control was enhanced by religion (see Chapter 14), which added the fears of postmortem judgment. Depending on the quality of one's activities in life one may face the prospect of being eternally consigned to the agonies of hell or to an endless cycle of painful reincarnations.

Riley (1983) observed that the point in the lifespan at which death normally occurs determines the meaning of life in a given culture. When death routinely interrupts people's lives prematurely and unexpectedly, it is viewed as being externally caused. This typically produces a fatalistic worldview. On the other hand, when death normally occurs in old age, after people have completed their role obligations and have lived a full life, the cultural ethos typically features autonomy and self-control. The lengthening of lifespans has been linked with a broad range of cultural changes: romantic love replacing arranged marriages, prolonged adolescence and greater parental emotional investment in children, the possibility of divorce, the confinement of bereavement to the elderly, occupational specialization, and the shift from ascribed to achieved roles as the basis of social stratification (Goldscheider 1976:184–186).

## CONCLUSION

In this chapter we began our inquiry into the human condition by considering the amount of free will underlying human motives and behaviors. This debate dates back to Plato, who claimed that human minds come equipped with innate ideas or inherited tendencies to think and behave in very specific ways. The opposite doctrine, associated with behaviorism, maintains that the mind is a blank slate at birth. Evidence shows that both views may be true.

Consideration of "inherited tendencies" leads to the sociology of the body, behavioral genetics, and human ecology. Some intriguing patterns can be seen in the ways in which genes and physical environments shape human behavior, attesting to our relationship with the animal kingdom. But unlike other creatures, humans are shapers of their environment and not mere responders to it; instead of leaving only skeletal or fossilized imprints of themselves, only humans leave remnants of what they have created. As far as we know, humans are the only species to live in moral pain and to have aesthetic impulses, to feel invincibility with lucky charms, to derive humor when reflecting on everyday experiences, to feel the need to be unique, to calculate ways of enhancing and restoring reputations, to die for reasons of shame and humiliation, to experience joy at simply being alive, and to have a choice in committing themselves to social groups.

On the other hand, as we have seen, many of our ways of perceiving and conceptualizing are "inherited tendencies" derived from our culture. There seems to be little question that body, mind, and culture are inextricably inter-related (Fausto-Sterling 1985:101). Perhaps the only true choice the individual has is in deciding whether or not to be a member of a society.

We concluded with a basic theme of this book: the centrality of death and sex in determining both the nature of human behavior and the course of social development. Admittedly, such a focus is not popular. As Huntington and Metcalf observe, the "introduction of 'death education' in the public schools is almost as controversial as the introduction of sex education" (1979:3). Never-theless, if the sex drive is not personally controlled, socially imposed death results:

> Without the prevention of childbirth by means of postponement of marriage or other contraceptive measures, the population must be limited by taking the life of living beings. And so societies have "invented" cannibalism, induced abortion, organized wars, made human sacrifice, and practiced infanticide (especially fe-male) as means of avoiding periodic famine and epidemics. (Riesman 1950:10)

In sum, the templates of the mind—the patterns by which individuals' thoughts, experiences, feelings, and drives are molded—are determined by ge-netic propensities, enculturation, and social experiences. Though this text focuses on the latter, in considering how social phenomena determine psycho-logical experiences, it cannot ignore the interactions between sociological, bi-ological, and cultural processes. In this chapter we examined the fundamental tension between nature and nurture in shaping the human condition. The next chapter explores a second: the tension between individual needs and social needs.

## REFERENCES

Barth, Fredrik. 1969. *Ethnic groups and boundaries: The social organization of cultural difference.* Boston: Little, Brown.

Benford, Robert, and Lester Kurtz. 1984. Performing the nuclear ceremony: The arms race as ritual. Paper presented at the annual meetings of the American Sociological Association, San Antonio, TX.

Berger, Peter, and Thomas Luckmann. 1966. *The social construction of reality.* Garden City, NY: Doubleday.

Bishop, Jerry. 1986, February 12. Researchers close in on some genetic bases of antisocial behavior. *Wall Street Journal*, pp. 1, 18.

Blauner, Robert. 1966. Death and social structure. *Psychiatry* 29:378–394.

Bock, Kenneth. 1980. *Human nature and history: A response to sociobiology.* New York: Columbia University Press.

Boorstin, Daniel J. 1989. *Hidden history: Exploring our secret past.* New York: Vintage.

Bronowski, Jacob. 1973. *The ascent of man.* Boston: Little, Brown.

Brozan, Nadine. 1982, July 12. Premenstrual syndrome: A complex issue. *New York Times*, p. C16.

Calhoun, J. B. 1962. Population density and social pathology. *Scientific American* 206(2):139–148.

CBS Evening News. 1981, March 4.

Chagnon, Napoleon. 1988. Life histories, blood revenge, and warfare in a tribal population. *Science* 239:985–992.

Condon, William S., and Louis W. Sander. 1974. Synchrony demonstrated between movements of neonate and adult speech. *Child Development* 45(2):456.

Davis, Wade. 1985. *The serpent and the rainbow.* New York: Simon and Schuster.

DeLong, Alton. 1981. Phenomenological space-time: Toward an experiential relativity. *Science* 213:681–683.

Derber, Charles. 1979. *The pursuit of attention: Power and individualism in everyday life.* New York: Oxford University Press.

Douglas, Mary. 1966. *Purity and danger: An analysis of concepts of pollution and taboo.* London: Routledge and Kegan Paul.

Douglas, Mary. 1973. *Natural Symbols.* New York: Pelican Books.

Eckholm, Erik. 1985, June 4. Premenstrual problems may beset baboons. *New York Times,* p. 19.

Elias, Norbert. 1939 [1978]. *The civilizing process,* vol. 1. Oxford: Basil Blackwell.

Ellis, Lee. 1983. Invasions and defense of sociological territory. *Contemporary Sociology* 12(1): 17–20.

Etzioni, Amitai. 1989, February 1. The "me first" model in the social sciences is too narrow. *Chronicle of Higher Education,* p. A44.

Evans-Pritchard, E. E. 1937. *Witchcraft, oracles and magic among the Azande.* Oxford: Clarendon Press.

Fausto-Sterling, Anne. 1985. *Myths of gender: Biological theories about women and men.* New York: Basic Books.

Feifel, Herman. 1959. *The meaning of death.* New York: McGraw-Hill.

Franklin, Jon. 1987. *Molecules of the mind: The brave new science of molecular psychology.* New York: Atheneum.

Freedman, J. L., S. Heshka, and A. Levy. 1975. Population density and pathology: Is there a relationship? *Journal of Experimental Social Psychology* 11:539–552.

Fromm, Erich. 1963. *The chains of illusion.* New York: Pocket Books.

Galle, Omer, Walter Gove, and J. Miller McPherson. 1972. Population density and pathology: What are the relations for man? *Science* 176:23–30.

Galvin, Ruth, and John Leo. 1977, August 1. Why you do what you do. *Time,* pp. 54–63.

Gay, Peter. 1983. *The bourgeois experience: Victoria to Freud,* vol. 1. *Education of the senses.* New York: Oxford University Press.

Geertz, Clifford. 1973. *The interpretation of culture.* New York: Basic Books.

Goldscheider, Calvin. 1976. The mortality revolution. In Edwin Shneidman (ed.), *Death: Current perspectives.* Palo Alto, CA: Mayfield.

Goleman, Daniel. 1986a, January 21. Clues to behavior sought in history of families. *New York Times,* pp. 17, 20.

Goleman, Daniel. 1986b, December 2. Major personality study finds that traits are mostly inherited. *New York Times,* pp. 17, 18.

Goodall, Jane. 1986. *The chimpanzees of Gombe.* Cambridge, MA: Harvard University Press.

Gorer, Geoffrey. 1965. *Death, grief and mourning.* Garden City, NY: Doubleday Anchor Books.

Greenberg, Michael, George Carey, and Frank Popper. 1987. Violent death, violent states, and American youth. *Public Interest* 87:38–48.

Griffitt, William, and Russell Veitch. 1971. Hot and crowded: Influences of population density and temperature on interpersonal affective behavior. *Journal of Personality and Social Psychology* 17(1):92–98.

Hall, Edward T. 1969. *The hidden dimension.* Garden City, NY: Doubleday Anchor Books.

Hall, Elizabeth. 1986, June. Profile: June Reinisch, new directions for the Kinsey Institute. *Psychology Today,* pp. 33–39.

Hallowell, Irving. 1955. *Culture and experience.* Philadelphia: University of Pennsylvania Press.

Harman, William. 1987. Reflections on what ritual does. *Key Reporter* 52(3):1–3.

Helsing, Knud, Moyses Szklo, and George Comstock. 1981. Factors associated with mortality after widowhood. *American Journal of Public Health* 71(8):802–809.

Huntington, Richard, and Peter Metcalf. 1979. *Celebrations of death: The anthropology of mortuary ritual*. Cambridge, England: Cambridge University Press.

Kleck, R., H. Ono, and A. H. Hastorf. 1966. The effects of physical deviance upon face-to-face interaction. *Human Relations* 19:425–436.

Kunz, P. R., and J. Summers. 1979–1980. A time to die: A study of the relationships of birthdays and time of death. *Omega* 10(4):281–289.

Lieber, Arnold, and Carolyn Sherin. 1972. Homicides and the lunar cycle: Toward a theory of lunar influence on human emotional disturbance. *American Journal of Psychiatry* 129:69–74.

Lindesmith, Alfred, Anselm Strauss, and Norman Denzin. 1977. *Social psychology* (5th ed.). Fort Worth, TX: Holt, Rinehart and Winston.

Lofland, Lynn. 1973. *A world of strangers: Order and action in urban public space*. Prospect Heights, IL: Waveland Press.

Lumsden, Charles J., and Edward O. Wilson. 1985. The relation between biological and cultural evolution. *Journal of Social Biological Structures* 8:343–359.

McClelland, David C. 1987. *Human motivation*. Cambridge: Cambridge University Press.

McGoldrick, Monica, and Randy Gerson. 1985. *Genograms in family assessment*. New York: Norton.

McHugh, Peter. 1968. *Defining the situation: The organization of meaning in social interaction*. New York: Bobbs-Merrill.

Malinowski, B. 1922. *Argonauts of the western Pacific*. New York: Dutton.

Meer, Jeff. 1985, September. The light touch. *Psychology Today*, pp. 60–67.

Meerloo, J. A. M. 1970. *Along the fourth dimension*. New York: John Day.

Moore, Sally, and Barbara Myerhoff (eds.). 1977. *Secular ritual*. Assen and Amsterdam, The Netherlands: Van Gorcum.

Muecher, Hans, and Hans Ungeheur. 1961. Meteorological influence on reaction time, flicker fusion frequency, job accidents, and use of medical treatment. *Perceptual and Motor Skills* 12:163–168.

Newman, Oscar. 1973. *Defensible space*. New York: Collier.

Peabody, Dean. 1985. *National characteristics*. Cambridge, England: Cambridge University Press.

Phillips, David. 1972. Death and birthday: An unexpected connection. In J. Tanur (ed.), *Statistics: Guide to the unknown*. San Francisco: Holden-Day.

Phillips, David, and K. Feldman. 1973. A dip in deaths before ceremonial occasions: Some new relationships between social integration and mortality. *American Sociological Review* 38:678–696.

Preti, G., W. B. Cutler, C. R. Garcia, G. R. Huggins, and H. J. Lawley. 1986. Human axillary secretions influence women's menstrual cycles: The role of donor extract of females. *Hormones and Behavior* 20(4):474–482.

Rabkin, Simon W., Francis Mathewson, and Robert Tate. 1980. Chronobiology of cardiac sudden death in men. *Journal of the American Medical Association* 244:1357–1358.

Reinisch, June. 1977. Prenatal exposure of human fetuses to synthetic progestin and estrogen affects personality. *Nature* 266(5602):561–562.

Rheingold, Howard. 1988. *They have a word for it: A lighthearted lexicon on untranslatable words and phrases*. Los Angeles: Jeremy P. Tarcher.

Riesman, David. 1950. *The lonely crowd: A study of the changing American character*. New Haven, CT: Yale University Press.

Rifkin, Jeremy. 1987. *Time wars: The primary conflict in human history*. New York: Henry Holt.

Riley, John. 1983. Dying and the meanings of death: Social inquiries. *Annual Review of Sociology* 9:191–216.

*San Antonio Express-News* [Cox News Service]. 1990, July 12. Females are segregated in Mexico subway. p. 6A.

Schmeck, Harold, Jr. 1987, March 31. Burst of discoveries reveals genetic basis for many diseases. *New York Times*, pp. 17–18.

Seyfarth, R. 1984. What the vocalization of monkeys means to humans and what they mean to the monkeys themselves. In R. Harré and V. Reynolds (eds.), *The meaning of primate signals*. Cambridge, England: Cambridge University Press.

Smith, Adam. 1776. *An inquiry into the nature and causes of the wealth of nations*, vol. 1. New Rochelle, NY: Arlington House (Classics of Conservatism).

Sommer, Robert. 1969. *Personal space: The behavioral basis of design*. Englewood Cliffs, NJ: Prentice-Hall.

Stone, Lawrence. 1985, July 8. Sex in the West: The strange history of human sexuality. *New Republic*, pp. 25–37.

Suarez, Manuel. 1985, February 8. Inquiry on early cases of sexual development. *New York Times*, p. 7.

Tellegen, Auke, David T. Lykken, Thomas J. Bouchard, Jr., Kimberly J. Wilcox, Nancy Segal, and Stephen Rich. 1988. Personality similarity in twins reared apart and together. *Journal of Personality and Social Psychology* 54(6):1031–1039.

Turner, Victor. 1982. *From ritual to theatre: The human seriousness of play*. New York: Performing Arts Journal Publications.

Ullman, Albert (ed.). 1965. *Sociocultural foundations of personality*. Boston: Houghton Mifflin.

*U.S. News & World Report*. 1987, August 10. Only your surgeon knows. p. 62.

van Gennep, Arnold. 1904[1960]. *The rites of passage* (trans. M. Vizedom and G. Caffee). Chicago: University of Chicago Press.

Visser, Margaret. 1988. *Much depends on dinner*. New York: Grove Press.

Wessel, David. 1987, May 22. Hair as history: Advantages seen in new methods for drug testing. *Wall Street Journal*, p. 17.

Wheeler, David L. 1989, February 1. Psychologist's view on race differences stirs controversy at meeting. *Chronicle of Higher Education*, p. A6.

Whorf, Benjamin. 1956. *Language, thought and reality*. Cambridge, MA: Technology Press of Massachusetts Institute of Technology.

Wilson, D. M., C. D. Hammer, P. M. Duncan, S. M. Dornbusch, P. L. Ritter, R. L. Hintz, R. T. Gross, and R. G. Rosenfeld. 1986. Growth and intellectual development. *Pediatrics* 78:646–650.

# 3

# Social Templates for Personal Motivations

♦ *The worst sin toward our fellow creatures is not to hate them, but to be indifferent to them; that's the essence of inhumanity.* *

In *The Wealth of Nations*, Adam Smith postulated how the unrestrained actions of selfishly motivated individuals can, because of the operation of an "invisible hand," collectively contribute to the well-being of society:

> Give me that which I want, and you shall have this which you want, is the meaning of every such offer; and it is in this manner that we obtain from one another the far greater part of those good offices which we stand in need of. It is not from the benevolence of the butcher, the brewer, or the baker, that we expect our dinner, but from their regard to their own interest. (1776:13)

In this chapter we will consider some of the dynamic interrelations between our needs as individuals and the needs of the social systems of which we are a part.

On the individual level, various needs are assumed to underlie personal drives and, hence, behaviors. A child's unsatisfied need for adult attention, for instance, may lead to deviant classroom behavior if his or her academic activities are not rewarded. Social systems have various "needs" as well. If we compare societies to complex organisms struggling to survive in potentially hostile environments (with each individual a single cell, linked with other cells to form the social whole), we can conceptualize a different order of needs—a realm of necessities quite apart from that of any individual.

The question of how personal needs come to be synchronized with those of a collectivity brings us to the problems of social motivation and social control, how personal impulses become transformed into such socially useful goals as heroism on the battlefield or loyalty in the workplace. Ideally, personal needs are "in sync" with the needs of the social system. Society's need for the procre-

---

*George Bernard Shaw

ation and socialization of new members, for instance, matches parents' need to care for and love their offspring. However, when these personal needs are not satisfied within a social system, the resulting frustration can lead to conflict, deviance, social withdrawal, or social change.

## NEEDS OF THE INDIVIDUAL

What drives underlie our behaviors? Are they animalistic impulses built into our biological being, like the urge to mate, or are they more social in origin, like the satisfaction of being praised? Is the basic human goal, as Adam Smith and generations of economists who followed him believed, no more than the desire to satisfy one's material wants? Are "higher-order," less self-serving drives, such as the desire to be a "good Christian" or a "patriotic citizen," actually disguised expressions of "lower-order" biological urges (e.g., to do well in school in order to get a good job in order to make lots of money in order to attract a desirable female in order to procreate)?

Studying the experiences of Polish peasants at the beginning of the century, W. I. Thomas and Florian Znaniecki postulated the existence of primary drives, which they referred to as "the four wishes." All human beings, they believed, were motivated by the desire for personal responses from others, for recognition, for new experiences, and for security (1927:73). As the century progressed and the social and biological sciences developed increasingly refined insights into the human condition, this list of primary needs was expanded and elaborated. New questions emerged. For example, what needs accounted for the desire of the Germans, Poles, Austrians, French, and, most recently, American skinheads to victimize the Jewish people? Were the individual needs of these various nationalities the same? Is there some need deprivation that accounts for such social pathology?

Toward the middle of the twentieth century, psychologist A. H. Maslow developed a frequently cited model of needs in which the basic goals of humans are related to each other and are arranged in a hierarchy. The hierarchy of needs begins with the physiological (food, shelter, sex), then moves to safety (security, health), love (affection, belonging, identification), esteem (self-respect, prestige, social approval), and, ultimately, the need for self-actualization. Maslow assumed that biologically linked "lower-level" needs dominate until they have been satisfied; only then do the more social "higher-level" needs become activated. The order in which these need states appear is progressive: When a given need is fairly well satisfied, the next "higher," less animalistic need emerges to dominate conscious life (1943:394).

Evidence for such a hierarchy of needs is mixed, however, and virtually nonexistent for the higher-order needs. In their study of managers, for instance, Hall and Nougaim (1968) found that higher-order needs are related to age and role rather than to the degree to which lower-order needs have been satisfied. Herskovits provides evidence that such "higher needs" as the desire for social status and prestige can displace unsatisfied "lower" needs. When studying the competitive yam-growing ethos of the Ponapean in Micronesia, Herskovits observed how "families of a man aspiring to great prestige may go hungry" (1960:462). Reflecting on such disconfirmations of Maslow's model,

Campbell notes that "this hierarchy of needs perspective . . . has strong over-tones of an evolutionary ethnocentrism, suggesting, as it appears to, that only in modern society do the 'highest' needs find proper expression" (1987: 237fn35).

Although the particulars of Maslow's model are in question, its logic is compelling, and not all researchers have abandoned a needs-based model of human motivation. Some psychologists, for instance, have focused on the needs of particular types of individuals within particular types of social set-tings. This has led to the insight that each need state has its own underlying tension. Corresponding with the need for the company of others, for instance, is the need for solitude. Where people fall on this continuum varies according to their personality and their social milieu.

More sociologically oriented scholars have focused on social motivation: how individual drives are changed from individual-level to social-level concerns. The tensions revealed by this approach is between the needs of individuals and the needs of social systems. The recognition that personal needs change with maturation and experience and that social needs change with cultural evolu-tion led to the insight that there are distinctive historical tensions between these need systems (Chapter 8).

## The Needs for Security and Challenge

The role of Maslow's physiological need states in determining the course of human action certainly cannot be questioned. Some theorists, like Karl Marx and Friedrich Engels (1846), accord primary status to the materialistic drives of humans. From their perspective, human behavior is motivated by nothing more than hedonistic pleasure seeking and the avoidance of pain. Underlying these motives is the sense of security from life-threatening situations.

***The Need for Security.*** Late in 1984 Bernhard Goetz was accosted in a sub-way by four black youths who threateningly asked him for five dollars. Goetz pulled out a revolver and fired, wounding all four. Bending over one slumped youth, he reportedly remarked that the injury was insufficient and then fired another shot, possibly crippling the youth for life. Goetz's defense was that he was acting out of absolute fear (Magnuson 1985).

The ultimate pain-avoidance motivation is the need for safety from life-threatening situations. Perhaps the central accomplishment of modern socie-ties has been to control untimely death. No longer are most premature deaths caused by the forces of nature (e.g., earthquakes, epidemics, starvation due to drought, or attacks by large predatory animals). Instead, most deaths of the nonelderly are caused by avoidable accidents, homicides, and suicides. In large part, modernization means that people can assume that the world is a safe place for those who follow the rules and that death can generally be avoided until old age.

Not surprisingly, when this need for security is not met, the psychological consequences are profound. When major catastrophes—earthquakes, airplane crashes, war—occur, the assumption of security dissolves. For victims and witnesses alike, basic trust and even the sense of self-worth are damaged.

The young are affected especially strongly by such catastrophic events. In a study of forty Cambodian teenagers who survived the Khmer Rouge death

To what extent does human civilization depend on the ability to satisfy the basic needs for survival? Here, an Iraqi Kurd refugee embraces his family's share of bread from a relief operation following the 1991 Persian Gulf war.

camps of the late 1970s, Kinzie and his associates (1984, 1986) found a host of psychological problems, including recurrent nightmares, inability to concentrate, depression, self-pity, and a pessimistic outlook on life. Two-thirds suffered from "survivor's guilt," deep remorse for having lived when other family members died.

The sociological consequences of such violations are equally destructive. When basic needs are not met, humans are often reduced to basic survival impulses. First to be destroyed is trust (Giddens 1984). When trust evaporates, an individual's commitment to collective needs is weakened, as one is no longer sure that others share this sense of duty. Without trust, there can be no sense of fairness, no faith that one will be treated by others as one treats them. Thus, in Chad, an inhospitable land where life was marginal to begin with, the drought of the 1980s unraveled the social fabric that had enabled civility to persist. In families, the men ate first, the women second, and then the children.

Parents let their sick children die so that there would be more for the survivors to eat (Kamm 1985).

A similar explanation can be given for why terrorism "works." When, for instance, a terrorist sprays bullets into a shopping mall, there is a sense of social violation and powerlessness. No longer is one's world benign; no longer is one willing to take risks. With the existence of such doubts comes lack of trust in "the system" and in other people. This can lead to increased demands on the political system to eradicate such threats, leading to a decrease in civil liberties.

**The Need for Challenge and Surprise.** On the other hand, humans also need surprise and challenge. If things were totally predictable, life would be extremely boring. It is the sense of mystery and wonder that triggers curiosity, which is one of humanity's greatest assets. The absence of challenge would be equally stultifying. The $210 billion legally wagered by some 110 million Americans in 1988 on gambling is evidence of the high degree of stimulation obtained by risking financial security to bet on chance events. See Figure 3.1 for lottery sales in 1987. In the extreme, wagering takes over the lives of compulsive gamblers.

Also invigorating are threats to life itself. Journalist Andy Rooney noted that people normally live at 50 percent whereas in times of war they live at 100 percent (ABC News 1987). The threat of death forces individuals to turn off their normal "autopilot controls" and become fully engaged in and aware of the details of life. Some individuals, in fact, must flirt with the possibility of death— by parachuting, hang-gliding, skiing at the limits of their ability, or climbing mountains—in order to "feel alive."

# The Need for Others

The second realm of needs that motivate behavior includes the desire for the company and attention of others and the fear of rejection (McClelland 1987). People's struggles to "connect" with others is a central theme of their life stories. Isolation and loneliness run contrary to human nature, which is perhaps why solitary confinement is considered one or the most severe forms of punishment.

Recent research indicates that the need for social contact is related to the biological needs described earlier. Studies of infants who have been deprived of physical contact reveal that mere touch releases brain chemicals that enhance the probability of survival. In a study of premature infants, those who were massaged for fifteen minutes three times a day gained weight 47 percent faster than those who were left alone in their incubators; on the average, massaged babies were released six days earlier than nonmassaged babies (Field 1986; Scafidi et al. 1986). The nervous systems of the massaged infants matured more rapidly, as could be seen in their greater activity and responsiveness to such things as a face or a rattle.

Loneliness is an acute problem for the elderly. In the United States, 41 percent of women over age 65 and 51 percent of those over 75 live alone (Ricklefs 1988). The consequences can be lethal. In a ten-year study of 37,000 Swedes, Finns, and Americans, House et al. (1988) found that isolated healthy people are twice as likely to die as people who have frequent contacts with friends and

In 1987, over $11 billion in income was made from ticket sales in the twenty-two states with lotteries. Per capita income from lottery ticket sales ranged from $183.78 in Massachusetts to $30.73 in Iowa. What social factors account for the sixfold difference in spending on lottery tickets from one state to another?

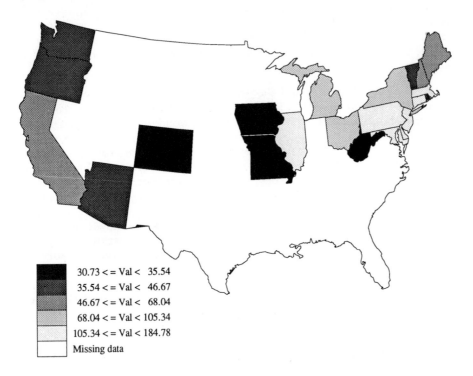

30.73 < = Val <  35.54
35.54 < = Val <  46.67
46.67 < = Val <  68.04
68.04 < = Val < 105.34
105.34 < = Val < 184.78
Missing data

Perhaps people spend more in less challenging environments. Indeed, per capital lottery income increases under the following conditions:

A decreasing proportion of the labor force is engaged in agriculture ($r = -.53$).
An increasing percentage of the state's population lives in urban areas ($r = .43$).
The state has a low rate of accidental death ($r = -.60$).
The state has a high median income ($r = .64$).
The state has a low suicide rate ($r = -.66$).

**FIGURE 3.1   Per Capita Expenditures for State-Administered Lotteries, 1987**

family. In fact, the ability of solitude to cause illness was found to exceed that of smoking: Although smoking increases the likelihood of all kinds of sickness by 1.6 times, social isolation doubles the probability.

***The Need to Belong.***   Americans are said to be of a nation of joiners; this is evidenced by their creation of and attraction to religious cults, weight-watchers' clubs, service organizations, communes, hobby groups, and many other types of groups and organizations.

The need to belong is a powerful drive, especially true in highly stratified societies. Members of many ethnic and racial minorities in the United States, for instance, feel like outsiders. They sense the presence of the social mainstream, but they feel that they are excluded from it. For Arturo Madrid, a noted Hispanic-American educator, such feelings kindled a lifelong drive to excel:

> We were the other. That was most acute for me in two places. One was school, where we had a sense of what that larger reality was, and the other one was church, because there were two kinds of churches, the American church and the Spanish church. . . . Two things happen. One is that you start putting up your defenses very quickly against being made to feel that you're not good enough, that you're different, that you're not part of that larger world. The second thing is, you start working very hard to incorporate yourself into that larger reality, to present yourself as well as you can, and in those areas where you're made to feel that you're not good enough, you make sure that you're not only good enough but even better. (Moyers 1989:213)

On the other hand, counterbalancing the need to belong are the needs for solitude and privacy. Joining groups is often a social production: One joins not because one wants to but because one has to in order to accomplish central goals, or feels compelled to in order to be socially accepted. In fact, privacy needs may be greater than ever in this era of urban life, continuous intrusions of telephones and beepers, and forced socializing.

***The Avoidance Motive.*** Perhaps equally potent is our need for others who represent the antithesis of ourselves. As we will see in Chapter 12, we define who we are partly in terms of who we are not. During the cold war, for instance, the American identity was understood partly in terms of not being communist. Other examples of the **avoidance motive** include the efforts of upper-class individuals to maintain physical and symbolic distance from members of the lower classes (see Chapter 10); the taboos prohibiting contact between Brahmins and Untouchables in India; the long history of American whites opposing racial integration; and the hostilities between Arabs and Israelis in the Middle East. In *The Need to Have Enemies and Allies* (1988), Vamik Volkan argues that the need for enemies is as normal as the need for love.

The avoidance motive also underlies the fear of failure, which for many individuals is greater than the desire to succeed. The fourth-grader who spends an inordinate amount of time on homework may be driven not so much by the need to master the subject matter but as by the fear of being "dropped" back into the nonspecial classes of "average" students.

## The Needs for Cognitive and Social Order

Humans are order-craving creatures. They are attracted to ordering principles the way fish are lured to light. The earliest known civilizations gave order to the random distribution of stars in the sky by creating the constellations. Perhaps part of the eternal appeal of storytelling is the way stories can give order to chaos, providing coherent beginnings and endings (Kakutani 1989).

Patterns are even inferred where none exist in fact. For instance, although clusters of events can occur randomly—such as a coincidence of airplane crashes, a few consecutive hot summers, or a string of bad luck—people believe that there is a pattern and look for explanations. And when four-year-olds throw tantrums if the foods on their plates are mixed, the same drive for order is at work.

The human need for order perhaps explains the fact that conceptualizations of randomness and disorder—such as quantum mechanics, relativity theory, and the science of chaos—were not developed until the modern era (see Gleick 1987). Order provides the possibility for knowing things with certainty, and the quest for certainty underlies philosophy and the numerous sciences. It has often been said that the last decades of Einstein's life were relatively unproductive as he refused to believe in the uncertainty principle of quantum physics (Lightman 1983), claiming that "God does not play dice."

The same need also explains the desire for social order. Only an ordered world is a predictable one, and the essence of society is the predictability of its members' actions. In a surprise-free world people feel a certain invulnerability, a sense that things are controllable or at least predictable.

During the twentieth century, fears of social disorder and radicalism have led to fascism and political witchhunts. For Italy and Germany, the end of World War I brought economic depression, strikes, and political chaos. Under these conditions Mussolini and Hitler were able to rise to power by promising to restore order and stability. Following World War II, anti-Communist hysteria broke out in the United States. Capitalizing on these fears, Senator Joseph McCarthy embarked on a political witchhunt that almost caused the suspension of the freedom of speech as suspected communists were hunted down and blacklisted.

**The Need for Self-Regulation.**  Not only do people need a sense of order in their social environment, they need a sense of order in themselves as well. As Chapter 7 will show, the very concept of identity entails various continuities in action and thought. For instance, to have a self includes having a sense of personal order through time, the ability to perceive one's autobiography as a continuously unfolding story. Moreover, both psychoanalytic and interactionist theorists assume that individuals are motivated to obtain an inner sense of consistency, a coherence in their attitudes toward themselves (see Turner 1988:43).

In addition to striving for a sense of personal coherence, people are motivated to appear as a consistent self to others. To be otherwise is to be either totally unpredictable or a sort of social chameleon who continually changes in order to blend into different social situations, and routinely acting in ways that are inconsistent with one's assumed core self may take a psychological toll in the form of diminished self-esteem (Turner 1988:44).

**The Need for Meaning and Purpose.**  Humans rely on symbols and labels to find purpose, value, and self-worth. They need an underlying sense of meaning in their lives in order to have a sense of trust. Humans cannot live long with doubt. And one function of society is to minimize doubt. The life-giving power of social purpose is demonstrated in Table 3.1.

As mentioned earlier, perhaps in no instance is this need greater than in matters of death. When a volcano erupts and covers a town with suffocating mud and ash, or when a nuclear weapon is detonated, all meaningfulness dissolves. Studies of survivors of the bombing of Hiroshima revealed that for them the world itself had died (Lifton 1967). One survivor of the Nazis' Buchenwald concentration camp, psychoanalyst Bruno Bettelheim, described how by stripping people of their identities one could also dissolve their core values and meanings (1943, 1960).

**TABLE 3.1  The Life-Giving Power of Social Purpose**

*Part of having a social purpose is having social responsibilities. Albert Bhak (1975) studied the monthly mortality rates for elderly men and women in small South Korean villages. The following data show the patterns of deaths, activity demands, climate, and food supply over one calendar year.*

| Month | Deaths (Percentage of Annual Total) by Month | | | Activity Demands | | | |
|-------|------|--------|-----|----------|----------|----------|-------------|
| | Male | Female | N | Male | Female | Climate | Food Supply |
| January | 8% | 7% | 7% | heavy | heavy | harshest | plentiful |
| February | 10 | 9 | 9 | nil | moderate | harsh | adequate |
| March | 7 | 14 | 10 | nil | nil | mild | low |
| April | 9 | 16 | 12 | slight | nil | great! | lowest |
| May | 9 | 11 | 10 | moderate | slight | mild | lowest |
| June | 5 | 5 | 5 | heavy | prime | unpleasant | dwindling |
| July | 6 | 6 | 6 | prime | prime | harsh | adequate |
| August | 10 | 7 | 8 | slight | slight | harshest | low |
| September | 5 | 5 | 5 | heavy | heavy | mild | dwindling |
| October | 6 | 5 | 6 | prime | heavy | great! | adequate |
| November | 9 | 9 | 9 | slight | slight | unpleasant | plentiful |
| December | 15 | 7 | 11 | nil | heavy | harsh | plentiful |
| Total (N) | 328 | 291 | 619 | | | | |

*It's obvious that monthly mortality rates are not equal. On average, we would expect by chance 27 male deaths (328/12) and 24 female deaths. Yet in December 78 percent more males die than would be expected, and in April nearly twice as many older women die than would be expected. It is also clear that there are profound gender differences in monthly death rates. In December, whereas elderly male death rates are three-quarters higher than would be expected by chance, female rates are almost 20 percent lower.*

**TABLE 3.1 Continued**

*To understand these variations, three hypotheses were tested: the availability of food, the climate, and activity demands for older men and women. Below are the correlations (Pearson's r):*

|  | Correlates of Monthly Death Rates of Older Men and Women | |
|---|---|---|
| *Variable* | *Males* | *Females* |
| Activity demands | −.71 | −.86 |
| Climate | −.39 | .43 |
| Food supply | .21 | −.57 |

*We see that activity demands are the strongest predictor of monthly mortality rates: The greater the demands, the lower the death rate. As the weather becomes increasingly harsh, old males are more likely to die and females less likely to die, perhaps indicating that the males work outside and females inside. As food supplies diminish, older females are more likely to die and males less likely; it seems that older males are the first to be fed.*

When people believe in a cause, the aforementioned relationship between material deprivation and social disorder may be counteracted. During the 880-day siege of Leningrad which coincided with one of the harshest winters ever recorded, the city's residents ate cats, dogs, rats, mice, sparrows, scraps of leather, gun grease, machine oil, and even wallpaper paste scraped from walls. But the social order survived. Ten miles from the front lines, a munitions plant continued to produce arms even though the workers, weakened by hunger, often died at their machines.

Having a cause also helps people survive when they have been separated from society. Some Japanese soldiers hid in the jungles of South Pacific islands for nearly thirty years after the end of World War II. Sixteen Yahi Indians, survivors of an 1870 massacre by white settlers, hid in a remote California canyon for forty-one years. A keen sense of purpose maintained the morale of both the soldiers and the Indians (Budiansky 1987).

**The Need for Disorder.** Aldous Huxley has observed that "too much consistency is as bad for the mind as for the body. Consistency is contrary to nature, contrary to life. The only completely consistent people are the dead" (1959:7). We need spontaneity and surprise as well as order (which may help explain our continuing fascination with the Loch Ness monster, UFOs, and the abominable snowman). In *Man's Rage for Chaos: Biology, Behavior and the Arts*, Peckham (1965) argues that a primary function of art is the dissolution of order and the introduction of chaos. And the desire of some people to experience altered states of consciousness may be an attempt to counterbalance excesses of order. There is only one known society that has not utilized some form of psychoactive substances. (The Eskimos had none until whites brought alcohol, but they still sought the feeling through rolling down snow hills, spinning around, and hyperventilating.)

In the extreme, however, lack of order and purpose can lead to **anomie,** a sense of normlessness, purposelessness, and isolation from (and apathy toward) the mainstream of social life. (See Table 3.2.) Anomie involves lack of regulation, failure to control individual aspirations, and the absence of social mechanisms for coordinating personal and social needs (Durkheim 1933 [1893]). This condition—the feeling that there is little rhyme or reason to life—is most likely to be found in areas of the social system in which individuals see little correspondence between following the rules and obtaining personal rewards. Often the outcome is deviant behavior. When, for instance, urban ghetto youth find that they can earn thousands of dollars a week in the drug trade, as opposed to going to school and working for the minimum wage in some socially approved enterprise, the temptation is often too great to resist.

## Symbolic Needs of the Self

One function of society is to produce identities and provide the bases for self-esteem. As Ernest Becker noted, the "function of culture is to make continued self-esteem possible, . . . to provide the individual with the conviction that he [or she] is an object of primary value in a world of meaningful action" (1962:81). This drive for self-worth and personal significance is arguably the primary social motive, so much so that the state of California created a Task Force to Promote Self Esteem and Personal and Social Responsibility and hundreds of American school districts have added self-esteem components to their curricula (Williams 1990). Without honor and respect, people will pine away and die not only from physical privation but from shame, humiliation, and loneliness (Harré 1980).

One foundation of self-esteem is the childhood sense of being wanted. If children feel that they are not valued by the larger society because of their race, ethnicity, gender, or social class, they may accept society's definition of them as lesser persons. Sometimes an individual refuses to accept such a definition. How often have we heard respected business people account for their success by saying "I was going to show all of the kids who were picking on me, who were making fun of me, that I was somebody, a 'big person,' a someone rich and famous!"

Another necessary condition for self-esteem is the attention of others. Not only must one receive attention from others, but there is a need for consistency in their responses. Only out of such regularity in behavior can meaning be deduced (Burton 1979).

Certainly one attention-getting strategy is to be unique in some way. But this is counterbalanced by the desire to be similar and to "fit in" with one's group. Ernest Becker (1973) views this as an essential dualism of human beings: We want to be part of something, such as winning teams, and yet to stand out, to be the star. The tension between conformity and uniqueness is a theme that will recur throughout this book.

The unequal ways in which attention is socially exchanged and controlled further evidence its value. As we will see in later chapters, attention is socially stratified, with higher-status people receiving attention and lower-status people giving it. Further, the very threat of being ignored, of having this precious commodity withdrawn, is a mechanism of social control. In South Africa, dis-

**Table 3.2    The Social and Personal Implications of Anomie**

*The concept of anomie includes the belief that others cannot be counted on for social and psychological support (Roberts and Rokeach 1956). To grasp some of the implications of this facet of anomie, consider responses to the following question:*

**Do think most people would try to take advantage of you
if they got a chance, or would they try to be fair?**

*Let us correlate responses to this question with responses to the following:*

*It's hardly fair to bring a child into the world with the way things look for
the future.*
*Are you a member of a service club?*
*How often do you attend religious services?*
*Do you think it will be best for the future of this country if we take an active
part in world affairs, or if we stay out of world affairs?*
*Do you smoke?*

*At issue is the significance of holding a basic sense of social trust in determining individuals' involvements with socially necessary activities (e.g., raising children and participating in service organizations), attitudes toward America's involvements in the emerging world system, and care for personal well-being (smoking).*

*From a 1988 survey of the American adult public (the General Social Science Survey of the National Opinion Research Center), we can see that those who view most other people as trying to take advantage of them are most likely to believe that it is hardly fair to bring a child into the world, less likely to belong to a community service group, less likely to attend church one or more times a week, less likely to believe that the United States should take an active role in world affairs, and most likely to smoke.*

**Implications of Feeling That Others Try to Take Advantage versus Try to Be Fair**

| Most People Try to | Percent Saying Hardly Fair | Percent Members of Service Clubs | Percent Attending At Least Once a Week | Percent Saying Take Active Role in World | Percent Who Smoke |
|---|---|---|---|---|---|
| Take advantage | 55 | 6 | 21 | 57 | 42 |
| Depends | 42 | 6 | 23 | 73 | 27 |
| Try to be fair | 37 | 15 | 29 | 74 | 31 |

sidents are silenced not only by incarceration but also by "banning." A banned individual cannot meet with more than one person at a time (except family members) and cannot publish anything or be quoted, even after death (Darton 1977).

The foundations for self-esteem are laid down in the family:

> Through love, stability, discipline, and laughter of parents and siblings, children learn that reality accepts them, welcomes them, invites their willingness to take risks. The family nourishes "basic trust." From this spring creativity, psychic

energy, social dynamism. If infants are injured here, not all the institutions of society can put them back together. (Novak 1976)

When the family fails in this task, several generations may be harmed. For instance, approximately one-third of people who were abused in childhood become child abusers in adulthood (Goleman 1989a). However, the best predictor of whether a person will become an abuser is not whether he or he was abused in childhood but whether he or she felt unloved and unwanted as a child (Altemeier et al. 1986).

If, on the other hand, basic trust and a sense of self-worth are instilled in a child, the individual's chances of entering into intimate relations with others as an adult are increased. In adulthood, McAdams and Bryant (1987) found such intimacies produce a sense of confidence and resilience for men—the emotional foundation many need before tackling the challenges of the broader society.

Again, however, there can be too much of a good thing—too much attention and too much esteem, as many Hollywood celebrities and political figures have found when their private lives became public news. In addition, according to psychoanalyst Judd Marmor:

> There is a terrific seduction of the spirit that takes place when you are surrounded by admiring throngs, when the red carpet is laid out for you. Unless you are aware of the blinding effect the adulation can have, your judgment can be impaired so that you begin to feel that you are immune to normal limits and penalties. (Cited in Goleman 1987:20)

Thus, underlying the downfalls of presidential candidate Gary Hart, television evangelist Jim Bakker, and Washington mayor Marion S. Barry, Jr., in the 1980s were narcissism (see Chapter 7) and the belief that the rules did not apply to them.

## Power Needs

In an intriguing experiment, Lefcourt (1976:3–6) gave two groups of adult subjects complex puzzles to solve and a proofreading chore to carry out. To make the task more challenging, there was a loud, randomly occurring distracting noise that included "a combination of two people speaking Spanish, one speaking Armenian, a mimeograph machine running, a desk calculator, a typewriter, and street noise—producing a composite, nondistinguishable roar." One group was simply told to work at the task, but members of the other group were given a button that they could push to turn off the noise. Although the button was never pushed, the second group solved five times the number of puzzles as the group without the button, and made far fewer proofreading errors.

As these results indicate, self-confidence and self-efficacy are related to people's beliefs about their ability to control or cope with specific situations. The need for control is also related to self-directedness, or the extent to which people feel that they are able to make decisions regarding their choice of activities and the manner in which they carry them out. Albert Bandura (1977)

## Table 3.3   Taking Responsibility for Oneself

*Soviet citizens were asked whether the state should be mainly responsible for people's success and well-being or whether people should look out for themselves and decide for themselves what to do to achieve success in life. Shown here, broken down by republic and by age, are the percentages of respondents saying that the state or individuals should be responsible for personal fates. As is evident, personal accountability is less acceptable in the Georgian republic than in the Baltic and Central Asian republics, and more acceptable among younger than among older respondents.*

|  | State Responsible | Individuals Responsible | No Answer | Total Percentage |
|---|---|---|---|---|
| Total | 46 | 45 | 9 | 100 |
| Russians | 46 | 45 | 9 | 100 |
| Balts | 39 | 52 | 9 | 100 |
| Georgians | 75 | 23 | 1 | 100 |
| Central Asians | 38 | 57 | 6 | 100 |
| Under 25 | 41 | 50 | 9 | 100 |
| 25–29 | 46 | 49 | 5 | 100 |
| 30–59 | 47 | 43 | 10 | 100 |
| 60 and older | 50 | 41 | 9 | 100 |

Source: Based on an Emory University survey of 2485 Soviet citizens interviewed in their homes in November and December 1989 by the National Center for Public Opinion Research in Moscow (cited in *New York Times* 1990).

argues that learning is a function not only of punishments and rewards but also of how people size up a situation and adjudge their own capacities.

From the experience of autonomy and control comes the sense of self-reliance and accomplishment; without it come hopelessness and fatalism. Thus, animals that are given unescapable random electric shocks develop "learned helplessness," becoming passive and ultimately even giving up (Seligman and Beagley 1975). In one experiment, rats were shocked under two conditions, one in which escape was possible and one in which it was not. Those that had no possibility of escape developed tumors. Feelings of helplessness are no less lethal for people. In their study of asthmatic children, Miller and Strunk (1989) found that the hopelessness spawned by abandonment, conflict-ridden families, and parental death or divorce increases the risk of a fatal asthma attack. Table 3.3 presents results of interviews of Soviet citizens on taking responsibility for oneself.

The issue of control is perhaps most evident among residents of institutional settings such as hospitals and nursing homes, who are often prevented from controlling their lives by well-meaning staff members (Rinaldi and Kearl 1990). The loss of control associated with lack of power to make decisions results in a loss of dignity (Krant 1974). When people living in convalescent homes are given a greater sense of control by being allowed to choose menus or decide how furniture should be rearranged, not only are they happier and more alert, but their mortality rate is dramatically reduced (Rodin 1986).

People with a high desire for control set more challenging goals for themselves and respond to challenging tasks with greater effort and persistence than those with less need for control (Burger 1985). When autonomy on the job is limited, and control opportunities thereby reduced or eliminated, workers are more likely to be dissatisfied (Deci and Ryan 1987) and to express their dissatisfaction through procrastination (Elizabeth Coote-Weymann, cited in Bennett 1988).

**Uncertainty and the Rabbit's Foot.**   In situations of uncertainty, humans often employ rituals or charms to compensate for their lack of control. For example, in his study of the Trobriand Islanders of the South Pacific, Bronislaw Malinowski observed that the natives employed magic when they ventured into the open sea to fish. Such magic was not used when the natives fished in a lagoon (where a poison was used, "yielding abundant results without danger and uncertainty"). Malinowski concluded that

> we find magic wherever the elements of chance and accident, and the emotional play between hope and fear have a wide and extensive range. We do not find magic wherever the pursuit is certain, reliable, and well under the control of rational methods and technological processes. Further, we find magic where the element of danger is conspicuous. (1926:81)

In a similar manner, college students and baseball players carry charms (e.g., a rabbit's foot) and conduct magic rituals (e.g., crossing themselves or closing their eyes in brief prayer) to influence events, boost their sense of control, and reduce anxiety when facing unpredictability and uncertainty. A shirt may become "lucky" if it was worn during a personal triumph; the ballpoint pen one used when making an unexpected A on a physics exam becomes a "secret weapon."

**The Needs to Dominate and to Be Dominated.**   In interpersonal relations the control need becomes a matter of dominance, with most individuals falling somewhere between the extremes of needing to dominate all others and needing to always be dominated. Where any given individual falls along this continuum is determined by a combination of innate predispositions and social learning (see Chapter 10). Males, for instance, are often taught that their social importance is a function of the amount of control they exercise over others and how much others depend on them. Those who desire influence for its own sake can be found where social power is concentrated, such as Washington, D.C., which attracts people with high power needs, including politicians, lawyers, and lobbyists (Goleman 1985).

On the other hand, there are individuals who need to be controlled by more powerful others; such individuals may willingly surrender their freedom of choice by joining radical cults or choose the role of slave in sado-masochistic relationships (Baumeister 1989). Lacking the environmental control they desire, these people seek relations with more powerful others who promise to compensate them for what they feel they lack.

Questioning the assumption that people want a maximum of freedom, political theorist Carl Friedrich argues that "it is much more nearly true to say that people want a minimum of freedom, rather than a maximum. Most people are very glad to leave a lot of things to other people" (1967:13). In Chapter 13 we will consider this issue in exploring why the masses have so often blindly followed dominant political leaders.

## Transcendent Needs

When social scientists speak of **transcendence,** they are referring to the ways in which people seek to escape from the various limitations imposed by their selves and their culture. These include attempts to transcend the physical nature of humanity—to be something more, whether spiritual, artistic, cultured, or simply self-controlled. They also include a hypothesized drive to transcend the limitations imposed by culture and to achieve **self-actualization.** Self-actualizing individuals are more autonomous and better able to resist the forces of enculturation and conformity, because they develop their own values and do not unthinkingly accept conventional goals merely because others do. For example, in decrying the state of education in America, Allan Bloom argues that "students have not the slightest notion of what an achievement it is to free oneself from public guidance and find resources for guidance within oneself" (1986:66).

Theorists have also argued that humans have a need to transcend themselves by identifying and merging with sacred forces (Becker 1973: 151–52). Those forces include the extraordinary, mysterious, and uncontrollable powers that are perceived to be acting against chaos and shaping the affairs of nature and humanity (Douglas 1966). Traditional Chinese folklore, for instance, views natural catastrophes as portending the end of dynasties, because they are understood to indicate the loss of heaven's mandate (Matthews 1976).

Finally, there is a need to somehow **transcend the inevitability of death** by leaving a mark on human society in the form of children, inventions, ideas, heroic deeds, or works of art (Becker 1973). When W. H. Auden accepted the National Medal for Literature in 1967, he remarked:

> To believe in the value of art is to believe that it is possible to make an object, be it an epic or a two-line epigram, which will remain permanently on hand in the world. . . . In the meantime, . . . we must try to live as E. M. Forster recommends that we should: "The people I respect must behave as if they were immortal and as if society were eternal. Both assumptions are false. But both must be accepted as true if we are to go on working and eating and loving, and are able to keep open a few breathing holes for the human spirit. (Cited in Laing 1967:49)

Unfortunately, the drive for immortality may also lie at the core of man's irrational nature and be the root of human evil (Becker 1975). Being a "loser" in life, John Hinkley sought immortality through infamy by trying to kill the President of the United States.

## From Needs to Desires

A number of cracks have appeared in the needs-based theories of human motivation, leading many social psychologists to doubt their utility (Wallach and Wallach 1983). First, as mentioned earlier, there are numerous disconfirmations of models in which biologically based needs must be satisfied before "higher-order" needs are experienced. A second difficulty involves the very conceptualization of a need, as often its existence is inferred from behavior. David McClelland asks, "Are needs to be thought of primarily in terms of the characteristic **mode of response** used to gratify them or in terms of the goal of behavior of any sort?" (1951:406). Might not differing combinations of drives have similar behavioral expressions? Conversely, could one need state be expressed through varying behavioral strategies? And are individuals conscious of their basic needs?

Third, there is a fundamental difference between seeking to satisfy needs and attempting to obtain pleasures. Theories of desires or wants are not equivalent to theories of needs. *Needs* are states of being, types of sensation. They arise out of states of deprivation and may be satiated; an example is the absence of hunger following a large meal. *Pleasure*, on the other hand, is not a state of being but, rather, a quality of experience, an agreeable reaction to sensory input (Campbell 1987: 60). *Desire* is the motivation to seek and experience pleasure. Unlike needs, desires are not satiable. "The difference is that need implies an object which satisfies the need, the object of the need being external to it; desire cannot be finally satisfied since desire is its own object" (Turner 1984:11).

The human capacity for pleasure may be infinite. When we consider people's motivations to collect beer cans or antique cars, to be the first on their block to own a pet rock or to be able to change the color of their eyes through irridology, we can begin to appreciate society's profound role in shaping and directing personal drives, many of which are unnecessary.

In affluent modern societies, in which most basic wants are absent, desires have replaced needs as the source of personal motivations. Accordingly, the "most inclusive statement that can be made about distinctive human nature," Newcombe writes, "is that humans have an enormous capacity for acquiring motives" (1950:144). When we consider the social availability of such motivations and how they have historically increased (George Washington did not have the opportunity to be a race car driver or a master of Nintendo), the social and historical relativity of personal drives is apparent.

## NEEDS OF SOCIAL SYSTEMS

Societies are human, not natural, constructions. As illustrated in *Lord of the Flies* (Golding 1959), various prerequisites must be met or the social fabric will be torn, perhaps beyond repair (Bell 1976). For instance, when Hurricane Gilbert slammed through the Caribbean in the fall of 1989, its physical devastation was matched in some areas by social devastation. On the island of St. Croix there was extensive looting. Civil authority broke down completely, and young men armed with rifles and machetes assaulted and burglarized tourists. Yet on other islands that were equally devastated, order prevailed.

Social systems emerge over time out of the regularized interactions of individuals. Each social system, be it a family, a bureaucracy, or a nation-state, comes to have a life of its own, governed by unique dynamics and having needs distinct from those of individuals. For instance, consider the spectrum of roles needed for contemporary American society to "work." People must be found and socialized to fill the positions of first sergeants, burn ward nurses, computer software writers, radio time salespeople, particle physicists, cattle inseminators, and janitors. Society does not emerge out of the collective role performances of individuals doing what their talents lead them to do; instead, the social structure determines what its role needs are. The social structure, for example, determines the need for more soldiers during times of war or fewer farmers as technology and economic forces reduce the numbers required to feed a nation. The irony is that even though society is a human product, individuals often experience it as being something external to themselves, an abstract force beyond their control that controls them.

We saw earlier that society is sometimes viewed as an organism, an organized system made up of parts that are stable and well integrated, each contributing to the welfare of the whole. Society has also been compared to a machine in which individuals are the cogs of various cogwheels, which themselves mesh and turn with other cogwheels; to a set of stages on which individual actors act out scripted roles; and to a series of ecological niches and territories within which individuals and groups compete to survive.

Talcott Parsons (1961) claimed that in order to survive, social systems must have mechanisms for social integration, adaptation, goal attainment, and management of latent problems. This entails such things as producing and socializing the next generation of social participants, reinforcing those who conform and punishing the deviants, and locating and nurturing the talented. When the social system is threatened by such "diseases" as selfishness, lack of cooperation, or chaos, it reacts violently to cast off the infection, often sacrificing individual rights for the good of the whole.

On closer inspection, these four mechanisms involve some very abstract and complex processes. The concept of social integration, for instance, involves the interrelationships among economic, political, religious, and artistic systems. At the social-psychological level, social integration also entails the ways in which social activities cognitively "hang together" and feel "natural" or "right" in the minds of individuals. Integration also requires a consensus regarding the common purposes and values toward which all members of society are oriented and around which all collective life is organized. Ideally, from society's perspective, such a consensus means that people are satisfied with their groups, voluntarily participate in civic activities, and respect the society's laws and norms.

If social systems are to meet their integrative needs, common values, interests, and goals must be instilled in the motivational structures of their members, or else coercion must be employed. People must orient their actions toward the welfare of others if a social system is to survive, and ideally (again, from society's perspective) such contributions to the common good stem from natural and automatic impulses. This was relatively easy in simpler societies, where individuals shared a common ancestry, religion, language, and occupation (see Chapter 8). In more complex societies, solidarity is derived from individuals' interdependencies with highly specialized others. Burton (1979) argues that this has led to a situation in which rules and norms have become more important than individual needs.

To attain their goals, societies create systems for rewarding "winners" and punishing "losers." The more challenges there are, the harder the society's members must work; the fewer life's challenges, the more likely individuals will slack off in their social duties. As Fehrenbach noted of the human condition, "If no disgrace is applied to failure, the glory of making it is dimmed" (1990:3-M).

Like personal needs, the needs of a society can be conceptualized as a set of tensions between extremes. There are, for instance, tensions between totalitarianism and anarchy, between deficiencies and excesses of freedom, and between forces directed toward the status quo and toward change.

In the past, civilizations have passed out of existence because they failed to develop cultural values that reflected human needs, or because they skewed values in favor of particular elites (Burton 1979:61). But some—such as many of the utopian communities that dotted the West during the mid-nineteenth century—have failed because of their members' failure to address basic social needs.

## MESHING PERSONAL AND SOCIAL NEEDS

In the city-states of classical Greece, each citizen was occupied in an "activity for which his or her soul [was] perfectly fitted," and the city integrated useful activities into a coherent whole. The bonds between individuals were based on their shared dedication to and understanding of "the good and the best as such" (MacIntyre 1988). In *Walden II* (1976), B. F. Skinner described a utopian community designed to maximize the collective good. There, and in the communes that Skinner's novel inspired, most property is held in common, what is earned or produced goes to the group, and cooperation rather than competition is valued (and reinforced).

Unfortunately, history is filled with instances in which social needs (at least as defined by a ruling elite) totally supersede personal needs. For instance, during the late 1920s and 1930s the Russian people made huge personal sacrifices under Stalin's massive modernization program. To guarantee a steady and predictable stream of food, Stalin imposed collectivization on the peasants. The grain they produced was exported in order to purchase the machinery needed by the new state. In the Republic of Georgia, people starved by the millions as requisition squads took all their food, even seed grain.

How can we best envision the interrelationships between the supposedly selfish needs of individuals and the collective needs of social systems? Are they the same as those between animals and nature (Ross 1901)? As we saw in the last chapter, there are serious limits to such an analogy. Talcott Parsons approached the issue with a different question:

> Will the personalities developed within a social system, at whatever stage in the life cycle, "spontaneously" act in such ways as to fulfill the functional prerequisites of the social systems of which they are parts, or is it necessary to look for relatively specific mechanisms, that is, modes of organization of the motivational systems of personalities, which can be understood in direct relation to the socially structured level or role behavior? (1961:31)

Parsons supported the latter approach, focusing on motivational systems as the way to understand how human desires come to coincide with social needs. It is society that transforms human needs into socially standardized goals and defines the means by which those goals may be obtained.

# Social Control

Common to all depictions of the social order is the inclusion of social control. As S. F. Nadel observed: "Social existence is controlled existence" (1953:265). Social control is what allows action to be regulated, patterned, and coordinated. Through its exercise, society suppresses or redirects the selfish and animalistic impulses of its members to obtain social cooperation and cohesion.

The issue of how social control should be exercised has shaped the course of history and continues to do so. For example, the tension between the two most powerful nations on earth is largely derived from philosophical differences dating back to the ancient Greeks and Romans. Democracy and communism are both experiments in devising an ideal social system. Erazim Kohák argues that communism grew out of the Byzantine ideal, which

> looked to true laws, codified by Emperor Justinian, and rigorous rule, embodied by a semidivine Emperor, to guard humans against their own nature. Not freedom, but obedience, the righteous rule of true faith, embodied its conception of authentic humanity. (1976:18)

Western states, on the other hand, "retained the ideal of a *res publica* of free equals [in which the state is] a guardian of liberties rather than a tutor of righteousness" (Kohák 1976:18).

The differences between these two views can be illustrated with reference to competitive sports. Sports are one way to keep a people disciplined, busy, and out of political mischief. In East Germany, sports were among the most important social institutions, serving that country's national identity by reducing its feeling of inferiority as "the other Germany" (Markham 1983). The state identified the athletically talented at the age of 4 or 5 and relocated them to sports camps where their talents could be polished. In the United States, on the other hand, athletes have to hustle for endorsements and financial support, since they are responsible for perfecting their own skills.

Social control thus can be conceptualized both as residing within social structure (e.g., in the form of systems of rewards and punishments, customs, and arenas for specified action) and as residing within the individual (e.g., in the form of guilt, loyalty, and minimization of risks). Society exists both "out there" and in our innermost being; the individual exists within society just as society exists within the individual.

## Models of Social Control from Within

Social systems depend on their members working for the common good. For humans, the conscious motivation to help others is the basic building block of altruism, social cooperation, and society itself.

In studying the internal motivations underlying helping action, psychologically oriented social psychologists have focused on *prosocial* behavior. Dennis Krebs (1970) defines three conditions for an act to be truly prosocial: The act must be performed *voluntarily*; the actor must *intend* to act for the benefit of another person or group; and the act must be performed as an *end in itself* and not as a means of fulfilling some ulterior motive. Thus, a 20-year-old male who stops his car to give a lift to an attractive 18-year-old female hitchhiker may not be engaging in a truly prosocial act.

Altruism is the purest form of prosocial behavior. The prototypical example of altruism is the unselfish and sacrificial behavior of parents toward their children. In addition, there are the Mother Teresas and Albert Schweitzers of the world, those rare individuals who have dedicated their lives to helping others. But what about those whose role is to be helpful, such as police, firefighters, social workers, and physicians? Their behavior is also defined as prosocial but is it altruistic? As Skinner (1971) noted, only when we do not understand why people do good deeds do we give them credit. Normally altruistic credit is not given to individuals whose prosocial behaviors are expected of them in their jobs.

Empathy for a person experiencing distress is a well-documented cause of purely altruistic behavior (Hoffman 1977). Even toddlers display sympathy and caring toward a friend who is crying. This ability to share another's emotions is a cornerstone of such socially valued states as compassion, friendship, and moral sensitivity. Its absence has been noted in criminal sociopaths, autistic individuals, and people suffering from chronic schizophrenia (Goleman 1989b). However, empathy is neither a necessary nor a sufficient cause of helping behavior. If empathy is not enough, what else is needed?

When considering Krebs' three conditions, doubt can be cast on whether any helping act is purely prosocial. First there is the issue of conscious intent. Sociobiologists view altruism not as a quality unique to humans but, rather, as a general genetic trait with evolutionary survival value. In all species evolution has favored the tendency to exchange benefits through prosocial acts. Konrad Lorenz and others have observed birds giving warning calls when a predator is sighted—a behavior that seems to serve the good of the species even though it may work to the detriment of the individual that sounds the alarm.

Psychoanalytic theories also shed doubt on the idea of altruistic intent and unselfishness underlying helping behavior. If one aids another person to alleviate superego-induced guilt, can we say that the prosocial act was performed as an end in itself? Research has found that people with high fear of embarrassment or sociopathic tendencies are less likely to help, whereas those with a high need for approval, a high degree of empathy, strong religious values, or confidence that the world is a just place (Lerner 1980) are more likely to help.

Social-exchange theorists have abandoned the notion of helping behavior as altruistic. Instead, they begin with the premise that each individual has needs and social resources with which to barter with others. Transactions between persons may be understood as economic relationships involving cost/reward ratios, with each person being motivated to maximize the returns on his or her investments. From this perspective, the altruistic motive derives from the desire for social rewards such as approval, increased self-esteem, and avoidance of self-blame and/or the criticisms of others.

A major norm governing social transactions is the **norm of reciprocity,** the idea that one should return in the same measure what one receives from others. This norm is implicit in moral codes, such as the Golden Rule (Gouldner 1960). It can also be seen in the fact that favors received often carry an implicit IOU: If you help me with my English composition, I can in the future be called on by you to share my expertise in mathematics. But what if you are an English major and it takes you only an hour to edit my composition? Although you have a certain knack for math, it takes you more time and energy to solve differential equations. Would two hours of my time on your math problems be a fair exchange? Here we get into the everyday calculus of exchanges involving **equity.** Unequal outcomes (I got a B on the composition while you got an A on the math problems that I solved) lead to a sense of inequality.

According to Adams (1965), if there is to be a sense of equity, the ratio of outcomes to inputs should be equal for both parties to the exchange. If I believe that my math is half as good as your abilities at composition, and I spent twice as much time on the numbers, distressed feelings of inequity result because I feel that my grade should have been the same as yours.

Consider the bartering exchanges that are engaged in as a strategy for avoiding income taxes. What quantity and type of dental work is equal to having the dentist's antique car refurbished by an auto mechanic? How much root canal work for a physician's family is equal to a coronary bypass operation? Such issues require that we focus on situational influences such as the normative structure of a social group, the relationship between helper and helped, the decision-making process of the helper, and the context of the behavior.

The proverbial "bottom line" of all models of social control from within concerns whether or not societies can produce individuals who internalize the "appropriate" (e.g., socially necessary) motivations, who willingly and energetically engage in prosocial activities, and who can agree on conditions of fairness for interpersonal exchanges. In later chapters we will explain in greater detail how this comes about, focusing on such matters as socialization, morality and guilt, the sources of self-esteem, and commitment to social beliefs.

On the other hand, perhaps the impetus for prosocial behaviors comes not from within the individual but rather from without. Perhaps social needs are addressed by virtue of the way in which the social organization of life leads even selfishly motivated individuals to perform prosocial acts.

## Models of Social Control from Without

By establishing rules by which people play the game of life, society determines the players' actions. The rules of the road, for instance, maximize the number of individuals who are able to reach their destinations in a given amount of time. Through driver education, people accept and internalize the expected routines and anticipate punishment if they violate them. Without these rules, there would be gridlock and chaos.

More sociologically inclined social psychologists have tended to focus on settings in which cooperation is shaped by mechanisms of social control. On the field of battle, soldiers must be trained to be willing to die for their compatriots; in the corporate world, subordinates must be willing to work to make their superiors "look good"; residents of communities must be willing to assist their neighbors when in need; in society in general, people should not victimize others for personal gain if the social order is to be preserved.

These social control mechanisms produce a spectrum of compliance forms. At one end of the continuum, individuals may be coerced to behave in certain ways and believe that they have been unwillingly forced to perform their social tasks. At the opposite end of the continuum, individuals willingly address society's needs and believe that the initiative is their own.

**Control through Coercion and Rewards.**   Among the world's repressive regimes we find the exercise of the most brutal forms of control. To maintain their power, totalitarian rulers have resorted to pogroms, torture, intimidation, and surveillance strategies. For instance, in Romania during the downfall of the communist regime of Nicolae Ceausescu, security forces were dispatched to suppress popular demonstrations. With tanks, armored vehicles, and helicopters, troops killed thousands of civilians. Though typically less brutal, external control through threats can also be found in prisons and mental hospitals. What's typically achieved is simply behavioral acquiescence; people continue to think one way and act in other. For instance, fearing their leaders and not trusting each other, Soviets have the habit of thinking one thing, saying another, and doing a third, according to exiled dissident Vladimir Bukovsky (1979).

Of course, social sanctions are not always negative. Behavior modification can also be achieved through environment design, as when society controls its members with positive reinforcements. In schools and workplaces, subordinates are regulated through the allocation of valued rewards—specifically high grades and large salaries.

**Normative Control.**   Consider the ways in which humans have altered the evolution of domesticated animals. Breeds of dogs have been designed to perform specialized activities; a good retriever, for instance, will locate and retrieve tossed balls and sticks until it drops from exhaustion. The domesticated pigeons that influenced Charles Darwin's thoughts on selective survival embodied the desired traits of generations of breeders.

Designing people to fulfill society's specialized needs is an idea that has a long tradition in fiction. As scientists make advances in recombinant genetics, science fiction writers can easily envision a competition among the nation's top research universities: Different institutions would field football teams with ideal creatures to fit each position—receivers with wings, 500-pound mammoths to man the front lines and so forth.

But the nature of social roles precludes such attempts. In fact, what has been engineered through calculated breeding is social bonds. Alliances between families, kingdoms, and nations have been dramatized by marriages and symbolically reaffirmed through their offspring. The preservation of religious and cultural traditions has been achieved through norms of **endogamy** which require that one marry a member of one's own faith or ethnic group.

The form of control arising from these social bonds is normative. When individuals become committed to a group they abide by its norms because they value their social membership. If their role performances fail to meet the expectations of the group, a host of negative sanctions can be activated, from others ignoring their presence or giving disapproving looks, to public degradations and outright expulsion from the group. (See discussion of how rules "work" in Chapter 9.)

**Thought Control.**   Though less insidious than fear of terrorism, the social strategies of thought control and surveillance are equally effective. A prime example is George Orwell's *1984*, in which the hero has a job falsifying records for the Ministry of Truth. Orwell's nightmare society is controlled by Thought Police, who persuade the society's members that ignorance is strength and war is peace.

Through propaganda, ideology, and socialization, political systems routinely work to shape the beliefs of their citizens. The primary belief that is shaped in these ways is belief in the legitimacy of the regime in power. In the Soviet Union, according to Urie Bronfenbrenner, state-sponsored education instills and develops the "socialist morality": "As soon as children are able to express themselves, they are given training in evaluating and criticizing each other's behavior from the point of view of the group" (1970:22). As we will see in later chapters, through control is not limited to politics. Religion instills morality, advertisers instill desires, and mass media shape commonly held stereotypes.

With the issue of thought control we have come full circle, to a point at which models of external control blend with those featuring internal controls. It also brings us to the processes that produce conformity.

**Conformity.**  Conformity is another means by which personal and social needs are synchronized as individuals orient their behaviors to the norms of the groups to which they belong. It involves the assumption that acting or thinking like others is more acceptable than acting or thinking differently. In all societies we find routine customs and patterns of interaction that allow life to proceed in orderly and predictable ways. They are followed not for personal gain or because of lack of free will but, rather, because "that's the way things are done."

Crutchfield (1955) found in various studies that businesspeople, homemakers, army officers, and students consistently agree with statements that they would reject if they were not told that other people believe them to be true. Hence, our acceptance of beliefs and ideas depends largely on the support given to them by others. As we will see in later chapters, conformity involves adherence to the socially expected standards of perception, cognition, and behavior. So powerful, in fact, is this form of social control that the perfectly socialized individual may never even conceive of alternative ways of understanding and doing things.

## The Duality of Self and Society

The examples of altruism given earlier shed doubt on the utility of selfish, hedonistic, and materialistic models of altruistic behavior or of behavior in general. If humans are such selfish creatures, how are they induced to put their lives on the line for total strangers? Why do one-third of those who are entitled to welfare benefits refuse their entitlements? Since people cannot be expected to change their behaviors without feeling that they have a choice in the matter, something else must be going on to explain such acts.

Admittedly, tensions exist between the needs of individuals and those of social systems—just ask the unwilling drafted foot soldier who must put his life on the line to defend social interests. But it is also true that one cannot exist without the other. In fact, it may be fallacious to view self and society as distinct entities. As Amitai Etzioni notes, "*The individual and the community make each other and require each other.* The society is not a 'constraint,' not even an 'opportunity,' *it is us.* . . . The I's need a We to be" (1988:9).

Basic motivations reflect the tension of being both an "I" and a "We." People's desires are evaluated against moral criteria (e.g., our right to benefit from the sacrifices of past generations and our obligation to sacrifice for future ones) and are then pursued in ways that ideally benefit others as well. The tension between these two selves is like having a devil at one ear and an angel at the other.

From this perspective, as George Herbert Mead (1934) noted, control occurs because individuals have learned to define situations from the standpoint of others and to know what others expect of them:

> Each individual aligns his action to the actions of others by ascertaining what they are doing or what they intend to do—that is, by getting the meaning of their acts. . . . [When taking the role of others] the individual seeks to ascertain the intention or direction of the acts of others. He forms and aligns his own action on the basis of such interpretation of the acts of others. (Blumer 1962:184)

These dynamics can be simulated in the game of Prisoner's Dilemma (Rapoport and Chammah 1965). Two individuals are arrested for a crime; the District Attorney knows that both are guilty. It being an election year, she wants to solve the case quickly and avoid a long and costly trial; she therefore is willing to deal leniently with the prisoners if they confess to the crime. The suspects are locked in separate cells and cannot communicate with each other. Separately, each is told that he can either confess or not confess. The D.A. has enough on them so that even if neither of them confesses she can lock them up for a year. If they both confess, they will each be given a moderate sentence of five years. If one confesses and the other does not, the one who does not confess will have the book thrown at him and be imprisoned for ten years, while the one who does confess will be released.

Collectively, it is in the prisoners' interest not to confess. But each individual is tempted to confess and thereby gain freedom while the other takes the rap. Sound familiar? Suppose this dilemma is translated into a game in which each pair of decisions is worth a certain number of points (e.g., both confess = −5 for each; both do not confess = 1 for each; one confesses and the other does not = 10 points for the confessor and −10 for the other). After twenty or thirty rounds are played, what would you expect to happen? The cooperative move would be not to confess, but this leaves one player vulnerable to the other player's making a competitive move and confessing. Each round reveals how much each player can trust the other, which becomes the basis of the next play. Generally, fewer than half of the plays made are cooperative, and cooperators are often exploited. Cooperation increases if the players know (McClintock and Neil 1967) or like (Swingle and Gillis 1968) each other.

**Individualism and Concentration of Social Power.** As the self becomes more important than relationships, community, and authority, society may be subverted. In extreme situations, excessive self-love (or narcissism) produces an ethos of self-fulfillment rather than self-denial, and grandiose visions of personal self-sufficiency rather than the appreciation of interpersonal interdependencies on which social solidarity depends (Lasch 1977).

Analogous to society's need to restrain individuals' egoistic impulses is individuals' need to restrain the tendency of social systems to limit personal freedom. According to Robert Michels (1949), in organizations with a hierarchy of authority, the advantages held by those at the top, together with the passivity and indifference of those at the bottom, causes power to become concentrated in fewer and fewer hands. Michels referred to this tendency as the *iron law of oligarchy.* Another social tendency that often runs counter to the well-being of individuals is bureaucratization. During the twentieth century huge, impersonal bureaucracies have emerged in politics and the workplace, reducing personal spontaneity, independence, and control. Within these organizational systems, individuals have become as replaceable and interchangeable as the nuts and bolts of a machine.

# CONSEQUENCES OF IMBALANCES BETWEEN SOCIAL AND PERSONAL NEEDS

When societies block or frustrate people's attempts to satisfy their needs or desires, violence results. Two forms of violence, aggression toward oneself (suicide) and aggression toward others (homicide), have received considerable attention in the social sciences.

## Suicide

Suicide is one of the clearest examples of the consequences of imbalances in the relationship between self and society. As with all theories of human behavior, scientists have located the cause of self-destructive behavior both within and outside the individual, depicting it as either a personal or a social pathology.

Historically, the causes of suicide have been located within the individual; suicide has traditionally been viewed as caused by imbalances of psychic forces, biochemical deficiencies, or metabolic disorders, Freud, for instance, talked of an alteration in the balance between the life force (Eros) and the death force (Thanatos). More recently, studies of people suffering from depression, alcoholism, schizophrenia, and personality disorders have detected abnormally low serotonin levels in those individuals. These deficiencies were found to be the critical factor in whether or not suicide is attempted (Greenberg 1982).

Instances of self-destruction can also be understood as resulting from imbalances in the relationship between individuals and their social system. As Durkheim (1964 [1892]) observed, if suicides stemmed from psychological or physiological factors, one would expect a relatively uniform distribution of suicides across various social groups. But such is not the case. Durkheim demonstrated that suicide rates were correlated with social phenomena: Protestants were more prone to commit suicide than Catholics, alienated urban dwellers more than rural inhabitants, and single individuals more than married people. Generalizing from these findings, he argued that suicides occur because of either excessive or insufficient social participation and/or regulation, or because of radical disruption in the nature of one's ties with society.

Durkheim suggested that varying levels of social integration and regulation yield four types of suicide: egoistic, anomic, altruistic, and fatalistic. Egoistic suicides result from too little social integration; an example would be the suicide of an unmarried, long-retired male. Excessive integration, on the other hand, can produce altruistic suicides (e.g., the action of Japanese kamikaze pilots in World War II). In cases of excessive regulation in conjunction with a high personal need to control one's environment, feelings of desperation and helplessness may result when goals become blocked, leading to fatalistic suicides (e.g., the suicide of a former high school whiz kid who fails his first examinations at a prestigious college). Finally, too little regulation or the shattering of accustomed relationships can lead to anomic suicides. Such suicides might result from the normlessness following economic collapse: suicides by poor individuals who have suddenly become wealthy or by wealthy people who have been suddenly impoverished are of this type. To illustrate these dynamics, Steven Stack (1986) demonstrated that the suicide rates of American 18- to 24-year-olds rose and fell between 1954 and 1978 along with divorce, unemployment, and church attendance rates.

Consider the information presented in Figure 3.2. In the early 1980s there were 12.3 suicides for every 100,000 Americans. In Austria the annual rate was more than double the U.S. rate, with 26 suicide victims per 100,000 population; in Italy, the suicide rate of 7.1 was nearly half the U.S. rate. If suicide's causes lie within the individual (e.g., abnormally low levels of serotonin), it would seem reasonable to expect similar rates in different countries (although biochemical imbalances could vary in different ethnicities), but such is not the case.

Figures 3.2a and 3.2b plot the national suicide rates of males and females of differing ages. It is evident that rates vary by both gender and age. In general, female suicide rates assume an upside-down U shape, starting out low in the early years, peaking in the middle years, and often declining among women age 75 and older. Male suicide rates, on the other hand, appear to increase with age, perhaps indicating a greater sense of normlessness in old age among males than among females. (See Chapter 8.)

When male suicide rates are standardized (i.e., divided) by the national rates for people age 75 and older (Figure 3.2c), we see that in Japan, Austria, Italy, and Sweden the suicide rates for those between the ages of 15 and 24 are less than 30 percent of the rates for the oldest males. Only in Poland are the suicide rates for men age 25–64 greater than the rates for men age 75 and older. From such trends, inferences can be made about the differing social satisfactions and tensions males encounter in their culture throughout the life cycle.

Gender differences are reflected in Figure 3.2d, in which male suicide rates for each age group are divided by the female rates for those age groups. In the United States, for instance, among people age 75 and older, males are over eight times more likely than females to take their own lives; in Japan, older females are almost as likely to commit suicide as older males. The U-shaped curve for the United States may reflect the fact that for males the highest degree of interaction with the social order occurs between the ages of 45 and 54 (the years when one is at the peak of one's career and has the greatest number of social involvements), whereas for females this phase of the life cycle represents the "empty nest" and other major role changes that may lead to anomic suicide.

## Aggression and Violence

One evening in April 1989, a 28-year-old female investment banker was brutally attacked and raped by a gang of 14- to 17-year-olds in Central Park, New York City. The youths apparently were hiding behind a bush and leaped out to strike

Suicide Rates for Selected Countries
for Males of Varying Age Groups

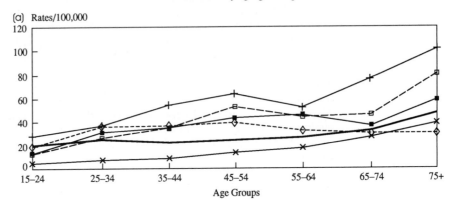

(a) Rates/100,000

Suicide Rates for Selected Countries
for Females of Varying Age Groups

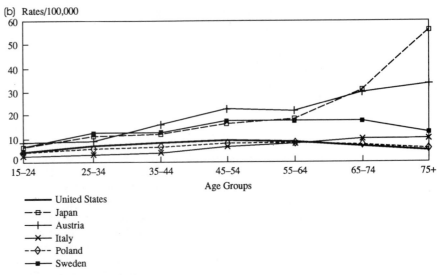

(b) Rates/100,000

- —— United States
- —⊟— Japan
- —+— Austria
- —✕— Italy
- --◇-- Poland
- —■— Sweden

**FIGURE 3.2   Suicide Rates by Country, Age Groups, and Gender**
Source: Statistical Abstracts of U.S., 1987.

the female jogger with a lead pipe as she passed by. There were reports that after being captured and imprisoned they laughed about the incident.

This apparently senseless incident of violence elicited an outpouring of social outrage. Social scientists were consulted for explanations of how such an act could have been committed. Undoubtedly, part of the explanation was peer pressure, the ways in which group dynamics lead individuals to do things that they either would never consider doing or would be too fearful to do alone. (See Chapter 12.) Another possible reason was that there was nothing constructive for the youths to do, that society had failed to provide them opportunities

Male Suicide Rates by Country
by Age Standardized by 75+ Rate

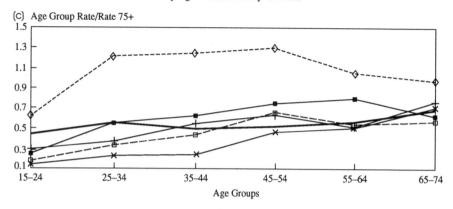

(c) Age Group Rate/Rate 75+

Age Groups

Male/Female Suicide Rates by
Country for Varying Age Groups

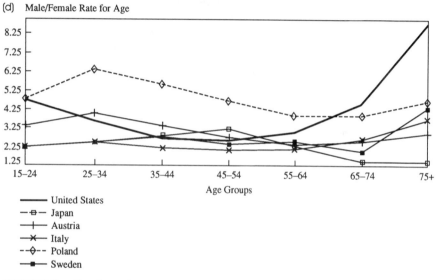

(d) Male/Female Rate for Age

Age Groups

——— United States
——⊟—— Japan
——+—— Austria
——✕—— Italy
--◇-- Poland
——■—— Sweden

**FIGURE 3.2** *Continued*

for socially meaningful action. Another was the absence of positive role models in the ghetto.

As in the case of suicide, theories of aggression run the gamut from Freud's death wish and Lorenz's aggressive-instinct explanation to the notion of a culture of violence. Distinctions have been made in terms of types of aggression—for example, passion-based (e.g., striking someone in an "uncontrollable" fit of anger), instrumental (e.g., a robber mugging a victim to obtain money), or sadistic (solely to inflict harm on another). They appear necessary given the spectrum of observed interpersonal relationships between aggressor and victim: In a study of killings that occurred in the United States between 1976 and 1985, researchers found that 13 percent involved spouses, former spouses, or lovers; 34 percent involved acquaintances; 8 percent involved other family members; 16 percent involved strangers; and the remaining 29 percent involved undetermined relationships (Maxfield 1989).

Psychologists have traditionally gravitated toward theories of violence:

1. The **frustration-aggression thesis,** which views violence as caused by the blocking of some need (Fromm) or goal-oriented behavior (Dollard et al. 1939).
2. The **social-learning thesis,** which views aggressive behavior as learned, reinforced, and then triggered by some social situation (Bandura 1973). Aggressive behavior has not been universally learned: The Arapesh of New Guinea, the pygmies of the Ituri rain forest, the Lepchas of Sikkim, and the Tasadays of the Philippines reportedly display no signs of violence.
3. The **interpretative-arousal thesis,** in which learned dispositions (e.g., when someone says something bad about my mother, I am to feel angry and insulted), coupled with a stimulus that produces arousal or excitation (such as in the heat of competition during a championship football game, an opposing lineman mentions how your grandmother should have aborted her daughter) leads one to define the emotion being experienced (since I feel the adrenalin flowing, this guy must really have insulted me) and the way it should be dealt with (therefore I better defend the honor of my family). (Zillman 1979)

More sociological explanations must be involved when we consider the huge national variations in homicide rates. (See Figure 3.3.) The United States is one of the most violent societies in the industrialized world. In New York City

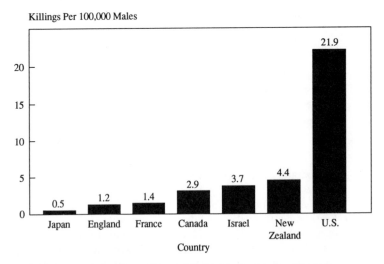

Killings Per 100,000 Males

**FIGURE 3.3  International Homicide Rates for Males 15–24 Years Old in 1986 or 1987**
Source: Rosenthal, 1990.

alone, more than twice the number of people are killed each year as in all of Japan. Homicide rates for American teenage males are from six to over forty times the rates in other industrialized nations (Otten 1989).

Those who focus on the dualities of self and society are more likely to locate the cause of aggression in some imbalance in synchronization of personal and social needs. Thus, Blau and Blau find that inequalities both within and between races are a significant predictor of differences in metropolitan homicide rates. They argue that these inequalities engender "alienation, despair, and pent-up aggression, which find expression in frequent conflicts, including a high incidence of criminal violence" (1982:126). At the bottom rungs of the social hierarchy, there is greater likelihood of a breakdown in social controls, an absence of supervision and socialization (Shaw and McKay 1942), and few opportunities for meaningful social engagements. "Reacting to the futility of his life," Poussaint notes, "the individual derives an ultimate sense of power when he holds the fate of another human being in his hands" (1972:72).

Personal esteem can become so precarious that a few words or a gesture can threaten its integrity. In cultures of violence such assaults invariably lead to aggressive retaliations. In the youth culture of Brooklyn, for instance, such insults even have a word: "dissed." There in 1990, a 15-year-old youth was shot simply because he had dissed another by refusing to reciprocate a "high five" (McKinley 1990). When categorizing the violent crimes of prison inmates and parolees, Toch (1969) found the most common form by far involved such preservations of self-esteem (41 percent), attacking those who insult or belittle one's identity.

# CONCLUSION

How and to what extent can the needs of the individual be meshed with the needs of society? As David Riesman phrased it: "What is the relation between social character and society? How is it that every society seems to get, more or less, the social character it 'needs'?" (1961:5).

In this chapter we explored these "personal" and "social" needs as a prelude to examining the processes by which social conventions become psychological necessities. We argued that when survival needs have been met, the motives underlying behavior are increasingly structured by the sociocultural milieu. On the other hand, cultural evolution is possible only when survival needs are no longer the primary concern of the individual. As Bonomi observed in relation to the first European settlers of the New World, in the struggle against hunger, disease, and Indian attacks, concerns about spiritual salvation became secondary (1986:15).

The question remains as to how malleable humans are and to what extent personal drives can be harnessed for social ends. Thomas Sowell (1985) contends that two divergent visions of humanity and society underlie the political, economic, and social conflicts of recent centuries. One is the "constrained vision," in which the human is seen as essentially a creature of self-interest; the other, the "unconstrained vision," sees humanity as progressing to ever higher reaches of selfless behavior. If the constrained vision is true, no matter what social strategies are undertaken to control or suppress human evil, other social ills are bound to be produced. All that can be hoped for is some prudent trade-off.

# REFERENCES

ABC News. 1987, April 9. *Our World* [the summer of 1944].

Adams, J. S. 1965. Inequity in social exchange. In L. Berkowitz (ed.), *Advances in experimental social psychology*, vol. 2. Orlando: Academic Press.

Altemeier, W. A., S. O'Connor, K. B. Sherrod, and D. Tucker. 1986. Outcome of abuse during childhood among pregnant low income women. *Journal of Child Abuse and Neglect* 10(3):319–330.

Bandura, A. 1982. Self-efficacy mechanism in human agency. *American Psychologist* 37(2):122–147.

Bandura, A. 1977. Self-efficacy: Toward a unifying theory of behavioral change. *Psychological Review* 84(2):191–215.

Bandura, A. 1973. *Aggression: A social learning analysis*. Englewood Cliffs, NJ: Prentice-Hall.

Baumeister, Roy. 1989. *Masochism and the self*. Hillsdale, NJ: Erlbaum.

Becker, Ernest, 1962. *The birth and death of meaning: A perspective of psychiatry and anthropology*. New York: Free Press.

Becker, Ernest. 1975. *Escape from evil*. New York: Free Press.

Becker, Ernest. 1973. *The denial of death*. New York: Free Press.

Bell, Daniel. 1976. *The cultural contradictions of capitalism*. New York: Basic Books.

Bennett, Amanda. 1988, August 15. When management professors gather, relevance sometimes rears its ugly head. *Wall Street Journal*, p 17.

Berger, Peter, and Thomas Luckmann. 1966. *The social construction of reality*. New York: Doubleday.

Bettelheim, Bruno. 1943. Individualism and mass behaviour in extreme situations. *Journal of Abnormal and Social Psychology* 38(4):417–452.

Bettelheim, Bruno. 1960. *The informed heart*. New York: Free Press.

Bhak, Albert. 1975. Social integration patterns and senile mortality. Paper presented at the annual meetings of the American Sociological Association, San Francisco, CA.

Blau, Judith R., and Peter M. Blau. 1982. Metropolitan structure and violent crime. *American Sociological Review* 47:114–128.

Bloom, Allan. 1986. *The closing of the American mind: How higher education has failed democracy and impoverished the souls of today's students*. New York: Simon and Schuster.

Blumer, Herbert. 1962. Society as symbolic interaction. In Arnold M. Rose (ed.), *Human behavior and social processes*. Boston: Houghton Mifflin.

Bonomi, Patricia U. 1986. *Under the cope of heaven*. New York: Oxford University Press.

Bronfenbrenner, Urie. 1970. *Two worlds of childhood: U.S. and U.S.S.R.* New York: Basic Books

Budiansky, Stephen. 1987, May 4. All by their lonesome. *U.S. News & World Report*, p. 71.

Bukovsky, Vladimir. 1979. *To build a castle: My life as a dissenter* (trans., Michael Scammell). New York: Viking Press.

Burger, Jerry. 1985. Desire for control and achievement-related behaviors. *Journal of Personality and Social Psychology* 48(6):1520–1533.

Burton, John. 1979. *Deviance, terrorism and war: The process of solving unresolved social and political problems*. New York: St. Martin's Press.

Campbell, Colin. 1987. *The romantic ethic and the spirit of modern consumerism*. New York: Basil Blackwell.

Crutchfield, David. 1955. Conformity and character. *American Psychologist* (10):191–198.

Darton, John. 1977, October 27. Banning: Unique South African punishment. *New York Times*, p. A8.

Deci, E. L., and R. M. Ryan. 1987. The support of autonomy and the control of behavior. *Journal of Personality and Social Psychology* 53(6):1024–1037.

Dollard, J., L. W. Doob, N. Miller, O. H. Mowrer, and R. R. Sears. 1939. *Frustration and aggression.* New Haven, CT: Yale University Press.

Douglas, Mary. 1966. *Purity and danger: An analysis of concepts of pollution and taboo.* New York: Frederick A. Praeger.

Durkheim, Émile. 1965[1915]. *The elementary forms of the religious life* (trans. Joseph W. Swain). New York: Free Press.

Durkheim, Émile. 1964 [1892]. *Suicide* (trans. John A. Spaulding and George Simpson). New York: Free Press.

Durkheim, Émile. 1933[1893]. *The division of labor.* New York: Macmillan.

Erikson, Kai. 1966. *Wayward puritans: A study in the sociology of deviance.* New York: Wiley.

Etzioni, Amitai. 1988. *The moral dimension: Toward a new economics.* New York: Free Press.

Etzioni, Amitai. 1961. *A comparative analysis of complex organizations.* New York: Free Press.

Fehrenbach, R. R. 1990, September 16. Educators still resist reforms. *San Antonio Express-News,* p. 3-M.

Field, Tiffany. 1986. Interventions for premature infants. *Journal of Pediatrics* 109(1):183–191.

Fisher, Lawrence M. 1989, October 14. For children, a first time for fear. *New York Times,* 10.

Friedrich, Carl. 1967. *An introduction to political theory.* New York: Harper and Row.

Giddens, Anthony. 1984. *The constitution of society: Outline of the theory of structuration.* Berkeley: University of California Press.

Gleick, James. 1987. *Chaos: Making a new science.* New York: Viking.

Golding, W. 1959. *Lord of the flies.* New York: Putnam.

Goleman, Daniel. 1989a, January 24. Sad legacy of abuse: The search for remedies. *New York Times,* pp. 19, 22.

Goleman, Daniel. 1989b, March 28. The roots of empathy are traced to infancy. *New York Times,* p. 13.

Goleman, Daniel. 1987, May 19. Sex, power, failure: Patterns emerge. *New York Times,* pp. 17, 20.

Goleman, Daniel. 1985, November 26. Emotional impact of disaster: Sense of benign world is lost. *New York Times,* pp. 17–18.

Gouldner, Alvin. 1960. The norm of reciprocity: A preliminary statement. *American Sociological Review* 25:161–178.

Greenberg, J. 1982. Suicide linked to brain chemical deficit. *Science News* 121(22):355.

Hall, D. T., and K. E. Nougaim. 1968. An examination of Maslow's need hierarchy in an organizational setting. *Organizational Behavior and Human Performance.* 3:12–35.

Harré, Rom. 1980. *Social being.* Lanham, MD: Littlefield Adams.

Herskovits, Melville J. 1960. *Economic anthropology: A study in comparative economics.* New York: Knopf.

Hoffman, M. L. 1977. Is altruism part of human nature? *Journal of Personality and Social Psychology* 40:121–137.

House, James, Karl Landis, and Debra Umberson. 1988. Social relationships and health. *Science* 241(4865):540–545.

Huxley, Aldous. 1959. Wordsworth in the tropics. In *Collected essays.* New York: HarperCollins.

Janoff-Bulman, Ronnie. 1989. Assumptive worlds and the stress of traumatic events: Applications of the schema construct. *Social Cognition* 7(2):113–136.

Kakutani, Michiko. 1989, May 31. Goodbye minimalists, hello tellers of tales. *New York Times,* pp. C15, C19.

Kamm, Henry. 1985, February 4. Drought weakens age-old social fabric in Chad." *New York Times,* p. 3.

Kinzie, David, W. H. Sack, R. H. Angell, S. Manson, and B. Rath. 1986. Psychiatric effects of massive trauma on Cambodian children. *Journal of the American Academy of Child Psychiatry* 25(3):370–376.

Kinzie, J. D., R. H. Fredrick, R. Ben, J. Fleck, and W. Karls. 1984. Posttraumatic stress disorder among survivors of Cambodian concentration-camps. American Journal of Psychiatry 141(5): 645–650.

Kohák, Erazim. 1976, August. Ancient enemies. *Harper's Magazine,* pp. 14–21.

Krant, M. J. 1974. *Dying and dignity: The meaning and control of a personal death.* Springfield, IL: Charles C Thomas.

Krebs, D. L. 1970. Altruism: An examination of the concept and a review of the literature. *Psychological Bulletin* 73:258–302.

Laing, R. D. 1967. *The politics of experience.* New York: Ballantine.

Langer, Susanne. 1942. *Philosophy in a new key.* Cambridge, MA: Harvard University Press.

Lasch, Christopher. 1977. *The culture of narcissism: American life in an age of diminishing expectations.* New York: Norton.

Lefcourt, Herbert M. 1976. *Locus of control: Current trends in theory and research.* Hillsdale, NJ: Erlbaum.

Lerner, M. J. 1980. *The belief in a just world: A fundamental delusion.* New York: Plenum.

Lifton, Robert. 1967. *Death in life: Survivors of Hiroshima.* New York: Random House.

Lightman, Alan. 1983, December. Weighing the odds. *Science 83,* pp. 21–22.

McAdams, Dan, and F. B. Bryant. 1987. Intimacy, motivation and subjective mental health in a nationwide sample. *Journal of Personality* 55(3):395–413.

McClelland, David. 1987. *Human motivation.* Cambridge, England: Cambridge University Press.

McClelland, David. 1951. *Personality.* Hinsdale, IL: Dryden.

McClintock, C. G., and S. P. McNeil. 1967. Prior dyadic experience and monetary reward as determinants of cooperation and competitive game behavior. *Journal of Personality and Social Psychology* 5:282–294.

McKinley, James C. 1990, January 10. A Brooklyn youth shot over a snub. *New York Times,* p. 16.

MacIntyre, Alasdair. 1988. *Whose justice? Which rationality?* Notre Dame, IN: University of Notre Dame Press.

Magnuson, Ed. 1985, April 8. Up in arms over crime. *Time,* pp. 28–39.

Malinowski, B. 1926. *Myth in primitive psychology.* New York: Norton.

Malinowski, B. 1922. *Argonauts of the western Pacific.* New York: Dutton.

Markham, James. 1983, August 1. East German sports: Politics everywhere. *New York Times,* p. 29.

Marx, Karl, and Freidrich Engels. 1846. *The German Ideology.* New York: International Publishers.

Maslow, A. H. 1943. A theory of human motivation. *Psychological Review* 50:370–396.

Matthews, Jay. 1976, July 31. "Will of Heaven" idea still stirs China. *San Francisco Chronicle,* p. 9.

Maxfield, Michael. 1989. Circumstances in supplementary homicide reports: Variety and validity. *Criminology* 27(4):671–695.

Merton, Robert. 1968. *Social theory and social structure.* New York: Free Press.

Michels, Robert. 1949. Political parties. New York: Free Press.

Miller, Bruce, and Robert C. Strunk. 1989. "Circumstances surrounding the deaths of children due to asthma. *American Journal of Diseases of Children* 143(11):1294–1299.

Moyers, Bill. 1989. *A world of ideas: Conversations with thoughtful men and women about American life today and the ideas shaping our future* (Arturo Madrid, pp. 212–220) (ed. Betty Sue Flowers). Garden City, NY: Doubleday.

Nadel, S. F. 1953, March. Social control and self-regulation. *Social Forces* 31:256–273.

National Opinion Research Center (NORC). 1989. *General social surveys 1988* (James A. Davis, principal investigator; Tom W. Smith, senior study director and co-principal investigator). Data distributed by the Roper Center for Public Opinion Research.

*New York Times.* 1990, March 29. Soviet views seen to split by region. p. A6.

Newcombe, Theodore M. 1950. *Social psychology.* Hinsdale, IL: Dryden Press.

Novak, Michael. 1976, April. The family out of favor. *Harper's Magazine,* pp. 37–46.

O'Leary, A. Self-efficacy and health. *Behavior Research and Therapy* 23(4):437–451.

Otten, Alan L. 1989, February 13. People patterns: Unnatural causes claim lives of more children. *Wall Street Journal,* p. B1.

Parsons, Talcott. 1961[1951]. *The social system.* New York: Free Press.

Peckham, Morse. 1965. *Man's rage for chaos: Biology, behavior and the arts.* Philadelphia and New York: Chilton.

Pouissaint, Alvin. 1972. *Why blacks kill blacks.* New York: Emerson Hall.

Rapoport, A., and A. M. Chammah. 1965. *Prisoner's dilemma: A study of conflict and cooperation.* Ann Arbor: University of Michigan Press.

Ricklefs, Roger. 1988, May 19. Adult children of elderly parents hire "surrogates" to oversee care. *Wall Street Journal,* p. 31.

Riesman, David. 1961 [1950]. *The lonely crowd.* New Haven and London: Yale University Press.

Rinaldi, Anoel, and Michael Kearl. 1990. The hospice farewell: Perspectives of its professional practitioners." *Omega* 21(4):1–18.

Roberts, Alan H., and Milton Rokeach. 1956. Anomie, authoritarianism, and prejudice. *American Journal of Sociology* 61:355–358.

Rodin, Judith. 1986. Aging and health: Effects of the sense of control. *Science* 233(4770):1271–1276.

Rosenthal, Elisabeth. 1990, June 27. U.S. is by far the leader in homicide. New York Times, p. A9.

Ross, Edward. 1901. *Social control: A survey of the foundations of order.* New York: Macmillan.

Scafidi, F. A., T. M. Field, S. M. Schanberg, C. R. Bauer, N. Veglahr, R. Garcia, J. Poirier, G. Nystrom, and C. M. Kuhn. 1986. Effects of tactile kinesthetic stimulation on the clinical course and sleep-wake behavior of preterm neonates. *Infant Behavior* 9(1):91–105.

Seligman, Martin, and G. Beagley. 1975. Learned helplessness in rats. *Journal of Comparative and Physiological Psychology and Supplement* 88(2):534–541.

Seligman, Martin, R. A. Rosellin, and M. J. Kozak. 1975. Learned helplessness in rats: Time course, immunization, and reversibility." *Journal of Comparative and Physiological Psychology and Supplement* 88(2):542–547.

Shaw, Clifford, and Henry McKay. 1942. *Juvenile delinquency and urban areas.* Chicago: University of Chicago Press.

Skinner, B. F. 1976. *Walden II.* New York: Macmillan.

Skinner, B. F. 1971. *Beyond freedom and dignity.* New York: Knopf.

Smith, Adam. 1776. *An inquiry into the nature and causes of the wealth of nations,* vol. 1. New Rochelle, NY: Arlington House (Classics of Conservatism).

Sowell, Thomas. 1985. *A conflict of visions.* New York: William Morrow.

Stack, Steven. 1986, May 28. A leveling off in young suicides. *Wall Street Journal,* p. 28.

Swingle, P. G., and J. S. Gillis. 1968. Effects of the emotional relationship between protagonists in the prisoner's dilemma. *Journal of Personality and Social Psychology* 8:160–165.

Thomas, William I., and Florian Znaniecki. 1927. *The Polish peasant in Europe and America.* New York: Knopf.

Toch, Hans. 1969. *Violent men: An inquiry into the psychology of violence.* Chicago: Aldine.

Turner, Bryan S. 1984. *The body & society.* New York: Basil Blackwell.

Turner, Jonathan. 1988. *A theory of social interaction.* Stanford, CA: Stanford University Press.

Useem, Bert, and Peter Kimball. 1989. *States of siege: U.S. prison riots, 1971–1986.* New York: Oxford University Press.

Volkan, Vamik. 1988. *The need to have enemies and allies: From clinical practice to international relations.* Northvale, NJ: Jason Aronson.

Wallach, Michael, and Lise Wallach. 1983. *Psychology's sanction for selfishness: The error of egoism in theory and therapy.* San Francisco: W. H. Freeman.

Williams, Lena. 1990, March 28. Feel well, do well: Self-esteem is tried as cure for social ills. *New York Times,* pp. B1, B8.

Zillman, D. 1979. *Hostility and aggression.* Hillsdale, NJ: Erlbaum.

# PART TWO

# The Social Patterning of Experience and Thought

One theme running through the first part of the book concerns the inherent arbitrariness and frailty of social reality. The order that we sense in our everyday social experiences is largely an assumption: We assume that there exists an ordered world external to ourselves, a world that existed before our birth and that will continue to exist long after our death; we assume that this world is largely as we perceive it; and we assume that others experience this order the same way we do.

In fact, much of what is perceived is inferred. The very notion of society is a social abstraction. One does not look out the window and "see" the United States or the state of Nebraska. The idea of society is akin to the large H's and L's that weather forecasters use to indicate barometric highs and lows. Behind the symbolism is an underlying model of how social groups or atmospheric phenomena work. What we see is not the direct event but, rather, a model that gives order and meaning to that which is sensed or felt.

But if the ordered "reality" that we take for granted does not exist somewhere "out there" but resides in our thoughts and experiences, how does this reality come to be experienced similarly by all of us? How do the feelings and experiences of separate individuals come to be synchronized?

In this section of the book we investigate the social determination of experience, feelings, and thought. According to Karl Marx, consciousness is determined by one's social being. In other words, society determines not only the appearance of its members' ideas, but their content as well. In the three chapters that follow, we will investigate how this occurs by considering how perception, cognition, and sentiment are shaped by the social milieu.

# 4

# Social Templates of Perception and Belief

People are more likely to accept as fact the stories of eyewitnesses than second- or thirdhand accounts. The ability of television to influence attitudes is derived from the assumption of viewers that they are seeing events "firsthand." In the legal system, jurors are most likely to be swayed by spectators' accounts.

However, when we compare the reports of several eyewitnesses to an identical event, our faith in such testimonies may be shaken. Studies have shown that the accuracy of eyewitness accounts in legal settings is influenced by the questions asked by lawyers and police and by the inability of many people to distinguish among members of other races, ethnicities, and even age groups.

To what extent is experience a function of mental activities (such as attention or interest) as opposed to qualities of the object experienced? What if "reality" is strictly in the eye of each beholder? Such questions challenge not only philosophers but social scientists as well. Admittedly the chair you sit on is "there," as is this book. But if the chair on which you sit was occupied by a great-grandparent seventy-five years ago or this book was purchased with the money you earned babysitting those kids from hell, these two objects suddenly become quite different to you than to others.

Even young children must grapple with the appearance–reality riddle that preoccupied ancient Greek philosophers. Make a red toy car appear black by covering it with a green filter and then show it to a 3-year-old and a 6-year-old. Let them hold and inspect the vehicle, then place it behind the filter again. Ask the children what color the car is. The 6-year-old will say red, the 3-year-old black (Flavell 1986). "Correct" insights into such experiences are not always guaranteed, even for adults. In this section we argue that the "reality" one perceives is largely inferred, and that the bases of inference are determined by one's social system.

In Chapter 3 we considered the need of both social systems and individuals to suspend doubt and minimize chaos. One of the doubts that is suspended is any question that things "out there" exist independently of their observers. In the *natural attitude*, individuals generally do not question that which they experience. Everything that is self-evident and "meaningful" to me, I know (or, at least assume until proven otherwise) is similarly self-evident and "meaningful" to you (Schutz 1973). Hence, throughout modern society people operate under the assumption that things and events external to themselves are as they appear, and that different observers can agree on precisely what exists. In our legal institutions, eyewitness testimony is the strongest evidence that can be brought against an accused. In the sciences, the strongest theories are determined by the observability of their predictions and the ability of independent observers to reliably obtain similar observations.

But we have all had experiences that cast doubt on the quality or stability of our perceptions: Initial impressions of a place seem incongruent with later observations; we realize that perception is selective when others point out what we don't see. Even in such fields as physics, the biases introduced through the sheer act of observing are recognized as distorting the phenomena being studied.

What if social reality is in actuality but a flux of chaotic events and that what appears to be self-evident is strictly a matter of consensus? If this is the case, then how is anything ever experienced similarly by a number of observers? And how do we explain the coherence of our consciousness, whereby discrete experiences are somehow transformed into a continuous, unfolding stream of consciousness?

## Personal Theories of Everyday Life

Psychologists (Kelly 1955; Wegner and Vallacher 1977) have approached such problems with a model in which the individual is a scientist of everyday life, continually trying to validate his or her own **construct systems,** or personal operating theories about types of people, types of settings, and types of events. When you think about it, many of our interactions with others involve the sharing, testing, and comparing of our personal models of the world. Such comparisons often take the form of a competitive game: "I told you this class would be boring"; "I knew they'd break up before the end of the year."

People have construct systems because of their reluctance to permit randomness and chance to enter their lives. They assume that there is an underlying meaning in every social situation that will eventually be revealed to its participants. Moreover, apparently unrelated things have underlying connections. This belief in order underlying apparent chaos may explain the appeal of the "connect-the-dots-and-see-the-picture" games of children.

With this assumption of order, actors can employ society's templates, or prescriptions for dealing with types of people in various types of situations. This is epitomized in bureaucratic organizations, where people's responses in specific situations (e.g., interacting with a client as opposed to one's immediate superior) are prescribed. As long as the prescriptions produce the expected results, they are applied without question. And the more one relies on acting

## Whose Templates to Use?
## On Anthropology's Distinction between Emic and Etic

Culture involves the "logico-meaningful" (Geertz 1973) domain of social life: the **cognitive-knowing,** the **normative-acting,** and the **expressive-feeling** dimensions of life. Culture, through its integration of skills, beliefs, values, and customs, services **social integration** by enculturating in its members a common subjective orientation to the social world. As defined by Sir Edward Tylor, the founder of academic anthropology:

> Culture . . . taken in its wide ethnographic sense is that complex whole which includes knowledge, belief, art, morals, law, custom, and any other capabilities and habits acquired by man as a member of society. The condition of culture among the various societies of mankind, in so far as it is capable of being investigated on general principles, is a subject apt for the study of laws of human thought and action. (1871)

In other words, culture is a system of cognition, a cognitive map. Individuals of the same culture come to internalize and share their culture's recipes for deciphering and dealing with reality.

When studying these cultural templates, as illustrated by the witchcraft logic of the Azande described in Chapter 2, anthropologists face the dilemma of whether to use their own reality models or those of the people being studied. Using *emic* analysis, observers employ concepts and distinctions that are meaningful and appropriate to the participants—in other words, the cognitive calculus of those being studied, such as what things they see as being meaningful, similar or different, or "appropriate." *Etic* analysis allows researchers to employ the concepts, classifications, and distinctions that are meaningful and appropriate to the observers. For instance, anthropologists may apply their notions of territoriality, ownership, religion, and kinship to a variety of cultural contexts to give order to their observations of an exotic culture.

in prescribed ways, the more likely one is to perceive oneself as a type of person for whom an entire life course "prescription" is available. *To the extent that people's construct systems are similar, their behavior should be similar as well*—a point to which we will return when considering the enactment of social roles.

***Personal Theories as Filters of Experience.*** The mind, Sherlock Holmes told Dr. Watson, is like an attic. "You have to stock it with such furniture as you choose. A fool takes in all the lumber of every sort that he comes across, so that the knowledge which might be useful to him gets crowded out." (Morrow 1990).

Young infants are easily startled. Over time they learn the sounds of familiar routines and can sleep through them undisturbed. When older, they learn that the sound of a garage door opening means that a parent will soon arrive with an embrace.

Personal theories work in analogous ways. Filtered out are experiences and information that are perceived to have no relevancy or meaning, leaving only "critical variables" to be attended to. In modern societies people are deluged by torrents of print, television images, and radio messages. One response to such information overload is simply to ignore the messages altogether.

The results of "discriminating obliviousness" (Morrow 1990) can be disastrous for individuals and social systems alike. For example, a Rand Corporation researcher traveling through Czechoslovakia in 1968 sensed that an oppressive action by the Soviet Union was imminent. He tried to warn the U.S. Embassy in Prague, which passed along the message to Washington, D.C., where the alarm was ignored because "it didn't fit the mind-set of the bureaucracy" (Menges 1989). Shortly thereafter, Soviet tanks rolled through the Czech capital and the country's new freedoms were suppressed.

## The Role of Conformity in the Practice of Everyday Science

In his development of the history of scientific paradigms, Thomas Kuhn argued that theories do not succeed by virtue of their truthfulness but rather by the extent of their popular support. This power of conformity, of accepting the viewpoint of "most others," similarly affects our personal operating theories. When there exists a conflict between personal modes of knowing and social modes of knowing often the latter wins out.

A classic illustration of such pressures was devised by Asch (1951, 1952, 1955). In an experiment using college undergraduates, seven confederates and one naive subject were asked to make a series of judgments about which of three comparison lines was equal in length to a standard line. The discriminations were far from difficult. For instance, in one test the subjects would be shown a stimulus line 10 inches long and comparison lines ten, eight, and twelve inches long. When they were tested alone, the naive subjects made correct judgments over 90 percent of the time. But strange things occurred when they found themselves in disagreement with others (i.e., the confederates).

In the second phase of the experiment, each of the subjects announced his or her judgment in turn. The naive subject was always the sixth or seventh person to present his or her assessment. On the first two rounds everything proceeded smoothly, with all the subjects presenting the same judgment. But the confederates had been coached to make obviously wrong choices in twelve of the eighteen measurements. When all of the confederates gave the same incorrect answer, approximately three-quarters of the naive subjects changed their estimates at least once to conform with the incorrect majority opinion. Nearly one-third of the subjects changed their estimates at least half of the time.

When Asch's conformity experiments were replicated in other countries, similar rates of conformity were found (e.g., 31 percent in Lebanon, 34 percent in Brazil, 32 percent in Hong Kong). By contrast, among the Rhodesian Bantu, whose culture emphasizes conformity and severely punishes deviant behavior, the conformity rate was 51 percent (Whittaker and Meade 1967). More recently, replications have reported lower rates of conformity in both the United States and Britain (Larsen 1974; Perrin and Spencer 1980).

To demonstrate the emergence of group norms and how these frames of reference come to be employed by individuals, Sheriff (1936) took advantage of a curious phenomenon called the autokinetic effect: When observing a stationary point of light without a frame of reference, as within a dark room, one sees the light move. In the first part of the experiment, people were led one at a time into a lightproof room and asked 100 times to indicate how far the light on the wall was moving. In this situation, without either a physical or a social frame of reference, the person can neither gauge how far the light is moving nor ask for the opinions of others. Sheriff found that after a few variable responses, each person's judgments became consistent. In other words, the people had formed their own frame of reference, or personal norm, and kept their judgments consistent with that norm.

In the experiment's next stage, Sheriff put groups of three people in a dark room at the same time and asked each to say out loud how far the light had moved. This is where social influence came into play. Ultimately, the judgments of people in the groups converged to produce a common social norm, usually a compromise based on individual norms. In separate posttests, each subject continued to give the group response, indicating that the subjects had truly changed their opinions and given up their personal modes of knowing in favor of the social mode.

In the sections that follow, we will discuss these issues in greater detail. We will begin with the spectrum of theories individuals employ to make sense of and predict social behavior. We then consider the ways in which these theories shape the processes of perception and how the resultant experiences are interpreted. Finally, we look at the relationships between thought and behavior—how, for instance, one's stereotypes are related to one's actions toward members of the stereotyped group.

## THEORIES EMPLOYED IN EVERYDAY LIFE

In Chapter 1 we considered such issues as the scope, determinacy, falsifiability, and formalism of theories, as well as differences in their assumptions about whether behavioral control resides within or outside of the individual. People's theories of everyday life also vary in terms of elaborateness, logical consistency, predictiveness, and amenability to testing. Both scientific and everyday theories seek to simplify chaos by organizing perceptions of the world into categories.

But here the similarities end. Whereas scientific theories generally expand in scope and decline in complexity as more general principles are uncovered and new paradigms overthrow the old ones, personal theories tend to work in reverse. In astronomy, for instance, the initial assumption was that the earth must be at the center of the cosmos, which is why nearly all of the stars move in circular patterns overhead. However, there were several wanderers in the night sky, which the Greeks called *planetes*, or planets. To account for their erratic orbits and still keep earth at the center of things, scientists created elaborate epicycles (like the motion of the earth's moon from the perspective of the sun) to account for planetary motions. Finally Copernicus simplified the model by putting the sun at the center. Initial personal theories, on the other hand, often begin simplistically and, with increasing age and experience, become increasingly complex. Rudimentary racial and ethnic stereotypes, for instance, become filled with qualifiers that take into account such matters as an individual's education, social class, age, and region of the country.

Another central difference between scientific and everyday theorizing lies in the way science is conducted. Ideally, scientific hypotheses arise out of impartial observation. However, everyday science normally works in reverse: Our expectations and preconceptions tell us what data to look for and how to interpret what we find; as a result, we are often immune to contradictory experiences. For this reason, social psychologists have long been interested in how attitudes, stereotypes, dogma, and ideologies determine human perception and behavior. Those who are more sociologically inclined have also been interested in the social genesis of such beliefs.

## Attitudes

In many ways, attitude is the most central concept of social psychology. Gordon Allport (1935) defined an attitude as a predisposition, a state of anticipation and readiness toward mental and physical activity. Attitudes are relatively enduring organizations of *affect*, or feeling, toward other persons, groups, ideas, and objects. They involve a proclivity to respond to something either favorably or unfavorably.

An attitude is a *collectively shared schema that one adopts.* For instance, Americans' attitudes toward socialism or the Islamic faith primarily derive from the perspectives of their social groups. Jaspers and Fraser (1981) note that this social nature of "attitudes" is often overlooked. In part, this is a because recent developments in attitude research and scaling techniques have led to the individualization of the study of attitude (Jaspers and Fraser 1981:116). On the other hand, there is mounting evidence that researchers need to take into account contextual variables—social microcontexts or situations—as well as the encompassing organizational and institutional conditions (Williams 1988:332). Like the subjects in the group condition of Sheriff's study of the autokinetic effect, people internalize the evaluative standards of their families, religions, political parties, unions, and community opinion leaders. Thus, instead of simply measuring the beliefs of isolated individuals, researchers need to consider how these frames of references evolve over time between regularly interacting individuals. (See Chapter 12's discussion of "group think.")

Attitudes can be conceptualized as ranging across at least two dimensions. The first is personal relevance. People hold attitudes that are relevant to their needs. According to Katz (1960), attitudes serve the following four basic personal functions:

1. **Adjustment:** Attitudes provide time-tested recipes for dealing with different types of situations or persons.
2. **Ego defense:** Attitudes "justify" one's emotions, behaviors, and self-worth. We like those whom we perceive as supporting our endeavors and tend to hold negative attitudes toward those whom we see as competing with or otherwise thwarting our objectives.

## Implications of Historical Ignorance

In the past few years, several studies have revealed a profound ignorance of historical matters among American students. For instance, in "What Do Our 17-Year-Olds Know?: A Report on the First National Assessment of History and Literature," Finn and Ravitch reported that 20 percent of the students thought the Watergate scandal had occurred before 1900 and only one-third could place the Civil War in the correct half-century (Fiske 1987). What are the implications of not having a historical perspective, and how can one measure these consequences?

To collect a sampling of arguments about the implications of historical ignorance, local historians were interviewed and a review of mass media articles on the topic was made. From these, a list of statements was devised, reflecting attitudes that were hypothesized to sharply distinguish between individuals with and without historical knowledge. Individuals were asked whether they "agree strongly," "agree somewhat," "disagree somewhat," or "disagree strongly" with each of the assertions. Following are examples of the statements used:

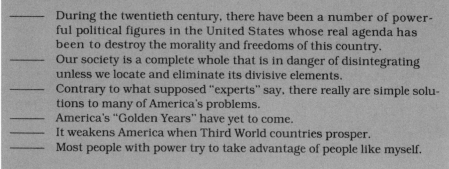

- \_\_\_\_\_ During the twentieth century, there have been a number of powerful political figures in the United States whose real agenda has been to destroy the morality and freedoms of this country.
- \_\_\_\_\_ Our society is a complete whole that is in danger of disintegrating unless we locate and eliminate its divisive elements.
- \_\_\_\_\_ Contrary to what supposed "experts" say, there really are simple solutions to many of America's problems.
- \_\_\_\_\_ America's "Golden Years" have yet to come.
- \_\_\_\_\_ It weakens America when Third World countries prosper.
- \_\_\_\_\_ Most people with power try to take advantage of people like myself.

To obtain a measure of individuals' historical knowledge, subjects were presented with a time line beside which were listed twenty-two historical events. Subjects were asked to place the appropriate letter next to the event on the time line. The events included the following:

- a. France loses her Indochina colonies when defeated in Vietnam.
- d. The Great Depression
- e. Austria and Hungary are separated, with much of their land going to Yugoslavia, Italy, Poland, and Czechoslovakia.
- n. American women receive the right to vote.

The subjects were 160 undergraduates attending a city college and a private liberal arts institution in 1989 and 1990. The extent of their historical ignorance was profound. Among other things, they believed that the Russian Revolution had occurred in 1970, that the first atomic device had been detonated in 1915, that manumission of American slaves had occurred as early as 1830 and as late as 1910, that the People's Republic of China had come into existence in 1790 and Israel in 1810, that the Napoleonic wars preceded the French Revolution, and that American women had received the right to vote as early as 1810!

Figure 4.1 plots the correlations between historical knowledge (scores recoded into quartiles) and some of the statements. As is evident (all correlations were statistically significant), with increasing knowledge, individuals are less likely to agree that the powerful take advantage of others, that there are simple solutions to many of America's problems, that America is weakened if the Third World prospers, and that divisive elements must be eliminated. Those with low historical knowledge demonstrate beliefs associated with **authoritarianism,** a personality type that will be described in Chapter 7.

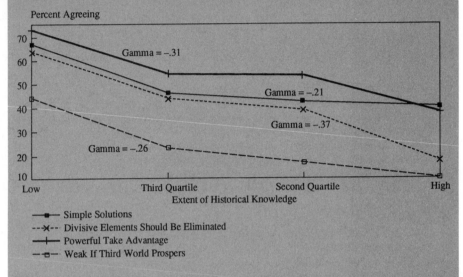

**FIGURE 4.1  Beliefs Associated with Historical Knowledge and Ignorance, by Level of Education**

Correlations were also found between historical ignorance and the beliefs that America's golden years have yet to come and that evil political figures have been working to destroy the morality and freedoms of this country. This brings to mind the social-psychological chemistry that gave rise to National Socialism in Germany in the 1920s and 1930s: Rising expectations were dashed and the dynamics of witchhunts and scapegoating were unleashed.

3. **Value expression:** Some attitudes express one's basic values, reinforcing one's self-image. Frustration at the demands of parents and teachers coupled with increasing needs for autonomy and self-assertion, for example, lead to adolescents' positive attitudes toward rock-and-roll music and its themes of defiance.
4. **Knowledge:** Without such beliefs, individuals would be overwhelmed by the complexity of their environment.

People also hold attitudes toward matters that have no personal relevance or are only indirectly relevant, such as attitudes toward communism, foreign aid to Zimbabwe, or tuna-fishing techniques that ensnare and kill dolphins. These attitudes often deal with things that are assumed to affect *social* functions, such as orientations toward morality and political action. On such issues, individuals take the perspective of their social system and evaluate things that are believed to affect the group as a whole.

The second dimension is actual personal knowledge about the matters underlying the attitudes. At one extreme, people hold attitudes toward issues and events about which they have next to no knowledge; this phenomenon is called **pluralistic ignorance.** Most Americans, for instance, hold attitudes toward euthanasia and nuclear energy even though none of their relatives or acquaintances have faced right-to-die issues or built nuclear reactors in their backyards. At the other extreme are attitudes toward phenomena with which individuals have considerable firsthand experience. Less subject to persuasion than those at the other end of the continuum, these individuals are also often looked upon as legitimate opinion shapers.

In sum, one's evaluative orientations emerge from one's interactions with significant others, although the basic templates (e.g., racial or ethnic prejudice) are probably laid down during one's early years. Only a portion of our attitudes derive from direct exposure to situations and persons rather than being received as secondhand information from family members, mass media, friends and acquaintances. First to be learned is sentiment; only later come the associated logic and norms that transform attitudes into full-blown belief systems. Some attitudes may be held exclusively by certain social groups and may even be the basis of their solidarity, as will be seen in Chapter 12.

## Stereotypes and Prejudice

Stereotypes are a special category of attitudes that deals with dispositions toward and beliefs about categories of people. Typically they are based on individuals' membership in a particular social group defined by a trait such as ethnicity, religion, age, or race.

Because they are collectively held, stereotypes do not emerge out of thin air. They are, in part, the products of history, legacies of the belief systems of past generations. They are a result of sociocultural forces. Arnold Rose (1948), for instance, locates the roots of anti-Semitism in early reactions against urbanization—which is characterized by increasing materialism, other-directedness, and depersonalization—and notes that Jews were often a symbol of city life. Prejudice is built into language; it is reaffirmed and legitimated every time one speaks. The word *black*, for instance, connotes evil, disorder, and lack of conformity to the social order (e.g., "He's the black sheep of his family"); the use of masculine pronouns and words like *mankind, chairman,* and *history* reaffirms male dominance. At the cultural level, stereotypes and prejudice are built into folk wisdom, children's stories, and religion.

At the individual level, stereotypes provide the schemata or templates by which our experiences of the behavior of others are parsed and interpreted. Often, what people "see" is a stereotype and not a unique phenomenon; they believe that their assessments are universally true for a category of persons (e.g., females, Chicanos, engineering majors).

## An Age of Organized Touchiness

Wendy's first 'Where's the beef?' television commercial is a small masterpiece of lunacy and perfect timing. But the Michigan Commission on Services to the Aging was not amused. The hamburger drama, said Commission Chair Joseph Rightley, gave the impression that "elderly people, in particular women, are senile, deaf and have difficulty seeing." . . .

To their credit, the Gray Panthers issued a statement declaring Wendy's innocent of ageism and announcing themselves pleased that the three women were not shown as quiet victims in the face of hamburger abuse. The Panthers, as it happens, have their own problems with overreaction, attacking the immortal Christmas song "Grandma Got Run Over by a Reindeer" (Grandma had too much eggnog and forgot her pills) and letting scriptwriters know that old people should not be shown with wheelchairs, canes, or hearing aids. . . .

In an age of organized touchiness, the goal of many lobbying groups is not so much to erase stereotypes but to reverse them so that there is never an image of any group that falls very far short of idealization. Infirm oldsters and ethnic criminals exist in the real world, but they are not to exist on screen. . . . Puerto Ricans and blacks sued to block the filming of *Fort Apache, The Bronx*, declaring it racist. Homosexuals tried to disrupt production of *Cruising*. Oriental activists protested a recent Charlie Chan movie, forcing the maker of the film into a preproduction whine about his respectful treatment of the famous Chinese detective. Sioux Indians demonstrated against the book *Huanta Yo*, which contained passages on the ferocity of the Sioux. . . . A New York coven of witches complained when ABC televised *Rosemary's Baby*.

Source: Leo, 1984.

## Personality Theories

A person's repertoire of attitudes and stereotypes is not simply a collection of unrelated schemas. Rather, they coalesce into distinctive patterns that provide operating models for deciphering reality. Individuals have operating theories about how these patterns are related—for instance, intelligent people are likely to be described as friendly and rarely as self-centered. We are surprised when attractive individuals like Theodore Bundy are linked with homicidal atrocities, or when religious leaders are caught in compromising situations in hotel bedrooms.

This calculus by which traits are assumed to be related is captured in **implicit personality theories** (Schneider 1973; Berman and Kenny 1976; Grant and Holmes 1981). The number of traits in these personality theories is limited. Rosenberg and Sedlak (1972) found that the schemas of college students frequently include only the qualities of intelligence, friendliness, self-centeredness, ambition, and laziness. Taken together, they provide a model of factors that are assumed to predict the behaviors of others.

Figure 4.3 presents one such model. Two salient dimensions underlying college students' theories of others are social and intellectual capacities. At the

## Education and Stereotypes

Education has the effect of liberalizing stereotypical attitudes toward social groups that are different from one's own. Let's consider how education affects attitudes toward the following questions:

FEHOME: Women should take care of running their homes and leave running the country up to men.

BLACKPRES: If your party nominated a black for President, would you vote for him if he were qualified for the job?

ATHSPK: There are always some people whose ideas are considered bad or dangerous by other people. For instance, somebody who is against all churches and religion. If such a person wanted to make a speech in your (city/ town/ community) against churches and religion, should he be allowed to speak, or not?

COMMSPK: Now, I should like to ask you some questions about a man who admits he is a Communist. Suppose he is teaching in a college. Should he be fired, or not?

To make our analyses a little more interesting, we will consider only the responses of those who could be assumed most likely to be prejudiced on such issues: males' attitudes toward FEHOME, whites' attitudes toward BLACKPRES, very religious persons' attitudes toward ATHSPK, and attitudes toward COMMSPK among those claiming to be moderately or strongly conservative politically.

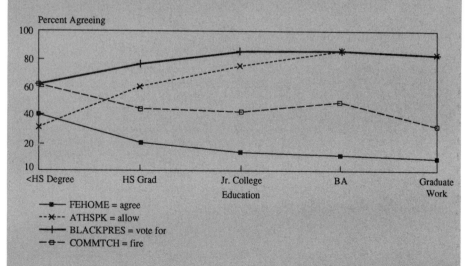

**FIGURE 4.2  Attitudes toward Females, Blacks, Atheists, and Communists, by Level of Education**

As is evident in the figure, as education increases, males are less likely to believe that a woman's place is in the home, whites are more likely to vote for a black President, very religious individuals are more willing to allow an atheist to speak, and political conservatives are less likely to demand that a Communist teacher be fired.

What is it about education that alters stereotypical views? Is it that people with more education are less likely to stereotype others on the basis of single-trait theory? More education may lead individuals to employ more complex and more numerous templates. For instance, "liberal arts" and "general education" curricula expose students to the operating models or worldviews of artists, writers, biologists, political scientists, and economists.

opposite ends of each dimension are opposing pair traits. The closer the traits are in this depiction, the more they are assumed to reside within the same individual.

Analogous to the implicit personality theories posited by psychologists is the **status expectation states** theory developed by more sociologically oriented social psychologists (Berger and Zelditch 1985). Here the traits considered are more purely sociological; they are based on individuals' social status. In small, task-oriented groups whose members are unequal in terms of their social standing in the broader society (i.e., black versus white, junior college versus

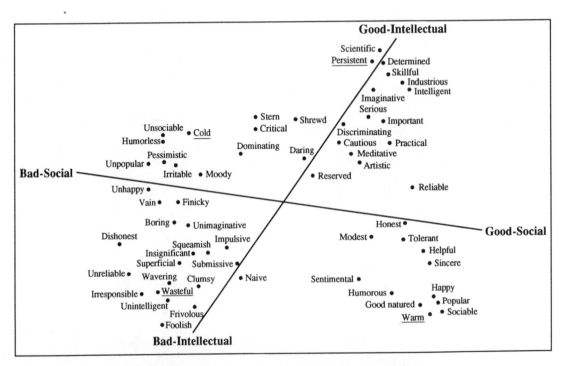

**FIGURE 4.3** Mental Map from Rosenberg, Nelson, and Vivekanathan (1968).

university student), even though an individual's status properties may be totally irrelevant to the task at hand, they are assumed to correlate with his or her power and prestige in the group. A self-fulfilling dynamic comes into play as high-status members talk more, are listened to more, and are more likely to become leaders.

## BELIEF SYSTEMS

Surveys conducted in the late 1980s revealed that two-thirds of American teenagers believe in the existence of angels and over 40 percent of American adults claim to have had contact with the dead (*Harper's Magazine* 1987). How can we account for such widespread certainty in empirically unverifiable phenomena?

Attitudes, stereotypes, and personality theories are but special cases of the more general phenomenon of **belief systems.** These relatively permanent schemas are sets of wide-ranging, interrelated ideas that provide broad explanations of aggregate phenomena such as political ideologies, religious dogmas, or the cultural myths that justify social inequalities. Whereas attitudes exist in a context of meaning, belief systems exist in a context of social organization as well, often serving moral and political purposes. Because of this, they are notions to which individuals and groups exhibit strong commitment: People may be willing to die for a religious dogma but never for a stereotype.

On the sidewalks of Harvard Square, a sidewalk preacher interacts with a representative of the anti-establishment punk movement. What personality assessments are being made by each man of the other? Why is this encounter attracting a crowd of amused onlookers?

It is important to appreciate the social context of beliefs. Belief systems emerge and change as groups adapt to social strains and disorders, as we saw in the case of the varying frequency of UFO sightings. Thus, the fall of the Eastern European countries after World War II and the Soviets' development of nuclear weapons frightened Americans, many of whom wanted an explanation of these events. In the 1950s, the John Birch Society emerged with an answer: There is an international Communist conspiracy that has been corrupting the moral foundations of the United States since the birth of the nation.

A second important facet of the social nature of belief systems is that the group, not any single individual, carries the "whole picture." Each member of the John Birch Society, for instance, assumes on faith that the international Communist conspiracy is, indeed, "real" and is so broad in scale that only the collective whole is able to appreciate its full scope.

## Components of Belief Systems

Borhek and Curtis (1973:25–38) have described how belief systems vary along several dimensions, including the following:

**Systematization:** A belief system may be an interrelated set of general statements applicable to all situations, or it may be little more than a set of prescriptions and proscriptions. Highly systematized beliefs feature logical rules linking one substantive belief with others. Sometimes this internal logic alone can move believers in unwanted or unanticipated directions. For example:

> Belief systems with a relatively high degree of system seem to rely on rather general internalized standards to maintain social control—standards such as generalized codes of ethics (science) or guilt, which is associated with a whole category of behavior such as pleasure (Puritanism). To learn part is to learn all. Belief systems with relatively low system . . . seem to depend on external sanctioning. (1973:27)

**Empirical relevance:** Belief systems vary in the degree to which they face the empirical world. For instance, for someone who believes that the spirits of the dead intervene in the affairs of the living, a string of bad luck may mean that it is necessary to appease those spirits. If the bad luck continues, obviously one's efforts at appeasements were not enough. Such logic helps explain why doomsday cults continue even when their predictions turn out to be incorrect.

**Willingness to accept innovation:** Belief systems vary in their ability to adapt to changing social situations. Religious beliefs, for instance, tend to be less pragmatic than scientific beliefs. On numerous occasions ideology and dogma have won out over truth.

**Tolerance for competing beliefs:** Why did much of Europe fail to develop during the "dark ages" while the cultures of the East flourished, producing advances in astronomy and mathematics? Largely because of Islam's receptivity to other knowledge systems (including that of classical Greece); it was based on contemplation and analysis rather than on miracles (Bronowski 1973:165–174).

**Degree of personal commitment demanded:** Personal commitment to a belief system may have little relevance to qualities of the belief system itself (e.g., its empirical relevance or logical tightness) but be due instead to demands of the social group. Obsessive commitment to beliefs that the group considers secondary or irrelevant causes the believer to be perceived as deluded. When they are seriously challenged, beliefs demanding low commitment tend to fade away, whereas those demanding total commitment produce "noisy apostates."

**Style of belief organization:** Beliefs provide perspective; they are the cognitive templates by which one's experiences are evaluated. One of the most common perspectives is provided by the relationship of the belief system and the social group to others (e.g., ally–enemy, capitalist–socialist, democratic–totalitarian). At a minimum, the perspective is merely encoded within a classification system. On the other hand, it may be contained in an elaborate ideology that is fully known only by the elite.

What determines the nature of these components for any given belief is the type of knowledge being addressed. Our criteria for empirical relevance, for instance, are considerably different for beliefs about the "greenhouse effect" than for beliefs about the entertainment industry. We are likely to accept the evidence presented by meteorologists and climatologists about changes in global weather patterns, but we may accept the gossip reported in the *National Enquirer* about the activities of Hollywood stars. According to Gurvitch (1966[1971]), this has to do with differences in the way different types of knowledge (e.g., perceptual knowledge of the external world, technical knowledge, political knowledge, philosophical knowledge) are perceived and understood. Those differences may be viewed in terms of five pairs of defining characteristics: mystical versus rational, empirical versus conceptual, positive versus speculative, symbolic versus concrete, and collective versus individual. In the contemporary United States, for instance, scientific knowledge is rational, empirical, speculative, and concrete—the antithesis of religious knowledge, which is mystical, conceptual, positive, and symbolic. Such differences between these two knowledge types are not inevitable, however. Their defining characteristics (e.g., religion being mystical versus rational) are derived as much from social factors as from any inherent quality of the knowledge itself. The larger the group (e.g., social classes, nations) carrying a knowledge system, the more likely its cognitive system predominates over those engendered by smaller groups.

## Attachment to Beliefs

During the twentieth century millions of people have died as a result of their devotion to political ideologies and religious beliefs. How do people come to be so firmly attached to their beliefs? The reasons are both psychological and sociological.

At a psychological level, personal needs for order, predictability, and meaning can lead to complete conviction in one's opinions. But rarely do social events unfold as expected or desired. Instead of leaving people to wrestle with problems involving good and evil or truth and falsity, ideologies and dogmas eliminate the need to make difficult distinctions. These belief systems create an artificial order and recast the shades of gray into black and white. As Arthur Schlesinger observes:

> Absolutism is abstract, monistic, deductive, ahistorical, solemn, and it is intimately bound up with deference to authority. Relativism is concrete, pluralistic,

## The Most Common Delusions

**Romantic Fixations.** The theme is one of being loved by someone of higher status, such as a celebrity. Fantasies are romantic rather than sexual and often lead to efforts to make contact through calls, letters, stakeouts, and the like, a source of harassment to most public figures.

**Grandiosity.** The person is convinced of having some extraordinary gift, power, insight, or prominence that has gone unrecognized. Typical forms are claims of being a relative of someone prominent, of having made startling scientific discoveries, or of having a mission.

**Jealousy.** The person is convinced, with no grounds, that a spouse or lover is unfaithful and may seize on trivialities as "proof," confront the partner, and try to prevent liaisons by spying or demanding that the partner stay home.

**Persecution.** The most common delusion, its theme is being the object of a plot and being spied on, followed, harassed, and so forth. The person takes small or imagined slights and setbacks as proof; may be obsessed with correcting some injustice, often by suing; and is typically, angry, hostile, and violent.

**Bodily fixations.** The person is convinced, contrary to all evidence, that there is something terribly wrong with his or her body, such as emitting foul odors, having the skin infested with insects, or being horribly misshapen or injured. Such people often go on a fruitless round of visits to doctors.

Source: Goleman, 1989.

---

inductive, historical, skeptical and intimately bound up with deference to experience. Absolutism teaches by rote; relativism by experiment. (1989:26)

In the extreme, beliefs become delusions when they are tenaciously held despite overwhelming counterevidence that would leave most others searching for alternative explanations.

Attachment to beliefs serves social functions as well, which is why social processes enter into the maintenance of belief commitment. As companies spend millions of dollars on advertising to create the beliefs that their products are needed and are superior, nations spend considerable funds on public education and propaganda to preserve the public's belief in the legitimacy of the regime in power—in other words, to identify the kingdom or state with its rule or rulers.

## The Social Bases of Belief Systems

One of the earliest sociologists, Henri de Saint-Simon (1825[1965]), observed that "the production of ideas occurs within the structure of every society." These ideas vary according to their social context, just as food crops flourish to different degrees, depending on soil and climate conditions. One major task of sociologically oriented social psychologists is to map the cultural and social

## The Pro-Life Movement

Evidence that attitudes toward euthanasia, abortion, and the rights of the terminally ill were coalescing into a coherent belief system in the minds of Americans was detected by Kearl and Harris (1981–1982). Using the 1977 and 1978 NORC General Social Science Surveys of the American adult public, they found that the following questions, listed in order of difficulty, produced a statistically significant, near-perfect Guttman scale (i.e., if a person agreed with question 4 and disagreed with question 5, then he or she also agreed with questions 1–3):

1. [Should it] be possible for a pregnant woman to obtain a legal abortion if the woman's health is seriously endangered by the pregnancy?
2. [Should it] be possible for a pregnant woman to obtain a legal abortion if there is a strong chance of a serious defect in the baby?
3. When a person has a disease that cannot be cured, do you think doctors should be allowed by law to end the patient's life by some painless means if the patient and his family request it?
4. Do you think a person has the right to end his or her own life if this person has an incurable disease?
5. Do you think a person has the right to end his or her own life if this person has dishonored his or her family?

The researchers argued that the unifying theme of these questions is the right of individuals to control the form and timing of death. With increasing permissiveness, one first accepts abortion, then the right to die, and finally suicide.

The best predictors of an individual's score on this scale were education (the greater the number of years of school, the more permissive the orientation), religiosity (the greater the degree of religiosity, the more restrictive the orientation), and personal attitudes toward the rights of women and homosexuals and the legalization of marijuana.

From the 1970s on, the abortion controversy has divided the American public like no other moral question since perhaps the time of slavery. Groups formed around both sides of the controversy, with the pro-life and pro-choice camps becoming among the broadest political coalitions in modern history (Shribman 1989). By the late 1980s, the pro-life movement had expanded its political belief system to challenge the growing right-to-die (euthanasia) movement. Even though legal experts claim that there is no link between laws governing abortion and euthanasia (Johnson 1990), a vital moral connection was seen by those in the abortion coalitions. On the one hand, the withdrawal of feeding tubes and the ending of the existence of the unborn were viewed as bestowing on individuals the power to take another's life. On the other hand, the decision to terminate a pregnancy or to mercifully end an unwanted existence were seen as decisions belonging to individuals and their families, not to the government. In 1987, the pro-life movement spawned the International Anti-Euthanasia Task Force.

factors that influence the production, dissemination, application, and internalization of these cognitive structures.

Gurvitch, for instance, has described how different types of social groups tend to favor different types of knowledge and, hence, different styles of thinking. A religious cult, for example, exerts a strong influence over its members' actions and thoughts. Perceiving the secular world as a source of evil, such groups tend to favor only knowledge about themselves, often, like the Amish, disdaining even work-saving technical and life-saving scientific knowledge.

The central templates of a social group act as magnets, attracting wide-ranging attitudes and theories held by the group's members. Such dominant beliefs are said to be **hegemonic.** A hegemonic belief is "an order in which a certain way of life and thought is dominant, in which one concept of reality is diffused throughout society, in all its institutional and private manifestations, informing with its spirit all tastes, morality, customs, religious and political principles, and all social relations, particularly in the intellectual and moral connotations" (Williams 1960:587).

Even supposedly impartial beliefs such as scientific theories are products of their times. The theory of natural selection, for instance, is as much a product of Victorian culture as it is of Darwin's mind (Gould 1990). Sociobiologists' focus on aggressive male behavior as determining the survival of particular genes may reflect not so much the dynamics of nature as the male dominance of organized science.

In sum, although it is tempting to understand consciousness and reasoning as internal, individual-level phenomena, they are largely social. Human thinking is always socially controlled (Durkheim 1912; Durkheim and Mauss 1903). The ways in which we experience, interpret, and ultimately act are all socially determined. As Douglas observed: "Classifications, logical operations, and guiding metaphors are given to the individual by society. . . . The sense of a priori rightness of some ideas and the nonsensicality of others are handed out as part of the social environment" (1986:10).

## Ideology and Propaganda

Sociologically oriented counterparts have focused on the roles of propaganda and ideology in shaping public logic and trust. Political regimes, for instance, control people either by force or by consent. The need to impose political will by force and/or continual surveillance, however, suggests that a regime has neither cultural nor social authority—it is not perceived to be legitimate. It is far preferable to find a noncoercive way to control how citizens think. This is where ideologies and propaganda come into play.

Ideologies differ from propaganda in the same way belief systems differ from stereotypes. As Table 4.1 shows, ideologies integrate theories and shape entire cognitive systems, while propaganda appeals to emotion rather than reason to shape specific attitudes. Marxist ideology, for example, perceives all social relationships in terms of class conflict. The contents of culture, educational curricula, and social-class difference in life expectancy, rates of mental illness, and even quality of sexual relations (see Chapter 10) are all seen as stemming from relations between oppressors and the oppressed.

Propaganda, on the other hand, attempts to produce desired behaviors using methods that take advantage of individuals' irrational persuadability.

**TABLE 4.1  Social-Psychological Differences between Ideologies and Propaganda**

| Characteristics of Ideology | Characteristics of Propaganda |
|---|---|
| 1. Unconscious adherence to patriotic norms, values. A singular set of beliefs, eliciting strong loyalties. | 1. Conscious manipulation of patriotic symbols, norms, values. Multiple sets of beliefs subject to rapid and radical alteration. |
| 2. Collectively established by the group over an extended period of time. Its purpose is defined by its message. | 2. Individually or corporately established over short period of time. Its purpose is to satisfy more basic needs external to itself. |
| 3. Techniques of persuasion in which persuaders are not intellectually distinguishable from persuaded. | 3. Technique of persuasion in which persuaders are intellectually distinguished from persuaded (myth-creator vs. myth-follower). |
| 4. Arises out of existing social conditions and relations in which community finds itself. | 4. Arises out of need to stimulate and revise artificially created standards of social cohesion and conflict. |
| 5. Shaping of "knowledge" and general theories of science and religion. | 5. Shaping of "opinion" and mass culture. |
| 6. Concerned with justification, rationalization of already accepted social behavior patterns. | 6. Concerned with multiplying stimuli best calculated to evoke desired behavior responses. |
| 7. Establishes systematic connections between theories (i.e., laws of historical change); a demand for "rational" motives of action. | 7. Establishes fixation of belief in relation to specific issues; willingness to defend or attack social structures in terms of "irrational" motives. |

Source: Horowitz, 1968:75.

According to the Institute of Propaganda, which was founded before the United States' entry into World War II, those methods include the following (Brown 1958):

**Name calling:** used to make people judge something without scrutinizing evidence.

**Glittering generalities:** the opposite of name calling; employs virtue words, effective use of the facts.

**Transfer:** a tactic used in legitimation, as in "In God We Trust."

**Testimonials:** like "transfers," testimonials employ prestige transfers, as when a respected tennis player publicly endorses a brand of cereal.

**Plain folks:** politicians, labor leaders, and businesspeople claim to be "ordinary people."

**Card stacking:** arguing unfairly in favor of a particular thesis when supposedly presenting a two-sided argument.

**Bandwagon:** "Everyone is doing it, so don't be left out."

Ideology and propaganda also differ in terms of their origins and the intent for which they are employed. Ideologies are broad social mindsets that emerge as part of a historical trend, whereas propaganda is intentionally constructed at a single point in time by, at most, a few individuals. The ideologist has total commitment to and certainty in his or her beliefs (Minogue 1985; Horowitz 1968); the propagandist does not. The former sees himself or herself as a vehicle for the beliefs in question, whereas the latter sees the belief as a vehicle for his or her own interests.

Events in Communist countries during the late 1980s and early 1990s demonstrate what happens when ideology fails. Marxism's view of private property as a form of theft rather than an object of personal motivation produced a politics of distrust and economics characterized by shoddy workmanship and inability to meet the needs of the people. No longer willing to tolerate the growing disparities between their standards of living and those of the West, one by one the Eastern European regimes collapsed to popular uprisings. In China, a growing public conception that the system was wallowing in corruption and that the leadership was arbitrary and unresponsive led to the mass demonstrations at Tiananmen Square in 1989 (Wallace 1989).

## THE SOCIAL PATTERNING OF PERCEPTION

We have argued that personal experiences are socially structured because of individuals' internalization and use of collectively held theories and beliefs. What we perceive is what we know, and what we "know" is largely secondhand knowledge taken from the advice of others.

Our awareness or perception of things around us varies considerably. Perception may be diverted. It may be focused or diffused. It is an active process rather than the passive receptor to stimuli in our environment.

Perception is largely a function of the interrelated processes of **anticipation, memory,** and **attention.** In this section we first consider each of these perceptual processes, focusing on both their psychological and sociological dynamics. We then turn to their consequences in decision making.

### Anticipation

Consider the situation in which two individuals interact with a young man who has a serious stuttering problem. Prior to their encounters, one individual is informed that the stutterer is a certified genius; the other is told he has never been quite "normal." To our first observer, the impression is perhaps that ideas come so fast and furious to the stutterer that he cannot blurt them out fast enough. The second interprets his utterances as evidence of a neurological defect.

The anticipations arising out of our stereotypes and beliefs often shape what we experience, producing **self-fulfilling prophecies.** If you think someone is lazy and stupid, that person will probably prove you correct. As Snyder notes, "Despite people's best intentions, their initial impressions of others are shaped by their assumptions about such characteristics" (1982). What we think about a person influences how we perceive that person. How we perceive another

## Anticipating Relief: The Placebo Effect

A fascinating example of how anticipation can determine subsequent experiences is the **placebo effect.**

When studying the efficacy of different drugs, a standard medical research practice is to give the control group a *placebo,* such as a sugar pill, instead of the medication that is given to the experimental group. Both groups thus share the faith that what they are taking is a potent pain- or symptom-relieving substance. Such anticipations are extremely potent.

Studies of pain victims show that placebos are half as effective as aspirin. For one-third of patients, the sugar pill is about half as effective as a standard dose of morphine. Although a standard dose of morphine was found to be only 54 percent effective for those who are insensitive to placebos, its effectiveness for those who respond to placebos increased to 95 percent (Evans 1974).

person influences how we behave toward him or her. And how we behave toward that person ultimately influences who that person becomes. As we will see in the following chapter, this opens up additional issues such as labeling theory, which deals with the role of classifications in shaping our anticipations.

Anticipations that are held collectively, such as widespread anticipation of an economic recession, can produce large-scale self-fulfilling prophecies. When economists make dire predictions about market trends, any subsequent downturn in economic indicators, however slight, can lead to panic selling and hoarding behavior. Because of the mass media's dissemination of economic knowledge, public anticipations play a major role in determining the direction of stock prices.

## Memory

Social beliefs not only shape anticipations and experiences but also determine what is remembered. People tend to recall only things that reinforce their personal theories. They also tend to forget things for which they have no schemas (Hamilton, Katz, and Leirer 1980). The reason most of us suffer from *childhood amnesia,* or inability to remember events during one's first years of life, is that our adult belief systems and theories of everyday life differ from the operating models we held as young children.

Even "concrete" memories like one's own autobiographical recollections have been found to be inaccurate. Barclay and Wellman (1986) found that people hold false memories because they reconstruct the past in terms of their current beliefs about themselves. Again personal theories (in this case, one's theories about oneself) shape what's perceived, how the experience is stored, and how the memory is retrieved.

Psychologically oriented social psychologists frequently focus on the fallibility of personal memories. For example, "mental blind spots" (Goleman 1985) are caused by the mind's attempts to preserve self-esteem. Psychoanalysts would claim that these are due to denial and repression, leading, for instance, to abused children failing to blame their parents for their abusive treatment. These blind spots can also result from reduced awareness of things that cause anxiety or stress, which is why people forget dental appointments. Flawed memories may also occur as a result of differences in attention. Because of the "weapons focus effect," for instance, viewers of two videotaped versions of an armed robbery varied in the accuracy of their recall of the event. When the robber's gun was hidden beneath a coat, "witnesses" were 40–50 percent more accurate in identifying the robber in a videotaped line-up than when the robber waved his gun during the holdup (Loftus 1984).

Although many people have trouble remembering what they had for lunch on the previous day, they can recall (or think they can) what the weather was like, what they were wearing, and whom they were with when they first heard that President John Kennedy had been assassinated in 1963 or when the Japanese attacked Pearl Harbor in 1941. Here we move into the interrelations between personal memories and social memories—for instance, how social memories trigger, reinforce, and frame the personal (e.g., I can't remember the year we were dating, but the song that was popular at the time was the Beatles' "Can't Buy Me Love."). It is important to appreciate the extent to which memory is actually social. Halbwachs (1950[1980]) argues that most of our memories are organized within a framework provided by the groups to which we belong. As individuals discover at high school reunions, not only are long-unseen faces linked with memories of past events, but the group itself revives and reorganizes the past experiences.

In addition, individuals carry social memories of events far removed in time and space from their own firsthand recollections. The past sets the collective agenda for the future. Americans either "know of" or are periodically reminded of social memories such as the American Revolution and the Civil War, George Washington and Abraham Lincoln, and the landing of the pilgrims. Periodically, these memories of social events are recounted. In the United States during the late 1980s, for instance, the mass media were filled with recollections of the tenth anniversary of the fall of Saigon, the twenty-fifth anniversary of John F. Kennedy's assassination, the seventieth anniversary of the "war to end all wars," the 125th anniversary of the American Civil War, and the bicentennial of the United States Constitution.

## Attention

Attention is the third component of perception. Given our discussions of anticipation and memory, it should come as no surprise that individual receptivity to stimuli is socially shaped as well.

Much consideration has been given by artists, psychologists, architects, and designers of military camouflage to the ways in which context (background) interacts with foreground. To perceive a person or object as an identifiable thing is to see it as a singular unit separated from its background. The greater its contrast, the more it stands out.

There is no way that the brain can process all the sensory input that impinges on it. To avoid cognitive overload, organisms are aware of only the features of the environment that affect their chances of survival. Information that is irrelevant to survival is typically filtered out. Research on the eye of the frog, for instance, has shown that it detects only four kinds of differences: fixed contrasts (e.g., bright water–darker land), sudden moving outlines, sudden decrease in light (e.g., an approaching hand trying to catch it), and small objects near the eye (e.g., a bug on a lily pad within reach) [Ornstein 1972:21–23].

Human awareness is similarly selective and efficient. In addition to the built-in programs that selectively determine what an organism perceives, human senses are further modified by their culture. As we saw in Chapter 2, these sensory frameworks are socially regularized, focusing individuals' attention on that which is predictable and meaningful. For this reason, children can be better perceivers than adults. In one demonstration, Neisser (1979) had both adults and children view a videotape of an action-packed basketball game. Afterward he asked the spectators to describe a woman who had walked through the game carrying an umbrella. Although almost no adult remembered seeing the woman, she was remembered by 22 percent of fourth-graders and 75 percent of first-graders.

Human senses are also modified by roles. An Audubon aficionado, a botanist, a cop, and a painter would experience Central Park in profoundly different ways. Each observer has sensory shorthands ("attention heuristics") to simplify the array of stimuli he or she encounters.

## SOCIAL AND COGNITIVE PATTERNINGS OF INFORMATION PROCESSING

Strictly speaking it is incorrect to say that the single individual thinks. Rather it is more correct to insist that he participates in thinking further what other men have thought before him. He finds himself in an inherited situation with patterns of thought which are appropriate to this situation and attempts to elaborate further the inherited modes of response or to substitute others for them in order to deal more adequately with the new challenges which have arisen out of the shifts and changes in his situation. (Mannheim 1936:3)

Just as individuals' theories of everyday life and perceptions of reality are shaped by social forces, so too are their judgments and decisions. The ill-fated decision to launch the space shuttle *Challenger* in January 1986 revealed that the social decision-making system was as much at fault as the individual decision makers. At the system level, experts' objections to the launch were overruled and kept from key decision makers because of the space agency's compartmentalized review process and "gung-ho, can-do" ethic (Boffey 1986), coupled with strong political pressure to meet launch schedules. For instance, when one engineer refused to give his approval for the launch, the agency went over his head and gained approval from his superior. At the personal level, commitment to the launch decision led to "freeze-think" (Kruglanski 1986), in which individuals abridged their search for information and options, particularly when contrary evidence was unavailable.

The motivations for maintaining commitment even to bad decisions include wishful thinking, psychological attraction to clear-cut answers and aversion to the ambiguity, and the belief that any decision is superior to indecision.

Among the few conditions that can counteract "freeze-thinking" are personal accountability for the decision ("the buck stops here") and "fear of invalidity," in which the costs of bad judgments become too high for the decision maker (Kruglanski 1986). In this section we will explore additional psychological and sociological dynamics underlying the ways in which individuals process data when making judgments and decisions.

## Inferences

Rather than using data to determine their hypotheses, people tend to use their hypotheses to determine what social data to process. Their observations are far from impartial, and the same is true of their interpretations of what is observed. People seem to be interested in evaluating how consistent the evidence is with the hypothesis they are testing; they fail to consider the possibility that it would support alternative hypotheses (Fischhoff and Beyth-Marom 1983). This is why people tend to seek out and remember cases that support their stereotypes and worldviews and to avoid, ignore, or forget those that do not (Hamilton and Rose 1980).

MAIER'S LAW: If the facts do not conform to the theory, they must be disposed of.

Individuals' impressions are influenced not only by commitment to hypotheses and beliefs but also by personal needs, desires, intentions, and emotions. In a famous study of how judgment is influenced by personal meanings, Bruner and Goodman (1947) asked ten-year-old children from different social classes to estimate the size of five coins. Poor children exaggerated their size; rich children did not. Similarly, people often believe themselves to be at the center of events: "Who are they talking about? It must be about me"; "I know that I am the reason for my parents' divorce"; "If I had only campaigned harder, Charlie would have been elected class president." These, in turn, can lead to ego-enhancing biases and illusions of control, in which people reinterpret events so as to put themselves in a favorable light: "If I hadn't been there, there's no way the sorority would have been ready for Parents' Weekend."

Biases are also introduced by the way the information itself was presented or acquired. Perhaps best known is the potency of **first impressions,** or the **primacy effect,** which disproportionately weights the first information encountered. When, for instance, a job applicant first meets a company's personnel officer, the latter quickly sizes up the candidate and interprets all subsequent impressions in ways that are consistent with the initial assessment. **Recency effects** have been detected as well (Jones and Goethals 1971). These can occur when subjects are told that they will be asked to recall specifics for each stimulus condition, which equalizes the otherwise decreasing attention given over time and taps the greater contents of short-term memory (Dreben, Fiske, and Hastie 1979). Thus, given the possible U-shaped relationship between memory and stimulus order, it is perhaps best for job candidates to be either first or last interviewed. Finally, there are **contrast effects.** When we are presented with two things, one after the other, and the second object is somewhat different from the first, our tendency is to perceive it as being more different than it really is.

# Which Template to Use?

Consider the following situation. You have been impaneled as a prospective juror on a case in which the accused is being tried for auto theft. The accused, a shabbily dressed 19-year-old white youth with long, unclean hair, claims that he was only borrowing the vehicle from an acquaintance. The acquaintance acknowledges talking about the car but is adamant about never having loaned the car to the individual. You are told that the defendant will not speak on his own behalf and that the case will revolve around his "intent."

The first decision is what schema to use for encoding your observations in the courtroom. We apply models that we perceive to be appropriate for deciphering particular social events. The readiness with which a schema is retrieved from one's repertoire of interpretative templates is referred to as its "construct accessibility" (Higgins and King 1981). Generally, it is the most accessible, not relevant, schema that is employed.

Once a schema is selected, its own internal logic further determines (and may bias) the ways decisions are made. Tversky and Kahneman (1973) propose that people form mental models based on similar past experiences and then "run" those models much like computer simulations to produce plausible scenarios. The researchers found that the easier a simulation outcome comes to mind, the more likely individuals are to believe that the outcome will occur in reality. For instance, in studying people's recollections and alterations of stories, Kahneman and Tversky (1982) found that to increase the tales' internal coherence people eliminate unexpected and surprising twists.

On the other hand, research indicates that successful corporate executives may have achieved their status through cognitive complexity (Streufert and Swezey 1986). These individuals remain open to new information and can anticipate a far wider range of possible scenarios, because they are not locked into a single interpretative framework.

# Selecting and Combining Inputs

Consider the difficulties faced by extremely obese people in finding jobs. And why is it the tallest candidate who usually wins the presidential election?

The schema selected largely determines *what* information is to be processed (**cue selection**) as well as *how*. As we have seen, a great deal of what is perceived is actually inferred. Often, negative or positive characteristics are assumed when only a single, dominant trait has been observed (the **"halo effect"** [Thorndike 1920]). The implicit personality and status expectations described earlier reveal how, using limited information, humans tend to make inferences (**illusory correlations** [Chapman 1967]) because of their assumptions about how personality and social traits are related.

As an illustration, consider the way physical attractiveness influences the fates of men and women in the work world. Attractiveness has been found to enhance gender characterizations, with attractive males perceived as more masculine than unattractive males and attractive females as more feminine than their less attractive counterparts (Gillen 1981). In one study, professional personnel consultants were presented with resumes differing only in terms of the applicants' gender; some were accompanied by photographs and others were not. Physical attractiveness was found to positively affect the consultants' decisions unless the applicants were seeking jobs considered inappropriate for their sex (Cash, Gillen, and Burns 1977). Pursuing the underlying inferences further, Heilman and Stopeck (1985) presented detailed resumes of corporate executives to a sample of men and women of various ages and a variety of occupations. Attached to each resume was a photograph of the individual. Again the resumes were nearly identical, varying only in terms of the applicants' gender (half were female), attractiveness (half were attractive, the other half not), and career progress (half were rapid climbers while the remainder had a normal rate of ascent up the corporate ladder). When the subjects were asked to account for the applicants' career progress in terms of ability, effort, political know-how, luck, and relations with higher-ups, attractive females were consistently judged as less capable than the unattractive female managers, and their success was less likely to be attributed to ability. Conversely, the success of attractive males was strongly attributed to their ability; they were viewed as being more capable than their unattractive counterparts.

Individuals, however, often hold not one but many attitudes that may be applicable in any given situation. How do some attitudes become more salient than others? How do they all coalesce? What are attitudes, anyway? Are they gut-level, automatic predispositions or consciously reasoned philosophies or merely orientations with minimal bearing on actions?

Consider students' attitudes toward particular classes. Often such opinions are publicly exchanged: A friend may ask a veteran of a particular course whether or not she should enroll; at the end of the semester, those enrolled may be asked for course evaluations. How do students pull together ten or fifteen weeks of academic experiences and derive a summary judgment?

Let's begin by examining how information may affect one's decision making, taking as an example a student's responses to statements on a university course evaluation.

*For each of the questions below, please indicate whether you strongly agree (+2), don't know (0), or strongly disagree (−2).*

| | |
|---|---|
| 1 | The professor's presentations are intellectually stimulating. |
| 1 | This course gave insights to many other classes I'm taking. |
| 2 | I like the professor personally. |
| 2 | I enjoy the subject matter of this class. |
| 1 | Examinations are graded fairly and objectively. |
| −2 | I learned many valuable ideas and/or skills. |
| −1 | This course inspired me to work hard. |
| −1 | The professor encourages class participation. |
| −1 | I expect to receive a good grade. |

In deciding whether a student will be more likely to tell a friend to take this course as opposed to another, we can simply add the scores given to the statements above for both classes and select the one with the highest total. The assumption of **additive model** of attitude formation is that overall impressions are determined by the sum effect of relevant attitudes. Despite the simplicity of this model, research indicates that individuals do not treat all attitudes equally; instead, they give more potency to some attitudes (e.g., fundamental moral beliefs or value orientations deemed central to one's self-concept) than to others. This insight has led to efforts to depict (and measure) the overall effect of attitudes by using **weighted models.** This method would take into account the student's responses toward the course evaluation categories in addition to the personal importance he or she places on each.

| | Personal Evaluation | Personal Importance | Evaluation × Importance |
|---|---|---|---|
| interesting lectures | 1 | 3 | 3 |
| course relevance | 1 | 1 | 1 |
| like prof | 2 | 1 | 2 |
| I like subject | 2 | 2 | 4 |
| exams fair | 1 | 3 | 3 |
| amount learned | −2 | 4 | −8 |
| worked hard | −1 | 2 | −2 |
| class style | −1 | 0 | 0 |
| good grade | −1 | 5 | −5 |
| Total Attitude | +2 (additive score) | | −2 (weighted score) |

Observe that according to the additive model the student's attitude toward the course is shown to be slightly positive, whereas according to the weighted model the student appears somewhat negative.

Researchers from the gestalt tradition point out another component of individuals' attitudinal calculus: Principles exist about how information or opinions are to be logically or casually related. Sometimes, when faced with a multiplicity of attitudes toward a particular situation, people become aware of their own attitudinal inconsistencies. Experiencing this dissonance as unpleasant, they seek a more consistent cognitive state. In the course evaluation example, note that the student reported liking the subject matter, viewed the exams as fair, and yet expected a low grade. This runs contrary to the assumption that one should do well when engaging in activities that one enjoys. What happens? According to **cognitive dissonance** (Festinger 1957) and **balance** (Heider 1958; Newcombe 1971) **theories,** there is a strong tendency to change one or more of one's attitudes to reduce dissonance: If one firmly believes that one likes the subject then the exams may, indeed, have been unfair; if the consensus of others is that the exams were fair, then perhaps one might reappraise one's interest in the subject matter and judge that it was really not that great.

## Attributions Made When Assessing Social Behavior

Out of the need to make sense of the world and gain some control over apparently random events (Kelley 1971), when social actors observe the behavior of others they infer meanings from the acts: "Why did Bill not return my wave?

He must not have acknowledged me because he is still steamed over my slip-up last Thursday night." To make such assumptions about underlying meanings, individuals must also make inferences regarding the causes of behavior: "But then again, perhaps Bill didn't even see me when I entered the cafeteria." Such **attributions** are of particular interest to social psychologists who study the ways in which people use their personal theories to interpret social action.

Our initial impulse is to infer stable characteristics in others on the basis of their overt behavior and to use them to explain future courses of action (Heider 1958; Jones and Davis 1965; Jones and Nisbett 1971). We assume that people do not behave in random and totally unpredictable ways, or that they are social chameleons, always changing to adapt to unique circumstances. Rather, we assume that individuals act in relatively consistent ways across a variety of situations. When viewing the fuller spectrum of our own actions, on the other hand, we typically see our behaviors as responses to situations in our environment. Thus, Bill thinks, "I wanted to wave to Margaret, but I just did not want to face the guys' snide remarks."

These assumptions lead to the **fundamental attributional error** (Ross 1977), whereby we tend to perceive our own behavior as occurring largely in response to various situations, whereas the actions of others are perceived as derived from their internal dispositions. In other words, there is a tendency to overestimate the importance of personal or dispositional factors and to underestimate situational or environmental factors when judging the behaviors of others. In part, this occurs because of the information available. Knowing our own thoughts and drives, we shift our focus to external factors when perceiving ourselves. Not having complete insight into the minds of others, we assume that their actions are personally motivated and not due to external forces.

Research has shown that we are not as accurate as we think we are even in deciphering our own inner states (Bem 1972). In one experiment, Valins (1966) had male students view nude female slides while simultaneously listening to what they thought were the amplified sounds of their heartbeats. The heartbeats they heard, however, were not theirs. Some images were accompanied by little rate of change in heart rhythm, while others were associated with increasing or decreasing rhythms. When asked to rate the attractiveness of the women, the males gave higher scores to those whose images were accompanied by higher heartbeat rates. They probably assumed that the increased rates were indicative of their inner feelings.

"Self-serving bias" (Miller and Ross 1975) may enter into the attribution process. Typically, the positive or successful behaviors of others are seen to be externally controlled, whereas their negative actions are seen as derived from internal dynamics. On the other hand, our own successful acts are seen as derived from internal traits while our failures are viewed as stemming from external factors. Such biases can lead to our **blaming the victims** for their fate. This is why the blame for poverty is so often placed on its victims rather than on the structural inequalities of society and why victims of rape so often receive so little public sympathy ("She must have asked for it").

There are, of course, numerous situations in which intentions cannot be inferred from behavior. Socially desirable acts are less likely to be seen as indicative of intent than socially undesirable acts. Nor are conventional actions; it is unconventional and unusual actions that provoke our need to identify a causal schema. Harold Kelley (1967) developed a mental calculus that takes into account not only the observed actor but also the social context and the target of his or her actions. For instance, consider the case in which a student makes disparaging remarks to a professor during class. The initial tendency is to view the student's motivations as internal: "He's just an abusive person." This attribution holds if the student is viewed to be similarly obnoxious in other classes (high consistency). However, if other students are similarly abusive toward the same teacher (high consensus) and the student in question acts this way only in this particular class (high distinctiveness), one infers that his action occurred because of external conditions.

One may ask, "So what? What difference does the cause of behavior make?" In large part it has to do with matters of free will and determinism. Consider how the issue of personal control enters into legal decisions such as whether or not a death is ruled a suicide or a person receives the death sentence for a capital crime. In 1979 the California Court of Appeals for the Fourth District ruled that an insane person could not commit suicide because such an individual "cannot form the intent to take his own life" (*New York Times* 1979). To be executed in the United States, individuals must be "mentally competent" at the time of death in order that they appreciate the ceremony and understand that they are about to be killed and the reason why.

Moreover, people will take more responsibility for their actions if they believe they have free choice. In the workplace, decentralization of decision making and increased worker autonomy lead to greater employee commitment, lower absenteeism, higher productivity, and better product quality. (See Chapter 15.) People who perceive themselves as having free choice may also be more satisfied with the direction their lives take because of their decisions.

## When a Template Is Inaccessible

When they encounter information that is irrelevant to their schematized world view, people tend to process it quickly and uncritically, often assuming it to be true. Why waste the cognitive effort? However, if the formerly irrelevant information later becomes relevant, it might not occur to the person that the facts might be incorrect. Alternative ways of thinking are unavailable.

As an illustration, consider the claims of parapsychological and extraterrestrial phenomena, events for which most people do not have interpretive schemas. Often such occurrences are accepted as fact with little verification. A 1987 survey found that college-educated Americans were more likely (by 57 percent to 46 percent) to believe in the existence of extraterrestrials than their counterparts who did not attend college (Gallup 1987). What could account for such a difference? Perhaps with higher education one is exposed to a broader range of schemas, resulting in greater cognitive flexibility.

The enhanced salience of information when schemas are weakly structured or underdeveloped has a number of sociological consequences. Smith and Caldwell (1973) found that a judge's admonishment to disregard inadmissible evidence was not always heeded. In cases in which the evidence presented was weak and inconclusive, the inadmissible evidence strongly influenced jurors' verdicts in simulated trials. When the evidence was sound, jurors were not biased by the inadmissible evidence. Apparently, when we think we have a solid foundation on which to make a judgment we do not feel a need to make use of additional information.

This chapter has been predicated on the cognitive psychological assumption that people have conscious control over their actions and that what they think has some bearing on what they do. Without such a correspondence, existing research on attitudes would be irrelevant and opinion research and public relations firms might as well close up shop. The assumption that by changing attitudes one can change behaviors also underlies federal campaigns to shape attitudes—for example, to reduce smoking or change sexual activities or driving behavior.

## The Attitude—Behavior Connection

For decades the relationship between attitudes and behavior has been debated. Some research has indicated that there is little connection between the two. For example, to gauge Americans' negative attitudes toward Asians during the 1930s, Richard LaPiere (1934) toured the United States with a Chinese couple. Of the 250 hotels and restaurants where they stopped, only one refused them service. Yet when LaPiere later wrote to the same establishments asking if they would accept Chinese patrons, half refused to answer, and of those that did, 90 percent refused them service. These results would seem to indicate that attitudes generally fail to predict behavior. However, this is not entirely true. Researchers have found that general attitudes predict general behaviors, whereas specific attitudes can predict specific behaviors. For instance, though we cannot calculate precisely how prejudiced persons will interact when in a face-to-face encounter with minority group members, we can predict they will be less likely than unprejudiced others to voluntarily seek out such engagements. Our accuracy increases when predicting their interference in the dating behavior of their daughters if we know the persons' attitudes toward having a close relative marrying someone from a particular ethnic or racial group.

Do attitudes cause behavior or does behavior affect attitudes? In general, research reveals the relationships to be modest at best (Hill 1981), with indications that causality goes both ways. In Ajzen and Fishbein's reasoned-action theory, behavior is conceptualized as being consciously controlled, with people first considering the implications of their actions (Fishbein 1967; Fishbein and Ajzen 1975; Ajzen and Fishbein 1980). Thus, the effects of one's private attitudes are indirect, being consciously weighted against their social appropriateness. (See Figure 4.4.) The restaurant personnel whom LaPiere studied, when faced by the researcher and his Asian guests, may have held negative attitudes toward Asians but also faced normative issues such as being unwilling to make an ugly scene and always being hospitable to well-dressed paying customers.

Reversing the causal connection between attitudes and behavior, Bem's self-perception theory (1967, 1972) views people as using their own behavior as a cue for understanding their own attitudes. Thus, a man might realize his sexist attitudes only upon recognizing that he interacts differently with women than with other men.

Applying this idea to America's racial problem, attempts were made to eliminate stereotypes and prejudice by placing people of different races together in military platoons, in the workplace, and in schools. The results sometimes

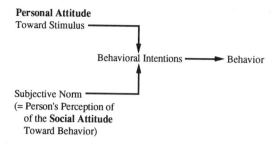

**Personal Attitude**
Toward Stimulus

Behavioral Intentions ⟶ Behavior

Subjective Norm
(= Person's Perception of
of the **Social Attitude**
Toward Behavior)

**FIGURE 4.4    Behavior as a Consequence of
Personal Attitudes and Constraints of Social
Attitudes and Contexts**

failed to go in the direction predicted. Reviewing studies of the effects of school desegregation, for instance, Stephan (1978) found that prejudice and interracial hostilities increased more often than they declined at desegregated schools. In her study of a desegregated school, Schofield (1986) found African Americans sensing that the white students considered themselves superior. Holding this view, it is not surprising that African Americans shunned offers of help by white students: The African American students interpreted the acts as condescending, and if the aid was accepted it would reinforce both white dominance and African American subordination. According to Allport (1954), such interpersonal contacts can actually reinforce prejudice unless the participants have equal power, participate together in cooperative endeavors, and get to know each other personally.

Consideration of how behaviors shape attitudes also gives us insight into how broad social forces can determine personal attitudes. In examining attitudes toward old age, for example, Kiesler (1981) first describes the social constraints, incentives, and pressures shaping individuals' behaviors (the "exogenous forces" in Table 4.2). Thus, the increasing age segregation of social activities has led to a situation in which the only older people with whom younger individuals have any meaningful interaction with are family members. Another illustration is the way society specifies the ages at which one should perform the roles of student, worker, or retiree.

## The Connection between Collective Action and Cultural Belief Systems

At a macro level, collective action also precedes cultural beliefs. Before a full-blown belief system comes into existence, replete with values and logic and worldview, there are cultural do's and don'ts. These, in turn, derive not from inner convictions but from social circumstances. Consider the changes in Western beliefs about the function of cemeteries. Before the tenth century in Catholic Christendom, cemeteries were simply undisturbed places were bodies would sleep (RIP = *requiescat in pace*) until Judgment Day. But with rising urbanization they became increasingly public places, asylums for residents of crowded cities. (So busy had they become that the church had to forbid gambling and dancing in cemeteries.) As urban areas became overpopulated and

**TABLE 4.2   How Broad Sociocultural Forces Determine Attitudes toward Old Age and Older People**

| Exogenous Forces → | Behavior | Attitudes |
|---|---|---|
| Demographic increases in older population | actual contact with older persons, as in family settings, in grocery stores, on the road, etc. | stereotypes of older persons as helpless and dependent or as exploiters of those in the labor force |
| Changes in older persons' standards of living | | |
| Social norms regarding old (e.g., rules of deference) | obligatory ritual actions toward the old | expectations of older persons in different social situations, such as being oblivious of others on the road or complaining of physical ailments in conversational settings |
| Geographic mobility of family members and less contact with grandparents | commitments to groups wherein old are found (e.g., civic, religious, and political groups) | |
| Increases in Social Security taxes on working population | age-related roles and expectations (e.g., 8-year-olds in school and not on factory assemble lines) | beliefs that the old are selfish, uncaring of younger generations |
| Changing media portrayals of older persons | | |

Source: Adapted from Kiesler, 1981.

additional land was needed for transportation systems and market areas, the world of the living had to be segregated from the world of the dead. Cemeteries were moved to the outskirts of town. To rationalize the change, the developing science of medicine sensitized the population to the health hazards of bodies floating to the surface and the stench of common graves; religious officials also began to portray contact with the dead as something indecent. At the same time, freed from the constraints of space and tradition, funeral architecture blossomed.

## Sociological Views of the Action–Belief Connection

A more sociological approach is to consider the social dynamics behind the idea that there is a connection between individuals' beliefs and their actions. This occurs when personal belief systems are expected to be publicly shared, so that when a social commitment is established, actors are expected to be responsible for doing what they say they will do.

In some spheres the connection between action and belief is taken for granted. For instance, religious leaders are expected to publicly express their doctrine and to act according to their precepts. To do otherwise, as in the notorious cases of televangelists such as Jim Bakker in the 1980s, is to run the risk of being accused of hypocrisy (the term is derived from the Greek *hypokrisis*, meaning "to pretend, to play a part on the stage"). To be hypocritical—to claim to others that one is acting on one's principles or beliefs when one really isn't—is to violate basic social trust. And if the ulterior motives are not known, the hypocrite's actions become uncertain, thereby violating the social need for predictability.

The latter situation is faced by many political regimes. Presidential candidates, for instance, present attitudes that are known to appeal to their audiences; if they present different attitudes on different occasions, they run the risk of being caught "flip-flopping." But the audiences know the game, and over time they come to expect a certain amount of variation in candidates' positions (Kinsley 1990). This can lead to loss of faith in the political leadership and even in the legitimacy of the political system.

## CONCLUSION

The perceived orderliness of the world turns out to be a function of the individual's interpretive capacities, together with willingness to suspend doubt. Such talents are not derived from biochemical programming but are learned from the social system and then internalized.

Social order requires at least some congruence between the templates—stereotypes, beliefs, and theories about behaviors—of its individual members. If every act were perceived to be idiosyncratic and unique by each social observer, neither personal nor social order would be possible. Instead, for the most part templates are held collectively. Through socialization, social actors come to assume that there exists a reciprocity of perspectives; they believe (until further notice) that social experiences are the same for all.

Culture itself can be understood as a collection of shared schemas for perceiving and interpreting the world. Out of the myriad of gestures, sounds, and feelings associated with one's social environment, it is largely culture that determines what one should pay attention to and how. Its function is analogous to that of a radio receiver: Social messages are carried on a broad range of frequencies; it is culture that selects the "sensory frequencies" that are to be noticed; it is culture that gives meaning to the meaningless, just as the radio makes sound out of silent radio waves.

Mythology provides an example of how cultural templates are used to interpret experience. As Joseph Campbell explains:

> Greek and Latin and biblical literature used to be part of everyone's education. Now, when these were dropped, a whole tradition of Occidental mythological information was lost. It used to be that these stories were in the minds of people. When the story is in your mind, then you see its relevance to something happening in your own life. It gives you perspective on what's happening to you. . . . These bits of information from ancient times, which have to do with the themes that have supported

human life, built civilizations, and informed religions over the millennia, have to do with deep inner problems, inner mysteries, inner thresholds of passage, and if you don't know what the guide signs are along the way, you have to work it out yourself. (1988:4)

Precisely how culture "works," how a common mental world comes to be, will be an underlying theme of the chapters to follow. In Chapter 5, for instance, we will note how words are the carriers of stereotypes and beliefs, and how, by thinking in terms of the same symbols, individuals come to share the same psychological realities. Even the most intensely personal, subjective experiences are recast and given meaning by these collectively held templates, as will be seen in the discussions of emotions in Chapter 6.

# REFERENCES

Ajzen, J. R., and M. Fishbein. 1980. *Understanding attitudes and predicting social behavior.* Englewood Cliffs, NJ: Prentice-Hall.

Ajzen, J. R., and M. Fishbein. 1977. Attitude-behavior relations: A theoretical analysis and review of empirical research. *Psychological Bulletin* 84:888–918.

Allport, G. W. 1954. *The nature of prejudice.* Garden City, NY: Doubleday.

Allport, G. W. 1935. Attitudes. In C. Murchison (ed.), *A handbook of social psychology.* Worcester, MA: Clark University Press.

Asch, Solomon. 1951. Effects of group pressure upon the modification and distortion of judgment. In H. Guetzkow (ed.), *Groups, leadership and men.* Pittsburgh: Carnegie Press.

Asch, Solomon. 1955, November. Opinions and social pressure. *Scientific American*, pp. 31–35.

Asch, Solomon. 1952. *Social psychology.* Englewood Cliffs, NJ: Prentice-Hall.

Barclay, C. R., and H. M. Wellman. 1986. Accuracies and inaccuracies in autobiographical memories. *Journal of Memory and Language* 25(1):93103.

Bem, D. J. 1972. Self-perception theory. In L. Berkowitz (ed.), *Advances in Experimental Social Psychology*, vol. 6. Orlando: Academic Press.

Bem, D. J. 1967. Self-perception: An alternative interpretation of cognitive dissonance phenomena. *Psychological Review* 74:183–200.

Berger, J., and M. Zelditch (eds.). 1985. *Status, rewards, and influence.* San Francisco: Jossey-Bass.

Berman, J. S., and D. A. Kenny. 1976. Correlational bias in observer ratings. *Journal of Personality and Social Psychology* 34:263–273.

Boffey, Philip. 1986, February 14. Analyst who gave shuttle warning faults 'gung-ho, can-do' attitude. *New York Times*, p. 11.

Borhek, James, and Richard Curtis. 1975. *A sociology of belief.* New York: Wiley.

Bronowski, Jacob. 1973. *The ascent of man.* Boston: Little, Brown.

Brown, Roger. 1958. *Words and things.* New York: Free Press.

Bruner, Jerome, J. J. Goodnow, and G. A. Austin. 1956. *A study of thinking.* New York: Wiley.

Bruner, Jerome, and Goodman. 1947.

Campbell, Joseph. 1988. *The power of myth.* New York: Doubleday.

Cash, T. F., B. Gillen, and D. S. Burns. 1977. Sexism and beautyism in personnel consultant decision-making. *Journal of Applied Psychology* 62:301–310.

Chapman, L. J. 1967. Illusory correlation in observational report. *Journal of Verbal Learning and Verbal Behavior* 6:151–155.

Douglas, Mary. 1986. *How institutions think.* Syracuse, NY: Syracuse University Press.

Dreben, E. K., S. T. Fiske, and R. Hastie. 1979. The independence of evaluative and item information: Impression and recall order effects in behavior-based impression formation. *Journal of Personality and Social Psychology.* 37:1758–1768.

Durkheim, Émile. 1912. *Les formes elémentaires de la vie religieuse: Le système totemique en Australie.* Paris: Alcan.

Durkheim, Émile, and Marcel Mauss. 1903. De quelques formes primitives de classification. *L'Année Sociologique* 6:1–72.

Etzioni, Amitai. 1988. *The moral dimension: Toward a new economics.* New York: Free Press.

Evans, Frederick. 1974, April. The power of a sugar pill. *Psychology Today*, pp. 55–59.

Festinger, Leon. 1957. *A theory of cognitive dissonance.* New York: HarperCollins.

Fishbein, M. 1967. Attitude and predictive behavior. In M. Fishbein (ed.), *Attitude theory and measurement,* New York: Wiley.

Fishbein, M., and I. Ajzen. 1975. *Belief, attitude, intention, and behavior: An introduction to theory and research.* Reading, MA: Addison-Wesley.

Fiske, Edward. 1987, September 8. Schools criticized on the humanities. *New York Times*, pp. 1, 7.

Fiske, Susan, and Shelley Taylor. *Social cognition.* Reading, MA: Addison-Wesley.

Fischhoff, B., and R. Beyth-Marom. 1983. Hypothesis evaluation from a Bayesian perspective. *Psychological Review* 90:239–260.

Flavell, John. 1986, January. Really and truly. *Psychology Today*, pp. 41–44.

*The Gallup report.* 1987, March. Rept. no. 258.

Geertz, Clifford. 1973. *The interpretation of cultures: Selected essays.* New York: Basic Books.

Gillen, B. 1981. Physical attractiveness: A determinant of two types of goodness. *Personality and Social Psychology Bulletin* 7:277–281.

Goleman, Daniel. 1989, June 27. Delusion, benign and bizarre, is recognized as common. *New York Times*, p. 10.

Goleman, Daniel. 1985. *Vital lies, simple truths: The psychology of self-deception.* New York: Simon and Schuster.

Gould, Stephen Jay. 1990, October. An asteroid to die for. *Discover*, pp. 60–65.

Grant, P. R., and J. G. Holmes. 1981. The integration of implicit personality schemas and stereotype images. *Social Psychology Quarterly* 44:107–115.

Gurvitch, Georges. 1966[1971]. *The social frameworks of knowledge* [trans. Margaret A. Thompson and Kenneth A. Thompson]. New York: Harper Torchbooks.

Halbwachs, Maurice. 1950[1980]. *The collective memory* (trans. Francis J. Ditter, Jr., and Vida Y. Ditter). New York: Harper Colophon.

Hamilton, D. L., L. B. Katz, and V. O. Leirer. 1980. Cognitive representation of personality impression: Organizational processes in first impression formation. *Journal of Personality and Social Psychology* 39:1050–1063.

Hamilton, D. L., and T. L. Rose. 1980. Illusory correlation and the maintenance of stereotypic beliefs. *Journal of Personality and Social Psychology* 39:832–845.

*Harper's Magazine.* 1987, March. Harper's index, p. 15.

Heider, F. 1958. *The psychology of interpersonal relations.* New York: Wiley.

Heilman, Madeline E., and Melanie H. Stopeck. 1985. Attractiveness and corporate success: Different causal attributions for males and females. *Journal of Applied Psychology* 70:(2):379–388.

Higgins, E. Tory, and Gillian King. 1981. Accessibility of social constructs: Information processing consequences of individual and contextual variability. In N. Cantor and J. F. Kihlstron (eds.), *Personality, cognition, and social interaction.* Hillsdale, NJ: Erlbaum.

Hill, Richard. 1981. Attitudes and behavior. In Morris Rosenberg and Ralph Turner (eds.), *Social psychology: Sociological perspectives.* New York: Basic Books.

Horowitz, Irving Louis. 1968. *Professing sociology: Studies in the life cycle of social science.* Carbondale and Edwardsville: Southern Illinois University Press.

Jaspers, J. M. F., and C. Fraser. 1981. Attitudes and social representations. In S. Moscovici and R. Farr (eds.), *Social representations.* Cambridge, England: Cambridge University Press.

Johnson, Dirk. 1990, July 31. "Right to die": Second battle for abortion foes. *New York Times*, pp. A1, A6.

Jones, E. E., and K. E. Davis. 1965. From acts to dispositions: The attribution process in person perception. In L. Berkowitz (ed.), *Advances in experimental social psychology*, vol. 2. Orlando: Academic Press.

Jones, E. E., and G. R. Goethals. 1971. *Order effects in impression formation: Attribution context and the nature of the entity.* Morristown, NJ: General Learning Press.

Jones, E. E., and R. E. Nisbett. 1971. The actor and the observer: Divergent perceptions of the causes of behavior. In E. E. Jones, D. E. Kanouse, H. H. Kelley, R. E. Nisbett, S. Valins, and B. Weiner (eds.), *Attribution: Perceiving the causes of behavior*. Morristown, NJ: General Learning Press.

Kahneman, Daniel, and Amos Tversky. 1982. The simulation heuristic. In Daniel Kahneman, Paul Slovic, and Amos Tversky (eds.), *Judgment under uncertainty: Heuristics and biases*. New York: Cambridge University Press.

Katz, D. 1960. The functional approach to the study of attitudes. *Public Opinion Quarterly* 24: 163–204.

Kearl, Michael , and Richard Harris. 1981. Individualism and the emerging 'modern' ideology of death. *Omega* 12(2):269–280.

Kelley, Harold H. 1971. Attribution in social interaction. In E. E. Jones, D. E. Kanouse, H. H. Kelley, R. E. Nisbett, S. Valins, and B. Weiner (eds.), *Attribution: Perceiving the causes of behavior*. Morristown, NJ: General Learning Press.

Kelley, Harold H. 1967. Attribution theory in social psychology. In D. Levine (ed.), *Nebraska symposium on motivation*. Lincoln: University of Nebraska Press.

Kelly, George. 1955. *The psychology of personal constructs*. New York: Norton.

Kiesler, Sara. 1981. The aging population, social trends, and changes of behavior and belief. In Sara B. Kiesler, James N. Morgan, and Valerie K. Oppenheimer (eds.), *Aging: Social change*. Orlando: Academic Press.

Kinsley, Michael. 1990, July 16. Is Bush nice? A contrarian view. *Time*, p. 88.

Kruglanski, Arie. 1986, August. Freeze-think and the Challenger. *Psychology Today*, pp. 48–49.

Kuhn, Thomas. 1970. *The structure of scientific revolutions* (2nd ed.). Chicago: University of Chicago Press.

LaPiere, R. T. 1934. Attitude vs. actions. *Social Forces* 13:230–237.

Larsen, K. 1974. Conformity in the Asch experiment. *Journal of Social Psychology* 94:303–304.

Leo, John. 1984, April 23. Essay: An age of organized touchiness. *Time*, pp. 85–86.

Loftus, Elizabeth F. 1984, February. Eyewitnesses: Essential but unreliable. *Psychology Today*, pp. 22–36.

Mannheim, Karl. 1936. *Ideology and utopia* [trans. Louis Wirth and Edward Shils]. New York: Harvest Books.

Menges, Constantine. 1989. *Inside the National Security Council: The true story of the making and unmaking of Reagan's foreign policy*. New York: Touchstone.

Miller, D. T., and M. Ross. 1975. Self-serving biases in the attribution of causality: Fact or fiction. *Psychological Bulletin* 82:213–225.

Minogue, Kenneth. 1985. *Alien powers: The pure theory of ideology*. New York: St. Martin's Press.

Morrow, Lance. 1990, March 5. Let us recuse ourselves awhile. *Time*, p. 72.

Neisser, Ulric. 1979. The control of information pickup in selective looking. In A. D. Pick (ed.), *Perception and its development: A tribute to Eleanor Gibson*. Hillsdale, NJ: Erlbaum.

Newcombe, Theodore. 1971. Dyadic balance as a source of clues about interpersonal attraction. In B. I. Murstein (ed.), *Theories of attraction and love*. New York: Springer.

*New York Times*. 1979, September 4. Coast court rules insane person may not be held to be a suicide. p. A25.

Ornstein, Robert. 1972. *The psychology of consciousness*. San Francisco: W. H. Freeman.

Perrin, S., and C. Spencer. 1980. The Asch effect—A child of its time? *Bulletin of the British Psychology Society* 32:405–406.

Rose, Arnold. 1948. Anti-semitism's root in city-hatred. *Commentary* 6:374–378.

Rosenberg, S. V., and A. Sedlack. 1972. Structural representations of implicit personality theory. In L. Berkowitz (ed.), *Advances in experimental social psychology*, vol. 6. Orlando: Academic Press.

Rosenberg, S. V., C. Nelson, and P. S. Vivekananthan. 1968. A multidimensional approach to the structure of personality impressions. *Journal of Personality and Social Psychology* 9: 283–294.

Rosenthal, R., and L. Jacobson. 1968. *Pygmalion in the classroom: Teacher expectation and pupil's intellectual development*. Fort Worth, TX: Holt, Rinehart and Winston.

Ross, L. 1977. The intuitive psychologist and his shortcomings: Distortions in the attribution process. In L. Berkowitz (ed.), *Advances in experimental social psychology*, vol. 10. Orlando: Academic Press.

Saint-Simon, Henri. 1825[1965]. La physiologie sociale, œuvres choisies. Paris: Presses Universitaires de France.

Schlesinger, Arthur, Jr. 1989, July. The opening of the American mind. *New York Times Review of Books*, pp. 1, 26.

Schneider, David J. 1973. Implicit personality theory: A review. *Psychological Bulletin* 92:294-309.

Schofield, Janet. 1986. Black-white contact in desegregated schools. In M. Hewstone and R. Brown (eds.), *Contact and conflict in intergroup encounters*. New York: Basil Blackwell.

Schutz, Alfred. 1973. *Collected papers I: The problem of social reality*. The Hague: Martinus Nijhoff.

Sheriff, M. 1936. *The psychology of social norms*. New York: HarperCollins.

Shribman, David. 1989, August 7. The anti-abortionists agree on one thing but not much else. *Wall Street Journal*, pp. A1. A4.

Ronald Smith, and Cathy Caldwell. 1973. Effects of inadmissible evidence on the decisions of simulated jurors: A moral dilemma. *Journal of Applied Social Psychology* 3:345–353.

Snyder, Mark. 1982, July. Self-fulfilling stereotypes. *Psychology Today*, pp. 60–68.

Stephan, W. G. 1978. School desegregation: An evaluation of predictions made in *Brown v. Board of Education*. *Psychological Bulletin* 85:217–238.

Streufert, Siegfried, and R. W. Swezey. 1986. *Complexity, managers, and organizations*. Orlando: Academic Press.

Thorndike, E. L. 1920. A constant error in psychological ratings. *Journal of Applied Psychology* 4:25–29.

Tversky, A., and D. Kahneman. 1973. Availability: A heuristic for judging frequency and probability. *Cognitive Psychology* 5:207–232.

Tylor, E. B. 1871. *Primitive culture: Researches into the development of mythology, philosophy, religion, language, art and custom*. London: J. Murray.

Valins, S. 1966. Cognitive effects of false heart-rate feedback. *Journal of Personality and Social Psychology* 4:400–408.

Wallace, James, with Dusko Doder. 1989, June 5. Behind China's anger: Privilege and corruption endure, as hard-liners win a power struggle. *U.S. News & World Report*, pp. 20–23.

Weber, Max. 1930. *The Protestant ethic and the spirit of capitalism*. London: Unwin.

Wegner, D., and R. Vallacher. 1977. *Implicit psychology: An introduction to social cognition*. New York: Oxford University Press.

Whittaker, R. M., and R. D. Meade. 1967. Social pressure in the modification and distortion of judgment: A cross-cultural study. *International Journal of Psychology* 2:109–113.

Williams, Gwyn. 1960. Gramsci's concept of *egemonia*. *Journal of the History of Ideas* 21(4):586–599.

Williams, Robin, Jr. 1988. Racial attitudes and behavior. In Hubert J. O'Gorman (ed.), *Surveying social life: Papers in honor of Herbert H. Hyman*. Middletown, CT: Wesley University Press.

# 5

# Language, Thought, and Society

♦ *What provides you with subject matter is your own language—and that's all. It sort of coils in your mind, that sort of thing, and dictates something to you. A writer is a tool of the language rather than the other way around.** *

Children often respond to verbal attacks with the familiar rhyme, "Sticks and stones may break my bones, but words will never hurt me." But words do hurt. Outright lies, innuendos, slander, and gossip have destroyed reputations. On the other hand, words are also the building blocks of social reality, which is why they are central to many myths. From the Bible we learn that "in the beginning was the word," and the lesson of the Tower of Babel is that a multiplicity of tongues creates chaos. We live in a symbolic world, a world largely created and maintained through words. Words are what makes life interesting. They also make society possible.

By studying language we pursue further the theme presented in Chapter 4: that human thought should be conceptualized as a social phenomenon rather than a solitary process. As Joseph Brodsky observed, we don't lead our language to where we want to go; rather, it leads us. When we think in the language of our culture, we think socially constructed thoughts (Rosenthal 1983).

In this chapter we will see that language is the central link between mind and society, connecting each level of social reality, from the biological to the cultural. At the physiological level, our senses and emotions are conditioned and directed by words. Psychologically, our vocabularies determine our anticipations, experiences, and memories; in other words, our perceptions are organized in terms of symbols. At the social-psychological level, language has a causal influence on social interaction: People must calculate what kinds of things to say to which people in various situations, and must decide what

*Joseph Brodsky, exiled Soviet poet and winner of the 1987 Nobel Prize in Literature (cited in Clines 1987)

message forms are appropriate in each situation. Sociologically, we see the significance of language when minority groups battle to preserve their language even at the risk of death. And culturally, we appreciate how language allows memories and ideas to be passed on from generation to generation.

## Psychological Lessons from Language Disorders

Thought is a continuous process, observed William James, but "the breach from one mind to another is perhaps the greatest breach in nature." This breach, or gap, is due to the physical impossibility of two sensory systems to occupy simultaneously the same point in space.

Some individuals can never cross this gap. For example, people suffering from **aphasia,** the loss or disturbance of the ability to use words as symbols of ideas (Gardner 1978), experience a problem of *semantics;* they cannot apply conventional rules about the relationship between symbols and the ideas or things they represent. Not knowing, for instance, the label "dog" for four-legged creatures that bark and wag their tails, they become confused when in the presence of such creatures. The internalized use of language normally allows humans to imagine objects and events that are removed in time and space. Aphasics, however, cannot conceptualize unseen persons or events. They can no longer project themselves into the point of view of others, an ability essential for social interaction (Lindesmith, Strauss, and Denzin 1988). In the extreme, aphasics are unable to perceive a stable world.

Spanning James's breach entails possible costs, however. In Great Britain during the late 1970s, there was an autistic girl who, at the age of five and one-half, had achieved an artistic ability surpassing Picasso's at the age of nine. With a moment's glance, say, at a galloping horse, she was able to draw the creature complete with the major muscle groups and flare of the nostrils. Art authorities acknowledged she was a genius. Yet, with language therapy her artistic genius dissolved. Genius was traded for happiness (Cronkite 1984).

Even an apparently facile use of language is no guarantee that full **intersubjectivity**—the ability to experience others' perceptions, to understand their ideas, and to empathize with their feelings—exists. Certain psychopaths, although intellectually understanding what they say, have no sense of the emotional significance of their utterances. Their problem may stem from physiological causes: Their language is controlled from both hemispheres of the brain and, unlike normal individuals, they do not exhibit increased pulse rates or sweating when expecting a mild electric shock (Hare et al. 1988).

## Sociological Lessons from Efforts at Language Control

History reveals numerous ways in which elites have attempted to control the masses by controlling language transmission. Before the American Civil War, for example, many southern states had laws forbidding the teaching of slaves to read and write. Whether by limiting the number of people who may gather together or by maintaining illiteracy, the intent of such policies is to control the subordinate group's ability even to question its plight, express feelings of frustration, and share ideas with others who might challenge the status quo.

Consider the history of elite control of writing, particularly in medieval times. In this period of European history, most people did not venture more than a few miles from their place of birth. It was a world without maps and without a refined sense of time. News was spread by traveling troubadours and poets, whose patrons often used them to spread propaganda (Burke 1985:98). It was a culture requiring considerable memory, as stories often were heard only once. Such oral cultures tended to be backward-looking, placing considerable emphasis on past achievements.

Oral messages could be forged or distorted, unlike a written document bearing its sender's mark. And in a context of illiteracy, strategies and conspiracies could be developed across great distances without anyone else knowing. Transcending these limitations had numerous advantages. Nobles therefore included in their households at least one individual who could read and one who could write (the two skills often did not go together) (Burke 1985: 102–105).

With the invention of the printing press, the ability to read remained a monopoly of the elite but became a basis for stratification between adults and children (see Chapter 8). Literacy did not immediately mean the liberation of the masses; instead, it was used to impose further controls on them. Simple verbal oaths of loyalty to a noble, which could always be denied, were replaced by written articles of loyalty with a binding signature.

## THE SOCIAL PSYCHOLOGY OF LANGUAGE EXCHANGES

When they go home for the holidays, many students report being tongue-tied at the dinner table. Concerned about ensuring that the four-letter words of student life do not slip out, they have difficulty easing back into family roles and language.

From a social-psychological perspective, a significant feature of language is its causal influence on social action. To communicate with another person is to interact symbolically, with each participant continually making decisions about how meanings are to be sent and received. This is no small problem, since individuals must fit their unique experiences, feelings, and ideas into socially standardized symbols—that is, words. Words, in turn, come with their own evaluative standards (Mead 1934). For instance, to label oneself as an alcoholic (see Chapter 12) is to admit socially a flawed identity and take on a new role, that of alcoholic seeking help.

Not surprisingly, encapsulating what is personally unique into socially typical symbols produces a translation that is far from perfect. Because every distinctive thing does not have a distinctive label, when unique experiences or insights are encoded linguistically much is lost. For instance, to an expectant mother, her novel sensations are special and unique, yet when sharing her condition with others she glosses over the particulars and simply says, "I'm feeling pregnant." Young lovers may feel an irresistible and inexplicable attraction, but when groping for words they can only say, "I love you."

The limitations of language do not act as insurmountable barriers. In fact, language itself can lead to new insights. We create new sentences all the time,

## Basic Sociolinguistic Concepts

**phonetics:** the sounds used in language

**morphology:** the way sounds are combined to form words

**semantics:** conventional rules about the relationship between symbols and the ideas they represent

**syntax:** conventional rules about the assembly of symbols to represent more elaborate ideas

**lexicon:** the vocabulary of a language and the sum of its classificatory systems

juxtaposing categories in novel ways to deal with novel situations. Languages allow us to combine a limited number of words into an infinite number of new messages; even to speak all the possible twenty-word sentences would take ten billion years. Each of us has the opportunity to say something totally original, a fact that allows us to share new technologies, ideas, or dreams.

Thousands of hidden rules govern how words are to be combined and under what conditions they are to be used. Before interacting with others, each of us must make several kinds of decisions, including the following:

*What things to say.* How does one select topics to talk about? In part, the situation and audience determine whether language is to be regulative, instructional, imaginative, humorous, or used to share feelings. It is the situation that establishes what topics are acceptable (see Chapter 9), such as private knowledge (i.e., stories about one's spouse and children) versus public knowledge (i.e., politics and the weather); the appropriateness of "small talk"; and the extent to which one can talk about oneself. The popularity of sports talk is derived in part from the fact that sports, like the weather, is a relatively "safe" topic. Compared with religion or politics, it entails less risk of offending others. (See Table 5.1.)

Further, the speaker must make calculations of common understandings and common histories with his or her audience. For instance, we all know those people who, out of the blue, share some story about an Aunt Jane or an Uncle Jack, going on and on about their doings with comments like "And you know about Jack's long-standing feud with Jane." The source of our irritation toward such conversation is that the speaker has failed to tailor his or her exchanges to the audience and to the situation. James's linking of the minds does not occur when too many sentences are laced with "you know's" despite the lack of common histories; when one's topic of conversation is irrelevant to the collective theme at hand; and when the speaker and the listener are operating at two different frequencies, neither attuned to the other.

*To what types of people.* All communicative interchanges are either symmetrical or complementary, depending on whether the participants have similar or unequal social status. If their status is symmetrical,

**TABLE 5.1   What Do People Talk About?**

A sample of 1000 adults were asked what subjects they had discussed during the previous week. Following are the percentages of men and women who said they had talked about the subjects listed:

| Men | | Women | |
|---|---|---|---|
| *Subject* | *Percent* | *Subject* | *Percent* |
| news events | 71 | food | 76 |
| work | 68 | health | 72 |
| television | 66 | television | 70 |
| money | 66 | money | 67 |
| sports | 65 | news events | 66 |
| food | 63 | work | 59 |
| health | 61 | movies | 57 |
| movies | 53 | personal problems | 52 |
| celebrities | 47 | celebrities | 49 |
| personal problems | 40 | sports | 42 |
| sex | 2 | clothes | 1.8 |
| clothes | 0.2 | sex | 0.8 |

Source: *U.S. News & World Report* 1989; data source: Bruskin Associates.

their language is characterized by equality and the minimization of differences; if it is asymmetrical, their language tends to maximize differences. Thus, whereas adults use many declarative statements among themselves, they switch to questions and commands when talking with children. In this way language simultaneously shapes interaction and reaffirms the status hierarchy; social superiors are expected to be assertive, whereas subordinates are expected to use verbal expressions of submissiveness.

*In what message forms.* When I was growing up, my family's holiday ritual included an elaborate meal with a lifetime friend of my grandmother's, a veteran of many decades in college English classes. So high was my family's regard for this individual that we all found ourselves tongue-tied out of fear of violating the rules of the language.

Part of our conversational calculus involves deciding not only what to say but *how*; this decision is based primarily on the speaker's inferences about his or her relationships with others. This determines such matters as the choice of pronouns, the degree of deference given, and the formality of the language spoken. In Spanish, for example, the distinction between *tú* and *usted* is used to reinforce the distinction between equals and subordinates. Here again we see language's causal influence on social behavior. When interacting with superiors, subordinates are more likely to speak a formal language (i.e., the language of the cultural elite) than when interacting with equals.

*In what kinds of situations.* When we consider the differences between the conversational topics and language used, for example, in locker rooms and in churches and synagogues, the effect of the setting on the substance and form of communication is evident. Once a situation has been defined, the topics selected are expected to be appropriate to that situation. Thus, confusion may result if a student encounters a respected faculty member making notes in a cafeteria. If the faculty member acknowledges the student and seems to expect interaction, what could the student say? Are the topics of conversation to be limited to academic matters or shared experiences (e.g., the hot weather), or can more personal matters be discussed?

Not only do social factors determine the substance and form of our interactions, but our interactions, in turn, reinforce our notions about the social order. The very act of speaking is a social ritual that reaffirms cultural beliefs and values and the social status hierarchy. In addition to conveying ideas, speakers are acknowledging their roles and their connections with others, their membership in a thought community, and their commitment to these relationships.

Finally, not only do we **encode** the messages we transmit but we also **decode** the messages we receive. Listeners make inferences not only from the message itself but also from assumptions about the speaker's decisions. Meaning is a function not only of what is said but also of how it is said, where it was said, and who said it.

## ENCODING

In this section we will first consider how private feelings and thoughts are encapsulated in symbols. Then we will look at how the encoding process produces special templates for perception and reasoning. To illustrate: The different processes used by the Romans and Arabs to encode numerical ideas produced entirely different mathematical systems. The Roman system focused on the sum of parts (e.g., 42 = XLII, or 10 from 50 plus 2), whereas in the Arab system the place where the symbol stood announced its value (e.g., 42 = 4 in the "tens" place and 2 in the "ones" place, which equals $4 \times 10^1 + 2 \times 10^0$). Roman numerals cannot readily be used in computations, but Arab numerals provided the foundation for Western mathematics.

## From Natural Signs to Conventional Symbols

To survive, our ancestors had to cooperate, plan, and coordinate. Unlike other advanced species like wolves, which also could cooperate and coordinate, humans could discuss their behaviors and seek ways to improve them. They could also discuss the behaviors and motivations of others far removed in space and time, envisioning the actions of their ancestors, of the gods, and of generations yet to be born.

All creatures respond to cues in their environment. As we saw in Chapter 2, the more evolved the species, the more choice it has in its manner of responding. The learned cues are "signs," each of which conveys a single fixed meaning. There are the *natural signs* of the environment, which creatures must learn if they are to survive, such as the scent of an enemy or the red glow indicating the heat of a burning ember. There are also *unnatural signs:* With classical conditioning, animals can be conditioned to respond to "unnatural" substitute stimuli, as when Pavlov's bell elicited the drooling behavior of dogs. If the sound of a bell meant food to a community of dogs and if the dogs knew to strike the clapper to cause food to be delivered, the dogs would be using *conventional signs.* Unlike those of natural signs, the means of conventional signs are totally arbitrary. They are **symbols;** their meanings are derived from social consensus. A middle finger gesture indicates anger; a red light means danger or warning. At American stock exchanges, hand signals are still used to convey transactions across large, crowded, and noisy floors. Informal at first, these signals became highly formalized over time, but each still has only one fixed meaning.

The role of social consensus in defining symbols brings us to the semantic realm of language, the social conventions specifying particular relationships between a set of symbols and a set of ideas. It also reveals the contractual nature of language, since all who use a symbol must assume that it means to others what it does to oneself. This aspect is captured in the very word *symbol,* which comes from the Greek *symbola,* meaning the two halves of a broken stick or coin kept by two parties as tokens of a contract or other social relationship. In fact, until late medieval times symbolic objects were routinely exchanged to represent a transaction. Knives were the favorite object, with the transactions recorded on the knife's handle. As Burke (1985:95) notes, it was the knife and not the inscription that symbolized the event.

This does not mean that all symbols hold exactly the same connotations for everyone. The American flag, for instance, means something considerably different to a first-grader learning the Pledge of Allegiance than it does to a military veteran who fought at Iwo Jima and saw his buddies die so that the stars and stripes could be raised over the island. Nevertheless, both assume that they know what the symbol means and that others share in at least part of that meaning.

With the evolution of the brain, conventional signs became multi-channeled symbols. Instead of automatically responding to the single fixed meaning of a sign, the perceiver of a symbol confronts a set of meanings. The perceiver emotionally feels those meanings and cognitively internalizes the implicit worldview. This complex processing requires an advanced right brain hemisphere (Ornstein, 1972; Lex, 1979:124–130; d'Aquili and Laughlin 1979:173–177; Davis-Floyd 1987).

Changes in the human brain occurred concurrently with cultural evolution. Cultural signs were superseded by cultural pictures. Pictures have a plurality of meanings and therefore must be scanned to derive their full message; in contrast, one can merely glance at signs, whose single meanings are typically commands. From the cave drawings of Lascaux, the hieroglyphics of Egypt, and the cuneiform markings of Babylon to the creation of the alphabet and binary computer codes, we see the progressive separation of pictures from their referents, an increasingly symbolic quality allowing increasing latitude of inference. Symbols became qualitatively different from the signs they superseded. This difference is explored in modern art: a painting on cloth of a flag is not a flag but a sign; yet a picture of a flag also incorporates the symbolic commands of the sign—an irony that is appreciated, as far as we know, only by our species.

At the most abstract level, the meanings activated by symbols carry the essence of a culture's worldview. For example, Allan Bloom observes that the French language existed not only "for the sake of conveying information, for communicating men's common needs; it was indistinguishable from a historical consciousness" (1987:53). Almost four centuries earlier, Francis Bacon pointed out that "words are the tokens current and accepted for conceits [ideas], as moneys are for values [material worth]. A word without a history bespeaks a concept without tradition or cultural jurisdiction."

In sum, our conceptions are organized in terms of symbols, and in this sense language is said to **objectify,** giving ideas and values an external reality that is as "real" as any object in the physical landscape. With the acquisition of language and conceptual thought, humans' reactions to external social and physical worlds become increasingly indirect. The inherent frailty of this indirectness is evident when we repeat a word over and over and it becomes nothing but meaningless sounds. On the other hand, it is because of language that humans are able to observe their own actions and can view themselves as objects in their own thought.

## Categorization

Consider the ways in which students symbolize their culture. When one asks a student what a particular course is like, instead of a lengthy summary of a semester's worth of insights and experiences one may be told that the course is "Mickey Mouse," a "gut," or a "barn-burner." Similarly, there are varieties of students (preppie, weenie, booker, jock) and varieties of professors. Observe that the language used is categorical, specifying the characteristics of groups of things.

Categories are a cultural shorthand used to make sense and order out of a world that otherwise would be chaotic and random. They are methods for organizing perceptions, knowledge, and moral relationships (Jayyusi 1984), permitting discrimination and generalization and reducing the need for constant learning. As Dewey noted, "a category . . . constitutes a point of view, a schedule, a program, a heading or caption, an orientation."

When an event cannot be categorized and identified, anxiety or panic may result. Let's say that you've experienced rapid weight loss, your corneas have turned yellow, and large orange blotches have broken out on your arms. You go to a physician and anxiously await the verdict. Nothing is quite as frightening as the statement, "I've never seen or heard anything about your condition." To have a label for your disease means that your condition is not unique, that at least some others have shared it.

## Implicit Classifications

The categories we employ create *contrast sets,* groupings of things that are assumed to be mutually exclusive and contrasting only in ways that are considered socially significant. For example, the classification of breeds of dogs by the American Kennel Association (e.g., working, nonworking, hounds, sporting, terrier, toy) has little basis in the genetic similarities or functions of the animals.

Contrast sets are further arranged in *hierarchical taxonomies.* Examples include the classification of courses according to the relative ease of making a good grade and the classification of the creatures of the animal kingdom in terms of evolutionary theory.

So potent are these classification systems that individuals often confuse them with the realities that they represent. Thus, Stephen Jay Gould notes:

> We seem driven to think in dichotomies. Protagoras, according to Diogenes, asserted that "there are two sides to every question, exactly opposite to each other." We set up our categories, often by arbitrary division based on tiny differences; then, mistaking names for moral principles, and using banners and slogans as substitutes for reason, we vow to live or die for one or the other side of a false dichotomy. (1990:78).

As an illustration, consider the categories of drugs. As drugs have become a major social problem over the past few decades, distinctions have been made between "good" and "bad" drugs. In addition, some drugs are taken for reasons of health and others for pleasure. Some, such as prescribed or over-the-counter substances, are legal; others are illicit and are sold by "pushers" instead of by pharmacists or bartenders. As the social debate over "substance abuse" continues, we discover the inherent arbitrariness of our categories. Take the case of cigarettes. During World War I they were associated with patriotism and were considered an indispensable part of the war effort (Troyer and Markle 1983:40). Antismoking crusades were viewed as unpatriotic; it was even suggested that those who espoused such crusades should be prosecuted under the Espionage Act. Three-quarters of a century later, the National Cancer Advisory Board has recommended that tobacco be classified as a drug and regulated by the Food and Drug Administration (*Wall Street Journal* 1989).

When individuals internalize their society's classification systems (and their associated moral connotations) we see how symbols direct personal thoughts through social channels. Social psychologists therefore devote considerable study to the relationship between language and thought. A shared language implies a shared criteria for evaluation and judgment. On the other hand, different languages lead their speakers to perceive and think about the world in profoundly different ways. Thus, the Apaches tend to see events and objects as related in fluid and unfixed ways, whereas speakers of English tend to categorize and compartmentalize events and objects in stable, fixed relationships. The shared criteria are the categories of one's language. Hence, even the most "private" thoughts of individuals are best conceptualized as social rather than personal phenomena. "By acquiring the categories of a language," C. Wright Mills observes, "we acquire the structured 'ways' of a group, and along with the language, the value-implicates of those 'ways' " (1963:433).

## Classifications of Time

To the casual observer, few phenomena seem more "real" than the passage of time. We talk about time bringing change, producing decay, or healing old wounds. Yet there is no "time" in nature, and time in and of itself "causes" nothing. Time is a socially constructed concept, emerging out of the routines of group life. It is a container for social activities and events (Melbin 1987).

## The Denotative and Connotative Aspects of Categorization

Categories not only specify similarities between groups of things but also often specify how one should feel toward such things. Hence, there are both **denotative** and **connotative** distinctions in the meaning associated with a given category. By using the *semantic differential,* researchers measure the emotional and ideological connotations triggered by particular categorical references, and see how broadly shared they are. For each stimulus word, subjects are presented with a list of adjective antonyms and asked to place the concept on each of the descriptive scales defined by the antonym pairs. For instance, consider the meanings invoked by the word *capitalism:*

*Note how you feel about the notion of capitalism on each of the scales below:*

| | | | | | |
|---|---|---|---|---|---|
| good — | — | — | — | — bad | |
| | +2 | +1 | 0 | −1 | −2 |
| peaceful — | — | — | — | — stressful | |
| | +2 | +1 | 0 | −1 | −2 |
| helpful — | — | — | — | — selfish | |
| | +2 | +1 | 0 | −1 | −2 |
| fair — | — | — | — | — unfair | |
| | +2 | +1 | 0 | −1 | −2 |
| democratic — | — | — | — | — totalitarian | |
| | +2 | +1 | 0 | −1 | −2 |

To determine how these connotations cluster, a statistical routine called **factor analysis** is employed. Words perceived as near synonyms produce statistically interrelated clusters. The underlying commonality (or factor) for each cluster is interpreted as a common meaning or feeling activated by the stimulus word.

Although days, months, and years have analogs in nature, the cycle of the week is totally arbitrary. The history of the seven-day week involves holy numbers, planets, and astrology. Some numbers are considered desirable, lucky, or holy in many nations. The number seven is one of these. This is one reason that there are seven days in the week (in fact, in many languages the word for "week" is the same as the word for "seven" [Zerubavel 1985].

One of the first acts of the French revolutionary government was to create the Thermidor, an entirely new temporal reality symbolizing individuality, secularity, and rationality. Each minute was composed of 100 seconds, each hour of 100 minutes, each day of 20 hours, and each year of 10 months (Zerubavel 1977). The names of months and days were changed to eliminate religious or superstitious connotations. Similarly, in 1929 the Russians created a five-day week on the pretext that such a rhythm would be better for work production; the real purpose was to curb religious observance.

# Metaphors

Metaphors are a powerful means of conveying feelings, changing attitudes, or explaining difficult theories. They are categorical strategies for describing or understanding something in terms of something else, a transfer (the Greek *metaphora* means "carrying over") from a literal to a figurative plane. For instance, we use our bodies as metaphors when we speak of hemorrhaging expenditures, infectious laughter, cancerous growths, and being a pain in the neck. Using nature, one might say that a scientist caught a wave that swept the scientific community of his day. Applying Darwin's theory of evolution to businesses, we metaphorically speak of the "survival of the fittest."

It can be argued that all knowledge is metaphoric (Brown 1977). Beyond being linguistic expressions, metaphors are concepts in themselves. They encapsulate the conceptual templates people use to interpret their everyday life. In fact, culture itself may be best conceptualized as an integrated metaphoric system.

As we will see in later chapters (especially Chapter 15), cultural mindsets are derived largely from the dominant form of work in a culture. New technologies give rise to new forms of work, producing not only new types of goods and services but also new styles of thinking. For instance, with the mastery of animal husbandry, pastoral societies were able to domesticate useful creatures and thereby guarantee a more constant food supply. It was during this stage of social evolution that Judaism and Christianity arose; not surprisingly, flocks are a central metaphor of these religions. Likewise, the machine metaphor underlying Sigmund Freud's depiction of personality and the computer-holographic imagery of cognitive theorists reflect the industrial and information-based contexts in which those theories were developed.

A society's energy sources also generate metaphors. In agrarian cultures, energy is seen as derived from nature itself. The life-giving forces of the soil and the sun are evident to people who are constantly in touch with their crops and herds. Nature is regenerative, as is demonstrated in the cycle of the seasons, and therefore time is viewed as a cyclical phenomenon.

In such societies, death is often intimately connected with rebirth (Kearl 1989). The logic of allowing dead plants to compost and enrich the soil for the next generation may have stimulated the notion of older generations sacrificing themselves to make room for their successors. Even the cycle of sleep and wakefulness seems to verify this logic: Each day we go through a mini-death (sleep), only to be resurrected (awaken refreshed) each morning.

In our own culture, on the other hand, the predominant form of work has little to do with the natural order. Our primary source of energy, fossil fuels, is not replaceable. Unlike the seed from one's crops or the growth of one's herds, the products of contemporary labor are not regenerative. Instead, they wear out and/or become obsolete; they are disposed of and then replaced. Here time has become linear and divorced from natural rhythms. Metaphorically, modern time can be captured in spatial terms: "We met a *long* time ago"; "Graduation is *far off* in the *distant* future"; "Billy, don't do your math assignment *in the* English period."

The clock ultimately runs down or breaks, and now so does human life. Death often means the end of existence, occurring to old people who are deemed obsolete by their culture.

The ways by which we communicate messages can be as potent as our encoding in shaping the meaning of those messages. As the adage goes, "it's not what you say, but how you say it." The channels through which messages are communicated range from nonverbal cues to the written page, from dance to music.

## Nonverbal Messages and Paralanguage

> He winketh with his eyes, he speaketh with his feet, he teacheth with his fingers.
> —Proverbs

Only a fraction of face-to-face human communication occurs through words. Much is communicated through *paralanguage:* the volume and speed of speech, pitch, stress, use of sighs, tone of voice, and silences. Moreover, feelings and thoughts are disclosed by facial expressions, gestures, and other kinds of "body language." In Japan, where cultural and racial homogeneity is so great that many unspoken values are commonly shared, words are not trusted. Instead, the Japanese rely on "a kind of visceral communication known as *Haragei* (ha-ra-GUY)" (Rheingold 1988:53–54).

As Nancy Henley (1977:7) has observed, nonverbal communication "becomes the yardstick against which words and intentions are measured." The units of this yardstick involve status differences between speaker and audience. What is reaffirmed through nonverbal channels are messages of dominance and subordinance:

> the trivia of everyday life—touching others, moving closer or farther away, dropping the eyes, smiling, interrupting—are commonly interpreted as facilitating social intercourse, but not recognized in their position as micropolitical gestures, defenders of the status quo—of the state, of the wealthy, of authority, of all those whose power may be challenged. (Henley 1977:3)

Some individuals are masters of the nuances of nonverbal communication and paralanguage. Ray Birdwhistell (1970) described how Fiorello LaGuardia, the popular mayor of New York City during the 1930s, could speak standard American English, Yiddish, and Italian. Not only was he able to change languages to fit the group to which he was speaking, but he was also able to change his nonverbal cues to suit the language he was using. So the hand gestures he used with Yiddish were different from those he used when speaking Italian.

Many more people are nonverbal klutzes. This is especially true when one travels outside one's own culture. To flash the "A-OK" sign in Japan means money; in France it means someone is a nothing, a zero; in Malta, it is an invitation to homosexual sex (*San Antonio Express-News* 1989). It is ironic, given the importance of such channels of communication, that we are so poorly socialized in the nuances of nonverbal language, receiving nothing like our formal education in verbal and written communication.

In an effort to specify the building blocks of nonverbal language, consider the following channels that are routinely used by humans.

**Movement and Gestures.**   Gestures, like words, are conventional signs (Birdwhistell 1970). As Fast observes: "We rub our noses for puzzlement, we clasp our arms to isolate ourselves or to protect ourselves. We shrug our shoulders for indifference" (1970:16).

Like those of words, the meanings of gestures depend on the interactional context. Movements of the hands, the head, or the entire body not only embellish what is spoken or reveal the speaker's feelings but also signify the speaker's status in the social hierarchy. High-status individuals, for instance, have greater license to move about in a setting and thereby attract the attention of others.

**Body Contact.**   From the strength of a handshake to pats on the back, kisses, and hugs, people simultaneously convey information about themselves and their relationships with those they touch. Not surprisingly, this language varies considerably from one culture to another. (See Table 5.2.) Among Africans and Arabs there is considerable bodily contact, whereas the British and Japanese are much more restrained.

Because touch entails the invasion of personal space, it is often initiated by higher-status people. For this reason, versatility in the use of body contact varies considerably within a given society, with those who are most likely to be touched being most adept. American women, for instance, can make distinctions between forms of touching that indicate warmth and friendship and those that indicate sexual desire (Nguyen, Heslin, and Nguyen 1975). For men, these two forms are interchangeable in meaning—they are "illiterate" in the language of touch.

**Proximity.**   As we saw in Chapter 2 in the discussion of proxemics, cultural norms specify distance rules for various types of social relationships. Subordinates, for example, must accept a superior's invasions of their territory. Violations of these norms have considerable meaning, but that meaning is largely inferred. An important inference is whether the infraction was intended or resulted from a misunderstanding. When a female stranger violates a young man's personal space, for example, he may think she likes him. Because one tends to like those who like oneself, the boy moves closer to the girl; she, on the other hand, attempts to avoid his advances, thinking it's too early in their relationship for outward signs of intimacy.

**Body Orientation.**   By sitting or standing side by side as opposed to facing each other, individuals reveal the nature of their relationship with those in proximity to them. Body orientation may communicate liking for others: Females tend to sit next to a person they like whereas males sit across from him or her (Byrne, Baskett, and Hodges 1971). Also communicated may be one's interactive relationship: Individuals who are in cooperative settings or are close friends tend to adopt a side-by-side position, whereas persons engaged in bargaining choose to face each other.

Information is also conveyed by the positions of various parts of the body. For instance, tilting the head signifies attentive listening for both humans and other creatures. Nierenberg and Calereo (1971) observed that women are socialized to make conscious use of this gesture when listening to a male whom they would like to impress.

***Appearance.*** Appearance is another nonverbal communication channel. Clothing is indicative of one's occupational and social status. In certain social settings, being "overdressed" may be interpreted as being ostentatious while being "underdressed" may be interpreted as a slight (as when a person wears jeans to a wedding or funeral). In the military, the press of one's pants, the shine on one's shoes, and the shortness and grooming of one's hair are interpreted by superiors as indications of the role adequacy and commitment of subordinates.

***Posture/Position.*** Erving Goffman (1959) noted that in medical staff meetings doctors often sat in undignified but comfortable positions, whereas nurses, residents, and social workers adopted a more dignified posture. High status confers the right to adopt a careless posture. Conversely, the lower one's status, the greater the degree of body control that is expected.

The required rigidity of lower-status individuals is, of course, uncomfortable and serves to reinforce their subordinate position. For instance, maintaining a rigid military bearing is equivalent to putting oneself at another's disposal. In Japan this relationship is conveyed by the bow: Women bow more often and longer than men; department store retailers are trained to bend 30 degrees when welcoming customers, 15 degrees when encouraging them to look around, and as much as 45 degrees when customers depart (Haberman 1985).

"The 'closed' positions of subordinates," Henley explains, "coats buttoned, faces grim, contracted bodies—are examples of the tightness required of them" (1977:126). She notes that women maintain closed leg positions and keep their arms close to their bodies, thereby "acting out female shrinking and male spatial expansion."

**TABLE 5.2  The Ways of Americans, through Vietnamese Eyes**

| American | Vietnamese |
| --- | --- |
| A. AFFECTION | |
| 1. Touching between members of the same sex is not acceptable. | One can see two men or women in the street holding hands. |
| 2. A man and a woman may hold hands or touch in public. | People do not do this in public. It looks "ridiculous." |
| 3. A man can touch a woman (putting an arm around her shoulder, hold her arm, kiss her cheek, etc.) | A man cannot do this for affection or friendliness. It is "insulting" to a woman. |
| 4. Kissing (between husband and wife, lovers) in public is usually acceptable. | It is a public offense. It has to be done in private quarters. No kissing in front of the children. |
| 5. Parents and children kiss each other. | Not at all except babies. |

TABLE 5.2 Continued

| American | Vietnamese |
|---|---|
| **B. DAILY HABITS** | |
| 1. All food is shared equally. | Preferred food is served to parents or to the elderly first. |
| 2. Americans do not make noise in appreciating good food. | Vietnamese sometimes make noise in appreciation of good food. |
| **C. GREETINGS** | |
| 1. Americans shake hands with the opposite sex. | Vietnamese do not shake hands with the opposite sex. They do not shake hands with old people or women unless the latter offer their hands first. Slightly bow the head and/or put the hands in front of the chest in order to show more respect. Two women do not shake hands. |
| 2. To slap someone on the back is a sign of friendship. | It is insulting to the Vietnamese to be slapped on the back; especially to women. |
| **D. MANNERS** | |
| 1. People may put their feet on tables or desks either at home or in the office. | It is considered impolite to do this. |
| 2. Talking directly about the main subject is preferable. | Vietnamese talk around the subject before coming to the point. |
| 3. Looking straight into someone's eyes in conversation shows honesty and frankness. | It is not an indication of respect to look into people's eyes. |
| 4. A smile means happiness. | A smile has many meanings: happiness or sorrow, agreement or disagreement, understanding or misunderstanding. |
| 5. Some people speak or laugh loudly in public. | This is considered bad manners, especially for women. |
| 6. Some people lose their temper in public. | It is considered impolite to lose one's temper in public. |

Source: Lack, 1978.

**Eye Contact.** In *Hitler: Memoirs of a Confidant*, Otto Wagener describes how he was mesmerized by Adolf Hitler's eyes:

> From the first, his eyes caught and held me. They were clear and large, trained on me calmly and with self-assurance. His gaze came, not from the pupil, but from a much deeper source—I felt as if it came from the infinite. It was impossible to read anything in these eyes. But they spoke, they wanted to speak. They did not ask, they talked. (Turner 1987)

These effects were caused by drugs. Hitler took Kola Dallmann in large quantities, and possibly belladonna, to enhance his magnetic effect on others.

There is a language of gaze behavior whose meaning again is inferred from its social context. Prolonged direct gazing at another person can convey intense concentration or strong attraction; it can also be interpreted as social incompetence (as when mental patients stare unblinkingly at visitors).

As predatory animals use their eyes to intimidate their victims, so the power of the "evil eye" has been employed by numerous cultures and religions to control behavior. This brings us to the ways in which gaze vocabularies are shaped by status differences. Since eye contact involves attention, it should not be surprising that low-status persons will spend more time looking at high-status individuals than vice versa. Women, for instance, engage in much more eye contact than men do. But eye contact can also mean violation of one's visual privacy, indicating surveillance and control. Exline (1963) referred to this as the "visual dominance behavior" of high-status persons. Thus, although students are expected to look at their professors during lectures, such attention is not always reciprocated.

***Facial Expression.*** Probably the most informative nonverbal messages are inferred from facial expressions, which include raised eyebrows, squints or wide-opened eyes, furrowed brows, and quizzical displays of the mouth. Cross-cultural studies reveal a high degree of consensus in interpretation of the facial expressions associated with such emotions as surprise, sadness, disgust, and anger.

One facial expression that has received considerable research is the smile. Smiles can mean many things, ranging from contentment to insult. The evolutionary advantage of smiling behavior is clear. Parents of young infants are reinforced by the baby's first smile. Noting the almost universal appearance of human smiles at around the third month of life, sociobiologist Melvin Konner notes that "[i]t is difficult to believe that natural selection could have left so important a signal to the vagaries of individual learning" (1987:42).

Smiles also are part of the nonverbal vocabulary of dominance and submission. Henley (1977:176–177) found that women returned smiles 89 percent of the time in social encounters. Men, on the other hand, reciprocated only 67 percent of the smiles from women and 58 percent of those from men. Goffman noted that in advertisements women are almost always shown smiling to show their deference to men (cited in Leo 1985).

## The Medium Is the Message?

Often it is the medium by which a message is transmitted that determines its meaning.

Consider long distance communications with professional colleagues. If one's message is sent on corporate stationery, numerous rules of format must be followed, including rules for salutations and closings and expectations of proper grammar and spelling. Often the appearance of the letter is as important as the words in conveying the significance of the message and the social status of its sender. A handwritten letter from a social superior means something considerably different than a handwritten message from a subordinate.

## The Lost Art of Conversation

It is a matter close to misery for me that there is so little conversation in the world these days. Of words we have a plentitude. The pour out at us in torrents from television, radio, and telephone. They overwhelm and drown us on a deluge of verbosity. But of conversation we have a growing paucity, for we seem to be forgetting the entertainment and warmth that there is to be had from talking to each other.

When some talk does occur between us, it is usually limited to sport or business, neither of which are subjects which promote either wit or imagination. . . .

The great blessing of conversation, its supreme virtue, is that it opens us up to each other. We warm ourselves in the glow of another's personality. One does not converse for information, but to enter into the being of others. Conversation diminishes our aloneness and it is of no small significance that the greatest literary figure of eighteenth-century England, Dr. Samuel Johnson, was known more as a conversationalist than he was as a writer.

Source: Wibberly, 1982.

When written messages are transmitted over alternative channels, such as computer networks, the format is considerably less formal. Spelling errors, for instance, are more acceptable, because the message is assumed to be more spontaneous and less permanent than a business letter.

If one's message is sent verbally by telephone, matters of spelling and appearance become irrelevant. How the telephone has altered human communication remains a matter of conjecture. Interactions are even more spontaneous, though some communicators still take care to create a good impression by using correct grammar and syntax. Recently, however, this medium has been changed by the advent of voice mail and telephone answering machines. These devices preserve verbalizations and allow them to be replayed for analysis.

## DECODING

Do you remember the excitement of beginning to learn how to read? In part, it is like having a coder/decoder set and being able to send and receive clandestine messages with a friend. Knowing how to read also enables one to peek into the adult world and learn its secrets.

Later, one learns that an author does not put meaning into his or her prose to be extracted by the reader. Instead, written works can be read in numerous ways, and what a reader takes out of a passage is directly linked to what he or she brings to it (Lipking 1989).

All symbolic messages must be decoded. As poets and writers know, words alone do not convey the meanings intended. People can say one thing and mean another, whether because of language deficiencies, the desire to deceive or avoid ruffled feathers, fear of persecution, or the assumption that the listener will "read between the lines."

## Deciphering Combinations of Nonverbal and Paralinguistic Messages

Part of the lore of the courtroom is that judges' attitudes toward defendants subtly affect juries' verdicts. Not only do judges know the law and have greater exposure to human wiles, but they also have information that is not available to jurors, such as knowledge of previous criminal records. To test how judges' nonverbal and paralinguistic messages can influence courtroom decisions, Blanck et al. (1985) videotaped five municipal judges as they read final instructions to jurors in thirty-four actual trials. The researchers scrambled the audio portion of the tape so that tones and inflections remained even though the actual words were unintelligible. They then showed the videotape to undergraduates and law students, who were asked to rate on a nine-point scale such qualities as the judges' warmth, honesty, anxiety, and open-mindedness. When the judges knew of a prior criminal record, they were scored as having less tolerance, warmth, and patience. Interestingly, defendants who had been arrested previously were twice as likely to receive a guilty verdict from juries.

In everyday life outside the courtroom, nonverbal and paralinguistic cues are also used to determine other people's "guilt," particularly deception. Premeditated lies are assumed to be accompanied by nervousness and shifty eyes. Paul Ekman tested these assumptions, focusing on the reliability of nonverbal signs that cannot be controlled voluntarily (i.e., how worry produces lifting of the inner part of the eyebrows, how eyebrows are raised and pulled together with fear, and how anger tightens and narrows the red margins of the lips [1982]). He found (1986) that many of the supposed clues to lying do not in fact reveal that a person is lying. Instead, lying behavior is normally accompanied by the following clues:

A prolonged smile or lingering look of amazement (nearly all authentic facial expressions fade after four or five seconds).
Out-of-sync body gestures and facial expressions, as when an angry face precedes by a few seconds banging on a table.
Crooked or asymmetrical facial expressions.
A slight rise in the pitch of the voice.
A dramatic decline in the speaker's normal use of gestures.

## LABELING THEORY

We have seen that people perceive the world in terms of personal theories, often seeing and remembering stereotypes rather than actual behaviors and events. And we saw in Asch's demonstration of how a stimulus word can alter personality inferences, that personal templates can be triggered by a single label. When categorizing personal experiences and meanings, one places them into symbolic systems that include evaluative frameworks. These frameworks, in turn, shape one's perceptions and expectations and lead to self-fulfilling prophecies. For instance, to categorize oneself as a "student" or a "friend" is to evaluate oneself as a certain type of individual; one then acts in ways that are typical of such individuals. This is the essence of **labeling theory.**

Let us consider a typology in which words vary in depth of meaning (Gurvitch 1971[1966]). At one end of this continuum are words referring to objects in our environment, things like lawnmowers and mountains, which are easy to observe and for which the connection between object and label is clear. The meanings of these words are relatively fixed. Next are words that label patterns of social interaction, like families and bureaucracies. They are somewhat more abstract than words labeling wagons and oranges, but the connection can still be observed. Still more abstract in their references are social symbols, which impose order on large-scale interactions: "economies," "political orders," "world system." Finally, at the other end of the continuum, are words referring to collective attitudes and belief systems such as communism, sexism, and ageism. Here, a word is just the tip of an iceberg of meaning.

In studying the power of expectations triggered by labels, Rosenthal and Jacobson (1968) gave teachers from eighteen elementary schools the names of students who had supposedly been identified by a new test, the Harvard Test of Inflected Acquisition, as "intellectual bloomers." In actuality, there was no such test and the students so identified had been selected at random. Nevertheless, by the end of the school year the students who had been labeled as intellectual bloomers showed greater gains in intellectual ability than others. The increase in IQ points for the selected students was more than double that for nonlabeled students. Among first-graders, the IQs of those expected to show gains in academic performance increased 27.4 points as opposed to 12.0 for the control group; among second-graders the increase was 16.5 points versus 7.0. Rosenthal called the phenomenon the **Pygmalion effect,** after the king of Greek mythology who fell in love with a statue he had sculpted, which eventually came to life as the woman of his dreams.

Pursuing this power of labels further, Hacking describes the ways in which society "makes up people" by labeling them and making sure that they conform to the labels (1986). He shows how new medical and psychological categories developed in the nineteenth century were applied and internalized, creating new kinds of people acting in new kinds of ways. Thus, on the social scene appeared drapetomaniacs (African Americans who rebelled against being slaves) and sufferers of revolutions (those disposed to rebelling against the king), neurasthenia (a male affliction similar to female hysteria), and onanists (those who masturbated when the act was deemed sinful). In *Psychopathia Sexualis* (1986), Richard von Krafft-Ebbing added the following labels for "psychopathological manifestations of sexual life in man": paradoxia (sexual excitement independent of any physiological stimuli); anathesia (the absence of sexual instinct, where stimuli fail to stimulate sexual interest); hyperesthesia (also called satyriasis, an abnormally increased susceptibility to sexual arousal); parathesia (perversions of the sexual instinct, such as masochism, fetishism, and antipathetic sexuality); and koprolagnia (disgusting acts of self-humiliation during masturbation).

The increase in the number of labels and the scope of their perceived applicability continues to increase. For instance, the number of mental disorders recognized by the American Psychiatric Association nearly doubled between 1952 and 1986, from 110 to 210 (*Harper's Magazine* 1986). Between 1977 and 1990, there was a 142 percent increase in the number of children identified as having "learning disabilities" (*Harper's Magazine* 1990).

## The Social Psychology of Names

Of what significance is it that of the thirty-seven Presidential elections where popular votes were recorded, in twenty-eight cases the major-party candidate with the longer name has won? And what can we make of the following observations?

> Consider that John Minor Wisdom, Pleas Jones, William Justice, and Learned Hand are judges. Russell Brain is a brain surgeon, William Dance is a dancing instructor, William Key is a jail warden, Cardinal Sin is an archbishop, Groaner Digger is an undertaker (Slovenko 1980:208–209).

Do people take on identities based on their names? Does one's name really determine one's fate, especially in politics?

Parents spend hours choosing names for their infants, believing that to name something is to shape its destiny. The idea is not new. "A good name smells sweeter than fragrant ointment," says the Bible (Eccles. 7:1). The Puritans believed that character or behavior could be manipulated through names. Accordingly, they gave their children names like Sindenie, Fear-not, Search-the-Scriptures, Flie-Fornication, Chastity, and Prudence.

Names can be extremely informative. Among other things, they reveal the following information about a person:

> *Gender:* Gender distinctions are given to family names in the Slavic languages. For example, in Polish a woman married to a man surnamed Lis is Mrs. Lisowa; if they have an unmarried daughter, she is Miss Lisowna. The Czech-born tennis star is surnamed Navratilova; her father is Mr. Navratil.
>
> *Family lineage:* In Hispanic cultures husbands and wives each keep their mother's and father's names. For example, a Latin-American man named José Lopez Rodriguez would have inherited the name Lopéz from his father and Rodriguez from his mother, and a woman named Maria Hernandez Dominguez would have received Hernandez from her father and Dominguez from her mother. If José and Maria married and had a son named Rafael, he would become Rafael Lopez Hernandez (Cherlin 1978).
>
> *Generation:* Names may indicate the historical period in which one was born. In the Soviet Union before the Bolshevik revolution, Russian Orthodox parents were required by their church to name their children according to the saints' days on which they were born. After the 1917 revolution, the church restrictions were lifted and nearly

three thousand new names were created. They ranged from the geographic (Himalaya, Ararat, Volga) to the horticultural (Oak, Birch, Daffodil) to the scientific (Radium, Helium—nicknames Radi and Heli) to the industrial (Hydroelectric Station, Diesel, Turbine, Electrification) to the political (Hammer-and-Sickle, and various twists on Lenin's name, such as Ninel [Lenin spelled backward]) (Mydans 1985). In California during the mid-1980s there appeared a generation with such names as Maybe, Breezy, Bambi, Cobra, Demon, and Mace (*San Antonio Express-News* 1987)

*Birthplace:* Following Arab tradition, Iraqi President Saddam Hussein al-Tikriti's second name was his father's. The last, Tikrit, is the name of his home village. In 1977 Hussein ordered Iraqis to drop their village surname in order to conceal the fact that so many high-level government positions were filled by Tikritis (*New York Times* 1990).

*Cultural assimilation:* For many immigrants to the United States, part of the experience of being Americanized was shortening their names. This form of cultural assimilation was developed into an art form by Hollywood stars, as can be seen in the following examples:

| | |
|---|---|
| Woody Allen | Allen Stewart Konigsberg |
| Fred Astaire | Frederick Austerliz |
| Charles Bronson | Charles Buchinski |
| George Burns | Nathan Birnbaum |
| Michael Caine | Maurice Micklewhite |
| Doris Day | Doris Kappelhoff |
| Kirk Douglas | Issur Danielovich Demsky |
| Karl Malden | Mladen Sekulovich |
| Walter Matthau | Walter Matasschanskayasky |
| Roy Rogers | Leonard Slye |

In recent years, however, stars have tended to keep their real names as stage names.

*Race and social class:* Roman numerals, for instance, rarely follow the monikers of the poor.

Three centuries ago Thomas Turner observed that "a name is a kind of face" (cited in Dunkling 1977:11). We feel as intimately bound to the sound of our name as to the reflection of our face in a mirror. To what extent does one's name shape one's social fate? Newman (1974) notes that college presidents and heads of foundations have more than their share of uncommon names, such as Kingman Brewster and McGeorge Bundy. Zweigenhaft (1977) found that people with unusual names have a significantly higher need for uniqueness. In the 1940s, B. M. Savage and F. L. Wells (1948) found that students with unusual names were more likely than their classmates to flunk out of Harvard. (See Table 5.3.)

Harari and McDavid investigated implicit stereotypes associated with different names. In one experiment (1966), groups of children were asked to rate a list of names according to how much they liked the sound of each name. Correlating this with a sociometric test of children's popularity, they found a strong relationship between name desirability and popularity status. In another experiment the researchers had a group of teachers grade essays written by fifth-grade students (1973). The names used to identify the authors were either desirable (Karen, Lisa, David, Michael) or undesirable (Elmer, Adelle, Bertha, Hubert). Essays supposedly written by Lisas and Davids were among those receiving the highest grades. As expected, the essays labeled with unpopular names generally received the lowest grades.

Like other labels, names are also mechanisms of social control. In the Bible, Adam's naming of the animals implied control over them. A creature unnamed is a creature untamed. When Moses asked God on Mt. Sinai how He should be referenced, God's reply was, "I am who I am" (implying that my name is none of your business). Among the Navaho, to know a man's name is to have power over him. Each man selects a name upon becoming an adult and never reveals it to anyone, using a public name instead.

**TABLE 5.3  What's in a Name?**

*To explore the extent to which names carry common stereotypical conceptions, the following lists of male and female names were given to eighty-five undergraduates at a predominantly white, upper-middle-class, private liberal arts college. Individuals were asked such questions as who they would expect to be least and most intelligent, most athletic, and most popular, and which individuals of each gender they thought they would most probably like.*

| Females | | Males | |
|---|---|---|---|
| 1. Alfreda | 11. Lisa | 1. Andrew | 11. Michael |
| 2. Bertha | 12. Margaret | 2. Bernard | 12. Paul |
| 3. Constance | 13. Mary Ellen | 3. Charles | 13. Percival |
| 4. Crystal | 14. Missy | 4. Dale | 14. Raymond |
| 5. Elizabeth | 15. Priscilla | 5. Eugene | 15. Richard |
| 6. Emma | 16. Rebecca | 6. Herbert | 16. Robert |
| 7. Gertrude | 17. Ruth | 7. Ivan | 17. Seymour |
| 8. Isadore | 18. Susan | 8. Jethro | 18. Stanley |
| 9. Janel | 19. Trudy | 9. Kirk | 19. Thomas |
| 10. Jennifer | 20. Violet | 10. Lawrence | 20. William |

*If sheer chance were at work, a given name would be expected to be mentioned 4.25 times (85 respondents/20 available names) for a given attribute. However, some names were mentioned ten (Jethro) and even thirteen (Bertha) times more often than could be expected by chance. Certainly for a given attribute, names that are mentioned three times more often than could be expected by chance (or by thirteen or more people) can be considered significantly correlated with the attribute in question.*

**TABLE 5.3  Continued**

|  | Most Expect to Be Old | Expect Least Intelligent | Most Likely to Like | Expect Most Athletic | Most Feminine |
|---|---|---|---|---|---|
| Andrew | 0 | 0 | 6 | 2 | 0 |
| Bernard | 6 | 6 | 0 | 0 | 4 |
| Charles | 3 | 1 | 3 | 2 | 1 |
| Dale | 1 | 3 | 2 | 12 | 7 |
| Eugene | 4 | 5 | 0 | 2 | **14** |
| Herbert | 9 | 3 | 0 | 0 | 1 |
| Ivan | 7 | 1 | 3 | 3 | 1 |
| Jethro | 3 | **42** | 3 | 2 | 0 |
| Kirk | 0 | 1 | 5 | **15** | 0 |
| Lawrence | 6 | 1 | 2 | 0 | 2 |
| Michael | 0 | 0 | **22** | 12 | 0 |
| Paul | 2 | 0 | 11 | 6 | 0 |
| Percival | **13** | 2 | 0 | 1 | **30** |
| Raymond | 1 | 3 | 0 | 3 | 6 |
| Richard | 0 | 0 | **14** | 1 | 1 |
| Robert | 0 | 0 | 7 | **13** | 0 |
| Seymour | **16** | 10 | 0 | 0 | 12 |
| Stanley | 10 | 6 | 2 | 1 | 6 |
| Thomas | 0 | 1 | 3 | 0 | 0 |
| William | 4 | 0 | 2 | 1 | 0 |

|  | Most Expect to Be Old | Expect Least Intelligent | Most Likely to Like | Expect Most Athletic | Most Obese |
|---|---|---|---|---|---|
| Alfreda | 2 | 3 | 1 | 6 | 4 |
| Bertha | 4 | 0 | 1 | 3 | **57** |
| Constance | 1 | 3 | 3 | 0 | 0 |
| Crystal | 0 | 5 | 4 | 1 | 1 |
| Elizabeth | 0 | 2 | 9 | 3 | 1 |
| Emma | **24** | 4 | 1 | 2 | 4 |
| Gertrude | **23** | 2 | 0 | 0 | 5 |
| Isadore | 11 | 1 | 0 | 1 | 0 |
| Janel | 0 | 0 | 3 | 5 | 0 |
| Jennifer | 0 | 2 | **16** | 9 | 0 |
| Lisa | 1 | 0 | **16** | 18 | 1 |
| Margaret | 1 | 1 | 6 | 4 | 1 |
| Mary Ellen | 0 | 1 | 9 | 4 | 2 |
| Missy | 1 | **29** | 1 | 3 | 0 |
| Priscilla | 2 | 4 | 0 | 0 | 2 |
| Rebecca | 1 | 2 | 5 | 5 | 0 |
| Ruth | 6 | 1 | 1 | 3 | 0 |
| Susan | 0 | 0 | 8 | 11 | 2 |
| Trudy | 2 | **17** | 1 | 7 | 2 |
| Violet | 6 | 8 | 0 | 0 | 3 |

# LINGUISTIC LINKAGES AMONG MIND, SELF, AND SOCIETY

The words we choose are determined not only by the thoughts we wish to express but also by social appropriateness, which comes from one's definition of oneself vis-à-vis others and one's definition of the social context. In this section we move one step further and consider how words channel our thoughts along culturally prescribed routes. Just as military strategists first move to control all ship canals and highways of commerce, so powerful social constituencies seek to control the thought channels known as words.

## Language as a Cultural System

There probably never will be a single international tongue. Language embodies a cultural perspective, a way of looking at the world. Throughout the world more than three thousand languages are spoken. Each of them allows different experiences of reality, which in turn, allow different types of knowledge to be socially developed. Thus, when a Mohawk Indian compares his language to English, he claims that Mohawk is like seeing a huge color screen unfold around oneself, whereas English is like watching a twelve-inch black-and-white screen.

As a species dies when its genes are not passed along, so a culture dies when its new generations do not learn its language. This genetic metaphor is appropriate in light of recent anthropological studies of American Indians and their origins. Based on language studies, Greenberg (1987) had argued that most Native American languages derived from one ancestral language. In 1990, using a methodology that allows researchers to trace maternal ancestry by analyzing mitochondrial genes, Douglas Wallace found that nearly 95 percent of American Indians, including the Mayans and Incas, were descended from four women who migrated from Asia to the Western Hemisphere across the Bering Strait between 15,000 and 30,000 years ago (*San Antonio Express-News* 1990).

## The Whorf–Sapir Theory of Linguistic Relativity

Language is the carrier and the embodiment of the features of a cultural environment. It singles out for specification the features that are common to a social group; its concepts are the means for preserving distinctions that are of practical importance to group life.

This idea that the reality one experiences is determined by the language one speaks is known as the **Whorf–Sapir hypothesis.** As Whorf explained:

> We dissect nature along lines laid down by our native languages. The categories and types that we isolate from the world of phenomena we do not find there because they stare every observer in the face; on the contrary, the world is presented in a kaleidoscopic flux of impressions which has to be organized by our minds—and this means largely by the linguistic systems in our minds. We cut nature up, organize it into concepts, and ascribe significance as we do, largely because we are

## Implications of Language Ignorance

Despite the increasing integration of the United States into the world economic system, enrollments in foreign-language courses are declining. This trend has significant implications. An international *faux pas* was created when President Carter, visiting Poland, spoke of "desire" and the word was translated as "lust" by an interpreter. Chase (1954) argues that similar misunderstandings may have led to the needless use of nuclear weapons in Japan. When Truman, Churchill, and Stalin called for the Japanese to surrender during their meeting at Potsdam, the Japanese responded with the word *mokusatsu*, which, in the context in which it was used, meant that they were reserving comment. Inaccurate translation led to the Allies' belief that the Japanese were ignoring their ultimatum.

Similar embarrassments caused by inaccurate translation have been experienced by American businesses. Chevrolet had difficulty marketing its Nova in Central and South America: in Spanish, *no va* means "no go." When Pepsi-Cola entered the Thai market, it employed its American advertising campaign slogan, "Come alive, you're in the Pepsi generation." The company later realized that the Thai translation it was using said, "Pepsi brings your ancestors back from the dead" (Gruson 1986).

parties to an agreement to organize it this way—an agreement that holds throughout our speech community and is codified in the patterns of our language. (1956:213)

Such parsings of reality produce a wider range of labels for phenomena that have practical significance for a culture. The Solomon Islanders, for example, have nine distinct names for coconut, specifying significant stages of growth. The Aleut Eskimos' thirty-three different words for snow allow them to make such distinctions as the snow's load-carrying capacity and the speed at which a sled can be run on its surface. And Otto Klineberg found that the Arabs have 6,000 names connected to "camel," including "names and classes of camels according to function—milk camels, riding camels, marriage camels, slaughter camels, and so forth; names of breeds of different degrees of nobility of lineage, derivation from different lands, and so forth; names of camels in groups, as several, a considerable number, innumerable; and with reference to their objectives—grazing, conveying a caravan, war expedition, and so forth; as many as fifty words for pregnant camels, states of pregnancy, stage at which movement of the foetus is first felt, mothers who suckle and those who do not, those near delivery, and so forth" (1954:50).

Certainly much can be inferred about a culture from an analysis of the phenomena for which it has labels and the categorical distinctions it makes for a given phenomenon. What can we learn about ourselves, for instance, from the fact that there are an estimated twenty-five hundred English expressions for being drunk (*Harper's Magazine* 1987), or about Tibetans, who have over 120 terms for distinctive states of consciousness (Leonard 1974)? One consequence of the fact that individuals are able to perceive and think only in terms of the categories of their language is a phenomenon called **metalinguistics.** This term refers to the restrictions imposed on a culture by the language itself.

## Language and Cultural Values

Cultural socialization occurs with the acquisition of language. When learning words one simultaneously learns the behaviors, thoughts, and emotions associated with them. An American child, for instance, learns that Mom's brother is an "uncle" as is Dad's brother. In the United States, children play the same role—that of niece or nephew—with both of these individuals because they have identical labels. In other cultures these two kin relations may have different labels (in many matrilineal systems, the mother's brother plays the authority figure role). Within the matrilineal descent system of the Crow Indians, one labels one's father's brother the same as one labels one's father; however, a different label exists for one's mother's brother. As a result, the child's role behavior with the mother's brother may differ from his or her behavior with the father's brother.

As illustrated by kinship designations, when learning words one also learns taxonomies, the interrelationships among things, and the reasons for which things are the way they are. This serves the important social goal of **legitimation.** In the example just given, a man can take charge of someone else's children because he is an uncle and uncles are expected to take care of their nieces and nephews. In other words, such conduct is legitimate because it is built into the language (Berger and Luckmann 1966:94).

Many other facets of social reality require legitimation. For instance, the reason Santa Claus visits only children in affluent families must be explained to children in poor families. Also requiring explanation is the fact that political leaders can affect personal lives by making decisions about war and taxes. Even to speak a language is to ritually reaffirm the social and cultural order.

Research on the relationship between language and cultural values often focuses on language shifts and the sociohistorical forces underlying such changes as well as their sociocultural consequences. New modes of expression produce new perceptions of reality. For instance, shifts in the cultural metaphors by which the natural order is understood (e.g., from a view of nature as an organic, regenerative whole to one in which nature is a complex machine that can be controlled by humans) are indicative of broad socioeconomic changes (i.e., from an agrarian to an industrial economy). C. Wright Mills (1963) argued that such semantic changes are to be understood as indicators of broad cultural conflicts. Two illustrations of such semantic change involve the social statuses of older people and women.

Fischer (1978) employed a historical analysis of semantic changes to challenge the hypothesis that industrialization contributed to the decline in the status of the old. He argued that their status did indeed decline but that this occurred prior to industrialization. The major cause was the end of the *ancien régime,* which was replaced by a world without veneration or condescension, a world without eldership or primogeniture. On the surface, the new order was characterized by greater equality, but beneath the surface a new form of inequality was developing.

In the late eighteenth century a new language emerged that expressed contempt for the elderly. There were changes in the meanings of old labels:

## They Have a Word for It

*bardo* (Tibetan, noun): The plane between death and birth.

*bonga* (Santali of India, noun): Spirit of place who must be dealt with.

*bricoleur* (French, noun): A person who constructs things by random messing around without following an explicit plan.

*farpotshket* (Yiddish, noun): Something that is all fouled up, especially as the result of an attempt to fix it.

*fucha* (Polish, verb): To use company time and resources for personal ends.

*ho'oponopono* (Hawaiian, noun): Solving a problem by talking it out.

*koro* (Chinese, noun): The hysterical belief that one's penis is shrinking.

*mamihlapinatapei* (Tieberra del Fuegan): Two people looking into each other's eyes, each hoping that the other will initiate what both want to do but neither chooses to commence.

*masa bodoa* (Javanese, adjective): Sociopolitically passive and unaware.

*maya* (Sanskrit, noun): The mistaken belief that a symbol is the same as the reality it represents. Maya relates not only to the endless play of forms and the void from which they spring, but to the dangerous attachments people tend to develop in relation to their conceptual maps of the world.

*mokita* (Kiriwana, New Guinea; noun): Truth everybody knows but nobody speaks.

*nârâchâstra prayoga* (Sanskrit, noun): Men who worship their own sexual organ.

*ngarong* (Dyak of Borneo, noun): A secret helper who appears in a dream.

*Radfahrer* (German, noun): Complicated paperwork involved in making a complaint.

*rêve à deux* (French, noun): A mutual dream or shared hallucination.

Source: Rheingold, 1988.

---

*gaffer* (formerly a title of respect, even endearment); *fogy* (before 1780, a wounded military veteran); *old guard* (a term of honor for Napoleon's soldiers, but by 1880 an expression used to describe reactionary, corrupt U.S. politicians). New words of condescension were invented: *codger* (probably derived from "to cadge," by 1796 had come to mean "stingy, miserly old fellow"); *old goad* (lecherous old man), *fuddy-duddy* (pompous old man) *granny* (weak old man), *mummy*, *geezer* (eccentric old man), *galoot* (uncouth old man), *bottlenose* (old alcoholic).

Kingston (1976) observes, "There is a Chinese word for the female *I*—which is 'slave.'" Although the English language is less explicitly oppressive in its treatment of women, it operates to place women in a subordinate position relative to men. The reactions of women are given less credence, accorded less worth, than the identical reactions of men. Consider the language of the workplace. As can be seen in the box below, this language denigrates the contributions of women and distorts the way their actions are perceived.

## How to Tell a Businessman from a Businesswoman

A businessman is dynamic; a businesswoman is aggressive.
A businessman is good on details; she is picky.
He loses his temper; she's bitchy.
When he's depressed, everyone tiptoes past his office; when she's moody,
    it must be her time of the month.
He follows through; she doesn't know when to quit.
He's confident; she is stuck up.
He stands firm; she's hard as nails.
He has the courage of his convictions; she's stubborn.
He is a man of the world; she's been around.
He can handle his liquor; she's a lush.
He isn't afraid to say what he thinks; she's mouthy.
He's human; she's emotional.
He exercises authority diligently; she is power mad.
He is closed-mouthed; she is secretive.
He can make quick decisions; she is hard to work for.
He climbed the ladder of success; she slept her way to the top.

Source: Author unknown, 1990.

As equality between the sexes has increased, however, there are signs of changes in the language as well. Publishers are attempting to use sex-neutral or gender-equivalent pronouns and labels: *chairperson* instead of *chairman*, *humankind* instead of *mankind*, and the like. In the 1970s, the tradition of giving hurricanes women's names was modified; today men's and women's names alternate as the hurricane season progresses.

## Language and Social Structure

We approach language from a more sociological perspective when we consider the relationships between language and the social organization of behavior. For example, there are words of power, which are used to control the behaviors and thoughts of others. There is a language signifying one's membership in a group, such as knowing the secret handshake of some fraternal order. And we will see in this section that language serves as a ritual acknowledgment of the social order and the speaker's place within it:

> As the child learns his speech . . . he learns the requirements of his social struc-
> ture. From this point of view every time the child speaks the social structure of
> which he is a part is reinforced in him, and his social identity develops and is
> constrained. The social structure becomes for the developing child his psychologi-
> cal reality by the shaping of his acts of speech. (Douglas 1970:46)

Use of deference terms when addressing adults, as when referring to a teacher as Mrs. Smith or a physician as Dr. Miller, signify and reinforce the child's lesser status. Such indications of social inequality establish limits as to the range of acceptable topics of discourse, the formality of language to be used, and the turn-taking rules of conversation.

### Words of Power.

> What a weird fate can befall certain words. At one moment in history, courageous, liberal-minded people can be thrown into prison because a particular word means something to them, and at another moment, people of the selfsame variety can be thrown into prison because that word has ceased to mean anything to them, because it has changed from the symbol of a better world to the mumbo jumbo of a doltish dictator. . . . The selfsame word can at one time be the cornerstone of peace, while at another, machine-gun fire resounds in its every syllable.—Vaclav Havel, president of Czechoslovakia (quoted in *U.S. News & World Report* 1990)

Insofar as vocabulary is an aspect of social conduct, it can also be said that language is an instrument for the control of behavior. In his famous book *1984*, George Orwell coined the term *Newspeak* to refer to the confusion and contradiction that is intentionally built into political language. People in his fictional totalitarian society were told that ignorance is strength, war is peace, and life was not bad but, rather, ungood. The author warned that "the worst thing you can do with words is surrender to them."

It is interesting to note that the word *dictator* originally meant "the one who gives the word." In modern society, many people have surrendered to the words of professionals. Physicians encode their descriptions and prescriptions in Latin for the same reasons that the Catholic priesthood did so: to distinguish themselves from the masses and to exercise power and control over others. Similarly, lawyers' use of "legalese," social scientists' "jargon," and the "gobbledygook" of government bureaucrats are all symbolic strategies for placing these professionals in an advantageous position relative to their clients.

Words are used not only to mystify but also to deceive. For example, political regimes routinely employ *euphemisms* and *double-talk* to cover up their lethal activities. When it required that seven million chickens be slaughtered to contain a virus in Pennsylvania, the federal government said the birds must be "depopulated." The multiwarhead MX missile is called the "Peacekeeper." In the late 1970s the Pentagon described the neutron bomb as a "radiation enhancement device." And to overcome civilian objections to homicide, the military socializes its recruits to "eliminate" or "neutralize" a dehumanized enemy that attacks in "hordes" or "herds."

### Language and Social Solidarity.

Desmond Morris (1967:139–143) observed that small talk is analogous to the grooming behaviors of chimps; both bring individuals together to attend to each other's need for contact. We feel comfortable, "at home," and "connected" when we hear the dialect and cadences of our childhood, when we understand the nuances of the speech of others. In parts of the American South and West, people who meet to discuss a work-related matter may spend the first half-hour sharing stories about their lives and families. To Northeasterners, such delays before "getting down to brass tacks" may appear to be a waste of time. But for a person from a rural Texan or Georgian culture small talk serves to acknowledge the wholeness and integrity of the self.

Part of language's ability to enhance social solidarity involves the experience of linguistic commonality. These commonalities emerge over time as people develop their own idiosyncratic systems of verbal and nonverbal codes, which have meaning only within the relationship. These private idioms come to serve as *shibboleths*, or passwords (the word "shibboleth" was, in fact, the password used by Gileadites to distinguish the Ephraimites, who could not pronounce the "sh" sound), devices by which one signals one's status as a linguistic insider and includes or excludes others from the group. To know the code is to be not only a linguistic insider but a social member as well.

Of all social memberships linguistically reaffirmed, perhaps the most central involves matters of one's social class. In George Bernard Shaw's *Pygmalion* (later made into the movie *My Fair Lady*), the lesson demonstrated by Eliza Doolittle was that even a poor, lower-class girl can pass for aristocracy if she knows the language. In American urban ghettoes, the new tribal language emerging also reaffirms status orders. Through "ranking," the constant stream of amiable jibes between gang members, personal loyalties to the group are reaffirmed and the relative status of group members defined.

Language serves not only to bond but also to separate peoples, preserving the identities of cultural minorities. In the United States, according to the 1980 census, one in nine people do not speak English at home; instead, they speak a variety of other languages, ranging from Arabic to Yiddish. The United States now has the seventh-largest Spanish-speaking population in the world (Large 1985). In the past two decades, as large numbers of immigrants have entered the country, a movement has arisen to ensure the primacy of English. In 1986, for example, California voters passed Proposition 63, which instructed the legislature to "take all steps necessary to insure that the role of English as the common language of the State of California is preserved and enhanced," and to pass no law that "diminishes or ignores" it. There has also been an intensification of the debate over bilingual education. From the perspective of newly arrived immigrants, bilingual education means the preservation of their culture as well as their native language. From the perspective of English-speaking Americans, it symbolizes a group's supposed refusal to assimilate into American society.

## How Social Structure Determines the Structure of Language

Given our discussion of the function of language as a ritual reaffirmation of the social order, it seems logical to assume that different types of codes will predominate in different kinds of groups. Basil Bernstein, a student of Whorf, demonstrated that different social classes have different linguistic systems, which emerge out of differing role relationships within families (1964, 1973). In working-class families relations between family members are often **role-centered** and characterized by hierarchy and dominance. For example, instead of treating a daughter as a unique person, parents treat her as the one in the oldest daughter role. Because each role is assumed to be linked with specific actions, the social order can be affirmed with a limited vocabulary. Hence, vocabularies in the lower classes can be very limited; in the United States they may include fewer than a thousand words. Syntax is simple and rigid, with some language understood only by members of the group. Children, for example, understand the grunt vocabulary of their father—one sound means it's time to hide; another is a sign of approval.

Bernstein labeled such speech **restricted codes,** referring to a language that is applicable only within a group and highly dependent on the context in which it is used. This "lower-class speech" is considerably less explicit in verbally communicating meaning and is a poor vehicle for abstract thinking. Its supposedly inferior status produces negative prejudices toward its speakers among teachers and employers.

In middle-class families, on the other hand, relations are often **person-centered** and characterized by cooperation instead of domination. In such families parents treat each of their children in unique ways, taking into account differences in personality, needs, and temperament. With no role recipes to guide interaction, there emerges an **elaborated code,** one that is richer in detail (and hence with a larger vocabulary). Elaborated codes are independent of context and highly explicit, and therefore it can be shared with people outside the family. Moreover, because they provide more possibilities for abstract thought and reasoning, they help explain why upper-class children fare so much better on standardized academic tests than children from lower-class backgrounds.

Of course, other factors besides role relationships shape the linguistic codes of families. Refining Bernstein's depiction of groups, Douglas (1970) focused on the solidarity relations between members of groups. Restricted codes occur when a group is characterized by high solidarity and many shared assumptions about the nature of the group. Elaborated codes develop in groups in which solidarity is weak and shared assumptions cannot be assumed; they are found in societies in which geographic and social mobility have removed individuals from the communities in which they were born and raised.

Group codes also vary according to the integration of the group itself with the broader culture. The isolation of a group from the majority culture, whether due to geographic isolation or to intended or enforced social remoteness, also produces restricted codes. In parts of rural Appalachia, for instance, Elizabethan English can still be heard. Drug dealers also have a group code, with terms like *horse, dog, cat, girl, shirt,* and *car* referring to drugs or quantities of drugs, and *picture* and *injection* referring to samples (DeStefano 1985).

## How Language Shapes Social Structure

So central is language to a culture and to the cultural identities of its members that throughout the world we observe social movements fighting to preserve particular languages. Language differences underlie the potential for civil war in Quebec, Latvia, Estonia, Lithuania, Belgium, and the Basque region of Spain. In each of these places linguistic minorities seek to resist the institutionalization of the language spoken by the majority. These minorities face a variety of challenges, such as being required to take proficiency tests in the majority language when seeking employment or public office. In the extreme, people have died for their language: In the 1980s, hundreds of ethnic Turks living in Bulgaria were killed for refusing to adopt Bulgarian names (Kamm 1985).

The Hispanic-American population grew five times faster than the rest of the public during the 1980s. The Spanish store signs and Latin rhythms on radio airwaves in numerous cities testify to the growing influence of Hispanic cultures on the broader American cultural ethos.

A dominant language is not always forcibly imposed on a people. Linguistic infiltration may occur because the ideas connoted by foreign words have no counterpart in the minority language. Lenin claimed that the Russian language (hence culture) was marred by the unnecessary use of foreign words. On the other hand, in the United States during the late 1950s, the use of the word "Sputnik" for "satellite" symbolized an affront to Americans' sense of technological superiority.

So significant are issues of language purity in France that there is a secretary of state for Francophone affairs; there is also what amounts to a language police, which patrols for violators of a 1911 law forbidding the use of English words in business where French equivalents exist (Doerner 1987). An area of particular concern is the language of data processing. General Becam, president of the Association of French-Speaking Computer Specialists, claimed that acceptance of such terms as *byte* and *networking* was equivalent to "submitting to the language of the conqueror" (Hudson 1985). Accordingly, in the 1980s French bureaucrats developed approved lists of French computer terms and outlawed their English counterparts.

The international dominance of English is due to its immense vocabulary (over 750,000 words), which permits great flexibility and subtlety; its ability to achieve technological precision (throughout the world English is used for air traffic control); its willingness to assimilate foreign words; and its ability to change with the times (Fehrenbach 1988a,b). Since 1966, an estimated 6.6 words have been added to the English language every day (*Harper's Magazine* 1988).

## Case Study: The Impact of Illiteracy

In the late 1980s, the Department of Education estimated that more than twenty-seven million Americans over the age of 17 cannot read or write well enough to perform the basic requirements of everyday life and that an additional forty-five million are barely competent in basic skills. In sum, nearly one out of three adults lack the reading and writing skills required to find work in an economy that requires ever greater levels of education. As a consequence, a steelworker misorders $1 million in parts because he cannot read well, and an insurance clerk who doesn't understand decimals pays a claimant $2200 instead of $22 (*San Antonio Express-News* 1988a).

As was the case in medieval times, language facility may once again determine a person's place in the social hierarchy. For many minority group members who lack schooling, their lower status may be reinforced and legitimated by their lack of language skills in an economy that is increasingly based on informational transactions (see Chapter 15).

Hans Enzensberger describes a typical "second-order" illiterate individual as follows:

> He has come a long way: The loss of memory from which he suffers causes him no suffering; he values his inability to concentrate; he considers it an advantage that he neither knows nor understands what is happening to him. . . . It contributes to the second-order illiterate's sense of well-being that he has no ideas that he is a second-order illiterate. He considers himself well-informed; he can decipher instructions on appliances and tools; he can decode pictograms and checks. . . . Simultaneous with the development of this problem, our technology has also developed an adequate solution. The ideal medium for the second-order illiterate is television. (1986)

To compensate for this trend, employers are restructuring jobs so that people do not have to read, write, or think—a phenomenon called "dumbing down" (*San Antonio Express-News* 1988b). On the cash registers at fast-food outlets, there are pictures of hamburgers and fries instead of digits; at grocery store checkouts, clerks use electronic scanners instead of punching in the prices; and at banks, automatic tellers are eliminating many personnel. Although dumbing down reduces training costs for companies, it means diminished opportunities for professional growth and job security for the employee.

# CONCLUSION

Society is possible only because of the intersubjectivity of its members, and it is language that makes intersubjectivity possible. Although words and gestures can never fully capture meanings or experiences, interacting individuals must assume that they do, for words are the common currency by which personally unique experiences are transformed into socially typical events. Words impose an order on the life-world, structuring both thought and action.

The cultural templates for perception and interpretation described in Chapter 4 are implicit within the symbols exchanged by the culture's members. For this reason, there can never be an international language. Built into each language is a culture's experience of time, space, cause and effect, appropriate foci of attention, and the nature of selfhood.

However, not all social relationships and interactions are based merely on shared intuitions (Chapter 4) and symbolic communication (Chapter 5). In addition, there are feeling states wherein the individual's social experiences are actually biologically felt. This is the realm of emotion, to which we turn in the next chapter.

# REFERENCES

Berger, Peter, and Thomas Luckmann. 1966. *The social constraint of reality.* New York: Doubleday.

Bernstein, Basil. 1973. A brief account of the theory of codes. In Hans Peter Dreitzel (ed.), *Recent sociology no. 5: Childhood and socialization.* New York: Macmillan.

Bernstein, Basil. 1964. Elaborated and restricted codes: Their social origins and some consequences. *American Anthropologist* 66(6):66–69.

Birdwhistell, Ray A. 1970. *Kinesics and context.* Philadelphia: University of Pennsylvania Press.

Blanck, P. D., R. Rosenthal, and L. H. Cordell. 1985. The appearance of justice: Judges' verbal and nonverbal behavior in criminal jury trials. *Stanford Law Review* 38(1):89–164.

Bloom, Allan. 1987. *The closing of the American mind.* New York: Simon and Schuster.

Brown, Richard H. 1977. *A poetic for sociology: Toward a logic of discovery for the human sciences.* Cambridge, England: Cambridge University Press.

Burke, James. 1985. *The day the universe changed.* Boston: Little, Brown.

Byrne, D., G. D. Baskett, and L. Hodges. 1971. Behavioral indicators of interpersonal attraction. *Journal of Applied Social Psychology* 1:137–149.

Chase, Stuart. 1954. *Power of words.* Orlando: Harcourt Brace Jovanovich.

Cherlin, Andrew. 1978, December. Hereditary hyphens? *Psychology Today,* p. 150.

Clines, Francis. 1987, October 23. A writer reflects on the fortunes of literature and the Russian language. *New York Times,* p. 8.

Cronkite, Walter. 1984, June 12. Universe. Public Broadcasting System.

d'Aquili, Eugene, and Charles Laughlin. 1979. The neurobiology of myth and ritual. In Eugene d'Aquili, Charles Laughlin, and John McManus (ed.), *The spectrum of ritual: A bio-genetic structural analysis.* New York: Columbia University Press.

Davis-Floyd, Robbie. 1987. Birth as an American rite of passage. In Karen Michaelson (ed.), *The anthropology of childbirth in America.* Bergin and Garvey.

DeStefano, Anthony. 1985, December 27. Drug agents turn linguist to plumb the criminal mind. *Wall Street Journal,* pp. 1, 6.

Doerner, William. 1987, September 14. Troubles of a tongue en crise. *Time,* p. 49.

Douglas, Mary. 1970. *Natural symbols.* New York: Random House.

Dunkling, Leslie. 1977. *First names first.* Detroit: Gale Research.

Ekman, Paul. 1986. *Telling lies.* New York: Norton.

Ekman, Paul (ed.). 1982. *Emotion in the human face* (2nd ed.). New York: Cambridge University Press.

Enzensberger, Hans M. 1986, October. In praise of illiteracy. *Harper's Magazine*, pp. 12–14.

Exline, Ralp. 1963. Explorations in the process of person perception: Visual interaction in relation to competition, sex, and need for affiliation. *Journal of Personality* 31:1–20.

Fast, Julius. 1970. *Body language.* New York: M. Evans.

Fehrenbach, T. R. 1988a, February 28. Precision puts English in lead. *San Antonio Express-News*, p. 3-M.

Fehrenbach, T. R. 1988b, March 6. English marked by acquisition. *San Antonio Express-News*, p. 3-M.

Fischer, David H. 1978. *Growing old in America.* New York: Oxford University Press.

Gardner, Howard. 1978, March. The loss of language. *Human Nature*, pp. 76–84.

Goffman, Erving. 1959. *The presentation of self in everyday life.* Garden City, NY: Doubleday Anchor Books.

Gould, Stephen Jay. 1990, Winter. Taxonomy as politics. *Dissent.*

Greenberg, Joseph L. 1987. *Language in the Americas.* Stanford, CA: Stanford University Press.

Gruson, Lindsey. 1986, December 2. U.S. working to close foreign-language gap. *New York Times*, pp. 1, 11.

Gurvitch, Georges. 1971. [1966]. *The social frameworks of knowledge*, New York: Harper & Row.

Haberman, Clyde. 1985, April 22. How Japan adds style to the bow. *New York Times*, p. 4.

Hacking, Ian. 1986. Making up people. In Thomas C. Heller (ed.), *Reconstructing individualism: Autonomy, individuality, and the self in Western thought.* Stanford, CA: Stanford University Press.

Harari, H., and J. W. McDavid. 1973. Name stereotypes and teachers' expectations. *Journal of Education Psychology* 65(2):222–225.

Hare, R. D., L. M. McPherson, and A. E. Forth. 1988. Male psychopaths and their criminal careers. *Journal of Clinical and Consulting Psychology* 56(5):710–714.

*Harper's Magazine.* 1990, March. Harper's index. p. 19.

*Harper's Magazine.* 1988, May. Harper's index. p. 15.

*Harper's Magazine.* 1987, March. Harper's index. p. 15.

*Harper's Magazine.* 1986, December. Harper's index. p. 13.

Henley, Nancy. 1977. *Body politics: Power, sex, and nonverbal communication.* Englewood Cliffs, NJ: Prentice-Hall.

Hudson, Richard. 1985, October 10. Computers threaten another tradition: The glory of France. *Wall Street Journal*, pp. 1, 22.

Hudson, R. A. 1981. *Sociolinguistics.* Cambridge University Press.

Jayyusi, Lena. 1984. *Categorization and moral order.* Boston: Routledge and Kegan Paul.

Kamm, Henry. 1985, August 7. Bulgaria slayings charged by Turks. *New York Times*, p. 7.

Kearl, Michael. 1989. *Endings: A sociology of death and dying.* New York: Oxford University Press.

Kingston, Maxine Hong. 1976. *The woman warrior: Memoirs of a girlhood among ghosts.* New York: Vintage.

Klineberg, Otto. 1954. *Social psychology.* Fort Worth, TX: Holt, Rinehart and Winston.

Konner, Melvin. 1987, March. The enigmatic smile. *Psychology Today*, pp. 42–46.

Krafft-Ebing, Richard von. 1886 [1925]. Psychopathia sexualis. New York: Physicians & Surgeons Books.

Lack, Pamela B. 1978, January 24. The ways of Americans, through Vietnamese eyes. *New York Times.*

Large, Arlen J. 1985, July 22. Proliferation of Spanish in U.S. inspires action against bilingualism. *Wall Street Journal*, pp. 1, 12.

Leo, John. 1985, January 14. Is smiling dangerous to women? *Time*, p. 82.

Leonard, George B. 1974, Language and reality. *Harper's Magazine*, pp. 46–52.

Lex, Barbara. 1979. Ritual and ontogenetic development. In Eugene d'Aquili, Charles Laughlin, and John McManus (eds.), *The spectrum of ritual: A bio-genetic structural analysis.* New York: Columbia University Press.

Lindesmith, Alfred, Anselm Strauss, and Norman Denzin. 1988. *Social psychology* (6th ed.). Englewood Cliffs, NJ: Prentice-Hall.

Lipking, Lawrence. 1989, October 2. Competitive reading. *New Republic*, pp. 28–35.

McDavid, J. W., and H. Harari. 1966. Stereotyping of names and popularity in grade school children. *Child Development* 37:453–459.

Mead, George Herbert. 1934. *Mind, self and society.* Chicago: University of Chicago Press.

Melbin, Murray. 1987. *Night as frontier: Colonizing the world after dark.* New York: Free Press.

Mills, C. Wright. 1963[1939]. Language, logic and culture. In C. Wright Mills (ed.), *Power, politics & people.* New York: Oxford University Press.

Morris, Desmond. 1967. *The illustrated naked ape: A zoologist's study of the human animal.* New York: Crown.

Mydans, Seth. 1985, February 16. In Russia, traditional names are popular again. *New York Times,* p. 18.

Newman, Edwin. 1974. *Strictly speaking: Will America be the death of English?* Indianapolis, IN: Bobbs-Merril.

*New York Times.* 1990, August 25. For the Iraqi ruler, variations on a name. p. A6.

Nierenberg, Gerald, and Henry Calero. 1971. *How to read a person like a book.* New York: Hawthorne.

Nguyen, T., R. Heslin, and M. L. Nguyen. 1975. The meanings of touch: Sex differences. *Journal of Communication* 25:92–103.

Ornstein, R. 1972. The psychology of consciousness. San Francisco: Freeman Press.

Rheingold, Howard. 1988. *They have a word for it: A lighthearted lexicon on untranslatable words and phrases.* Los Angeles: Jeremy P. Tarcher.

Rosenthal, Peggy. 1983. *Words and values: Some leading words and where they lead us.* New York: Oxford University Press.

Rosenthal, R., and L. Jacobson. 1968. *Pygmalion in the classroom.* Fort Worth, TX: Holt, Rinehart & Winston.

*San Antonio Express-News* [AP]. 1990, July 27. Study traces American Indians to 4 women. p. 4-A.

*San Antonio Express-News* [AP]. 1989, February 12. Insular American learns to edit his body language. p. 6-M.

*San Antonio Express-News* [AP]. 1988a, February 28. Illiteracy: America's economic time bomb. p. 8-K.

*San Antonio Express-News* [AP]. 1988b, February 18. "Dumbing down" helps firms cope with illiteracy problem. p. 8-K.

*San Antonio Express-News* [AP]. 1987, April 23. In California, the name game is not the same.

Savage, B. M., and F. L. Wells. 1948. A note on singularity in given names. *Journal of Social Psychology* 27:271–272.

Slovenko. 1980. On naming. *American Journal of Psychotherapy* 34(2):208–219.

Stevens, William K. 1985, March 15. Black and standard English held diverging more. *New York Times,* p. 10.

Troyer, Ronald, and Gerald E. Markle. 1983. *Cigarettes: The battle over smoking.* New Brunswick, NJ: Rutgers University Press.

Turner, Asby. 1987. *Hitler: Memoirs of a confidante.* New Haven, CT: Yale University Press.

*U.S. News & World Report.* 1990, February 26. The word as arrow. p. 38 [from acceptance speech for the Peace Prize of the German Booksellers Association, October 15, 1989].

*U.S. News & World Report.* 1989, May 15. Talk, talk, talk. p. 73.

*Wall Street Journal* [AP]. 1989, February 9. Classification, regulation of tobacco as drug urged. p. B4.

Whorf, Benjamin. 1956. *Language, thought and reality.* Cambridge, MA: Technology Press of Massachusetts Institute of Technology.

Wibberly, Leonard. 1982, June 13. The lost art of conversation. *San Antonio Express-News,* p. 6H.

Zerubavel, Eviatar. 1977. The French republican calendar: A case study in the sociology of time. *American Sociological Review* 42:868–877.

Zerubavel, Eviatar. 1985. *The seven day circle: The history and meaning of the week.* New York: Free Press.

Zweigenhaft, Richard. 1977. The other side of unusual first names. *Journal of Social Psychology* 103:290–302.

# 6

# The Social Psychology of Emotions

Their fight was triggered by the issue of fairness in the household's division of labor. As the wife insisted that she made the greater contribution, the husband became angry and irrational. Words were said that were not meant, and heard as if they were. Tones of voices became louder and more heated. Accusations were exchanged as if the fight were a game of tennis, each volley more intense than the last. Weeks of noncommunication had dammed up misperceptions, perceived slights, and negative feelings, and feelings now surged like flood waters pushing past a failing dike. The course of events following such a scenario can go many ways. Some relationships seem to thrive on cycles of bitter arguments and passionate makeups. For other couples, this may be their first major confrontation; it could lead to negotiation and compromise, mutual disengagement, or even violence.

In the search for general models of human behavior, the role of emotions has been given short shrift. "Primal emotions," are viewed as vestiges of our bestial ancestry, obscuring the more central, meaningful, and socially conditioned drives. Economists, for instance, frequently rely on a "rational" paradigm in explaining economic activities—a model that has no place for such "irrational" feelings as greed, envy, desire for attention. In American popular culture, this model is epitomized by "Star Trek's" Mr. Spock, the brilliant science officer from a planet of totally rational beings, a highly evolved people with no emotions to distort their thoughts.

Many social psychologists have likewise devoted little attention to emotions. They view emotions as derived from the unconscious, an unobservable realm of unmeasurable forces. Emotions are typically viewed as the source of irrational behavior and hence, as something that must be actively suppressed, as in "control your emotions!"

On the other hand, would society be possible if there were no feelings of love, compassion, kindness, or happiness? We think not. We believe that emotional predispositions provide the foundations for moral behavior. We believe that ignoring feeling states in any depiction of the human condition leaves out a sizable portion of the story.

But incorporating emotions into models of behavior raises a host of methodological and theoretical issues. Do we take an objective approach, looking at outward (and measurable) appearances, or the subjective approach, focusing on inner (and therefore less measurable) experiences? If emotions are included in social-scientific paradigms, human nature must be understood as grounded in subjectivity, feeling, and reflection, and shaped through direct experience (Denzin 1984). This approach also goes against the more typical perspective in which modernization results in greater rationality, materialism, and secularism—and emotions, along with mysticism, intuition, and superstition, are swept under the proverbial rug.

For social psychologists with a psychoanalytic perspective, emotions involve the urges arising out of the unconscious and the restraints imposed by the ego and superego, which determine personality and, hence, behaviors. The intensity with which emotions are experienced, for instance, may vary according to the individual's personality, determining such traits as susceptibility to mob behavior or need for a powerful leader. Behaviorists might focus on the actual or anticipated experiences associated with positive or negative reinforcements. Cognitive theorists would most likely be interested in how people interpret their inner feeling states and how they act on them. And symbolic interactionists would probably consider how people label their emotions and, in sharing those labels with others, create emotional self-fulfilling prophecies. As we will see, these have indeed been the starting points of research on emotions. But in the 1980s some startling findings have pointed to some interesting theoretical convergences and some entirely new lines of inquiry.

## THE ROOTS OF EMOTIONS

Charles Darwin (1872[1965]) believed that basic emotions such as fear and anger are biologically determined *universals*, visceral states that proceed from instinct rather than from intellectual motivation. Evidence for such a model comes from developmental studies of the young. Steiner (1973), for instance, found newborns crying, smiling, and showing signs of disgust. The presence of expressions of disgust even in brain-damaged newborns also seems to affirm the genetic origins of emotions.

Research indicates that 6-week-old infants experience their worlds in terms of the feeling evoked by objects, people, and events, and that they already have strong visual preferences (Stern 1990). With time (see Table 6.1), a full panoply of emotions unfolds, producing an intimate interplay between feeling and thought.

In addition to the regular developmental progression of different emotional states, Ekman and Oster (1979) claim that there is "unambiguous evidence for universality" in the ways in which at least five basic emotions are expressed. In their cross-cultural studies of people's judgments of photographed emotional displays, they found that even aboriginal groups from New Guinea, who had never had contact with the pictured people from Western countries, recognized the expressions of happiness, anger, disgust, sadness, and combined fear/surprise.

The ability of certain chemical substances to create or mimic various emotional states also seems to validate the biological roots of emotion. Humans have discovered that depression can be dissolved pharmacologically and that euphoria can be generated with narcotics. Cocaine, for instance, works directly on the pleasure center of the brain that responds to such pleasurable sensations as sex and food. As a physician said about his $1000-a-week cocaine habit: "It made my conversation seem sparkling, music sound better, made me feel good. . . . In the beginning, I felt I was communicating with God. In the end, I thought I was God." (*Time* 1983). Such sensations are a result of neural transmissions triggered by the release of a chemical called dopamine. Once the nerve endings on adjacent cells have been activated, the transmitting cell draws the dopamine back inside for reuse. Cocaine, however, prevents the reclamation of dopamine, thereby allowing the pleasurable sensation to be transmitted long after it would have normally ended.

### TABLE 6.1   When Feelings Arrive

*Emotional capacities present at birth: pleasure, surprise, disgust, and distress*

| | |
|---|---|
| By 6–8 weeks: | anger, fear, and joy |
| By 4 months: | sadness |
| By 12–18 months: | tender affection |
| By 18 months: | shame |
| By 2 years: | pride |
| By 3–4 years: | guilt |
| By 5–6 years: | the social emotions, including insecurity, humility, confidence, and envy |
| By adolescence: | romantic passion, philosophical brooding |

# Connections between Emotional and Biological Well-Being

Nearly a century ago, Sir William Osler wrote that "the care of tuberculosis depends more on what the patient has in his head than what he has in his chest" (cited in Brody 1983). Only recently, however, have researchers begun to understand how the mind affects health and healing. Emotional reactions either suppress or stimulate the release of hormones and neurotransmitters, which, in turn, affect a host of physiological processes. For example, psychoneuroimmunologists have discovered that pain can lead to the release of endorphins, a class of opiates whose quantity may account for the variance in pain thresholds of different individuals. Endorphins can also be released through exercise and meditation; thus, they constitute an example of a biological process that is potentially influenced by social phenomena. (See Chapter 2.)

Numerous connections between states of mind and physical well-being have been documented. The stress of academic examinations has been linked with declines in the production of interferon, which reduce one's ability to fight infection and disease (Kiecolt-Glaser et al. 1984). Likewise, feelings of depression have been found to correlate with genital herpes among students (Kemeny 1984) and with depressed lymphocyte responses among recently widowed men (Schleifer et al. 1983). Those who are unable to suppress feelings of anger and distress have more positive immune responses to serious skin cancers than those who are able to repress those feelings (Temoshok et al. 1985). And when comparing the chemical composition of tears produced by emotional states with those produced by eye irritation, Frey (1985) found higher levels of protein and manganese (a mineral linked to mood alterations) in the former. Crying may serve an exocrine function and, like urination and exhaling, remove toxic substances from the body.

The connection between affect and physiology is not simply a matter of emotional states directly causing biological processes. The individual's cognitive awarenesses and level of control over feelings are part of the dynamic. For instance, with behavioral therapy, responses to stress can be diminished, enhancing the survival chances even of people at high risk for developing lung cancer or heart disease. And individuals who can keep the proverbial "stiff upper lip" may not be aware of their inner stresses because they tune out distressing feelings. As a result, they pay a biological price for their emotional stiflings.

Even death has been linked to suppression of emotions. In a study of 57 mastectomy outpatients, researchers at London's King's College Hospital found a significant correlation between women's emotional response three months following their surgery and their rate of survival a decade later. (See Table 6.2.)

## Express It and Feel It

The physical display of emotion may lead to the feelings associated with that emotion. Edgar Allen Poe wrote in *The Purloined Letter* that to discover how wise, stupid, good, or evil a person is or what he might be thinking at the moment, "I fashion the expression of my face, as accurately as possible, in accordance with the expression of his, and then wait to see what thoughts or

**TABLE 6.2   Reactions to Cancer after Ten Years**

| Psychological response three months after operation | Percentage Alive, No Recurrence | Percentage Alive with Cancer | Percentage Dead | Total (N) |
|---|---|---|---|---|
| Denial: "Despite the operation, I don't believe I really ever had cancer." | 50 | 0 | 50 | 10 |
| Fighting spirit: "I'm going to conquer this thing." | 60 | 10 | 30 | 10 |
| Stoic acceptance: "Keep a stiff upper lip; don't complain." | 22 | 3 | 75 | 32 |
| Helplessness, hopelessness: "There's nothing to be done. I'm as good as dead." | 20 | 0 | 80 | 5 |

Source: *New York Times* (Goleman), 1985.

sentiments arise in my mind or heart" (cited in Ekman et al. 1983). Paul Ekman and his associates (1983) tested this notion experimentally and found that facial displays of different emotions (such as anger, fear, sadness, surprise, and disgust) indeed produce distinctive effects on the automatic nervous system. But how does this occur? Is our emotional wiring so primitive that we smile when happy and feel happy when we smile? Zajonc (1985; et al. 1989) argues that the physiological processes are more complicated, involving the ways in which various expressions affect the quantity of blood reaching different areas of the brain. The tightening of the facial muscles to produce a smile, for instance, has a tourniquetlike effect, decreasing the amount of blood flowing to the brain. Particularly affected is the hypothalamus, which not only helps shape emotional life but also regulates the temperature of the body and brain. This is why we shiver with fear and sweat when we are anxious.

## Communicating Emotional States

People tend to mimic the expressions of those around them. Given the ways in which emotional expressions produce the associated feelings, the mirroring of others' expressions leads to a transference of their emotions. Such emotional contagion is evident when a 1-year-old, seeing the tears on the face of an older brother or sister after an accident, begins to cry and seeks solace as if he were the injured one. An extreme example of such empathetic arousal is the **couvade syndrome**, in which husbands experience the morning sickness, backaches, food cravings, and weight gains of their pregnant wives.

Such mimicking, extended over many years, may actually cause long-married individuals to resemble each other. To test the idea, Zajonc et al. (1987)

presented undergraduates with photographs of twelve couples, showing each individual at the time of marriage and twenty-five years later. Half the students were asked to judge man-woman pairs for physical resemblance; the other half were asked to indicate the likelihood of each pair's being married. The researchers found significant similarities of appearance only among couples who had been married a long time. They hypothesized that years of unconscious mimicking of the spouse's expressions produce shared sentiments and similar faces.

In sum, there is an emotional language that is both visibly and viscerally shared. People go to a party, see others smiling, find a smile on their own faces, and have an enjoyable evening themselves. This logic may explain how the theater shapes audience emotions and why smiles in advertisements are effective. "The perception of another face is not just an information transfer," notes Ekman, "but a very literal means by which we feel the sensations the other feels" (cited in Schmeck 1983).

## A Dual Memory System?

The ability of emotions to override rational thought may have a physiological basis. Research on how the brain works reveals that the seats of thought and emotion have little physical connection. Our emotional life is regulated by the limbic system, which apparently is centered in the amygdala. The thinking part of the brain is the cerebral cortex, whose focal point seems to be the hippocampus. When sensory information is received by, say, the eye, neural signals are sent to the thalamus, whence the messages are sent to the sensory decoding portions of the neocortex. It was formerly thought that the hippocampus was part of both the limbic and the cognitive systems, and that the amygdala received information only after it had been processed by the neocortex. However, LeDoux (1989) discovered nerve pathways going directly from the thalamus to the amygdala. Thus, it is possible that emotional responses do not follow from cognitive understanding. Instead, humans appear to have a dual memory system, one for thoughts and the other for emotions.

Some social psychologists anticipated these findings, contending that emotions are just as central as cognition in determining behavior. Zajonc (1985) noted that cognitive psychologists usually assume that cognitions hold primacy over emotions because they occur first, and that emotions are merely reactions to thoughts: "Once I realized that I was being made fun of, I really got mad." He presented the possibility that the logic works in reverse, that emotions might precede thought: "Boy, I really feel mad. I wonder why her presence upsets me so much." These findings also appear to support the contention of psychoanalytic theory that there exists an unconscious mind that affects mental life.

## EMOTIONS AND COGNITION

In the wake of Ronald Reagan's victory in the 1984 presidential election, psychologists found feelings to be three or four times as potent as issues or party identification in determining how people vote (Abelson 1985; Adler 1988). But successful politicians have known this all along. In 1968, Richard Nixon won the election by promising what Americans wanted to hear after the murders of Robert Kennedy and Martin Luther King, the burnings of inner-city ghettoes, and polarization over the war in Vietnam: His themes were law and order, peace, security, and "bring us together." He appealed to the patriotic and hawkish white working middle class, which he called the "forgotten Americans," the "silent majority." President Saddam Hussein of Iraq also demonstrated the effectiveness of appealing to a combination of pride, hope, anger, and fear. Despite the international condemnation of his country's military takeover of Kuwait, the Iraqi leader's standing among poor Arabs grew as he prepared for a showdown with the United States. Despite his bloodthirsty reputation, he stirred pride among a people long disgraced by foreign intervention:

> Make it clear to your rulers, the emirs of oil, as they serve the foreigner; tell the traitors that there is no place for them on Arab soil after they humiliated Arab honor and dignity. (cited in Friedrich 1990:26)

As we saw in the discussion of attitudes in Chapter 4, perceptions and beliefs have a strong affective component. This is particularly evident in situations of social chaos or disaster, in which personal decisions and behaviors are strongly influenced by emotional states and impulses (Shibutani 1961:384). In everyday life, according to **affect control theory** (Heise 1987), individuals seek to maintain and confirm their initial feelings just as they seek to make their experiences conform with their personal schemas of everyday life.

Emotions also affect cognitive processes, which is why it is hard to concentrate when one is upset, angry, or involved in a new romance. Affect has a measurable effect on decision making. Alice Isen et al. (1987) compared subjects who had just watched a comedy film of television "bloopers" with subjects who had watched a film on math or who had exercised. They found the comedy condition produced the most creative solutions. Isen concluded that "the mind associates more broadly when people are feeling good after hearing a joke. They think of things they ordinarily would not and have access to a broader range of mental material. And the more ideas present in your mind, the more ways you see to connect things; you're able to see more solutions" (cited in Goleman 1987a).

Cognitive flexibility and creativity are a function not only of humor but also of the magnitude of one's emotional experiences. People who live emotionally intense lives have more varied goals, seek greater novelty and complexity, and structure their goals in order to maximize their affective experiences (Emmons and Diener 1986; Emmons and King 1989).

It has long been appreciated that learning is more likely to be imprinted on the mind when it occurs in an emotionally charged context (Davis-Floyd 1987:156). This connection, again, results from a physiological chain of events:

> Highly charged emotional experiences . . . are transferred electro-chemically (acetylcholine is the neurotransmitter) through the hippocampus which acts as a bridge between the limbic system and long-term memory storage. If events are not perceived as carrying value or significance to the individual the data are kept approximately seven hours, never to be encoded in long-term memory storage. (Peterson and Hehl 1984:194)

## Changing Emotions through Reverse Psychology

**Paradoxical therapy** is a technique for modifying a person's commitment to initial emotions (Frankl 1960). Consider the tantrums staged by 4-year-olds when they cannot have their own way. Often these outbreaks occur at embarrassing times and places. But instead of insisting that the youngster give up the tantrums (i.e., "Stop that or you will not live to see your sixth birthday"), the parent could say that it is all right to have them but only in a special "tantrum place" at home. Later, the child may be told that tantrums are acceptable only during a specified time of day. Often the behavior is extinguished within a few weeks.

One reason paradoxical therapy works is that by prescribing the symptom (e.g., instructing the child to do what you want him or her to stop doing), one causes involuntary emotions to become deliberate and voluntarily controlled. Another reason is the Tom Sawyer effect: By reshaping the individual's perspectives—as in telling others that it is a privilege and not a chore to whitewash the fence—one causes negative emotions to become positive. Finally, defiance to change can be used to promote change: If a child refuses to eat his beans, claiming that he hates them, the parent might say, "Of course you don't like them; you are not old enough" (Lobsenz 1987).

The difficulty of eliminating prejudice stems from the dual memory-response system built into the mind. As Thomas Pettigrew observed: "The emotions of prejudice are formed early in childhood, while the beliefs that are used to justify it come later. Later in life you may want to change your prejudice, but it is far easier to change your intellectual beliefs than your deep feelings" (cited in Goleman 1987b).

Conversely, cognitive processes may determine the emotions one experiences. The premise of Albert Ellis's rational-emotive therapy, for instance, is that disturbed emotions arise not only out of one's life events but also out of the way one interprets them:

> People do not *get upset* but instead *upset themselves* by insisting that (a) they should be outstandingly loved and accomplished, (b) other people should be incredibly fair and giving, and (c) the world should be exceptionally easy and munificent. (Ellis 1973:15)

## Emotionally Charged Social Symbols

Emotional states can be generated by the manipulation of social symbols. Every culture has words that capture its central values, hopes, and fears. In the United States, besides *mom* and *apple pie*, such words as *death, cancer, patriotism,* and *God* evoke intense feelings; indeed, their very sounds affect the galvanic skin responses of listeners. These words activate deep-seated belief systems and strong emotions. Just listening to the four-millisecond subliminal message "Mommy and I are One" improves not only emotional well-being but even dart-playing performance (Weinberger and Hardaway 1990). And as we saw in Chapter 5, failure to understand and feel the emotional significance of words is linked with psychopathology.

Architecture also invokes certain emotional states. Consider the sentiments produced by viewing mausoleums (e.g., the Taj Mahal) and monuments (e.g., the Lincoln Memorial or the Eiffel Tower). Sometimes architecture is explicitly designed to arouse emotions. Hitler knew how to employ monumental architecture to intimidate and direct the masses. Medieval clergy were aware of the emotional power of cathedrals, whose dominating spires remind one of religion's place in life and whose interiors produce the feelings of awe associated with encountering the sacred.

Political and religious regimes have also tapped the emotional power of color, as have manufacturers, retailers, and advertisers. To convey a feeling of purity, for instance, cigarette packs feature large areas of white with light-colored lettering (Toufexis 1983). Consumer confidence has been gauged by the colors women wear: A positive mood is reflected by such "happy colors" as yellow and rosy pink, whereas troubled uncertainty is reflected in earth tones like the drab khakis in vogue during the recession of the 1970s (Solomon 1987). The restraining cells of some community prisons are painted pink because of the color's curious enfeebling effects. And black uniforms make American athletes appear and actually act meaner (Frank and Gilovich 1988): Between 1970 and 1986, the most penalized teams of the National Hockey League and the National Football League were those with black uniforms.

## Consequences of Social Sharing of Feeling States

Most of us have had the experience of having to "get something off our chest," of having to tell someone about something and feeling better as a result. Sometimes the information we feel compelled to share is good, as when a stroke of good fortune makes us feel as if we will "burst" unless we tell someone about it. Sometimes the information is bad, producing an equally strong need to confide in one's priest or therapist.

When you think about it, this ability to discharge emotional intensity by simply sharing one's feelings with another person borders on the miraculous. And because of the physiological basis of emotion, the sharing of feeling states has demonstrable impacts on biological well-being. Lin et al. (1979) found that social support contributes significantly to the diminution of illness symptoms. Pennebaker and Beall (1986) demonstrated that *not* confiding causes damaging internal tensions and increases the likelihood of stress-related illness.

How does the sharing of feelings reduce the harm caused by "keeping things bottled up"? Psychoanalysts would point to the cathartic function of talk, claiming that confiding reduces the inner stresses caused by anxiety or guilt. Behaviorists might claim that externalizing personal transgressions provides release from the tension created by the anticipation and fear of negative feedback from others. Cognitive theorists may argue that the tension is generated by the dissonance between one's self-concept and one's past actions. Valins and Nisbett (1972) suggested that the individual who confides receives social-comparison information from empathetic others. Confiding also helps one organize, structure, and find meaning in stressful circumstances (Silver and Wortman 1980). The therapeutic effect of religious confessionals (see Chapter

14) lies in their ability to allow individuals to preserve their self-template while being ritually absolved of the deviant act.

Symbolic interactionists would focus on how, by giving words to inner turmoil, one can externalize the sources of anxiety and address them objectively. Talking puts feelings outside of oneself; the externalized feelings can then become objects for collective scrutiny, with diffusion of responsibility. The need to share feelings may be intensified as our culture becomes increasingly other-directed (see Chapter 8).

Capitalizing on this strategy for coping with negative emotions, a myriad of support groups have come into existence during the past few decades. These groups are composed of people with shared characteristics, such as the recently bereaved (Widow-to-Widow programs, parents of SIDS, and AIDS victims), people who must cope with a difficult family problem (support groups for spouses of Alzheimer's victims), or those who have had a traumatic experience (support groups for Vietnam veterans or Cambodian refugees).

An intriguing insight into the therapeutic value of socially sharing one's troubles was reported by Spiegel et al. (1989). These researchers unexpectedly found that women with metastic breast cancer lived twice as long if they participated in a psychotherapy support group than if they did not. In their study of eighty-nine women receiving normal medical care for breast cancer, half of the subjects were randomly assigned to special therapy groups while the others were not. After ten years all but three of the women had died, but those in the therapy groups had lived, on average, thirty-seven months after the beginning of the study, whereas those who were not in therapy groups had lived a mean of nineteen months. Not only did the women in the experimental group live longer, but they also reported less depression, anxiety, and pain, and they seemed to make more constructive use of the limited time remaining to them.

## Determining One's Emotions from Social Cues

To investigate the extent to which people's definitions of their own feeling states can be manipulated by external influences, Schachter and Singer (1962) conducted a creative experiment involving the injection of epinephrine (adrenalin), which stimulates the sympathetic nervous system and produces palpitations and feelings of jumpiness. To create the various control conditions, subjects were injected either with epinephrine or with an inert placebo. Some were correctly informed about what reactions to expect; others were incorrectly informed (they were told to expect itchiness and numbness in their feet); a third group was told nothing at all. To alter the influence of the social environment, some subjects were accompanied by a confederate and others were not. Those exposed to a confederate either saw the confederate interpret the symptoms euphorically and engage in bouts of laughter, or saw the confederate express anger and hostility.

If emotions are a consequence of biological factors, the arousal effect should be experienced equivalently by all subjects; push the same button and people will feel the same thing. Any advance information or environmental cues (actions of a confederate) should have little effect on the emotions the subjects actually experience. On the other hand, if emotions are shaped by culture, these amorphic subjective feelings should be influenced by both information and social environment. The researchers found evidence to support both hypothe-

## Vocabularies of Emotion

*amaeru* (Japanese, verb): To presume upon another's love, to act like a baby in order to be treated as a dependent

*conmoción* (Spanish, noun): Emotion held in common by a group or gathering

*curo contento* (Italian, noun): The way a happy, even-tempered person feels. Literally, a "happy heart."

*Feierabend* (German, noun): Festive frame of mind at the end of the working day

*nadi* (Balinese, noun): The feeling a person retains for someone he or she once loved

*razbliuto* (Russian, noun): The feeling a person retains for someone he or she once loved

*sabsung* (Thai, verb): to slake an emotional or spiritual thirst, to be revitalized

*sbottonarsi* (Italian, verb): To open up, reveal one's opinion or feelings

*Schadenfreude* (German, noun): Joy that one feels as a result of some else's misfortune

*ta* (Chinese, verb): To understand things and thus take them lightly

*Weltschmerz* (German, noun): A gloomy, romanticized world-weary sadness, experienced most often by privileged youth

*yoin* (Japanese, noun): Emotional reverberation that continues to move one long after the initial external stimulus has ceased

*zanshin* (Japanese, noun): A state of relaxed mental alertness in the face of danger

Source: Rheingold, 1988.

ses: Subjects' evaluations were influenced by all three factors. However, only with a narrow range and at low levels of arousal could individuals be induced to mislabel their emotional states.

## Emotional Self-Objectification

Humans' tendency to understand and define their emotive states using social cues leads to a model in which individuals first register some internal state of arousal and then use a cultural emotional logic to interpret the feeling state. This interpretative system defines the feeling, specifies its social source, and indicates whether it is good or undesirable. Cultural criteria also specify how the feeling state is to be managed (Rosenberg 1987). Thus, the arousal one senses when opening the envelope containing one's report card is taken as a sign of the importance one places on education. The feelings experienced when seeing a column of A's or F's are interpreted as the emotion of either pride or humiliation. And whether one displays this emotional state by rushing into the street to share one's news with strangers or by heaping guilt upon oneself is a matter of cultural prescription.

## The Concept of Happiness

O happiness, our being's end and aim
Good, pleasure, ease, content! Whatever thy name
That something still which promptest eternal sigh
For which we bear to live, or dare to die.—Alexander Pope

The Declaration of Independence states, "We hold these truths to be self-evident—that all men are created equal; that they are endowed by their Creator with certain unalienable rights; that among these are life, liberty, and the pursuit of happiness."

But what is **happiness**? Is it synonymous with pleasure, satisfaction, or well-being? Can one experience happiness if one has never experienced its antithesis? Is happiness a state that one can maintain for days, weeks, or even months, or can there be too much of a good thing? Does one really know when one is happy, or is the condition of happiness realized only in reflection? Is happiness a specific biological-psychological condition, such as the condition created by release of the bodily produced opiates called endorphins, or is it a socially defined subjective state?

Given the fact that people constantly seek happiness, it is curious that the topic of happiness was not even indexed in *Psychological Abstracts International* until 1973 (Swanbrow 1989). Recent research has revealed that rather than happiness being the opposite of unhappiness, the two are distinctive feeling states that can rise and fall independently of each other (Diener et al. 1991).

Happiness involves both the sense of subjective well-being and the capacity to enjoy life. Such capacities, according to psychoanalysts, stem from the **pleasure principle** and are influenced by personality factors such as one's ability to filter out the unpleasurable, to receive joy from creating art or solving scientific equations, or to feel intense appreciation for others because of being loved by another.

From a stimulus-response perspective, happiness may entail receipt of the proper amount of positive reinforcement—neither too much, which leads to satiation and diminishing levels of satisfaction, nor too little.

Cognitive theorists may view happiness as a personally defined state. For instance, an individual may be socialized to believe that happiness is derived from helping and giving to others. Thus, the feeling one obtains by giving to charity is interpreted as happiness. In addition, according to the research of Reich et al. (1988), happiness is gained not only from what one does but also from one's perceived influence over pleasurable outcomes.

In subsequent chapters we will explore how this feeling state is distributed across the social landscape—comparing, for instance, the highly and sparsely educated and the upper and lower classes.

This point is illustrated by Becker's (1953) study of drug effects. Becker found that marijuana smokers must *learn* how to achieve a "high." Novice smokers often report feeling no effects, either because of faulty smoking technique or because false expectations caused them not to notice the drug's effects.

Once the proper technique is learned and effects are perceived, the novice learns from others how to interpret the experiences as being pleasurable. When these experiences are shared with others, an ideology emerges about how the drug enhances one's experiences and how its less desirable symptoms can be managed.

Returning to the case of voodoo death, it may be "the victim's cognitive apprehension of the meaning of witchcraft" that brings about the state of fright that leads to lethal physiological changes (Lex 1974:821–822). The victim feels a sense of hopelessness, helplessness, and stress, and both he and other members of his culture believe that he is doomed. Lachman (1982–1983) argues that the biological disturbance caused by psychological factors may be a learned response to certain emotional stimuli. When studying voodoo practices among the Australian aborigine, Eastwell (1982) found that resultant deaths involved deviant activities—such as adultery, murder, and desecration of ceremonial land—and perhaps spurred fears of retribution. If the victim is to suffer death, a self-fulfilling prophecy must be established. The victim must first assume the role of victim, which is then reinforced by the behaviors of family and community members toward him.

The examples just given suggest that emotions can be conceptualized as a dimension of intersubjectivity. In addition to providing shared memories, beliefs, and cognitions, words and gestures can also produce shared feeling states that touch people's innermost beings. In the next section we turn to the question of how these cultural criteria are socially constructed—that is, how emotional expressions come to be socially standardized and how their subjective experiences come to be socially learned.

# THE SOCIAL CONSTRUCTION OF FEELING STATES

Sociologists who study emotion have focused on feelings arising out of social processes. At the beginning of the century, Charles Horton Cooley believed in the universality of emotions. But he saw them as arising not out of shared biological traits, such as brain structures and functioning, but, rather, out of shared social dynamics. The emotions arising out of social life are every bit as "primordial" as those arising out of the limbic system. Intimate groups, Cooley noted, give rise to "sympathy and the innumerable sentiments into which sympathy enters, such as love, resentment, ambition, vanity, hero-worship, and the feelings of social right and wrong. . . . Always and everywhere men seek honor and dread ridicule, defer to public opinion, cherish their goods and their children, and admire courage, generosity, and success" (1909:28). The social need for individuals to exercise self-control turns out to involve emotional control as well.

Many of the affective states considered by more sociologically inclined social psychologists turn out to be qualitatively different from the immediate, sensual qualities of the emotions considered earlier in this chapter. Feelings of love, resentment, and disgrace are not only triggered and maintained when people interact with others but are longer in duration and change with time. For these reasons, Gordon distinguishes the "relatively undifferentiated body arousal[s]" of emotions from the more social **sentiments**, which are "combinations of bodily sensations, gestures, and cultural meanings that we learn in enduring social relationships" (1981:563).

Kemper (1987) argues that sentiments, or "secondary emotions," are derived from four physiologically grounded primary emotions, which are socially modified. He hypothesized that these primordial emotions include fear, anger, depression, and satisfaction. Fear, for instance, can be learned without the involvement of the cortex (Goleman 1989)—it is the basic "gut reaction." While physiologically experiencing one of these emotions, individuals learn from socializing agents how to label and define these states. Out of anger arises shame; out of fear comes guilt; and from satisfaction evolves pride. Moreover, these emotional meanings are derived largely from social relationships—specifically, the social power and status of the experiencer. For instance, the exercise of power arouses fear and the retraction of status arouses anger (Kemper 1978).

## Social Control and Personal Motivations

Societies routinely shape, reinforce, or reject various feeling states. Addressing the individual's need to "feel good" both physically and psychologically, society has evolved a repertoire of feeling states that, like the cognitive templates and language discussed in the previous chapters, turn out to be additional mechanisms of social control.

Perhaps the most basic of these emotions of social control is fear. As we will see in Chapter 8, according to at least one theory of moral development the fear of punishment is the first stage of moral reasoning. Fear may also be one of the first controlling emotions in the evolution of societies; it is typically used by early leaders to consolidate their power. To this day, many political and religious regimes employ fear to stifle dissent and enforce obedience. Primary among these fears is the fear of death, whether of oneself or of loved ones. Thus, in response to the increasing political and economic competition provided by African Americans at the turn of the century, particularly during times of inflationary shifts in the price of cotton, white southerners employed the fear of lynching to control blacks.

Related to fear of death is fear of torture, historically an effective means by which regimes have obtained confessions from those they suspected of challenging or betraying basic principles (see Figure 6.1). In addition to fears of dying and injury, religions have developed fear of one's fate after death. (See Chapter 14.) Indeed, one of the most powerful mechanisms for ensuring social cooperation and self-sacrifice is the fear of eternal damnation, not being resurrected, or being reincarnated in an undesirable form. On the other hand, the control of fear brings a sense of security and well-being, out of which emerge self-confidence, self-reliance, optimism, and trust. A young child, for example, learns that its parent is still present while out of sight and with this confidence begins to explore its world and to take risks.

In addition to fear, several other socially inculcated emotional states contribute to the meeting of various social needs:

> In the family, romantic love ideally leads to parenting and stable relationships, instilling trust in other social institutions.
> In religion, worshipers develop a sense of awe toward sacred things, from which is derived subservience to higher principles.

In this chart, from *The Emergency Public Relations Manual* for officials involved in "crisis management" and "disaster public relations," public perceptions of various risks are plotted on two axes, degree of personal familiarity (vertical) and the relative degree of dread (horizontal). According to the manual, "understanding the emotions at work" can help officials develop "communications strategies that stabilize tense emotional strategies."

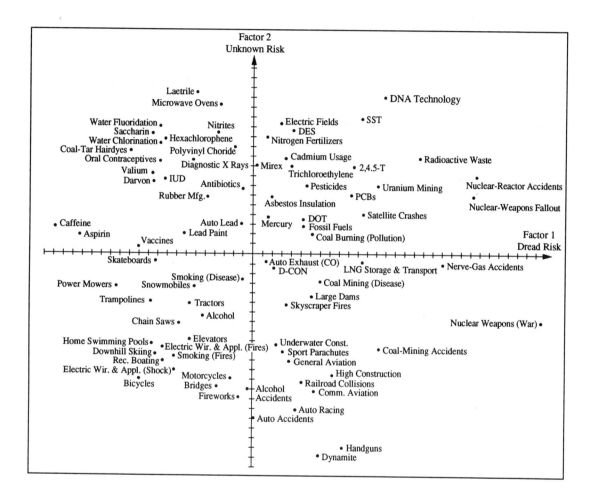

From the third edition of *The Emergency Public Relations Manual*, a handbook for corporate and government officials involved in "crisis management" and "disaster public relations," published by Pase, Incorporated. This chart, created by psychologist Paul Slovic, attempts to measure the public perception of various risks according to two criteria. The location of each risk along the horizontal axis shows the relative degree of dread associated with it; the location along the vertical axis shows the relative degree of familiarity. "Understanding the emotions at work" can help public-relations officials develop "communications strategies that stabilize tense emotional situations."

**FIGURE 6.1   Axis of Fear**
Source: Reprinted in *Harper's Magazine*, 1987.

Both religion and law depend on the emotions of guilt and fear of violating moral or legal principles.

Political regimes inculcate patriotism and fear and hatred of adversaries.

Educational systems ideally stimulate excitement and curiosity in learning so as to produce the next generation of workers.

## The Sentiment of Social Belonging

From society's perspective, perhaps the most central emotional state involves the sentiment the society's members feel toward their primary groups: the sense of loyalty, affection, and belonging. Acknowledgments of such bonds appear early in life. A 5-year-old comes to the defense of his 2-year-old brother, telling off the older neighborhood kids for taunting him. Maybe at home the older brother can call his brother a "baby," but that is not a prerogative of the other kids on the block.

For hundreds of generations the primary human bonds have been tribal. For most individuals, being in the company of one's own people is all that really matters. This feeling is especially pronounced in tribal cultures, but even in the United States the special bonds one feels with the city of one's birth and childhood may cause one to root for the hometown football team even though one moved out of state thirty years earlier. The resurgence of ethnic identity (and language) movements throughout the world reveals the failure of political regimes to replace traditional tribal loyalties, at least within a period of two or three generations.

People are likely to feel empathy toward someone whom they perceive as being similar to themselves, and altruism results from that empathy. Sociobiologists may argue that the propensity to help others evolved from early humans who, not knowing precisely who their relatives were, tended to assist those with whom they shared physical similarities or who were members of their in-groups (Krebs 1975). As human interdependencies have expanded from family to tribe to community to city to nation-state and, finally, to the world-system, humans have recognized commonalities and shared concerns with an increasingly broad range of others. Thus, David Riesman notes that with modernization comes "a general tendency, facilitated by education, by mobility, by the mass media, toward an enlargement of the circles of empathy beyond one's clan, beyond even one's class, sometimes beyond one's country as well" (1950[1961]:xxi).

***Apathy and Engagement***.  Boredom has been called America's most prevalent disease (Ramey 1974). From society's perspective, this feeling is a possible source of mischief. One of the sources of terrorism and criminal mischief, for instance, is unemployment and the absence of social engagement. The restraints of normal sentiments evaporate when rootless and victimized individuals accept an ideology that attacks the perceived source of their lifelessness or when they identify with a leader who makes them feel vital or whole.

## The Moral Sentiments

Would crime rates go down if we made public spectacles of deviants? What if moral violators were put in highly visible cages in shopping malls to be subjected to public ridicule? What if malls were also a setting for public lashings, where one could see blood flowing from the backs of serious offenders, simultaneously empathizing with their pain while feeling the satisfaction of retribution?

Social systems depend on various sentiments of moral integration. Among these are the emotional checks one feels when one is not in sync with the moral order. Recall that in the Asch experiments on conformity, in which subjects were asked to select one of three lines that was equal in length to a standard line, only one-quarter of the naive subjects did not go along with the unanimous wrong decisions of the group. What was not mentioned in Chapter 4 is the fact that all the subjects, both those who remained independent and those who went along with the group, exhibited anxiety, doubt, and confusion. Such are the emotional consequences when one's perceptions or ideas come into conflict with what "everyone else" sees or knows. This is particularly true with respect to moral consensus (Sabini and Silver 1982).

The continuing distress and pain felt by American military who participated in the atrocities and slaughter of the Vietnam War is another example of what happens when one violates fundamental moral principles. The symptoms of such "moral pain" include feelings of victimization, inability to love or trust, estrangement from one's own feelings, guilt, and need for absolution (Marin 1981).

Guilt has been referred to as both a destructive form of self-hate and the guardian of social goodness (Adams 1979). As Willard Gaylin explains,

> We are so constructed that we must serve the social good—on which we are dependent for our own survival—and when we do not, we suffer the pangs of guilt. . . . Guilt is the guardian of our goodness. . . . Guilt then is a form of self-disappointment. It is the sense of anguish that we did not achieve our standards of what we ought to be. (1979:55, 52)

Laboratory experiments reveal that the higher their level of guilt, the less likely college students are to have been involved in sexual, delinquent, aggressive, or drug-related behaviors (Mosher 1973; Gerrard 1982).

Guilt is an auditory notion: One can "confess" one's guilt or live with its "nagging" effects. It is also an economic notion, a debt owed by the offender to society or the victim. In this sense, guilt is related to fear—specifically, fear of being punished for a forbidden act. In a guilt-based system of social control punishment is the repayment, as when one "pays one's debt to society" (French 1984). Guilt can also instigate helping behavior: The contributions of churchgoers were found to be greater for those who had not confessed than for those who had (Harris, Benson, and Hall 1975).

***Attraction and Repulsion.*** The emotions that serve to integrate a people depend not only on sentiments of attraction but on sentiments of repulsion as well. The latter may range from the food taboos of a religious group to national loathing of foreign enemies. Georges Bataille argues that attraction toward that which is repulsive and taboo became the basis of social solidarity:

> Early human beings were brought together by disgust and by common terror, by an insurmountable horror focused precisely on what originally was the central attraction to their union. (1988:106)

But for some, that which is taboo also evokes curiosity and excitement. Criminals report that they gain a feeling of excitement and adventure when committing their crimes (Frazier and Meisenhelder 1985). Underlying the workings of paradoxical therapy is the tendency to think and dwell on unwanted or forbidden thoughts (Wegner 1989), or to feel the opposite emotion to that which is socially expected. One study, for instance, found that women with strong feelings of guilt about sexual behavior or feelings have stronger physiological reactions to erotic videotapes than women with low sexual guilt, yet are unaware of those reactions (Morokoff 1985).

## Sentiments of Personal Worth

Related to the moral sentiments are feelings derived from one's sense of whether or not one "measures up" to the moral demands of one's group and/or the social requirements of one's role. Those feelings include shame, guilt, embarrassment, pride, and self-esteem.

Scheff (1988, 1990) depicts shame as the master emotion, a private feeling of self-loathing that is capable of inhibiting most other emotions and is perhaps the most difficult to discharge. Experienced as embarrassment or humiliation, shame involves one's basic sense of self and social worth. Because this is a uniquely human trait, as Darwin noted (1872[1965]), only humans blush.

Shame is a more primitive emotion than guilt. It precedes guilt in the individual's psychological development (see Table 6.1) and in the evolution of social emotional controls. (See Chapter 8.) It is more of a visual than an auditory notion, as is evidenced by early cultures branding the foreheads of deviants and publicly displaying moral transgressors in stockades, as well as by the symbol of shame worn by Hester Prynne in *The Scarlet Letter* (French 1984). To hide their state, those who are shamed attempt to cover or turn their faces.

This feeling of personal shortcoming or impropriety, the belief that one has not behaved in the socially approved way, produces heightened self-consciousness (Izard 1977) and loathing of one's whole self. A cross-cultural study of children from six countries in grades three through nine (an age when identity is not yet established) found fear of personal humiliation or embarrassment to be more troubling than many other concerns (Yamamoto et al. 1988).

The antithesis of shame is pride, which also first appears during the second year of life. Both emerge with the development of a sense of self and from the emotional messages received from others. Shame and humiliation result if the child learns he or she displeases others. On the other hand, if the child learns that he or she pleases others, that one is successfully in control of their desirable feedback, then pride and dignity emerge.

Related to the emotions of shame and guilt is embarrassment. Although the feeling may occur in situations in which individuals feel overrewarded given their ability or contribution (Anderson et al. 1969), embarrassment normally follows from failure to meet the expectations of a particular situation. For such individuals the result is often a loss of self-control, which is taken as a sign of "weakness, inferiority, low status, moral guilt, [and] defeat" (Goffman 1967:101–102). Such behaviors of embarrassed individuals are an "important class of acts which are usually quite spontaneous and yet no less required and obligatory than one self-consciously performed" (Goffman 1967:111).

On the other hand, when one's actions match the framework of social obligations, social actors may find the audience actually enhancing their performance. Singers, actors, and public speakers, for instance, describe special times when they can "feed off" their audience's positive reactions to their presentation and feel a sense of total composure and control.

## Socially Constructed Feeling States

To generate and reinforce the sentiments of solidarity and connectedness with others, societies have traditionally employed ritual. Collective rituals generate the emotional energy that binds together a community's members. One such ritual involves the mourning obligations of various categories of kin. In a review of mourning in seventy-three societies, Rosenblatt, Walsh, and Jackson (1976) discovered incredible variations in the form and intensity with which grief is expressed. In all but one of the societies studied, people weep at death (the Balinese, the only exception, say that they laugh to avoid crying). There were gender differences in crying in sixty of the societies; in thirty-two, both sexes cried equally, and in twenty-eight women cried more than men. In eighteen societies, members of both sexes attempt self-injury (such as cutting a finger off at the joint); in twelve, women are more likely than men to mutilate themselves. Not only do the ritual expressions of grief vary across cultures, but the lower one's status in the social hierarchy, the greater the expected emotional display (in only 17 percent of the societies were males expected to cry the most, and in none were they expected to mutilate themselves more than women did).

In analyzing such phenomena, Durkheim noted that the sentiments occasioned by loss are actually socially constructed:

> Mourning is not a natural movement of private feelings wounded by a cruel loss; it is a duty imposed by the group. One weeps, not simply because he is sad, but because he is forced to weep. It is a ritual attitude he is forced to adopt out of respect for custom, but which is, in a large measure, independent of his affective state. . . . It is the social organization of the relations of kinship which has determined the respective sentiments of parents and children. (1965 [1915]:442–443)

Further, by publicly expressing the appropriate emotion, people come to actually feel the culturally appropriate sentiment, thereby enhancing social integration. As Durkheim's student A. R. Radcliffe-Brown noted in discussing ritual weeping,

> Ceremonial customs are the means by which the society acts upon its individual members and keeps alive in their minds a certain system of sentiments. Without the ceremonial those sentiments would not exist, and without them the social organization in its actual form could not exist. (1922[1964]:324)

For these reasons, **state funerals** are a traditional strategy used by political regimes to reaffirm their legitimacy. When Ayatollah Khomeini died in 1989, hysterical throngs of Iranians took to the streets of Tehran. So frenzied was the crowd that Khomeini's body toppled to the street, where its shroud was torn away by mourners seeking a relic of their beloved leader. Though more controlled, the public mournings of Americans over the deaths of presidents

Political regimes often fan and focus sentiments with public rituals, intensifying the feelings of collective bonds between a people. In the Japanese state funeral for Emperor Hirohito, the solemnity of the attendants ensures that alternative emotions do not challenge the theme of grief.

Roosevelt and Kennedy produced an equally intense emotion of communal grief.

Opponents of political regimes also tap the emotional power of death to communicate their cause. In South Africa in the mid-1980s, **political funerals** became such an effective rallying point for the anti-*apartheid* movement that South African authorities limited the number of mourners to 200 and banned all placards and all speeches by anyone except clergy.

***Feeling Rules.*** In *The Managed Heart*, Hochschild (1983) describes the **feeling rules** required by certain occupational roles. To satisfy these rules of emotional expression, workers must perform **emotion work**, either evoking or suppressing their private feelings on demand so as to experience the sentiments required by their jobs. In bureaucratic contexts, for instance, one is expected never to let one's emotions show to a client and rarely, if ever, to reveal them to superiors. To be "professional" means not only to control professional knowledge but also to be able to exercise control over personal urges.

Most of our work takes place in bureaucratic settings, places where activities are rationally programmed and individuals interact with others in terms of their roles in the system. Here people are understood to be distinct from the roles they occupy, and private selves are separate from public selves. (The admonition "Don't take things so personally" means that one has failed to separate oneself from one's organization role.) In service occupations such as flight attendant or salesperson, one must force oneself to be equally nice to all customers, even obnoxious ones. The expression of unauthorized emotion reflects poorly on the individual, who has "acted unprofessionally," and on the organization, whose representative has presented a poor corporate face to the public. Hochschild estimates that one-third of American workers are required to perform such emotional labor.

When what individuals actually feel is synchronized with the sentiments that are socially expected, the fusion of self and society is complete. The pride of a worker in a job well done meshes with the economic need for quality workmanship; a parent's love of a child creates unselfish dedication to socializing the next generation. In the periods of public mourning mentioned earlier, personal grief coincided with the grief of the entire nation, and Americans' sense of solidarity has rarely been greater.

Such synchronizations are not guaranteed. When workers are forced to present the company image, individuals are denied control over their own mannerisms and emotions. In Hochschild's (1983) study of flight attendants, she found that requiring them to put aside all emotions except joy and to treat all passengers as if they were guests could cause them to become alienated from their own true feelings. Without the right to show exhaustion, exasperation, anger, or boredom, they pay a psychological price. Glick et al. (1974) liken such mismatches between psychological feelings and ill-fitting ritual to sticking a sore foot into a shoe two sizes too small.

## EMOTIONS IN CROSS-CULTURAL AND HISTORICAL PERSPECTIVE

Like language and beliefs, emotions are cultural artifacts (Geertz 1973:81) that are conditioned by group life. In the course of social evolution, new emotions emerged out of traditional tribal sentiments. As Kemper notes, "As long as society differentiates new situations, labels them, and socializes individuals to experience them, new emotions will continue to emerge" (1987:263).

There is a myth that individuals in "primitive" cultures were more in touch with their emotions than people in modern societies, that they were more "innocent" and less likely to fake emotions. However, rarely do we find social approval being given to the expression of *spontaneous*, idiosyncratic emotions. Gerth and Mills argue that such individual emotional displays have historically occurred only during times of great social transformation, such as during the collapse of the feudal order and the American and French Revolutions. With the eventual establishment of a new social order, spontaneity once again gives way to convention, "often to the point of . . . rigidly prescribed forms of etiquette" (1964[1953]:62–63).

Over time, social control has shifted from externally to internally exercised. Dreitzel explains this as a two-stage process:

> At first the norms of behavior become more and more rigid, formalized, and ritualized. Manners of everyday behavior are now formally prescribed . . . The second stage is the internalization of these formal norms of good behavior via socialization procedures. The control of body and emotions now becomes semiautomatic. The external sanctions against rule-breaking behavior are eventually replaced by psychic reactions like embarrassment, shame, and finally, guilt feelings. (1981:213)

In other words, the exercise of social control has historically shifted from bodily punishment to emotional manipulations, which are considerably more potent.

Such differences in social control may still be found in the American class structure. Social control through corporal punishment is more likely to be found in the lower and working classes, whereas the middle and upper classes are more likely to rely on emotion management (see Figure 6.2). Arlie Hochschild (1979) found middle-class parents controlling their children through appeals to feeling, whereas working-class parents tend to control their offspring through appeals to behavior. Similarly, Melvin Kohn, a long-time observer of social-class differences in socialization, notes that

> middle class mothers are far more likely to punish their son physically for what they call loss of temper than for behavior defined as wild play. They appear to find the child's loss of temper, but not his wild play, particularly intolerable . . . The distinction between wild play and loss of temper was most often made in terms of the child's presumed intent, as judged by his preceding actions . . . If his actions seemed to stem from the frustration of not having his own way, they were judged to indicate loss of temper. (1963:308)

## Defining the Emotional Meanings of Sex

The feelings produced by sexual impulses provide undeniable evidence of the biological roots of emotion. The power of these urges was so great that Freud put them at the center of his psychoanalytic paradigm, with the id producing the energy that drives the entire personality system. So great is the power of sexual suggestion to command attention and elicit excitement that advertisers routinely employ sexual images to draw attention to their products.

From society's perspective, such a powerful force cannot be left unrestrained. To control it is to harness a source of energy that, instead of threatening social relationships, can be used to enhance them. Throughout history, communities, churches, and political regimes have sought to control sexual urges: the community to avoid civil disorder arising out of rape or seduction, the church to reinforce its moral codes by regulating the direction and meaning of sexual passion, and the state to replenish its warriors and producers.

Historical changes in the nature of social bonds have been associated with changes in the social control of sexual drives. When, for instance, the status of males far exceeds that of females, often sexual pleasure becomes an exclusive male privilege. Operations such as clitoridectomies are used to reduce females' sexual pleasure; clitoridectomies are still performed on hundreds of thousands of women in more than twenty developing countries.

The wide range of emotional meanings attached to sexual activities in different cultures are derived not only from differing views of the sex act itself but also from differences in the significance of marriage and the strength of cultural connections between sex and marriage. Some Christians, for instance, believe that sex between spouses for any purpose other than procreation is immoral. In the fourth century A.D., St. Jerome claimed that "nothing is more impure than to love one's wife as if she were a mistress" (Stone 1985:26).

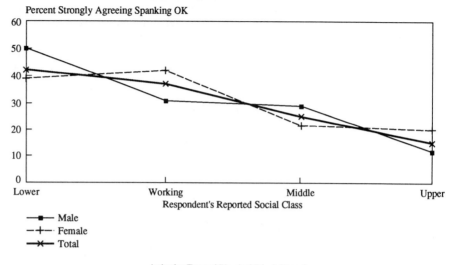

Attitudes Toward Physical Discipline of
Children, by Social Class and Gender

Percent Strongly Agreeing Spanking OK

Respondent's Reported Social Class

— ■ — Male
— + — Female
— ✕ — Total

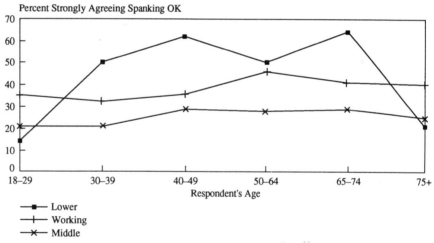

Attitudes Toward Physical Discipline of
Children, by Social Class and Age

Percent Strongly Agreeing Spanking OK

Respondent's Age

— ■ — Lower
— + — Working
— ✕ — Middle

Social-class differences in attitudes toward physical punishment can be gauged by responses to the statement "It is sometimes necessary to discipline a child with a good, hard spanking." The following table presents the percentage of individuals of different social classes who agreed strongly with this statement in the 1989 NORC General Social Science Survey. For both males and females, the higher the reported social class, the lower the percentages concurring. These results are presented in graphic form.

**FIGURE 6.2 Attitudes toward Physical Discipline of Children, by Social Class and Gender**
Source: NORC 1988.

# The Social Construction of Love and Anger

With modernization, the basic social unit has shifted from the family to the individual. Instead of being economic coalitions, as they were through most of history, families have become emotional networks. And as love replaced authority and economic cooperation as the cement of family relations, and as ultimate loyalties shifted from kinship to political and economic ties (it is now the state, not one's family, that is ultimately responsible for one's care in advanced old age), a new realm of recognized emotional states and disorders emerged.

In nineteenth-century America, romantic love became a sufficient precondition for marriage (Campbell 1987:27). In part, this occurred because the family no longer organized daily life: It had lost its traditional economic functions when industrialization removed work from the home, had lost its traditional procreative functions when children no longer were an economic asset, and had lost its traditional social integration with the community. The rise of romantic love was also related to the need of an increasingly mobile society to have its members make quick, spontaneous attachments (Solomon 1982). In the traditional arranged marriages of India, on the other hand, there are few exceptions that love will develop between a husband and wife, because the union is based on a financial compact in which assets are transferred from the bride's family (the dowry) to the groom's.

With the evolution of romantic love occurred changes in cultural orientations toward anger. This coincidence was not accidental, since love and anger are not opposites on an emotional continuum but are actually closely related. Thirteen percent of all homicides in the United States involve spouses, former spouses, and lovers, and an additional 8 percent involve other family members (Malcolm 1990). An assumption of our times is that anger is something that must be expunged from the psychophysiological self, whether through dissipation, channeling, or denial. But such is not always the case. Stearns and Stearns (1986) chronicle a history of increasing restraint of (and ambivalence toward) anger in the United States.

In the country's early days, there were strategies for diverting angry behavior, such as using verbal insults instead of physical violence against one's neighbors or reserving full emotional ventings for outsiders. Anger did not become a social problem until an enhanced value was placed on family life and the ideal of rationally controlling impulses was internalized. The ability to control anger would not become a valued trait until the second half of the 1800s. Injunctions against displays of temper and feelings of anger began appearing, first focusing on the family (where anger was seen as an obstacle to marital love) and later becoming part of the emotional standards of work and politics required in a society experiencing increasing urbanization and economic interdependency.

As greater emotional expectations were placed on marriage, traditional community emotional supports declined, and as it came to be expected that external frustrations were to be resolved within the "private sphere" of the home, the family became a cauldron for emotional turmoil. Eventually, according to Carol and Peter Stearns (1986), Americans began seeking to regulate not only angry behavior but the feeling of anger itself. With such prohibitions, one of the few remaining channels for dissipating anger was to direct it inward toward oneself, producing guilt. The Stearnses also speculate that the participation of Victorian wives in social protest movements may have served as an outlet for marital anger.

In the twentieth century anger was recognized as an inherent drive that must be carefully manipulated and dissipated over time to avoid destructive outbursts. In their content analysis of women's advice columns on marital love and anger appearing in popular magazines between 1900 and 1980, Francesca Cancian and Steven Gordon (1988) found a "continuous trend towards modern norms encouraging emotional expression, individualism, and flexible gender roles." However, the rate of change varied over time, accelerating in the 1920s, reversing in the 1930s through the 1950s, and accelerating markedly in the 1970s. The authors point to the importance of cultural ferment and economic conditions in explaining these patterns.

## A Conceptual Model of the Relations between Social Structure and Emotions

In their study of the meaning of sexuality, D'Emilio and Freedman (1988) devised a framework that allowed them to make connections between historical patterns of cultural and social organization. In general, emotional meanings (i.e., the recognized and labeled categories, and the legitimacy and underlying ideology of one's feeling states) are shaped by the ways in which emotions are regulated and by the emotional politics controlling their definition. Thus, over time social regulation has shifted from external and social (e.g., shame) to internal and psychological (guilt and anxiety). Emotional politics involve the competition for control of emotional meanings and are shaped by changes in regulation. For instance, in the United States the sense of guilt experienced by women considering abortion has weakened owing to the increasing power and involvement of women in the economic realm.

Finally, changes in social bonds are themselves products of demographic, economic, and traditional forces. (See Figure 6.3.) For instance, the bonds between parents and children profoundly changed as a result of declines in childhood mortality. To avoid emotional attachments with their children, who so often died, New England Puritan parents often did not name them until they

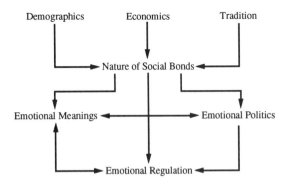

**FIGURE 6.3  Linking Emotional States with Sociohistorical Dynamics**

## A Twelfth-Century Methodology for Determining Whether You Are in Love

The clarity and boundaries of such emotions as shame, disgust, and contempt have shifted over the centuries. Social constructionists assume that emotions are determined largely by social norms for emotion, or "feeling rules," and that social actors must define situations before emotions will be experienced. Take, for example, the emotion of love.

In the West before the fifteenth century, the romantic bond was generally nonexistent, or at least was not culturally recognized. Many domestic households in Europe were casual cohabiting affiliations, not *families* as we know them, centering on the husband-wife role relationship. But a new emotional state—love—was beginning to be recognized as spousal bonds became more clearly defined and legitimated. In *The Rules of Courtly Love*, Andreas Capellanus presented a checklist for the diagnosis of love. He wrote that love is a form of suffering derived from the sight of and excessive meditation on the beauty of the opposite sex, causing the lover to wish above all things the embraces of the beloved. Among Capellanus's rules for recognizing love are the following:

i.      Marriage is no real excuse for not loving.
ii.     He who is not jealous cannot love.
iii.    No one can be bound by a double love.
iv.     It is well known that love is always increasing or decreasing.
v.      That which a lover takes against the will of his beloved has no relish.
vi.     Boys do not love until they arrive at the age of maturity.
vii.    When one lover dies, a widowhood of two years is required of the survivor.
viii.   No one should be deprived of love without the very best of reasons.
ix.     No one can love unless he is impelled by the persuasion of love.
x.      Love is always a stranger in the home of avarice.
xi.     It is not proper to love any woman whom one would be ashamed to seek to marry.
xii.    A true lover does not desire to embrace in love with anyone except his beloved.
xiii.   When made public, love rarely endures.
xiv.    The easy attainment of love makes it of little value; difficulty of attainment makes it prized.
xv.     Every lover turns regularly pale in the presence of his beloved.
xvi.    When a lover suddenly catches sight of his beloved his heart palpitates.
xvii.   A new love puts to flight an old one.
xviii.  Good character alone makes any man worthy of love.
xix.    If love diminishes, it quickly fails and rarely revives.
xx.     A man in love is always apprehensive.
xxi.    Real jealousy always increases the feeling of love.
xxii.   Jealousy, and therefore love, are increased when one suspects his beloved.
xxiii.  He whom the thought of love vexes eats and sleeps very little.
xxiv.   Every act of a lover ends in the the thought of his beloved.

reached the age of 6 or 7, and sent them to live with relatives or friends, ostensibly for discipline (Stannard 1976).

## Opportunities for Emotional Release

Inappropriate guilt, fear, anger, or joy can be equally destructive to the self and to society. Similarly destructive are feelings that are inappropriately intense. Following the equilibrium models of psychoanalytic theory, we believe that if such intensely felt emotions are not appropriately dissipated or rechanneled they will surface elsewhere. Demos (1970), for instance, argues that the frequent reports of anger between neighbors in the Plymouth colony compensated for the emergent norm of restraint of familial anger in an era when familial affection was being encouraged. More recently, Elisabeth Kübler-Ross (1979) recommended that hospitals and other institutions provide "screaming rooms" in which patients and staff can privately vent their fears and frustrations.

Differing opportunities for emotional release may be one reason that the Norwegian suicide rate is approximately one-third the rate in Denmark and Sweden, even though these countries are very similar ethnically and culturally (Farberow 1975). Norwegian children are raised with greater independence and more culturally sanctioned opportunities for emotional venting. Their parents are more actively involved in child rearing, producing a supportive family environment that, combined with strong religious and moral traditions, produces a low rate of suicide.

## CONCLUSION

In this section of the book we have considered the ways in which individuals perceive, experience, and interpret social experiences. Our analyses have taken us across a number of disciplinary domains, from physiological investigations into the workings of the brain to the evolution of sentiments as studied by social historians.

In this chapter we have seen how, given the profound physiological impact of emotions as well as the social potential to activate these feeling states, society can indeed penetrate the individual. Social systems depend on the construction and maintenance of a variety of emotional states, such as the feeling of love to cement the most crucial of social relationships, or the feeling of patriotism when a society must go to war. As social needs shift over time, new forms of socially reinforced emotion appear, as do new normative systems for controlling their expression. Thus, as individualism increasingly replaced collectivist identities, new emotions appeared that increasingly focused on the self (i.e., self-love, self-hate), superseding many traditional sentiments of social attachment.

Emotions play a role in shaping personal motivations toward socially required goals and in countering self-centered or antisocial temptations. This holds true for either model of the connection between social setting and emotional feeling states:

setting → autonomous feeling state → application of social rules → emotional expression

or

setting → application of social feeling rules → emotional expression → feeling state

As we have seen, social situations determine the expression of emotions and, in varying degrees, the ways in which they are subjectively experienced.

Emotions are currently an active area of social-scientific research. Physiologically oriented social psychologists are conducting research on how socially induced feeling states can have biological ramifications. Historically oriented social psychologists are studying how sociohistorical contexts produced such emotions as anger and anxiety. Social psychologists engaged in cross-cultural research are looking for evidence indicating whether emotions are culturally specific or universal. Psychologically oriented social psychologists, acknowledging the inevitability of human irrationality and error, are examining how anger, greed, envy, happiness, and hope shape cognitions and decision making. And for the more sociologically inclined, emotions are the ways in which one truly feels one's social bonds.

In the following chapter we will consider how emotion-feeling selves are socially produced—for instance, how the family shapes the emotional systems of the young and how morality is thereby instilled. In Chapter 8 we consider how emotional feelings and controls change with age and maturity and with social evolution.

# REFERENCES

Abelson, Robert P. 1985. The role of affect in public response to political stimuli and meeting. *Bulletin of the British Psychological Society* 38:A53.

Adams, Virginia. 1979, September 30. The best and worst of guilt. *San Antonio Express-News* [New York Times Service], p. K-1.

Adler, Valerie. 1988, November. Heart votes. *Psychology Today*, pp. 61, 64.

Anderson, B., J. Berger, M. Zelditch, and B. P. Cohen. 1969. Reactions to inequity. *Acta Sociologica* 2:1–12.

Bataille, Georges. 1988. Attraction and repulsion I: Tropisms, sexuality, laughter and tears. In Denis Hollier (ed.), *The college of sociology (1937–39)* (trans. Betsy Wing). Minneapolis: University of Minnesota Press.

Becker, Howard S. 1953. Becoming a marijuana user. *American Journal of Sociology* 59:235–252.

Brody, Jane. 1983, May 24. Emotions found to influence nearly every human ailment. *New York Times*, pp. 17, 19.

Burton, Sandra. 1990, May 14. Straight talk on sex in China. *Time*, p. 82.

Campbell, Colin. 1987. *The romantic ethic and the spirit of modern consumerism.* New York: Basil Blackwell.

Cancian, Francesca. 1987. *Love in America: Gender and self-development.* New York: Cambridge University Press.

Cancian, Francesca, and Steven Gordon. 1988, September. Changing emotion norms in marriage: Love and anger in U.S. women's magazines since 1900. *Gender & Society.* 2(3):308–342.

Capellanus, A. 1183[1941]. *The art of courtly love.* New York: Columbia University Press.

Cooley, C. H. 1909. *Social organization.* New York: Scribner's.

Darwin, Charles. 1872[1965]. *The expression of emotions in man and animals.* Chicago: University of Chicago Press.

Davis-Floyd, Robbie. 1987. Birth as an American rite of passage. In Karen Michaelson (ed.), *The anthropology of childbirth in America.* South Hadley, MA: Bergin and Garvey.

D'Emilio, John, and Estelle B. Freedman. 1988. *Intimate matters: A history of sexuality in America.* New York: HarperCollins.

Demos, John. 1970. *A little commonwealth: Family life in Plymouth Colony.* New York: Oxford University Press.

Denzin, Norman K. 1985. Emotion as lived experience. *Symbolic Interaction* 8:223–240.

Denzin, Norman K. 1984. *On understanding emotion.* San Francisco: Jossey-Bass.

Diener, Edward, Edward Sandvik, and William Pavot. 1991. The social psychology of subjective well-being. Fairview Park, New York: Pergamon Press.

Dreitzel, H. P. 1981. The socialization of nature: Western attitudes towards body and emotions. In P. Heelas and A. Lock (eds.), *Indigenous psychologies: The anthropology of the self.* London: Academic.

Durkheim, Émile. 1965[1915]. *The elementary forms of the religious life* (trans. Joseph Swain). New York: Free Press.

Eastwell, H. D. 1982. Voodoo death and the mechanism for dispatch of the dying in East Arnhem, Australia. *American Anthropologist* 84:5–18.

Ekman, Paul, Robert W. Levenson, and Wallace V. Friesen. 1983. Automatic nervous system activity distinguishes among emotions. *Science* 221:1208–1210.

Ekman, Paul, and H. Oster. 1979. Facial expressions of emotion. *Annual Review of Psychology* 30:527–554.

Ellis, Albert. 1973. *Humanistic psychotherapy: The rational-emotive approach.* New York: Julian Press.

Emmons, Robert A., and E. Diener. 1986. An interaction approach to the study of personality and emotion. *Journal of Personality* 54:371–384.

Emmons, Robert A., and Laura A. King. 1989. Personal striving differentiation and affective reactivity. *Journal of Personality and Social Psychology* 56:478–484.

Epstein, Seymour. 1984. Controversial issues in emotion theory. In Philip Shaver (ed.), *Review of personality and social psychology*, vol. 5. Newbury Park, CA: Sage.

Erdmann, Gisella, and Werner Janke. 1978. Interaction between physiological and cognitive determinants of emotions: Experimental studies on Schachter's theory of emotions. *Biological Psychology* 6:61–74.

Farberow, Norman. 1975. *Suicide in different cultures.* Baltimore: University Park Press.

Frank, Mark G., and Thomas Gilovich. 1988. The dark side of self- and social perception: Black uniforms and aggression in professional sports. *Journal of Personality and Social Psychology* 54:74–85.

Frankl, Viktor. 1960. Paradoxical intention: A logotherapeutic technique. *American Journal of Psychotherapy* 14:520–525.

Frazier, Charles E., and Thomas Meisenhelder. 1985. Exploratory notes on criminality and emotional ambivalence. *Qualitative Sociology* 8:266–284.

French, Peter. 1984, November 14. It's a damn shame. Trinity University Lennox Lecture.

Frey, William. 1985. *Crying: The mystery of tears.* Minneapolis: Winston Press and Harper and Row.

Friedrich, Otto. 1990, August 27. He gives us a ray of hope. *Time*, pp. 26–29.

Gaylin, Willard. 1979. *Feelings: Our vital signs.* New York: HarperCollins.

Geertz, Clifford. 1973. *The interpretation of cultures.* New York: Basic Books.

Gerrard, M. 1982. Sex, sex guilt, and contraceptive use. *Journal of Personality and Social Psychology* 42:153–158.

Gerth, Hans P., and C. Wright Mills. 1964 [1953]. *Character and social structure: The psychology of social institutions.* Orlando: Harcourt Brace Jovanovich.

Glick, Ira, Robert Weiss, and C. Murray Parkes. 1974. *The first year of bereavement.* New York: Wiley.

Goffman, E. 1967. Embarrassment and social organization. In E. Goffman (ed.), *Interaction ritual.* Garden City, NY: Doubleday.

Goleman, Daniel. 1985, October 22. Strong emotional response to disease may bolster patient's immune system. *New York Times,* pp. 13, 18.

Goleman, Daniel. 1987a, August 4. A sense of humor found to aid creativity and social ties. *New York Times,* pp. 17, 20.

Goleman, Daniel. 1987b, May 12. Useful modes of thinking contribute to the power of prejudice. *New York Times,* pp. 17, 20.

Goleman, Daniel. 1989, August 15. Brain's design emerges as a key to emotions. *New York Times,* pp. 15, 19.

Gordon, Steven L. 1981. The sociology of sentiments and emotions. In Morris Rosenberg and Ralph M. Turner (eds.), *Social psychology: Sociological perspectives.* New York: Basic Books.

*Harper's Magazine.* 1988, May. Axis of fear. p. 31.

*Harper's Magazine.* 1987, March. Harper's index. p. 15.

Harrè, Rom (ed.). 1986. *The social construction of emotions.* New York: Basil Blackwell.

Harris, M. B., S. M. Benson, and C. Hall. 1975. The effects of confession on altruism. *Journal of Social Psychology* 96:187–192.

Heise, David. 1987, April. Affect control theory. *Sociology of Emotions Newsletter,* p. 2.

Hochschild, Arlie. 1983. *The managed heart: Commercialization in human feelings.* Berkeley and Los Angeles: University of California Press.

Hochschild, Arlie. 1979. Emotion work, feeling rules, and social structure. *American Journal of Sociology* 85:551–575.

Isen, Alice M., K. A. Daubman, and G. P. Nowicki. 1987. Positive affect facilitates creative problem-solving. *Journal of Personality and Social Psychology* 52:1122–1131.

Izard, Carroll. 1977. *Human emotions.* New York: Plenum.

Izard, Carroll. 1972. *Patterns of emotions: A new analysis of anxiety and depression.* Orlando: Academic Press.

Izard, Carroll, and Sandra Buechler. 1979. Emotion expressions and personality integration in infancy. In Carroll Izard (ed.), *Emotions in personality and psychopathology.* New York: Plenum.

Kemeny, Margaret. 1984. Psychological and immunological predictors of recurrence in the Herpes Simplex II. Paper presented at the 92nd Annual Meeting of the American Psychological Association, Toronto, Ontario, Canada.

Kemper, Theodore. 1987. How many emotions are there? Wedding the social and the autonomic components. *American Journal of Sociology* 93:263–289.

Kemper, Theodore. 1984. Power, status, and emotions: A sociological contribution to a psychophysiological domain. In Klaus R. Scherer and Paul Ekman (ed.). *Approaches to emotion.* Hillsdale, NJ: Erlbuam.

Kemper, Theodore. 1981. Social constructionist and positivist approaches to the sociology of emotions. *American Journal of Sociology* 87:336–362.

Kemper, Theodore. 1978. *A social interactional theory of emotions.* New York: Wiley.

Kiecolt-Glaser, Janice, Ronald Glaser, C. Speicher, G. Penn, J. Holliday, and R. Glaser. 1984. Psychosocial modifiers of immunocompetence in medical students. *Psychosomatic Medicine* 46:7–14.

Kohn, M. L. 1963. Social class and the exercise of parental authority. In Neil Smelser and William Smelser (eds.), *Personality and social systems.* New York: Wiley.

Krebs, Dennis. 1975. Empathy and altruism. *Journal of Personality and Social Psychology* 32:1134–1146.

Kübler-Ross, Elisabeth. 1979. Trans-disciplinary care for terminally-ill patients and their families. Speech presented at Trinity University, San Antonio, TX.

Lachman, S. J. 1982–1983. A psychophysiological interpretation of voodoo illness and voodoo death. *Omega* 13:345–360.

LeDoux, Joseph E. 1989. Cognitive-emotional interactions in the brain. *Cognition and Emotion* 3:267–289.

Lester, D. 1972. Voodoo death: Some new thought on an old phenomenon. *American Anthropologist* 74:386–389.

Lex, W. L. 1974. Voodoo death: New thoughts on an old explanation. *American Anthropologist* 76:818–823.

Lin, N., W. M. Ensel, R. S. Simeone, and W. C. Kuo. 1979. Social support, stressful life events, and illness: A model and an empirical test. *Journal of Health and Social Behavior* 20:109–119.

Lobsenz, Norman. 1987, Nov. 22. Don't eat those peas. *Parade Magazine*, pp. 22–23.

Malatesta, Carol, and Carroll Izard (eds.) 1984. *Emotion in adult development*. Newbury Park, CA: Sage.

Malcolm, Andrew H. 1990, February 5. Study of domestic violence fails to find path to killings. *New York Times*, p. A10.

Marin, Peter, 1981, November. Living in moral pain. *Psychology Today*, pp. 68–80.

Morokoff, Patricia. 1985. Effects of sex guilt, repression, sexual "arousability," and sexual experience on female sexual arousal during erotica and fantasy. *Journal of Personality and Social Psychology* 49:177–187.

Mosher, Donald. 1973. Sex differences, sex experience, sex guilt, and explicitly sexual films. *Journal of Social Issues* 29:95–112.

National Opinion Research Center (NORC). 1990. *General Social Surveys 1972–1989* (James A. Davis, principal investigator, Tom W. Smith, senior study director and co-principal investigator). Data distributed by the Roper Center for Public Opinion Research.

Pennebaker, J. W., and S. K. Beall. 1986. Confronting a traumatic event: Toward an understanding of inhibition and disease. *Journal of Abnormal Psychology*. 95:274–281.

Peterson, Gayle, and Lewis Hehl. 1984. *Pregnancy as healing: A holistic philosophy for pre-natal care* (2 vols.). Berkeley, CA: Mindbody Press.

Radcliffe-Brown, A. R. 1922[1964]. *The Andaman Islanders*. New York: Free Press.

Ramey, Estelle R. 1974, November. Boredom: The most prevalent American disease. *Harper's Magazine*, pp. 12–22.

Reich, John W., Michael McCall, Robert Grossman, Alex Zautra, and Charles Guarnaccia. 1988. Demands, desires, and well-being: An assessment of events, responses, and outcomes. *Journal of Community Psychology* 16:392–402.

Rheingold, Howard. 1988. *They have a word for it: A lighthearted lexicon on untranslatable words and phrases*. Los Angeles: Jeremy P. Tarcher.

Riesman, David. 1950[1961]. *The lonely crowd*. New Haven, CT: Yale University Press.

Rosenberg, Morris. 1987, April. Emotional self-objectification. *Sociology of Emotions Newsletter*, pp. 4, 6.

Rosenblatt, Paul, R. Patricia Walsh, and Douglas Jackson. 1976. *Grief and mourning in a cross-cultural perspective*. New Haven, CT: Human Relations Area File Press.

Sabini, John, and Maury Silver. 1982. *Moralities of everyday life*. New York: Oxford University Press.

Schachter, Stanley, and Jerome Singer. 1962. Cognitive, social, and physiological determinants of emotional states. *Psychological Review* 69:379–399.

Scheff, Thomas. 1990. *Micro-sociology: Discourse, emotion and social structure*. Chicago: University of Chicago Press.

Scheff, Thomas. 1988, June. Shame and conformity: The deference-emotion system. *American Sociology Review* 53(3):395–406.

Scheff, Thomas, and Ursula Mahlendorf. 1988. Emotion and false consciousness: Analysis of an incident from *Werther. Theory, Culture, and Society* 5:57–79.

Schleifer, Steven J., Steven E. Keller, Maria Camerino, John C. Thornton, and Marvin Stein. 1983. Suppression of lymphocyte stimulation following bereavement. *Journal of the American Medical Association* 250:374–377.

Schmeck, Harold. 1983, September 9. Study says smile may indeed be an umbrella. *New York Times*, pp. 1 and 16.

Shibutani, T. 1961. *Society and personality: An interactionist approach to social psychology.* Englewood Cliffs, NJ: Prentice-Hall.

Silver, R. L., and C. B. Wortman. 1980. Coping with undesirable life events. In J. Garber and M. P. Seligman (eds.), *Human helplessness: Theory and applications.* Orlando: Academic Press.

Solomon, David. 1987, May 27. And we thought that hemlines were the best economic indicators. *Wall Street Journal,* p. 29.

Solomon, Robert C. 1982, February 13. Violets are red, roses are blue. *New York Times,* p. 19.

Spiegel, David, J. R. Bloom, H. C. Kraemer, and Ellen Gottheil. 1989, November 14. Effect of psychosocial treatment on survival of patients with metastatic breast cancer. *Lancet,* pp. 888–891.

Stannard, David. 1976. Death and the Puritan child. In David Stannard (ed.), *Death in America.* Philadelphia: University of Pennsylvania Press.

Stearns, Carol Zisowitz, and Peter Stearns. 1986. *Anger: The struggle for emotional control in America's history.* Chicago: University of Chicago Press.

Steiner, J. E. 1973. The human gustofacial response. In J. F. Bosma (ed.), *Fourth symposium on oral sensation and perception.* Rockville, MD: U.S. Department of Health, Education and Welfare.

Stern, Daniel N. 1990. *Diary of a baby.* New York: Basic Books.

Stone, Lawrence. 1985, July 8. Sex in the West: The strange history of human sexuality. *New Republic,* pp. 25–37.

Swanbrow, Diane. 1989, July-August. The paradox of happiness. *Psychology Today, pp. 37–39.*

Temoshok, Lydia, Bruce W. Heller, Richard W. Sagebiel, Marsden S. Blois, David M. Sweet, Ralph J. Di Clemente, and Marc L. Gold. 1985. The relationship of psychosocial factors to prognostic indicators in cutaneous malignant-melanoma. *Journal of Psychosomatic Research.* 29(2):139–153.

*Time.* 1983, April 11. "I Thought I Was God." p. 26.

Toufexis, Anastasia. 1983, July 18. The bluing of America. *Time,* p. 62.

Valins, S., and R. Nisbett. 1972. Attributional processes in the development and treatment of emotional disorder. In E. E. Jones, D. E. Kanouse, H. H. Kelley, R. E. Nisbett, S. Valins, and B. Weiner (eds.), *Attributions: Perceiving the causes of behavior.* Morristown, NJ: General Learning Press.

Wegner, Daniel. 1989. *White bears and other unwanted thoughts: Suppression, obsession, and the psychology of mental control.* New York: Viking.

Weinberger, Joel, and Richard Hardaway. 1990. Separating science from myth in subliminal psychodynamic activation. *Clinical Psychology Review* 10(6):727–756.

Yamamoto, Kaoru, A. Soliman, J. Parsons, and O. L. Davies. 1988. Voices in unison: Stressful events in the lives of children in 6 countries. *Journal of Child Psychology and Psychiatry* 28(6):855–864.

Zajonc, Robert. 1985. Emotion and facial efference: A theory reclaimed. *Science* 228:15–21.

Zajonc, R. B., Pamela K. Adelmann, Sheila T. Murphy, and Paula M. Niedenthal. 1987. Convergence in the physical appearance of spouses. *Motivation and Emotion* 11(4):335–346.

Zajonc, Robert, Sheila Murphy, and Marita Inglehart. 1989. Feeling and facial efference: Implications of the vascular theory of emotions. *Psychological Review* 96(3): 395–416.

Zimbardo, Philip, Paul Pilkonis, and Robert Norwood. 1975, May. A shrinking violet overreacts: The social disease called shyness. *Psychology Today* pp. 69–72.

# PART THREE

# The Self

The social product that is of greatest interest to social psychologists is the self. But what is the self?

Of all the things about which we have knowledge, what could we possibly "know" any better than our own selves? But the self is not a simple, singular phenomenon. When one "talks to oneself," for example, is it the same self that does the talking and the listening? Does an amnesia victim have a self even if all past memories are forgotten? Are we one self or many? Is the self something that one "has" (and therefore can lose), or is it something that one "is"? Are selves basically the same with age, or do individuals become different selves at different ages?

The quest for a definition of the self underlies many human endeavors, including psychological studies. Social-psychological interest in such self-based notions as **consciousness** and **self-esteem** are undoubtedly derived from theologians' interest in the **soul** and philosophers' inquiries into **free will.**

In Chapter 7 we summarize the various theoretical notions of selfhood and then explore the self's social genesis, from the impact of birth order in the family to the effects of schooling. In Chapter 8 we look at the self's encounters with time, considering the developmental models of psychology, sociology's perspective on how individuals pass through a series of age-graded roles, and the ways in which selves are shaped by social history.

# 7

# The Self-System and Its Social Genesis

In the early 1970s, 19-year-old newspaper heiress Patty Hearst was kidnapped by members of the radical Symbionese Liberation Army. While negotiating for her release, the group allegedly had brainwashed Patty. Six weeks later, Patty had become Tanya; she was later seen participating in the holdups of a bank and a sporting goods store. On a tape-recorded message Patty informed the world that she was an urban guerrilla. What had happened? Was her susceptibility to brainwashing due to the lack of a firm self-concept?

Although the concept of self is one of the oldest and most enduring depictions of human nature, social scientists themselves have yet to reach consensus on precisely what the self is. Do we understand personality *as a cause of behavior* or do we see personality *as the effect of behavior* (or at least as the effect of others' reinforcements)? Is it no more than a set of unique, identifying characteristics, and if so, from whose perspective: that of the actor or that of others? In other words, is our true self known only to ourselves, or is it a conception held by significant others?

Gordon Allport questioned whether the concept of self is even necessary, observing that "for two generations psychologists have tried every conceivable way of accounting for the integration, organization, and striving of the human person without having recourse to the postulate of a self" (1968:25). Walter Mischel (1968) argued that a personality trait varies so greatly across situations that the concept is practically useless for understanding behavior. If different types of people do not behave in predictably different ways, why bother with the distinction?

Despite such doubts, two facets of selfhood cannot be doubted: its uniqueness and its innate tendency to preserve its integrity. The body self, for instance, is like no other; each individual's DNA and fingerprints are unique. To protect its integrity, it has a built-in defense system that destroys viral invaders and rejects transplanted organs. Analogously, there is the self that is experienced psychologically, which is one's own and is like no other. And there is a social self, the self that can be identified by others owing to its distinctive attributes.

"Know thyself," said Socrates; in *Hamlet,* Polonius advised, "Unto thine own self be true." The question "Who and what am I?" echoes throughout intellectual history. Yet the nature of the self remains mysterious and murky. Immanuel Kant was the first philosopher to analyze both the *subjective* (the self as knower or conceiver) and the *objective* (the self as known or conceived) aspects of the self, and this subject/object duality is still a central theme of philosophy, psychology, and sociology.

Within the social sciences, psychology and sociology have devoted more than a century to analyzing the nature of the self, its development over time, its social and psychological determinants, and its personal and social outcomes. Numerous distinct conceptual and methodological approaches have emerged from this analysis. The most frequently encountered of these approaches are described here.

## Psychological Traditions

***Psychoanalytic Portrayals.*** As was briefly noted in Chapter 1, Freudian analyses of the self focus on the internal dynamics among the ego, id, and superego. The central legacy of this perspective is the assumption that certain **types of selves** conduct themselves in distinctive ways in a variety of situations. In other words, there is considerable faith in the proposition that by understanding an individual's **personality system**, researchers can predict the course of his or her behaviors.

Some psychoanalytic researchers have taken an **idiographic approach** toward understanding specific selves, focusing on the interrelationships between a person's early socialization experiences and his or her characteristics as an adult. One can see this approach in psychobiographies of people like Howard Hughes, Richard Nixon, and Lyndon Johnson. For example:

> Howard Hughes Jr. was the child of a hearty, extroverted but often absent father and a quiet, softspoken mother who focused her full attention on her only child. (Fowler 1986:24)

This approach does not lead to comparisons between individuals; instead, it produces rich case studies.

The **nomothetic approach**, on the other hand, assumes that although the self has numerous facets, some are so central that many secondary traits coalesce around them in predictable ways. This approach thus focuses on one predominant trait and sees each self as having a certain "amount" of it, such as being highly compulsive or not very gregarious. Some personality types are categorized in terms of central motives, others in terms of what the person typically thinks or does. "Type A" personalities, for instance, are assumed to take broader responsibility for the social events of which they are a part. This happened in the case of Robert McFarlane, one of President Reagan's advisers, who attempted to take his own life out of guilt for the unfolding of the Iran-Contra scandal.

One way of approaching these central personality traits is to conceptualize them as dominant personal needs. In terms of our inventory of these needs in Chapter 3, some of the resultant personalities include the following.

**Machiavellians**, for whom power needs predominate. These are individuals who hold such personal credos as "It's safer to be feared than to be loved," "Ends justify means," and "Humility is not only of no service but is actually harmful." They see people as objects to be manipulated for personal ends. For example, in one experiment groups of three persons, one of whom scored high on a scale of Machiavellianism while the others scored medium and low, were given the task of dividing $10.00 between two of the three members. The mean amounts obtained by the three individuals were $5.57, $3.14, and $1.29, respectively (Christie and Geis 1970).

**Narcissists**, for whom esteem needs predominate. Typical of this personality type is an inflated sense of self-importance, self-assuredness, and self-absorption, and a strong need for the admiration of others.

The **achievement-oriented** personality, who has a high need for control. According to cross-cultural research by McClelland et al. (1953), the prosperity of civilizations is due to the prevalence of this personality type. These individuals are self-reliant. They seek situations in which they are responsible for finding solutions; they set moderate goals for themselves; and they always want feedback about how well they are doing.

**Authoritarians**, whose need for order is their central motivation. To help explain the attraction of fascism during the second quarter of the twentieth century, a group of social psychologists identified a personality type that is prone to prejudice and regimentation. In the preface of *The Authoritarian Personality*, Theodor Adorno and his associates described the type as follows: "In contrast to the bigot of the older style, [the authoritarian] seems to combine the ideas and skills of a highly industrialized society with irrational or anti-rational beliefs" (1950:3). Highly authoritarian people are rigidly conventional, have an exaggerated need to uncritically submit to others, favor stern discipline, are antiintellectual, and have a tendency toward superstition and stereotyping. They are the products of traditional families in which "children were seen but not heard" and had restricted rights, and in which both parents were themselves authoritarian, each with clear-cut roles.

The continuing influence of psychoanalytic thought can be seen in the many ways in which people gauge personality types as a way of predicting behavior. For example, for years European firms have used *graphology* to evaluate potential employees. Supposedly more than three hundred personality traits can be assessed from handwriting. Such traits as enthusiasm, imagination, ambition, for example, are gauged from the size and slant of the script, how the *t*s are crossed, and whether the *m*s and *n*s are round, pointed, or wedge-shaped.

**Cognitive Perspectives**   Unlike psychoanalysts, who assume that individuals are not necessarily aware of their selves or of their innate drives, cognitive theorists focus on individuals' perceptions of themselves and how these self-definitions affect behavior. A greater measure of free will enters the equation as cognitive theorists argue that having a clear sense of identity helps one make choices. Action is dependent on one's knowledge of oneself.

From this perspective, attention is directed toward such matters as individuals' perceived locus of self-control (Rotter 1966), i.e., their ego involvements, their rules for reasoning, as well as their structures of values and priorities. Muzafer Sherif and Hadley Cantril (1947) define the ego as this system of attitudes.

These attitudes are not, of course, present at birth. The infant probably is unable even to distinguish itself from its environment: The moving arms, the mobile overhead, and the bottle are all part of the self. With maturation, the child comes to understand its distinctive and limited place on the social stage. Only later (and only true in more developed societies) does one achieve a full understanding of oneself as a unique individual with unique thoughts.

To illustrate the way cognitive theorists link self-concept with behavior, consider the phenomenon of **learned helplessness**. Individual potentiality involves having a realistic personal goal and sufficient self-esteem to believe one can reach that goal. But sometimes one's perceived potentiality becomes severely curtailed. In such situations one comes to feel that outcomes are independent of one's actions and that one is dependent on others. For instance, many nursing-home residents are defined by staff members as incapable of managing their own lives. As a result, residents come to understand themselves in these terms.

## SOCIAL ASPECTS OF THE SELF

Out of these psychological traditions have arisen conceptions of the self as a system of aptitudes, attitudes, temperament, emotional stability, motivations, extroversion, sociability, aggressiveness, practicality, self-sufficiency, and self-assuredness, and with cognitive styles of varying complexity. Although such conceptualizations of the self have inspired much research, they fail to account for the sociological bases of the self-system.

As physicists were discovering the constituent processes that make up matter—for example, how interacting systems of molecules, atoms, nuclei, protons, mesons, and quarks come to appear as rocks and golden retrievers—social scientists were discovering parallel processes that make up selves: culture, society, institutions, large-scale organizations, small groups, social encounters, language, symbols, and meaning. In other words, the self-system is totally enmeshed in a variety of other systems that emanate from social life.

To better understand the social dimensions of the self, we will explore the contributions of several theorists whose work has had a significant influence on modern social psychology.

### Self as Symbolic System

What distinguishes sociological from psychological approaches to the self is the former's focus on the ways in which identity is negotiated with others. The foundations of the sociological approach are built largely on the philosophical ideas of George Herbert Mead. Mead's contribution to the study of self was his understanding that society (culture, institutions, role structures, language, objects, and acts) precedes symbolic thought (which he termed *minding*) which, in turn, precedes the development of selves.

**Society** is built up from significant symbols and their shared meanings. It contains an immense variety of differentiated social forms, either abstract categories or concrete groups. **Acts** are social constructions that may involve a plurality of actors. They include impulse, images of desired goals, intention, attention, perception, emotion, imagination, motivation, reasoning, role-taking, and inferring the interpretations of other participants (Meltzer 1964). Acts may be very brief (e.g., shaking hands with an acquaintance or driving to the store) or may extend over most of a lifetime (e.g., becoming a skilled physician or a good spouse).

**Gestures** are the building blocks of social acts. They are symbolic movements or words drawn from what the actor believes is the common culture of the participants. They are used to signify a desired (but not automatic) interpretation on the part of another participant. In Mead's words:

> Gestures, if carried back to the matrix from which they spring, are always found to inhere in or involve a larger social act of which they are phases. In dealing with communication we have first to recognize its earliest origins in the unconscious conversation of gestures. Conscious communication—conscious conversation of gestures—arises when gestures become signs, that is, when they come to carry for the individuals making them and the individuals responding to them, definite meanings or significations in terms of the subsequent behavior of the individuals making them. (1934:69n)

Mead's approach to the development and utilization of *minding*, or **mind**, involves the highly selective and creative construction of **objects** in the social and physical environment, drawing heavily on the culture and language of the person. Objects (including physical entities, social situations, and any person, including the self) are creatively constituted and endowed with meaning by the individual, through selective use of all the cultural and cognitive resources available, and in response to particular phases of anticipated social acts. For example, suppose that in a new work situation, B is introduced to A as a potential work-team member, a rival for a key promotion, a superior, or a subordinate. The meanings assigned by A to B, the cues attended to, and the gestures employed will be very different according to these situational identities. In addition, the texture and coloration of gestures and meanings will change if either A or B begins to infer changes in the orientation of the other (e.g., judgments of hostile intent or sexual interest).

Mead's view of object constitution became the cornerstone of symbolic interactionism. An important aspect of this approach is its emphasis on the role of language. Mead emphasized that **language** is a system of potentially shared meanings and images on which interactants can draw to construct discourses that call out in others meanings sufficiently alike for interaction to proceed and be coordinated. Mead stated that symbols must have meanings that are "identical" for all interactants, but this should be understood as "cognitively close enough for practical purposes." (Mead consistently ignored the importance of variation in emotional shadings of concepts for different individuals.) Following are Mead's core statements on the power of language to go beyond the nonsymbolic gesturing of animals to uniquely human symbolic communication that makes finely coordinated interaction possible:

> What language seems to carry is a set of symbols answering to certain content which is measurably identical in the experience of the different individuals. If there is to be communication as such the symbol has to mean the same thing to all individuals involved. . . .
>
> The human animal, however, has worked out a mechanism of language communication by means of which it can get this control. Now, it is evident that much of that mechanism does not lie in the central nervous system, but in the relation of things to the organism. The ability to pick these meanings out and to indicate them to others and to the organism is an ability which gives peculiar power to the human individual. The control has been made possible by language. It is that mechanism of control over meaning in this sense which has, I say, constituted what we term "mind." . . .
>
> Language as made up of significant symbols is what we mean by mind. The content of our minds is (1) inner conversation, the importation of conversation from the social group to the individual, and (2) imagery. Imagery should be regarded in relation to the behavior in which it functions. (1934:54,133,190–191)

Mead viewed **role-taking** as the essential element in social intelligence, in how social control is exerted over individual interaction, and in how social selves are developed. Role-taking is the process by which one person imaginatively tries to interpret his or her own gestures from the perspective of the other participant(s) in the social act, and to infer what their categorizations and judgments of him or her might be:

> It is generally recognized that the specifically social expressions of intelligence, or the exercise of what is often called "social intelligence," depend upon the given individual's ability to take the roles of, or "put himself in the place of," the other individuals implicated with him in given social situations; and upon his consequent sensitivity to their attitudes toward himself and toward one another. These specifically social expressions of intelligence, of course, acquire unique significance in terms of our view that the whole nature of intelligence is social to the very core—that this putting of one's self in the places of others, this taking by one's self of their roles or attitudes, is not merely one of the various aspects of expressions of intelligence or of intelligent behavior, but is the very essence of its character. (1934:141)

This process of role-taking is the key to understanding Mead's contribution to the analysis of **self-systems**. Mead argues when very young children merely *imitate* actions they see around them, they do so without thinking of self and other in a reflexive way. In other words, each child is not yet taking into account others' perspectives in acting (hence play is "parallel" as opposed to being interactive) or how his or her behavior and identity is being interpreted by others. This *imitative stage* is best captured by the line "Monkey see, monkey do."

In the *play stage* an internal reflexive conversation with a single other-role occurs. At this stage the child is just past the imitative stage but is not yet

Socialization largely occurs through imitating the behaviors of significant others. Moreover, basic values and rituals are passed along through such mimicries, ensuring the cultural order survives despite the deaths of its older members.

engaging in organized games. Instead, the child is *playing at being* first one and then the other role in a two-role system:

> Play in this sense, especially the stage which precedes the organized games, is play at something. A child plays at being a mother, at being a teacher, at being a policeman; that is, it is taking different roles, as we say. . . . When a child does assume a role he has in himself the stimuli which call out that particular response or group of responses. . . . In the play period the child utilizes his own responses to these stimuli which he makes use of in building a self. The response which he has a tendency to make to these stimuli organizes them. He plays that he is, for instance, offering himself something, and he buys it; he gives a letter to himself and takes it away; he addresses himself as a parent, as a teacher; he arrests himself as a policeman. He has a set of stimuli which call out in himself the sort of responses they call out in others. He takes this group of responses and organizes them into a certain whole. Such is the simplest form of being another to one's self. (1934:150–151)

Finally, in the *game stage* the child engages in internal reflexive conversions with multiple and organized other roles. As soon as the child begins to play organized games, he or she must learn to visualize skills and action sequences from the standpoint of a variety of other roles. For example, when the youngest or least skilled child is told to play right field in baseball, he or she must try to understand the different roles of all the team members (pitcher, catcher, infielders, other outfielders) and also the roles and purposes of the members of the other team, one of whom is now the batter. The child must also try to take the standpoint of each of these various other roles to infer what each wants and expects from him or her as right fielder. In Mead's formulation:

> If we contrast play with the situation in an organized game, we note the essential difference that the child who plays in a game must be ready to take the attitude of everyone else involved in that game, and that these different roles must have a definite relationship to each other.
>
> This organization is put in the form of the rules of the game. Children take a great interest in rules. They make rules on the spot in order to help themselves out of difficulties. Part of the enjoyment of the game is to get these rules. Now, the rules are the set of responses which a particular attitude calls out. You can demand a certain response in others if you take a certain attitude. (1934:151–152)

Out on one's internal symbolic interaction with various organized composite others emerges the **generalized other**. Young ball players soon learn to interpret their intended actions from a more generalized and composite perspective rather than only from that of each teammate. They develop some level of "game sense" about aspects of smart play that they can take with them to any new baseball (or life) situation. They also develop generalized self-conceptions about their capacities for the various roles available ("poor pitcher or catcher but really good at shortstop or second") and about qualities that may well carry on into adult life: "talented but lazy"; "very competitive but not very well coordinated"; "loyal and reliable but not a big star."

Mead focused on ways in which the generalized others associated with various communal social activities provide the basic reflexive conceptions of the developing person:

> If the given human individual is to develop a self in the fullest sense, it is not sufficient for him merely to take the attitudes of other human individuals toward himself and toward one another within the human social process, and to bring that social process as a whole into his individual experience merely in these terms: he must also, in the same way that he takes the attitudes of other individuals toward himself and toward one another, take their attitudes toward the various phases or aspects of the common social activity or set of social undertakings in which as members of an organized society or social group, they are all engaged; and he must then, by generalizing these individual attitudes of that organized society or social group itself, as a whole, act toward different social projects which at any given time it is carrying out, or toward the various larger phases of the general social process which constitutes its life and of which these projects are specific manifestations. (1934:154–155)

Finally, Mead tied this process into the major concept of **social control** and showed that social control is actually self-control. Mead thus conceptualized self as a *process* rather than as a substance or "thing," and held that "I" and "me" are phases of that process:

> The self is not so much a substance as a process in which the conversation of gestures has been internalized within an organic form. This process does not exist for itself, but is simply a phase of the whole social organization of which the

individual is a part. The organization of the social act has been imported into the organism and becomes then the mind of the individual. It still includes the attitudes of others, but now highly organized, so that they become what we call social attitudes rather than roles of separate individuals. This process of relating one's own organism to the others in the interactions that are going on, in so far as it is imported into the conduct of the individual with the conversation of the "I" and the "me," constitutes the self (1934:178–179)

The "I" phase, according to Mead, is active, spontaneous, and to a large degree autonomous. In addition, the "I" evaluates the "me" by imaginatively interpreting the responses of other interactants. The "me" phase consists of the self-conceptions generated from others (and from the generalized other); the "I" phase interprets and judges these me-conceptions. An element of unpredictable action occurs in this process as the I continuously interprets the me-conceptions with the available opportunities in different situations.

***Construction of Self and World through Discourse.***  Mead's view of selves being self-reflective and socially exchanged systems of symbols and meanings continues to inspire social-psychological inquiry. A promising recent development is the interlinking of the **social construction** perspective in sociology and social psychology with **discourse analysis** derived from linguistics and literary analysis. A key contribution was *The Social Construction of Reality* by Peter Berger and Thomas Luckmann (1966), in which it was argued that each person's speech (both reflexive and nonreflexive) makes more "real" the self-reality that they experience. In other words, "Men must talk about themselves until they know themselves."

**Grammar about self:** The vast majority of languages contain a grammatical split between self as subject ("I") and self as object ("me") (Potter and Wetherell 1987). This language form allows speakers the world over to generate accounts of themselves in which they claim credit and praise themselves for valued actions ("I talked myself into doing it, even though it was hard"). This split also allows easy production of excuses and justifications to minimize blame for actions seen as less than desirable ("I didn't mean to do that" or "I had to do that because my boss ordered me to"). (See Chapter 9.)

**Self as ideological system:** Kenneth Gergen focuses on the ways in which interest groups (including professional social psychology) tend to offer ideologies to justify or warrant their own particular political, economic, professional, and interpersonal self-interests. Ideologies, as we discussed in Chapter 4, are schemas that give order (gestalt) and meaning to wide-ranging and disparate events. In addition to the social-level ideologies (e.g., those provided by religion and politics) there are personal-level ideologies employed in everyday discourse.

Gergen argues that when certain discourse strategies become effective in justifying their users' ideological positions they become *hegemonic* (e.g., supportive of those groups and individuals currently in power). For this reason, both groups and individuals attempt to use the most successful ones to warrant their particular interests. As Gergen notes:

> the mental world becomes elaborated as various interest groups within the culture seek to warrant or justify their accounts of the world. In effect, our vocabulary of self shifts as pragmatic exigencies dictate. . . . This is all by way of illustrating the vast importance in social life of hegemony in world construction. If one's linguistic

construction of the world prevails, the outcomes may be substantial. Failure to achieve intelligibility in construction is to have little role in the coordinated set of daily activities from which life satisfactions are typically derived. (1989:72–73)

Gergen identifies five major explanatory strategies ("conventions of warrant") commonly used to furnish rationales and justifications as to either why one's self or group should be given precedence or why opponents' "warranting claims" should be discredited:

> *Experience*: "I am very familiar with this kind of thing, and have an excellent track record."
> *Rationality*: "I have good reasons and a clear view of it; they are biased and irrational."
> *Intention*: "I have the good of the group at heart; they are selfish and greedy."
> *Passion*: "We are committed and caring; they are unfeeling, detached, and coldly calculating."
> *Moral values*: "Our values are sincere, and derived from the groups we all love; their values are foreign and opposed to our ways." (adapted from Gergen 1989:74–75)

In devising their warrants, individuals use whatever discourse strategies are culturally available. By so doing, both selves and societies become symbolically reaffirmed:

> In effect, as warrants are developed, disputed and elaborated in defense, the result is a rich and variegated language of the self along with sets of supporting institutions and practices. What we take to be the dimensions of self in the present era may be viewed, in part, as the accumulated armamentarium of centuries of debate. They are symbolic resources, as it were, for making claims in a sea of competing world constructions. (Gergen 1989:75)

And so people develop knowledge about themselves through their discourses with others. All experience is reflexively organized into a very complex system of self-referential meanings that can be expressed by "signs of the self" (Singer 1982). Out of one's symbolic encounters, according to Perinbanayagam, arises a motivationally active "maxisign of the self" that controls most personal conduct:

> The self therefore is an assemblage of signs, a more or less coherent text that the mind claims as its own and identifies as a presence in the world of others. . . . This does not mean that the self is achieved once and for all, petrified forever after in the life of the body and mind. Rather, the mind and other minds conceive of and handle it as if it were fixed and stable, although it is continually being altered, enriched, impoverished, beclouded, and qualified in and through interactions and discourses. . . . Once constituted, the maxisign of the self will achieve its own power and demand sovereignty over all its acts. The acts that issue from it thereafter will add further dimensions to the already constituted self, thereby allowing it to grow, expand, and enrich itself or diminish and impoverish it. The signs of the self may have a certain stability at any given moment in its career, but in the long run the self is unstable insofar as it is capable of accepting new signs and

abandoning old ones. The self develops by temporally and logically related moves from moment to another, thus achieving a narrative status for itself until death. (1991:12–13, 10)

## Self as Role System

Mead's ideas of role-taking being a central dimension of self-systems (and of social control) stimulated several generations of sociologically oriented social psychologists. Indeed, individuals' actions seemed better predicted by the roles they were playing than by the personality characteristics described by psychologists (which, perhaps, are better predictors of the *style* by which people perform their roles). Moreover, in describing their selves to others, people typically define themselves in terms of the roles they occupy (e.g., parent, worker, service volunteer, and so forth). Finally, the concept of role specifies a clear way in which self and society are fused.

Ralph Turner focused on the interconnection of role and self, defining both so that strong links are forged between personality, situation, social structure, and culture. According to Turner, role-taking is a very active and creative process involving much more than conformity to behavior expectations:

> The unity of a role cannot consist simply in the bracketing of a set of specific behaviors, since the same behavior can be indicative of different roles under different circumstances. The unifying element is to be found *in some assignment of purpose or sentiment to the actor.* (1962:28, emphasis in original)

Turner makes it clear that roles can be connected to culturally defined values, informal interactive positions, or positions embedded in formal organizations:

> By *role* we mean a collection of patterns of behavior which are thought to constitute a meaningful unit and deemed appropriate to a person occupying a particular status in a society (e.g., doctor or father), occupying an informally defined position in interpersonal relations (e.g., leader or compromiser), or identified with a particular value in society (e.g., honest man or patriot). We shall stress the point that a role consists of behaviors which are regarded as making up a meaningful unit. The linkage of behaviors within roles is the source of our expectations that certain kinds of action will be found together. When people speak of trying to "make sense" of someone's behavior or to understand its meaning, they are typically attempting to find the role of which the observed actions are a part. (1956:316–317)

In a 1968 essay Turner connected role to socialization and, thus, to self-conception (see also Gordon 1972). During the socialization process, the individual tends to adopt a repertoire of role relationships as a framework for his or her own behavior and as a perspective for the interpretation of the behavior of others. Socialization is therefore partly a matter of learning culturally standardized role conceptions and partly a matter of learning to constitute the social world through enactment of role processes. Following up these ideas, Turner (1978) has developed the further dimension of *merger between role and person,* by which he means the question of whether attitudes and behaviors associated with one role and its typical situations carry over into other situations. Observable criteria of role-person merger would include spillover from a role into unconnected situations, resistance to giving up the role when a desirable alternative is available, and acquisition of a full complement of attitudes and beliefs connected to the role.

## Self as Esteem-Seeking System

Neither Mead's ideas of how social control is actually self-control or developments in role theory fully address the problem developed in Chapter 3 about how personal needs become synchronized with social needs. Selves come across as being opportunists rather than moral agents. To counter this perceived difficulty one approach has been to address *motivation*, or how social control occurs in the form of personal drives—for example, how individuals become self-regulating participants in the maintenance of social order. In particular, focus has been placed on *esteem*, a phenomenon existing in the realm where sociology blurs with psychology. **Self-esteem** is something that one cognitively grasps and emotionally feels and is something whose bases and standards of adequacy derive from society's moral order.

About a century ago, philosopher and psychologist William James (1842–1910) viewed the self primarily engaged in the business of obtaining esteem. This entails constantly balancing the self that one desires to be with the self that garners the attention and approval of others.

James divided the self into the following constituents:

1. *Material me*—body and clothes styles, immediate family, home, and work products, along with strong desires to cherish and protect these.
2. *Social me*—recognition from others: "A man has as many social selves as there are individuals who recognize him and carry an image of him in their minds" (1892:179). But since these individuals are divided into classes or groups, "we may practically say that he has as many different social selves as there are distinct groups of persons about whose opinion he cares" (p. 179). The person acts differently in each group, and often does not want one group to know how he or she performs in another.
3. *Spiritual me*—"The entire collection of my states of consciousness, my psychic faculties and dispositions taken concretely" (p. 181). Especially important here are emotions, desires, and other feeling states of consciousness.

The feelings and emotions that the constituents of the self aroused are referred to as *self-appreciation*. They include *self-complacency*—"pride, conceit, vanity, self-esteem, arrogance, vainglory"—and *self-dissatisfaction*—"modesty, humility, confusion, diffidence, shame, mortification, contrition, the sense of obloquy, and personal despair" (p. 182).

The **acts** resulting from these feelings and emotions include **self-seeking** and **self-preservation** behaviors. *Bodily self-seeking* consists of eating and defense, fear and anger, acquisitive activities, and so forth. *Social self-seeking*

is carried on directly through our amativeness and friendliness, our desire to please and attract notice and admiration, our emulation and jealousy, our love of glory, influence, and power, and indirectly through whichever of the material self-seeking impulses prove serviceable as means to social ends. . . . Under the head of spiritual self-seeking ought to be included every impulse towards psychic progress, whether intellectual, moral, or spiritual in the narrow sense of the term. It must be admitted, however, that much that commonly passes for spiritual self-seeking in this narrow sense is only material and social self-seeking beyond the grave." (pp. 184, 185)

James also emphasized the interconnections among self-conceptions, aspirations, social outcomes, and the resulting changes in self-evaluations. He noted that many desired selves must be put aside, while only certain of the potential selves (characters) that the person might develop actually receive attention and energy:

> Such different characters may conceivably at the outset of life be alike *possible* to a man. But to make any one of them actual, the rest must be suppressed. So the seeker of his truest, strongest, deepest self must review the list carefully, and pick out the one on which to stake his salvation. All other selves thereupon become unreal, but the fortunes of his self are real. Its failures are real failures, its triumphs real triumphs, carrying shame and gladness with them. (p. 186)

On the basis of this analysis of the self, James formulated what is known as the *law of self-esteem*:

$$\text{Self-esteem} = \frac{\text{Success}}{\text{Pretensions}}$$

But this "law" did not allow for the impact of other people's judgments of our successes (or lack of them) and other people's unwillingness to allow us to repeatedly lower our pretensions. Significant others, especially employers and spouses, may simply not allow us to give up goals of economic and social success without major forms of turmoil (such as getting fired or divorced).

Charles Cooley (1864–1929) focused more than did James on *self-feeling* as the core of subjective self-apprehension and on the *reflected appraisals of significant others* in shaping that self-feeling. It is in the context of social interaction in primary groups (family, peer groups, friends, etc.) that the forms of symbolic communication occur that develop an individual's self-ideas and feelings toward one's self. Here Cooley used the metaphor of the **looking-glass self**, the images of one's self that one imagines personally significant others hold:

> Our ideals of personal character are built up out of thoughts and sentiments developed by intercourse, and very largely by imagining how our selves would appear in the minds of persons we look up to. (1902:242)

The personal importance of these appraisals of one's self derive from the significance of individuals' *group identification* (family, friendship group, university, nation, etc.) to their self concepts.

Following the tradition of James, Cooley, and Mead regarding the reflexive character of the self, Morris Rosenberg added a strong emphasis on the *determinative power* of the *self-image*:

There are few topics so fascinating both to the research investigator and the research subject as the self-image. It is distinctively characteristic of the human animal that he is able to stand outside himself and to describe, judge, and evaluate the person he is. He is at once the observer and the observed, the judge and the judged, the evaluator and the evaluated. Since the self is probably the most important thing in the world to him, the question of what he is like and how he feels about himself engrosses him deeply. This is especially true during the adolescent stage of development. (1965:vii)

Rosenberg defined self-image as the "attitude toward the self." He also applied the full range of major aspects of attitude study to self-image:

We conceive of the self-image as an attitude toward an object. (The term "attitude" is used broadly to include facts, opinions, and values with regard to the self, as well as favorable or unfavorable orientation toward the self.) . . .

A number of dimensions by which attitudes toward any object in the world can be classified have evolved. Attitudes may differ in content, in direction, in intensity, in importance, in salience, in consistency, in stability, and in clarity. (1965:5–6)

Rosenberg selected *direction* (i.e., evaluation, positive or negative) as the central aspect of attitudes and developed what has become the most frequently used measure of self-esteem. The Rosenberg Self-Esteem Scale has ten questionnaire items, with the response categories Strongly Agree, Agree, Disagree, Strongly Disagree:

1. On the whole, I am satisfied with myself.
2. At times I think I am no good at all.
3. I feel that I have a number of good qualities.
4. I am able to do things as well as most other people.
5. I feel I do not have much to be proud of.
6. I certainly feel useless at times.
7. I feel that I am a person of worth, at least on an equal plane with others.
8. I wish I could have more respect for myself.
9. All in all, I am inclined to feel that I am a failure.
10. I take a positive attitude toward myself. (1965:17–18)

In a study of over five thousand high school students from New York State, Rosenberg (1965) found low self-esteem to be associated with higher levels of anxiety as well as with plausible intervening variables such as instability of self-image, a sense of often presenting a false front to others, vulnerability, and social isolation. The self-esteem score also was found to relate with the students' interpersonal attitudes and participation in school activities, and with many aspects of occupational orientations. A variant of the self-esteem score was used in a study of African American and white schoolchildren in Baltimore, and again this variable showed important relations to social-structural factors, even demonstrating that African American students (especially in predominantly African American contexts) had somewhat *higher* self-esteem than did whites (Rosenberg and Simmons 1972:25).

In further studies of self-concept, Rosenberg (1979) drew on William James' idea of self-seeking: Persons generally seek to increase their self-esteem and will direct considerable energy toward doing so. Goal-directed striving and the attainment of symbolically defined success is certainly one means of increasing self-esteem (as James pointed out), but another is to defend oneself energetically against attacks on one's self-esteem. Such defense is accomplished by means of various defense mechanisms:

1. *Rationalization*: finding a socially acceptable explanation of our behavior.
2. *Compensation*: efforts to overcome failure in one area by extraordinary accomplishments in another.
3. *Projection*: attributing to others some negative characteristics or wishes that are actually true of ourselves but that would be damaging to self-esteem if admitted.
4. *Displacement*: asserting superiority over others upon being humiliated or frustrated by those who are more powerful.
5. *Reaction formation*: adopting conduct that is the opposite of deeply felt emotions to avoid having to face them.
6. *Repression*: pushing impulses into the subconscious so that they cannot damage self-esteem.

**When Selves Are Socially Defiled.**  In studying what happens to the self in highly structured social settings, Erving Goffman developed the concept of **total institutions**. He defines a total institution as "a place of residence and work where a large number of like-situated individuals, cut off from the wider society for an appreciable period of time, together lead an enclosed, formally administered round of life" (1961:xiii). Prisons and concentration camps, of course, meet this definition, but so do a wide range of institutions such as monasteries or nunneries, military training camps, lumber or mining camps, ships at sea, residential schools, reformatories, survival training programs, isolated clinics, "political reeducation camps," mental hospitals, and so forth. Goffman examined the more extreme forms of such organization to obtain a deeper insight into the inner world of inmates' self-conceptions.

Goffman found that four critical dimensions of the self are systematically "mortified" as the person becomes an inmate of a total institution:

1. *Destruction of the previous outside-world self.* The barrier between the outside world and the total institution produces a clear curtailment of self, and the impossibility of going outside to take care of business or to have visitors come in means that serious role dispossession occurs. Extended periods of time lost from one's occupation, education, interaction with friends and relatives, sexual partners, and so forth, can never be recovered. Storage or destruction of all previous identity pegs speeds the process of destruction of the former self: Clothing, jewelry, hair, and personal effects of all kinds are likely to be removed, literally leaving a naked person. Personal pride may also be destroyed by such practices as "medical" or "security" examinations that expose the recruit's body to others, using common sleeping rooms and open toileting facilities, cells with bars instead of walls, being kept naked in perpetually lit rooms "for one's own protection," and the like.
2. *Construction of a disvalued inside identity.* Category names such as "swab" or "boot" are used to make it clear the new person is not only

one of the lowly inmates (in relation to staff) but also among the lowest of the low for being a new recruit and ignorant in the ways of the institution. Ill-fitting clothing, a number instead of a name, a dehumanizing haircut, a dirty cell, a bad bed, terrible food, and so forth, also serve to define all new inmates as alike, thus eradicating as much as possible of the sense of individual identity.

3. *Curtailment of "adult" self-determination, autonomy, and freedom.* Official admission procedures commonly involve forced stripping, searching, fingerprinting, bathing, disinfecting, rectal and vaginal examinations, and the like, all of which take over actions that inmates had previously performed for themselves (if at all). The unofficial admission procedures may be even more harsh, involving staff members requiring the new inmate to stand rigidly at "attention" and shout "Yes, Sir!" over and over, or to engage in other forms of verbal or gestural profanations of the self to show that he "agrees" to be obedient to institutional commands. Such "breaking of the will," accomplished through a combination of psychological pressure, physical pain, and deprivation of sleep, food, and normal toileting privileges, is extremely detrimental to any self-conception of autonomy and pride.

4. *Destruction of the sense of personal security.* This is accomplished through punishments and tortures administered by the institution's staff. These actions may include beatings, branding, loss of limbs, lobotomy, electroshock "therapy," surgery, and so forth. In addition, forced exposure to the other inmates may threaten other forms of injury, such as homosexual gang rape (which also can destroy even the sexual identity of inmates).

5. *Reduction of the sense of competence and efficacy.* This is achieved by such institutional practices as straitjackets, handcuffs, leg irons, and being chained in a group with other prisoners. The sense of competence is also crushed by being pushed and pulled around, having to "beg" for a cigarette or a light, and the like.

6. *Weakening the sense of self-worth.* Goffman uses the term *experiential mortification* to summarize a wide range of ways in which the worth of inmates is shattered, such as forcing them into close proximity with others whom they find socially contaminating by reason of age, ethnic group, class, or other characteristics. He reports a case in which one prisoner in a concentration camp was left tied in a bed with another inmate who had died during the night.

7. *Identification with the institutional ideology.* Occasionally recruits identify so completely with the ideology of the total institution that they interpret each "degradation practice" as a step away from an undesired previous self and as a step toward a new, noble, or pure self that is defined totally within the cognitive and emotional framework of the institution. This situation occurs most frequently within religious contexts (where the former sinner self is put aside in favor of the newly emerging brother or sister identity within the church), but it can also occur among mental patients who fervently believe that the clinic or great doctor can "cure" them and lead them to healthy new selves.

# Self as Integrity-Seeking System

Thus far our model of self process portrays people engaging in role-taking and self-evaluation, continually adjusting their symbolic responses as they interact with others in their search for self-esteem. The final system-based notion of selfhood that we will consider is the seemingly constant image that individuals carry of themselves over time. This returns us to the matter described above of the tendency of life systems to preserve their uniqueness and integrity. In the case of humans, this preservation drive involves various processes: biological (e.g., the rejection of transplanted organs), psychological (e.g., experiencing one's biography as a continuously unfolding whole story), and sociological (e.g., as will be explored in Chapter 8, society requires various coherent biographical summaries like job resumes).

Jack Douglas, a leader in the field of existential phenomenology, argues that the basic tenor of the individual's "unique sense of being" at any given time can be either secure or insecure, trusting or mistrustful, optimistic or pessimistic. He provides a vibrant depiction of the essential part played by our strongest emotions and values:

> No human being can live for long, except in a state of total dependency, without a reasonably stable but slowly evolving sense of inner self. The sense of inner self, as I shall try to show, is the highest-order centrally integrating sense that our mind has of our overall being-in-the-world. It is this sense of inner self that partially orders the vastly complex subsystems of our mind and orients us continually toward acting in the vastly complex and changing situations we face in everyday life.
>
> Our need for a sense of inner self seems to spring directly from our sense of time, from our immense memories, from the vast complexity and pluralism of our human mind (with its immensely complex interrelations among subsystems), from our awareness of the many potentially conflicting basic emotions and values that might push us in different directions in life at any given time, and from the necessity we face of choosing plans of action to satisfy (optimally) these conflicting emotions and values over relatively long periods of time.
>
> It is our sense of inner self that gives a partially unifying, but changing, form (a general, meaningful gestalt) and an overall sense of slowly shifting direction, of evolving intentionality, to our lives. Without a basically secure sense of self, however taken for granted it is, we are continually threatened by a sense of being formless, meaningless, lost, disintegrated, confused, and shattered, and life becomes constricted, tyrannized by anxiety, dread, and panic. With a basically secure sense of self, one that is largely taken for granted in everyday life, we are free to grow, to expand joyfully in meaningful conquest and creation. (1984:69)

Douglas further notes how self-integrity becomes threatened by the dread of death or self-degradation. He argues that such threats lead to extreme self-awareness.

Rosenberg (1979) stresses the desire to maintain self-consistency by acting in accord with existing self-conceptions. This desire can interact in different ways with the desire for self-enhancement. If self-esteem is high, there is no problem; both desires lead to attempts at difficult actions that probably will lead to valuable symbolic rewards. But if self-esteem is low and the person feels that he or she probably is not able to succeed (especially when the situation is competitive), self-consistency pressures will block effective action, even when self-enhancement desires press for strong effort.

With Howard Kaplan, Rosenberg makes one of the strongest motivational statements in the literature about the self:

> Finally, it is important to stress that the self-concept includes not only cognitions and emotions but motives as well. These motives refer to certain impulses to act in the service of the self-concept. In fact, much of human striving represents an effort to achieve a satisfying self-concept. People have strong preferences about the various constituents of their self-concepts. They prefer high self-esteem to low; clear, crystallized self-pictures to vague and ambiguous ones; stable self-concepts to shifting ones; consistent self-concepts to inconsistent ones; high feelings of efficacy to feelings of ineffectuality; low self-conscious to high; and so on. The self-concept, then, is an arena of passionate involvement, not detached neutrality. It motivates behavior, interaction, perception, attention, valuation, or virtually anything else that enters the human experience. (1982:9)

Ralph Turner (1968) went one step further, distinguishing between the slowly accruing *self-conceptions* that are relatively stable over time with the situational *self-images* that are formed through immediate evaluative feedback from those present in face-to-face interaction. Turner here focuses on self-conception as containing (among many other elements) a highly selective organization of *evaluative standards* concerning individuals' highest potentials, the objectives toward which they strive, and what they potentially could be under the most favorable conditions and incentives. The subjective presence of these evaluative standards allows the individual to make direct comparisons between *desired self-conceptions* and self-images constructed from imputed responses of others in the interaction situation. The results of such internal comparisons produce assessments of credit or blame, elation or dejection as the self-images engendered in current interaction episodes surpass or fall short of cherished self-conceptions.

## Self as Impulsive System

Given these various self-systems and their social contexts, wherein lies the **true self**? In the early 1970s Turner became interested in discovering the situations in which persons feel most "truly themselves" (Turner 1976; Turner and Schutte 1981; Turner and Gordon 1981). He discovered that many people identify themselves with their *impulses* rather than with the *institutions* that provide their major roles. In Turner's analysis, the real self is revealed when one is doing something out of desire to do so, not when one is living up to a high institutional standard even in the face of temptation. Impulsives view the true self as something to be discovered; institutionals see true self constructed in selecting and completing difficult projects of action. For the impulsive, true self is revealed when inhibitions are dropped; for the institutional the real self is shown when the person is in full control of his or her energies and actions. Impulsives typically adopt a present time perspective, whereas institutionals make commitments for the future. Both try to resist social pressures, but impulsives try to avoid being controlled by arbitrary rules and false goals, while institutionals seek to avoid pressure to drop standards and slip toward mediocrity.

Turner's concept of the impulsive anchorage of self is clearly parallel with Douglas's depiction of the strongly emotional features of the existential self:

> Most of our basic, positive emotions are felt by most people to be the *vital* aspects of our sense of self. Each of these basic emotions constitutes a dynamic core of feeling, which, when aroused and willed (not successfully repressed), orients our self toward the world by orienting our perceptions and thoughts toward acting in the world to fulfill and enhance itself. The more powerful the emotion, the more the self is oriented, until, at the extreme, the entire sense of self is pervaded by, over-ridden by, completely in the grip of the emotion. These powerful emotions of love, sex, joy, excitement, exultation, curiosity, and so on fill us with life. When they pervade our being we feel totally alive; when they are lacking, we feel deadened (and, at the psychotic extreme of feelinglessness, may even believe we are dead). Our "peak experiences" in life are those dominated by these powerful emotions of vital-ity, those in which the emotion becomes the focal point of our whole life, the aspect of our self is then identified with the consuming emotion, as when we feel that "My love *is* my life!" (1984:85–86, emphases in original) . . .
>
> Loving-and-fusing with the other self is a precondition of the vitality, the growth, and the wholeness of the individual self. This loving-and-fusing is the "natural" and normal orientation of the human self. (Douglas 1984:91)

## THE SOCIAL CONTEXTS OF SOCIALIZATION

How does society produce a person whose wants and needs correspond with those that are socially approved of and who aspires to the goals demanded by that society? How does one produce a child who is oblivious to the historical prejudices of racism, sexism, and ageism? What skills are to be inculcated in a person who may work in low earth orbit or 10,000 feet below the surface of the ocean? It is through the process of socialization that social needs become fused with personal needs and mind and self are synchronized with society.

This process takes the form of **primary socialization**, in which a new member of a society is molded to the needs and requirements of that society, and **secondary socialization**, in which an individual learns specific new roles.

### Primary Socialization

In primary socialization the structure of the self-system is laid down as new members of the society interact with significant others. Through this process one's place in the social order becomes internalized: lower-class children absorb the lower-class worldview; males and females learn socially approved gender roles; and so forth. (See Chapter 10.) As Bernard Malamud observed: "One is conditioned early in family life to an interpretation of the world. And . . . no matter how much happiness or success you collect, you cannot obliterate your early experiences" (quoted in Gray 1986).

## The Social Psychology of Toys

Part of the socialization process in contemporary societies involves playing with toys. Through toys and games children learn about their culture and adult ways of life. The game of Monopoly, for instance, instructs in the logic and incentives of capitalism; with toy kitchen sets and yard appliances, children learn how to spend leisure time. Concern for this didactic function of toys was reflected in a 1983 survey conducted by the National Association for Female Executives. Fully three-quarters of the 10,000 women surveyed felt that there are not enough toys that "provide a positive role for the executive woman." Among the toys suggested were doctors' bags, lawyers' briefcases, and business clothing for dolls.

Toys and games also reflect broad cultural trends. For instance, the resurgence of religiosity was accompanied by the Patty Prayer doll, which kneels and says a bedtime prayer. During the 1980s, when militarism was "in" (as reflected in the popularity of the *Rambo* movie sequels), sales of war toys increased 600 percent (*San Antonio Express News* 1987). The lesson of aggressive maleness has also been reinforced by twenty-five years of G.I. Joe; during this period 200 million G.I. Joe figures and 100 million G.I. Joe tanks, trucks, and planes have been sold (Pereira 1989).

Toys did not make an appearance in Western cultures until childhood was recognized as a distinctive stage of the life cycle. (See Chapter 8.) For most of human history children were not socialized primarily with others of their age group. Rather, they were included in collective life, engaging with others of all age groups in work and communal ceremonies. In fact, it was not until the early phase of industrialization, when both mothers and fathers left the home to become factory workers, that toys began to proliferate. Eventually toys became products of mass production, envisioned—along with compulsory education—as a means of keeping unruly children out of mischief. Play became increasingly controlled by adults—for example, through the creation of playgrounds, organized sports (e.g., Little League), and civic programs (e.g., Brownies, Bluebirds, Cub Scouts, Boy Scouts).

According to Brian Sutton-Smith (1985), with the advent of mechanical and computerized toys imaginative physical play has increasingly been replaced by games of information and strategy, and collective play has been replaced by isolated entertainment. This is evident in the top-selling toys of the 1990 Christmas shopping season; seven of the top twenty were computer-based entertainment.

1. Nintendo Entertainment System
2. Super Mario 3 (Nintendo)
3. Barbie
4. Game Boy (Nintendo)
5. Teen-Age Mutant Ninja Turtles
6. Tetris (Nintendo)
7. Magic Nursery
8. Teen-Age Mutant Ninja Turtles (Ultra/Konami)
9. Super Mario Brothers 2 (Nintendo)
10. My Pretty Ballerina
11. Go-Go, My Walking Pup
12. Final Fantasy (Nintendo)
13. Mega Man II
14. Genesis (Sega)
15. Scattergories
16. World Wrestling Federation figures
17. Cabbage Patch Kids
18. New Kids on the Block
19. Baby Alive
20. Little Tykes Workshop

Source: *Toy & Hobby World*, cited in Ramirez, 1990.

Among the factors influencing primary socialization are parental influence and birth order.

***Parental Influence.*** From all sociological and psychological perspectives, parent–child relationships are central to socialization. Psychoanalytic theory sees the emergence of the ego as resulting from infants' relationships with their parents; learning theory points to the reinforcements children receive by imitating the behaviors of parents; in symbolic interactionism, parents are viewed as the most significant of significant others. As Michael Novak has noted:

> The family is the primary teacher of moral development. In the struggles and conflicts of marital life, husbands and wives learn the realism and adult practicalities of love. Through love, stability, discipline, and laughter of parents and siblings, children learn that reality accepts them, welcomes them, invites their willingness to take risks. The family nourishes "basic trust." From this spring creativity, psychic energy, social dynamism. If infants are injured here, not all the institutions of society can put them back together. (1976:44)

The United States currently witnesses another major historical shift in parent–child relationships as adult male and female roles change in the broader society. In particular, the trend has been toward increasing parental absence. The increasing labor force participation of women with young children (over one-half of women with infants and toddlers now work outside the home) and the increasing number of female-headed households (which now account for over one-quarter of all households with children under 18) have fundamentally altered parent–child relationships. The likely consequences in terms of the types of selves emerging from socialization in the family are a matter of considerable speculation.

One area of parental influence that has been extensively studied is the impact of divorce. In studying how children of divorced parents fare as adults, Glenn and Kramer (1985) analyzed the NORC General Social Surveys for eight years. On eight indicators of psychological well-being (e.g., happiness, health, and satisfaction with life activities), female children of divorced parents scored as adults significantly lower on six measures and males lower on three.

***Birth Order.*** The more siblings there are in a family, the less attention the parents can give to each child. Thus, Judith Blake (1989) found that children from families in which there are three or fewer children have higher IQs and greater verbal ability and go further in school than children from larger families.

Research on the relationship between birth order and personality has produced some intriguing findings. Of the first 23 American astronauts, 21 were firstborn children; of the 102 Supreme Court justices appointed between 1789 and 1985, 56 were firstborns or only children (only 38 could be expected by chance) (Weber 1984). The achievement orientation of firstborns may be a result of high levels of parental attention early in life and the desire to maintain this attention in the face of competitive demands from later-born siblings. Later-borns, on the other hand, are reported by parents and teachers to be friendlier and more popular (Steelman and Powell 1985). Supposedly having lower need for approval, they are also reported as being less conforming to the status quo than firstborns. In Frank Sulloway's study of 2,784 researchers and their role in twenty-eight scientific controversies, later-borns were more likely to challenge the accepted paradigms. (See Table 7.1.) As tantalizing as these

**TABLE 7.1  Birth Order of Scientists and Their Support for Controversial New Theories**

| Controversy | Support among Firstborns | Support among Later-borns |
| --- | --- | --- |
| Relativity theory | 30 | 76 |
| Quantum hypothesis | 43 | 82 |
| Darwinian revolution | 20 | 61 |
| Harvey and the circulation of blood | 30 | 76 |
| Continental drift | 36 | 68 |

Source: Sulloway, cited in Goleman, 1990.

findings are, however, the evidence for a connection between birth order and personality is mixed. Of forty-five published scientific investigations of birth order effects in 1988 and 1989, more than one-third found no effect (Goleman 1990).

## Secondary Socialization

Secondary socialization involves all forms of socialization in which the individual is inducted into new areas of society and assumes new roles. One's experiences in school and work, with peers, and with the mass media are all varieties of secondary socialization. From these experiences there eventually emerges a **generalized other**, a frame of reference abstracted from the roles and attitudes of specific others to the roles and attitudes of people in general.

*Schools.* Educational systems are an essential component of modern societies. With industrialization and the rise of nation-states, schools have become places where nationalism is instilled, where young people are taught necessary skills for living in a highly specialized and knowledge-intensive workplace, and where people are sorted and certified in terms of their worthiness for entry into professional roles. In the United States, schools historically have also functioned as assimilation machines, making "Americans" out of the children of immigrants from a multitude of cultures.

This institutional agenda of education has profound implications for self-definition. As we will see in Chapter 10, personal "worthiness" in the United States is often determined less by personal ability than it is by the child's location in the stratification hierarchy (e.g., his or her social class, ethnicity, and race). Thus, for instance, although members of the working class comprise about one-half the population, they constitute only about 12 percent of medical students. In sum, it is in school that a child first learns how well he or she will fit into the broader social system and forms his or her expectations for the future.

Among the types of selves that primary and secondary school produce, whether intentionally or not, are the following:

> *Bureaucratic selves.* Students learn that they are members of bureaucratic categories (e.g., second-grader, "special ed," "accelerated,"

etc.). These determine the types of students with whom they attend class, the intellectual challenge of the subject matter discussed, and the institutional privileges to which they are entitled. Ideally, from society's perspective, they internalize the bureaucracy's norms of order, obedience, self-control, and uniformity.

*Student selves.* Related to the bureaucratic self is the degree to which young people internalize the student role and derive esteem in its performance. For many, this role self may be stronger than family roles, as when a child is more reinforced by the praise of a teacher than by that of a parent. Variants of student roles include "class clown," prom queen, and jock.

*Citizenship selves.* Required courses in state and national history, government, and civics illustrate the role of schools in creating a sense of citizenship. Through such rituals as the Pledge of Allegiance, students are given a sense of membership in the overarching in-group: the United States.

*Subculture selves.* Schools create status hierarchies in such areas as popularity, athletics, intellectual achievement, and extracurricular activities (pep squad, band). One's self-definition is derived from one's position within these hierarchies as well as from one's membership in one or more of the distinct student subcultures.

**Peers.** In the United States, children increasingly find themselves in the company of their age-mates, or peers. Secondary selves may be the products of one's friendship circle (Chapter 11), youth gangs (Chapter 12), civic groups (e.g., Boy Scouts and Girl Scouts), sports groups (e.g., baseball and basketball leagues), hobby clubs, and other groups. Out of these arise **peer cultures** featuring their own norms, values, and criteria for establishing self-worth.

**Television.** The average American child spends far more time in front of a television than in a classroom, watching 5000 hours of TV by the time he or she enters first grade and 19,000 hours by the end of high school (Zoglin 1990). What effect does such a high level of exposure have on self-concept, especially given a medium whose goal is to "create unreality" for profit (Moyers 1989)?

On one level, television provides models of various selves that provide standards against which one can judge the adequacy of one's own self. One may ask "How pretty or handsome am I?" and gauge oneself against televised standards of cultural beauty and good looks. Or one may ask "How interesting am I as a person?" and compare one's wit and engaging qualities with those of talk-show guests. According to Jay Martin (1988), the "fictive personalities" providing such standards flood the popular culture; in popular tabloids and television shows about Hollywood personalities, performers' biographies are thoroughly interwoven with their characters in soap operas and program series. Some audience members adopt these fictive selves. An example is Mark David Chapman, whose identification with J. D. Salinger's Holden Caulfield supposedly inspired him to assassinate musician John Lennon.

By virtue of television's visual focus, it leads to the definition of selves in terms of appearance and actions. For instance, television emphasizes the sexual self as an aspect of overall self-conception. Each year the average viewer watches an estimated nine thousand scenes of suggested sexual intercourse or innuendo on prime-time TV (Wallis 1985), scenes involving primarily attractive, "successful" characters. Television also conveys the implicit lesson that who one is a function of what one owns—a theme that is ritually repeated on the forty thousand or so commercials watched by the average viewer each year (Parenti 1986).

## CONCLUSION

The concept of self is a complex and multifaceted one. From the psychological perspective, the self is typically understood in terms of innate personality factors such as aptitudes and interests, values and drives, genes, impulse and self-control, temperament, and orientations toward dominance and submission. A central assumption is that different types of selves have differing propensities to act in certain ways on the basis of internal personality dynamics (psychoanalytic theory) or because of the ways in which they process the stimuli coming from their environments (cognitive theory).

The sociological tradition, on the other hand, views the self as contextually bound to its social environment, as an entity that is experienced in social interaction and is continuously negotiated with others. As radical feminist Jill Johnson observed, "Identity is what you can say you are according to what they say you can be" (cited in Kitzinger 1989:82). From this perspective, the self involves a host of external, socially defined characteristics—including ascribed statuses (e.g., gender and race) and achieved statuses (e.g., career or parenthood)—which together place a person in hierarchical relationships with other selves and define his or her moral worthiness in terms of dominant cultural ideologies. The sociological approach alerts us to not only the effects of society on individuals but also to the effects of self-systems on social structure and processes (Turner 1988).

In Chapter 8 we add the temporal component of the self, examining ways in which selves change as they pass through the life cycle, cognitively "maturing" and encountering different historically shaped, age-related social expectations and opportunities. In Chapter 9 we examine more fully what happens when different selves interact, setting the stage for discussions of the social psychology of inequality (Chapter 10), interpersonal relationships (Chapter 11), and group dynamics (Chapter 12).

## REFERENCES

Adorno, T. W., Elsie Frenkel-Brunswik, Daniel J. Levinson, and R. Nevitt Sanford. 1950. *The authoritarian personality*. New York: Harper.

Allport, Gordon. 1968. Is the concept of self necessary?" In Chad Gordon and Kenneth Gergen (eds.), *The self in social interaction*. New York: Wiley.

Berger, Peter, and Thomas Luckmann. 1966. *The social construction of reality*. New York: Doubleday.

Blake, Judith. 1989. *Family size and achievement*, vol. 3: *Studies in demography*. Berkeley, CA: University of California Press.

Christie, R., and F. L. Geis. 1970. The ten dollar game. In R. Christie and F. L. Geis (eds.), *Studies in machiavellianism*. New York: Academic Press.

Cooley, Charles H. 1902. *Human nature and the social order.* New York: Scribners. (Page references here are to the 1964 Schocken Books edition, ed. Philip Rieff.)

Douglas, Jack. 1984. The emergence, security, and growth of the sense of the self. In Joseph A. Kotarba and Andrea Fontana (eds.), *The existential self in society.* Chicago: University of Chicago Press.

Fowler, Raymond. 1986, May. Howard Hughes: A psychological autopsy. *Psychology Today,* pp. 22–33.

Gergen, Kenneth. 1973. Social psychology as history. *Journal of Personality and Social Psychology* 26:309–320.

Gergen, Kenneth. 1982. *Toward transformation in social knowledge.* New York: Springer-Verlag.

Gergen, Kenneth. 1989. Warranting voice and the elaboration of the self. In John Shotter and Kenneth J. Gergen (eds.), *Texts of identity.* London: Sage.

Glenn, Norval, and K. B. Kramer. 1985. The psychological well-being of adult children of divorce. *Journal of Marriage and the Family* 47(4):905–912.

Goffman, Erving. 1961. *Asylums: Essays on the social situation of mental patients and other inmates.* New York: Doubleday.

Goleman, Daniel. 1990, May 8. The link between birth order and innovation." *New York Times,* pp. B1, B9.

Gordon, Chad. 1972. Role and value development across the life-cycle. In John A. Jackson (ed.), *Sociological studies 4: Role.* London: Cambridge University Press.

Gray, Paul. 1986, March 31. Transcending denomination. *Time,* p. 73.

James, William. 1892. *Psychology: The briefer course.* New York: Henry Holt.

Kitzinger, Celia. 1989. The discursive construction of identities. In John Shotter and Kenneth Gergen (eds.), *Texts of identity.* Newbury Park, CA: Sage.

McClelland, D. C., J. W. Atkinson, R. A. Clark, and E. L. Lowell. 1953. *The achievement motive.* New York: Irvington.

Martin, Jay. 1988. *Who am I this time? Uncovering the fictive personality.* New York: Norton.

Mead, George Herbert. 1934. *Mind, self and society* (ed. Charles W. Morris.). Chicago: University of Chicago Press.

Meltzer, Bernard N. 1964. Mead's social psychology. In B. N. Meltzer, *The social psychology of George Herbert Mead.* Center for Sociological Research, Western Michigan University. Reprinted (pp. 15–27) in Jerome Manis and Bernard Meltzer (eds.), *Symbolic interaction: A reader in social psychology* (3rd ed.). Boston: Allyn and Bacon.

Mischel, Walter. 1968. *Personality and assessment.* New York: Wiley.

Moyers, Bill. 1989. *The Public Mind series: Illusions of news.* Public Broadcasting Service.

Novak, Michael. 1976, April. The family out of favor. *Harper's Magazine,* pp. 37–46.

Parenti, Michael. 1986. *Imagining reality.* New York: St. Martin's Press.

Pereira, Joseph. 1989, February 6. After 25 years, toy maker enjoys fortune of soldier. *Wall Street Journal,* pp. A1, A12.

Pereira, Joseph. 1987, July 27. Toy industry faces a lackluster year. *Wall Street Journal,* p. 4.

Perinbanayagam, R. S. 1991. *Discursive acts.* New York: Aldine de Gruyter.

Potter, Jonathan, and Margaret Wetherell. 1987. *Discourse and social psychology: Beyond attitude and behavior.* London: Sage.

Ramirez, Anthony. 1990, December 6. Toy business not all fun and games. *New York Times.*

Rosenberg, Morris. 1979. *Conceiving the self.* New York: Basic Books.

Rosenberg, Morris. 1965. *Society and the adolescent self-image.* Princeton, NJ: Princeton University Press.

Rosenberg, Morris, and Howard B. Kaplan. 1982. *Social psychology of the self-concept.* Arlington Heights, IL: Harlan Davidson.

Rosenberg, Morris, and Roberta G. Simmons. 1972. *Black and white self-esteem: The urban school child.* Washington, DC: American Sociological Association.

Rotter, J. B. 1966. Generalized expectancies for internal versus external control of reinforcement. *Psychological Monographs 80* (Whole No. 609).

*San Antonio Express-News* [AP]. 1987, November 18. Rambo mentality motivates warriors. p. 5-F.

Sherif, Muzafer, and Hadley Cantril. 1947. *Psychology of ego-involvement: Social attitudes and identifications.* New York: Wiley.

Singer, Milton. Signs of the self. In Milton Singer (ed.), *Man's glassy essence*. Bloomington, IN: Indiana State University.

Steelman, Lala C., and Brian Powell. 1985. The social and academic consequences of birth order: Real, artifactual, or both? *Journal of Marriage and Family* 47:117–124.

Sulloway, Frank. 1990, February. Presentation at the Annual Meetings of the American Association for the Advancement of Science. Cited in Daniel Goleman, The link between birth order and innovation. *New York Times* (May 8, 1990): B1, B9.

Sutton-Smith, Brian. 1985, October. The child at play. *Psychology Today*, pp. 64–65.

Turner, Ralph, H. 1988. Personality in society: Social psychology's contribution to sociology. *Social Psychology Quarterly* 51:1–10.

Turner, Ralph H. 1978. The role and the person. *American Journal of Sociology* 84:1–23.

Turner, Ralph, H. 1976. The real self: From institution to impulse. *American Journal of Sociology* 81:989–1016.

Turner, Ralph H. 1968. The self-conception in social interaction. In Chad Gordon and Kenneth Gergen (eds.), *The self in social interaction*, vol. I: *Classic and contemporary perspectives*. New York: Wiley.

Turner, Ralph H. 1962. Role-taking: Process versus conformity. In Arnold M. Rose (ed.), *Human behavior and social processes: An interactionist approach*. Boston: Houghton Mifflin.

Turner, Ralph H. 1956. Role-taking, role standpoint and reference group behavior. *American Journal of Sociology* 61:316–328.

Turner, Ralph H. 1947. The navy disbursing officer as bureaucrat. In Robert K. Merton (ed.), *Reader in bureaucracy*. Glencoe, IL: Free Press.

Turner, Ralph H., and Jerry Schutte. 1981. The true self method for studying the self-conception. *Symbolic Interaction* 4: 1–20.

Turner, Ralph, H. and Steven L. Gordon. 1981. The boundaries of the self: The relationship of authenticity to inauthenticity in self-conception. In M. Lynch, A. Norem-Hebeisen, and Kenneth Gergen (eds.), *The self-concept: Advances in theory and research*. Cambridge, MA: Ballinger, Springer.

Wallis, Claudia. 1985. December 9. Children having children. *Time*, pp. 78–90.

Weber, Paul J. 1984. The birth order oddity in Supreme Court appointments. *Presidential Studies Quarterly* 14:561–568.

Zoglin, Richard. 1990, October 5. Is TV ruining our children? *Time*, pp. 75–76.

8

# The Self in Time

Have you ever studied the family photo album and compared yourself with your parents, your grandparents, or perhaps even your great-grandparents when they were your age? Maybe you noticed how much older a grandmother looked at age 50 than your mother did. Not only did the grandmother look more weathered by time, but she may have dressed like an older person, wearing black granny shoes and a baggy black dress instead of Adidas and a pastel jogging suit.

Our encounters with time are affected by biological, psychological, social, and historical timetables. As we age biologically, there are predictable changes in our bodies: The amount of light reaching the retina of an 80-year-old is less than one-third that reaching the retina of a 20-year-old; some 40 percent of the taste buds are lost by the sixties, with the sweetness receptors going first; during menopause, women lose between 0.5 and 1.5 percent of their peak bone mass each year; and between the ages of 20 and 95, individuals can be expected to experience a 30 percent decline in cardiovascular output and a 45 percent decline in their maximum breathing rate. As we age psychologically, fluid intelligence (the ability to solve new problems and reason abstractly) declines somewhat, but crystallized intelligence (e.g., knowledge, verbal abilities) generally increases throughout most of the lifespan. Sociological aging entails entry into such roles as grandparent, mentor, gatekeeper, and moral arbitrator. Finally, there are the rhythms of social history, such as the cycles of political liberalism and conservatism, war, and economic cycles. The experience of old age is certainly different if one perceives oneself as having lived during the best of times than if one feels that one has experienced excessive disruption and hardship.

In any one of these "clocks," unexpected variations can occur that fundamentally alter people's biographies: 11-year-old victims of progeria die of biological old age; people may become psychologically "old" at age 30 following a major trauma, or they may remain psychologically "young" at age 70; there are grandparents in their twenties and 70-year-old fathers of infants; sometimes history regresses as a culture is swept by nostalgia, and sometimes it lurches into the future owing to major technological breakthroughs. Because of differences in individual "clocks," coupled with the effects of social conditions (e.g., being an elderly African American female in an ageist, racist, and sexist culture), human aging is a process that produces increasingly unique individuals over time.

In this chapter we begin by considering the social psychology of the lifespan, exploring the contributions of psychologists and sociologists to the study of how self-systems change with increasing age. We then take a broader, more sociohistorical perspective and discuss how changes in social structure have been accompanied by changes in the self. Like leaves floating on a stream, the currents of history have taken individuals into unimaginable situations, which, in turn, have produced novel thoughts, concerns, behaviors, and selves. In illustrating the ways in which self-systems are shaped by both developmental and historical processes (see Smith 1977), we will consider how greater social complexity has led to increasing complexity in individual identity, how the sense of self has changed in the West over the past 1000 years, and how childhood and old age were "invented" and became socially accepted stages of the lifespan. Finally, we will explore the notion of **generations,** noting how social history leaves its imprint on the identities of people born around the same time. As C. Wright Mills noted:

> The biographies of men and women, the kinds of individuals they have become, cannot be understood without reference to the historical structures in which the milieux are organized. Historical transformations carry meanings not only for individuals, but for the very character—the limits and possibilities of the human being. (1959:175)

## THE SELF ACROSS THE LIFESPAN

When looking over a kindergarten or first-grade classroom, one is often struck by the similarities among the children. With time, however, people become increasingly dissimilar in appearance, cognitions, and personality. Why does this happen?

Among the reasons that people attend school reunions is the desire to see where the currents of time have taken their classmates. Will individuals be extensions of their earlier selves, or will they be totally different? Did the class

By juxtaposing her present self with a photograph of herself as a young bride, this older woman freezes two periods in her journey through time. To what degree are these two selves the same? Perceiving themselves in terms of earlier self-conceptions, elderly individuals are often the last to discover they are "old" and learn of this status only from interactions with others.

bully evolve into a criminal or did he become a professional athlete? Did the star of the debating team become a lawyer or a professor, or something totally different? What about those who were not part of an "in" crowd in high school or college but "blossomed" later on? Will they present their new selves at the reunion, or will they be relegated to their former lowly statuses.

## Psychological Perspectives

Psychologists often locate the source of change within the self. As a plant develops through distinctive stages, so selves are seen as unfolding over the lifespan. In this section we briefly capture the flavor of various models of psychosexual, psychosocial, intellectual, and moral development before turning to the ways in which these psychological dynamics interact with sociohistorical processes.

***Psychoanalytic Perspectives.*** How important are early childhood experiences in the shaping of adult personality? From a psychoanalytic perspective, they are crucial. In his theory of psychosexual development, Freud hypothesized that instinctual sexual energy is the central motivator of human behavior and that individuals pass through an unvarying and universal sequence of stages in dealing with this force. Each stage involves not only the individual's focus of erogenous satisfactions (progressing from oral to anal satisfactions and finally to the genital areas of the body) but also personality traits that are derived from the conflicts that occur during that stage.

As individuals pass through this series of stages, the ego and superego first emerge out of the infant's experience of need deprivations and satisfactions when interacting with caregivers. The id, the source of irrational impulses, strives toward selfish gratification. When these impulses (the "pleasure principle") are frustrated, the ego emerges, mediating the tensions between inner needs and outer reality and propelling the individual toward realistic social goals (the "reality principle"). Initially conforming out of fear of punishment, at about 6 years of age the child begins to identify with its parents and to internalize their standards. Such identification occurs in relation to the child's sexuality. In the case of males, this identification depends on successful resolution of the Oedipal conflict (the desire to eliminate the father in order to monopolize the attentions and affections of the mother); for females, identification occurs with resolution of the Electra complex. By age 6, the nature of the individual's major drives and interpersonal relationships has been established, and this organization of the self endures throughout life; later changes are only elaborations and variations of the basic themes established in childhood.

Many of Freud's students and intellectual heirs challenged his biologically based paradigm of human behavior, which portrayed personality development as basically ending in adolescence. They concentrated on interpersonal and cultural influences on the development of the self, while retaining a role for unconscious mental forces. Carl Jung, for instance, viewed personality development as continuing throughout adulthood, being shaped by age-linked changes in the balances between extraversion–introversion and masculinity–feminity. With increasing age, the extraversion of young adults (perhaps required for securing a mate and career) shifts to increasing introversion owing to the need to explore personal feelings toward aging and death. Also with age, Jung believed, basically androgynous selves are freed from the demands of cultural sex roles, allowing the expression of suppressed parts of the personality. As a result, men become more feminine and females more masculine.

Erik Erikson, another student of Freud, formulated a set of psycho*social* stages of development from birth through adulthood and old age. This view of development was based on Freud's system of psycho*sexual* stages from infancy through adolescence, but Erikson expanded the frame of reference to include both immediate social relationships and the circumstances of culture and history. All of these factors are interrelated within a single systemic perspective based on the **epigenetic principle:**

Whenever we try to understand growth, it is well to remember the *epigenetic principle* which is derived from the growth of organisms *in utero*. Somewhat generalized, this principle states that anything that grows has a *ground plan*, and that out of this ground plan the *parts* arise, each part having its *time* of special ascendancy, until all parts have arisen to form a functioning whole. . . . In the sequence of his most personal experiences the healthy child, given a reasonable amount of guidance, can be trusted to obey inner laws of development, laws which create a *succession of potentialities for significant interaction* with those who tend him. While such interaction varies from culture to culture, it must remain within the *proper rate and the proper sequence* which govern the *growth of a personality* as well as that of an organism. Personality can be said to develop according to steps predetermined in the human organism's readiness to be driven toward, to be aware of, and to interact with, a widening social radius, beginning with the dim image of a mother and ending with mankind, or at any rate that segment of mankind which "counts" in the particular individual's life. (1950:52)

In Erikson's developmental model (Table 8.1), each psychosocial stage has positive as well as negative components, and the sequence of stages is invariant. Vestiges of former stages can be found in individuals who failed to successfully resolve the crises or challenges posed at those stages. During the first stage, for instance, infants learn the extent to which their basic needs will be satisfied; the challenge is to develop trust in others. Resolution of this crisis occurs when the infant feels secure enough so that it no longer feels anger, rage, or fear when separated from its caregivers. Out of this resolution arises hope and an appreciation of one's interdependencies with others. If the crisis is not resolved, the person does not trust others late in life.

At the second stage, toddlers (ages 1–2) begin exploring their worlds. Their range increases as they progress from crawling to walking, and their curiosity is often insatiable. As parents begin establishing boundaries and rules (e.g., toilet training), defiance emerges; one of the first words spoken is "no!" Excessive demands and constraints, according to Erikson, can lead to a sense of worthlessness and shame, countering the motivations for autonomy and self-direction. The resolution of this crisis creates will and, ideally, acceptance of the cycle of life.

Erikson is best known for his use of the epigenetic perspective on the distinctive drama of late adolescence in developed Western countries (especially the United States). In a striking passage, he has crystallized the process of *identity formation* in late adolescence:

The integration now taking place in the form of the ego identity is more than the sum of the childhood identifications. It is the inner capital accrued from all those experiences of each successive stage, when successful identification led to a successful alignment of the individual's *basic drives* with his *endowment* and his *opportunities*. In psychoanalysis we ascribe such successful alignments to "ego synthesis"; I have tried to demonstrate that the ego values accrued in childhood culminate in what I have called a *sense of ego identity*. The sense of ego identity, then, is the accrued confidence that one's ability to maintain inner sameness and continuity (one's ego in the psychological sense) is matched by the sameness and continuity of one's meaning for others. (1950:89)

**TABLE 8.1  Erikson's Stages of Psychosocial Development**

| Stage (Approximate Age) | Psychosocial Crisis | Significant Relations | Psychosocial Strengths from Successful Resolution | Lessons for Old Age |
|---|---|---|---|---|
| **I Infancy** (infants) | basic trust vs. mistrust | maternal person | hope | appreciation of interdependence and relatedness |
| **II Early Childhood** (1–2 years) | autonomy vs. shame and doubt | paternal person | will | acceptance of the cycle of life, from integration to disintegration |
| **III Play Age** (3–5 years) | initiative vs. guilt | basic family | purpose | humor, empathy, resilience |
| **IV School Age** (early school years) | industry vs. inferiority | school and neighborhood | competence | humility; acceptance of course of one's life and unfulfilled hopes |
| **V Adolescence** | identity vs. identity confusion | peer groups and out-groups; leadership models | fidelity | sense of complexity of life; merger of sensory, logical, and aesthetic perception |
| **VI Early Adulthood** | intimacy vs. isolation | partners in friendship, sex, cooperation, and competition | love | sense of complexity of relationships, value of tenderness and loving freely |
| **VII Adulthood** | generativity vs. stagnation, self-absorption | divided labor and shared household | care | caring for others, empathy and concern |
| **VIII Old Age** | integrity vs. despair | "humankind," "my kind" | wisdom | existential identity; sense of integrity strong enough to withstand physical disintegration |

Source: Erikson, 1982 and Goleman, 1988.

Erikson uses the evocative concept of a *psychosocial moratorium* (provided by away-from-home college experiences) to explain how societies structure the process of identity formation in late adolescence:

[In current American adolescence] the sexually matured individual is more or less retarded in his psychosexual capacity for intimacy and in the psychosocial readiness for parenthood. The period can be viewed as a *psychosocial moratorium* during which the individual through free role experimentation may find a niche in some section of this society, a niche which is firmly defined and yet seems to be uniquely made for him. In finding it the young adult gains an assured sense of inner continuity and social sameness which will bridge what he *was* as a child and what he is *about to become*, and will reconcile his *conception of himself* and his *community's recognition* of him. (1956:111)

Self-development does not, according to Erikson, conclude with early adulthood. During the middle years many individuals give back to society, serving as mentors and teaching members of younger generations. In old age, the crisis is between giving way to despair at the prospect of death and attempting to give order and meaning to one's biographical experiences (wisdom). Among the many possible outcomes are suicide and the writing of autobiographies and memoirs.

Each developmental stage builds on the preceding stages, encompassing ever broader ranges of significant others. Failure to resolve any particular psychosocial crisis reduces the likelihood of resolving subsequent ones, whereas if a particular crisis is resolved, future challenges are more likely to be faced successfully.

In his later years Erikson expanded his epigenetic stage theory in two directions. First, he applied the themes of fidelity, love, hope, care, and wisdom that had emerged in his study of American adolescence to his analysis of Mahatma Gandhi's career and the ways in which Hindus conceptualize the stages of life, particularly the transitions to young adulthood (1969). Although he found many differences between the Hindu and American cultures in these respects, he also found that the general epigenetic approach was applicable in both settings.

Second, in his last major work Erikson extended his consideration of major value themes such as love, care, wisdom, generativity, and integrity to the furthest reaches of old age, as can be seen in Table 8.1. These themes operate in all areas of life, but they can also be seen in varying interpretations of death. As Erikson wrote,

> It seems that the stage of generativity, as long as a threatening sense of stagnation is kept at bay, is pervasively characterized by a supremely sanctioned disregard of death. Youth, in its own way, is more aware of death than adulthood is; although adults, busy as they are with "maintaining the world," participate in the grand rituals of religion, art, and politics, all of which mythologize and ceremonialize death, giving it ritual meaning and thus an intensely social presence. Youth and old age, then, are the times that dream of rebirth, while adulthood is too busy taking care of actual births and is rewarded for it with a unique sense of boisterous and timeless historical reality—a sense which can seem somewhat unreal to the young and to the old, for it denies the shadow of nonbeing. (1982:79–80)

***Psychological Perspectives on Early Adulthood.*** Age 18 marks the point at which young men and women are deemed old enough to join the armed forces, to vote, and to make valid contracts regarding property ownership; at age 21 they are officially allowed to ingest society's approved psychoactive chemical, alcohol. But two even more significant role acquisitions actually bring about the transition from adolescence to early adulthood. Freud put it best when he was asked what a normal person should be able to do well: "Lieben und arbeiten," he said, "to love and to work" (quoted in Erikson 1950:89).

Entry into an occupation (or graduate school, in preparation for a future occupation) usually occurs after completion of high school or college. Entry into marriage or some other stable living arrangement also tends to happen around age 20, but like first occupations, these connections may prove temporary. Occupation and marriage roles are not necessarily the only opportunities for working and loving, but they are among the most solid bonds between the individual and society. For both men and women, occupation will establish social-class position (both directly through the characteristics of the work and indirectly through the resulting income). It will determine the rhythm and content of everyday activities, shape the characteristics of associates, and determine the degree of autonomy in decision making. Living arrangements will go a long way toward determining the level of emotional as well as economic security.

Orville Brim (1966) made a strong case that adult socialization is predominantly concerned with teaching the content and technique of overt role conduct, rather than with instilling basic values or motivations, which are the main emphases of childhood socialization. Brim also points out that adult socialization tends to center on acquiring and polishing new combinations of previously learned responses, on practical realism in role prescriptions rather than on idealism, on mediation between conflicting role demands, and on the learning of specific patterns that apply to only a few situations.

Yet there are also important areas of *anticipatory socialization* in which the major values and some of the behavior patterns of members of significant reference groups are learned as a prelude to possible membership (Merton 1957:265ff). For example, new workers take the opportunity to observe those above them in the organizational hierarchy, and when couples learn that they are expecting a child, they often interact more with friends who already have babies.

Socialization for the intimacy of the marital relationship and sexual bond is less institutionalized in contemporary urban America than is the socialization for any other major role. Young people typically have only the emotion-laden models of their own parents, a little advice from married friends, romantic moonbeams or horror stories from the mass media, and a bewildering array of "how to" books on everything from sex to cooking. Socialization for the intimacy of parenthood is a good deal more thorough and multifaceted in that both partners have been children themselves, have probably helped care for younger brothers or sisters, will get much more practical advice from relatives and friends, and will have access to much better advice in the form of manuals like the famous books by Dr. Benjamin Spock.

A central dilemma of early adulthood is the interplay between *self-determination* and *connection*. Even when such factors as ethnicity, social class, education, geographic location, and personality are taken into account, the range of possible occupations and marriage partners available to almost any young adult is very large. How to maintain the maximum level of self-directed choice while establishing necessary and/or rewarding, stable, and binding connections to the larger social order is an intensely private and frequently painful problem. The problem is magnified because some occupations, such as the professions, make demands that put severe strains on the marriage bond, while the obligations of marriage and parenthood may be overwhelming. Most people probably do not reach a thoroughly satisfactory resolution of this dilemma, as is suggested by the demand for specialized *agencies of resocialization* in the key areas of occupation (adult education, employment counseling, job training), marriage (social work, marriage counseling, psychiatry and other psychotherapies), and parenthood (nursery schools, Head Start programs).

A focused commitment to work that is personally fulfilling, allows sufficient self-determination, and pays well enough to support the family unit, together with increased assistance to the marital partners in sharing the burdens and the joys of child rearing, is doubtless the ideal solution. However, it is unlikely to be found very frequently under present economic and political circumstances.

As usual, Erikson has framed the problem with evocative clarity:

> Young adults emerging from the adolescent search for a sense of identity can be eager and willing to fuse their identities in mutual intimacy and to share them with individuals who, in work, sexuality, and friendship promise to prove complementary. One can often be "in love" or engage in intimacies, but the intimacy now at stake is the capacity to commit oneself to concrete affiliations which may call for significant sacrifices and compromises.
>
> The psychosocial antithesis to *intimacy*, however, is *isolation*, a fear of remaining separate and "unrecognized"—which provides a deep motivation for the entranced ritualization of a, now genitally mature, "I-you" experience such as marked the beginning of one's existence. A sense of isolation, then, is the potential core pathology of early adulthood. (1982:70–71)

***Cognitive Approaches.*** Cognitive approaches place more emphasis on cognition and free will in depicting the development of selves. From this perspective, judgments and conduct are the conscious attempts of individuals to apply learned rules to novel situations. Accordingly, cognitive theorists point to the need to identify the situational factors that influence individuals' decision making.

As we saw in Chapter 3, perhaps the most important facet of socialization from the point of view of society is the development of morality. Morality is a multidimensional concept, involving behavioral, affective, and cognitive processes.

Although moral standards vary from one culture to another, within a society, people must agree on what's right and what's wrong. Therefore, the moral training of youth has high priority on society's political agenda. In communist societies, for example, the primary objective of education is not the teaching of subject matter but, rather, the development of "socialist morality." In the West, there is greater emphasis on the nature of individuals' own morality in their search for justice and liberty.

Given the sociological significance of morality, it is not surprising that social scientists have been interested in how moral values are inculcated. One question pursued by social scientists is the extent to which moral behaviors emerge from reason as opposed to emotions such as empathy and basic caring, which may be innate (Alper 1985). For instance, at roughly the age of 1 year children react to another's distress; for example, they may cry when watching their mother receive a shot.

Jean Piaget was the first modern psychologist to attempt to explain moral development in children. He directed his attention to the development of increasingly abstract reasoning and intellectual capabilities in children. Like Erikson's theory, Piaget's model is an orderly sequence of stages, from an infant's exploration of simple objects to a teenager's capacity for logical thought. The revolutionary aspect of Piaget's thinking is his rejection of the concept of the child as a miniature adult and his insight that the child is not simply a vessel into which knowledge is poured.

Piaget believed that children's social maturation, including the ability to make moral decisions, depends on two factors: the acquisition of the rules and patterns governing behavior, and the ability to reason and solve problems using these rules. He postulated a two-stage development progression. In the stage of *heteronomous reasoning,* children judge the severity of an act in terms of the resultant damage rather than in terms of its underlying intent. Thus, one who trips and breaks twelve plates is judged as being worse than one who trips and breaks only one. Piaget believed that this occurs because young children are self-centered, unable to see another's perspective, and because they do not yet have the cognitive skills to understand the purpose of society's rules. At this stage, the stage of moral realism, the child also accepts rules as derived from authority and believes that rules are sacred and unalterable and that actions are either completely right or completely wrong.

In *autonomous morality* there is moral independence; the individual believes in modifying the rules to fit the needs of the situation. In this stage we find autonomous moral judgments and the ability to use abstract reasoning. Moral judgments consider intent as well as results. Cooperation and reciprocity are important at this stage, and rules are viewed as capable of being modified by agreement or according to human needs.

## Sociological Perspectives

To a sociologist, selves are little more than the roles they perform (MacKay 1973). In this section we consider the changing structure of the roles played by individuals as they pass through the lifespan. Since sociologists view identity as a social product that is never achieved once and for all, it is important to study not only its *creation* but its *maintenance* as well.

***The Riley Model of Age Stratification.*** To conceptualize the ways in which people are linked to society, Matilda Riley (1971, 1977; Riley et al. 1972) begins by distinguishing between people and roles. Roles involve the normative expectations, facilities, rewards, and deprivations of individuals located in particular social statuses. With modernization, these roles have become increasingly age-graded. Hence, one's location in the age structure is a central determinant of one's attitudes, behaviors, and self-concepts.

Riley's model takes into account **age strata** and **age-related acts and capacities** (see Figure 8.1). Age strata involve the relative proportions of people in different age groups in a given society, as illustrated by demographers' population pyramids. Distinctive bulges and concaves can appear in these pyramids because of the existence of a "baby boom" cohort or because of large-scale, age-specific deaths (i.e., the deaths of young male adults in war). Age groups vary in the contributions they can make to society because of age-related differences in physical capacities and personal motivations.

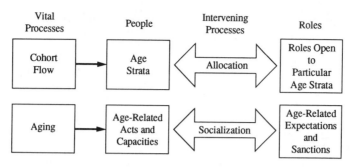

**FIGURE 8.1   Riley's Model of Age Stratification Systems**

These individuals become linked to the **age structure of roles** through social allocation mechanisms. Children are assigned to educational roles; young adults may be drafted; the role of retiree is normally allocated to people in their seventh decade of life. However, there are times when there are too few members of a particular age group to fill the positions required for the social order to function. For instance, in Germany during the closing months of World War II, so many men in their late teens, twenties, and thirties had been killed or captured that 12-year-olds and 50-year-olds were recruited or drafted. In the United States in recent years, as the number of teenagers and young adults has decreased, fast-food franchises have increasingly been staffed by older workers.

Finally, through socialization, age-related capacities are transformed into age-related expectations and sanctions. Hence, newborns are not expected to be toilet-trained, and diapered 5-year-olds normally cannot be enrolled in primary school. However, actual or assumed capacities also turn out to be quite variable. As we saw in Chapter 2, the age at which women are capable of giving birth has declined over the past few centuries. And as the primary requirements for work have become less physical, the ability of older individuals to be effective workers has increased. If demographic projections of labor shortages in the next two decades hold, the elderly may be expected to work until later ages before being required to retire.

In sum, Riley's model suggests two parallel conveyor belts moving together through time, though not necessarily at the same rates. Associated with the aging process are role complexes, which also change in a nonstatic society. Each of these roles, in turn, comes with its own implicit timetable. As we will see shortly, these timetables become the basis of self-esteem.

***Temporal Outlooks across the Lifespan.***   In addition to the available role repertoires at different stages of the life cycle, another temporal factor shaping the self is the perceived gap between one's actual self and one's ideal self. College students, for instance, may feel that they are in the process of *becoming*. Octogenarians, on the other hand, may refer to themselves in terms of what they *have been* (e.g., "I am a retired engineer").

The ultimate constraint on such appraisals is, of course, death. Raymond Schmitt and Wilbert Leonard (1986) argue that as the prospect of extinction becomes more real, self-concerns shift toward one's *postself*, the self one will leave for posterity. As R. D. Laing asks, "Who is not engaged in trying to impress, to leave a mark, to engrave his image on others and on the world—graven images held more dear than life itself?" (1967:48).

Let us take a closer look at the temporal outlook of people at different points in the lifespan.

*Early Adulthood.* In American culture, early adulthood is viewed as the "best years of life" (see Table 8.6). Being far removed from the possibility of death gives one the sense of limitless opportunities and limitless time to enjoy them. Thus, with increased life expectancy there has been a prolongation of adolescence and dependency.

If, as was the case until but a century or two ago, one saw that most people die before their thirtieth birthday, why would one choose to remain in school for sixteen or more years? Why would one wait until one's twenties to marry? Nowadays, of course, women can pursue a career and postpone childbearing until their late thirties or early forties. Students can become the legendary "perpetual students," pursuing graduate education until their thirties before seeking entry into the full-time work force.

This time-rich mindset is conditioned not only by age but also by social class. (See Chapter 10.) Members of the upper classes can afford to retard their social aging by remaining longer within educational systems (physicians nearly all come from upper-middle-class families), by delaying marriage and childbearing, and by postponing retirement.

*The Middle Years.* For the middle-class American, the first symptom of one's own mortality often occurs after the age of 35. It may be precipitated by a serious illness or a premature heart attack. This is the time of life when the first member of one's friendship circle dies of "natural causes," when one witnesses the deaths of one's parents and their friends, when one purchases life insurance, and when one begins to read obituaries.

Middle-aged people have a unique perspective on the lifespan by virtue of being in a position to see the flow of generations. They watch their parents' generation leave the world as that of their grandchildren enters it. One day a middle-aged woman may tend to the needs of her bedridden mother; on the next day she may care for her new grandchild. Nevertheless, the death of one's parents means that one's own generation is the "next up to bat" and that one's own countdown has begun. People tend to start thinking in terms of how much time they have left as opposed to how long they've lived (Erikson 1963; Jacques 1965; Levinson et al. 1978).

*Old Age.* In old age the sense of a future dissolves as one's time runs out. It is the old who are most likely to think about and discuss death and who are least likely to be frightened by it. But the stigma of death associated with this phase of the lifespan has transformed what should be understood as one of the greatest social accomplishments—the near guarantee at birth of being able to live a full, complete life—into a socially problematic stage in a culture that values youth.

Old age is a time of losses: of spouse and friends, job, health, standard of living, and future time. With each of these losses, there is a partial death. With the death of significant others, for instance, the distinctive selves that each of these people brought out are gone as well; with the loss of one's job, one loses the frame of reference provided by one's coworkers. For the institutionalized elderly in hospitals or long-term care facilities, there is the loss of independence

## The Old as Society's Fittest

The next time you encounter some old-timer doddering along as though he or she might not make it to the end of the block, back off and take another look, for what you are seeing is one of the fittest members the human species has ever produced. Improbable as that sounds, it's so. Darwin wrote a book about it.

Look at it this way: The oldsters around us, at least those over 70, many of whom are not the least bit decrepit, have somehow survived the deadliest perils known in this century, ones we are most warned about today.

Nowadays hardly a week passes that we are not made aware of newly discovered hazards that have been lurking around all these years to do us in—things in the air, things in the water, things in the ground, things in the food we eat.

Well, somehow these old folks have about made it through these mine fields and did so before cautionary labels and warning signs were posted. . . .

It's too glib to attribute their longevity just to advancements in medical science, especially since the "medical science" of their earlier years was one of the things they had to survive.

And don't go attributing their success in this to some notion that they grew up in a more pristine and less polluted environment than the one we have today.

The fact is that their earlier environment was crowded with pollutants, contaminants, poisons, bacteria, viruses, and other threats to health that many people today aren't even familiar with.

Indeed, some of them have been so outlawed—such as smallpox—that they don't exist anymore, not anywhere in the world. No, there have to be other explanations for why they have been able to hang in there so long.

Consider that these people survived a time when tuberculosis, The Great White Plague, was still killing more Americans a year than did cancer, heart disease, or any other malady known then or now.

For sure, they lived through the big influenza epidemic in the autumn of 1918 that killed 548,000 Americans, far more than this nation had killed in all the battles fought in World War I, World War II, the Korean conflict, and Vietnam, combined.

These are the people who survived the times when all the toothpaste came in a lethal lead tube, all store-bought paint came laced with lead, and lead pencils were just that.

Chlorine wasn't used to purify the often wiggler-filled water they drank and no public health authority certified the healthfulness of most public water supplies.

A community drinking cup was still chained to many public water fountains, as on some trains, and the spittoon abounded wherever men gathered.

Outdoor privies were commonplace, not just in rural areas but also behind some of the old shotgun tenements in major cities. They could be placed anywhere one wanted on his own property, right uphill from a neighbor's or the community's well, if that was the choice.

These are people who slept for years with a big two-bell alarm clock with a radium-painted dial placed right beside their heads.

When the fluoroscope came out they treated it as a novelty, as when shoe stores used it to let customers see just how their new shoes fit, and anyone dropping in could take turns staring into those x-rays to see how his bones moved when he wriggled his toes.

How come these survivors didn't succumb to the horrendously foul air that lay like a pall around many factories and all freight yards when locomotives burned coal? Or to the kerosene and gas heaters that were unvented to the outside? Or to the asbestos pads placed over the burners on most kitchen ranges?

Maybe it was just dumb luck that they weren't blown away by the 110 volt open wall sockets in their homes, or the ungrounded electrical appliances they used, or the deadly firecrackers they played around with, or that Pittsburgh water heater that could take the side and roof of the house off.

But how do you explain that they were not done for by the unpasteurized and unrefrigerated milk they drank or the mayonnaise that spoiled on the way to the picnic?

Talk to any old-timer and he will speak with intimate knowledge about measles, mumps, diphtheria, pneumonia, whooping cough, chicken pox, worms, dysentery, typhoid fever, blood poison, and maybe malaria, mastoiditis, Bright's disease, yellow jaundice, or scarlet fever.

Source: Schmidt, 1989.

and, often, of dignity. In sum, the old now die a number of social deaths before physically expiring. Such losses produce the common experiences of loneliness, grief, depression, despair, anxiety, helplessness, and rage.

Old age is also a time of reflection and reminiscence. This turning inward, coupled with social and psychological disengagement from life, can diminish the sense of loss as attachment to the things of this world is lessened. Old age is also a period when, as Robert Butler and Myrna Lewis observe, "the sins of omission and commission for which an individual blames himself weigh even more heavily in light of approaching death" (1981:37). (See Table 8.2.)

***Continuity of the Self over Time.*** Cultural mythologies are replete with formulas that represent the life cycle. We can see the assumption of life cycle stages in the riddle of the sphinx, in the "seasons of man," and in our demarcations of early or late adolescence and old age. However, because the biological process of aging is continuous, how do distinctive stages come to be recognized? How are changes in the self over time made socially meaningful, and how do those meanings change when the life cycle itself is modified?

In modern societies chronological age has become the criterion by which role complexes are linked together (Eisenstadt 1956). Age is the referent by which we can compare a 3-year-old to 5-year-old, by which we can claim that an individual is too young to be married or too old to be working full time. The ways in which these age-linked stages of life are typified provide a standardized timetable by which one can gauge the "correctness" of one's life trajectory.

From the individual's perspective, to be "on time" is to be socially synchronized. This implies awareness of social-structural time (Glaser and Strauss 1971, 1965) and reveals the social bases of projects that make up one's **life plan**

**TABLE 8.2   When Do People Become "Old"?**

*In 1974 Louis Harris and Associates interviewed a large national sample
(n = 4254) to gauge the myths and reality of old age in America. When individuals were asked when an average man and an average woman become
"old," about half specified a fixed age. As can be seen in this table, over half
believed that old age begins at a specific age, less than one in four claimed
that "it depends," and only one in twenty was not sure.*

|                                    | Average Man | Average Woman |
|------------------------------------|:-----------:|:-------------:|
| Under 40                           | 1%          | 1%            |
| 40–49 years                        | 4           | 5             |
| 50–59 years                        | 11          | 11            |
| 60–64 years                        | 12          | 10            |
| 65–69 years                        | 11          | 8             |
| 70–74 years                        | 10          | 9             |
| 75–79 years                        | 3           | 3             |
| 80 and older                       | 1           | 2             |
| Never                              | 2           | 2             |
| It depends                         | 22          | 23            |
| When he/she stops working          | 4           | 2             |
| When his/her health fails          | 11          | 13            |
| When she can't have babies anymore |             | 2             |
| Other                              | 3           | 3             |
| Not sure                           | 5           | 6             |

(Berger, Berger, and Kellner 1973:73). The life plan is shaped by the timetables of the roles that the individual assumes to be central to his or her self-concept. Those roles also serve as the basis for comparisons with others. We are continually contrasting our present selves with our former selves and with the biographies of significant others when they were at a similar stage. Having been tracked with people of similar ages through school, Little League, Girl Scouts, and the like, and in our occupational careers, we ritually compare our biographical development with that of our age-mates in Christmas cards and alumni magazines and at class reunions and professional meetings. Such biographical comparisons have social as well as psychological consequences.

As is evident in Table 8.3, social institutions often require various kinds of biographical summaries. When one shapes one's history in such "institutionally relevant" ways, one is simultaneously maintaining the meanings on which one's symbolic identity depends. In retirement ceremonies, for example, one's work history is described in the context of the company's history. Institutions thus provide a symbolic order within which individuals realize a continuity of self through life. In sum, both social and personal orders depend on coherent biographies.

Such biographical coherence has become increasingly problematic. The traditional continuities provided by one's lifelong roles (e.g., a single career and

**TABLE 8.3  Biographical Timetables Implicit in the Life Plan**

| Institutions | Forms of Biographical Summaries | Rituals for Biographical Reviews of Self and Institution |
| --- | --- | --- |
| Family | Diaries, scrapbooks, memorabilia | Anniversaries, holidays, reminiscences of the old, funerals |
| School | Report cards, alumni magazines, applications for admittance | Annual award ceremonies, graduations, class reunions |
| Work | Job vitae, portfolios of work histories, promotions and demotions | Annual evaluations and reviews, company indoctrination sessions when entering job, retirement ceremonies |
| Economy | Credit histories, canceled checks, possessions | Tax preparations |
| Religion | Rank in church hierarchy (deacon, elder, young adult, etc.) | Confessionals, Christmas and Easter, baptism, funerals |

Source: Kearl, 1980.

a single marriage) have disappeared. Moreover, these roles are synchronized in different ways. For instance, instead of beginning careers and families simultaneously, many middle-class Americans postpone marriage and child rearing; mothers in their early forties now find themselves with preschoolers at the same point in the life cycle when their mothers were experiencing the "empty-nest syndrome."

Since the 1970s there has been a proliferation of popular and professional literature addressing such perceived discontinuities of the self. We are informed that the sensation of periodic *crises* associated with the unfolding of personal biographies is no longer pathological but normal, a regular event requiring "typical treatment" (e.g., Levinson 1978; Sheehy 1974). One of the best known of these crises is the so-called "midlife crisis." In the past, such disjunctures of the life course were not left to be resolved by the individual or treated by medical and psychiatric therapists. Rather, they were managed collectively through rites of passage.

***Rites of Passage.*** Even to argue that there are different kinds of people such as children, adults, and the elderly is to imply that one passes through a series of distinct kinds of being. Cultures often develop specific social rituals to assist individuals undergoing these transformations of identity. **Rites of passage** are rituals that symbolically recast individuals' social identities during times of significant biographical change, when there are considerable discontinuities between past and future role expectations. Through these rites, social systems transform events that are personally unique into events that are socially typical, thereby making them socially meaningful and personally less frightening. When such role changes correspond with biological change—for example, when initiation into "manhood" corresponds with puberty—they seem more "natural," legitimate, and "real."

Much of our thinking about rites of passage is shaped by the turn-of-the-century works of anthropologist Arnold van Gennep (1960 [1908]). Van Gennep saw **regeneration** as the law of life and the universe: The energy that is found in any system gradually becomes spent and must be renewed at intervals. Just as summer spends itself only to be renewed in spring, individuals become worn out and must be ritually "recharged" and given opportunities to shed a used-up self.

To be between roles or in some way outside of them is to be socially polluting. People in this position are often seen as having uncontrolled, dangerous, and disapproved powers. As Mary Douglas has written, "It seems that if a person has no place in the social system and is therefore a marginal being, all precaution against danger must come from others" (1966:117). This condition calls for rites that will incorporate the individual into the group and return him or her to the customary routines of life.

Life passages and the ceremonies that accompany them involve the *social structuring of time*. First, they help mark seasons of life—what Neugarten, et al. (1965) has called "the normal, predictable life-cycle." Second, each transition has, within itself, a predictable sequence of events. Van Gennep saw rites of passage as having three subphases: separation, transition, and reincorporation. Third, they provide some "lee-time," or time when the normal course of activities is interrupted, allowing all the actors to realign their interactions, perceptions, and expectations.

## CHANGING SOCIETIES, CHANGING SELVES

On the *USS Enterprise* of "Star Trek" fame, a classification system is applied to various planets to categorize their inhabitants' degree of sociocultural development. Such a model would explain how some societies, like Japan during the twentieth century, evolve faster than others, while others, like the classical Hindu culture of India, "get stuck" at a particular level of development.

Although such a model has yet to be fully worked out in the social sciences, several "evolutionary" trends in human societies are evident. First, there is a trend toward increasing specialization and differentiation of both groups and selves. Whereas, for instance, the family system was basically a self-sufficient unit, over time many of its functions have come to be managed by specialized agencies such as educational institutions, daycare and nursing-home facilities, and the workplace. Selves similarly have undergone such specialization, which is why we hear so little about "Renaissance men" or "jacks-of-all-trades." In the workplace, the artisan has been replaced by people with specialized roles, each contributing a component of the total product. As we will see in Chapter 15, this has done little for self-esteem: Whereas in the past the death of any community member was an irreplaceable loss, nowadays one is simply replaced by an interchangeable other. To ensure that modern social systems are minimally disrupted by the deaths of their members, roles are made more important than their occupants.

A second broad trend is the shift from *Gemeinschaft* to *Gesellschaft* solidarities (Töennies 1963[1887]—from the era in which the "social gravity" binding a people consisted of the intimate bonds between homogeneous residents of small communities where individuals knew one another, to the impersonal bonds now linking heterogeneous and yet interdependent strangers in large urban areas (see Chapter 16). *Gesellschaft* relationships are based not on mutual affection but, rather, on the achievement of complementary goals. Interpersonal relationships are largely secondary and role-based; total selves are irrelevant to most social interactions. (See Table 8.4.) The high rates of economic productivity achieved in *Gesellschaft* societies come at a cost: Such contexts have been shown to be related to high rates of homicide, suicide, juvenile delinquency, divorce, child abuse, and alcoholism (Naroll 1983). On the other hand, as Michiko Kakutani notes, let us not be overly nostalgic for the small towns of the past:

> Often these places were a repressive, fatalistic—and often stultifyingly provincial—way of life. The dominant emotions are of a sense of suffocation, of lost innocence, and of time past intruding ineluctably upon time present. It is also peculiarly

**TABLE 8.4  Primary Social Contexts Underlying the Genesis of Personality Types**

|  | Moral Communities (*Gemeinschaft*) | Mass Communities (*Gesellschaft*) |
|---|---|---|
| **Attachments to significant groups** | high sense of belonging; identification | sense of being cut off; alienation |
| **Moral unity** | high sense of oneness as people share blood ties, tradition, common values, and shared geographic space; sense of pursuing common goals | low sense of oneness; moral fragmentation due to divergence of individuals' goals |
| **Personal connectedness with moral order** | involvement; sense of personal responsibility toward others | disengagement; sense of being detached, that others' affairs are irrelevant to self |
| **How others are viewed** | as whole persons of intrinsic worth | segmentation; others are merely a means to an end |
| **How others are dealt with** | through sentiment, owing to collective conscience | laws and contracts |
| **Sense of personal identity** | collectivism, being but a part of a larger whole that existed before one's birth and will continue after one's death | individualism |

hermetic, full of the sort of social backbiting that obtains among people of all classes in an isolated community. Gossip is a primary activity. (1985:15)

In sum, each phase of social evolution implies new relationships between individuals and society. And given the interdependencies between the two, it is not surprising that new selves arise as a result of momentous social change. Paralleling the work of psychologists and psychiatrists seeking to understand how children's cognitions and identities unfold are the efforts of anthropologists and historians to identify patterns in the ways in which self-systems have changed over time. Indeed, their studies reveal that the personal self that we know and take for granted is a very recent creation.

## The Collectivist Mindset

For most of human history, the basic unit of society was not the individual but the social group, such as the clan or tribe. Even in the 1990s, approximately 70 percent of the world's population continues to live in collectivist cultures where personal goals are subordinate to group goals.

In the West before the rise of individualism, identities were largely programmed, remaining relatively stable throughout the lifespan. This was possible because of the static social context; one could look at one's parents or grandparents and see oneself in the future. Similarity and conformity were valued (Baumeister 1986). Because the self was yet to be discovered, the loss of self through death was accepted without question or concern (Ariès 1974) as long as one's people survived. It was the clan or tribe that extended like a ribbon through time, with the self being but a small snippet of that ribbon.

In part, selves remained stable because they were largely ascribed. And identities were largely fixed in geographic terms, since people rarely strayed far from the place of their birth. This lack of geographic mobility had collective and social implications as well. Mary Douglas (1988:103), for instance, has observed how much the Biblical labels of Judean, Nazarene, or Samarian revealed about a people. She cites Lawrence Rosen's observations of contemporary Moroccans, among whom the self is more likely to be understood in terms of the geographic groups than in terms of occupation or age:

> A very considerable part of an individual's character is constituted by the social milieu from which he draws his nurture. To Moroccans, geographical regions are inhabited spaces, realms within which communities organize themselves to wrest a living and forge a degree of security. . . . Their main focus is on the identity of persons *in situ* because the site itself is a social context through which an individual becomes used to ways of creating a lived in space. To be attached to a place is, therefore, not only to have a point of origin—it is to have those social roots, those human achievements, that are distinctive to the kind of person one is. (Rosen 1984:23)

Collectivist cultures are often associated with **traditionalist identities.** The collectivity consists not only of those now living but also of generations long dead and those yet to be born. In other words, tradition-directed individuals live in a timeless present, entrenched in a world in which ritual and routine were defined by previous generations. Theirs is a world of honor, in which identity is "firmly linked to the past through the reiterated performance of prototypical acts" (Berger et al. 1973:91).

## Collectivism in Japan

A collectivist mindset may be found in Japan, a racially and culturally homogeneous society that was isolated for centuries from the individualizing influences of the West. When American baseball players were hired by Japanese teams, the players thought that in this alien society at least the ball field would seem like home. It did not. The Japanese ethos had changed the game even though the rules remained intact.

In Japan, teams play not to win but to tie. The best game is one in which the teams tie (a time rule allows for this possibility)—that way no one loses and all can save face. Players cannot stand out either, for that detracts from the group. American ball players on "hot streaks" find the strike zones expanding until their statistics float back down to the level of others.

U.S. companies trying to break into Japanese markets are similarly frustrated by the different rules by which the game is played. For example, to convince a Japanese distributor that he should purchase from an American company is similar to asking him to cease doing business with his brother-in-law. Business relationships are based on family ties.

The commitment of the Japanese to their primary groups is legendary. Consider the Japanese soldier who was found on a remote South Pacific Island in 1989 still fighting World War II. Or the Japanese worker socializing with his coworkers in a local bar: When he was asked what his personal goals were, a quizzical look came over his face; no one had ever asked him the question before. So thoroughly interwoven are personal and collective ambitions that the question was meaningless.

Source: *Frontline, 1989.*

# The Rise of Individualism

During the late Middle Ages and the Renaissance, people became more geographically mobile and therefore were more likely to come into contact with radically different cultures and selves. It was in this context that the concept of identity developed. An inner self was postulated, a self that gave individuals *personal* interpretations of the world and unique emotional experiences. This was the era when the vendetta system began disappearing as one's kin were no longer seen as being equivalent to oneself. The discovery of the unique self was accompanied by the appearance of epitaphs on tombstones containing abridged biographies, which were now meaningful as all lives were no longer taken to be equivalent. In the arts, there were the first portrayals of individual states of emotion. There was renewed interest in drama, wherein the distinctions between the person and the role were explored. There was concern with sincerity and whether or not one's behavior reflected one's true self. As a result, there was heightened concern with one's distinguishing characteristics, coupled with interest in biographies.

The relatively recent emergence of the concept of identity is perhaps not surprising, considering that human commonalities far outweigh human differences, that there is a universal human nature, generally remains as a personal bias. As Emerson observed, "The wise man shows his wisdom in separation, in gradation, and his scale of creatures and of merits is as wide as nature. The foolish have no range in their scale, but suppose every man is as every other man" (quoted in Krauthammer 1983).

With the rise of industrialization and urbanization during the late eighteenth and early nineteenth centuries, social roles became increasingly differentiated and specialized. Religion retreated from everyday life. No longer was there a cultural model for the "correct" life; no longer did individuals automatically live up to their "God-given" potential. So people groped for new models of fulfillment: love, creativity, personality. Self and society were assumed to be in conflict, a conflict that was dramatized in the "noble savage" myth of the time (see Torgovnick 1990). At the same time, it was assumed that society could be reformed to assist individuals in realizing their potential. Personality became recognized as the revelation of an inner self. This period also saw the rise of privacy, in which unique, *private* selves could be cultivated.

During the Victorian era the perceived conflict between self and society became more acute. There was less optimism about the possibility of reforming society. Among the outcomes were transcendentalism, anarchism, progressivism, and emphasis on home and family. As the bifurcation between public and private selves became more complete, individuals became increasingly enigmatic to themselves. The notion that it is possible for others to know you better than you know yourself emerged, to be elaborated in the Sherlock Holmes stories and the development of psychoanalysis.

***Inner-Directedness.*** During the eighteenth and nineteenth centuries a new personality type developed as immigrants struck out from the established centers of civilization to colonize the American West. According to David Riesman, this was the **"inner-directed"** self for whom identity was no longer automatically provided by the primary group (1950). Living in novel situations bereft of recipes for action, these individuals had to decide what to do—and therefore what to do with themselves. Their culture stressed self-discipline and personal accountability. Deviant behavior was viewed as resulting from a flaw or weakness in one's character.

Traces of this historic personality type remain in remote agrarian communities throughout the United States. The traditional family farm requires considerable self-sufficiency. As the family sits down to eat, most of the meal is a product of their own efforts. In urban areas, on the other hand, the family meal is a reminder of the family's interdependence with a host of others. Instead of eating peas that one planted, tended, harvested, and shelled, one places a plastic pouch of preseasoned peas in the microwave for a few minutes.

***Other-Directedness.*** By the mid-twentieth century, with the increasing bureaucratization and rationalization of everyday life, when production outdistanced consumption and fewer people worked the land, and when shorter work hours and declining birthrates meant increasing leisure time for the middle classes, a new personality type emerged: the **other-directed** individual. In a setting that allowed considerable social and geographic mobility, where the rates of change in knowledge and values are phenomenal, Americans shifted their reference groups from family to peers. The other-directed self operates out of the need to be approved and accepted by peers, friends, coworkers, classmates, and neighbors. Riesman argues that social approval has considerably more reward value in contemporary society than it did a century ago:

> What is common to all the other-directed people is that their contemporaries are the source of direction for the individual—either those known to him or those with whom he is indirectly acquainted, through friends and through the mass media. This source is of course "internalized" in the sense that dependence on it for guidance in life is implanted early. The goals toward which the other-directed person strives shift with that guidance: It is only the process of striving itself and the process of paying close attention to the signals from others that remain unaltered throughout life. (1950:20)

Table 8.5 provides a typology of historical selves.

The modern individual, buffeted by the rapid and dramatic changes both in cultural values and in the means by which to obtain them, never "knows" himself or herself. The frequent results are anomie and anxiety. According to David Kallen, "the other-directed individual seeks both the goal and the goal pathway from those around him rather than from himself" (1963:76). A fixed, rigid sense of morality is no longer a useful guide. Instead, other-directed individuals are characterized by moral flexibility. Moral behavior is determined more by what peers expect than by what parents teach.

This personality type is, in part, a product of permissive child-rearing practices. Instead of controlling children with authority and self-assurance, parents employ reason or manipulation. As a result, notes Riesman, "it depends less on what one is and what one does than on what others think of one—and

**TABLE 8.5    A Typology of Historical Selves**

| Personality Type | Sociohistorical Characteristics | Clarity of Cultural Goals | Clarity of Cultural Means to Obtain Goals | Emotional Control over People | Metaphor for How Social Control Is Experienced |
|---|---|---|---|---|---|
| Tradition-directed | *Gemeinschaft* solidarities | + | + | shame | divine wrath |
| Inner-directed | | + | ? | guilt | gyro or compass |
| Other-directed | *Gesellschaft* solidarities, high urbanization, rapid social change, high moral pluralization | ? | ? rapid role obsolescence, greater interdependence with others | anxiety | radar or sonar |

Source: Riesman, 1950.

how competent one is in manipulating others and being oneself manipulated" (1950:45).

***Character and Personality.*** The twentieth century has featured increasing economic interdependence between individuals. The relationship between self and society continues to deteriorate. The individual self is devalued: Broad, abstract social forces are seen as the major determining factors of social life; hero worship is replaced by critical and iconoclastic biographies of powerful or successful figures.

Whereas the nineteenth-century character structure emphasized self-discipline, delayed gratification, and restraint, the twentieth-century self features materialism and cynicism. With the emergence of a "culture of abundance," according to Warren Susman (1985), there was a shift of emphasis from the romantic ideal of "character" to an ideal of "personality." Whereas character involves matters of integrity and duty, personality involves the ability to make friends. In consequence, the self has shifted from being judged in terms of its morality to one whose social adequacy is evaluated merely in terms of its popularity.

# CHANGING PATHWAYS THROUGH TIME

The great demographic and social changes of the past few centuries produced not only new kinds of selves but also new ways in which selves pass through time. Corresponding with the increasing differentiation and specialization of the social order was an increasing differentiation of the life course. The recognized stages of life became less a matter of biology (e.g., menarche or the appearance of gray hair) and more a matter of social rhythms, particularly those emanating from the division of labor. More precisely, the age strata that serve as the major basis for social organization and determine individuals' life experiences fluctuate as society changes. Moreover, given the interrelationships between the meanings of different stages of life (e.g., the meaning of the teenage years is determined by the meanings of childhood and adulthood), change in any one stage affects the meanings of all others.

Over the past century, age norms have become increasingly important attributes of both identities and social structure. Before 1850, age distinctions played little role in social organization (Ariès 1962; Chudacoff 1989). The distinction between the mid- and post-adolescent stages, for example, was nonexistent fifty years ago, just as the distinction between the old-old (those 85 and older) and the young-old (those 65–74) was nonexistent two decades ago. But specific characteristics of different age groups were noted by educational, medical, and psychological specialists (Chudacoff 1989). These characteristics were broadly disseminated in popularized versions, producing increasing age consciousness and more crystallized age norms.

When a particular age group becomes associated with a major social problem, as when "urchins" harassed urban adults in the late nineteenth century, agencies of welfare and social control become involved. Eventually, the age group becomes institutionalized as legislation is passed on its behalf and new organizations (schools, YMCAs, etc.) are created to deal with its special needs (Hareven 1976).

# The Social Construction of Childhood

Middle-class parents who, after a day at the office, play games with and read stories to their offspring during "quality time," participate in creating a form of childhood that did not exist until relatively recently. Over a century ago, it was the child who participated in the adult world, not vice versa. Children often were expected to perform their share of the family's work in an era when the family was a unit of production rather than a unit of consumption. For instance, on the farm, children had chores that simply must be done—the cow could not wait to be milked, nor could the hay wait to be harvested. Play was devised by the children themselves, with imagination transforming blocks into trains or the local woods into a medieval kingdom.

As small adults, children were assumed to have adult concerns, including such emotions as guilt and terror. As David Stannard (1977) has explained,

> James Janeway's *A Token for Children*, a book designed for reading to and by children, had as its sole purpose to remind children of the ever-nearness of death and its possible consequences. It may have been exceeded in popularity only by the New England Primer; but even as they learned the alphabet from this latter book, Puritan children were instructed with such rhymes as:
> **G**—As runs the *Glass*/Man's life doth pass;
> **T**—*Time* cuts down all/Both great and small;
> **X**—*Xerxes* the great did die/and so must you & I
> **Y**—*Youth* forward slips/Death soon nips. (p. 65) . . .
> And Cotton Mather, once again, in words directed to the "many children, the *Small People*" in his congregation, advised that the "Go into *Burying*-Place, CHILDREN; you will there see *Graves* as short as your selves. Yea, you may be at Play one Hour; Dead, Dead the next." (p. 66)

Neil Postman observes that "unlike infancy, childhood is a social artifact, not a biological category" (1982). Similarly, in *Centuries of Childhood* Ariès shows how childhood was "invented" in the West as a distinctive stage of the life cycle. The appearance of children as shrunken adults wearing small adult clothing in Renaissance paintings, for instance, was not a failure by the artists but a result of how children were perceived. Until the seventeenth century, there wasn't even a word for "child" in French, English, or German; the term *child* referred to kinship rather than age. Ariès found that during the Middle Ages people in every age group dressed in similar ways. Distinctive costumes for children did not become generalized throughout the European upper classes until the end of the sixteenth century, with boys' clothing appearing first.

As infant mortality rates declined, for the first time in human history parents could expect to raise their children to maturity. As a result, new cultural conceptions of this stage of social life developed. The emergence of this socially defined stage as a distinctive phase of the life cycle accompanied the rise of industrialization (with its segregation of work from the home) and the evolution of the notion of social class (Ariès 1962). In the United States, childhood was first "discovered" by middle-class urban families in the early nineteenth century, when sentiment (as opposed to economic interdependence) was becoming the basis of familial relationships (Hareven 1980).

# The Social Construction of Old Age

If we were able to bring William Shakespeare back to life and deposit him in contemporary Orlando, Florida, he would be amazed at the large number of older people living there. Old age is a major accomplishment of modern society. The Biblical allotment of three score and ten years has practically become a right of citizenship in the United States. However, because of the relative novelty of this life stage, appropriate cultural adjustments have not yet appeared. As Erikson observed:

> As we come to the last stage (old age), we become aware of the fact that our civilization really does not harbor a concept of the whole of life. . . . Any span of the cycle lived without vigorous meaning, at the beginning, in the middle, or at the end, endangers the sense of life and the meaning of death in all those whose life stages are intertwined. (1964:132–133)

Wilbert E. Moore (1963) observed that the increasing longevity of people in postindustrial societies has disrupted the centuries-old synchronization between the temporal order of social systems and the temporal order of biological humans. Our contemporary "social problem" orientation to old age and our anxieties about death may exist in part because we outlive the traditional lifespan "recipes" and no longer "know" how to grow old and die. One can now be alive biologically yet socially dead, disengaged from most of one's central social roles.

There is nothing inherently problematic about the biological inevitability of growing old. But old age has become a marginal condition of social life. Americans go to great lengths to obscure their own aging (e.g., with cosmetics and hair dyes) and to segregate the elderly in old-age communities or nursing homes.

A nationwide survey of Americans age 18 and older was conducted in 1974 to gauge myths about old age. As shown in Table 8.6, only 2 percent of the public viewed the sixties and seventies as the best time of life, while more than one-third saw those years as the worst. If indeed the basis of society is the production of meaningful identities and the maintenance of self-esteem, this pattern, in which everything is perceived as "downhill" from the thirties on, must be explained. If there is no "cash-in" value for maturity, for years of social contribution and social experiences, why grow old (Butler 1975)?

To legitimate the evaporating roles and diminishing status of the old, a new life cycle stage evolved: retirement. Culturally, retirement provides a buffer against the disruptions caused by death and allows new generations to bring new perspectives to old problems. From the perspective of management, upward mobility within organizations must be possible for the young in order to maintain their corporate loyalty; because hierarchical organizations have fewer positions at higher levels, by retiring the old one makes room for the young. To justify forcing people to surrender so central a component of self-concept as their work, a culturally acceptable rationale had to be created.

Retirement has become a time of life that one supposedly earns after years of social contribution, a time of true leisure for those with diminished energies. But as we will see in Chapter 15, leisure (which is different from "free time") is

**TABLE 8.6** The Perceived Best and Worst Years of Life according to a 1974 Survey of Americans 18 and Older

| | Best Years of Life | | Worst Years of Life | |
| --- | --- | --- | --- | --- |
| | *Respondents Age 18–64* | *Respondents Age 65 +* | *Respondents Age 18–64* | *Respondents Age 65 +* |
| *Years of Life* | | | | |
| Teens | 16% | 7% | 20% | 10% |
| 20s | 33 | 17 | 5 | 7 |
| 30s | 24 | 22 | 3 | 5 |
| 40s | 13 | 17 | 3 | 3 |
| 50s | 3 | 8 | 6 | 4 |
| 60s | 1 | 6 | 12 | 14 |
| 70s | * | 2 | 21 | 21 |
| Other | 1 | 2 | 6 | 7 |
| Wouldn't choose any | 7 | 15 | 17 | 22 |
| Not sure | 2 | 4 | 7 | 7 |

Source: Harris, 1975.

something most Americans know very little about and for which they have little anticipatory socialization. As Arlie Hochschild argues:

> Leisure is not quite leisure when you don't have work. Ironically, the old are more likely than the young to base their pride squarely on work. . . . To many of the old, the "fun ethic" and even the culturally sophisticated use of leisure is an ideological veneer for the growing scarcity of jobs. (1973:19–20)

Inherent in the ideology of leisure is the notion of individualism and its associated myths of self-fulfillment and self-actualization. As Daniel Callahan notes, however, such ideas often mean little:

> The price we pay for our individualism in an aging society is that our culture provides neither the elderly nor anyone else with a clear picture of what they should be able to hope for from society in their old age or of the way they might make social sense of their illnesses and eventual death. Given the great importance of meaning for the aged—meaning in their lives and about their place and value in society— there is a harm in the implicit relativism of the diversity itself. There is at present no meaning for the aged unless they can supply it for themselves. . . . The great danger is self-absorption, the embracing of service to self or the "rewarding" of oneself as a way of warding off, or attempting to compensate for, the death that is to come. (1987:60, 50)

In sum, as childhood emerged as a consequence of industrialization, so today old age is a product of postindustrial, service-oriented economies. One of the largest of these service industries is medicine (see Chapter 16), for which the old are—by virtue of their diminished health and proximity to death—ideal consumers. If the elderly are "generational pioneers," then the physician has become their trail guide (Kearl 1985).

# THE INTERSECTION OF BIOGRAPHY
# WITH SOCIAL HISTORY

In rapidly changing societies populated by increasingly long-lived individuals, the interfaces between biography and history become more numerous and complex. At any given time there may be four, five, even six lineal generations of individuals with distinctive identities, outlooks toward life, and agendas for social change. For this reason, according to Alvin Toffler (1970), time has replaced space as a basis for commonality between people.

As a result of the accelerating pace of change during the last century (see Chapter 16), different age groups have come to hold distinctive outlooks toward life. Each group grows old in unique ways; each has its own values and life plans, its own sense of common membership and common goals. Social scientists refer to such self-conscious cohorts as **historical generations.** According to Robert Wohl:

> A historical generation is not defined by its chronological limits or its borders. It is not a zone of dates; nor is it an army of contemporaries making its way across a territory of time. It is more like a magnetic field at the center of which lies an experience or a series of experiences. . . . [W]hat is essential to the formation of a generational consciousness is some common frame of reference that will distinguish the members of the generation from those who follow in time. (1979:210)

With modernization, the number of these "magnetic fields" has increased—there are as many as four per century. (Judging from the number of songs from the 1960s and 1970s on the radio, college students in the 1990s still feel the magnetic influences of America's postwar baby boom generation.) Following Mannheim (1952[1926]), we believe these generational outlooks are instilled by the historical context of their entry into adulthood—when a cohort's members are "old enough to participate directly in the movements impelled by change, but not old enough to have become committed to an occupation, residence, a family procreation, a way of life" (Ryder 1965).

Demographics play a role in the development of a historical generation. Richard Easterlin (1980), for instance, shows the bearing of cohort size on personal well-being. Comparing "baby bust cohorts" (cohorts born when birthrates are low) with "baby boom cohorts" (cohorts born when birthrates are high), he argues that members of baby bust cohorts generally experience an ordered, productive, and satisfying life course, whereas members of baby boom cohorts find their life course comparatively disordered, tough, and stressful. According to Easterlin, the unique problems facing members of baby boom cohorts include the following:

> The economic fortunes of young workers are adversely affected as their numbers exceed available work roles and salaries are reduced because of surplus laborers.
>
> Young adults are hesitant to marry, unable to afford the life-style of their parents at a comparable age.
>
> High levels of marital strain; high divorce rates.
>
> High levels of psychological stress and feelings of alienation among young adults.

There are various cyclical theories concerning the appearance of different generations. One of the most recent was constructed by two baby boomers who wondered if generations like theirs had occurred before. They found four. They also detected a four-generation pattern that repeats itself over time.

According to William Strauss and Neil Howe (1991), this pattern of generations is the product of two dynamics. The first involves styles of parenting. Strauss and Howe assume that parents tend to raise their children in a way opposite to that in which they themselves were raised; nurturing styles therefore shift from relaxed and underprotective to rigid and overprotective. The second dynamic is sociohistorical. As the political pendulum oscillates between liberalism and conservatism, a cycle is created in which "secular crises" (such as the Civil War and World War II) are followed by "spiritual awakenings" (e.g., the Puritans in the seventeenth century, the transcendentalists in the nineteenth, and the consciousness-raising movement of the late 1960s and early

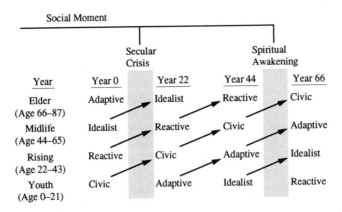

A dominant, inner-fixated *idealist generation* grows up as increasingly indulged youths after a secular crisis; comes of age inspiring a spiritual awakening; fragments into narcissistic rising adults; cultivates principle as moralistic midlifers; and emerges as visionary elders guiding the next secular crisis.

A recessive *reactive generation* grows up as underprotected and criticized youths during a spiritual awakening; matures into risk-taking, alienated rising adults; mellows into pragmatic midlife leaders during a secular crisis; and maintains respect (but less influence) as reclusive elders.

A dominant, outer-fixated *civic generation* grows up as increasingly protected youths after a spiritual awakening; comes of age overcoming a secular crisis; unites into a heroic and achieving cadre of rising adults; sustains that image while building institutions as powerful midlifers; and emerges as busy elders attacked by the next spiritual awakening.

A recessive *adaptive generation* grows up as overprotected and suffocated youths during a secular crisis; matures into risk-averse, conformist rising adults; produces indecisive midlife arbitrator-leaders during a spiritual awakening; and maintains influence (but less respect) as sensitive elders.

**FIGURE 8.2 Strauss and Howe's Cycle of Generations**
Source: Strauss and Howe, 1991, pp. 74, 75.

1970s). From a combination of these two trends, "adaptive," "idealist," "reactive," and "civil" generational types arise. (See Figure 8.2.)

Such broad theories are, of course subject to a host of criticisms. Undoubtedly variations exist across social classes, ethnicities, and geographic regions. Nevertheless, Strauss and Howe have provided an imaginative integration of life cycle, generational, and historical processes.

# CONCLUSION

In the preceding chapter we saw that self and society are inseparable and that personal order depends on individuals' sense of social order and vice versa. In this chapter we considered the interactions between self and society across the lifespan and in relation to social history. In the trajectory from birth to death profound interplays occur among biological, psychological, and sociological processes; these suggest that self-systems are best understood as dynamic systems rather than as relatively unchanging structures. This is not to deny that selves seek some consistency through time and across social encounters. We reflect on our life stories as if they were continuously unfolding, coherent biographies, not a series of discrete, unrelated episodes.

In the chapters that follow, we will focus on the specific social contexts in which selves are molded, altered, and reaffirmed. We will study the ways in which they become linked with other selves and how, through their interactions, new social orders arise.

# REFERENCES

Alper, Joseph. 1985, March. The roots of morality. *Science 85*, pp. 70–76.

Ariès, Philippe. 1974. *Western attitudes toward death.* Baltimore: Johns Hopkins University Press.

Ariès, Philippe. 1962. *Centuries of childhood: A social history of family life* (trans. Robert Baldick). New York: Vintage.

Baumeister, Roy. 1986. *Identity: Cultural change and the struggle for self.* New York: Oxford University Press.

Berger, Peter, Brigitte Berger, and Hansfried Kellner. 1973. *The homeless mind: Modernization and consciousness.* New York: Random House.

Berger, Peter, and Thomas Luckmann. 1966. *The social construction of reality.* New York: Doubleday.

Brim, Orville G., Jr. 1966. Socialization through the life cycle. In Orville Brim and Stanton Wheeler, *Socialization after childhood: Two essays.* New York: Wiley.

Butler, Robert. 1975. *Why survive? Being old in America.* New York: HarperCollins.

Butler, Robert, and Myrna Lewis. 1981. *Aging and mental health: Positive psychosocial and biomedical approaches.* St. Louis, MO: C. V. Mosby.

Callahan, Daniel. 1987. *Setting limits: Medical goals in an aging society.* New York: Simon and Schuster.

Chudacoff, Howard P. 1989. *How old are you? Age consciousness in American culture.* Princeton, NJ: Princeton University Press.

Douglas, Mary. 1988. *How institutions think.* Syracuse, NY: Syracuse University Press.

Douglas, Mary. 1966. *Purity and danger: An analysis of concepts of pollution and taboo.* London: Routledge and Kegan Paul.

Easterlin, Richard A. 1980. *Birth and fortune: The impact of numbers on personal welfare.* New York: Basic Books.

Eisenstadt, S. N. 1956. *From generation to generation.* New York: Free Press.

Elder, Glen. 1974. *Children of the Great Depression: Social change in life experience.* Chicago: University of Chicago Press.

Elder, Glen. 1985, September. Life course analysis in the 1980s: Some trends and reflections. Paper presented at the Conference on Trends in Sociology, sponsored by the Committee on Scholarly Communication with the People's Republic of China, National Academy of Sciences, Airlie House, Washington, DC, pp. 23–25.

Erikson, Erik. 1982. *The life-cycle completed: A review.* New York: Norton.

Erikson, Erik. 1975. *Life history and the historical moment.* New York: Norton.

Erikson, Erik. 1969. *Gandhi's truth: On the origins of militant nonviolence.* New York: Norton.

Erikson, Erik. 1964. *Insight and responsibility.* New York: Norton.

Erikson, Erik. 1956. The problem of ego identity. *Journal of the American Psychoanalytic Association* 4:56–121.

Erikson, Erik. 1950. Growth and crises of the healthy personality. In M. J. E. Senn (ed.), *Symposium on the healthy personality, supplement II.* New York: Josiah Macy Jr. Foundation. Reprinted in Erik Erikson, *Psychological issues: Identity and the life cycle.*

*Frontline.* 1989, June 27. American game, Japanese rules. PBS.

Glaser, B., and A. Strauss. 1971. *Status passage.* Chicago: Aldine Atherton.

Glaser, B., and A. Straus. 1965. Temporal aspects of dying as a non-scheduled status passage. *American Journal of Sociology* 71:48–59.

Goleman, Daniel. 1988, June 14. Erikson, in his own old age, expands his view of life. *New York Times,* pp. 13, 16.

Gordon, Chad. 1976. Development of evaluated role identities. *Annual Review of Sociology,* vol. 2, pp. 405–433.

Gordon, Chad. 1972. Role and value development across the life cycle. In John A. Jackson (ed.), *Sociological studies IV: Role.* London: Cambridge University Press.

Hareven, Tamara. 1980. Life course: Integrative theories and exemplary populations. In Kurt Back (ed.), *AAAS selected symposium 41.* Boulder, CO: Westview Press.

Hareven, Tamara. 1976, Fall. The last stage: Historical adulthood and old age. *Daedalus,* pp. 13–27.

Harris, Louis. 1975. *The myth and reality of aging in America.* Washington, DC: National Council on the Aging.

Hochschild, Arlie. 1973. *The unexpected community.* Englewood Cliffs, NJ: Prentice-Hall.

Hogan, Dennis. 1988. Review of Sorensen et al. (eds.) 1986. Human development and the life course: Multidisciplinary perspectives. *Contemporary Sociology* 17:694–695.

Jacques, E. 1965. Death of the mid-life crisis. *International Journal of Psychoanalysis* 46:502–514.

Kakutani, Michiko. 1985, November 30. Review of Ronald Blythe's *The visitors. New York Times,* p. 15.

Kallen, David J. 1963. Inner direction, other direction, and social integration setting. *Human Relations* 16:75–87.

Kearl, Michael. 1985. The aged as pioneers in time: On temporal discontinuities, biographical closure, and the medicalization of old age. In Charles Gaitz, George Niederehe, and Nancy Wilson (eds.), *Aging 2000: Our health care destiny,* vol. II: *Psychosocial and policy issues.* New York: Springer-Verlag.

Kearl, Michael. 1980. Time, identity, and the spiritual needs of the elderly. *Sociological Analysis* 41:172–180.

Krauthammer, Charles. 1983, August 15. Deep down, we're alike, right? Wrong. *Time,* pp. 30–32.

Laing, R. D. 1967. *The politics of experience.* New York: Ballantine.

Levinson, D., C. Darrow, E. Klein, M. Levinson, and B. McKee. 1978. *The seasons of a man's life.* New York: Ballantine.

Lifton, Robert J. 1970. *History and human survival.* New York: Random House.

MacKay, Robert. 1973. Conceptions of children and models of socialization. In Hans Peter Dreitzel (ed.), *Recent sociology no. 5: Childhood and socialization.* New York: Macmillan.

Mannheim, K. 1952[1926]. The problem of generation. In P. Kecskemeti (ed. & trans.), *Essays on the sociology of knowledge.* London: Routledge and Kegan Paul.

Merton, Robert K. 1957. *Social theory and social structure.* New York: Free Press.

Mills, C. Wright. 1959. *The sociological imagination.* New York: Oxford University Press.

Moore, Wilbert E. 1963. *Man, time and society.* New York: Wiley.

Naroll, Raul. 1983. *The moral order: An introduction to the human situation.* Newbury Park, CA: Sage.

Neugarten, Bernice, Joan W. Moore, and John C. Lowe. 1965. Age norms, age constraints and adult socialization. *American Journal of Sociology.* 70(6):710–717.

Postman, Neil. 1982. *The disappearance of childhood.* New York: Delacorte Press.

Riesman, David. 1950. *The lonely crowd: A study of the changing American character.* New Haven, CT: Yale University Press.

Riesman, David, and Daniel Lerner. 1965. Self and society: Reflections on some Turks in transition. In David Riesman, *Abundance for what? and other essays.* New York: Anchor.

Riley, Matilda. 1977. Age strata in social systems. In R. H. Binstock and E. Shanas (eds.), *Handbook of aging and the social sciences.* New York: Van Nostrand Reinhold.

Riley, Matilda. 1971. Social gerontology and the age stratification of society. *Gerontologist* 11(1, Part 1):79–87.

Riley, Matilda, Margaret Johnson, and Ann Foner. 1972. Elements in a model of age stratification. In M. Riley, M. Johnson, and A. Foner (eds.), *Aging and society,* vol. 3: *A sociology of age stratification.* New York: Russell Sage.

Rosen, Lawrence. 1984. *Bargaining for reality: The construction of social relations in a Muslim community.* Chicago: University of Chicago Press.

Rosenberg, Morris. 1979. *Conceiving the self.* New York: Basic Books.

Ryder, N. 1965. The cohort as a concept in the study of social change. *American Sociological Review* 30:843–861.

*San Antonio Express-News.* 1987, February 22. Teen dad needn't pay support yet, p. 7A.

Schmidt, Fred. 1989, January 8. Old-timers are really fittest members of human society. *San Antonio Express-News,* p. 4-M.

Schmitt, Raymond, and Wilbert Leonard II. 1986. Immortalizing the self through sport. *American Journal of Sociology* 91:1088–1111.

Sheehy, Gail. 1974. *Passages: Predictable crises of adult life.* New York: E. P. Dutton.

Smith, Brewster. 1977. A dialectical social psychology? Comments on a symposium. *Personality and Social Psychology Bulletin* 3:719–724.

Stannard, David. 1977. *The Puritan way of death. A study in religion, culture, and social change.* New York: Oxford University Press.

Strauss, William, and Neil Howe. 1991. *Generations: The history of America's future, 1584 to 2069.* New York: William Morrow.

Susman, Warren I. 1985. *Culture as history.* New York: Pantheon.

Töennies, Ferdinand. 1963[1887]. *Community and society.* New York: HarperCollins.

Toffler, Alvin. 1970. *Future shock.* New York: Random House.

Torgovnick, Marianna. 1990. *Gone primitive: Savage intellects, modern lives.* Chicago: University of Chicago Press.

van Gennep, Arnold. 1960[1908]. *The rites of passage* (trans. M. Vizedom and G. Caffee). Chicago: University of Chicago Press.

Wohl, Robert. 1979. *The generation of 1914.* Cambridge, MA: Harvard University Press.

# PART FOUR

# *Negotiating Reality with Others*

Now that we have explored the concept of the self and its thorough dependency on social encounters, the stage is set for a discussion of social interaction. In this section we explore how new levels of reality emerge from the interaction of different selves. This new reality is governed by dynamics whose principles cannot be reduced to biological or psychological sources. When individuals' interactions become routinized and patterned, there arise group processes, organizational structures, institutional realms of religion and work—indeed, an entire sociocultural order. Often the workings of these social systems are independent of their members' intentions and contrary to their desires.

The social order is considerably more than the sum of its parts. The academic disciplines of sociology and anthropology, in fact, are predicated on the assumption that this realm of the human condition cannot be theoretically reduced to genes or to the individual psychological characteristics. Instead, such processes as conformity and intergroup conflict derive from the dynamics of this realm of reality, shaping the templates of consciousness and self-conception. The irony is that even though this reality is created by human actors, it comes to be perceived by those actors as a force external to themselves.

# 9

# Interaction between Self and Others

After an elegant dinner that capped a long day of interviewing, the wife of the job candidate kissed the company's managing director on the lips. She thought the gesture would contribute to her husband's good impression. The director thought it inappropriate and began to wonder whether the applicant had put her up to it. With the director obviously taken aback by the kiss, the wife suddenly realized that corporate etiquette in New York City was not the same as the norms of behavior in her Kansas country club. She began to blush, and for the first time she realized how out of place she had been all evening.

The meaning of the wife's nonverbal communication in this incident was shaped by the setting, the identities of the participants and their relative social status, and the participants' understanding of their relationships with one another. To complicate matters further, with the blurring of social and business etiquette, corporate kissing is reportedly becoming more frequent (Hughes 1988). But many people witnessing this trend feel awkward and confused. Who kisses whom, and when and how? If the wife had been interviewing and the managing director had been female, would it have been more or less appropriate for the husband to kiss his wife's potential boss on the cheek?

As this example shows, **social order** is created through human interaction. But before interaction can occur, the social game board must be negotiated so that players know which rules apply. Is the interaction to be competitive, as in a game of Monopoly, or is it to be cooperative? Social power enters into the process, since some individuals have a greater say in how the situation is to be defined, as when an older brother determines the nature of play with his younger siblings. Once the rules have been agreed on, the players assume their roles and the game unfolds.

Normally all of this occurs quite naturally, almost automatically. But when it doesn't—for example, when dealing with strangers in novel settings—the social order becomes visible and social actors become conscious of the social frameworks structuring their interactions with others. This chapter focuses on some of the dynamics that come into play when individuals interact with one another.

# The Moral Templates of Action

> The real rule guiding human behavior is this: "What everyone else does, what appears as norm of general conduct, this is right, moral and proper. Let me look over the fence and see what my neighbour does, and take it as a rule for my behavior." . . . And the lower [the average member's] level of cultural development, the greater stickler he will be for good manners, propriety, and form, and the more odious to him will be the non-conforming point of view.—Malinowski (1922: 326–327)

For 99 percent of human history, people have lived in small groups as hunters and gatherers. The social routines that ensured survival were handed down from generation to generation. Over time, these routines crystallized into specific rules of behavior called **norms,** which are recipes for negotiating reality with family members and members of one's community and with strangers— they organize social behavior the way genes organize physiological processes. Taken together, these routines are the social DNA that we inherit; they make up the **normative order** of a culture.

The ability of norms to control behavior derives not only from their specifications of action but also from the sense of their being right or proper. This sense of correctness derives from **values,** the shared ideas that justify norms. Together, these values comprise a culture's **moral order.** From the perspective of social actors, morality is an external force that is experienced physically. It is the source of the boiling outrage one feels when witnessing an adult brutally beating a helpless child or the emotional distress felt when one does something one shouldn't do. Moralities are what commit us to others, entailing an unwritten social contract among all interacting individuals. This contract specifies the basic considerations that must be accorded to others, such as shaking another person's hand or in other ways giving social approval upon first meeting. This contract also defines the appropriate degree of attachment and emotional feeling one is to have to whatever reality emerges out of one's encounters with others.

Morality is both an inhibitor and a stimulator of action. Morality checks the impulses to behave in ways that are not considered right and serves as a stimulus to behave in ways that are approved; it determines both the goals of one's actions and the means by which they are to be achieved. Accordingly, changes in values invariably are accompanied by changes in norms.

With these matters of morality in mind, we turn to three broad traditions by which interacting selves have been conceptualized.

# SOCIAL INTERACTION AS NEGOTIATED REALITY

> If men define situations as real, they are real in their consequences.—W. I. Thomas

Society can be envisioned as a collection of stages on which individuals act out various roles in their quest for social approval. These stages are totally arbitrary, as are the scripts that are acted out on them. College freshmen, for instance, may view college as an arena for intellectual, career-launching, social,

## Defining Situations of Self Sacrifice and Death

Of all the situations that society must create, perhaps that in which it calls on its members to give up their lives is the most challenging. Eric Hoffer describes how in preparing for war a new reality system is created, one with a highly theatrical quality:

> Dying and killing seem easy when they are part of a ritual, ceremonial, dramatic performance or game. There is need for some kind of make-believe in order to face death unflinchingly. To our real, naked selves there is not a thing on earth or in heaven worth dying for. It is only when we see ourselves as actors in a staged (and therefore unreal) performance that death loses its frightfulness and finality and becomes an act of make-believe and a theatrical gesture. . . . Uniforms, flags, emblems, parades, music and elaborate etiquette and ritual are designed to separate the soldier from his flesh-and-blood self and mask the overwhelming reality of life and death. (Hoffer 1951: 64–65)

or athletic pursuits. Each of these definitions of the situation carries with it implied role definitions: Being "successful" in an intellectual context may mean understanding the connections between nineteenth-century European culture and social structure and the appearance of impressionism in art and literature; being "successful" in a social context may mean having many good friends or sexual liaisons. Thus, each definition of the situation carries definitions for the self, which, in turn, carry criteria for personal behavior and role judgments (e.g., grade point average, athletic statistics, the number of invitations to parties).

But are individuals simply puppets of social situations, assuming predetermined roles, being guided by internalized norms and goals, and conforming to the expectations of others in attempting to obtain a positive self-image? To what extent are these social situations, themselves, predetermined? What happens when different individuals come to a setting with differing definitions?

Such difficulties in defining situations are evident when examining the pattern of play of 5-year-olds, who are shifting from "parallel play" to interactive play. Often the children spend considerable time arguing about what the play should be, how the game is to be defined ("No, let's pretend we . . . "), and who is to play what role ("You're always the good guy. It's your turn to be the alien!") Or consider the possible confusion of definitions when a college class is held outdoors, when one finds oneself bowling with one's pastor, or when a young professor joins a student party.

In a classic article, Joan Emerson (1970) describes the risk of conflicting definitions of the situation when a woman is examined by a male gynecologist. The procedure runs the risk of being interpreted in romantic, as opposed to medical, terms, since in American society people do not normally submit to the touching of their private parts by a member of the opposite sex unless the relationship is sexual. To ensure that such confusion does not occur, the setting is medicalized. Instead of soft lighting and background music, there are scientific props: The sterile examining-room walls are adorned only with the medical degrees of the practitioner, which serve to legitimate his actions. And instead of referring to body parts in everyday parlance, the physician utilizes medical labels. The female nurse acts as referee to guarantee that no deviation from the official definition of the situation occurs.

Only when the definition of the situation is mutually agreed on can role acting begin. And this, notes Peter McHugh, "is possible only when physical space and chronological time are transformed into social space and time. . . . Failure of definition will cause failure in interaction" (1968:3). How, then, are such shared definitions derived?

## Assumptions of Standardized Social Settings and Roles

In many ways, humans are creatures of habit. Unlike those of most species, the habits of humans are socially constructed and are learned through social routines. "We live in a world," observes Henley, "that tells us what to do—moves us through it in preordained fashion, tells us what to think of others and ourselves, and indicates how to act in each setting" (1977:55). So thorough is our social programming that familiar situations trigger ingrained behavior patterns, such as stopping at a red light or shaking a hand that is extended toward us.

The familiar situations that activate such automatic behavior are recognized in terms of their meanings. Actors assume that there is a meaning system underlying each situation and that it will become evident over the course of interaction (McHugh 1968:37). Sometimes there exist props to reinforce a particular meaning. We assume, for instance, that a space with stained-glass windows depicting Biblical stories and a crucifix on the wall behind a pulpit will not house slot machines or bowling lanes, nor is it a place where off-color jokes are appropriate.

Randall Collins (1986) claims that there are but three basic types of situations that determine individuals' interaction strategies: work/practical, ceremonial, and social situations. These have been described by Jonathan Turner as follows:

> Work/practical situations involve the expenditure of conversational energy and capital to establish one's place in the group and its authority hierarchy, division of labor, and ranking system. Ceremonial situations revolve around the deployment of conversational energy and capital to emit appropriate rituals that can increase one's sense of group involvement and membership. And social situations evidence the use of resources to enhance standing in groups, to promote authority as well as prestige, and to secure favorable coalitions. (1988:52)

For each of these basic situations there are corresponding roles. These roles carry behavioral scripts for interacting with different types of others (See Table 9.1). Young children beginning school, for instance, learn that familial roles and relations are inappropriate in this new setting. And even though a child may slip and call the teacher "Mom," he or she clearly understands that the teacher has a different kind of authority and a different kind of relationship with children. As time passes, children learn that there are different types of students ("teacher's pet," "good students," "bad students," etc.) and different ways of playing the student role. They also learn that others are to be acted

**TABLE 9.1   Influence of Situations on Behavior toward Others**

| | Type of Situation | | |
| | Work/Practical | Ceremonial | Social |
|---|---|---|---|
| Categories | Others as functionaries whose behaviors are relevant to achieving a specific task or goal and who, for the purposes at hand, can be treated as strangers | Others as representatives of a larger collective enterprise toward whom highly stylized responses are owed as a means of expressing their joint activity | Others as strangers toward whom superficially informal, polite, and responsive gestures are owed. |
| Persons | Others as functionaries whose behaviors are relevant to achieving a specific task or goal but who, at the same time, must be treated as unique individuals in their own right | Others as fellow participants of a larger collective enterprise toward whom stylized responses are owed as a means of expressing their joint activity and recognition of each other as individuals in their own right | Others as familiar individuals toward whom informal, polite, and responsive gestures are owed |
| Intimates | Others as close friends whose behaviors are relevant to achieving a specific task or goal and toward whom emotional responsiveness is owed | Others as close friends who are fellow participants in a collective enterprise and toward whom a combination of stylized and personalized responses are owed as a means of expressing their joint activity and sense of mutual understanding | Others as close friends toward whom informal and emotionally responsive gestures are owed |

Source: Turner, 1988:154.

toward only in terms of the roles they occupy and not as whole persons with whom are shared facets of one's own self outside the purview of one's own role.

If the assumed existence of such basic situations is so crucial in the maintenance of social order, what happens when their unspoken routines are violated? To investigate, Garfinkel (1967) employed a set of creative strategies; his students assumed the role of boarders with their families, or handed out money to strangers on city streets. These behaviors produced dramatic results: The parents of "boarders," for instance, employed a variety of strategies to get their children back into their normal role and to restore the definition of the situation to one in which they interacted as family members: "Did you have a bad day at school?" "Are you on drugs or something?" "Don't be silly. Come down and help me with dishes." Unless their children returned to their roles as sons and daughters, the parents could not play their parental roles and the entire family order was threatened with collapse. In sum, despite their taken-for-granted quality, social assumptions turn out to be quite frail and people go to considerable lengths to maintain them.

# Emergent Definitions of Situations

Mead observed that it is the ability to define situations from the standpoint of others that makes a shared reality possible (1934:152–164). But how does this occur? We know that situations are understood in terms of types, such as work, a class session, family, leisure, or "good times" and bad. Moreover, we know that there are types-of-others whose standpoint in a particular situation must be understood if interaction is to be possible, since all roles are reciprocally related. "Each individual aligns his action to the actions of others by ascertaining what they are doing or what they intend to do—that is, by getting the meaning of their acts" (Blumer 1962:184). This meaning turns out to be highly contextual.

Harold Garfinkel (1967) observes that the relationship between setting and meaning is **reflexive:** Every act is at once both in a setting and at the same time creates the setting in which it appears and from which it derives its meaning. For instance, in Chapter 5 we saw how people carry out a conversational calculus that specifies what kinds of things to say, in what message forms, to what kind of people, and in what kinds of situations. Depending on one's decisions for each of these phases of encoding, and on how others decipher one's message, a definition of the situation emerges. Concurrently, individuals are held accountable for orienting their actions toward this definition.

In addition to being reflexive, action is also **indexical,** conveying far more information than surface appearances would suggest. Each act is understood to be indexing or referencing some broad underlying theme, which, in turn, underlies a host of other acts and gives a unifying meaning to them all (Shearing 1973). For instance, in recent decades it has become easier to unintentionally insult another: A man may receive an ugly stare from a woman as he opens the door for her; a scout who offers to help an old woman across the street may be icily told, "I can get along just fine, thank you." Traditional courtesies are often interpreted as sexist, racist, or ageist.

# Emergent Social Roles

Assuming that a situation's definition is mutually agreed on, it is tempting to conceptualize interaction as people acting out the prescribed scripts associated with a situation's built-in roles. Such a viewpoint, however, misses several important dynamics. How, for instance, are roles even allocated? And where do these supposedly prescribed scripts come from?

The roles available for any individual are not infinite. Instead, they are determined by his or her position in the **status order.** Status is a structural concept; it involves the rights and duties associated with a particular niche in the stratification hierarchy (Linton 1936). A role consists of the activities normatively expected of one in a given status position (Goffman 1961:85).

Sometimes statuses can be clearly defined but their associated roles are not, such as being an emeritus professor or the recipient of an honorary degree. Sometimes it is the role that is clear but the status that is vague, such as being a rebel or the class cutup (Rosow 1976:462–469). Indeed, the normative guidelines even for such institutionalized roles as those of family members, where both status and role are supposedly clearly defined, are far from complete. For instance, in dealing with the woman who lives with me and calls herself my wife, I am forced to assume the role that she sees me playing, namely, that of her husband. Now most husbands and wives have not read manuals on how to play their spousal roles. They undoubtedly have *role models,* such as their parents or the Cleavers on television, who provide some clues to what husbands and wives do. However, novel situations may emerge that were not encountered by earlier generations of spouses (such as commuter marriages, being a "war bride," or a "mail order bride" in the Old West). So how does one play the role if there is no script?

Although it seems to us that we are stepping into preexistent roles, we are in fact creating the roles we play. For instance, when one assumes the role of college student, one does not receive extensive instruction how to perform that role. Instead, one rehearses the role in one's mind and does what one thinks college students do. On the bases of self and feedback from others, one adjusts one's behavior. Inevitably novel situations arise, forcing one to improvise and redefine one's roles. This indeterminate nature of roles has led some researchers to focus not on roles but rather on the underlying rules in order to better understand social interaction.

## Emergent Rules and Their Internalization

Underlying the definitions of situations are rules that govern events and determine how they are experienced. These rules emerge in the course of social encounters, controlling affect, determining what should be attended to and what is irrelevant, and shaping the structure of action.

People act as if they were applying general rules to specific situations. But reality is a little more complicated than that. In law, for instance, cases are argued partly on the basis of precedent, whereby unique events are captured and transformed into types of situations for which there exist types of rules. Categorizations are constructed, not automatic. Thus, to otherwise portray social behavior as merely conforming to rules is to ignore the contextual features of the situation and the involvement of actors in deciphering those features.

Studies of jurors who unanimously distinguish between first- and second-degree murder, and of data coders who reliably match events with pre-established categories, demonstrate that rules alone cannot explain the convergences observed. Rules are too general to be applicable to unique situations, and actors never apply them directly; instead, they employ them to orient themselves (Garfinkel 1967). As Cicourel explains:

> The rule provides the actor with a basis for rejecting or reducing a range of possible meanings to a collapsed typification of the social structures. The rule instructs the actor to reject or recognize particular instances as acceptable representations of a more general normative set. (1970:35)

Thus decisions are made not by selecting among a set of possibilities but by acting in what appears to be a rational manner. There are also decision-making rules by which one justifies one's actions and in the course of making justifications one often "discovers" the rules governing a situation.

## Case Study: Norms of Grocery Shopping

As mundane as the activity may seem, shopping in a supermarket serves to illustrate the processes involved in arriving at a definition of the situation. There is a customer role to be played in grocery stores. There generally is a standard of orderliness. Shoppers are not seen pushing each other out of the way, picking things out of each other's shopping carts, or sitting on the floor eating from a recently opened can. How does one "know" how the role of customer is to be played? Aside from the "No Shirt, No Bare Feet" sign on the door and the "You Must Be At Least 21 To Purchase . . .". sign by the cash register, there is no clear listing of shopping rules.

Evidence of the implied existence of such rules can be found in the way people react to a fellow shopper dressed in a gorilla suit or to someone who violates the norms for waiting in line at the checkout counter. One may feel that rules are being broken when one finds oneself standing in line with melting ice cream behind a grandmother who takes out her grandchildren's photographs to show to the clerk. Such behavior violates the norms of universalism (all customers are to be treated equally) and efficiency; the grocery store is not a context in which one shares one's private self with others, particularly anonymous others.

Commitment to a rule entails commitment to a sense of order and a sense of self. Judicial rules and procedures, for instance, "invite the juror to see himself as a person who can act in accordance with the official line" (Garfinkel 1967:111) and to perceive situational definitions without recourse to "habitual rules of social judgments" (p. 112) "A person is 95 percent juror before he comes near the court" (p. 110).

***Rules of Conduct.*** A special class of rules consists of rules governing conduct. These are behavioral guides that are culturally recommended not because they are efficient but because they are suitable or just. In Japan, for instance, rules of courtesy are deeply ingrained. Good manners lubricate interaction at all levels of Japanese society. Columnists John A. Cicco, Jr., and Richard D. Snyder observe that courtesy may be "the most subtle, but most powerful, weapon in Japan's management arsenal" and that

> even the most senior executive, phoning an associate, will patiently spend several minutes asking how he is, how the family is, or how his back feels before dealing with whatever business reason may have prompted the call—regardless of its seeming urgency. As the Japanese explain it, whatever the problem may be, it's the relationship with the other person that will be the basis of its solution. So the relationship, not the problem, deserves primary attention. (1985)

Besides being behavior guides, these rules of conduct also govern the standards by which others make appraisals of the actions of a social performer. As we argued in Chapter 7, the self is primarily engaged in seeking esteem in social encounters, trying to promote and sustain internal self-con-

## Defining and Managing Sexual Harassment

In late 1990 the Associated Press (AP) ran a story about the new sexual harassment code at Amherst-Pelham Regional High School in Massachusetts. "High-schoolers who beam sexually charged stares at their classmates or exchange snippets of intimate gossip in the halls could run afoul of new guidelines designed to curb sexual harassment among students," AP asserted. What follows is one journalist's reflections on the story and its implications.

I telephoned the superintendent of schools, Gus Sayer. Is there a serious harassment problem at the school? No, he said, we just thought these rules were a good idea. How much gazing or leering would it take to be brought up on sexual-harassment charges? There is no time limit, he said; a single stare might do it. And what if a friend told a friend, " I think Marcie and Allen have something going"? "That would qualify as sexual harassment," he replied.

This expansive view of harassment is in the air these days. Driven by feminist ideology, we have constantly extended the definition of what constitutes illicit male behavior. . . . In Swarthmore College's rape-prevention program, "inappropriate innuendo" is actually regarded as an example of acquaintance rape. At the University of Michigan, sexual-harassment charges were filed against a male student who slipped the following joke under the door of a female student: Q. How many men does it take to mop a floor? A. None, it's a woman's job.

A small irony [of the Amherst-Pelham code] is that gossip is the primary means by which an informal social group, such as a class or a student body, creates and maintains norms. Beneath the titillation of gossip, approval and disapproval are constantly being doled out, and behavior is being modified. A male who treats females badly is far more likely to be brought into line by peer-group gossip than by a huffy administration imposing rules from above.

There is another ominous aspect to the Amherst rules. In listing "the spreading of sex gossip" as a school offense, they impose, rather casually, what is apparently the first speech code at an American high school. . . .

[At American colleges] the new speech police have successfully imposed codes to defend the sensibilities of sexual, racial and ethnic groups. The mopping joke was a violation of the University of Michigan code, which, by the way, has since been found unconstitutional. But many other colleges have installed these dubious programs.

Source: Leo, 1990.

ceptions that are as favorable as possible in terms of the given situation. Each situation features ritual ways different selves are to be presented. If people ritually acknowledge that they understand the definition of a situation and know their place within it (e.g., by giving deference to higher-status others or by not acting like those of lesser status), their credibility as social members will be acknowledged.

It is individuals' attachments to these rules that creates constancy in the patterning of behavior. These rules are, according to Goffman (1956), of two kinds: *substantive* (or instrumental, like law, morality, and ethics) and *ceremonial* (or expressive, like etiquette). Ceremonial messages may be linguistic (labels, intonation), gestural (physical deportment—insolent or obsequious), spatial (e.g., who goes through a doorway first), or part of the communication structure (who speaks most receives the most attention?) Ceremonial rules of conduct are experienced either as **obligations,** which can be met without much feeling, or **expectations,** that can be pleasant (these are known as privileges, or rights) or unpleasant (e.g., necessary evils). These obligations and expectations can be symmetrical, as is the case of common courtesies, or asymmetrical when people of unequal status interact, as when jurors and lawyers stand for the arrival of the judge.

When individuals become involved in the maintenance of a rule, they tend also to become committed to a particular self, and the way they are treated by others will express their conception of that self. "In establishing himself as the sort of person who treats others in a particular way and is treated by them in a particular way, he must make sure that it will be possible for him to act and be this kind of person" (Goffman 1956:475).

***Deference and Demeanor.*** In social action, one does not participate as a total person but, rather, in terms of one's special capacity or one's status. The lower one's status, for instance, the greater the expectation that one will act with circumspection. The pecking order must be continually reaffirmed; otherwise the entire agreed-upon social order comes into doubt. By examining the ceremonial rules of deference and demeanor we can see how both the self and the status order of a situation are ritually acknowledged.

**Deference** is the symbolic means by which appreciation is regularly conveyed by subordinates to superiors, for example, as when English prep school students stand for the entry of their instructor and collectively say "Good morning." Through such rituals actors confirm their relationships with the recipient of their deference.

Goffman (1956) detected two broad types of deference rituals: avoidance and presentational. Avoidance rituals involve ceremonial distance; examples may be found in traditional Indian cultures in which extensive and elaborate taboos forbid contact with members of lower castes. We avoid persons of higher status out of concern for self-protection. Avoidance rituals also give the higher-status individual room to maneuver, enabling him or her to present only a self that is worthy of deference. At the same time, avoidance makes it easier for lower-status individuals to assure themselves that the deference they have shown is warranted.

Presentational rituals involve the messages subordinates must give concerning how they regard their superiors and how they will treat them in forthcoming interactions. These include salutations, invitations, compliments, and minor services for others. The rules regarding these presentational rituals involve prescriptions, not proscriptions, as is the case with avoidance rituals.

Displays of deference by subordinates are reciprocated in the demeanor of superiors. This form of ceremonial behavior is conveyed through dress and bearing. The well-demeaned individual is a good sport, has a good command of speech and behavior, exercises control over emotions and habits, and *controls the information that others can have about him or her.* Through their demeanor, superiors create an image that justifies and compensates for the deference

## Case Study: The Use of First Names

In the late 1880s any form of familiarity between individuals on the first few encounters was considered bad style. Observed Jane Aster (1881), "Familiarity arises either from an extreme excess of friendliness or a deficiency of respect. The latter is never pardonable"; it gives an impression of imprudence and impropriety.

In the 1920s and 1930s in so-called "smart circles," people called each other by their first names much earlier in their acquaintance than did people in other walks of life ("Next door neighbors often addressed each other as Mr. and Mrs. all their lives" [Wilson 1937:277].) If one had been accepted whole-heartedly into a group whose members called each other by their first names, after a certain point it would be too conspicuous to continue to call them by their last names. But how could one know when that point had been reached? The solution was to wait until someone from the group had referred to one informally (Wilson 1937:276–280).

By the 1950s and 1960s the use of first names was so widely accepted that even recently introduced strangers readily employed first names. The only exceptions in etiquette rules were for one's superiors in business, older persons, individuals of high status (Post 1969), and business dealings with customers and clients. During the 1980s, however, as illustrated in the editorial below, even these exceptions were evaporating.

#### I'm Mr. Jones To You

The note to my husband attached to the mortgage form said "Ralph, please review the. . . ." There it was again—a first name being used by an utter stranger. A month before, a bank employee nearly half my age, who had never before seen my face, peered over my application for a certificate of deposit and quietly cooed, "Now, Jill, let me explain how this works."

After several years of this first-name nonsense, my cool collapsed. "I don't believe I have invited you to use my first name. I am Dr. or Mrs. to you." She blanched. . . .

Why am I distressed at the use of first names? Their use, after all, is a sign of acquaintance, informality and warmth. . . . In dealing with one another, we need cues to signal behavior. The nonsense about the bank teller or the dental technician using first names lies in the false premise that an acquaintance or stranger is in an informal or caring relationship. They are not. . . . Why this has occurred among paraprofessionals and clerks is an interesting question and one that has to do with the larger issue of relationships in such situations—power relationships.

Women have long known about the use of first names as an expression of power relations. Every visit to a gynecologist was an experience in first name nonsense. He called out "Sheila," "Donna," or "Sue" while you properly responded "Doctor"— as did his nurse and secretary. His was a position of knowledge and, therefore, authority.

In an era of mass society and anonymity, the business community attempts to stroke and manipulate us with feigned friendliness.

Source: Norgren, 1986.

that subordinates are obliged to express toward them. Like rules of deference, rules of demeanor can be either symmetrical or asymmetrical.

In sum, the rules of conduct that tie actors and recipients together are the bonds of society. The rules of deference and demeanor are complementary, ritually lubricating encounters between people of unequal status so that interaction can progress.

***The Significance of Motives.*** Over the Thanksgiving dinner table a respected grandparent directs your way the anticipated question: "So what courses are you taking this semester?" Upon detailing your class schedule you leave yourself open to the follow-up query: "I thought you were majoring in engineering. Why are you taking a course in social psychology?" Since those gathered are perhaps paying a sizable chunk of your bills, a reply like "It was the only course open at 2:30 P.M. and I try to avoid the morning classes" would probably not go over well. Perhaps the course qualifies as one that satisfies a required understanding or experience in your institution's liberal arts curriculum. In this case, you may have to develop the rationale of liberal arts education and the importance of having broad experiences in the arts, humanities, and the social and natural sciences. Perhaps you believe that the course would give you a greater understanding of human nature and that possibly your future holds a managerial position where such insights could prove useful. As you develop your response, slowly a general career plan begins to unfold, producing a heightened awareness of the motives underlying your student-self and their connection with an eventual career-self.

One way to see how rules "work" in helping to define a situation is to consider the motive talk of individuals. When responding to such questions as "What are you doing?" actors attempt to make their behaviors appear meaningful. To appear meaningful, actors' explanations must acknowledge the rules of the situation and demonstrate how their behaviors are normatively appropriate (Blum and McHugh 1971:98–100). Here is where things get interesting: In giving an accounting we often discover new reasons that legitimate a particular course of action (like taking a social psychology course) and we come to influence both ourselves and others (Mills 1973 [1940]).

Observe how different this sociological approach to motives is from typical psychological depictions of motives being "subjective 'springs' of action" somehow fixed "in" a self-system (Mills 1973:439). Instead, when one imputes personal motives there occurs a balancing of self-image with the appraisals of others. By applying to oneself the motives that are appropriate in a given situation (e.g., aspiring for high grades in college), one is acknowledging one's personal acceptance of the situations' norms and rules. One is also specifying how his or her social conduct contributes to the definition of the situation and how it is integrated with the conduct of others.

In sum, sociologists view motives as ways of conceiving and justifying action. Motives are neither individual nor selfish. They are explanations in which one reaffirms group goals and acknowledges the means used to obtain them. For this reason, as Gerth and Mills (1953) argued, the availability of a suitable normative language is as much a constraint on individuals' freedom of action as more concrete forces. Further, the reasons we give for an action are among the conditions for its continued performance; by winning acceptance, motives strengthen the individual's will to act.

## Situations over Time

Once situations are defined and individuals routinely interact within them, new processes emerge. Over time, the identities and meanings of the past influence the identities and meanings of the present. Actions become less spontaneous and more routinized and ritualized. A collective memory is developed. Students enrolled in a year-long course, for instance, accumulate shared memories of classroom events. Certain role-types emerge: the class clown, the brain, the classroom leader. As the context and performances become regularized, individuals come to be viewed as "out of character or role" if their actions are not consistent with the expectations that have been developed over time. Paralleling this is the actors' recognition of their obligation to be consistent in their actions, as otherwise their social competencies become questioned or social order itself becomes threatened.

This collective memory may sometimes be employed to restore or invigorate waning group solidarity and fading definitions of the situation. When the students return for their twentieth reunion, for example, their collective history is pieced together by the group. Of the ten women who thought they had married the school's quarterback, nine find out that they did not. Precisely what happened when the earthquake hit during lunchtime is determined. Also reactivated may be the shared emotions felt during major events, such as when the *Challenger* blew up or when President John Kennedy was assassinated.

---

## SOCIAL INTERACTION AS SOCIAL EXCHANGE

"Don't you realize that he's using you?" said the concerned friend. "You've allowed an intimate relationship to develop with Bill, and I just don't see what you're getting out of it. The guy is married and there's no way he's going to leave that rich wife of his."

"It's funny that you said that," Mary replied. "Just the other day, Bill told me that his therapist told him that I was using him. There's no question that Bill opened doors for me. If it hadn't been for him, there's no way I could have gotten that job at the museum."

"Well, then I guess I don't know who is using whom."

Another way of conceptualizing social interaction is to view it as a set of exchanges. From this perspective, the focus of attention is on the benefits people receive from their encounters with others. Interactions continue because actors find themselves participating in a system of reciprocally reinforcing actions.

People enter into exchange relationships because of their desire for social rewards, such as prestige, approval, or power. The more similar a situation is to past occasions when one was reinforced with such rewards, the more likely one is to participate in it; the more often a behavior sequence was rewarded in the past, the more likely it is to be repeated (Homans 1961:33–37).

Interaction proceeds as long as all participants find it rewarding, in other words, as long as their contributions to others (their "costs") are commensurate with the benefits (the "rewards," positive reinforcements, or valued outcomes) they derive from the interaction (Blau 1964; Emerson 1981). However, as mentioned in Chapter 1, continued interaction has an inflationary quality; repeated receipt of a given benefit produces satiation and diminished utility for the recipient, leading to a desire for greater benefits from future interaction.

## Equity and Distributive Justice

In the mid-1980s a number of industries began to employ two-tier wage structures. Unions were given an unappealing choice: Either there would be layoffs or those entering the labor force would be paid less than their predecessors. In 1984, for instance, the Post Office began hiring new workers at pay levels 20 percent below the wages of previous hirees (Keller 1984). A year later, Pan Am flight attendants were hired at $784/month; the previous starting pay was $1236 (Noble 1985). What happened was predictable: recently hired workers resented their more senior colleagues. The problem was one of perceived injustice. George Homans describes the situation:

> A man in an exchange relation with another will expect the profits of each to be directly proportional to his investments, and when each is being rewarded by some third party, he will expect the third party to maintain this relation between the two of them. If the investments of two men, or two groups, are equal, their profits should be equal, and if their investments are unequal, the one with the greater investment should get the greater profit. (1961:244)

When social unequals interact, the benefits of the interaction are not equally distributed. Part of the moral equation entails conceptions of *distributive justice* and the belief that higher-status individuals deserve disproportionately more for their efforts. When individuals see others receiving more than they do even though they are perceived as social equivalents, the rules of fairness are seen to be violated and feelings of *relative deprivation* occur. These feelings, in turn, may create anger or guilt, cognitive change, or the choice of a different referent for comparison. The recently hired postal workers and flight attendants may feel resentment over being short-changed when comparing themselves with earlier generations of employees, or they may accept their fate (after all, one at least has a job in a tight economy), or use other recent hirees as their frame of reference for gauging self-worth.

The concept of relative deprivation was inspired by Robert Merton's (1968[1957]:288–304) analysis of soldiers in World War II. When interviewed upon being inducted into service, married men were more likely than their single counterparts to maintain that they should have been deferred. Comparing themselves with unmarried draftees, the married soldiers felt that they sacrificed more by entering the Army. When asked "Do you think a soldier with ability has a good chance for promotion?" soldiers in a branch of the service where rates of promotion were high, indicated less satisfaction with their perceived chances for promotion than those in branches in which promotion rates were relatively low. The researchers concluded that a high rate of promotion among soldiers in a particular branch of the service created excessively high expectations for promotion. These soldiers' rapidly advancing reference group led to personal senses of frustration and impatience at still remaining in their current ranks.

## SOCIAL INTERACTION AS STRATEGIC GAMES

Certain interactions can be likened to game playing (Goffman 1961, 1969). These "games" involve tactics by which individuals attempt to alter their social bonds (e.g., make coalitions or sever a relationship), increase their power or status (or minimize the power or status of others), and reveal (or not reveal) their true identities and intentions in a given situation.

**Information Games.** One category of strategic encounters entails those in which individuals control information about themselves (see "The Presentation of Self" below) while attempting to decipher others' controlled information about themselves.

According to Goffman (1974:7, 10–11), people employ organizing principles called "frames" (for frames of interpretation) to assess the actions of others directed toward themselves. For instance, when a person approaches you at a party and tells you that he can make you a Hollywood star, numerous calculations must be made as to whether this person can really come through. Using every possible clue—the person's appearance, behaviors toward others, ingratiation techniques, eye contact, self-serving motives, and so forth—you look for any discrepancies between claimed and actual identities to determine whether this person is really a sincere movie agent who can be trusted (frame 1) or simply some fraud with secret ulterior motives (frame 2).

To illustrate how frames play out, consider what you would do if you were a junior professor and discovered that a recently hired senior professor has a criminal record. To make matters more interesting, let's say that the professor came with some impressive credentials, which he flaunts, and that he routinely treats you as a social inferior. What would you do with this information? Would you even let the professor know that you are aware of his secret?

If you went to the professor and promised to withhold disclosure for a price—say, a glowing letter of recommendation or an opportunity to meet others in your field who are normally inaccessible—society would frame the encounter as blackmail. If you went to the president of the college, in effect exchanging the exclusive information for a possible salary increase for being a loyal and tactful worker, we would say you were being "political," or possibly a "backstabber," "tattletale," or "snitch." If you shared the information with a colleague, who told you in exchange an equally juicy story about another professor, we would call it gossip. And if you sold your story to a newspaper, we would call it journalism or whistleblowing.

Perhaps the enduring popularity of poker derives from the fact that the game captures the essence of informational strategies. Often it is to one's advantage for others not to know what one knows or how one feels. Revealing one's dislike for a colleague may have negative consequences: The person to whom you revealed your feelings may share this information with the disliked individual, who, in turn, may use it against you in some strategy to "get even"; your inability to get along with others may become common knowledge, canceling any possibility of promotion to a supervisory role. By keeping quiet, you increase your chances of bluffing others, which can be parlayed into increased status and prestige.

*Power Games.* In games of power, actors attempt to maximize their influence over others through displays of dominance or distortions of information. These "games" take a variety of forms, some of which are described below.

**Intimidation games:** To maintain their control over others, high-status persons employ a variety of tactics to either put others down or keep others in their place. In face-to-face situations, they feel free to violate subordinates' space and to behave aggressively. They often control the interaction from beginning to end, controlling both the setting (which typically takes place on their "turf") and the conversation.

**Deception games:** Often control of information is the source of power, and to enhance their power individuals will either withhold or present false information about themselves to others.

**Laying traps:** To derail attempts by others to challenge one's status or prestige, one may intentionally "set them up" for public embarrassment. When one is asked for a prized recipe, one may intentionally leave out an ingredient. To make a fellow student who gets good grades without attending class "look bad," one may not warn him about a forthcoming test.

**Backstabbing:** Individuals often stab from the back, with negative information, the reputations of others whose power they wish to see diminished. The victims are lulled into security by positive signals in face-to-face interactions. Behind their backs, the conspirators do all they can to damage their victims' credibility.

*Status Games.* Related to power games are the games by which individuals attempt either to improve their position in a status hierarchy or to reassert their superior station.

**One-upmanship:** We all know individuals who, whenever you tell them about an adventure or achievement, always counter with a tale that eclipses yours. If you climbed Mr. Rainier, they've climbed Everest; if you kayaked on the Connecticut River, they've done the white waters of the Colorado; if you received an A after studying only three hours for the test, their A was obtained without even cracking the book.

**Pulling rank:** To "pull rank" is to publicly demonstrate one's superior status and the perquisites it entails. Sometimes it may take the form of a command that a subordinate cannot make, as when a boss tells his or her secretary to make coffee. On a commercial airliner, first-class passengers pull rank by being able to get on and off the plane first. When rank is pulled, subordinates are reminded of their relatively lower status.

**Put-downs:** As a student at an isolated, all-male undergraduate institution, one author looked forward to "co-ed week," when females on spring break would visit the campus and attend classes. It was a time when machismo could be displayed and various "shows" could be put on. One ritual show involved a psychology professor who customarily saved his lecture on sexual deviance for this particular week. As his lecture became more lurid, the women's blushes became more evident.

The professor noted one young woman who seemed unaffected as she calmly listened while knitting. Frustrated, he said, "Young lady, you do know that knitting is a form of masturbation." Her response was a classic strategy for putting one in his place: "Sir, you do it your way and I'll do it mine."

**Joking:** According to a 1990 Pentagon study of sexual harassment in the military ($n = 20,249$), over one-half of females (compared to only 13 percent of males) reported being victims of denigrating teasing and jokes (Schmitt 1990).

***Expressive Games.*** Expressive games are played in order to control emotional information. They may take the form of deceptive feedback, as when one feigns enjoyment when viewing a friend's home movies or feigns boredom at the stellar performance of a rival. Instead of being fraudulent, the feedback may be simply exaggerated, as when one laughs at a superior's poor joke.

**Playing interested and intense:** As we say in our discussion of nonverbal behavior, lower-status individuals are obligated to give attention (e.g., more direct eye contact) to superiors. To signal that one is receptive to a superior's performance, one can nod or tilt one's head or ask questions (even if one is not interested in the answers). Superiors, on the other hand, can reaffirm their standing by acting impassive and making their lessers earn any approving response.

**Keeping a poker face:** As noted earlier, there are times when it is advantageous to not let others know what one knows or feels. The less they know about how one really feels, the less able they are to anticipate one's future action; this gives one a strategic advantage.

**Flirting:** This game features information ambiguity coupled with the emotional intensity of a potential sexual encounter.

***Solidarity Games.*** This final category of interaction involves the means by which people affirm or reaffirm their connectedness with others and how much they value their relationships. Competitive games and task-oriented activities are suspended so that individuals may simply enjoy the company of others.

**Acting modest:** In some situations individuals may wish to present themselves in ways emphasizing modesty or lack of a particular accomplishment rather than offering signs of wealth, talent, achievement, or other attributes. This "underplaying" is often done by people who wish to establish or maintain bonds of loyalty, affection, or love to others who are not as fortunate as themselves along these dimensions. Examples would include showing loyalty to friends from an old school or job situation by not bragging about one's achievements, and playing down one's knowledge or skills in order not to frighten off a prospective date (Goffman 1959:38–39).

**Making light of a situation:** During an elaborate dinner party, one of the older male guests began berating his wife. On a roll, he turned his venom on all the women at the table, exclaiming "All you b . . . s are the same!" The host may attempt to turn the occurrence into a nonevent or recast it ("Are we having fun? Didn't I see this routine on I Love Lucy?").

**Small talk:** As mentioned in Chapter 5, small talk is like the grooming behaviors of chimpanzees, bringing individuals together to attend to each other's need for contact and spontaneous exchange. Discussions of the weather and sports may lead to revelations of the selves behind the roles, increasing individuals' sense of connectedness.

**Checking in:** Individuals reaffirm the importance of others in their lives in various ways. They may do this with a daily phone call or just "drop by" with no other agenda than to see how one is doing.

**Using intermediaries:** Mary, the president of a small computer software firm, wants Harry to know that his creative efforts for the corporate logo were awful. Harry, a good graphic designer, has been freelancing on his own for several years and enjoys a near monopoly over design work in town.

Mary cannot inform Harry of her dissatisfaction directly because he would take offense and tell her to do her own designing. So she tells Mike, Harry's good friend and longtime business associate, to relay her message to Harry (e.g., "You can tell Harry that his ideas were terrible"). Here one's disappointment is still communicated but with the emotional and nonverbal components filtered out.

So important is this function that certain individuals routinely come to serve in the intermediary role. Mike, a computer retailer, by virtue of residing within a large number of professional and friendship circles may frequently find himself serving in the role of information conduit. Sometimes the intermediary role is institutionalized; examples include the realtor role in negotiations between buyer and seller or the lawyer who acts as intermediary between husband and wife in divorce proceedings.

## THE PRESENTATION OF SELF

Many individuals are a tad uneasy in this era of video and movie cameras. Perhaps your father is continually pointing the camera at you and telling you to do something for the family anthology. You do something stupid, and for years afterward you cringe in embarrassment every time the tape is shown. In fact, the spectators of that captured moment may eventually include people you did not know at the time, such as new friends, one's future spouse, and perhaps even your children.

Why does one often feel awkwardness when one knows that one is being videotaped? Aren't other people always watching us and remembering what they see and hear? This is so, but the "video clips" that others have of you might be recorded over by subsequent events. In any case, the tapes are edited by perception and memory and are easily distorted.

Unlike the traditional photograph, the recorded self is accountable not only visually but auditorily, and over considerable periods as opposed to a fraction of a second. (This has had an interesting effect on the political process. Candidates, realizing that every utterance may be captured and available for replay if their actions veer from what they promise, have become more self-conscious, more guarded, and perhaps less willing to take chances.) We take on faith that what we see on television is fact, not some memory and interpretation by an eyewitness. So when we see and hear ourselves as others do—without the thoughts and feelings that, for us, were also part of the recorded situation—an uncomfortable detachment occurs. We see, for instance, how little of ourselves really "gets through," how little of the self-image that we thought we were transmitting was really being conveyed. By watching ourselves on television, we see the normally invisible qualities of ourselves: We did not appreciate how many "uhs" and "ums" had infected our speech; we did not know that we made so many goofy gestures and facial expressions when we talked; we did not know that this was the self that we were presenting to others.

With new technologies, individuals can now view themselves as others see them. Employing such feedback, self-presentation industries now train executives to control their expressions, gestures, and unconscious twitches so as to enhance their persuasiveness when dealing with others.

## The Management of Self-Image in Social Interaction

People continually attempt to manage their self-image. Through designer jeans, serious expressions, gestures, joking behavior, and other devices, we present images of ourselves that we wish others to accept and to respect. With cosmetics, veils, sunglasses, and beards, we mask all or part of ourselves either to disguise ourselves or to compensate for feelings of powerlessness.

The attention individuals give to impression management is, in part, a function of personality. High self-monitors, for instance, are particularly sensitive to the self-presentations and expressions of others. They are adept at making good impressions in a broad range of social situations, acting as if they are different persons in each. To satisfy their strong need to "fit in," these individuals determine what others expect of them and manage their appearance accordingly (Snyder 1986).

More significantly, impression management is a function of social setting. Erving Goffman (1955) refers to these activities as "face-work." He begins by taking the perspective of one of the interactants, and interprets the impact of that person's performances on the others and on the situation itself. He considers being *in wrong face, out of face,* and *losing face* through lack of tact, as well as *savoir-faire* (diplomacy or social skill), the ways a person can attempt to save *face* in order to maintain *self-respect,* and various ways in which the person may harm the "face" of others through *faux pas* such as gaffes or insults. These conditions occur because of the existence of self-presentational rules. These rules, in turn, are determined by how situations are defined. For

## Dressing for Power

Clothes make the man. Naked people have little or no influence in society.
—Mark Twain

Appearance plays a significant role in the presentation of self; an important way of physically expressing oneself is through the clothes one wears. To ensure that their definitions of the situation are maintained, schools, clubs, and restaurants use dress codes as mechanisms of social discipline. These codes are based on the premise that certain kinds of dress preclude certain kinds of behaviors (and certain kinds of individuals). Again, the greater the degree of social control required, the greater the degree of body control expected. Through the physical constraints of clothing—such as the corsets worn by women in the nineteenth century, the strait jacket used to restrain the mentally ill, or the restrictive cut of business suits—the wearer's subordinate status is reaffirmed. The restraining effects of neckties, those suffocating badges of respect worn around the necks of white-collar workers and boys in private schools, similarly differentiate levels of those in the social hierarchy: Blue collar workers and students in public schools don't wear them (Morrow 1978). In 1987, an inspector for the Federal Bureau of Alcohol, Tobacco, and Firearms was fired for refusing to wear a necktie in a photo for his new agency ID card (Edelson 1988).

The power of clothing is also evident when organizations require their employees to wear uniforms, believing that workers so garbed are more obedient, responsive, and productive and that they are more loyal to organizational goals. Nearly one-quarter of all American workers—more than 23 million—wear such "career apparel" (Solomon 1987). To be uniformed is to display one's group loyalty and one's position within the organization. And though they suppress individuality, uniforms allow us to interact with others in ways that might otherwise be considered deviant (Joseph 1986). They are important props that "put us in role" and inform our audience that our role behaviors are legitimate.

instance, there is greater latitude in social situations than in task-oriented situations. Situations also dictate available roles and how much self-importance people can sustain.

Consider the norms of impression management at a swimming pool. There are various poolside roles (e.g., swimmers, waders, sunners, machos, gawkers). Three are also poolside norms. There may be negative sanctions if one is fully clothed, norms for where and how superfluous clothes are to be removed, rules pertaining to the distance between selves (for instance, it is permissible to publicly rub another person when applying suntan lotion), and norms about displaying one's body.

Against this definition of the situation are matched the matters of personal motivations discussed in Chapter 3. Individuals must decide what type of self they are to be in a given situation. For instance, you think of yourself as a humorous, well-rounded, and outgoing person, but you also suspect that other students see you as a humorless, shy bookworm. You have a strong need to be liked by others. An invitation to a party may give you the opportunity to present a different self from the one projected in the classroom, to be the "wild and crazy" person that you perceive yourself to be outside the student role.

***"Selling" a Self-image.*** Goffman (1969) portrays everyday interactions as strategic encounters in which one is attempting to "sell" a particular self-image—and, accordingly, a particular definition of the situation. The presenting individual generally tries to offer an idealized version, to try to convince the audience that he or she represents and supports the "officially accredited" values of the society (cleanliness, competence, integrity, etc.), a version that frequently contains claims for a higher social status than he or she might otherwise be accorded. This is termed **impression management.** In particular, performers tend to conceal activities, facts, or motives that are incompatible with the idealized version of themselves that they are trying to project, and to foster the impression that their relation to this audience is somehow "special."

When an individual plays a part, he or she implicitly requests that others take the performance seriously and believe in the impression being presented:

> When an individual projects a definition of the situation and thereby makes an explicit or implicit claim to be a person of a particular kind, he automatically exerts a moral demand upon others, obligating them to value and treat him in a manner that persons of his kind have a right to expect. (Goffman 1959:13)

At one extreme, an individual can believe in his or her own act (we recognize such people as being "sincere"); at the other, he or she does not believe in it (we consider such people to be "cynical"). A person whose image presentation is successful is said to be "in face"; one who is not successful must resort to a repertoire of "face-saving" devices.

Although the audience is obliged to "buy" the self-image presented, at least initially, deception is always a possibility in everyday situations. According to Goffman, in modern life the emphasis is frequently on negative possibilities, partly because in seeking to convince others of our own self-worth we often try to diminish the self-worth of others:

> Secret derogation seems to be much more common than secret praise, perhaps because such derogation serves to maintain the solidarity of the team, demonstrating mutual regard at the expense of those absent and compensating, perhaps, for the loss of self-respect that may occur when the audience must be accorded accommodative face-to-face treatment . . . [Actors] are treated relatively well to their faces and relatively badly behind their backs. (1959:171, 175)

Audience members will read from the performer many features of the "front" that he or she presents to them, a front that includes anything used in the way of setting, props, appearance, and manner. The performer's front will be read by the audience for the signs that are given both intentionally and unintentionally. Intentional signs include those that apparently are under the performer's voluntary control and that he or she selects for the developing performance: the manner and content of speech or writing, facial expressions, gestures, selection of clothing, insignia of rank, posture, hairstyle, vehicle, and props of various kinds. Unintentional signs include those that apparently are *not* under voluntary control: sex, age, race, body type, physical conditions that a person presumably would not voluntarily choose (e.g., unusual combinations of height and weight, deformities and disfigurements, handicaps), sweating and shaking that may be used to infer nervousness, and forms of appearance and manner that are not valued by the interactants. Audiences generally use information gleaned from such signs to check the credibility of the signs that are under voluntary control.

The result of all this performance effort and audience interpretation is the development of a "working consensus" in which audience members tend to engage in "tactful" *protective practices* to help the performance along, such as overlooking small disruptions, or interpreting them in unserious ways. The performer uses *defensive practices* to try to enhance his or her credibility (those practices include discipline and circumspection, information control, wise choice of team members, control over access to the back region, etc.) and also various ways of attempting to increase the consistence and credibility of the presentation: selective presentation, management of the given-off signs, mystification, use of sincerity signs, and so forth.

***Rules of Self-Disclosure.*** Why are some individuals more likely to reveal their "true selves" to bartenders and hairdressers than to coworkers or even to spouses or friends? The ability to confide in others has considerable implications for emotional and biological well-being. Perhaps only through such self-disclosures do we come to know ourselves (Jourard 1971). On the other hand, revealing too much can give others potential power over oneself since they know one's weaknesses and "skeletons in the closet."

There are norms regarding how much or how little of oneself is to be revealed to others. These norms involve the nature of one's relationship to others and the setting. We may be taken aback, for instance, if a new acquaintance tells us about his urinary tract infection or his experiences as a child following the divorce of his parents. These norms also have a temporal dimension. For instance, good or bad personal news is not revealed early in a conversation. If one has known another person for a time and considers him or her a "friend," one may become obligated to make incremental self-revelations. Such obligations increase if one has any major negative characteristics; withholding such information poses a danger to the identities of those you interact with, who may become "infected" in the eyes of others by being connected with a morally flawed self.

From the dramaturgical perspective, revelations of true selves are normally confined to "backstage" regions (Goffman 1959). What is presented to an audience when an actor is "onstage" and "in role" is the finished product, which has been rehearsed outside of public view in some private area. A professor, for instance, may appear extremely authoritative if she delivers a brilliant lecture without notes. Students assume her expertise to be great owing to the apparent spontaneity of the performance. The effect would be lost if they knew that the professor had rehearsed the lecture for hours.

This is not to deny that an occasional "stepping out of role" can be an effective strategy of self-revelation. When, for instance, a professor admits in class that he feels that a work that is generally considered a masterpiece is "hogwash," students may feel closer to him because he has shared a professional secret. Shakespeare often let the audience in on such secrets, by having an actor go to the edge of the stage and deliver an "aside" (McCauley 1987).

***Management of a Flawed Self.*** Certain facets of self may cause an individual to become stigmatized, that is, to have a flawed self. Observes Goffman:

> While the stranger is present before us, evidence can arise of his possessing an attribute that makes him different from others in the category of persons available for him to be, and of a less desirable kind—in the extreme, a person who is quite thoroughly bad, or dangerous, or weak. He is thus reduced in our minds from a whole and usual person to a tainted, discounted one. Such an attribute is a stigma, especially when its discrediting effect is very extensive; sometimes it is also called a failing, a shortcoming, a handicap. It constitutes a special discrepancy between virtual and actual social identity. . . . The term stigma, then, will be used to refer to an attribute that is deeply discrediting, but it should be seen that a language of relationships, not attributes, is really needed. (1963:2–3).

Stigmas sometimes discredit the person immediately; examples include physical deformities or the "tribal stigmas" of race, nation, and religion that can be instantly recognized. Others are *potential* stigmas in that they concern "blemishes of individual character" that are only revealed if certain information comes to light ("weak will, domineering or unnatural passions, treacherous and rigid beliefs, dishonesty, . . . mental disorder, past imprisonment, addiction, alcoholism, homosexuality, unemployment, suicidal attempts, and radical political behavior" [1963:4]).

The stigmatized person will seek but never be sure of "acceptance," may try to "correct" the problem (e.g., by joining an alcoholism recovery programs), or may reassess the conceptual and emotional limitations of "normal" individuals. If the problem is potentially stigmatizing information, he or she will try to control it and to "pass" as a person without stigma. If the problem is immediately discrediting, he or she may try to avoid normals or may become a spokesperson for the stigmatized group. Regardless of these efforts, other people may turn away from the stigmatized person, and he or she may come to hold their standards:

> The stigmatized individual tends to hold the same beliefs about identity that we do; this is a pivotal fact. . . . Further, the standards he has incorporated from the wider society equip him to be intimately alive to what others see as his failing, inevitably causing him, if only for moments, to agree that he does indeed fall short of what he really ought to be. Shame becomes a central possibility, arising from the individual's perception of one of his own attributes as being a defiling thing to possess, and one he can readily see himself as not possessing. The immediate presence of normals is likely to reinforce this split between self-demands and self, but in fact self-hate and self-derogation can also occur when only he and a mirror are about. (Goffman 1963:7)

Finally, as Goffman argues, there are norms regarding the ways individuals with flawed identities can exert information control:

> Apparently in middle class circles today, the more there is about the individual that deviates in an undesirable direction from what might have been expected to be true of him, the more he is obliged to volunteer information about himself, even though the cost to him of candor may have increased proportionately, . . . [unlike] the Old

West, where apparently one's past and one's original name were defined as rightful private property. (1963:64)

## When Self-Presentations Fail

Many factors may disrupt the favorable definition of the situation that has been presented, just as a sour note can spoil a musical performance. Those factors include disclosure of "secrets," unmeant *faux pas* (indicating incapacity, impropriety, disrespect), open lies, and disagreement among members. What happens if the routine fails and the working consensus in an important situation is disrupted? Goffman suggests three outcomes:

1. The immediate interaction screeches to a halt, leaving the performer and the audience members feeling "awkward, flustered and, literally, out of countenance."
2. Audience members come to doubt the capacity of the performer to handle this (or perhaps any other) routine and doubt is also cast on his team members.
3. The individual (especially when deeply identified with the particular part, establishment, and group) may find his self-conception as a competent performer severely damaged and perhaps discredited (1959:242–243).

Each person is potentially accountable every time he or she agrees to participate in a socially defined situation. There exists an implicit social contract that each person is responsible for the consequences of his or her actions even if they unintentionally become negative. Whenever unanticipated disruptive events occur that stem from the individual's actions, the audience affected usually attempts to decide who was responsible, determine whether the consequences were intentional, and then repair the violated situation so that action can proceed. Often this requires the guilty party to make certain amends, to give an account that bridges the gap between expectations and action (Scott and Lyman 1968).

The more negative the action and the clearer the link between the performance and a particular individual, the greater the likelihood that the individual will make **excuses** or **justifications.** In the case of excuses, the perpetrator acknowledges the negative qualities of the act but refuses to accept full responsibility. Justifications, on the other hand, are accounts in which individuals accept full responsibility but deny the negative qualities of the acts in question (Scott and Lyman 1968:47).

Excuses employ the motive vocabularies described earlier. Let's say that you failed miserably on a test for a course in your major. If the instructor inquires about your performance, how do you respond? To preserve a positive self-image, you are unlikely to say you're stupid or that the material had no personal relevance. You may choose the strategy of shifting blame, saying that your roommate was partying all night and made it impossible for you to study or sleep. To reaffirm your commitment to the motives expected, you might argue that you were reading too much into the questions and became sidetracked. Of course, there's the old standby: "I wasn't feeling well and couldn't concentrate." In sum, individuals go to considerable effort to divorce themselves from their bad performances.

To justify a normally negative act, on the other hand, the guilty party must argue that in special cases the questioned behavior is acceptable, such as killing another person in self-defense or contending that others have committed worse deeds without reproach.

In addition to their face-saving function, excuses and justifications serve as a "social lubricant" (Snyder 1984). If we acknowledge that our perceived failures were not intentional (or situationally acceptable), that we still observe the rules of a situation and value our participation within it, we are allowed to resume our interactions with others despite our fallibility. Accounts help us take chances and push the limits, knowing that possible failure need not destroy our status or membership in a group.

Not everyone, of course, faces such accountability, for entailed is the relative social status of the actor's role vis-à-vis that of his or her audience. Military officers do not have to explain tactical blunders to their subordinates just as parents often do not have to account for their improprieties to their young children. When, on the other hand, one is not immune to others' questionings there is the possibility that the role identity of the blundering individual is on the line and might have to be renegotiated: The 16-year-old who has just totalled the family car may have to switch identities and once again accept the nondriver role and the chauffeuring of his parents.

## Levels of Personal Involvement

There are various levels of personal involvement in any interaction. One can, for instance, be engaged emotionally, cognitively, or socially. At one extreme, individuals can become so self-conscious that they experience only themselves. Such people are accused of being in his or her "own little world" and are viewed as nonparticipants in the course of events. Being self-conscious can also mean being overly sensitive to the expectations of one's audience. When, for instance, musicians receive enormous public attention, they may become overly self-conscious, a condition that may result in less creative energy and more attention to detail.

On the other hand, we are all familiar with occasions when we become so absorbed in a situation that we lose our sense of self and sense of time. Such phenomena can be very important for a social system, for example, when in the midst of a religious service one's sense of self becomes fused into the sense of communion with others.

In more structured interactions, such as that between a bureaucrat and a client, one's "real" self can also be lost. This can occur either when the self becomes absorbed into the role it happens to be playing (e.g., when a jazz musician "gets into" his performance) or when one becomes totally divorced from the situation, as often occurred among concentration camp guards during the Third Reich.

Finally, the self can become lost by behind **deindividualized.** When one becomes an anonymous entity among many in an emotionally charged and ambiguous situation, self-awareness is minimized. In part, this loss of self-awareness entails the absence of the normal emotional controls of guilt, shame, or fear (Zimbardo 1970) as one focuses exclusively on the outside world (Diener 1980).

## THE NATURE OF SOCIAL POWER AND INFLUENCE

As we saw in Chapter 3, human beings have strong needs for affiliation. We join churches, lodges, fraternities, and social groups to satisfy our needs to belong. But in exchange we often find ourselves being seduced, cajoled, persuaded, intimidated, or completely transformed—in other words, we make ourselves susceptible to the power and influence of others. When a sample of university students were asked "Who tries to persuade you in the course of your everyday life" and "Whom do you try to persuade in the course of your everyday life?" Rule and her associates (1985) found that individuals see more people trying to persuade them than they, themselves, try to persuade.

On the other hand, social influence is the process that makes social order possible. Through socialization, indoctrination, authority systems, and role models, members come to perceive their social world in similar ways, to share its basic values, and to be motivated to address the spectrum of society's needs. Because some individuals have greater influence than others, they have the power to determine and establish their definition of the situation over competing definitions. For instance, they are most likely to dominate a conversation by focusing the interaction on themselves. They are also most likely to control the attention given by interrupting others and monopolizing the conversation.

Often assumed but rarely expressed is what, precisely, is being socially influenced. Ultimately, it would seem to be behavior. Bayer hopes that its commercials will influence people to purchase their product. Big Brothers and Big Sisters programs hope that by providing same-sex role models they will influence children to shun gangs and other forms of deviance and, instead, pursue socially valued goals.

However, we've seen how, through classical or operant conditioning, individuals can be induced to do all kinds of things. Personal volition therefore must be considered in determining the extent of social influence. For instance, we argue that more social influence is being exerted when a child who dislikes beans is induced to eat them because he thinks he wants to than when he is made to eat the vegetable through force or bribery. Social influence is greatest when external surveillance is unnecessary, when people are induced to do things out of personal motivation. Thus, to understand social influence, one must take into account cognitive factors and consider how they are socially manipulated.

At the lowest level, social influence involves the shaping of emotions. Prejudices and stereotypes may be the most deep-seated of impulses, but they are frequently checked by social norms. As social influence increases, people's perceptions are altered. Now the stimuli that they process cognitively become more standardized, increasing the likelihood that they will behave in similar ways. At higher levels, social influence entails the structuring of beliefs. This can lead to changes in one's primary relationships, as when members of a religious cult give up their interactions and identification with their families. Finally, at the extreme, social influence can change a person's concept of self, as when political prisoners are thoroughly "brainwashed." In such cases social influence creates an entirely new self with new values, desires, drives, and behaviors.

**The Concept of Social Power.** Social influence occurs whenever an individual's behavior, feelings, or attitudes are altered by what others say or do. To have power over others is to be able to determine their behaviors, perceptual schemas, and beliefs, and their sense of the social order and their place within it. In the political realm, power entails the ability to make and enforce rules and laws.

In general, social power derives from control over valued resources, specifically, symbols and things that address individuals' needs and desires. As Blau observed, whoever "commands services others need, and who is independent of any of their commands, attains power over others by making the satisfaction of their need contingent on their compliance" (1964).

In social systems, power is generally centered not in the person of the powerful individual but, rather in his or her social position (Mills 1956). Individuals in powerful positions are known as **authority figures.** People defer to legitimate authority figures because the judgments of such individuals are understood to be society's final word. Authority may be based on tradition, such as that of the British monarchy, or may have a legal or bureaucratic basis, such as being the chief executive officer of a corporation or a bishop in the Catholic church (Weber 1946).

**The Impetus to Control Others.** One episode of *Twilight Zone* featured two astronauts on a distant planet where an advanced civilization of ant-sized humans had been discovered. One astronaut became obsessed with his ability to control the projects of this tiny society, threatening to step on its cities unless a huge statue of himself was constructed. Drunk with power, he waved off his fellow astronaut's orders to leave when the launch window arrived, preferring the loneliness of his power to the company of his own kind.

Why do some individuals seem so driven in their quest for power? Are subordinates' displays of deference exceptionally reinforcing? Are these individuals' needs for order and predictability so great that only by controlling others do they feel secure? Or is the obsession with power an eventual consequence of being in powerful social roles (along the lines of Lord Dalberg-Acton's [1887] maxim "Power tends to corrupt, absolute power tends to corrupt absolutely")?

In developing any taxonomy of personality types, a dimension that is always considered involves a person's need to either control or be controlled by others. This basic orientation determines whether one aspires to be a leader or a follower, to dominate or be passive in social gatherings, and whether or not one is assertive and initiates group action.

We must not forget that social power is a relational concept, not something that one either has or has not. There are, for instance, chronic bullies and chronic victims. Studies of school-age bullies, for instance, note a curious complicity in their victims. Simple fear of a bully may lead some to become overly compliant and passive. They send a message of vulnerability, which is picked up on by the bully, who often himself is such a victim when at home. Observes Nathaniel Floyd: "It is striking to see a sort of choreography of victimization. A dance goes on. It is as if they court each other, and often it seems as if neither can leave the other alone" (1985).

People also exercise power because of the nature of the roles they occupy. The power of a teacher, for instance, is derived from his or her expected control over the definitions of the situation, behaviors of students, and over scarce valued resources (grades).

*Influence as a Mutual Process.*  At the interpersonal level, social influence is a mutual process. Even when the interaction is between a parent and a young child, not only does the adult socialize the infant but the child socializes the adult. To be more powerful than another means to be able to influence that person more than he or she influences you. Indeed, power exists because parties in an exchange relationship are unequally dependent on each other (Emerson 1962).

French and Raven (1959) explored the ways in which people are motivated to comply with the wishes of another. They identified six forms of power:

> **Coercive power,** which stems from desire to avoid punishment. To suppress dissent, for instance, leaders may hold threatening potential critics with imprisonment or even death.
>
> **Reward power,** in which compliance results from the desire for rewards. For instance, the desire for resurrection or a desirable reincarnation has motivated religious individuals to live moral lives.
>
> **Referent power,** or power derived from dependence and identification. This power can be exercised when the target of influence desires to be similar to the influencer, whether it be an individual (role model) or a group (reference group). The referent group becomes a yardstick against which one evaluates oneself.
>
> **Legitimate power,** the power of physicians and legal institutions, arises out of social values that dictate that the source has a legitimate right to influence others and that those others have an obligation to accept its influence.
>
> **Expert power,** which is based on the belief that the source has relevant knowledge and that if one wants to do the right thing one must attend to his or her message.
>
> **Informational power,** or power based on the *content* of a message. Attitudinal or behavioral changes occur as result of cognitive reorganization or insight; individuals comply out of the desire to appear rational.

In considering social influence, we need to take into account the individual's willingness to be influenced. It is one thing to be forced to do something that goes totally against one's principles and self-concept; it is quite another to be induced to do something about which one has no feelings one way or the other or that perhaps will make one feel better about oneself.

## Direct Attempts to Influence Behavior and Thought

When dealing with others one often acts in response to direct and indirect attempts to influence one's behaviors or beliefs. Judges, parents, teachers,

# The Milgram Study of Obedience to Authority

During the 1960s, the trial of Adolf Eichmann provided an international morality play like few others. How could any individual oversee the programmed extermination of hundreds of thousands of men, women, and children? Eichmann was one of the most notorious concentration camp butchers, but, as Hannah Arendt (1964) noted, this personification of evil was a disappointment. He was a colorless bureaucrat who argued that he was merely doing what he was told to do.

To investigate the "banality of evil," Stanley Milgram (1974) conducted an experiment designed to see how far people would go in carrying out the orders of an authority figure. The subject enters a laboratory, where he meets another subject (actually a confederate) and the experimenter. The experimenter informs both subjects that he is conducting a scientific investigation of the effects of punishment on learning. In a rigged drawing, the subject "wins" the role of teacher and the confederate becomes the "learner." Both subjects are taken into an adjacent room, where the learner is strapped into a chair and has electrodes affixed to his arms. After being strapped in, the learner shyly mentions that he has a heart condition.

The teacher is told first to read a list of word pairs to the learner and then to test the learner's recall. If an incorrect response is made, the teacher is to administer an electric shock (the teacher is given a sample shock of 45 volts, the only actual shock delivered). The shock generator has thirty calibrations, labeled from 15 to 450 volts. Beneath the voltage readings are descriptions, ranging from "SLIGHT SHOCK" to "DANGER: SEVERE SHOCK" (at 375 volts) to "XXX" (at 435 volts). The teacher is told to begin with the mildest shock and, with each incorrect response, to increase the shock intensity by one unit. He is also told to treat each failure to respond as a wrong answer.

The teacher returns to the outer room and the experiment begins. The confederate has been trained to show increasingly painful reactions to his predetermined wrong answers: At 150 volts he cries out, "Experimenter, get me out of here! I won't be in the experiment any more! I refuse to go on!" At 270 volts the learner gives agonized screams; from 300 to 330 volts the learner refuses to give answers and now shrieks in pain. From 330 volts on, the learner is no longer heard.

What happened? Invariably, the teachers attempted on several occasions to stop the experiment, but were told by the experimenter to continue. Refusals were met with the experimenter saying, "You must continue. You have no other choice." In this version of the experiment, 65 percent of the subjects obeyed to the end, ultimately delivering 450-volt shocks. In a variant in which the subject did not actually administer the shock (another confederate did) but performed an essential related task, 90 percent remained with the experiment until the 450-volt shock was given. On the other hand, when the subject was standing next to the learner and had to press the learner's hand to the shock plate, only 20 percent obeyed to the end. Milgram commented:

> A commonly offered explanation is that those who shocked the victim at the most severe level were monsters, the sadistic fringe of society. But if one considers that almost two-thirds of the participants fall into the category of "obedient" subjects,

and that they represented ordinary people drawn from working, managerial, and professional classes, the argument becomes very shaky. . . . Ordinary people, simply doing their jobs, and without any particular hostility on their part, can become agents in a terrible destructive process. Moreover, even when the destructive effects of their work become clear, and they are asked to carry out actions incompatible with fundamental standards of morality, relatively few people have the resources needed to resist authority. (1974:5–6)

propagandists, and advertisers continually attempt to induce others to perform certain acts or think certain thoughts. When people change their thoughts or behavior in response to the direct commands of others they are said to obey. Those whom one obeys normally have greater social status than oneself; they are persons of authority who can grant rewards or persons of power who can exercise coercion.

**Compliance** is another type of response to direct attempts to influence behavior, but in this case behavior is changed because one agrees to behave the way others wish one to behave. Individuals who comply change their behaviors in order to conform to widely accepted beliefs or standards. Instead of doing something because they were ordered to do so, compliant individuals have a sense of personal freedom and control over their own actions.

The feeling that one is voluntarily and publicly performing a particular action makes possible various forms of manipulation. In the **foot-in-the-door technique,** people who comply with a small request are more likely to comply with larger ones. In one study, for instance, subjects were contacted at their homes and requested to display a small sign or to sign a petition supporting a safe-driving campaign. A few weeks later the experimenters returned as representatives of Citizens for Safe Driving. The subjects were asked if the group could place in their front yards a large, poorly lettered sign saying "Drive Carefully." Of those who had not been previously approached, only 17 percent agreed, compared with 76 percent of those who had agreed to display the small safe-driving sign (Freedman and Fraser 1966).

Similarly, in the **low-ball technique,** individuals' initial commitment to an action increases the likelihood that they will perform the activity even if the costs are later increased. When introductory psychology students were asked if they were willing to participate in an experiment, the control group was told (before being given the opportunity to agree) that the experiment would begin at 7:00 A.M. Members of the experimental group (i.e., the group being low-balled) were asked about their willingness to participate before being informed of the hour of the experiment. While 24 percent of the control group arrived at the appointed hour, 53 percent of the low-ball group were there at the crack of dawn (Cialdini et al. 1978).

The compliance obtained through voluntary and public avowals of intent is amplified when influence is exerted collectively. In the case of political socialization, for instance, national allegiance is instilled through repetition and ritual, through mass rallies, loyalty oaths (such as the Pledge of Allegiance), patriotic songs, and political youth groups (such as the Soviet Pioneers and the Hitler Youth).

In addition to obedience and compliance, social influence may involve persuasion. Plato claimed that persuasion is the key to power. Its workings can be formal or informal, conscious or unconscious, open or hidden. Plato's student, Aristotle, identified three factors that determine an individuals' ability to influence others: *ethos*, characteristics of the speaker that enhance the persuasive impact of the speech; *pathos*, emotional reactions of the audience that facilitate or inhibit the speech's persuasive impact; and *logos*, qualities of the message itself, such as the logical patterns of argument.

History is filled with accounts of individuals possessing an uncanny ability to influence others. As Halbwachs observed, "The whole art of the orator probably consists in his giving listeners the illusion that the convictions and feelings he arouses within them have come not from him but from themselves, and he has only divined and lent his voice to what has been worked out in their innermost consciousness" (1950:45). In part, the source of their power resides within their **persona,** which includes their appearance (attractive individuals are more persuasive than unattractive ones [Dion and Stein 1978; Chaiken 1979], size (the taller candidate invariably wins the U.S. presidential election), sincerity, and charisma. **Ethos** is also a function of the communicator's position and authority in the social structure, which, in turn, determines his or her credibility and perceived legitimacy to persuade (Hovland et al. 1953). While the influence of high-ethos sources on attitude change is significantly greater in the short term than that of low-ethos sources, over time the effectiveness of high-ethos sources wanes whereas that of a low-ethos source can increase (Hovland and Weiss 1951).

Persuasiveness also involves various learned skills, notably the ability to "read" others, understanding their central desires, drives, and feelings and seeing through their statements or actions to the contrary. Influential persons also can "read" situations, immediately sensing who the key actors are. The communicator's perceived ulterior motives also enter into the equation. A communicator is more effective when apparently arguing against his or her own interests than when arguing for them; the audience views this as a sign of trustworthiness (Walster, Aronson, and Abrahams 1966).

Coupled with ethos in determining of persuasiveness are qualities of the message itself (logos). Facts do not always speak for themselves, nor does logic always overcome emotion. Studies have focused on the number of arguments presented and whether they are one- or two-sided, the amount of repetition, the comprehensibility of the message, personal rewards implicit in the message, and the arousal or reduction of fear. They have found that the more rapid one's speech, the more intelligent and objective one is perceived to be and the greater the audience's susceptibility to persuasion (Miller et al. 1976). They have also shown that fear-arousing messages do not always produce significant attitudinal or behavioral change. A study of strategies to promote proper dental care found that pictures of advanced gum disease were less effective than messages with lower levels of fear arousal in promoting behavioral change (Janis and Feshbach 1953).

The persuasiveness of a message is, in part, a function of the audience. One-sided arguments are more effective when the audience is in basic agreement with the speaker or is uninformed about the issue; two-sided arguments are more persuasive if the audience is opposed to the speaker's standpoint or knowledgeable about alternative positions (Karlins and Abelson 1970; Sawyer

1973). Although highly intelligent individuals may be more resistant to persuasive communications by virtue of having more highly refined personal schemas and standards of belief verification (see Chapter 4), they are also more likely to be influenced by complex messages than those of lower intelligence (Eagly and Warren 1976).

In addition to intelligence and knowledgeability about the issues, pathos also involves matters of emotion. Nearly one-half century ago, Dale Carnegie (1936) argued in his influential book *How to Win Friends and Influence People* that "when dealing with people we're dealing with creatures of emotion, creatures bristling with prejudice and motivated by pride and vanity." But different personality types undoubtedly respond differently to the emotional buttons being pushed.

## Indirect Sources of Social Influence

By "indirect," we mean situations in which instead of occurring because of the intentional designs of a persuader, cognitive or behavioral changes are instigated by individuals themselves. This realm of social influence arises out of our participation in and identification with groups.

Consider the influence of **role models,** people who exemplify one's goals and ideals, personal heroes who epitomize what one aspires to be. When one adopts the behaviors or thoughts of such individuals one is said to *identify* (Kelman 1958) with them. Commercial sponsors make use of this process when they hire Olympic medalists to use their products.

Some role models, such as parents, may consciously control their own actions, knowing that they will influence others. Other individuals may not know or appreciate their role as influencers of others. Society may come down relatively hard on unaware role models who are expected to uphold central values; this explains the highly publicized punishments of professional athletes accused of substance abuse.

Perhaps the most potent indirect source of social influence is the **reference group.** A reference group is a group to which individuals orient themselves (Hyman 1942, 1960). The individual views himself or herself through the eyes of the reference group, using its standards to judge his or her adequacy as a whole self or as a role player.

The concept of a reference group is related to Erikson's "radius of significant others" and Mead's "generalized other" (see Chapters 7 and 8), whose scope increases with age and maturity. During the formative years, the infant's first reference point is (usually) its mother. Its set of significant others gradually expands to include other kin (father, siblings, grandparents, etc.), peer group, and other groups in the community and workplace.

These groups do not directly impose their standards and vantage points on the individual. Nor do individuals query all the members of a reference group and determine their opinions on all matters. In fact, one does not even have to be a member or participate in a group to internalize a reference group's perspective.

In addition to these "positive" reference groups, which represent the values and goals one aspires to internalize, there are negative reference groups. For instance, in studying the negative images Americans hold of the old, Robert

Kalish (1979) observed that the dominant stereotype depicts elderly persons as least healthy, least capable, and least well-off. A large national survey revealed that this "new ageist" stereotype is shared by both the young and the old (see Table 9.2), whereas most of the elderly view themselves as exceptions. In addition, older persons who saw themselves as being better off than most other people over 65 had higher life satisfaction scores (Kearl 1981–1982).

**TABLE 9.2   Problems of Older Americans: Stereotype and Actuality**

*In 1974, a random sample of 4254 individuals was surveyed by Lou Harris and Associates for the National Council on Aging. Among the questions asked was a series of questions like the following: "How serious a problem do you think not having enough money to live on is for most people over 65: a very serious problem, somewhat serious problem, hardly a problem at all, or are you not sure?" On no issue did more than 1 percent of respondents say that they were not sure.*

| | Percent saying problem is "very serious" for "most people" over 65 | | Percent saying problem is personally "very serious" | |
|---|---|---|---|---|
| | *Respondent's Age* | | *Respondent's Age* | |
| | *18–64* | *65+* | *18–64* | *65+* |
| Not having enough money to live on | 63 | 59 | 18 | 15 |
| Loneliness | 61 | 56 | 7 | 12 |
| Not feeling needed | 56 | 40 | 5 | 7 |
| Fear of crime | 50 | 53 | 15 | 23 |
| Poor health | 50 | 53 | 10 | 21 |
| Not enough job opportunities | 47 | 32 | 11 | 5 |
| Not enough medical care | 45 | 36 | 9 | 10 |
| Not enough to do to keep busy | 38 | 33 | 4 | 6 |

*As can be seen in the rightmost column, those older and younger than 65 years are, with the exception of health (where the difference is 11 percent), nearly indistinguishable with regard to their low likelihood of reporting these problems as being personally "very serious." These two age groups are likewise similar in their high rates of agreeing that these problems are "very serious" for most people over 65, with the percentages rarely differing by more than 10 percent. In other words, most older persons see themselves as exceptions to the problem-oriented stereotypes of old age. As Kearl (1981–1982) demonstrated, instead of internalizing the negative stereotypes of their age group, most older persons instead use these images as a negative reference group and feel relatively advantaged (with higher life satisfactions) as a result.*

# CONCLUSION

We began with the problem of how situations are defined and concluded with the internalization of reference group perspectives. As the processes involved were explored, it became clear that situational definitions are to groups what personal theories are to individuals. Both shape the individual's perspective, giving order to what is perceived and remembered, giving meaning to emotions felt and activities seen, and serving as a basis for prediction.

In actuality, the personal theories and belief systems described in Chapter 4 are the same as the group perspectives described here. In fact, the broadest and most encompassing reference group in any society is what we call "culture." Individuals acquire their worldviews by interacting and sharing their perceptions with others. As Tamotsu Shibutani notes:

> The socialized person is a society in miniature; he sets the same standards of conduct for himself as he sets for others, and he judges himself in the same terms. He can define situations properly and meet his obligations, even in the absence of other people, because . . . his perspective always takes into account the expectations of others (1955:564)

When we change our groups, we notice things that were previously overlooked, see connections between things that were formerly thought to be unrelated, and hold emotional attachments to values and beliefs of which we were previously unaware.

In the next chapter we will consider how one's position in the social hierarchy determines one's psychological reality. Each rung on a social ladder provides a distinctive worldview for its occupants, who, in turn, develop a shared identity by virtue of the jobs they hold, the messages they receive about their social worth, similarities in their reference groups, and similarities in their experiences when interacting with people of greater or lesser social standing.

In Chapter 11, we will explore the forces that bring individuals together. Definitions of situations are not self-sustaining, and in this chapter we will also explore how people work to maintain their bonds with others and how, when they fail, social interactions and relationships are terminated.

Chapter 12 elaborates on another process introduced in this chapter: how regular encounters between individuals can become routinized interaction sequences (called role behaviors) that occur independently of the particular actors involved. For instance, despite the changing personnel in an office setting, similar patterns of behavior occur there. And just as individuals learn, through personal development and experiences, how to be aware of themselves as actors, to remember their past actions, and to see themselves from the vantage point of others, so, too, do interaction networks. Routinely interacting individuals come to view their interaction system as a group and their roles within it as those of group members.

# REFERENCES

Arendt, Hannah. 1964. *Eichmann in Jerusalem: A report on the banality of evil.* New York: Viking.
Aster, Jane. 1881. *The habits of good society.* New York: G. W. Carleton.

Becker, Howard S. 1960. Notes on the concept of commitment. *American Journal of Sociology* 66: 32–40.

Blau, Peter. 1964. *Exchange and power in social life.* New York: Wiley.

Blum, Alan, and Peter McHugh. 1971. The social ascription of motives. *American Sociological Review* 36:98–109.

Blumer, Herbert. 1962. Society as symbolic interaction. In Arnold M. Rose (ed.), *Human behavior and social processes.* Boston: Houghton Mifflin.

Carnegie, Dale. 1936. How to win friends and influence people. New York: Simon & Schuster.

Chaiken, S. 1979. Communicator physical attractiveness and persuasion. *Journal of Personality and Social Psychology* 37:1387–1397.

Cialdini, R. B., J. T. Cacioppo, R. Bassett, and J. A. Miller. 1978. Low-ball procedure for producing compliance: Commitment then cost. *Journal of Personality and Social Psychology* 36: 463–476.

Cicco, John A., Jr., and Richard D. Snyder. 1985, June 13. Japan's "secret" weapon. *New York Times,* p. 29.

Cicourel, Aaron. 1970. Basic and normative rules in the negotiation of status and role. In Hans Dreitzel (ed.), *Recent sociology no. 2: Patterns of communicative behavior.* New York: Macmillan.

Collins, Glenn. 1986, May 12. Studying the behavior of bully and victim. *New York Times,* p. 13.

Collins, Randall. 1986. Interaction ritual chains, power, and property. In J. Alexander, Richard Munch, Neil J. Smelser, and Bernard Geissen (eds.), *The micro-macro link.* Berkeley, CA: University of California Press.

Dalberg-Acton, John Emerich Edward. 1887, April 5. In *Letter to Bishop Mandell Creighton.*

Diener, Edward. 1980. Deindividuation: The absence of self-awareness and self-regulation in group members. In P. Paulus (ed.), *The psychology of group influence.* Hillsdale, NJ: Erlbaum.

Dion, K. K., and S. Stein. 1978. Physical attractiveness and interpersonal influence. *Journal of Experimental Social Psychology* 14:97–108.

Eagly, A. H., and R. Warren. 1976. Intelligence, comprehension, and opinion change. *Journal of Personality* 44:226–242.

Edelson, Nathan. 1988, June 27. The case for sanity in Men's business dress. *Wall Street Journal,* p. 16.

Edgerton, Robert B. 1985. *Rules, exceptions, and social order.* Berkeley: University of California Press.

Emerson, Joan P. 1970. Behavior in private places: Sustaining definitions of reality in gynecological examinations. In Hans P. Dreitzel (ed.), *Recent sociology no. 2; Patterns of communicative behavior.* New York: Macmillan.

Emerson, Richard. 1981. Social exchange theory. In Morris Rosenberg and Ralph H. Turner (eds.), *Social psychology: Sociological perspectives.* New York: Basic Books.

Emerson, Richard. 1962. Power-dependence relations. *American Sociological Review* 27:31–41.

Floyd, Nathaniel. 1985. Pick on somebody your own size. *Pointer* 29(2):9–17.

Freedman, J. L., and S. C. Fraser. 1966. Compliance without pressure: The foot-in-the-door technique. *Journal of Personality and Social Psychology* 1:155–161.

French, John R. P., Jr., and Bertram H. Raven. 1959. The bases of social power. In D. Cartwright (ed.), *Studies in social power.* Ann Arbor: University of Michigan Press.

Garfinkel, Harold. 1967. *Studies in ethnomethodology.* Englewood Cliffs, NJ: Prentice-Hall.

Goffman, Erving. 1974. *Frame analysis: An essay on the organization of experience.* New York: HarperCollins.

Goffman, Erving. 1969. *Strategic interaction.* New York: Ballantine Books.

Goffman, Erving. 1963. *Stigma: Notes on the management of spoiled identity.* Englewood Cliffs, NJ: Prentice-Hall.

Goffman, Erving. 1961. *Encounters.* Indianapolis: Bobbs-Merrill.

Goffman, Erving. 1959. *The presentation of self in everyday life.* Garden City, NY: Doubleday.

Goffman, Erving. 1956. The nature of deference and demeanor. *American Anthropologist* 58:473–502.

Goffman, Erving. 1955. On facework: An analysis of ritual elements in social interaction. *Psychiatry* 18:213–231.

Halbwachs, Maurice. 1980 [1950]. *The collective memory* (trans. J. Francis Ditter and Vida Ditter). New York: Harper & Row.

Harris, Louis, and Associates. 1975. *The myth and reality of aging in America*. Washington, DC: National Council on the Aging.

Henley, Nancy M. 1977. *Body politics: Power, sex and nonverbal communication*. New York: Simon & Schuster.

Hoffer, Eric. 1951. *The true believer*. New York: Harper.

Hollingshead, August, and Frederick Redlich. 1958. *Social class and mental disorder*. New York: Wiley.

Homans, George. 1961. *Social behavior: Its elementary forms*. Orlando: Harcourt Brace Jovanovich.

Hovland, C. I., I. L. Janis, and H. H. Kelley. 1953. *Communication and persuasion*. New Haven, CT: Yale University Press.

Hovland, C. I., and W. Weiss. 1951. The influence of source credibility on communication effectiveness. *Public Opinion Quarterly* 15:635–650.

Hughes, Kathleen. 1988, July 6. Kissing in the workplace poses dilemma. *Wall Street Journal*, p. 21.

Hyman, H. H. 1942. The psychology of status. *Archives of Psychology* 269.

Hyman, H. H. 1960. Reflections on reference groups. *Public Opinion Quarterly* 24:383–396.

Janis, I. L., and S. Feshbach. 1953. Effects of fear-arousing communications. *Journal of Abnormal and Social Psychology* 48:78–92.

Johnson, Allan. 1986. *Human arrangements: An introduction to sociology*. Orlando: Harcourt Brace Jovanovich.

Joseph, Nathan. 1986. *Uniforms and nonuniforms: Communication through clothing*. Westport, CT: Greenwood Press.

Joseph, Nathan, and N. Alex. 1972. The uniform: A sociological perspective. *American Journal of Sociology* 77:719–730.

Jourard, Sidney M. 1971. *Self-disclosure*. New York: Wiley.

Kalish, Robert. 1979. The new ageism and the failure models: A polemic. *Gerontologist* 19:398–402.

Karlins, M., and H. I. Abelson. 1970. *How opinions and attitudes are changed* (2nd ed.). New York: Springer.

Kearl, Michael. 1981–1982. An inquiry into the positive personal and social effects of old age stereotypes among the elderly. *International Journal of Aging and Human Development* 14: 277–290.

Keller, Bill. 1984, July 26, Postal officials plan to impose 2-tier pay scale. *New York Times*, pp. 1, 30.

Kelman, H. C. 1958. Compliance, identification and internalization. *Journal of Conflict Resolution* 2:51–60.

Leo, John. 1990, August 13. What qualifies as sexual harassment? *U.S. News & World Report*, p. 17.

Linton, Ralph. 1936. *Study of man*. New York: Appleton-Century.

Lurie, Alison. 1981. *The language of clothes*. New York: Vintage.

McCauley, Lawrence. 1987. Public noontime lecture series. Trinity University.

McHugh, Peter. 1968. *Defining the situation: The organization of meaning in social interaction*. New York: Bobbs-Merrill.

McHugh, Peter, and Alan Blum. 1971. The social ascription of motive. *American Sociological Review* 36:98–109.

Malinowski, B. 1922. *Argonauts of the western Pacific*. New York: E. P. Dutton.

Mead, George Herbert. 1938. *The philosophy of the act*. Chicago: University of Chicago Press.

Mead, George Herbert. 1934. *Mind, self and society*. Chicago: University of Chicago Press.

Merton, Robert K. 1984. Socially expected durations: A case study of concept formation in sociology. In W. W. Powell and R. Robbins (eds.), *Conflict and consensus*. New York: Free Press.

Merton, Robert K. 1968 [1957]. *Social theory and social structure*. New York: Free Press.

Merton, R. K., M. Fiske, and A. Curtis. 1971. *Mass persuasion: The social psychology of a war-bond drive*. Westport, CT: Greenwood Press.

Milgram, Stanley. 1974. *Obedience to authority*. New York: HarperCollins.

Miller, N., G. Maruyama, R. J. Beaber, and K. Valone. 1976. Speed of speech and persuasion. *Journal of Personality and Social Psychology* 34:615–625.

Mills, C. Wright. 1974[1940]. Situated actions and vocabularies of motive. *American Sociological Review* 5(6):904–913. Reprinted in *Power, Politics, and People: The Collected Essays of C. Wright Mills* (ed. Irving Louis Horowitz). New York: Oxford University Press: pp. 439–452.

Mills, C. Wright. 1956. *The power elite*. New York: Oxford University Press.

Morrow, Lance. 1978, July 24. The odd practice of neck binding. *Time,* p. 80.

Morrow, Lance. 1977, July 11. A nation without last names. *Time,* p. 43.

Noble, Kenneth. 1985, April 2. Lower starting wage is reported in Pan Am and Teamster accords. *New York Times,* pp. 1, 13.

Norgren, Jill. 1986, April 5. Please stop using my first name. *New York Times,* p. 15.

Post, Emily. 1969. *Etiquette* (12th rev. ed.). New York: Funk and Wagnalls.

Rosenberg, Morris. 1979. *Conceiving the self.* New York: Basic Books.

Rosow, Irving. 1976. Status and role change through the life span. In Robert H. Binstock and Ethel Shanas (eds.), *Handbook of aging and the social sciences.* New York: Van Nostrand Reinhold.

Rule, B. G., G. L. Bisanz, and M. Kohn. 1985. Anatomy of a persuasion schema: Targets, goals, and strategies. *Journal of Personality and Social Psychology* 48:1127–1140.

Sabini, John, and Maury Silver. 1981. *Moralities of everyday life.* New York: Oxford University Press.

Sawyer, A. 1973. The effects of repetition of refutational and supportive advertising appeals. *Journal of Marketing Research* 10:23–33.

Schmitt, Eric. 1990, September 12. 2 out of 3 women in military study report sexual harassment incidents. *New York Times,* p. A12.

Scott, Marvin, and Stanford Lyman. 1968. Accounts. *American Sociological Review* 33(1):46–62.

Shearing, C. D. 1973. Towards a phenomenological sociology. *Catalyst* 7:79–14.

Shibutani, Tamotsu. 1955. Reference groups as perspectives. *American Journal of Sociology* 60:562–569.

Snyder, C. R. 1984, September. Excuses, excuses. *Psychology Today,* pp. 50–55.

Snyder, Mark. 1986. *Public appearances, private reality.* New York: Freeman.

Solomon, Michael. 1987, December. Standard issue. *Psychology Today,* pp. 30–31.

Turner, Jonathan. 1988. *A theory of social interaction.* Stanford, CA: Stanford University Press.

Walster, E., E. Aronson, and D. Abrahams. 1966. On increasing the persuasiveness of a low prestige communicator. *Journal of Experimental Social Psychology* 2:325–342.

Warner, Richard. 1986, June. Hard times and schizophrenia. *Psychology Today,* pp. 50–52.

Weber, Max. 1946. *From Max Weber: Essays in sociology* (trans. and eds.) H. H. Gerth and C. Wright Mills,. New York: Oxford University Press.

Wilson, Margery. 1937. *The new etiquette.* New York: Frederick Stokes.

Zanna, Mark (ed.). 1987. *Social influence* (papers from Ontario Symposium on Personality and Social Psychology). Hillsdale, NJ: Erlbaum.

Zimbardo, P. G. 1970. The human choice: Individuation, reason, and order versus deindividuation, impulse, and chaos. In W. J. Arnold and D. Levine (eds.), *Nebraska symposium on motivation, 1969.* Lincoln: University of Nebraska Press.

# 10

# The Social Psychology of Oppression and Inequality

♦ *"There are two kinds of people in this world: pianos and piano players."*

As the hot, sultry days of summer arrive in Wichita, Kansas, the children of two families anticipate their summer vacations. One is an 11-year-old African American boy named Diamond Roynel, known as D. R. by his friends. D. R. lives in his grandmother's house, along with his brother, his Aunt Bea, three cousins (two of Aunt Shirley's kids and Aunt Bea's 16-month-old girl), an uncle, and, occasionally, his Grandpa Jack. Each morning at 6 A.M., Aunt Shirley comes over and watches the children while Grandma goes to work managing the home of a white professional couple. For D. R., summer means no school, sandlot ball, "hangin' out" with friends, and an occasional weekend picnic either at the zoo or at a park on an Air Force base (Grandpa is retired from the military). A highlight of the previous summer was the day Grandma's white family came by and picked up D. R. and his brother to join them at a Wichita Aeros baseball game. The low point was when Uncle Jeffrey (Grandma's oldest son) was murdered in Fort Worth. Of all of the grandkids, only Janice, who was 13, "got to go" on the bus to Texas with Grandma for the funeral.

In another part of the city lives 11-year-old Lindsey Pines. For her, summer means a partial break from ballet and piano lessons and a chance to have fun in the sun beside her family's pool. This year, the family trip will take advantage of Uncle Mac's move to his company's Singapore branch: a week in Japan, another in Hong Kong, before arriving for a ten-day stay with Uncle Mac and Aunt Cindi. Coming home, Lindsey talked her folks into stopping over in

Honolulu so she can see her best friend, Jane. Last summer, supposedly because she did so well on her basketball team and her brother made it to the state level in judo competition, Dad, "out of the blue," took the family to Disney World. This, on top of the trip to Switzerland and Austria, had made that summer the best ever.

A 1979 Carnegie study (de Lone) found that position in the status hierarchy determines a child's future. Consider the fates of Bobby and Jimmy, two second-graders, who both pay attention and do equally well in the classroom and have nearly identical IQs. Bobby is the son of a successful lawyer, while Jimmy's father works infrequently as a custodial assistant. Despite their early similarities, the difference in their social-class backgrounds makes it **twenty-seven times more likely** that when he is in his late forties Bobby will hold a job that pays him an income in the top tenth of all incomes in this country. Jimmy, on the other hand, has about one chance in eight of earning the median income.

In this chapter we will elaborate on the interpersonal power games introduced in Chapter 9, focusing on the processes underlying all such interactions. We will see how individuals' positions in the stratification hierarchies of class, gender, and race shape their psychological realities.

## The Social Needs for Stratification Orders

Humans invariably exist within stratification hierarchies like the pecking orders of chickens, which guarantee unequal satisfaction of individuals' needs and desires. What precisely is stratified is the social allocation of scarce resources such as wealth, power, and prestige (Weber 1946, 1947). The unequal distribution of these scarce resources creates profound differences in the identities, beliefs, perceptions, behaviors, and life experiences of people at different levels of the hierarchy.

Some social theorists argue that stratification systems emerge out of various *social needs*, such as the need for order and the need to reinforce those who most contribute to that social order. Davis and Moore (1940), for instance, viewed this need being addressed by creating the desire in talented individuals to fill the most socially necessary (or functional) roles and the motivation to perform them. For example, in compensation for their numerous years of education and apprenticeship required to master the medical arts, society gives greater prestige and wealth to physicians than it does to secretaries.

Conflict theorists (e.g., Marx and Engels 1967 [1848]; Dahrendorf 1959) view stratification systems as the product of more selfish impulses. Persons high in social hierarchies are seen as taking advantage of their position to exploit those in lower positions and thereby secure greater rewards. From their perspective, subordinates must be kept "in their place." In particular, those who are denied an equal share of scarce resources such as wealth or prestige must be convinced, seduced, or forcibly coerced to accept their station in life. This goal is achieved through a broad spectrum of strategies, ranging from control over the dominant cultural ideology and the mechanisms of socialization to manipulation through fear and the use of violence.

From the perspective of the oppressed, a central problem is how to break out of the self-fulfilling prophecies that reinforce their subordinate position.

This involves difficult changes in thought and behavior, such as seeing through and rejecting the belief of personal inferiority that has been internalized since childhood. It means challenging centuries-old cultural stereotypes and overcoming the emotions of fear and self-doubt.

In between these two perspectives, Lenski (1966) argues that stratification systems are largely determined by the amount of surplus resources produced by a society which, in turn, is determined by the degree of evolution of their economies (e.g., hunting and gathering versus agricultural versus industrial). Though this surplus wealth is initially allocated largely in the way conflict theorists say, with mature industrialism and postindustrialism the middle class expands as the lower classes contract because more jobs are produced requiring ever greater skills. In consequence, also produced are societywide personal drives for (and expectations of) upward mobility.

Regardless of the genesis of stratification systems, the fact remains that the division of labor produces a spectrum of jobs that vary considerably in desirability. A number of these are tasks that most members of society are unwilling to perform because they are dangerous, physically demanding, or devoid of prestige. If no lower class is available or willing (even after being coerced) to perform these needed duties, wealthy societies will import one. Thus, during the twentieth century the Germans brought in Turks; the French, North African Moslems; and the English, East and West Indians (Fehrenbach 1988). In addition to doing the dirty work, the poor can be made to absorb the economic and political costs of change and growth. They can be sacrificed in battle when the social system must defend itself; thus, although they make up less than 12 percent of the U.S. population, African Americans accounted for more than one-third of the casualties in the Vietnam War. And to uphold the legitimacy of dominant norms and reaffirm the moral order, the poor can be ritually demeaned. For instance, the unemployed may be forced to publicly reveal their status by having to exchange stigmatizing food stamps for produce to survive.

At the social psychological level, stratification systems provide the frameworks for definitions of the situation as well as the bases for the interpersonal comparisons from which social identity and self-esteem are derived. Poverty, for instance, helps to guarantee the status of those who are not poor, providing a negative reference group that allows others to feel relatively advantaged.

# THE SOCIAL PSYCHOLOGY OF CLASS

What is **social class**? According to Max Weber (1946), the notion involves a group of people who, by virtue of their position in the stratification order, have a number of shared life experiences. These shared experiences include life-style, family events, emotional well-being, desires, and beliefs. Social class, for example, determines the likelihood that an individual will suffer from mental illness. Hollingshead and Redlich (1958) found schizophrenia to be eleven times more common among the lowest classes than among the highest in New Haven, Connecticut. (Of course, issues of labeling theory may be involved here. Lower classes are more likely to be diagnosed as schizophrenics by upper-middle-class professionals. Whether they are or not in any absolute sense is impossible to ascertain because the diagnosis itself is a social construction heavily bound up with class and power issues.)

Depending on the structure of a society, one's position in the class system may be ascribed (determined at birth) or achieved (earned by personal efforts). An example of an ascribed status is the traditional caste system of Hinduism. Castes are rigid positions within the Indian society's social hierarchy, determining what occupations one can have and where higher-caste persons hold power over those in lower castes. The caste into which one is born is the caste in which one will die. With social evolution, status becomes increasingly a function of income, which, in turn, is determined by one's occupation. Gilbert and Kahl (1987) identified nine variables that determine a person's place in the class structure: occupation, income, wealth, personal prestige, association, socialization, power, class consciousness, and mobility. Using these variables, they defined the following classes: capitalist (those whose income comes largely from returns on assets), upper-middle (university-trained professionals and managers), middle (those who follow the orders of the upper-middle class), working (individuals who are less skilled than those in the middle class, usually working in routinized, closely supervised manual and clerical jobs), working-poor (laborers and service workers in low-paying jobs), and underclass (those who rarely participate in the labor force).

## Social Class and the Quality of Life

Stratification systems allocate the resources that largely determine individuals' ability to successfully manipulate the world and to publicly dramatize self-worth (Della Fave 1980). Although modernization has narrowed the gap between the haves and the have-nots, considerable disparities remain. In the United States, 70 percent of households have no discretionary income (*Wall Street Journal* 1989), and the richest 1 percent of Americans had nearly as much after-tax income in 1990 as the bottom 40 percent. Between 1978 and 1987, the poorest fifth of American families became 8 percent poorer while the richest fifth became 13 percent richer.

Social class determines not only the quality but quantity of life (see Table 10.1). People at lower levels of the class structure are more likely to die prematurely as a result of homicide, accidents, and inadequate medical care than people at higher levels (Kearl 1989). Thus, in London in 1830 the average age at death for the gentry was estimated to be 44 years, dropping to 25 years for tradespeople, clerks, and their families and 22 for laborers and their families (Morley 1971: 7). In the United States in 1900, the life expectancy of African American males was only 71 percent of that of white males; ninety years later, white men still live seven years longer than African American men and the infant mortality rate of African Americans is more than double that of whites. African American men living in Harlem in New York City are less likely to reach the age of 65 (40 percent) than men in Bangladesh (55 percent) (McCord and Freeman 1990).

In the course of social evolution, the basic material needs related to personal survival are increasingly guaranteed. Concurrently, however, other desires and needs become profoundly stratified in terms of opportunities to meet those needs. In Figure 10.1, for instance, the "unalienable right" of happiness clearly is not satisfied equally at all levels of society.

**TABLE 10.1   Income, by Deaths due to Heart Disease in Los Angeles County, 1979–1981**

*Both the quality and the quantity of life are determined by the individual's location in the stratification system. In Los Angeles County between 1979 and 1981, for instance, there were 40 percent more deaths due to heart disease among individuals making less than $13,601 a year than among those making more than $28,500. Frerichs et al. (1984) found the discrepancy to be even greater for African American males, among whom the poor were 53 percent more likely to die than those in the highest income level.*

| Annual Income | Heart-Disease Deaths per 100,000 Population |
|---|---|
| $13,600 or less | 460.1 |
| $13,601–18,750 | 404.6 |
| $18,751–22,600 | 393.0 |
| $22,601–28,500 | 377.6 |
| $28,501 + | 329.5 |

Source: Frerichs et al., 1984.

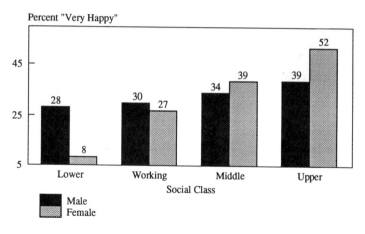

**FIGURE 10.1   Social Class, by Reported Happiness**
Source: NORC, 1989.

## Class and Self-Esteem

People's sense of self-worth is derived not only from comparisons with those who are perceived to be of equal status but also with those who have more or less status. Self-worth is also derived from power and the ability to satisfy most of one's desires and achieve most of one's goals.

Members of the lower classes feel powerless compared to members of the middle and upper classes, in that they are unable to influence their fate. This fatalism can breed self-hatred and low self-esteem. Self-worth may be derived from one's ability to imitate at least some facets of the lives of people in higher classes, such as through the clothing one wears, the automobile one drives, or the organizations to which one belongs.

Those at the top of a class or status hierarchy, in contrast, are the standard setters. Often this is accomplished through what is known as "conspicuous consumption." As Thorstein Veblen (1953 [1899]) pointed out, in modern societies self-esteem is based on one's demonstrated capacity to acquire and conspicuously consume material goods. In other words, the wealthy do not accumulate wealth in order to consume goods; rather, they consume goods in order to display their accumulation of wealth:

> But it is only when taken in a sense far removed from its naive meaning that consumption of goods can be said to afford the incentive from which accumulation invariably proceeds. The motive that lies at the root of ownership is emulation . . .
> The possession of wealth confers honor; it is an invidious distinction. Nothing equally cogent can be said for the consumption of goods, nor for any other conceivable incentive to acquisition, and especially not for any incentive to the accumulation of wealth. (Veblen 1953 [1899]: 35)

## Class and Attention

The subordinate and poor are socially invisible. They are not noticed, never stand out; their needs or interests are not attended to. So unseen have African Americans and Hispanics become that the phenomenon has come to be known as the "invisible minority syndrome" (Armas 1990). In 1980, for instance, the Census Bureau admitted having missed as many as 30 percent of Hispanics (or some 6 million people) when tallying the nation's population, and one out of two who were missed were African American (*Harper's Magazine* 1990a).

In Chapter 5 we observed that subordinates must give attention while superiors receive it. The allocation of attention is built into roles. Women in a sexist society, for instance, are expected to occupy the mother role, "the archetypical attention-giving role in which women must give attention without expecting an equal measure in return" (Derber 1979: 44). Women learn not only to give attention but also to "experience some degree of doubt, fear, or guilt when taking it or accepting it for themselves" (55).

Observing with disdain the slow progress of integration in the United States, James Meredith, who as a young man in 1962 was the first African American to enter the University of Mississippi, commented:

> I'd rather be lynched than ignored and treated like I didn't exist. It used to be whites would exploit blacks for cheap labor, even slave labor. Now you don't see blacks picking the fruit or cotton or waiting tables. Whites don't even want to exploit black labor. I'd rather be exploited than ignored. (*San Antonio Express-News* 1985)

The receipt of attention, on the other hand, is one of the hidden privileges of socially dominant classes. Fame, wealth, and power translate into the ability to define oneself as having greater worth and, hence, as deserving attention (Derber 1979: 64). Moreover, the attention received does not have to be reciprocated by attention given:

## "For the Right Price, Just About Anything Can Bear Your Name"

Most people would rather not have their name on bathroom walls. Gary Horowitz isn't most people.

Mr. Horowitz, a professor and administrator at Alfred University in Alfred, New York, donated $5000 for renovations at the school last year and got his name on a plaque. It reads "Everyone Has to Be Remembered Somehow!" and is mounted on one of the most scrutinized walls on campus, just across from the toilet in the first floor men's room of Alumni Hall.

"I could have bought a window for $7500," he says. "But I wanted to be remembered in a different way."

To name an endowed chair at Columbia University costs $1.5 million, but naming a plastic chair at the school's football stadium costs just $1000. Carnegie Hall will name a grand staircase for $500,000 and a loading dock for $250,000; for $75,000, you can have your name on a stagehand's office. Sutter General Hospital in Sacramento, California, is putting plaques on a wide range of equipment, from $127,200 ultrasound devices to $1254 baby scales and $170 tuning-fork kits.

For years, well-heeled philanthropists have donated their spare millions to get their names on entire buildings. But these days, new buildings are so expensive—or tycoons so cheap—that few individuals pick up the entire tabs anymore. . . .

No one would accuse the Michigan Theater of lacking imagination. In its "Buy a Piece of the Michigan" restoration fund drive last year, the 1800-seat performing arts center in Ann Arbor solicited donors for such items as aisle signs ($100 each), light fixtures ($250 apiece), seats ($500 each), stage rigging ($6000), a boiler ($10,000), and the concession stand ($12,000).

Some items went unsold, but the theater did raise $1.8 million, in part by getting donations for some 800 seats, the mezzanine railing at $12,000 and six toilets and two urinals at $400 a pop. "The plaques went right above the fixtures," says Sue E. Sasic, the theater's program coordinator.

Hospitals are also proving increasingly adept at the naming game. The Westmoreland Hospital in Greensburg, Pennsylvania, will memorialize an elevator lobby or nurses' station for $10,000, a patient room for $5000, or the ambulance driver's basement office for $3000.

Source: Fuchsberg, 1987.

---

As Hegel observed in the early nineteenth century, it is an ancient aristocratic prerogative to be seen by the lower orders without having to look at them in turn. Tilting his chin high in the air and gazing down at the world under hooded eyelids, the aristocrat invites observation while refusing to look back. (Solomon 1988)

In recent years there has been a proliferation of *Who's Who* compilations, which help meet individuals' need to be noticed and considered important. Sometimes entries are free, but the publisher may offer an expensive framed acknowledgment of inclusion. For instance, the *International Register of Profiles*, produced by the International Biographical Centre in Cambridge, England, produced the following advertisement:

> The number of entries is strictly limited to a thousand, each one occupying a whole page including a portrait photograph. Each contributor ordering a copy of the Luxury Edition will receive a handsome Diploma of Inclusion for exhibition in study, office or home.
>
> Congratulations on being invited to provide biographical information for inclusion in a leading Who's Who to be published by the IBC. . . . Price for a Luxury Edition: $295.00, for a Standard Edition: $167.50.

## Class and Alienation

Alienation is another subjective phenomenon that varies at different levels of the status order. Alienation—the sense of powerlessness, normlessness, meaninglessness, and despair, in which people no longer feel connected with society—has been linked to mental illness, deviance, and suicide.

The French sociologist Émile Durkheim developed the notion of *anomie*, or normlessness, to describe situations in which people are motivated by personal desires rather than by social norms. William Rushing notes that normlessness involves "the tendency to accord legitimacy to individual self-interest rather than to honesty and the norms, rules, and laws of society" (1972: 9). A central cause of anomie in the United States is the cultural focus on monetary success and the inability of the socially disadvantaged to achieve this goal through culturally acceptable means (Merton 1968).

Leo Srole (1950; cited in Merton 1968: 218–19) measured the following subjective outlooks among people experiencing anomie:

> The perception that community leaders are indifferent to one's needs.
> The perception that little can be accomplished in a society that is seen as basically unpredictable and lacking order.
> The perception that one's life goals are receding rather than being realized.
> A sense of futility.
> The conviction that one cannot count on personal associates for social and psychological support.

As is evident in Figure 10.2, when these measures are correlated with social class, anomie is greater at lower levels of the social hierarchy.

## SOCIAL-CLASS INFLUENCES ON PERCEPTION AND THOUGHT

Owing to their distinctive needs, socialization, and interaction experiences, members of different social classes live in dissimilar psychological realities. Among the differences that have been detected are differences in the personal

Measures of Alienation

Worse Off: In spite of what some people say, the lot (situation/condition) of the average man is getting worse, not better: 62% agree.

Unfair: It's hardly fair to bring a child into the world with the way things look for the future: 39% agree.

Uninterested: Most public officials (people in public office) are not really interested in the problems of the average man: 68% agree.

Excitement: In general, do you find life exciting, pretty routine, or dull? 45% exciting, 50% routine.

Advantage: Do you think most people would try to take advantage of you if they got a chance, or would they try to be fair? 34% say take advantage, 61% be fair.

Trusted: Generally speaking, would you say that most people can be trusted or that you can't be too careful in dealing with people? 39% say can trust, 57% be careful.

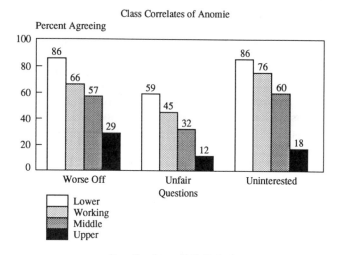

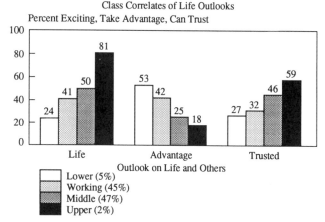

**FIGURE 10.2  Social Class, by Measures of Anomie**
Source: NORC, 1988.

theories and beliefs through which social events are understood and differences in the concept of time.

## Class Differences in Time Orientation

People at different levels of the social hierarchy have different temporal orientations. Class-based differences in present versus future orientation, willingness to delay gratification, and sensitivity to time and schedules have been detected (Coser and Coser 1963; Henry 1965). The higher one's social class, for instance, the more social commitments one has and the greater the need to adhere to schedules. Whereas the American middle class is future oriented, the poor live largely in the present. The present-time orientation of the lower classes is derived from their tendency toward fatalism—their belief that since things don't work out as planned it is useless to worry about the future (Goleman 1986).

This world without past or future is revealed in the language of the streets: "What's happening?" "Where's it at?" It is also revealed in behaviors that do not take account of future consequences. Lower-class adolescent couples, for example, engage in unprotected sexual intercourse without fully appreciating the long-term implications of starting a family (Stark 1986).

When the children of the urban poor attend school, they are handicapped by the temporal requirements of the institution. Having been raised in temporally unstructured homes, they find themselves baffled by the "time-slotted" school environment (Norton 1978). Their crayons are taken away before their drawings are completed because it is no longer "art time" but rather "math time." One clinical psychologist has observed that "the structured situation makes them feel powerless. It feels arbitrary, senseless, and imposed because at home there is no predictability and rigidity" (Jeree Pawl, cited in Taylor 1989).

## Relative Deprivation and False Consciousness

In *The Communist Manifesto* (1967 [1848]: 57–58), Karl Marx showed how subordinate mentalities have historically been achieved and maintained. He argued that under capitalism, the bourgeoisie (entrepreneurs) own the means of production and exploit the proletariat (the laboring class) in their quest for profit. For instance, when workers are paid the minimum wage to produce a product or service that is sold for several times the amount it cost to make it (thereby creating "surplus value"), the owner of the means of production profits at the expense of the workers. The workers do not object to such inequities, either because they are unaware of their exploitation or because they are too unorganized to do anything about it. In part, this ignorance and lack of organization occur because the bourgeoisie controls the ideas of the proletariat and uses these ideas as tools of domination. In part, it has to do with the propensity of humans to identify with their oppressors under extreme conditions.

Some of the stories coming out of the Nazi concentration camps told of prisoners identifying so thoroughly with their guards that they even dressed and acted like them. According to Bruno Bettelheim (1969: 170–175), such behaviors were more likely to occur among the "old prisoners," those who managed to avoid the ovens by learning how not to stand out:

> Bad behavior in the labor gang or in the barrack endangered the whole group. To become conspicuous was always dangerous, and usually the group to which the conspicuous person belonged at the moment would be singled out by the SS for special attention. (p. 170)

To survive, old prisoners adopted the goals and values of the SS, as well as their attitudes and aggressive behaviors toward prisoners. Even when obeying the most inane rules, these inmates firmly believed them to be desirable standards of behavior in the prison setting.

In less extreme situations people may be frustrated when they compare their lot with that of people at higher levels of the stratification order. The deprivations experienced are relative rather than absolute. As Marx and Engels noted: "Our desires and pleasures spring from society; we measure them, therefore, by society and not by the objects which serve for their satisfaction. Because they are of a social nature, they are of a relative nature" (1955: 94).

To prevent revolution, such inequities must be explained, and the explanations must be accepted by those who are relatively disadvantaged. This is termed **legitimation.** It involves telling people not only why they should perform one action and not another but also why things are the way they are. Legitimation is carried out in a variety of ways. As Berger and Luckmann (1966: 92–104) have shown, legitimation can take the following forms:

> Explanations that are built into the language, such as the use of masculine pronouns and references in a sexist society.
> Rudimentary theoretical propositions of everyday life, such as proverbs, maxims, folk wisdoms, and legends.
> Explicit theories of religion and political regimes, which provide a fairly comprehensive frame of reference (e.g., the traditional Hindu legitimation of the caste system).
> Theoretical traditions comprising a cultural ethos, integrating all realms of action and thought into a coherent whole (e.g., the ideology of capitalism allows the accumulation of private property, which encourages individuals to maximize their efforts which, in turn, produces larger quantities of products than under alternative economic systems).

It is clearly in the interest of the upper classes to have the "social losers" blame themselves, as opposed to the social system, for their fate. For the ruling classes, such lower-class beliefs relieve any feelings of responsibility or guilt. For the lower classes, the choice is between accepting the fiction that the world is just and denying "the moral validity of the claims of those above you, asserting in their place grounds for prestige which favor those like yourself" (Campbell 1987: 53–54). An example of the latter is the belief that "the meek shall inherit the earth." For these reasons, Marx viewed such ideas as tools of domination, producing a "false consciousness" that dupes the dominated classes into contributing surplus value for the benefit of the ruling classes. False consciousness entails "the lack of awareness of and identification with one's own objective interests. . . . [These] 'objective interests', refer to those **allegiances** and **actions** which would have to be followed if the **accepted values** and desires of the people **involved in given strata situations** are to be realized" (Mills 1946). A study of how Americans identify their "class" is shown in Table 10.2.

An example of false consciousness can be found in the lowest rank of the lowest caste in India, the chamars, who are descended from carcass handlers. In traditional Hindu culture, one is born into a caste and one's caste determines the nature of one's contribution to the social order. But rights, privileges, and wealth are unequally distributed among the various castes. Members of the lowest castes have been socialized to believe that they are beneath everyone else, despite the fact that their social contributions may be as great or even greater than those of members of other castes. For centuries they have automatically and unquestioningly served those above them on the Hindu social ladder.

Feagin (1972) presented a national sample with three explanations of poverty—individual, societal, and fatalistic. He found that most Americans attribute poverty to individual causes; that is, the poor are thought to be responsible for their fate. Similarly, in a review of psychological studies of African

**TABLE 10.2  What Social Class Do You Belong To?
the Middle Class, of Course**

*Aristotle viewed the middle class as a compromise between the extremes:*

*The best political community is formed by citizens of the middle class, and ... those states are likely to be well-administered, in which the middle class is large, and stronger if possible than both the other classes, or at any rate than either singly; for the addition of the middle class turns the scale, and prevents either of the extremes from becoming dominant. (1943:192)*

*The likelihood of class conflict is diminished when there is a large and prosperous middle class. This is so because the middle class is loyal to the status quo and unlikely to take sides, sharing the same aspirations as the upper classes and the same roots as the lower classes.*

*According to the 1989 NORC General Social Science Survey, nearly one-half of American adults identify themselves as members of the "middle class."*

| Household Income | Lower | Working | Middle | Upper | Row Total |
|---|---|---|---|---|---|
| $10,000 | 18% | 42% | 37% | 3% | 16% |
| $10–20,000 | 6 | 61 | 30 | 2 | 23% |
| $20–35,000 | 2 | 50 | 46 | 1 | 26% |
| $35–50,000 | 0 | 33 | 65 | 2 | 16% |
| $50,000 + | 0 | 21 | 68 | 11 | 19% |
| Column Total | 5% | 43% | 48% | 4% | 1380 |

Americans, Caplan and Nelson (1973) found that in over 80 percent of the cases African Americans attributed their condition to themselves rather than to circumstances.

Any social-psychological model of legitimation must address the processes of conflict that give rise to the need for the rationales used to stabilize the social order (Berger and Luckmann 1966). In addition, social psychologists must determine how such rationales are internalized, allowing for the perpetuation of the stratification order. "Any theory of legitimation," Della Fave observes, "must ultimately answer the question of how legitimations of stratification become part of the consciousness of the individuals who make up society" (1980: 959).

## Class Differences in Belief Systems

The lower an individual's position in the class structure, the more likely he or she is to subscribe to conservative views of work, family, and patriotism. As is evident in Figure 10.3, this lower-class conservatism extends to matters of sexuality, the traditional separation of the sexes, euthanasia, and punishment. Moreover, the lower their class status, the more likely people are to believe that one gets ahead by luck as opposed to effort, and the less likely they are to believe that poor people should take responsibility for themselves. It may be the case that the poor have a very accurate view of their life chances. Such a view, however, if adhered to strongly, may also hinder them from trying to transcend their limitations. Further, the perspective that it might require government to *structurally* improve their life chances (recall the difference in the likelihood that Bobby and Jimmy will earn a high income) might be extremely realistic.

Perhaps the greatest class differences in beliefs are seen on the issue of abortion. Each year there are roughly 1.6 million abortions in the United States. Chances are that one woman in two will have an abortion sometime in her life. A 1988 national survey conducted by the Alan Guttmacher Institute revealed that women who are young, poor, and members of minority groups are most likely to have abortions. Ironically, support for legalized abortion increases at higher levels of the class structure. For instance, a *Wall Street Journal*/NBC survey of Americans found class support for abortion to be divided as shown in Table 10.3 (Shribman 1989).

Luker (1984) found that social class is the single most important predictor of attitudes toward abortion. She found that the typical pro-life activist is a nonworking, undereducated mother: Twenty percent of the pro-life respondents in her survey had six or more children; 63 percent did not work at paid jobs; and 40 percent either had never gone to college or had not completed a college education. Working-class women view abortion as a challenge to their identity:

> By giving women control over their fertility, [abortion] breaks up an intricate set of social relationships between men and women that has traditionally surrounded (and in the ideal case protected) women and children. . . . [It] is wrong because it fosters and supports a world view that deemphasizes (and therefore downgrades) the traditional roles of men and women. (Luker 1984: 162)

| Premarital Sex | If a man and a woman have sex relations before marriage, do you think it is always wrong, almost always wrong, wrong only sometimes, or not wrong at all? (**% always wrong**) |
|---|---|
| Women Work | Do you approve or disapprove of a married woman earning money in business or industry if she has a husband capable of supporting her? (**% disapproving**) |
| Help Poor? | Some people think that the government in Washington should do everything possible to improve the standard of living of all poor Americans; they are at point 1 on this card. Other people think it is not the government's responsibility, and that each person should take care of himself; they are at point 5. Place yourself on this scale. (**% government only**) |
| Spanking | Do you strongly agree, agree, disagree, or strongly disagree that it is sometimes necessary to discipline a child with a good, hard spanking? (**% agreeing strongly**) |
| Euthanasia | When a person has a disease that cannot be cured, do you think doctors should be allowed by law to end the patient's life by some painless means if the patient and his family request it? (**% yes**) |
| Get Ahead? | Some people say that people get ahead by their own hard work; others say that lucky breaks or help from other people are important. Which do you think is most important? (**% luck only**) |

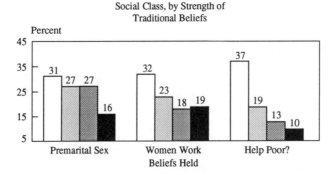

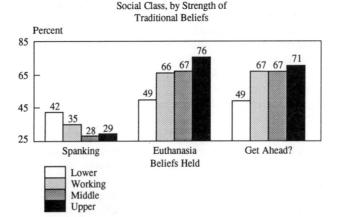

**FIGURE 10.3  Social Class, by Strength of Traditional Beliefs**
Source: NORC, 1989.

**TABLE 10.3  Percent Favoring Legalized Abortion**

| Household Income | Percent Favoring | Educational Level | Percent Favoring |
|---|---|---|---|
| $0–20,000 | 52 | < high school | 47 |
| $20–50,000 | 68 | high school diploma | 65 |
| $50,000 or more | 74 | college | 72 |
| | | postgraduate work | 79 |

# SOCIALIZATION AND SOCIAL CLASS

Through socialization, children learn the identities and mindsets associated with their social-class position. From their families, lower-class children learn the lower-class worldview, just as upper-middle-class youths learn and internalize the outlook of the upper middle class.

Kohn (1969) observed that membership in the middle class requires the ability to deal with others, solve problems, and manipulate symbols. Middle-class parents therefore stress self-direction, curiosity, imagination, and creativity. The working class, on the other hand, tends to stress obedience. Middle-class parents are more likely to emphasize the motivations underlying behavior and, when responding to the behavior of their children, to focus on its intent. Members of the working class are more concerned with behavior itself, and parents are more likely to respond to the child's behavior and its consequences.

Middle-class parents appear to be more supportive of their children and place more emphasis on psychological satisfaction. Working-class parents are more likely to stress conformity, obedience, and neatness. Such class-based differences are evident in Table 10.4. The results of a 1989 national survey of Americans revealed that individuals identifying themselves as members of the lower class are seven times more likely than those identifying themselves as members of the upper class to mention obedience as "the most important [thing] for a child to learn," and less than half as likely to mention thinking for oneself. The explanation for this is that to survive, lower-class individuals must know how to obey and to defer to others.

Class differences also extend to punishment. Whereas members of the lower classes are more likely to employ corporal punishment, members of the upper classes are more likely to use reason and emotional manipulation. As part of their cognitive training, children of the middle and upper classes learn to take the perspective of and empathize with the victims of their transgressions, and to internalize guilt.

Children in affluent families have more clothes, a wider range of food, and greater number of games, toys, and hobbies than children in less affluent families. They obtain instruction not only at a school but in such pursuits as tennis, swimming, horseback riding, and music. They observe that newspapers, radio, and television offer news not only about unknown others but also about neighbors, friends, and acquaintances of their parents. Their parents' authority outside the home is matched within the home, as when children observe their parents giving orders to servants and service providers.

**TABLE 10.4 Class-Based Differences in Socialization**

*If you had to choose, which thing on this list (to obey, to be well-liked or popular, to think for oneself, to work hard, and to help others when they need help) would you pick as the most important for a child to learn to prepare him or her for life?*

| Self-Reported Social Class | Obey | Popular | Think for Self | Work Hard | Help Others |
|---|---|---|---|---|---|
| Lower | 42 | 0 | 33 | 14 | 12 |
| Working | 23 | 1 | 47 | 16 | 13 |
| Middle | 22 | 1 | 51 | 13 | 12 |
| Upper | 7 | 0 | 70 | 11 | 14 |

Percent Saying Most Important

Source: NORC, 1989.

Class differences are carried over into the schools. Ray Rist (1970) observed a group of black children in an urban ghetto school, from the time they began kindergarten in the fall of 1967 until the end of the second grade. He found that teachers determined which children would succeed on the basis of social-class criteria; by the second week they had identified "fast" and "slow" learners. These initial judgments remained with the students throughout their schooling, often acting as self-fulfilling prophecies. Thus, a 1990 Rand Corporation study of 1200 private and public schools found that African American and Hispanic children—those assumed to be members of the lower and working classes—are often placed in classrooms with students of lesser abilities (*New York Times* 1990a).

---

## SOCIAL CLASS AND PERSONAL IDENTITY

In view of the processes just described, it is not surprising that the class structure produces distinctive personal identities as well. To be a member of the lower class, for instance, is to have a stigmatized self, a self that is felt to be on the sidelines of society. In the case of Hispanic Americans, American educator Arturo Madrid describes the experience of being "defined out of" the mainstream:

> When I looked at movies and television, I saw that the Latinos in those movies were not Americans, but Mexicans or Latin Americans. So my experiences and the people around me were not to be found in public life, and they were not to be found on TV or in the movies. In that sense, I was defined out of reality. . . .
>
> In some cases, people fight against being defined out. In some cases, people accept it. In many other cases, people are not even aware of the fact that they're being defined out, and function fairly normally. (Moyers 1989: 213, 214)

## Experts Dispute Effects Of Culture on Learning

The reemergence of a theory that many black and white children learn differently because of their different cultural backgrounds has set off a political and intellectual debate among New York officials and educators.

The debate, at a time of increasing frustration over the high dropout rates of minority-group students in many cities around the country, is often confusing and contradictory, evoking charges of racism from both sides.

On one side, educators said the theory could be used to segregate minority-group children and give them inferior educators. On the other side, advocates said the existing system was racist, by not acknowledging the differences among children.

The controversy erupted in the fall of 1987 with the publication of a Board of Regents booklet on increasing the percentage of students who complete high school. Among the "qualities noted in African-Americans," the booklet included "a preference for inferential reasoning, rather than deductive or inductive reasoning" and "a tendency to approximate space, number, and time, instead of aiming for complete accuracy."

Source: Rimer, 1988.

In the extreme, the upper class not only makes the subordinated classes socially marginal but actively destroys their personal identities. For instance, before physically destroying their Jewish victims, the Nazis first systematically dissolved every aspect of their social identity. As the Nobel Prize–winning writer Elie Wiesel observed:

> The Nazis' aim was to make the Jewish universe shrink—from town to neighborhood, from neighborhood to street, from street to house, from house to room, from room to garret, from garret to cattle car, from cattle car to gas chamber. And they did the same to the individual—separated from his or her community, then from his or her family, then from his or her identity, eventually becoming a work permit, then a number, until the number itself was turned to ashes. . . . The disorder seems total: Children are like old men and women; adults—stripped of authority, impotent, vulnerable—conducted themselves like children. (1984: 1, 23)

## "Welfare Mentalities"

As mentioned earlier, people in lower socioeconomic groups often do not feel good about themselves. One alternative to blaming and hating oneself is to take on the status of victim, attributing one's shortcomings to the unfairness of society or history. In American society, to be certified as a legitimate victim entitles one to the benefits of the welfare state. But to assume this status often means to handicap oneself.

## India's Lowest of the Low Start to Cry "Enough"

The fifty or so people who live in one small cluster of mud-walled houses in Gaura Kalan, India, in the heart of India's lush Ganges plain call themselves simply, in Hindi, "Hum log"—"We people."

Many other Indians would know them as chamars, the lowest rank of Hindu untouchables: outcasts, historically the lowest of the low, descendants of the handlers of carcasses.

But across the country today there is a new restiveness among rural untouchables, a people that Mohandas K. Gandhi dubbed harijans, or children of God. For the first time in centuries, they no longer bow automatically to the will of those above them on the Hindu social ladder, or do their bidding slavishly, or allow themselves to be used with impunity.

For a generation, the harijans have been encouraged by official government policy to think of themselves as the equals of everybody else. Special preference has systematically been given them in higher-education and government jobs. Mass communication and increasing literacy have raised their expectations for a better life.

Source: Stevens, 1984.

When analyzing the failures of welfare programs in the United States, some have focused on the ways in which the system has reduced people's ability and willingness to take control of their lives, leading to the abdication of personal responsibility (Murray 1986). Murray (1988) argues that in the United States poverty has only recently become synonymous with despair, immorality, and social chaos. The reason lies, in part, in the inability to envision a better future.

The resultant "welfare mentalities" are characterized by lack of self-respect, sense of accomplishment, and sense of community. Sometimes antipoverty programs have produced passive or antisocial reactions. Thus, native populations leading lives of welfare dependency suffer some of the highest suicide rates found anywhere. This is true of Canadian Indian and Eskimo communities, where the traditional hunting and trapping life-style has given way to irregular wagework, unemployment, and welfare. It is equally true for Australian aborigines.

## CLASS CONSCIOUSNESS

Historically, the poor have rarely challenged the status quo. Before this can occur, a new mindset must emerge. The role of victim must be transformed into that of aggressor, and fear must be transformed into anger. The sense of isolated impotence must be turned into a feeling of collective omnipotence.

This new mindset is based on the recognition of relative deprivation. In part, this includes recognizing that one's low status is not due to personal limitations or to an immutable, preordained fate. Next, subordinated individuals must be able to view themselves as members of a particular stratum or class, and to see others as belonging either to the same stratum or to others higher or lower in the stratification hierarchy. If a feeling of belonging to the same class occurs, as when one interacts with others and identifies with their worldview and commitments, a collective definition of the social situation may arise. This shared belief system or ideology is internalized, and the stratum or class then becomes a reference group. Under these conditions "class consciousness" is said to exist. And class consciousness is the prerequisite for collective class action (Morris and Murphy 1966).

Class consciousness and the experience of relative deprivation have far-reaching political significance. In *The Homeless Mind,* Berger et al. develop the concept of "conscientization," meaning "the entire transformation of the consciousness of the people that would make them understand the political parameters of their existence and the possibilities of changing their situation by political action." According to this definition, one becomes freed from ideological domination by the elite; for oppressed people to become liberated, "they must first become liberated from "the patterns of thought imposed [on them] by the oppressors" (Berger et al. 1973: 176).

## CLASS AND BEHAVIOR

Given the impact of social class identity, thought, and belief, it should come as no surprise that individuals' position in the class structure should determine their behaviors as well. As we will see in this section, social class structures the nature of one's encounters with others, including sexual activities.

### Interactional Reaffirmation of the Status Hierarchy

As we saw in Chapters 5 and 9, status hierarchies are reaffirmed and maintained in the course of everyday social interactions. For instance, rituals of deference shape the meaning and tone of interaction between subordinates and superiors. Such rituals include bows, eye contact, distance rules, and the language used. (In the not-too-distant past, "Mr." was a title reserved for whites. African Americans were called by their first names or simply "boy.") Since such communications often occur through nonverbal channels, subordinates must develop sensitivity to nonverbal cues:

> Greater social sensitivity itself may well be the special gift—or burden—of subordinates, for example, women in a male-dominated society, or blacks in a white-dominated one. Pam English has noted that slaves were described by early writers as having an acute judgment in discriminating the character of others, and believes this quality may refer to an aptitude for interpreting nonverbal signals, common to slaves and women alike. (Henley 1977: 14)

***Spatial Reaffirmations of Subordinate Status.*** High-status individuals also affirm their standing by using spatial props and waiting strategies to control how situations are defined. This is achieved in part through the physical design of situations. Spatial distance, for instance, ensures that leaders are physically (and symbolically) set apart from the masses: Hence the elevated seat of the judge in the courtroom or the king in the throne room, or the fixed seats in classrooms angled so that seated students must look at a standing professor.

In corporate America, the chief executive officer typically has the highest office in a building, along with his or her own parking space and keys to the executive washroom. In stark contrast to the public work zones of most subordinates, the CEO's space is normally invisible, behind closed doors guarded by a zealously protective secretary. When interactions with subordinates do occur, they are often scheduled appointments on the boss' turf. When invited into the office, the subordinate sees all the props reaffirming the superior status of its occupant and is invited to sit opposite the boss, separated from his or her by a large, impressive desk.

High-status individuals are also given greater territorial mobility. In large manufacturing plants, for instance, the color of one's identification badge determines where one can go on the shop floor. Whereas the orange-badged lathe and drill press workers may not leave the orange zones painted on the floor, the blue-badged supervisors may go wherever they wish. They also have the right to invade the personal spaces of lower-status workers.

### Temporal Reaffirmations of Subordinate Status.

> Don't you know they're talking about a Revolution
> while they're standing in the welfare lines
> crying at the doorsteps of those armies of salvation
> wasting time in the unemployment lines,
> sittin around waiting for a promotion. . . .
> Poor people are going to rise up and get their share,
> Poor people are going to rise up and take what's theirs.
> —Tracy Chapman, "Talkin' About a Revolution"

Because it is a scarce resource, time is often used to exercise power over others. Queueing and waiting, for instance, are two ways in which situations force the poor or powerless to recognize the definitions of the situation established by the elite or powerful. When President Roosevelt made a bank president wait half an hour outside his White House office (as he, himself, had previously been made to wait by the bank president), the message conveyed was that the banker was in a lower-status position. Because of their presumed greater social value, privileged individuals don't have to wait. Further, the more important a person is, the greater his or her license to violate rules of punctuality and the longer the waiting period subordinates must accept without showing impatience. Thus, in many universities there is an unwritten code in which students allow assistant professors to be ten minutes late before leaving the classroom, whereas associate professors are given twenty minutes and full professors thirty (Levine 1987: 28).

Often such waiting increases the value of the eventual encounter. For instance, which physician would you have more confidence in, one for whom you are the only patient, or one who has a filled waiting room? The more important the person, the more valuable his or her time becomes and the further into the future he or she is "booked in advance."

When a subordinate finally is "given time" by a more powerful individual, temporal factors continue to reaffirm his or her lesser status. For instance, one may be given only a few scheduled minutes to be with the superior other. When the superior answers a phone call or accepts the interruption of an equally powerful other, the subordinate is reminded that this interaction time is not his or her own and he or she can be put "on hold."

## Class and Sex

Class dynamics even determine what takes place in the bedroom. The greater the status discrepancy between men and women, the less likely women are to enjoy sexual activity. This status discrepancy is greater, for instance, in rural areas where traditional life-styles are more likely observed than in cities. (See Chapter 16.) Thus, in Liu Dalin's study of the sexual activities of Chinese couples ($N = 23,000$), 34 percent of rural couples said that they engaged in a minute or less of foreplay, compared with 17 percent of those living in cities (cited in Burton 1990).

Compared to the lower classes, in which sex tends to be unsophisticated and male-dominated, the upper classes are more likely to engage in a greater variety of sexual activities while the middle classes tend to be "provident and inhibited [in their sexuality], an attitude consonant with their thrifty and calculating economic behavior" (Stone 1985:28). After World War II, Alfred Kinsey et al. (1948) found that only 15 percent of married men who had not attended college ever engaged in cunnilingus, compared to 45 percent of their college-educated counterparts. In general, the higher their social class, the less likely they are to say that premarital sex is always wrong and the more likely they are to claim that homosexual relations are not wrong at all.

Closely tied to social class are the attributes of gender and race. These additional dimensions of stratification also affect how situations are defined and interactions are negotiated. When they are combined with class and age, increasingly distinctive selves result as the status characteristics associated with each attribute are either magnified or become a source of **status inconsistency.** In other words, one status does not override the other: Being old does not diminish the significance of race in determining how one perceives oneself or how others will interact with one. For example, the deference received by successful physicians and the sense of personal consistency they experience is altered for those who are not upper-class white males.

## THE SOCIAL PSYCHOLOGY OF FEMALE SUBORDINATION

In addition to age, gender is one of the universal dimensions on which status differences are based. Women have always had lower status than men, but the extent of the gap between the sexes has varied. Throughout history there has been a trend toward increasing subjugation of women. Numerous theories have been proposed to explain why women's status declined as civilization progressed. One important factor seems to be that men always did the fighting, possibly because pregnancy and physical weakness prevented women from being effective warriors. As civilizations evolved, the warrior class nearly always ended up with the political power. Another factor is that civilization developed in cities, where women were routinely excluded from many aspects of life.

In primitive societies women enjoyed nearly equal status with men (Tannahill 1980). On the basis of archaeological evidence, Marija Gimbutas (1982a:9) argues that between 7000 B.C. and 3500 B.C. Europeans lived in peaceful agricultural societies characterized by egalitarianism, matrifocal and matrilineal kinship systems, and worship of the Great Goddess. The Great Goddess, Campbell (1988:167) notes, represents the earth. As the earth gives birth and nourishment to plants, so do women to their infants. Although the division of labor was determined by gender, with the men hunting and building while the women headed clans and controlled religion, one sex did not dominate the other.

Lacking a warrior class, this egalitarian system was overthrown in the fourth millennium B.C. by Semite invaders, who had formerly been hunters and had become herders of goats and sheep. For them, life's central metaphor was not regeneration and procreation but, rather, death. In the resulting wars, conquered men were killed and women and children were enslaved and exploited. Gerda Lerner (1986) argues that the enslaved peoples were the first form of property and that the property status of women was the origin of status distinctions based on gender.

Lerner (1986) locates the cultural invention of patriarchy, or male domination, in the Middle East between 3100 B.C. and 600 B.C. In his view, patriarchy was a product of social necessity and mutual consent. With lifespans of less than 28 years and with infant mortality rates between 70 and 75 percent, women had to be pregnant almost continuously if the tribe was to survive. Tribal needs also included intertribal exchanges of women. Because of such practices, men were ultimately viewed as having rights that were not shared by women.

Although modernization has generally produced greater political and legal equality between the sexes, vast discrepancies remain. Women continue to work longer and harder than men. In the United States, as a result of increasing rates of divorce and growing numbers of single-parent families, poverty has increasingly become feminized over the past few decades.

## Maintenance of the Gender Order

The gender order is maintained in a myriad of ways, including gender biases in language, differences in socialization (see Chapter 7), institutionalized prejudice and ideological justifications, and outright harassment. We have seen how social reality is created and maintained through interaction; here, too, the subordination of women is affirmed. In addition to receiving nonverbal messages of subordination (see Chapter 5), women have difficulty even "getting the floor" to put forth their ideas. In face-to-face interactions, men make between 76 and 96 percent of the interruptions (Zimmerman and West 1975). In a study of attempts to either start or maintain conversation, one study found men succeeding in twenty-eight out of twenty-nine attempts, whereas women succeeded in only seventeen of their forty-seven ventures (cited in Pfeiffer 1985).

The gender order is also affirmed by the notion of femininity. Femininity is associated with displays of incompetence, helplessness, passivity, and non-competitiveness (Sontag 1979). Women learn early in life not to aspire to high achievement. Coleman (1971) detected this tendency in high school, where girls learn that popularity depends not on brains but on looks, clothing, and being chosen by a successful male. As a result of these experiences, a **fear of success** is instilled in women (Horner 1970). A related lesson is the devaluation of female achievement. In one experiment (Goldberg 1971), college women were asked to rate a series of manuscripts, supposedly written by both men and women, dealing with either traditionally masculine fields (e.g., law) or traditionally feminine ones (e.g., dietetics). Regardless of the gender orientation of the topics, the results were the same: The manuscripts that were supposedly written by women received lower ratings.

Even if women do excel in school, their success is not internalized. In a longitudinal study of high school valedictorians, salutatorians, and honor students, researchers found that at graduation 23 percent of the men and 21 percent of the women believed they were "far above average" in intelligence. As college sophomores, only 4 percent of the women still held that belief, whereas 22 percent of the men continued to rate themselves that way. By the senior year in college, none of the women reported feeling far above average, compared with 25 percent of the men (cited in Epperson 1988).

## Ideological Justifications of the Subordination of Women

It can be argued that gender distinctions are determined not so much by biology as by ideology and social control (Epstein 1988). In the course of social evolution, civilizations developed ideologies to explain the status quo. Religious and other justifications for women's inferior status multiplied. In ancient Greece, for example, the story of Pandora's box featured a woman who introduced misfortune and suffering to the world. In the Christian version of the myth (Phillips 1984), Eve committed the original sin that condemned humanity to toil and pain instead of paradise.

By the time of Columbus, women were viewed as particularly susceptible to evil, owing to an excessive sexual drive and weak moral constitution: According to a manual on witchcraft, the *Malleus Maleficarum* (1486), "All witchcraft comes from carnal lust, which in women is insatiable" (cited in Phillips 1984).

Similar cultural images of female depravity reappeared during the late nineteenth century, again stressing their autoerotic tendencies and their inability to differentiate spiritual passion from lust. In the emerging market society where "every man was for himself" there was little room for women; not coincidentally, females during the mid-Victorian period were being illustrated with consumptive looks and dying beautiful deaths. With the closing of the frontier, the transformation of work from independent farming to the collectively controlled labor of the assembly line (wherein women were interchangeable with men), and the rise of women's rights movements, the very underpinnings of masculinity were evaporating. According to Bram Dijkstra's (1986) analysis of artistic motifs of the century, such changes produced reactionary shifts in the depictions of women, from sentimentalist images of their soul-healing power to more base and misogynist portrayals—reflected in such painting titles as *Bondage* (Ernest Normand 1895), *A Martyr of Fanaticism* (José [de] Brito 1895), and *The Source of Evil* (Giovanni Segantini 1897), and in the female vampire and prostitute motifs of the period. There also arose the mythology of therapeutic rape and the idea that "women love to be beaten." The theory of evolution also contributed to the perception of women as occupying a lower evolutionary rung along with the "primitive" races being discovered by anthropologists.

As the twentieth century comes to a close, scientific research into gender differences and their origins continues to legitimate the traditional inequalities. Recent research has focused on the brain. Tanenbaum (1989), for instance, claims that owing to their stronger left-hemisphere functions, men tend to divide up tasks into component parts and deal with each as it occurs; this explains their superiority in mathematical and spatial reasoning. By virtue of their stronger right-hemisphere brain functions, women are more likely to grasp a holistic overview of the situation and to be more adept at verbal fluency and comprehension. And since emotions are more closely associated with the right hemisphere, women also have greater ability to relate to others.

## Violence and Sexual Harassment as Mechanisms of Social Oppression

Violence or the threat of violence against women permeates American society. Physical abuse by men is the primary source of injury to women. According to FBI reports, a woman is beaten every eighteen seconds, and between three and four million women are battered by spouses or partners each year (Pisano 1990). In addition, there are symbolic and psychological forms of abuse. A 1990 Pentagon study of sexual harassment in the military found that nearly two-thirds of the women in uniform had been harassed either directly, by being pressured to grant sexual favors, or indirectly, by being subjected to catcalls, teasing, and the like (Schmitt 1990). (See Table 10.5.)

The most demeaning and devastating form of violence against women is rape. One out of ten American women will be raped at some time during her lifetime. A study of women living in Los Angeles county ($n = 248$) revealed that for one-quarter the first experience of intercourse occurred through rape (Wyatt

TABLE 10.5   Forms of Sexual Harassment in the U.S. Military

|  | Percent Women | Percent Men |
|---|---|---|
| Teasing, jokes | 52 | 13 |
| Looks, gestures | 44 | 10 |
| Touching, cornering | 38 | 9 |
| Pressure for sexual favors | 15 | 2 |
| Actual or attempted rape, sexual assault | 5 | 1 |

Source: *New York Times* (Schmitt), 1990.

Numerous are the ways by which males intimidate or otherwise demonstrate their power over females. Here, in the workplace, a man confines a woman coworker between his planted arms. While he may perceive his nonverbal message as conveying a message of caring and "openness," the tilt of her body reveals a possible interpretation of sexual harassment.

1988). A study conducted in the late 1980s found that half of a sample of male junior high school students in Rhode Island believed it is acceptable to rape a woman if the man had spent more than $15 on her, and one out of twelve college men admitted to having committed rape (Holtzman 1989).

According to Susan Brownmiller (1975), rape is a political tactic used by men to intimidate women. A study of 646 Philadelphia rapes found that half were pair or gang rapes (Amir 1971). Among adolescent males, gang rape serves as a ritual of male bonding as well as a rite of passage, particularly in militaristic and violence-prone cultures in which men have little involvement in child rearing (Sanday 1981) and masculinity is equated with dominance and sex with violence.

For the victims of rape, the ordeal violates and destroys many aspects of the self, including the sense of invulnerability, trust, control, self-esteem, and self-confidence. A tendency to blame the victim is evident in court cases, in which the victim often becomes the defendant as her sexual history is publicly scrutinized. In 1975, for instance, Britain's law lords (the equivalent of the United States Supreme Court) ruled on a case involving the wife of a sergeant who had supposedly been raped by three Royal Air Force men. The husband had invited them to have intercourse with her and had told them to ignore her protests, which he said she had produced for her own sexual stimulation. On appeal, the British law lords ruled 3 to 2 that a man cannot be convicted of rape as long as he thought he was really acting as the woman wanted him to, no matter how unreasonable his belief and despite any protests the woman might have made.

## THE SOCIAL PSYCHOLOGY OF RACIAL SUBORDINATION

It has been said that race is the plague of civilization. Even in supposedly race-blind societies such as Israel, the specter of racism raises its head. In the Caribbean islands, social stratification corresponds almost perfectly with skin pigmentation. Hitler called the United States a "mongrel nation" because of its racially heterogeneous population. Nearly half a century later, the prime minister of Japan, Yasuhiro Nakasone, boasted that the source of Japan's strength is its "racial homogeneity." Nakasone remarked that the average level of intellectual achievement among Americans is lower than that of the Japanese because of the large proportions of African Americans and Hispanics in the U.S. population.

African Americans are the only group to have arrived in the United States against their will and to have been forcibly stripped of their culture. During World War II, the noted Swedish economist Gunnar Myrdal (1944) observed in *An American Dilemma* that the racial problem cut to the very core of the definition of Americans as a people. He saw that even though the nation was founded on the ideals of individual liberty and personal dignity, white Americans could not, through law or social practice, treat the descendants of slaves as their equals. Today, although some legal progress has been made, prejudice and inequality remain prevalent in American society.

### Racism

> Sometimes I wonder if they [civil rights leaders] really want what they say the want. Because some of those leaders are doing very well leading organizations based on keeping alive the feeling that they're victims of prejudice.—Ronald Reagan (cited in Rosenthal 1989)

As the 1980s came to a close, the United States witnessed a resurgence of racism. Residents of Brooklyn were appalled when a 16-year-old African American youth was ambushed and killed by a white gang. In Louisiana, a former Ku Klux Klan leader was elected to the state's House of Representatives. A Dallas

## The 1950 UNESCO Statement on Race

According to present knowledge, there is no proof that the groups of mankind differ in their innate mental characteristics, whether in respect of intelligence or temperament. The scientific evidence indicates that the range of mental capacities in all ethnic groups is much the same.

## Reaffirmations of Racism in the Naming of Things

Names such as "Nigger Creek" and "Dead Negro Draw" should be wiped off the Texas map, says an NAACP chapter president, Gary Bledsoe, who is making the first concerted effort in the nation to change an entire state's racially offensive geographic names.

"My guess is we don't have 'Caucasian Mountain' or 'Japanese Mountain,'" he said. "It does lead one to believe that one group is being treated differently because of their skin color."

Many locations have been tagged with racial names because Blacks have lived there.

One example: The "Colored Subdivision" in Pflugerville, an area that locals say was given to Blacks after the Civil War.

There are six "Negro Creeks" in Texas, a "Negro Crossing" in Green County near San Angelo, and "Negroes Liberty Settlement," "Negro Bend," and "Negro Gully," in Liberty County east of Houston.

"Negro" was substituted for "nigger" in a comprehensive 1962 name switch by the Board of Geographic Names in Reston, Va. The board decides which names are used on all maps produced in the United States.

The Travis County Commissioners Court has worked for months to change "Nigger Creek" and "Niggerhead Hill" to "Warbler Creek" and "Warbler Hill."

Those new names are awaiting a nod from the Board of Geographic Names to decide such requests.

Source: Hightower, 1990.

---

judge ruled that a high school (80 percent white and 10 percent African American) could continue to use Confederate symbols for its sports team, including a flag resembling that of the Confederacy and a fight song sung to the tune of "Dixie."

As will be shown in the following chapter, proximity plays a large role in determining social bonds. Consequently, racial segregation maintains the isolation of minority groups from the mainstream of society. Demographers report that neighborhoods in many of the nation's largest cities in the Northeast and Midwest have become "hypersegregated," with Chicago being the most segregated city, followed by Detroit, Cleveland, Milwaukee, Newark, Gary, Philadelphia, Los Angeles, Baltimore, and St. Louis (Massey and Denton 1989). Members of different races rarely interact outside of the workplace. Whites do not support equal opportunity or equal treatment when it could lead to close or prolonged social contact between the races.

According to the Community Relations Service of the Justice Department, reports of racial incidents throughout the nation increased by more than 400 percent between 1980 and 1987 (Gup 1988). Even college campuses were not immune. Whereas the old racists believed African Americans were inferior to whites, the new racists, though not subscribing (at least publicly) to such beliefs, still treat African Americans differently than whites. Contempt of African Americans is expressed in such racially charged symbols as affirmative action, riots, crime, and fair housing laws (Murray 1984).

Prejudice is rampant even in the medical establishment, supposedly a bastion of rationality. In the late 1980s studies showed that African American patients waited 59 percent longer (14 months versus 8.8 months) for kidney transplants, even though the federally funded distribution center was supposed to be color blind and not based on ability to pay (San Antonio Express-News 1990). Even when white and African American heart patients were equally able to pay, whites were significantly more likely than African Americans to receive such treatments as angiographies and coronary bypass surgery (Wenneker and Epstein 1989).

## The Toll of Centuries of Prejudice

As a result of the experience of slavery, African Americans were severed from their past and their African culture for many generations. Some memories of life in the pre–Civil War South survived in the oral histories collected during the Depression by the Federal Writers' Project of the Works Progress Administration. They include stories telling how African Americans were whipped for learning to read or for praying out loud for freedom (Mellon 1989).

It is hard for many young people to believe that only a generation ago many southern cities had segregated restrooms, water faucets, and even theater entrances. NBC had to cancel the "Nat King Cole Show" because sponsors refused to pay for African Americans to appear on TV. When, in 1961, ABC television presented a documentary featuring the African American perspective, the show's sponsor, Bell and Howell, was boycotted. As late as 1970, some public stations in the South declined to carry the children's series "Sesame Street" because of its racially integrated cast.

In 1986 the Census Bureau reported that the median net worth of white households was over eleven times greater than that for African American households, one-third of which had no wealth at all (Kilborn 1986). As the proportion of white Americans living in poverty declined toward the end of the 1980s, the proportion of African Americans in poverty increased (Tolchin 1988).

Nearly half of all African American children are born out of wedlock, and many live in single-parent families. Whereas in 1970 58 percent of African American children lived with both parents (compared with 85 percent for all races), by 1990 that figure had declined to 37 percent (compared with 73 percent for all races). Between 1925 and 1987, the percentage of prison inmates in the United States who were African American doubled, from 23 to 46 percent (Harper's Magazine 1988). By 1989 there was a one in four chance that a African American male in his twenties was either in prison, on parole, or on probation (U.S. News & World Report 1990).

Strongly influencing these figures is the situation of many African Americans living for several generations in the deteriorating cores of major cities. These individuals are defined less by their income than by their behaviors. Theirs is a culture marked by an increasingly distinctive language (e.g., hip-hop words), music (e.g., rap), teenage pregnancy (nearly one-half of African American females are pregnant by the age of 20), undereducation (high school dropout rates exceed 50 percent in many inner cities), chronic unemployment (only

## Exposure to the Culture of Violence

In 1989, one of the questions in the NORC General Social Survey of the American public age 18 and older dealt with firsthand knowledge of a homicide victim:

> Within the past 12 months, how many people have you known personally that were victims of homicide?

Nine percent of whites personally knew one or more victims, compared to over 23 percent of African Americans. In fact, as shown in Figure 10.4, nearly 40 percent of African Americans between the ages of 18 and 29 knew someone who had been murdered during the previous year. These victims were not distant acquaintances: 29 percent were either family members or lovers, and 42 percent were personal friends.

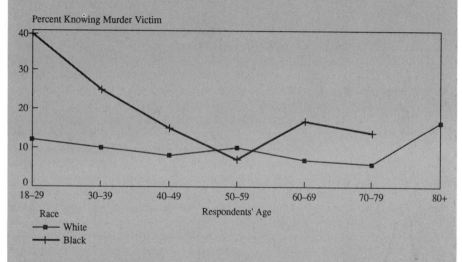

**FIGURE 10.4   Personally Known Murder Victims, by Age and Race**
Source: NORC, 1990.

What are some of the social implications of knowing a person who is murdered, particularly for those in the age group most affected? Following are data indicating changes in orientation toward some of the measures of anomie presented in Figure 10.2 for African Americans and whites between the ages of 18 and 29:

| | Whites | | African Americans | |
|---|---|---|---|---|
| | *Percent Knowing Recent Murder Victim* | *Percent Not Knowing* | *Percent Knowing Recent Murder Victim* | *Percent Not Knowing* |
| **Unfair** Percent agreeing that it's hardly fair to bring a child into the world | 17% | 37% | 44% | 62% |
| **Advantage** Percent agreeing that most people try to take advantage of others | 60 | 48 | 82 | 62 |
| **Life Excitement** Percent finding life exciting | 61 | 51 | 33 | 31 |
| **Trust** Percent saying most people can be trusted | 44 | 29 | 9 | 19 |

These data indicate that knowing a recently murdered individual increases the likelihood of believing that most people try to take advantage of others. However, contrary to what might be expected, it also decreases the likelihood of agreeing that it's hardly fair to bring a child into the world. Moreover, knowing a murder victim slightly enhances the feeling that life is exciting. The races diverge on matters of trust: Among whites, those who know a murder victim are 52 percent more likely than those who do not know a victim to agree that most people can be trusted; the relationship is reversed for African Americans.

Such analyses do not take into account social class, which, as was evident in Figure 10.2, is highly correlated with both anomie and homicide. To control for this, we modify the table so as to contrast those who identify themselves as members of the "lower" and "working" (L-W) classes with those who identify themselves as members of the "middle" and "upper" classes (M-U).

| Class: Know Murder Victim? | Percent Whites | | | | Percent African Americans | | | |
|---|---|---|---|---|---|---|---|---|
| | L-W | | M-U | | L-W | | M-U | |
| | Yes | No | Yes | No | Yes | No | Yes | No |
| **Unfair** (Percent agreeing) | 50 | 47 | 7 | 27 | 50 | 50 | 33 | 83 |
| **Advantage** (Percent agreeing) | 80 | 53 | 47 | 45 | 100 | 53 | 60 | 83 |
| **Life Excitement** (Percent exciting) | 25 | 36 | 71 | 64 | 33 | 30 | 33 | 33 |
| **Trust** (Percent can trust) | 10 | 22 | 67 | 35 | 0 | 20 | 20 | 17 |

> Now a more intriguing picture emerges. Knowing a murder victim diminishes young adults' sense of unfairness (agreeing that "it's hardly fair to bring a child into the world") only among the middle and upper classes, and more so for whites than for African Americans. Knowing a murder victim increases the belief of lower- and working-class whites and African Americans that people always try to take advantage of others; the reverse holds true among middle- and upper-class African Americans.

half of the African American men in the ghetto have jobs), drug use, and long-term welfare dependency (40 percent of African American children are dependent on public assistance) (Stengel 1988). Further, the cycle is self-perpetuating: Nearly two-thirds of the daughters of single women on welfare end up on welfare themselves (Stengel 1988).

The culture of the urban lower-class African Americans also features violence. Although African Americans account for approximately 11 percent of the American population, over 40 percent of all murder victims are African American. Homicide has become the leading cause of death for African American males between the ages of 15 and 39; the homicide rate among this group is over six times greater than the rate among white males in the same age group.

Being raised in and living with such chaos has many social-psychological implications. Unlike white children in affluent families, who learn that death normally occurs among older people because of natural causes, those who are raised in inner-city ghettos learn that death often comes violently and prematurely. Theirs is an environment of fear in which parents cannot even assume that their children can walk to school safely. In a 1990 survey of more than one thousand middle and high school students living in Chicago's inner city, the Community Mental Health Council found that 74 percent had witnessed a slaying, shooting, stabbing, or robbery, and nearly one-half had personally been victims of violent crimes (Starks 1990). In sections of Los Angeles, social workers counsel children who exhibit all the psychological traumas found in war zones.

For these children, the social message that their lives are relatively cheap is conveyed in a variety of ways. For instance, whereas only one in five billboards in white neighborhoods of Baltimore advertises alcohol and tobacco, the figure is 76 percent in the African American neighborhoods (*Harper's Magazine* 1990b). Many African Americans view such ads—along with the drug epidemic and crack wars—as a form of intentional genocide (Bayles 1989). Even the AIDS epidemic is sometimes seen as an antiAfrican American conspiracy. By late 1989, African Americans accounted for nearly 30 percent of all diagnosed cases of AIDS, and 55 percent of all cases among children under the age of 13 (*New York Times* 1990b).

## CONCLUSION

In this chapter we have seen that social structure directly influences the self. The individual's position in the stratification system strongly influences one's self-concept, self-esteem, core beliefs, ambitions, emotions, and sense of time.

So different, in fact, are the outlooks of people at different levels of the status hierarchy that considerable doubt is shed on social-psychological research based on college-age, white, middle- and upper-middle-class subjects.

Precisely specifying how sensory and cognitive processes (psychological experiences) are influenced by society is the social-psychological style of consciousness that is being advocated by this book. Sometimes this social-psychological connection is direct, as we saw how emotions could be directly triggered by social environments and precede any cognitive processing. More often, the connection is indirect, modified by the self and its beliefs: Stereotypes, for instance, shape what people perceive; the self-esteem bound up with self-consciousness also filters what individuals perceive, with ego-threatening events being ignored and forgotten.

This self, as we saw in the previous chapter, is strongly determined by its interactions with other selves. Out of these interactions arise socially standardized definitions of situations, which specify the cast of social actors as well as the form and objectives of their interactions. In this chapter, we have considered how the structure of these interactions are, in turn, determined by societies' stratification orders that arise out of historical and economic factors. This, in turn, produces a reinforcing cycle: A subordinate finds himself or herself kowtowing, smiling, or otherwise displaying culturally standardized signs of deferences. How we act determines how we think and focus on the world. Seeing ourselves acting in deferential ways and observing the displays of status superiority of others toward us, we can come to see ourselves as lesser persons. Assuming the social roles available to them, people of subordinate status internalize and pass on to their children the mindsets, emotions, and life-styles of lower-status persons.

This logic underpins the social-psychological strategy of mapping precisely how social factors shape cognitions, beliefs, emotions, selves, and the interactional contexts wherein selves create and maintain social realities with other selves. But before examining how people are shaped by the broadest of social forces (e.g., the psychologies of religion, work, or mass media), another intermediary link between mind and society must be considered: individuals' bonds with others and emergent group dynamics, the topics developed in the following two chapters. Thereafter, we will observe how social inequalities determine the nature of individuals' relationships and, further, how their influence is modified by such social institutions as religion and work, and how it buffers one from the forces of modernization.

# REFERENCES

Amir, Menachem. 1971. *Patterns in forcible rape.* Chicago: University of Chicago Press.

Aristotle. 1943. *Politics* (trans. Benjamin Jowett). New York: Modern Library.

Armas, José. 1990, March 28. Invisible people have no future. *San Antonio Express-News*, p. 18-A.

Bayles, Martha. 1989, August 21. Crying wolf about racism. *Wall Street Journal.*

Berger, Peter, and Thomas Luckmann. 1966. *The social construction of reality.* New York: Doubleday.

Berger, Peter, Brigitte Berger, and Hansfried Kellner. 1973. *The homeless mind: Modernization and consciousness.* New York: Random House.

Bettelheim, Bruno. 1969. *The informed heart.* New York: Free Press.

Brownmiller, Susan. 1975. *Against our will: Men, women, and rape.* New York: Simon and Schuster.

Burton, Sandra. 1990, May 14. Straight talk on sex in China. *Time*, p. 82.

Campbell, Colin. 1987. *The romantic ethic and the spirit of modern consumerism*. New York and Oxford: Basil Blackwell.

Campbell, Joseph, with Bill Moyers. 1988. *The power of myth*. Garden City, NY: Doubleday.

Caplan, N., and S. D. Nelson. 1973. On being useful: The nature and consequences of psychological research on social problems. *American Psychologist* 28:199–211.

Chafe, William H. 1977. *Women and equality: Changing patterns in American culture*. New York: Oxford University Press.

Coleman, James. 1971. *Adolescent society*. New York: Free Press.

Coser, Lewis, and Rose Coser. 1963. Time perspective and social structure. In A. W. Gouldner and H. P. Gouldner (eds.), *Modern sociology*. Orlando: Harcourt Brace Jovanovich.

Dahrendorf, Ralf. 1959. *Class and class conflict in industrial society*. Palo Alto, CA: Stanford University Press.

Davis, Kingsley, and Wilbert E. Moore. 1940. Some principles of stratification. *American Sociology Review* 10:242–249.

de Leon, Richard. 1979. *Small futures: Children, inequality, and the limits of liberal reform*. Washington, D.C.: Carnegie.

Della Fave, Richard. 1980. The meek shall not inherit the earth: Self-evaluation and the legitimacy of stratification. *American Sociological Review* 45:955–971.

Derber, Charles. 1979. *The pursuit of attention: Power and individualism in everyday life*. New York: Oxford University Press.

Dijkstra, Bram. 1986. *Idols of perversity: Fantasies of feminine evil in fin-de-siècle culture*. New York: Oxford University Press.

Epperson, Sharon E. 1988, September 16. Studies link subtle sex bias in schools with women's behavior in the workplace. *Wall Street Journal*, p. 19.

Epstein, Cynthia Fuchs. 1988. *Deceptive distinctions: sex, gender, and the social order*. New Haven, CT: Yale University Press.

Feagin, Joe R. 1972. Poverty: We still believe that God helps those who help themselves. *Psychology Today* 6:101–129.

Fehrenbach, T. R. 1988, August 28. Society wants its underclass. *San Antonio Express-News*, p. 3-L.

Frerichs, R. R., J. M. Chapman, and E. F. Maes. 1984. Mortality due to all causes and to cardiovascular-diseases among 7 race-ethnic populations in Los Angeles Co. *International Journal of Epidemiology* 13:291–298.

Fuchsberg, Gilbert. 1987, September 21. For the right price, just about anything can bear your name. *Wall Street Journal*, pp. 1, 14.

Gilbert, Dennis, and Joseph A. Kahl. 1987. *American class structure: A new synthesis* (3rd ed.). Belmont, CA: Wadsworth.

Gimbutas, Marija. 1982. *The goddesses and gods of old Europe: 6500–3500 BC myths and cult images*. Berkeley: University of California Press.

Goldberg, Philip. 1971. Are women prejudiced against women? In Athena Theodore (ed.), *The Professional Woman*. New York: Schenkman.

Goleman, Daniel. 1986, December 30. Perception of time emerges as key psychological factor. *New York Times*, pp. 15, 16.

Gup, Ted. 1988, October 17. Racism in the raw in suburban Chicago. *Time*.

*Harper's Magazine*. 1990a, January. Harper's index to the 1980s. p. 41.

*Harper's Magazine*. 1990b, April. Harper's index. p. 17.

*Harper's Magazine*. 1988, August. Harper's index. p. 11.

Henley, Nancy M. 1977. *Body politics: Power, sex & nonverbal communication*. New York: Simon and Schuster.

Henry, Jules. 1965, March-April. White people's time, colored people's time. *Trans-action* 2:2.

Hightower, Susan [AP]. 1990, April 15. Racially labeled Texas towns may undergo name changes. *San Antonio Light*, p. A16.

Hollingshead, August, and Frederick Redlich. 1958. *Social class and mental disorder*. New York: Wiley.

Holtzman, Elizabeth. 1989, May 5. Rape—the silence is criminal. *New York Times*, p. 27.

Horner, Matina S. 1970. Femininity and successful achievement: A basic inconsistency. In J. Bardwick, E. Douvan, Matina Horner, and D. Gutmann (eds.), *Feminine personality and conflict.* Belmont, CA: Brooks/Cole.

Kearl, Michael. 1989. *Endings: A sociology of death and dying.* New York: Oxford University Press.

Kilborn, Peter. 1986, July 19. U.S. whites 10 times wealthier than blacks, census study finds. *New York Times,* pp. 1, 26.

Kimmel, Michael. 1987, April. Women-hating in perspective. *Psychology Today,* pp. 71–72.

Kinsey, Alfred C., Wardell B. Pomeroy, and Clyde E. Martin. 1948. *Sexual behavior in the human male.* Philadelphia: W. B. Saunders.

Kohn, M. L. 1969. *Class and conformity.* Homewood, IL: Dorsey Press.

Lenski, Gerhard. 1966. *Power and privilege: A theory of social stratification.* New York: McGraw-Hill.

Lerner, Gerda. 1986. *The creation of patriarchy.* New York: Oxford University Press.

Levine, Robert. 1987, April. Waiting is a power game. *Psychology Today,* pp. 24–33.

Lewis, J. David, and Andrew J. Weigert. 1981. The structures and meanings of social time. *Social Forces* 60:432–462.

Luker, Kristin. 1984. *Abortion and the politics of motherhood.* Berkeley: University of California Press.

McCord, Colin, and Harold Freeman. 1990 January. *The New England Journal of Medicine.*

Marx, Karl, and Friedrich Engels. 1967[1848]. *Communist manifesto.* New York: Pantheon.

Marx, Karl, and Friedrich Engels. 1955. Wage, labor and capital. In *Selected works in two volumes.* Moscow: Foreign Languages Publishing House.

Massey, Douglas, and Nancy Denton. 1989, August. Hypersegregation in U.S. metropolitan areas: Black and Hispanic segregation along five dimensions. *Demography,* pp. 373–391.

Mellon, James (ed.). 1989. *Bullwhip days: The slaves remember.* New York: Weidenfeld and Nicolson.

Merton, Robert. 1968. *Social theory and social structure.* New York: Free Press.

Mills, C. Wright. 1946. The middle classes in middle-sized cities. *American Sociological Review* 2:520–529.

Morley, John. 1971. *Death, heaven and the Victorians.* Pittsburgh: University of Pittsburgh Press.

Morris, Richard T., and Raymond J. Murphy. 1966. A paradigm for the study of class consciousness. *Sociology and Social Research* 50:297–313.

Moyers, Bill. 1989. *A world of ideas: Conversations with thoughtful men and women about American life today and the ideas shaping our future* (Arturo Madrid, pp. 212–220) (ed. Betty Sue Flowers). New York: Doubleday.

Murray, Charles. 1988. *In pursuit of happiness and good government.* New York: Simon and Schuster.

Murray, Charles. 1986. *Losing ground: American social policy 1950–1980.* New York: Basic Books.

Murray, Charles. 1984, December 31. Affirmative racism. *New Republic,* pp. 18–23.

Myrdal, Gunnar. 1944. *An American dilemma: The Negro problem and modern democracy.* New York: HarperCollins.

National Opinion Research Center (NORC). 1990. *General Social Surveys 1989* (James A. Davis, principal investigator, Tom W. Smith, senior study director and co-principal investigator). Data distributed by the Roper Center for Public Opinion Research.

*New York Times* [AP]. 1990a, September 20. Racial harm is found in schools' 'tracking.'

*New York Times* [AP]. 1990b, March 23. U.S. health gap is getting wider. p. A8.

Norton, Dolores. 1978. *Dual perspective: Inclusion of ethnic minority content in the social work curriculum.* Alexandria, VA: Council on Social Work Education.

Pfeiffer, John. 1985. Girl talk–boy talk. *Science* 85:58–63.

Phillips, J. A. 1984. *Eve: The history of an idea.* New York: HarperCollins.

Pisano, Marina. 1990, September 30. Domestic violence: The silent epidemic: *San Antonio Express-News,* pp. 1K and 3K.

Pomeroy, Sara B. 1975. Goddesses, whores, wives, and slaves: Women in classical antiquity. New York: Schocken Books.

Rimer, Sara. 1988, June 24. Experts dispute effects of culture on learning. *New York Times,* p. 11.

Rist, Ray. 1970. Student social class and teacher expectations: The self-fulfilling prophecy in ghetto education. *Harvard Educational Review* 40:411–451.

Rosenthal, Andrew. 1989, January 14. Some rights leaders exaggerate racism, President suggests. *New York Times,* pp. 1, 7.

Rushing, William A. 1972. *Class, culture, and alienation: A study of farmers and farm workers.* Lexington, MA: D.C. Heath/Lexington Books.

*San Antonio Express-News* [Scripps Howard Service]. 1990, August 19. Study: Blacks wait longer for transplants, p. 17-A.

*San Antonio Express-News* [Washington Post Service]. 1985, February 24. Black activist from '60s labels integration a "sham." p. 9A.

*San Antonio Light* [UPI]. 1977, March 5. Klan's try uprooted. p. 3.

Sanday, Peggy. 1981. The sociocultural context of rape—A cross-cultural study. *Journal of Social Issues* 37:5–27.

Schmitt, Eric. 1990, September 12. 2 out of 3 women in military study report sexual harassment incidents. *New York Times*, p. A12.

Schwartz, Barry. 1975. *Queuing and waiting: Studies in the social organization of access and delay.* Chicago: University of Chicago Press.

Schwartz, Barry. 1974. Waiting, exchange, and power: The distribution of time in social systems. *American Journal of Sociology* 79:841–871.

Shribman, David. 1989, April 26. Better paid and better educated are more apt to favor abortion. *Wall Street Journal*, p. A8.

Solomon, Jack. 1988. *The signs of our time.* New York: Perennial Library/HarperCollins.

Sontag, Susan. 1979. The double standard of aging. In J. H. Williams (ed.), *Psychology of women.* New York: Norton.

Srole, Leo. 1956. Social integration and certain corollaries: An exploratory study. *American Sociological Review* 21:709–716.

Stark, Elizabeth. 1986, October. Young, innocent and pregnant. *Psychology Today*, pp. 28–35.

Starks, Tamara. 1990, September 29. Brutal scenes in Chicago depressed inner-city children. *Birmingham Post-Herald* [AP]. p. 4A.

Stengel, Richard. 1988, October 10. The underclass: Breaking the cycle. *Time*, pp. 41–42.

Stevens, William. 1984, October 29. India's lowest of the low start to cry "Enough." *New York Times*, p. 4.

Stone, Lawrence. 1985, July 8. Sex in the West: The strange history of human sexuality. *New Republic*, pp. 25–37.

Tanenbaum, Joe. 1989. *Male and female realities: Understanding the opposite sex.* Sugar Land, TX: Candle.

Tannahill, Reay. 1980. *Sex in history.* New York: Stein and Day.

Taylor, Elizabeth. 1989, February 27. Time is not on their side. *Time*, p. 74.

Tolchin, Martin. 1988, September 1. Minority poverty on the rise as white poor decrease in U.S. *New York Times*, p. 9.

*U.S. News & World Report.* 1990, March 12. A bleak indictment of the inner city. p. 14.

Veblen, Thorstein. 1953[1899]. *The theory of the leisure class: An economic study of institutions.* New York: Mentor/New American Library.

*Wall Street Journal.* 1989, June 7. People patterns.

Weber, Max. 1947. *Max Weber: The theory of social and economic organization* (trans. A. M. Henderson and Talcott Parsons). New York: Oxford University Press.

Weber, Max. 1946. *From Max Weber: Essays in sociology* (trans. and ed. H. H. Gerth and C. Wright Mills). New York: Oxford University Press.

Wenneker, Mark B., and Arnold M. Epstein. 1989. Racial inequalities in the use of procedures for patients with ischemic heart-disease in Massachusetts. *Journal of the American Medical Association* 261:253–257.

Wiesel, Elie. 1984, August 19. All was lost, yet something was preserved. *New York Times Book Review*, pp. 1, 23.

Wyatt, Gail. 1988. The relationship between child sex abuse and adolescent sexual functioning in Afro-American and white American women. *Annals of the New York Academy of Sciences* 528:111–122.

Zimmerman, Don H., and Candarce West. 1975. Sex roles, interruptions and silences in conversation. In Nancy Henley and Barrie Thorne (eds.), *Language and sex: Difference and dominance.* Rowley, MA: Newbury House.

# Creating, Maintaining, and Ending Interpersonal Bonds

Think of a time when, at the prodding of friends or associates, you have attended a social function that you never would have considered going to alone. Perhaps it was a coven of witches, a gathering of victims of UFO abductions, or a monthly meeting of Uglies Unlimited or the Triskaidekaphobia Illuminatus Society. In such a novel setting, your social radar is on full alert. Members are scanned as you look for shared identifying characteristics. Simultaneously, you may wonder how you appear to them, whether or not they see you as "fitting in." Not to fit in means to somehow "stand out," so that your presence may be questioned and your motives queried. You notice the nonverbal messages conveying how members regard each other—for example, whether encounters are initiated with hugs, handshakes, or "high fives." You listen to the topics of conversation and perhaps detect a different, shared vocabulary. If individuals refer to one another as "Brother" or "Sister," a familial relationship is implied; this may mean that these individuals have known each other for some time and in ways extending beyond casual acquaintanceship. You wonder, "Who are these people and what brought them together in the first place? What is the social glue that continues to bond them together?"

In the preceding chapters we've seen how mind, self, and society emerge out of the interactions between individuals in various micro social environments. Absent from these analyses was discussion of what factors determine that these encounters even occur. Here we will consider the chemistry of interpersonal attractions and the various kinds of interpersonal bonds which can result. We will further examine how these relationships are maintained over time, and in what ways they are ended.

## Searching for a Match in a Mismatched World

"Do you believe in traditional family values? Search continues for that special Christian gentleman. I am nonsmoking, mid-50s, professional. Enjoy Austin, bluebonnets, jogging, walking, dancing, children, etc. Write, with photo."

"Fun-loving, hardworking single dad, 35, white, 5'7", 130, enjoys C&W dancing and evenings at home. Like to meet female 28–35 for honest relationship. Reply with photo."

"Alluring artist, SWF 21, likes films, British comedy, novels, and the occasional adventure among others. Seeks intelligent, sensitive, yet creative SWM 19–30 with sense of humor. Photo/note/phone."

"GWJF with parental instincts and sense of humor sought by warm, caring GWJM, 37, for friendship, marriage, kids."

"European F 25, with enormous hunger for love, needs a man with pure ideals who loves classical literature and music, who longs for exclusively monogamous deep intimacy with one woman. For lifetime. No overweight, please."

"Are you a SF who wants to make the world a better place and enjoys doing so? Can you take ordinary activities and make them exciting? If so, I might be the person for you. I am a SM, 29, doctoral student in sociology, politically left, serious, calm, sensitive, and a good listener."

## Needs Addressed by Affiliating with Others

Studies of the effects of isolation show clearly that most people cannot handle being alone. It goes against the inherent sociability of humans; hence older people's fear of loneliness and criminals' fear of solitary confinement. But people do not affiliate with anyone who happens to be available. Instead, the bonding process is guided by psychological and sociological characteristics, including individuals' self-definition and motivations and the opportunities for interaction provided by society.

From the perspective of reinforcement theory, attraction is derived from individuals' needs for belonging and approval. Prime candidates for gang membership, for instance, are youths with low self-esteem who lack structure in their lives. For them, gangs provide rules, a sense of belonging, and the opportunity to be part of something larger than themselves.

Albert and Bernice Lott (1974) claimed that if an individual is in any way rewarded when in the presence of another person, liking for that person increases. The connection between the liked individual and the reward received does not have to be direct. This was demonstrated experimentally by Griffitt and Guay (1969). In one variation of their study, the creativity of a group of subjects was evaluated by an outsider, while in another variation the outsider was simply present during an evaluation by the experimenter. In both situa-

The sharing of a common culture and belief system is a potent catalyst for interpersonal attraction, particularly when they are challenged by outside agencies. Here, the Islamic Society of Boston condemns American involvement in the Persian Gulf war, bringing together individuals who may otherwise have never interacted had they remained in their homelands.

tions, the group members liked the outsider better after a positive evaluation than after a negative one.

Social-exchange theorists view social interaction as the result of individuals cooperating to obtain numerous ends. When, for instance, personal needs or desires cannot be obtained alone, one often seeks others with whom to cooperate. Examples include support groups such as Alcoholics Anonymous, Spouses of Alzheimer's Victims, and Widow to Widow programs. In addition, as is evidenced by the myriad of hobby clubs ranging from model railroaders and breeders of racing pigeons to collectors of Civil War artifacts, we gravitate toward those who share our interests.

According to social-comparison theory, in the absence of a physical or objective standard of correctness we seek others as a means for evaluating ourselves. From this perspective, one returns to his or her twentieth high school reunion to see those with whom one shared one's formative years and to evaluate one's subsequent biography from the standpoint of this reference group.

Personality theories attribute the propensity to attract or be attracted to the affiliative motives of various types of selves. Firstborns, for instance, apparently have a greater need to affiliate with others when they are anxious (Schachter 1959). Narcissists need their admiring throngs, Machiavellians their dupes, extraverts their audience, and introspectives their privacy. Those with a high need for affiliation are more sensitive to affiliative cues (Atkinson and Walker

1956), make more telephone calls (Boyatzis 1973), pay more visits to friends (Lansing and Heyns 1959), and possibly have greater fear of rejection (Schachter 1959).

## Social Needs Addressed by Affiliation

Our species continues to exist because of the ability of numerous individuals to coordinate their activities in addressing both collective and personal needs. Unlike most other species, however, we do not do this automatically through instinct. Over the course of human social evolution, the value of close individual ties has been affirmed and societies have increasingly come to depend on the cooperative activities of voluntary associations and interest groups. (See Figure 11.1.)

Out of interpersonal attraction emerge commitments and obligations to others. Consider, for instance, the massive expenditures of time and energy required to care for the infirm elderly. In a study of employees at Travelers Corporation ($n = 739$; cited in Collins 1986), over one-quarter said that they spent an average of 10.2 hours a week caring for relatives or friends over the age of 55. Some full-time employees spent as many as eighty hours at this task. The social need for such commitment, despite the personal sacrifices necessary (80 percent said that this responsibility interfered with other family obligations and with their own social and emotional needs), is evident. If families either refuse or cannot accept this responsibility and friends do not step in, government agencies must do so.

In the *Gemeinschaft* social systems described in Chapter 8, similarities of ancestry, ethnicity, religion, and occupation provided social cohesion. Three centuries ago, Thomas Hobbes could not envision the possibility of an ethnically diverse society avoiding anarchy. But as a result of massive migrations, increasingly differentiated and specialized divisions of labor, and ever more complex social organization, modern societies require cooperation among increasingly heterogeneous peoples. Thus, one of the major problems facing the United States is to find ways to bring together individuals of varying ethnicities, cultures, religions, social classes, and generations.

## FORMS OF CONNECTEDNESS

Living in convention towns, the authors see a wide range of associations, from the Society of Small People to the American Petroleum Association, the Southern Baptists, Jesters, Parents Without Partners, Hospice Volunteers, and the Southern St. Bernard Association. The bonds linking Americans together are numerous, including occupation or profession, religion, political views, service activities, life-style, shared beliefs, and hobbies. When 10,000 members of the American Barbershop Quartet Association descended on our city, passersby often stopped on the sidewalk to strike up a tune. The sounds of four-part harmony even emanated from behind the doors of hotel restrooms.

Connectedness has many dimensions. There are the bonds of loving, liking, commitment, closeness, task interdependency, emotional interdependency, identity interdependency, interdependency of instrumental needs (e.g.,

In the 1989 NORC General Social Science Survey, respondents were asked about the groups and organizations they belong to. Figures 11.1a and b present a life-cycle model of association membership. For instance, after a slight decline between the ages of 18 and 49, there is a general increase in individuals' membership in church groups. From age 30 on, there is a decline in involvement in sports groups. For the remainder of the groups, the pattern is one of consistent participation, with roughly 10 percent of Americans involved in those groups. Corresponding with Erikson's theory (Chapter 8), we note a slight peak at midlife in the percentage of people age 40 and older who belong to service clubs.

In Figure 11.1b, the role of social class in determining the density of involvements is clear. Of the sixteen kinds of groups and organizations included, lower-class men belong to 1.16 while their upper-class counterparts belong to 2.76. The class effect is even more pronounced for women, with the mean number of memberships of upper-class women over four-and-one-half times that of lower-class women.

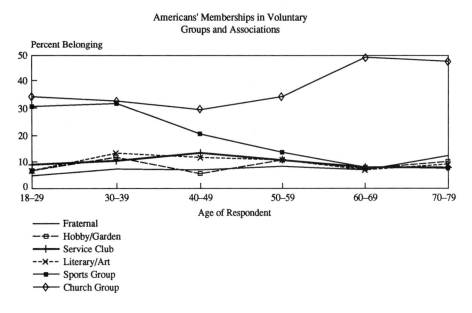

Americans' Memberships in Voluntary
Groups and Associations

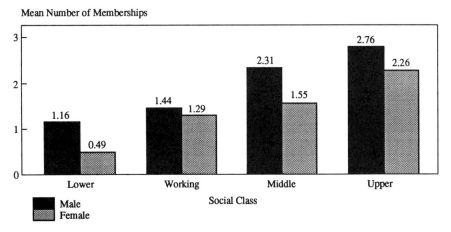

Mean Number of Group or Association
Memberships, by Gender and Class

**FIGURE 11.1  Membership in Voluntary Associations, United States, 1989**
Source: NORC ,1989.

we'll be friends as long as I need what you have to offer), and so forth. There are also variations in the degree to which one's whole self becomes committed to a relationship. Out of these various types of interpersonal relationships emerge different types of affiliation.

Relationships can be envisioned as spaces within the three-dimensional axis shown in Figure 11.2. Close friendships, for instance, would be located in the forward (whole self known), upward (total concern for), and rightmost (expressive) zone, whereas interactions with a bureaucrat at the Department of Motor vehicles would be located in the lower (little or no concern for), back (anonymous), leftmost (instrumental activity) zone.

## Primordial Tribal Bonds

For the vast majority of human history, the bonds linking individuals together were based primarily on kinship. So significant was the power of kinship that before the era of industrialization political ties between families in the ruling elite were often sealed by exogamous marriages. Even in the early twentieth century, the ruling aristocracies of Europe's most powerful nations were no more distantly related than second cousins.

Intermarriage outside of one's ethnicity, race, or religion remains a central mechanism of cultural assimilation. According to the 1980 census, over 60 percent of native-born Americans born after 1960 had mixed ancestry, compared with 31.4 percent of Americans born before 1920. Among those of Italian descent, only 8 percent of those born before 1920 had mixed ancestry, compared with 70 percent of those born after 1970. However, this assimilation mechanism has yet to merge the races: 99 percent of African American women and 97 percent of African American men still marry within their race, as do 72 percent of Asian Americans (Collins 1985).

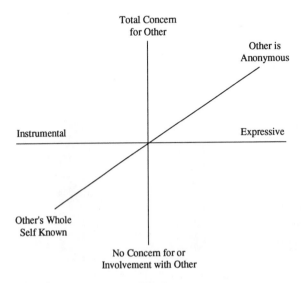

**FIGURE 11.2  Types of Affiliation**

As we saw in Chapter 8, the ties between family members have altered as the family unit has changed from a unit of production to a unit of consumption. In terms of Figure 11.2, whereas relationships traditionally covered the breadth of the instrumental-expressive dimension, in modern societies this zone has contracted and shifted toward the expressive end.

Nevertheless, as is evident in Figure 11.3 married individuals are happier than their never-married, divorced, separated, or widowed counterparts across the entire lifespan. Approximately 90 percent of Americans marry at some time in their lives, and of those who divorce, 80 percent eventually remarry. The family has become the sphere of the "private self." In an era of massive, imper-

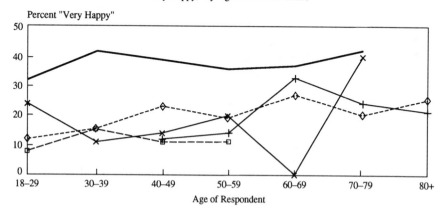

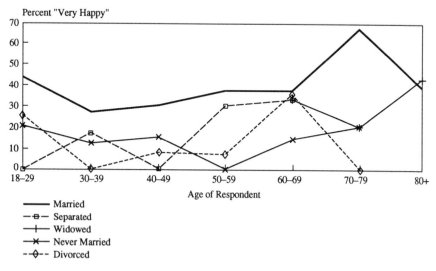

**FIGURE 11.3 Percent "Very Happy" by Marital Status, Age, and Gender**
Source: NORC, 1987.

sonal bureaucracies, the family is the only institutional sphere of life in which individuals can shape their own reality (Berger and Kellner 1964). Though some interpret the high rate of divorce as an indication that the family is falling apart, an alternative perspective is that the relationship has become so important that partners expect more of each other.

The shared genes and shared experiences of family members produce commonalities that are rarely approached even between the best of friends. The effect of such bonds often leads to the assumption that basic loyalties and primary beliefs are also shared. During the McCarthy era in the United States, for instance, individuals were held responsible for the views of their relatives. One such person was a brilliant individual whose father had been a member of the International Workers of the World. Even though the father died before the son reached the age of 2, the government never gave the son a security clearance.

## Relations with Family Members versus Unrelated Others

The 1985 NORC General Social Science Survey included a series of questions dealing with social networks. Respondents were first asked the following question:

> From time to time, most people discuss *important matters* with other people. Looking back over the last six months—who are the *people* with whom you discussed matters important to you? Just tell me their first names or initials.

Much can be read into this question, but here we will interpret it as indicating the individuals with whom one shares one's innermost thoughts, fears, and concerns.

The researchers pursued these relationships further, using the following question:

> Here is a list of some of the ways in which people are connected to each other. Some people can be connected to you in more than one way. For example, a man could be your brother and he may belong to your church and be your lawyer. When I read you a name, please tell me *all* the ways that person is connected to you. [The connections included spouse, parent, sibling, child, other family member, coworker, group member, neighbor, friend, and professional adviser.]

Table 11.1a summarizes the relationships *mentioned first*, broken down by social class. Several qualifications should be made in relation to this table. Because they could select a number of ways in which the person mentioned was connected to them, respondents could say that their spouse or parent was also a friend, adviser, and fellow group member. To control for such difficulties, familial relations were separated from the other categories. Second, the category "friend" includes all cases in which "friend" was mentioned in combination with other categories. Thus, if a person was both a coworker and a friend, that individual was coded only as a friend. With these qualifications in mind, observe that, in all, 60 percent of the first-mentioned individuals were family members.

**TABLE 11.1a    First Person Mentioned as Being One with Whom Respondent Had Discussed Important Matters, by Social Class**

| Closest Relationship Mentioned[1] | Social Class | | | | |
|---|---|---|---|---|---|
| | Lower | Working | Middle | Upper | Total |
| Spouse | 13 | 29 | 32 | 27 | 30 |
| Parent | 11 | 12 | 9 | 13 | 11 |
| Sibling | 7 | 9 | 6 | 5 | 7 |
| Children | 2 | 6 | 8 | 5 | 7 |
| Other Family | 11 | 6 | 6 | 4 | 6 |
| **Total Percent Family** | **43** | **61** | **60** | **55** | **60** |
| Friend | 50 | 33 | 36 | 45 | 35 |
| Coworker | 2 | 6 | 5 | 5 | 5 |
| Group Member | 2 | 5 | 9 | 4 | 7 |
| Adviser | 11 | 6 | 4 | 9 | 6 |
| Total | 46 | 621 | 664 | 55 | 1386 |

[1]Column totals do not sum to 100 percent because of overlaps in coworker, group member, and adviser categories.

Table 11.1b reveals how social class affects the relationship between the respondent and the first person mentioned. If, for instance, individuals first mentioned their spouse or sibling as being one with whom they had had a serious discussion, upper-class respondents were more likely to also say that their spouse (80 percent) or sibling (67 percent) was also a friend. Among those who first mentioned a nonfamilial friend, for lower-class respondents that individual was at least twice as likely to be a neighbor (39 percent) than was the case for respondents in other social classes.

**TABLE 11.1b    Impact of Social Class on Relationship Categorization**

| If Mentioned First: | Spouse[1] | Spouse | Parent | Sibling | Friend | Coworker[2] |
|---|---|---|---|---|---|---|
| **Percent Also Saying Person =** | Friend | Adviser | Adviser | Friend | Neighbor | Friend |
| **Class:** | | | | | | |
| Lower | 50 | 17 | 20 | 33 | 39 | — |
| Working | 67 | 21 | 24 | 55 | 13 | 74 |
| Middle | 57 | 20 | 24 | 65 | 20 | 81 |
| Upper | 80 | 27 | 43 | 67 | 16 | 100 |

[1]Among those currently married, not separated or divorced.
[2]Among only those working full time.
Source of Data: NORC, 1985.

# Friendships

Consider the people whom you think of as your friends. What determines your relative liking of those individuals? Do you have different kinds of friends with whom you share different kinds of experiences? Some people prefer as friends those who are clones of themselves, whereas others' friendships include many different types of individuals. Are there some people whom you like more than they like you? Does the degree of your friendship determine the degree to which you are willing to make sacrifices for those individuals or the degree to which you feel that you can depend on them? Must you interact frequently with another person for that person to be considered a "best friend"?

Relationships can be categorized on the basis of closeness. One distinguishes among one's relationships, rating them along a continuum from stranger through acquaintance to close friend. Close friends express a high degree of concern, caring, and trust for each other. Their interactions include frequent self-disclosures. The term *close*, when used in reference to relationships, is "virtually synonymous with *influential;* people in close relationships have a great deal of impact on each other" (Kelley et al. 1983:13). Jeffrey Young (1986) has noted that degrees of closeness translate into four types of relationships (see Table 11.2), which are determined by the extent to which the self is involved. Intensity of self-involvement, in turn, is a function not only of the extent of caring and trust but also of frequency of contact, the longevity of the relationship, and its expected duration.

Friendships fulfill needs in three basic areas: material, cognitive, and socioemotional. Perhaps the most important need met by friendship is the need for emotional intimacy, which, according to Joseph Newirth, means "being willing to be affected by someone else's feelings, [and] to be aware of the nuances

**TABLE 11.2  Young's Typology of Friendships**

| Characteristics of Friendships | Level AA | Level A | Level B | Level C |
|---|---|---|---|---|
| Brief designation | check-in, best friend | close friend when available | companion, good buddy | acquaintance |
| History and expected duration | high | high | moderate | low to moderate |
| Frequency of contact | daily or almost daily | variable, depends on distance and time | moderate (once every two weeks) | low, occasional |
| Disclosure, caring, and trust | very high | high to very high | moderate | low |
| Shared interests | moderate to high | moderate to high | moderate to high | moderate |

of their inner meanings and their moods" (quoted in Goleman 1987). It also means feeling able to disclose oneself and feeling that one is understood (Solano 1986:235). Doug McAdams and Fred Bryant (1987) found that emotional intimacy is equally important for both sexes in determining their happiness. Using 1957 and 1976 national surveys of mental health, they also found that intimacy plays an increasingly important role as a determinant of personal fulfillment.

Friendship also entails a relatively high degree of self-disclosure. Friends are the individuals with whom one's biographical story is shared, who are privy to one's backstage self and accept one with full knowledge of one's strengths and weaknesses. The results of survey concerning the formation of new friendships is presented in Table 11.3.

Significant gender differences in friendship and emotional intimacy have been reported. Karen Roberto and Jean Scott (1986) found that women report more emotionally intense relationships with their friends and hold greater expectations for them, whereas men have more structured relationships with their friends and express greater satisfaction with them. Men gain a sense of closeness with others when sharing enjoyable activities, whereas women receive a satisfying sense of intimacy through emotional self-disclosure

### TABLE 11.3 Percentage of New Friendships

*In the spring of 1990 the Gallup poll asked 1202 Americans the following question:*

**How long ago did you most recently make a new friend?**
*The following table presents information about the percentages of those who said "within the past year":*

| **Total** | 65% $(n = 1202)$ |
|---|---|
| **Age** | |
| 18–29 | 82 |
| 30–39 | 64 |
| 50 and older | 55 |
| **Race** | |
| White | 66 |
| Nonwhite | 58 |
| **Education** | |
| Not high school graduate | 52 |
| High school graduate | 65 |
| Some college | 74 |
| College graduate | 71 |

*As is evident in these figures, Americans' lives are frequently enriched with new friends. However, the likelihood of befriending others generally decreases with age and increases the higher individuals are in the stratification order.*

Source: DeStefano, 1990:33.

(Goleman 1987). Whereas intimacy may lead directly to happiness for women, for men it provides a sense of security, confidence, and resilience (McAdams et al. 1988).

## Relations with Anonymous Others

At the opposite end of the continuum of emotional closeness from friendships are relationships with strangers. As societies have undergone modernization, the proportion of individuals' interactions that involve anonymous others has increased dramatically. In more traditional societies, people knew each other as whole persons because they were raised together, grew old together, and shared many experiences. In such a society a stranger would stand out as a unique individual and might eventually become part of the community. With urbanization and massive economic interdependency, however, individuals often interact only as role functionaries, often with the assumption that they will never see each other again. Under such conditions a stranger is unlikely to be treated as a whole person.

As we have seen in earlier chapters, when people lack information about the identities of others, they are prone to stereotyping. If the stranger is obviously a member of a minority group or bears a visible stigma, or is clearly higher in social status, all the interaction rituals of status unequals (e.g., distancing rules and nonverbal messages of deference and demeanor) come into play.

## The Density of Interpersonal Networks

To the extent that a person's interaction networks overlap, his or her self-concept will be reinforced by others' shared views of that person. On the other hand, if one's networks of acquaintances do not overlap, one is less likely to encounter a common, controlling definition of one's identity.

The NORC social-network survey presented in Tables 11.1 included a tally of the number of people with whom respondents had had a "discussion of important matters" in the previous six months. This information is presented in Table 11.4.

Shown in Table 11.5 are the results of correlating the number of such affiliations with some of the dimensions of social stratification. It is apparent that the higher the respondent's social class, the greater the number of relationships. Whites have more relationships than African Americans, members of the upper classes more than members of the lower classes; differences between the sexes are not significant.

These data have several implications. Relative lack of density in relationships may contribute to the general invisibility of the lower classes. The data may also indicate differences in degree of social *engagement*. It is hypothesized that the greater an individual's degree of social engagement, the lower the level of anomie experienced by that person. This is supported by the data in the second column of Table 11.5, where one measure of anomie—whether individuals consider their life dull, routine, or exciting—is positively related to the number of persons mentioned (gamma = .25). The relationship persists even

**TABLE 11.4 Number of Others with Whom One Had Discussed "Serious Matters" by Percent Finding Life "Exciting"**

| Number of Significant Relationships Mentioned | Percent of Total | Percent Finding Life "Exciting" |
|:---:|:---:|:---:|
| 0 | 8.9 | 28 |
| 1 | 14.9 | 40 |
| 2 | 15.3 | 41 |
| 3 | 21.0 | 47 |
| 4 | 15.2 | 58 |
| 5 | 19.2 | 58 |
| 6+ | 5.5 | 57 |
| Total | 1531.0 | |

Source: NORC, 1985.

when we control for class (conditional gamma = .40 for the lower class, .18 and .21 for the working and middle classes, and .64 for the upper class).

Class determines not only the number of relationships mentioned but also the degree to which individuals know each other. As mentioned earlier, the more one's networks overlap; the more one's self-concept is reinforced. Consider responses to the following survey question:

**Some people have friends who mostly know one another. Other people have friends who don't know one another. Would you say that all of your friends know one another, most of your friends know one another, only a few of your friends know one another, or none of your friends know one another?**

**TABLE 11.5 Social Class, Race, and Gender, by Number of Important Relationships**

| | Number of Relationships Mentioned | |
|:---|:---:|:---:|
| | *One or Less* | *Five or More* |
| **Social Class** | | |
| Lower | 43% | 15% |
| Working | 26 | 19 |
| Middle | 21 | 29 |
| Upper | 15 | 46 |
| **Race** | | |
| White | 22 | 26 |
| African American | 41 | 15 |
| **Gender** | | |
| Male | 26 | 25 |
| Female | 22 | 24 |

**TABLE 11.6   Percent Saying That "All" or "Most of" Their Friends Know One Another**

| | Gender | | |
|---|---|---|---|
| | *Male* | *Female* | *Total* |
| **Social Class:** | | | |
| Lower | 54 | 54 | 54 |
| Working | 61 | 62 | 62 |
| Middle | 61 | 61 | 61 |
| Upper | 72 | 59 | 64 |
| **Race:** | | | |
| White | 63 | 62 | 62 |
| African American | 46 | 56 | 52 |
| Total | 61 | 61 | 61 |

In total, 61 percent of the respondents claimed that "all" or "most" of their friends knew each other. As is evident in Table 11.6 the differences between the sexes and the working, middle, and upper classes are negligible. However, upper-class males were 33 percent more likely than lower-class males to say that their friends are part of the same network, and white males were 37 percent more likely to say this than black males.

Are people whose friends are part of the same network happier than those whose friends do not know one another? The "Total" column of Table 11.7 provides weak support for this hypothesis: Those for whom "all" of their friends know each other are 35 percent more likely to report being "very happy" than those for whom "none" of their friends know each other. Interestingly, as evidenced by the conditional gamma correlations (between friendship network and happiness within each social class), this relationship between friends knowing one another and happiness is greatest within the lower ( = .23) and upper ( = .29) classes.

**TABLE 11.7   Percent of Respondents Saying They Are "Very Happy," by Friendship Network and Social Class**

| | Social Class | | | | |
|---|---|---|---|---|---|
| | *Lower* | *Working* | *Middle* | *Upper* | *Total* |
| Friends Know One Another? | | | | | |
| All | 20 | 32 | 26 | 62 | 31 |
| Most | 18 | 24 | 36 | 57 | 31 |
| Few | 16 | 24 | 28 | 30 | 26 |
| None | 0 | 29 | 23 | — | 23 |
| Conditional Gamma$_{\text{network, happy}}$ | .23 | .02 | .07 | .29 | |

Source of data: NORC, 1985.

The various configurations of personal and social needs do not alone determine the formation of relationships. A number of factors act as catalysts; they include sheer proximity and the presence of outgoing individuals who bring others together at parties and other social functions. The emotional intensity of shared experiences has a unifying effect as well, as can be seen in the relationships formed between soldiers in combat or between strangers waiting for their loved ones in hospital emergency rooms.

## Conceptualizing Social Attraction

There are several metaphors by which we can conceptualize the forces that draw individuals together. There may, for instance, be a social force similar to gravity, in which individuals gravitate toward large gatherings of people just as meteors are attracted to the mass of the earth. And as large celestial bodies affect the time-space continuum, so too do social gatherings: When in the company of others, one's sense of self can be lost and one's conception of time warped. ("I've had such a great time with you folks that I don't know where the evening went.")

Another metaphor might be magnetism, whereby individuals find themselves drawn to others whose personal strengths complement their own weaknesses. A related concept is that of exchange: "You scratch my back and I'll scratch yours," or "Since I have what you want and you have what I desire, let's talk." Instead of conceptualizing the process as one of attraction, we could imagine that individuals are simply pushed together, using the metaphor of fusion. Thus, *A Report From Iron Mountain* (1967), which discusses possible international implications of peace, presents the idea that society is possible only as long as there exists a collective fear of some deadly external threat.

All of these metaphors illustrate the fact that the nature of the bonds between individuals determines the structure of the social whole. That whole may resemble the tightly interconnected latticework of a crystal, or a collage of loosely connected and unrelated pieces.

## The Binding Power of Similarity

How do we choose the people with whom we affiliate? Is it really a matter of choice, or do we subconsciously gravitate toward people like ourselves?

Researchers have found that similarity goes a long way toward explaining attraction between individuals. We tend to be attracted to people whom we perceive to be akin to ourselves, that is, who share socially significant characteristics and a common worldview. Nevertheless, physical similarity remains one of the strongest forces of attraction. Consider the bonds between individuals who are similar in race or body size (e.g., the Tip Toppers and the Society of Small People). So potent is the binding power of physical similarity that Native American tribes would transform the appearance of their members by flattening and sloping the foreheads of infants or inflicting body scars during rites of passage.

Next in potency is the binding power of a shared culture. Culture is to the social self what skin and facial features are to the biological self: a defining attribute of one's social identity. As we saw in Chapter 2, ethnocentrism is a common feature of the human condition, entailing not only a preference for one's own group but also disdain, if not outright hostility, toward other groups. For example, despite their physical similarities, Koreans are treated as outcasts in Japan because of their different culture. Facing job discrimination and opposition to intermarriage with Japanese citizens, most Koreans hide their origins by using Japanese aliases (Makihara 1990).

Culture is embedded in language. We feel comfortable and "at home" with those who talk like us. The Georgian at Harvard becomes increasingly southern as he drives home for summer break. His self metamorphoses with each state he drives through, as do his accent and the metaphors of his speech.

Attraction may also be based on similarities of social class, age (or generation), race, gender, and occupation. The effects of such similarities are evident in the results of the social-network survey questions discussed earlier.

Table 11.8 summarizes some of these shared attributes. Again the first person mentioned (as being one with whom one had "discussed important matters"), *if that person was not a family member,* is categorized by social class. The first two columns show mean differences in age. Lower-class women, for instance, were an average of 7.4 years older than the person they mentioned in their network, whereas upper-class women were 7.3 years younger. In terms

**TABLE 11.8   Social Class, by Similarity of Attributes of Unrelated First Person Mentioned**

| | Mean Age Difference | | Percent Same Gender | | Percent Same Education |
|---|---|---|---|---|---|
| | *Male* | *Female* | *Male* | *Female* | |
| **Class:** | | | | | |
| Lower | −3.1 | 7.4 | 82 | 73 | 20 |
| Working | .5 | 1.5 | 80 | 67 | 37 |
| Middle | 2.2 | 1.1 | 84 | 67 | 35 |
| Upper | −2.2 | −7.3 | 73 | 86 | 40 |

| | Percent Same Race | | | |
|---|---|---|---|---|
| | African Americans | | White | |
| | *Male* | *Female* | *Male* | *Female* |
| **Class:** | | | | |
| Lower | 100 | — | 86 | 100 |
| Working | 78 | 87 | 95 | 93 |
| Middle | 75 | 75 | 96 | 94 |
| Upper | — | — | 100 | 83 |

Source: Data from NORC, 1985.

of gender similarities, roughly 80 percent of the men mentioned another man, while approximately 70 percent of the women mentioned another woman. Upper-class men and women were most likely to mention a relationship with a woman.

Perhaps most striking are commonalities in education. Educational level was coded into categories based on number of years of schooling received. Whereas among the upper class, 40 percent of the people mentioned first were in the same educational category as the respondent, the figure was only 20 percent for members of the lower classes. Finally, the racial similarities are considerable, with few differences across social classes. The likelihood of mentioning someone outside of one's race increases with the social class of African Americans and white females; the reverse is true for white males.

The absence of perfect correlations in Table 11.8 indicates that the precise ways in which similarities result in interpersonal attractions and interactions are complex. Various types of affiliations probably result from different combinations of similarities. Marital unions, for instance, involve similarities in social class, ethnicity, age, intelligence, values and attitudes, interests, and religion (Buss 1984), whereas political unions often entail only similar economic interests. In addition, personality differences determine the number and importance of the similarities required for one person to be attracted to another. Situational features also affect interpersonal attraction: Two Americans, who otherwise have nothing in common, may meet on a Greek island and become close companions. Generalizations about which similarities produce the greatest interpersonal attraction are further complicated by life cycle differences in individuals' affiliative needs. For modern adults, for instance, social similarities increasingly supersede physical similarities as the central bases for attraction.

## Shared Time and Space as a Basis for Attraction

Shared space, or **proximity,** and activities, such as the daily routines of family and work, are well-documented sources of unity and companionship. In a study of friendship patterns in a married-student housing complex, many more friendships were found between couples living on the same floor than among those living on different floors of a twenty-two-story building (Festinger, Schachter, and Back 1950). Among those living on the same floor, the closer the apartments, the more friendly the tenants. Next-door neighbors were four times as likely to interact socially as people who lived at opposite ends of the hall. Indeed, nearly half of all Americans live within fifteen minutes of their best friends (*Harper's Magazine* 1989).

Proximity creates the **mere exposure effect** (Zajonc 1968): Frequency of exposure to a stimulus increases a subject's liking for that stimulus. As George Homans (1950) explained, proximity increases the possibility of interaction, and the more individuals interact, the greater the positive sentiment between them.

In addition to shared space, shared time also leads to interpersonal attraction. Friendships between people in different groups are rare because of the relatively few opportunities for them to interact. Through day care, school, scouts, and sports we are tracked with our agemates through time. Social

## "Love Is Sharing a History Together"

There's a good interview with talk-show host Larry King in this month's *Lear's* magazine, in which he is quoted as saying, "I never think about age. But I could never go to bed with anyone who didn't know who Adlai Stevenson was."

Is he kidding? I could never go to bed with anyone who didn't *vote* for Adlai Stevenson. It's called the comfort factor.

We tend to "hang out" with people who have lived through our own war, wear our same morality, and get tired the same time we do. Our bodies fall at the same rate; our ailments are in sync with our age. We want to have our children when our friends are having theirs and deal with the same problems as a group.

When we try to mix the generations, we end up with a family tooling down the highway singing the only song all of them have in common: "Row, row, row your boat, gently down the stream. . . . "

My own history is important to me. And surviving it with someone adds to its dimension. The crying babies my husband and I held in our arms at the social room of the church as they got their first inoculation against dreaded polio. Sobbing together over the assassination of a president and the greatest black leader of our times, and wondering what we had become. . . .

It doesn't mean we shut out other generations or don't relate to them. But generations are like high school classes. Each one has its own members, reputation, and personality. It's probably why we go to reunions. We go to walk once again with our friends in the world we created that is unique to us. No one else understands us better.

Source: Bombeck, 1989.

institutions generally separate the old and the young, and these groups rarely interact outside the family. One result is negative stereotypes. To counter such trends, a number of programs have been designed to connect the generations. In Pittsburgh, Generations Together organizes phone links between older people and latchkey children. In Cambridge, Massachusetts, the Stride Rite Corporation has set up a day care facility for both the old and young, with areas where the generations may intermingle (Ludtke 1990).

According to Alvin Toffler (1970), in rapidly changing societies time, not space, has become the primary divider of social actors. Whereas in the past a 20-year-old Vermonter may have had more in common with a 60-year-old Vermonter than with a 20-year-old Californian, nowadays the two 20-year-olds have more in common.

## Attraction to Desirable and Threatening Others

Individuals are also attracted to individuals who possess socially or personally desirable attributes. We are attracted to people who are pleasant or agreeable, who like or approve of us (Berscheid and Walster 1978; Kenny and Nasby 1980), and whom we perceive to be like ourselves but having greater power (Bales 1970). Given the tendency to attribute positive personality traits to attractive individuals (see Chapter 4) and the status enhancements that come from being associated with such persons (Kernis and Wheeler 1981), physical beauty plays no small role in attraction and liking (Walster et al. 1966; Byrne, London, and Reeves 1968).

Stephen Nowicki and Carolyn Oxenford (1989) found individuals' popularity to be related to their ability to read nonverbal cues. Using tests in which 9- to 11-year-olds judged emotions on the basis of slides and audiotapes, the researchers found that those with the lowest scores tended to be the least popular in their classes and, despite equal intelligence, to be academic underachievers. These children misinterpret the feelings of others and are unaware of the often negative nonverbal messages they themselves send.

More intriguing is individuals' attraction to abusive and even life-threatening others, as when battered children remain loyal to their abusive parents. Sometimes victims of violent and prolonged hostage-taking incidents develop emotional bonds with their captors and come to agree with their kidnappers' views. The phenomenon is called the Stockholm syndrome (see Fuselier 1988) after a 1973 incident in which four bank employees were held for five terrifying days in a bank vault with their captors. Afterward, two of the female captives developed close relationships with the terrorists.

## Social Bonding Zones

The similarities mentioned earlier are perhaps necessary but not sufficient conditions for interpersonal attraction. If individuals are to interact, they must be brought together. This is where sociological dynamics come into play: They create the conditions under which similar people have the opportunity to interact.

As we saw in Chapter 10, one such opportunity occurs because of the nature of residential segregation based on race and social class. Since young children are most likely to play with children living nearby, and since those living nearby generally are of the same social status, the proximity $\rightarrow$ interaction $\rightarrow$ liking causal chain described by Homans (1950), coupled with the binding power of similarity, often guarantees that they will be attracted to one another. To ensure that their children do not bond with (and possibly even marry) members of lower social classes, the elite often send their offspring to private schools. (A latent function of college, in fact, is to serve as a marriage market. As graduates discover later in life, never again will they be in proximity to so many individuals who are similar to themselves.)

The workplace, too, provides fertile ground for meeting similar others. In fact, outside of their families, many individuals have only their workmates to network and socialize with. In the 1985 NORC study, among people who work full time, 22 percent of men and 19 percent of women first mentioned a coworker as the person with whom they discussed serious matters. (See Table 11.1b.)

In addition to the neighborhoods, school, and workplace, there are various socially defined places in which individuals may meet others. In England, for instance, there is the pub, where members of a community regularly get together to talk politics or share gossip. Often these individuals already have a number of common bonds by virtue of having been born and raised in the same community and having grown older together. The United States, too, has bars and taverns. They differ from the British pub, however, owing to Americans' greater geographic mobility and weaker sense of community. Instead of the community pub, there are taverns and nightclubs for people with a common marital status (e.g., singles bars), the same occupation (e.g., bars adjacent to factories), and similar social class (country clubs).

Churches also provide social opportunities for their members, allowing people with similar moral values and outlooks to bond. To bring together individuals with similar life-course experiences, for instance, churches sponsor parents-without-partners and widow-to-widow programs. In addition, there are the various voluntary associations mentioned previously. In our NORC survey, among those who first mentioned a friend as being one with whom serious discussion was shared, approximately one-quarter were fellow group members.

## Attractions among Large Numbers of Individuals

Why during the 1980s and 1990s—a period of relative prosperity during which national economies were increasingly absorbed into the world economic system—were there so many revivals of national and ethnic identity? What caused the international epidemic of ethnic hatred, directed against the Koreans in Japan, Arabs in France, Turks in Bulgaria, Hungarians in Romania, Armenians in Azerbaijan, African Americans in America? Such events run counter to modernization theory's prediction that ethnic and national identities will eventually evaporate as nations become increasingly similar in social and economic terms.

Beyond the dynamics of interpersonal attraction there are forces of large-scale attraction that produce *communal identities.* For culturally and racially heterogeneous nation-states, the need to create a national identity that either subsumes or replaces familial, ethnic, racial, and geographic identities is a significant problem (Smith 1981).

Anthony Smith (1981) argues that during times of rapid social change, ethnic identities become submerged into class identities. When social conditions are stabilized, ethnicity reemerges because the bonds of ethnic sentiment are stronger than those of social class. However, as was evident in the late 1980s when the former communist societies underwent major political and social upheavals, collective ethnic identities are also spawned when political orders lose their legitimacy.

Among the reasons for the resurgence of ethnic identity is a growing collective consciousness (see Chapter 10) of ethnic-based exploitation, analogous to the way in which class conflict creates heightened class consciousness (Cohen 1985). When people feel threatened, they establish clear-cut lines drawn between themselves and their perceived enemy. If members of a particular ethnic group do not have many crosscutting loyalties, ethnicity provides a more comprehensive and unambiguous form of social grouping than almost any other. Ethnicity provides a variant of the tribal bonds of common ancestry linking family members together. The effect is enhanced if members also share a common culture and a language distinct from that of the dominant culture, and if ethnic status happens to be the primary basis of social stratification, determining the roles one can play and the personalities one can assume (Barth 1969:15–17).

## STRATEGIES TO ASSIST INTERPERSONAL ATTRACTION

Social systems have devised numerous strategies to encourage interpersonal bonding among their members. To intensify the bonds between students, for instance, private colleges and universities select a relatively homogeneous population. To magnify the effects of similarity and propinquity, freshman roommates—who may be required to live on campus in dormitories reserved for freshmen—are often matched in terms of interests and life-style. Students also find themselves in communal eating, studying, and leisure areas. In addition, there may be matriculation rituals, hazings, meals with faculty members, and the like. Bonding is also encouraged through the creation of a common identity, a we-feeling, through sporting events, T-shirts, bumper stickers, and campus traditions.

In part, the effectiveness of the German Wehrmacht during World War II and the contemporary success of the Japanese in manufacturing can be explained by the forging of primary-group relationships. Appreciating that soldiers fight best for their buddies, the Germans organized their military into small platoons within which soldiers remained throughout their military careers. Platoon members shared the most intense of all life experiences. The unifying effect of such experiences is described by an American mercenary who fought in Vietnam:

> This is really going to sound strange, but there's a love relationship that is nurtured in combat because the man next to you—you're depending on him for the most important thing you have, your life, and if he lets you down you're either maimed or killed. If you make a mistake the same thing happens to him, so the bond of trust has to be extremely close, and I'd say this bond is stronger than almost anything, with the exception of parent and child. It's a hell of a lot stronger than man and wife—your life is in his hands, you trust that person with the most valuable thing you have. (Dyer 1985:104)

### Rituals Dramatizing Connectedness

The greater the degree to which relationships are institutionalized, the more formal the rituals used to dramatize connectedness.

At one end of the continuum of formalized rituals are those of friends. To signify the specialness of their friendship bond, Tom Sawyer and Huck Finn became "blood brothers" by cutting their thumbs and letting their blood commingle. In *Coming of Age in New Jersey*, Michael Moffat (1989) describes the different signals students use to express friendship, including "busting on" one another. To "bust on" someone is "to deflate their pretensions by means of aggressive verbal mockery." But only friends are "busted on," and to be the recipient of such jibes means that one has the trust of others.

Midway along the continuum are the bonding rituals of groups such as youth gangs and fraternal organizations. As will be discussed in Chapter 12, these social units may employ hazing rituals to dramatize their interpersonal bonds and accentuate their significance. The more severe the hazing, the more initiates will value their membership in the group. ("If I am willing to go through such humiliation and pain, this must be really important to me.")

For highly institutionalized unions, such as when a man and woman become husband and wife, there are typically full-blown rites of passage in which whole selves are symbolically redefined as parts of a larger social unit. In the case of marriage, one is no longer "single" but, rather, part of a "couple."

## MAINTAINING SOCIAL RELATIONSHIPS OVER TIME

The bonds we form with others are, in part, a function of their expected duration. Extensive self-disclosure and deep intimacy do not normally occur with individuals with whom we do not expect to have a lasting relationship. Even the bonds that we expect and desire to last are far from guaranteed. Close ties with high school friends, for instance, may not survive one's college years. Without routine maintenance, all but the strongest relationships dissolve with time. See Figure 11.4.

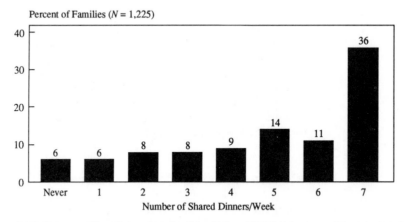

Percent of Families (N = 1,225)

**FIGURE 11.4  A Declining Family Ritual: The Obsolescence of the Nightly Family Dinner**

One of the few routine ritual occasions when all family members come together and reaffirm their collective bonds is the nightly dinner. However, as this chart shows, such communion is no longer a daily occurrence.
Source: Adapted from data by Gallup, 1990; cited in U.S. News, 1990.

## Staying in Touch

The primary way of maintaining relationships is through continued interaction. Bonds between an out-of-state college student and his or her parents may initially be maintained through frequent telephone calls and letters. Over time, however, the frequency of such communications may decline. Instead of sharing day-to-day activities and concerns, the infrequent correspondent may employ more global summaries. Instead of sharing the names of friends and faculty members and descriptions of everyday activities, the student relates only significant events, often in such a highly abridged form that the parents no longer understand or empathize with their offspring's experiences (see Figure 11.5)

## Creating Social IOUs

From the perspective of exchange theory, relationships are maintained through cycles of mutually obligating exchanges. Years before they formally run for the presidency, presidential hopefuls make speeches throughout the country on behalf of everyone from mayors and governors to senators and representatives. Parents lend their children money to make the down payment on their first home. Whether the motivations of the politicians and parents are selfless or self-serving, the consequence for the recipients is a sense of indebtedness.

This sense of indebtedness can be eliminated by reciprocating with something of equal value or thoughtfulness. The sense of obligation can also be transferred to the original giver. For instance, perhaps you start a personal tradition of giving "a little something" to a friend for Christmas and do not inform the friend of your new ritual. Feeling the obligation to reciprocate, the friend counters, perhaps a few days late, with a gift a notch or two better than what you consider appropriate. The years pass and you and your friend live on opposite sides of the country, but the gift exchange continues—no, it expands to include the person your friend eventually marries and, later, their children. These mutually obligating exchanges are not only reinforcing cycles of reciprocating acts but also symbolic reaffirmations of social bonds.

The gift, of course, needn't have monetary value to be personally priceless—knickknack shelves are filled with such items. "The gifts between two associations may have little value, yet they are visible emblems of social solidarity, and the act of giving evokes latent feelings of solidarity, unity, and interdependence" (Warner 1945:242). Thus, in their study of middle- and working-class Chicago residents, Csikszentmihalyi and Rochberg-Halton (1981:281) found that over 40 percent of adults' most treasured possessions had been received as gifts.

On occasions such as birthdays and holidays, people often seek to reaffirm the social bonds that matter to them, sometimes to ease guilt for letting relations wane or to reinforce valued relationships about which they are insecure (Csikszentmihalyi and Rochberg-Halton 1981:37). If an individual was on the gift list last year and now is not, it means that the relationship is expected to weaken or end during the following year (Caplow 1982).

Feelings of social obligation can even be provoked by the sending of Christmas cards (Kunz and Woolcott 1976). In the mid-1970s, Phillip Kunz mailed some six hundred cards to Midwestern families randomly selected from

Figures 11.5a and 11.5b plot the percentages of males and females who replied "Never" to these questions. As is evident, the higher the respondents' social class, the lower the percentage claiming that they never engage in such activities.

Among the questions asked of respondents in the 1989 NORC General Social Science Survey was one dealing with socializing activities.

Would you use this card and tell me which answer comes closest to how often you do the following things...

Spend a social evening with someone who lives in your neighborhood?
Spend a social evening with friends who live outside the neighborhood?
Go to a bar or tavern?
Spend a social evening with a brother or sister?

| Almost every day | About once a month | About once a year |
| Once or twice a week | Several times a year | Never |
| Several times a month | | |

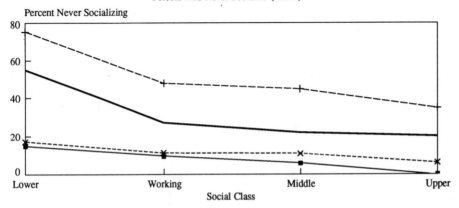

Percent Who Never Socialize (Males)

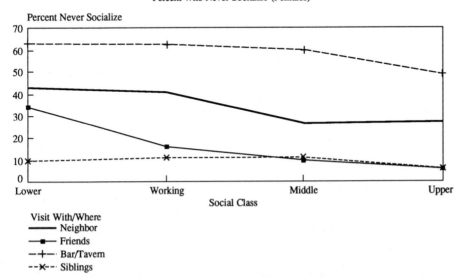

Percent Who Never Socialize (Females)

Visit With/Where
——— Neighbor
—■— Friends
—+— Bar/Tavern
--✗-- Siblings

**FIGURE 11.5  The Social-Class Factor in Socializing Activities**
Source: NORC, 1989.

telephone books. The cards were reciprocated by nearly 20 percent of the families. Two "old friends" asked whether they could stay with the Kunz family during forthcoming holiday trips. Some had difficulty establishing their relationship with the researcher's family but did so nevertheless. One person responded how the researcher's name did not initially register and asked to be forgiven for having been so stupid, especially as he and Kunz's father had been such good friends!

## WHEN RELATIONSHIPS END

Nowadays few relationships survive across the lifespan and nearly all roles have temporal limits. The increasing rates of divorce, religious conversions, job changes, and retirements occurring within increasingly long lifespans provide evidence that role careers are increasingly concluded not by death but by design. However, modern society lacks a cultural consensus over exactly how endings—whether from work, the family or from life itself—should ideally be conducted. As a culture, Americans do not know how to say good-bye.

Individuals who are "in exit"—at the conclusion of their life or role career—no longer need to conform to the norms of their roles. They can say what they like, since there is nothing to lose. Further, it is assumed that endings occasion special insights. Approaching conclusions are generally the only social occasions when individuals are compelled to derive a sense of coherency and meaningfulness from their encounters with time. The awareness of one's own mortality at middle age is a time of introspection, stocktaking, and life reviews (Butler 1963). Task deadlines and annual self-evaluations can be seen as artificial attempts to capture the life review process observed among people approaching death (Kearl 1980).

There is little doubt that some endings are better than others. Society now distinguishes between "good" and "bad" divorces, retirements, and deaths. According to Glaser and Strauss (1971), good endings are normally predictable, scheduled, voluntary, and often collective. Thus, common grief reactions to the experiences of widowhood, divorce, separation, unemployment, and property damage following a natural disaster have been observed (Lynch 1977; McLeod 1984).

Given the increasing prevalence of role careers ending by design (as opposed to death, as was the case in the past), Ebaugh (1988) observes in *Becoming an Ex* that society coins terms to denote types of exiters: *divorcee, retiree, recovered alcoholic, widow,* and *alumnus.* Others are simply referred to with the *ex* prefix: ex-doctor, ex-executive, ex-nun, ex-convict, ex-cult member, ex-athlete. Often such *ex-* labels are the source of stigma.

Death, of course, is the most absolute and emotionally profound of all relationship endings. When death occurs, survivors mourn, in part, for the portions of themselves that have died as well, for the aspects of the self that will never again be activated because of the absence of the deceased individual.

In many ways, death provides the central metaphor for understanding all endings. Consider the parallels between people with an illness that has been diagnosed as terminal, workers who have "given notice," or neighbors who put up a "for sale" sign in their yards. All go through feelings of loss analogous to Elisabeth Kübler-Ross's (1969) stages of the dying trajectory: denial, anger, bargaining, depression, and, possibly, acceptance.

In their anticipatory grief, those remaining behind or "surviving" often distance themselves from the departing individuals. The worker who resigns or is fired may be treated as if he or she is socially dead. Communication dries up either because individuals do not know what to say or because they and the departing person lack a shared future.

## Endings of Familial Relationships

*Widowhood.* Of all the relationships affected by death, it is the death of a spouse that most changes the social identity of the bereaved person. Indeed, society recognizes them as different people, which is why they are labeled "widowers" and "widows." (Observe there are no comparable changes in the labels, and hence social status, of other bereaved individuals.) Further, given the tendency of men to marry women younger than themselves, coupled with the fact that women live an average of eight years longer than men, widowhood carries the stigmas of sexism (Lopata 1971) and ageism. An estimated 80 percent of all married American women can expect to be widowed, outliving their husbands by an average of sixteen years (Lawson 1990).

So great can be the emotion of grief at the death of a spouse that survivors quite literally forget who they are. They are drained of energy and develop a sense of distance and imperviousness to others. There are overwhelming surges of intense and often conflicting emotions: love for the deceased coupled with profound anger at having been left behind; loneliness coupled with lack of desire for the company of others. If the dying process was long and taxing, the sense of relief and even joy that the survivor experiences can lead to guilt.

Effects are compounded for women who filled the traditional role of a nonworking wife and whose identities were thoroughly interwoven with those of their husbands. Their world may be shattered. After forty or fifty years of role continuity, one faces the prospect of having to assume a new self. As is evident in Figure 11.6, the extent to which widowhood has this effect increases with education (Lopata 1973).

Directly related to this change in the self are changes in the feedback one receives from society. In a couple-oriented society, widows often find that they are rejected by couples who were formerly friends. This is particularly true for the first woman in a friendship circle who becomes a widow: Friends do not know what to say; other wives do not want to be reminded of their eventual fate and may also fear that they will lose their husbands to the newly single woman.

Bereavement may be more lethal for widowers than for widows. One study of over four thousand widowed spouses found that while bereavement had no impact on the mortality rate of widows, widowers were 26 percent more likely to die than their married counterparts. Among widowers 55 to 64 years of age, in fact, the mortality rate of widowers was 61 percent higher than that of a matched control group of married men (Helsing, Szklo, and Comstock 1981).

*Divorce.* Today, for the first time in history, a marriage is as likely to be concluded by divorce as by death (Weitzman 1985). Over one-third of marital unions fail within the first four years (Otten 1989). In 1984, 54 percent of

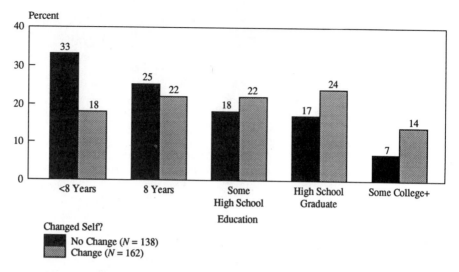

**FIGURE 11.6  Perceived Change in Self with Widowhood, by Education**
Source: Adapted from data in Lopata, 1973.

divorces involved dependent children (*Wall Street Journal* 1989), and more than half of all American children are likely to experience the dissolution of their parents' marriage before they are 18.

Divorce can exact a greater and in many cases longer-lasting emotional and physical toll on the former spouses than virtually any other life stress, including widowhood. In marital dissolutions, the normal, expected progress through the life course is disrupted—there is no "right time" to get divorced, nor is there any culturally defined sequence for exiting from marriage. The partner who initiates the dissolution has the advantage, normally having the time to go through a sequence of changes that reverses the transition into marriage. Those changes include emotional withdrawal from the relationship, giving up the attachment to the marital role, disrupting the routines of everyday living, and severing the bonds of shared experience and interdependencies (Vaughn 1988).

In an analysis of the results of a national telephone survey (n = 2387) conducted by Louis Harris and Associates, Sheldon Cohen (cited in *San Antonio Light* [AP] 1989) found that the stresses of divorce are inversely related to social status: They are greater for women than for men, for blue-collar workers than professionals and managers, and for African Americans than for whites. Associated with the stresses of divorce are more symptoms of illness, more visits to physicians, and higher rates of smoking. In a 1988 divorce trial, a Houston woman won a civil award of $500,000 for the "severe emotional distress"—she called it "emotional terrorism"—her husband had caused (Phillips 1988).

Children, too, often suffer long-term effects of divorce. In Wallerstein and Blakeslee's (1989) study of 131 individuals who were between 2 and 18 years old at the time of their parents' divorce, 60 percent felt rejected by at least one parent. As young adults, two-thirds of the females reported becoming deeply

## Giving Ritual to Divorce

When the United Church of Christ published the new edition of its "Book of Worship" [in 1986], it introduced a section on prayers suitable for anyone going through a divorce.

Similar prayers have been introduced by many other denominations over the past decade, including the Lutheran, United Methodist, Episcopal, and Presbyterian churches and the Unitarian Universalist Association. The Reform movement of Judaism is discussing a similar concept. . . .

Ministers say these new prayers and their accompanying rituals are being included as congregations seek ways to ease the sense of personal failure and alienation from religious life that their members seem to experience as they go through divorce. . . . "Although we had centuries-old ways of giving support at other critical moments of life, we were finding the church had nothing to offer at this very painful time," said Hoyt Hickman, the director of worship resource development for the United Methodist Church in Nashville.

These new rituals carry no legal ramifications. Thus they should not be confused with the annulment tribunals of the Roman Catholic Church or the divorce tribunals of Orthodox Judaism. . . .

The new prayers are clearly well intentioned, but members of the clergy say that so far there has been little demand for them, at least not in their current form. Modifications are already being discussed.

A major deterrent right now is that the divorcing couple are expected to recite the prayers together, usually in the company of friends or relatives, as is traditional in the celebration or sanctification of many other major events in life. The problem is that such recitations require a spirit of unity that might not be possible.

For example, the new service of the United Church of Christ called "Recognition of the End of a Marriage" assumes both partners are present and offers responsive reading by an "informal gathering of members and friends."

The model created for Unitarian congregations around the country by the Rev. Rudolph Nemser, the minister of the Unitarian Church in Cherry Hill, New Jersey, goes even further. It is patterned after a marriage ceremony. It gives the couple a chance to recite words of respect and lay aside bitterness through responsive readings led by a minister in front of invited guests. Marriage vows are repealed. The couple hand their wedding rings to the minister. The service ends with a pronouncement from the minister that the marriage is dissolved, and the couple shakes hands.

Source: Brooks, 1987.

anxious and unable to commit themselves to lasting relationships. Many of the males failed to develop independence, confidence, or a sense of purpose.

***Leaving Home.*** Leaving home, as when one departs for college or moves into one's first apartment, marks a formal change in both family systems and family roles. For the departing offspring, it means the end of childhood and the beginning of adult autonomy; for the remaining younger siblings, it means moving up a notch in the family hierarchy; and for parents whose last child has left, it means an "empty nest" and the end of their active parenting roles, which can be especially traumatic for women whose identity is considerably bound up in the mother role.

## The Need for Ending Rituals

Related to the personal needs for order and meaningfulness is the need for closure. For a new self to emerge, the old self must be ritually destroyed. This may explain why divorce can have a more devastating impact than widowhood. The greater individuals' involvement and identification with their lost roles, the greater their need for rituals to assist in their identity transformations.

## CONCLUSION

In this chapter we have explored some of the facets of social integration, what it means in social-psychological terms to be bonded to others and how such bondings occur. From the perspective of society, integration is generally inversely related to deviance. When their interests are meshed with those of a group, individuals' selfish impulses are constrained by mutual interests. From the perspective of individuals, through participation in social networks one becomes plugged into the social order, which protects one against the experience of anomie. The possibility of such integration is strongly determined by the individual's position in status hierarchies.

The following chapters explore the social structures arising out of individuals' interactions and how they, in turn, act as external forces that further shape identities, behaviors, emotions, and thoughts.

## REFERENCES

Atkinson, J. W., and E. L. Walker. 1956. The affiliation motive in perceptual sensitivity to faces. *Journal of Abnormal and Social Psychology* 53:38–41.

Bales, Robert F. 1970. *Personality and interpersonal behavior.* Fort Worth, TX: Holt, Rinehart and Winston.

Barth, Fredrik. 1969. *Ethnic groups and boundaries: The social organization of cultural difference.* Boston: Little, Brown.

Berger, Peter, and Hansfrid Kellner. 1964. Marriage and the construction of reality. *Diogenes* 45:1–25.

Berscheid, E., and E. Walster. 1978. *Interpersonal attraction* (2nd ed.). Reading, MA: Addison-Wesley.

Bombeck, Erma. 1989, June. Love is sharing a history together. *Dallas Times Herald.*

Boyatzis, R. E. 1973. Affiliation motivation. In D. C. McClelland and R. S. Steele (eds.), *Human motivation: A book of readings.* Morristown, NJ: General Learning Press.

Brooks, Andree. 1987, August 31. Finding solace: Prayers accepting divorce. *New York Times,* p. 20.

Buss, D. M. 1984. Toward a psychology of person-environment (PE) correlation: The role of spouse selection. *Journal of Personality and Social Psychology* 47:361–377.

Butler, Robert. 1963. The life review: An interpretation of reminiscence in the aged. *Psychiatry* 26:65–76.

Byrne, D., O. London, and K. Reeves. 1968. The effects of physical attractiveness, sex, and attitude similarity on interpersonal attraction. *Journal of Personality* 36:259–71,

Caplow, Theodore. 1982. Christmas gifts and kin networks. *American Sociological Review* 47: 383–392.

Cohen, Anthony. 1985. *Symbolic construction of community.* New York: Routledge, Chapman and Hall.

Collins, Glenn. 1986, January 6. Many in work force care for elderly kin. *New York Times*, p. 18.

Collins, Glenn. 1985, February 11. A new look at intermarriage in the U.S. *New York Times*, p. 16.

Csikszentmihalyi, Mihaly, and Eugene Rochberg-Halton. 1981. *The meaning of things: Domestic symbols and the self.* Cambridge and London: Cambridge University Press.

DeStefano, Linda. 1990. Pressures of modern life bring increased importance to friendships. *The Gallup Poll Monthly* 294:24–33.

Dyer, Gwynne. 1985. *War.* New York: Crown.

Ebaugh, Helen Rose. 1988. *Becoming an ex: The process of role exit.* Chicago: University of Chicago Press.

Festinger, L., S. Schachter, and K. Back. 1950. *Social pressures in informal groups: A study of human factors in housing.* New York: Harper.

Fuselier, G. Dwayne. 1988. Hostage negotiation consultant: Emerging role for the clinical psychologist. *Professional Psychology: Research and Practice* 19:175–179.

Glaser, Barney, and Anselm Strauss. 1971. *Status passage.* Chicago: Aldine Atherton.

Goleman, Daniel. 1987, November 30. Worries about intimacy are rising, therapists find. *New York Times*, pp. 17, 21.

Griffitt, W., and P. Guay. 1969. "Object" evaluation and conditioned affect. *Journal of Experimental Research in Personality* 4:1–18.

*Harper's Magazine.* 1989, July. Harper's index. p. 15.

Helsing, Knud, Moyses Szklo, and George Comstock. 1981. Factors associated with mortality after widowhood. *American Journal of Public Health* 71:802–809.

Homans, George. 1950. *The human group.* Orlando: Harcourt Brace Jovanovich.

Kearl, Michael. 1980. Time, identity, and the spiritual needs of the elderly. *Sociological Analysis* 41:172–180.

Kelley, Harold, Ellen Berscheid, Andrew Christensen, John H. Harvey, Ted L. Huston, George Levinger, Evie McClintock, Letitia A. Peplau, and Donald R. Peterson. 1983. *Close relationships.* New York: Freeman.

Kenny, D. A., and W. Nasby. 1980. Splitting the reciprocity correlation. *Journal of Personality and Social Psychology* 38:249–256.

Kernis, M. H., and L. Wheeler. 1981. Beautiful friends and ugly strangers: Radiation and contrast effects in perceptions of same-sex pairs. *Personality and Social Psychology Bulletin* 7: 617–620.

Kübler-Ross, Elisabeth. 1969. *On death and dying.* New York: Macmillan.

Kunz, Phillip R., and Michael Woolcott. 1976. Season's greetings: From my status to yours. *Social Science Research* 5:269–278.

Lansing, J. B., and R. W. Heyns. 1959. Need affiliation and frequency of four types of communication. *Journal of Abnormal and Social Psychology* 58:365–372.

Lawson, Carol. 1990, August 30. Try to tell a widow that life still goes on. *New York Times*, pp. B1 and B2.

Lopata, Helena. 1971. Widows as a minority group. *Gerontologist* 2:67–70.

Lopata, Helena. 1973. Self-identity in marriage and widowhood. *Sociological Quarterly* 14:407–418.

Lott, A. J. and B. E. Lott. 1974. The role of reward in the formation of positive interpersonal attitudes. In T. L. Huston (ed.), *Foundations of interpersonal attraction.* Orlando: Academic Press.

Ludtke, Melissa. 1990, April 16. Getting young and old together. *Time*, p. 84.

Lynch, James. 1977. *The broken heart: The medical consequences of loneliness.* New York: Basic Books.

McAdams, Dan, Renee M. Lester, Paul A. Brand, and William J. McNamara. 1988. Sex and the TAT: Are women more intimate than men? Do men fear intimacy? *Journal of Personality Assessment* 52:397–409.

McAdams, Doug, and Fred Bryant. 1987. Intimacy motivation and subjective mental health in a nationwide sample. *Journal of Personality* 55:395–413.

McLeod, Beverly. 1984, October. In the wake of disaster. *Psychology Today*, pp. 54–57.

Makihara, Kumiko. 1990, May 28. No longer willing to be invisible. *Time*, p. 36.

Mauss, Marcel. 1954[1925]. *Essay on the gift: An archaic form of exchange* (Ian Cunnison, trans.). London: Routledge and Kegan Paul.

Moffat, Michael. 1989. *Coming of age in New Jersey: College and American culture.* New Brunswick, NJ: Rutgers University Press.

National Opinion Research Center (NORC). 1990. *General social surveys 1985, 1989* (James A. Davis, principal investigator, Tom W. Smith, senior study director and co-principal investigator). Data distributed by the Roper Center for Public Opinion Research.

Nowicki, Stephen, and Carolyn Oxenford. 1989. The relation of hostile nonverbal communication styles to popularity in preadolescent children. *Journal of Genetic Psychology* 150:39–44.

Otten, Alan. 1989, June 23. People patterns: Marriages that fail often do so early on. *Wall Street Journal*, p. B1.

Phillips, Carolyn. 1988, February 2. Divorce case marks first time a spouse wins civil award for emotional distress. *Wall Street Journal*, p. 29.

*A report from Iron Mountain: On the possibility and desirability of peace* (introduction by Leonard Lewin). 1967. New York: Dial Press.

Roberto, Karen A., and Jean P. Scott. 1986. Friendships of older men and women: Exchange patterns and satisfactions. *Psychology and Aging* 1:103–109.

*San Antonio Light* [AP]. 1989, May 21. Study: Stress decreases when income, age increase. p. F5.

Schachter, Stanley. 1959. *The psychology of affiliation: Experimental studies of the sources of gregariousness.* Stanford, CA: Stanford University Press.

Smith, Anthony. 1981. *The ethnic revival.* New York: Cambridge University Press.

Solano, Cecilia. 1986. People without friends: Loneliness and its alternatives. In Valerian J. Derlega and Barbara Winstead (eds.), *Friendship and social interaction.* New York: Springer-Verlag.

Toffler, Alvin. 1970. *Future shock.* New York: Random House.

*U.S. News & World Report.* 1990, April 23. News you can use: Piecemeal dinners, p. 78.

Vaughn, Diane. 1988. Uncoupling: The social construction of divorce. In Candace Clark and Howard Robboy (eds.), *Social interaction: Readings in sociology* (3rd ed.). New York: St. Martin's Press.

*Wall Street Journal.* 1989, March 3. People patterns: Divorce often breaks more than a marriage. p. B1.

Wallerstein, Judith, and Sandra Blakeslee. 1989. *Second chances: Men, women, and children a decade after divorce.* New York: Ticknor and Fields.

Walster, E., E. Aronson, D. Abrahams, and L. Rottman. 1966. Importance of physical attractiveness in dating behavior. *Journal of Personality and Social Psychology* 4:508–516.

Warner, W. Lloyd. 1945. *The living and the dead: Yankee City series no. 5.* New Haven, CT: Yale University Press.

Weitzman, Lenore. 1985. *The divorce revolution.* New York: Free Press.

Young, Jeffrey. 1986. A cognitive-behavioral approach to friendship disorders. In Valerian J. Derlega and Barbara Winstead (eds.), *Friendship and social interaction.* New York: Springer-Verlag.

Zajonc, R. B. 1968. Attitudinal effects of mere exposure. *Journal of Personality and Social Psychology Monographs* 9 (2, part 2):1–27.

# Social Groups

Individuals perform their noblest and their most ignoble deeds in groups. In the mid-1960s, for example, a class of California high school students questioned how the German people could sit by while the Nazis committed the atrocities of the Holocaust. To demonstrate the workings of totalitarian regimes, their teacher began discussing the virtues of discipline. He had the students sit stiffly in their chairs. He then made them practice entering the classroom quickly and silently, collectively assuming the required sitting position within five seconds. Other new rules of behavior were introduced, such as beginning every sentence with "Mr. Jones" and exchanging cupped hand salutes when passing fellow class members on campus. There were class slogans, such as "strength through discipline" and "strength through community." What was to be a day-long experiment spilled into the rest of the week, fueled by student enthusiasm. To locate those who did not play along and conform to the new rules, the teacher selected three student informers. The selection proved unnecessary, as half the class ended up acting as informants. In general, the students' classroom attention and performance improved significantly.

The experiment was contagious. Enrollment swelled to eighty as other students cut their classes to join the movement. A noontime rally was announced, featuring a televised press conference in which a nationwide movement based on the class's principles was to be announced. Two hundred students arrived in time to work up an emotional fervor by chanting slogans and giving salutes. However, the television screen remained blank. Eventually the students were shown clips of a Nuremberg rally and the war trials at which individuals charged with monstrous crimes pleaded innocent (Salgado 1976).

Building on Chapter 11's portrayal of social bonds as personal-level attractions, we now conceptualize relationship structures in terms of their functions and organization. Here we find ourselves at a crossroads in our study of the human condition. At this juncture the traditional scope of psychological social psychology merges with the sociological.

In this chapter we consider the ways in which the thoughts and behaviors of individuals are determined both by their positions within groups and by group-level processes. Those processes represent an entirely different kind of social phenomena than the face-to-face interactions between individuals. Groups come into existence to address various social and personal needs. They survive as long as they are effective in attaining their task-related objectives while simultaneously satisfying their members' needs (Barnard 1938). As we will see, however, groups are greater than the sum of their parts.

## CHARACTERISTICS OF GROUPS

In the strictest sense, a group is a collection of people interacting together in orderly ways on the basis of shared expectations about each other's behavior. When interactions continue over time, a **social system** takes form, structuring behavior and social relationships into predictable and enduring patterns. Social systems have a dynamism of their own, often beyond the control of and contrary to the intentions of their members.

Groups are arrangements of individuals just as living organisms are arrangements of cells: Both are systems of independent units working in concert to form unique wholes (Thomas 1974). These unique wholes have their own distinctive agendas and needs. To survive in a competitive environment, a group must protect its boundaries against other groups, seek feedback from the outside world, maintain memories of past assaults and successful strategies for coping with them, and monitor and coordinate the activities of its members. To regenerate itself when founding members depart, it must recruit and transform outsiders into insiders. In sum, groups take on a life of their own, their workings often remaining unchanged despite changing membership.

Recognition of this emergent order is what, in part, distinguishes sociological from psychological social psychology. For instance, instead of describing a group's ability to attain its objectives in terms of the averaged competency scores of its members, sociologists may focus on the group's internal structure and its regulative norms. They seek to understand the ways in which these properties of a group depend on its purposes, as well as on the ways in which the environment has either accommodated or frustrated them.

### Dynamics of Group Size

In analyzing the significance of numbers in social life, Simmel (1955) illustrated how changes in group size lead to qualitative transformations in group interaction. Small groups of two or three people possess characteristics that differ from those of groups of four or more people. For instance, sentiments are emphasized more in two-person groups, or *dyads*, than in larger ones. Add just one person, creating a *triad*, and not only does the number of dyadic relationships increase to three but a new dynamic becomes possible: coalitions of two against one, such as mom and dad versus baby or mom and baby versus dad.

With further increases in size, a group eventually reaches a threshold at which informal qualities become more formal as members begin to establish explicit rules and regulations. Another threshold involves optimal sizes for accomplishing various collective tasks. Productive student work committees, for example, commonly end up with five, seven, or nine members, whereas

T-groups and sensitivity training groups lose their effectiveness after the addition of the fifteenth member.

## Groups as Temporal Systems

Although the concept of a group often has spatial connotations, as can be seen in the different neighborhoods of a city or the "turf" of a street gang, it is more accurate to characterize groups as temporal systems. Members of work groups, for instance, cross the temporal boundary between family and work when they "punch in" at the company time clock. They are reminded of the pressures of group existence through exhortations such as "Don't waste time" and "Time is money."

Groups are temporal arrangements that emerge because of the synchronized interactions of their members. The processes of group life determine the sequence, duration, rate, rhythm, recurrence, routine, and synchronization of social action (Moore 1963). As mentioned earlier, what makes time seem so real is the fact that it is a container for group activities and events.

The time people experience is not their own but, rather, that of the groups of which they are a part. As Pitirim Sorokin and Robert Merton (1937) observed:

> Systems of time reckoning reflect the social activities of the group. Their springs of initiation are collective; their continued observance is demanded by social necessity. They arise from the round of group life, are largely determined by the routine of religious activity and the occupational order of the day, are essentially a product of social interaction (pp. 620–621).

A prerequisite for group membership is internalization of the group's time perspective.

## Communication Channels in Groups

In most groups, not all members interact with everyone else, nor are all interactions equal in terms of either quantity or quality. If one keeps a tally of who talks with whom within a group (see box "Establishing a Group's Communication Structure Through Conversational Analysis"), the resultant totals typically disclose the hierarchical structure of the group.

Conversational analysis also reveals **communication networks,** which ultimately affect a group's ability to accomplish tasks and maintain its members' satisfaction. Consider a five-person group, focusing on members who interact frequently. Several possible structures are diagrammed in Figure 12.1. The Equal Communication model is a rare form, because networks invariably evolve into simpler forms. Much of the activity of the Equal Communication and Circle networks were found to focus on the development of efficient hierarchies (Guetzkow and Dill 1957). Eventually, often one person becomes a communications hub, and some individuals come to occupy peripheral positions where they are linked to the network through only one other person. The closer individuals are to central communication positions, the greater their enjoyment of the group.

### Establishing a Group's Communication Structure Through Conversational Analysis

An interaction matrix can be used to record observations of who talks to whom within a group. If, for instance, person 2 is observed telling person 3 something, one would place a 1 in the appropriate cell. If a person addresses the group as a whole, that would be recorded in the "To All" column. When the observations are complete, row and column totals are calculated and the group's members can be rank-ordered in terms of interactions initiated and received. The row totals, or totals of interactions individuals have initiated, are correlated with the amount of power they have tried to exercise. The column totals, or totals of interactions individuals have received, are related to their social status.

| From: | To: 1 | 2 | 3 | 4 | 5 | Acts Initiated to All | Sum to Individuals | Total Initiated |
|---|---|---|---|---|---|---|---|---|
| 1 | x | | | | | | | |
| 2 | | x | | | | | | |
| 3 | | | x | | | | | |
| 4 | | | | x | | | | |
| 5 | | | | | x | | | |
| Sum received | | | | | | | | |

The data become more interesting when, for instance, one compares an individual's totals of interactions initiated versus received. In general, one receives more interactions from persons of lower status than one gives to them. Lower-status individuals, seeking to legitimate or improve their position, address those who are thought to agree with them and who also have greater power. Thus, group leaders can be readily identified, since they are the recipients of the most communication.

Those who are more likely to address the group as a whole also prove to be distinctive and predictable players. When they speak, they do so impersonally and have little to say to specific members. Robert Bales found such behaviors to be "the earmark of the person who thinks of himself . . . as the embodiment of the whole group and the group norms. In the extreme, such a person may not even feel the need to elicit overt agreement or comments from others at all—he assumes the role of invited and respected lecturer" (1970:79).

Whereas the Circle pattern is slower and more inefficient than the Wheel, it also allows for more internal corrections of errors and produces greater socioemotional satisfaction for participants (Leavitt 1951). In general, the progression of patterns from Circles to Chains to Y's to Wheels is associated with increasing leadership, organization, and task efficiency, but diminishing enjoyment (Leavitt 1951).

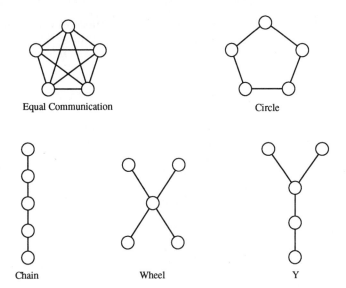

Equal Communication

Circle

Chain

Wheel

Y

**FIGURE 12.1   Patterns of Communication**

## Stable Differentiation of Roles and the Emergence of Hierarchy

When individuals routinely interact with others, their behaviors become increasingly formal and less spontaneous. Rules and roles emerge. Such canned behaviors occur out of the need to know what others will do in a given situation so that one can act accordingly. To avoid surprise, people literally engage in a trade-off: Individuals act in expected, patterned ways so that others will do the same; others follow suit because they, too, expect their own predictability to be reciprocated.

Out of emergent communication channels and routinized role activities arises a hierarchical order. This entails such matters as the distinctions between leader and followers, the length of the chains of command, the number of levels in the pecking order, and the relative numbers of individuals at each level. Distinctive structures arise out of the number and nature of the functions addressed. Peter Blau (1973), for instance, found that the greater the number of units in an organization, the larger its administrative component will be.

## Control over Group Activities

Like their members, groups vary along a continuum in terms of the degree of control they exercise over their own activities. Groups with low autonomy, for instance, often do not produce the affective bonds of more independent groups, because members feel relatively little commitment to the group's goals.

The failures of the centralized bureaucracy in the Soviet Union provide evidence of what happens when power is overly centralized. When the groups running factories and farms have no control over their activities, a devil-may-care attitude sets in, leading to inefficiency and shoddy products. However, centralized bureaucracies are effective in times of war. Thus, Stalin, despite inferior technology and massive opposition, prevailed against the Nazis because of his centralized control over the Russian military forces.

## Effects of Changes in Group Functions

Changes in the functions of the family can be used to illustrate the effects of group functions on role structure. In colonial America, families were "little commonwealths," miniature versions of the larger society that performed vital services for the community as a whole (Demos 1986). The family was responsible for the rearing and education of children and performed a variety of economic functions (Degler 1980, 1984). However, with the increasing differentiation and specialization of society, in which the world of work was increasingly separate from the world of the family (see Chapter 15), both the functions and structure of the family changed.

For instance, because families are no longer units of production, the role (and value) of children has changed. Instead of being understood as an economic asset, as more hands for the farm or a source of social security for the parents in old age, children are now viewed as an economic liability. And as the family is no longer responsible for educating children, it now functions primarily to provide caring relationships for its members, a place where one retreats to lick one's wounds. The "glue" bonding family members together is no longer economic interdependency but, rather, emotions. As a result, Demos (1986) notes that contemporary cultural depictions of the family are as some kind of "encounter group."

As a result of these changes, coupled with women's increasing participation in the labor force, the roles of husband and wife have changed considerably. The clear differentiation of gender roles that characterized nineteenth-century families—when work was the male sphere and home the sphere of women—have increasingly blurred. Approximately two-thirds of women with children under the age of 18 work outside the home (*Wall Street Journal* 1988). Among nearly one-quarter of all couples, the wife is the chief breadwinner (Hays 1987), and many men have become "househusbands." (The term *homemaker* is used to refer to both women and men who devote themselves to housework and child care.)

It takes time to get used to such profound changes, and traditional beliefs about men's and women's roles may still be found in certain sections of society. Figure 12.2 summarizes Americans' reactions to the following question: "Do you agree or disagree with this statement? Women should take care of running their homes and leave running the country up to men." Twenty-one percent of Americans 18 years of age and older agreed with this statement, with no statistical difference between the sexes. When the results are broken down by age and education, both generational and educational differences are evident. The likelihood of agreement generally increases with age and decreases with education. And across the life cycle, with the exception of women 65 years of age and older who have at most a high school education, men are more likely than women to agree.

Group dynamics change over time, and increasingly social scientists are taking a longitudinal view of group processes. The quality of husband–wife relationships, for instance, changes through the life cycle. Some researchers

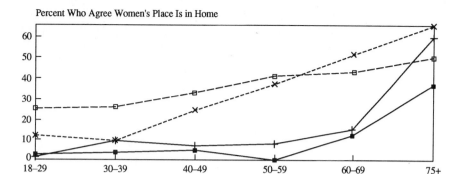

Percent Who Agree Women's Place Is in Home

Gender/Education
—▫— Male: ≤ High School Grad
—+— Male: Post High School
--✗-- Female: ≤ High School Grad
—▪— Female: Post High School

**FIGURE 12.2  Attitudes toward the Idea That Women's Place Is in the Home, by Age, Gender, and Education**
Source: NORC, 1988.

(e.g., Blood and Wolfe 1960) have found that marital satisfaction declines with age. Lowenthal, Thurnher, and Chiriboga (1976) found that marital dissatisfaction tends to peak during the period preceding the empty-nest stage and then declines to levels close to those of the newlywed phase. Some of the findings in this area are summarized in Table 12.1, which reveals both life-stage and gender differences. Whereas men are likely to describe their spouse in positive (+) terms at all three stages of the relationship, during middle age women are as likely to describe their husbands in neutral or ambivalent (0) terms as in positive terms, becoming more positive during the preretirement years.

These findings require considerable qualification. First, these are not longitudinal studies of the same individuals; rather, they are studies of differ-

**TABLE 12.1  Perceptions of Spouses Across the Lifespan**

|  |  | Newlywed | | Middle Age | | Preretirement | |
|---|---|---|---|---|---|---|---|
|  |  | M | F | M | F | M | F |
| Description | + | 72% | 76% | 85% | 42% | 82% | 82% |
| of spouse | 0 | 24 | 16 | 15 | 42 | 18 | 18 |
|  | − | 4 | 8 | 0 | 16 | 0 | 0 |
| Male dominant |  | 64% | 75% | 54% | 44% | 41% | 50% |
| Egalitarian |  | 36 | 17 | 31 | 26 | 44 | 10 |
| Female dominant |  | 0 | 8 | 15 | 30 | 15 | 40 |

Source: Lowenthal, Thurnher, and Chiriboga, 1976:27.

ent age groups at different times. Second, there are undoubtedly generational differences in the nature of the relationship between spouses. For those married in the 1920s, for instance, the meaning of marriage and the expectations associated with the roles of husband and wife may vary considerably from the meanings and expectations held by those marrying in the 1990s. And finally, the historical recency of the divorce revolution produces a distinctive sample of once-married couples in old age.

Another profound change in the family involves the increasing longevity of the husband–wife union. A century ago, when life expectancy was forty-six years, marriages lasted an average of little more than twenty-five years before one of the spouses was widowed. Nowadays, marriages may last half a century or more.

## Group Tasks and Integration

Why do individuals allow themselves to be absorbed into an entity that has a dynamic of its own and that may do things that are contrary to their interests? What's in it for the 14-year-old guard of a gang leader at a school dance, who is there to "take the rap" if guns appear and police arrive? Although the youth cannot be held and tried as an adult, he still faces detention and the possibility of being sent to a reform school.

The major return to individuals for their contributions to the group is satisfaction of their socioemotional needs. Groups give their members solidarity with others, a sense of belonging, and a feeling of self-worth. They offer the individual a place in the broad scheme of things. The 14-year-old finds that in the gang he can be more important, that others may depend on *him* and he can be *someone*, than in the adult world, which treats him as a child.

Robert Bales (1958) described group processes as featuring both tension and harmony as the group works to fulfill its instrumental (or task) goals while simultaneously working to satisfy its members' socioemotional needs. He was influenced by the human-relations theory of administration that was popular in the 1930s and 1940s. This theory held that productivity is influenced not simply by monetary rewards but also by the social relationships among workers. In Bales's view, task-oriented activities give rise to tensions in the socioemotional area. But when the group turns its attention to those issues, neglect of task performance gives rise to task-related tensions. Thus, the group oscillates between its instrumental and socioemotional concerns and is continually trying to reach an equilibrium that will keep tension to a minimum.

According to Bales's "phase-movement hypothesis," a typical problem-solving group goes through three patterned sequences of task-related activities: (1) a high amount of task-oriented activity at the outset, with a decline in the relative amount of such activity thereafter; (2) a (relatively) high amount of mid-course task evaluation activity compared to the preceding and following phases; and (3) a steady rise in the amount of control exercised over task activities during the course of the group's work. Bales also posited an increase in both positive and negative socioemotional activities (with a slight downturn in negative ones and an upturn in positive ones toward the end of the session).

To test these ideas, Bales and his associates constructed the *interaction process analysis* for use in coding each verbal and nonverbal unit of behavior observed in a small, task-oriented group. Coders were instructed to base their classifications on the presumed significance of a message for the individual transmitting it.

As noted in Figure 12.3, four broad categories underlie the twelve items in Bales's index. The extreme groups describe the socioemotional problems arising out of the group's task endeavors (D) and the socioemotional strategies used to preserve the group's harmony and integration (A). The intermediate groups (B and C) are emotionally neutral; they are oriented toward the tasks confronting the group. When the number of acts in each of the twelve categories is determined, profile scores can be computed for both individuals and groups. Group scores are assumed to reflect such factors as degree of orientation toward tasks, amount of interpersonal tension, and degree of group harmony.

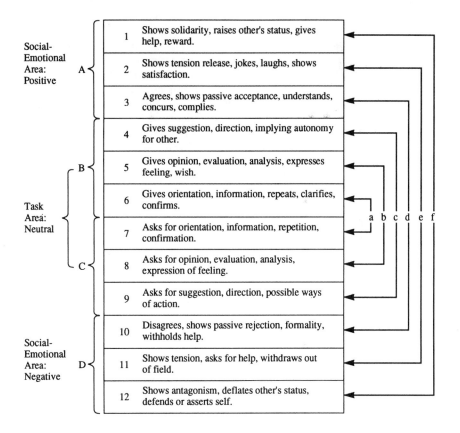

a–Problems of Communication
b–Problems of Evaluation
c–Problems of Control
d–Problems of Decision
e–Problems of Tension Reduction
f–Problems of Reintegration

A–Positive Reactions
B–Attempted Answers
C–Questions
D–Negative Reactions

**FIGURE 12.3. Categories of Action Coded in Bales's Interaction Process Analysis**

Descriptions of the internal structures and processes of groups are analogous to anatomists' depictions of organisms. But these fail to take into account the interactions between groups and their environments. For instance, just as the metabolic processes of a hare are accelerated when it is stalked by a fox, so group dynamics are intensified when the group is threatened by other groups.

Ecology provides a useful perspective for examining the relationships between groups. According to some social scientists (e.g., Hannan and Freeman 1989), the same ecological dynamics that govern fox and rabbit populations apply to the geographic distribution of retail establishments and service organizations. Similarly, the relationships between ethnic groups can be approached by looking at the distinctive economic niches they occupy. In the past, German immigrants to the United States became brewers; the Chinese found work as launderers; and Italians grew fruits and produced wines. Today we find Greeks concentrated in the pizza business, Koreans in the fruit and vegetable trade, Soviet and Nigerian emigrés in the taxi industry, and Arabs in grocery stores. Group interactions may be minimal, as when two ethnic groups occupy two clearly distinct niches and do not compete for resources. They may be symbiotic, as when groups provide important goods and services for each other and become closely interdependent. Or groups may compete with each other for resources or markets. Such situations sometimes lead to violence, as has occurred between Portuguese and Asian fishermen in Boston.

## Self-Definition by Groups

In parts of Pennsylvania and Kansas, one can have a direct encounter with the nineteenth century. Here live the Amish, a religious group that eschews what members consider the evils of modernization. Amish farmers, for instance, refuse to comply with state regulations requiring indoor plumbing in all new houses for which construction permits are granted, as well as in schools and other public buildings. The farmers insist that their outdoor privies are quite adequate and that modern flush toilets would violate their religious commitment to a simple life.

Like individuals, groups define themselves in terms of features that distinguish them from others. This is most true of autonomous groups. In nonautonomous groups such as military regiments, the group defines itself in terms of a broader ideal.

## Groups as Boundary-Maintaining Systems

Just as wolves mark their spatial territories, juvenile gangs maintain their turf by "tagging" the boundaries with spray-painted names, symbols, or slogans. During the 1980s and 1990s, American cities were increasingly adorned with such graffiti. A single gang name on a wall typically means that a gang is operating nearby. When one gang's name is written over another, it means that they are enemies and boundaries are being reestablished (Edwards 1990).

Social groups create boundaries in both space and time. Amish families preserve their nineteenth-century lifestyles amid the materialistic temptations of the present.

Kai Erikson (1966) noted that groups are boundary-maintaining systems, expending energy to preserve their own "space." Unlike animal groups, human groups mark their boundaries not only in geographic space but in time as well. Parents' attempts to have all family members present at dinnertime are designed to create a family time that does not overlap with play time, work time, or TV time. Moslems are reminded of their collective membership five times a day, when they simultaneously bow down toward Mecca, the birthplace of Mohammed. Some groups actually use time as a basis for self-definition; this can be seen in labels like "Sixties radicals" or "the class of '34" (Johnson 1986).

The secret handshakes between members of fraternal groups are an example of the way groups also define themselves in cultural terms (Erikson 1966). Many other examples can be given. In cities near the Mexican border and in the Caribbean, Hispanic groups battle for time on the radio airwaves so that they can hear their language and music. The nonverbal messages exchanged between customers in a gay bar are used to determine who is and who is not a member of the homosexual community. If the new patron recognizes the boundaries, it implies that he shares the group's standard for evaluation and judgment (Barth 1969).

### Boundary Maintenance Rituals

Members of a community inform one another about the placement of their boundaries by participating in the confrontations which occur when persons who venture out to the edges of the group are met by policing agents whose special business it is to guard the cultural integrity of the group (Erikson 1966:11)

The greater the importance of boundaries to a group's self-definition and ability to control its members, the less permeable those borders become. Particularly when they feel threatened, groups close themselves off from the outside world, carefully guarding against people and ideas crossing their borders. For instance, after the fall of Saigon in 1975, to guard against Western influences the North Vietnamese gathered up all the books, records, and films in the city. When media networks began televising professional sporting events on Sundays, various religious leaders protested the encroachment of secular pursuits on the sabbath.

When a group is threatened, either by some external threat or by a growing lack of moral consensus among its members, it will increasingly confront members on its moral fringes. Deviance that was formerly tolerated now becomes the object of ritual prosecution. For example, although the Bill of Rights guarantees freedom of speech and socialism has had supporters in the United States since at least the turn of the century, after World War II the fear of infiltration by communist revolutionaries gave rise to McCarthyism and the blacklisting of talented individuals with socialist leanings as well as of many people with only the vaguest links to such individuals.

Group boundaries are also maintained through rituals of inclusion. The more restrictive its membership rules, the more likely a group is to dramatize ritually the selection and initiation of its new members. Consider the hazing rituals of college fraternities. Although they are often demeaning and painful for the initiates, they cause the newcomer to value membership highly. For older members, such rituals increase their solidarity: If recruits are willing to accept such suffering, the group must truly be important.

## Relations with Other Groups

People tend to like their own group (*in-group*) and to dislike competing or opposing groups (*out-groups*). Individuals with strong group identification are especially prone to favor the in-group and to hold negative sentiments toward out-groups. This attitude is termed **ethnocentrism** (Sumner 1924).

As we saw in Chapter 11, the history of society is in part a story of the progressive weakening of individuals' identification with kinship and tribal bonds and the strengthening of their identification with broader groups such as social classes and nation-states. Throughout history individuals and groups have formed alliances in opposition to perceived threats, thereby intensifying in-group sentiment. The American colonies coalesced in opposition to the British. Under pressure from neighboring Germans, Lithuanian tribes united in the thirteenth century to become a medieval state. Stalin owed his success in consolidating his repressive regime partly to the creation of non-Communist out-groups that were depicted as enemies of the people who would fight to the death.

Groups can be placed on a continuum in terms of their accommodation or hostility toward other groups. Among religious groups, for example, sects exist in hostile relationships with the secular world, whereas churches are more accommodating. However, the most intense in-group dynamics occur among groups that are in direct competition with other groups.

***Competition and Conflict between Groups.*** Intergroup conflict is a situation in which groups take antagonistic actions toward each other in order to control some valued outcome. Because such confrontations tend to invigorate the group, they are highly tenacious and resistant to restraining efforts. A legendary illustration of such persistence is the feud between the Hatfields and the McCoys, mountain families who for generations had lived peacefully on opposite sides of a narrow river. The conflict was triggered by Floyd Hatfield's moving his pigs to the McCoy side of the river. Randolf McCoy, Floyd's brother-in-law, accused Floyd of stealing the pigs. More than a hundred persons lost their lives in the course of the feud, which lasted from 1873 until 1928.

Conflict initially arises when groups have directly opposing goals or when one group suddenly threatens or deprives another and provokes an aggressive reaction, or when members of one group act in prejudicial ways toward members of another group. Even when an underlying opposition of interests is not present, the mere awareness of an out-group can provoke discriminatory responses by in-group members. According to the Santa Barbara Peace Resource Center, of the thirty-two wars that were in progress during 1988, twenty-five had a significant ethnic, racial, or religious dimension (Schlesinger 1989).

As distrust and hostility grow, individuals develop increasingly antagonistic attitudes toward out-group members and feel increasing cohesion with members of their own group. Concurrently, boundary maintenance activities increase. Penalties for deviance become harsher as the enforcement of norms stiffens. Tolerance for dissent declines as the focus of group activities shifts from the rights and welfare of members to the task of winning the conflict.

Boundary reaffirmations also produce a heightened sense of in-group identity. This, in turn, leads to an expansion of the issues under dispute as members endow their cause with additional significance and increase their commitment to the group (Coser 1956). Contacts with members of the opposition diminish, leading to distorted stereotypes of out-group members and overblown conceptions of the worthiness and power of the in-group.

## TYPES OF GROUPS

A variety of efforts have been made to classify social groups to better understand how group function determines group processes and how those processes, in turn, determine group structure. The resulting categories, although somewhat arbitrary, can serve as a starting point for an examination of the vast variety of human social groups.

### Identity Groups

In the movie *The Big Chill*, a group of close college friends meet several years after graduation to attend the funeral of one of their classmates. The friends had gone separate ways and had largely lost touch with one another. At the funeral, each discovers how far he or she has drifted from the group's shared

## Lessons from Alcoholics Anonymous

Alcoholics Anonymous is one of the best-known identity transformation groups. A central task of this group is teaching individuals to view themselves and their lives from the perspective of sober others. To accomplish this, individuals become members of a new reference group, one comprised of others sharing a socially defined problem and a desire for change.

Alterations in life-style are viewed as requiring a different matrix by which reality is approached, one replete with new values, new roles, and new self-conceptions. Individuals must first recognize that, because of alcohol, their entire self-systems are out of kilter and that they are negatively impacting others. They must publicly acknowledge that they are "alcoholics." To recognize new options and attitudes, these contaminated identities must first be destroyed and then replaced by alternative identities, such as "recovering alcoholic." Groups like Alcoholics Anonymous (AA) supply both the tools and support for such transformations.

AA provides members with a vocabulary that will appear to themselves and others to be an adequate motive and a frame of reference for experience. Because motives are most significant when one is forced to account for actions that do not seem meaningful (see Chapter 9), an accounting of motives and reflection of the group will integrate the individual into the group, adding to group solidarity and social order. The recovering alcoholic may then begin to draw a meaningful identity and a set of role recipes from significant others in the resocialization process.

youthful ideals. Each has lost a little self-esteem; each had missed the reinforcement of being told that he or she is a great person. Like the family, primary groups like this group of friends involve the whole self and help meet their members' identity needs.

*Identity Reaffirmation.*    Groups are often formed by people who share common passions, beliefs, life-style, or social stigma (such as blindness, obesity, or old age) that are central to their identities. Such groups offer an "intellectually worked-up version of their point of view" (Goffman 1963:25), legitimating and reaffirming the significance of such bases of self-conception.

There can be a dark side to such groups. Deep-seated emotions and reaffirmations of identity, for instance, bind groups based on hate, such as the Ku Klux Klan and neo-Nazi groups, which subsist on antiblack and anti-Semitic feelings. Such groups are spawned during times of economic and political uncertainty and attract individuals who feel left out of the mainstream, often young adults. As of 1990, there were between four and five thousand neo-Nazi groups in the United States (Irving Spergel, cited in Mydans 1990).

*Identity Transcendence.*    People also perceive themselves as belonging to groups whose members never meet. These groups can include individuals long dead or yet to be born. These central reference groups, such as families and religious groups, provide their members biographical continuity and meaningfulness, giving order to discrete life experiences and a sense of integration between their own lives and those of their ancestors and successors (Back 1981:327).

***Identity Transformation.*** Many organizations are dedicated to the reconstruction of personal identities. Among them are Alcoholics Anonymous, consciousness-raising groups, sensitivity groups, Weight Watchers, Synanon, and new religious movements. There are an estimated five hundred thousand self-help groups meeting the needs of some 15 million Americans (Kerr 1982). They are referred to as "identity transformation groups" (Greil and Rudy 1984).

Prominent among the strategies employed by such groups is the sharing of feelings and public statements by members in which they describe their limitations or sins. For a new self to be constructed, the old self must be disassembled, analyzed, and ritually destroyed. For the new self to persist, group members must frequently interact to reinforce the new identity and the new behaviors associated with it.

## Groups Whose Members Share a Common Collective Identity

A second broad category of groups consists of those whose members have a shared identity by virtue of living in the same community, sharing central cultural traits (ethnic and racial groups) and moral outlooks (religious groups), or occupying the same position in the stratification system (social classes, unions). As with identity groups, membership in these groups is highly valued and provides a central component of identity. Unlike identity groups, these groups, such as the ethnic identity movements described in Chapter 11, exist to reaffirm and maintain the identity claims of collectivities rather than individuals, providing collective causes that bind members together. Often allegiance to such collective causes places these groups in opposing relationships with others; the resulting conflicts typically are waged in the political realm. As we will see later in the chapter, the existence of threatening out-groups often serves to crystalize the sense of collective consciousness among members of groups with a shared social fate.

## Integrative Groups

Between identity- and task-oriented groups are large-scale voluntary associations that contribute to the integration and continuity of society (Simmel 1955). Members of such groups are only partly involved in the group, and the bonds between them are limited. They include fraternal associations, which offer a sense of belonging and an arena for self-expression (Schmidt 1980). Also included are service and membership groups such as the American Association of Retired Persons and the Veterans Association. (See Table 12.2.) Between 1975 and 1990, the number of such groups increased by 77 percent, to 23,000, and 70 percent of Americans belong to at least one such association (*U.S. News & World Report* 1990).

**TABLE 12.2  The Largest Membership Groups in the United States**

| Association | Membership |
| --- | --- |
| American Automobile Association | 29.0 million |
| American Association of Retired Persons | 28.0 |
| YMCA of the U.S.A. | 14.0 |
| National Geographic Society | 10.5 |
| National Right to Life Committee | 7.0 |
| National PTA—National Congress of Parents and Teachers | 6.1 |
| National Wildlife Federation | 5.1 |
| National Committee to Preserve Social Security and Medicare | 5.0 |
| 4-H Program | 4.8 |
| Boy Scouts of America | 4.8 |
| Women's International Bowling Congress | 3.7 |
| American Bowling Congress | 3.3 |
| American Farm Bureau Federation | 3.3 |
| Girl Scouts of the U.S.A. | 3.1 |
| National Rifle Association | 3.0 |
| American Legion | 2.9 |
| International Friendship League | 2.8 |
| Little League Baseball | 2.5 |
| National Alliance of Senior Citizens | 2.2 |
| Veterans of Foreign Wars | 2.1 |

Source: American Society of Association Executives; *U.S. News & World Report,* 1990.

## Task-Oriented Groups

The U.S. Navy has asked you to select the crew of a nuclear submarine. What criteria would you use to put together a team that can live peacefully in a metal container, under water, for months at a time yet always be prepared to work together effectively during times of crises? Would you want all the crew members to be close friends? What kind of captain would you choose? One who is considered a friend by the crew, or a person who is feared and yet respected?

Such are the issues that arise when one considers groups whose function is the coordinated pursuit of a collective goal. As the competitiveness of the United States in the world economy has declined, a great deal of research has been directed toward ways to enhance the creativity, productivity, cooperation, and efficiency of work groups. (See Chapter 15.)

The epitome of the task-oriented interactive group is the professional sports team. During the 1970s and 1980s, fifty or more state and local governments spent at least $6 billion to build or refurbish stadiums in order to attract or keep professional baseball and football teams. Taxpayers, whether fans or not, contributed to the building of these community temples. This nations' "sports syndrome," as commentator Howard Cosell (1986) labeled it, may be derived from the games' ability to dramatize the central values of a culture. Sports also serve to enculturate social neophytes. Gunther Barth (1981), for

**TABLE 12.3 Symbolic Dramatization of Blacks' Position in Society in the Sport of Baseball**

| Percentages of Major-League Baseball Players Who Were Black, 1986 | | | |
|---|---|---|---|
| Catcher | 0 | Second base | 25 |
| Pitcher | 6 | Shortshop | 20 |
| First base | 29 | Third base | 11 |
| | | Outfield | 48 |

Source: Rosellini, 1987.

instance, observed that the rise of baseball corresponded with cities' need to show rural immigrants how competition could flourish under the influence of rules and regulations, control and authority.

Sports reaffirm a culture's central concerns. For example, increasing urbanization and specialization in the world of work are mirrored in the popularity of games against time (football, hockey, basketball) as opposed to traditional games like baseball. Concurrently, spectators' preferences have also shifted toward increasingly aggressive sports.

From sports one learns basic lessons such as how the whole can be greater than the sum of its parts and a team of individual superstars can lose if there is no "team play." Sports also reaffirm cultural messages dealing with gender, age, and race. In a sexist society, sports requiring team players are reserved primarily for males; celebrated female athletes are found primarily in sports like golf, tennis, or gymnastics. In a youth-oriented society, the physical games of the young are preferred. And in a racist society team roles may be segregated along racial lines.

During the 1986 major league baseball season, although one-quarter of the players were black, none of the head coaches and only 9 percent of the assistant coaches were black. And the positions blacks occupy on the field tend to be peripheral. In baseball the tempo and action of the game are controlled by the pitcher and the catcher. Table 12.3 shows that these key defensive positions are most likely to be held by whites. In general, the farther one is from the central action of the game, the more likely one is to be black (Rosellini 1987).

**Formal Organizations.** The formal organization ranks among our species' greatest innovations. Unlike groups in the animal kingdom, formal organizations are deliberately created for the achievement of specific goals. In these groups function determines structure. Within an organization subgroups conduct parallel but separate business. An advertising division, for example, might include groups devoted to market research (requiring statisticians, samplers, interviewers, media watchers, data coders, and keyboard operators), graphics, internal media, domestic media, international media, and corporate as opposed to product advertising. This division of functions is termed **rationalization.**

Rationalization creates roles that are distinct from their occupants. Role activities come to be defined in terms of the rules and procedures set forth in job descriptions. They exist within hierarchies of authority (e.g., assembly-line worker, supervisor, manager, director, junior vice-president, senior vice-president, chief executive officer), with each level responsible for overseeing an increasing proportion of the total process.

## Why Business Meetings Often Fail

*The usefulness of a meeting is in inverse proportion to the attendance.*
—Lane Kirkland, President, AFL-CIO

In the workplace, the higher one is on the organizational ladder, the more time one spends in meetings. Oppenheim (1991) found that top managers spend an average of twenty-three hours a week in meetings and middle managers an average of eleven. Much of that time is wasted.

Several conditions have been correlated with productive use of time in business meetings. First, there must be a balance between the members' sense of group solidarity and their focus on the task at hand. Second, the participants must assume that there is a worthwhile agenda with clear-cut objectives. When meetings are called just because there are supposed to be biweekly meetings, or the convener simply wants to exercise his or her power or put on a show for higher management, participants will either tune out or sabotage the meeting in some way.

Third, the task or objectives must be appropriate to the group. For instance, when innovative brainstorming or problem solving is required, individuals working alone may be more effective than a group (Bouchard, Barsaloux, and Drauden 1974; Dunnette, Campbell and Jaastad 1963). The reasons are varied: they include apprehension about the opinions of others, a temptation to "get a free ride" when members' ideas are pooled and analyzed at a group level, and the simple fact that only one person can speak at a time (Lamm and Trommsdorff 1973). In fact, Diehl and Stroebe (1987) found that the latter reason is the most likely explanation of groups' inferior brainstorming capacities. When they established working conditions that allowed individuals to verbalize their ideas when they occurred, the number of ideas doubled compared to the condition in which individuals must wait their turn to talk. The researchers concluded that groups are more successful when they perform an evaluative function than when they attempt to produce ideas.

Fourth, as Lane Kirkland noted, there may be too many people present. Oppenheim (1991) found that not only the "right" people need to be in attendance but the "wrong" individuals need to be absent. An overly zealous, domineering "eager beaver," for example, can destroy the group's harmony and coordination. Williams and Sternberg (1988) found that the groups that came up with the most creative solutions to two written problems were those whose membership included at least one person with high intelligence (as opposed to a high average IQ among all the members). Those groups also had high average scores on persuasiveness, expressiveness, and assertiveness; and their members were characterized by a diversity of experiences and points of view.

Once established, formal organizations take on a life of their own. This can be seen in several tendencies of such organizations. For instance, organizations often acquire a "preservation motive" (Selznick 1949), which perpetuates their existence even after their original basic goal has been satisfied. Further, according to the **iron law of oligarchy,** over time power tends to become concentrated in the hands of a few members because of the group's need for a hierarchy of authority and because of the tendency of underlings to passively defer to leaders (Michels 1967 [1911]).

In addition, organizational rules and regulations have a tendency to become more important than the organization's goals, resulting in **goal displacements,** as when people go to great lengths to document that their each and every move was performed "by the rules." Finally, internal competition can lead to antagonism: Instead of working together for the common good, members engage in bureaucratic infighting.

## Masses

The largest and most omnipotent of all human groups is the nation-state. Political regimes have mobilized millions for war, harnessed individuals' reproductive urges, and created laws that govern the behaviors of all, superseding all local statutes, norms, and mores. Through the nation-state, individuals can envision and accomplish goals that were rarely even imagined one century ago, such as developing space stations to orbit the earth, bombarding the nuclei of atoms with subatomic particles propelled at nearly the speed of light, or, as in Maoist China, organizing a billion people to eradicate the common fly.

## Factors Underlying Distinctions among Types of Groups

The distinctions among the types of groups described in this section go beyond differences in group size. Also involved is the degree of involvement of members in the group (Back 1981). This turns out to be equivalent to the degree of personal attraction between members of the group and inversely related to the amount of pressure overtly exercised by the group on its members (Gurvitch 1941). Groups vary in the degree to which their members are controlled and organized to work together to meet the challenges faced by the group.

At one end of the continuum are associations that involve the whole self, in which interpersonal attraction is greatest, and in which members' sense of fusion with the group is most intense. Because individuals' participation is voluntary, group control over their behavior is minimal.

By "fusion with the group," we mean the extent of the individual's psychological participation in the group and the extent to which their identities are subsumed in that of the group. On this dimension, groups can range from the **membership groups** to which one belongs only in name (e.g., being a card-carrying member of the National Geographic Society) to **reference groups** whose norms, goals, and identities are internalized by the individual (e.g., one's coworkers and family).

At the other end of the continuum are groups that involve only a small portion of the self, in which there is the least attraction between members and a minimal sense of participating in the group. To survive, some of these groups (such as the military) may require involuntary membership, which invariably places limits on members' ability to make decisions. When individuals are forced to become members, commitment to the group is low. This, in turn, entails the greatest degree of group pressure on members. Nations, for instance, monopolize all legitimate forms of violence to ensure that their laws are obeyed.

# THE GROUP WITHIN THE INDIVIDUAL

Not only do individuals do things in groups that they would never consider doing alone, but group dynamics can alter the ways in which individuals perceive the world. Such perceptual changes run the gamut from becoming totally oblivious to the outside world, as when group members become overly absorbed with each other, to becoming hypersensitive to certain stimuli, as when members of a religious sect view the secular world as hostile and corrupt.

Among the best-known impacts of group participation on behavior and decision making are the audience effect, diffusion of responsibility, "groupthink," and polarization.

***The Audience Effect.***   The sheer presence of others facilitates social performances. Since the turn of the century, when Triplett (1897–1898) observed bicyclists going faster when racing head-to-head than when racing alone, social scientists have recorded numerous instances in which audiences affect individuals' behaviors, enhancing well-rehearsed performances and inhibiting others (Zajonc, Heigartner, and Herman 1969). When the audience is made up of members of a highly valued group, the show one puts on is motivated by more than the need for attention. (See Chapter 3.) Also involved is the desire to demonstrate that one is a valuable role player and that one is willing to do anything to please the group. (See box entitled "Sexual Rampages by Athletes.")

***Diffusion of Responsibility.***   When one participates in collective action with others, accountability for that action becomes diffused. Thus, when sharing a task with others, individuals face the temptation to work less hard than when they are working alone. With accountability spread out, the relationship between personal effort and outcome fades, and "social loafing" (Williams, Harkins, and Latané 1981) often results.

On the other hand, groups can also remove burdens from certain individuals and disperse their obligations among all their members, as when members of a community all feel responsible for the socialization of everyone's children. Such commitment is an integral component of the sense of interdependency and trust on which all groups depend.

***"Groupthink."***   One consequence of the pressure for conformity is the possibility that individuals will become locked into the frame of reference of their group and fail to realistically perceive and appraise alternative courses of action. In their efforts to preserve group harmony, they neglect detailed critical thought, inspection of alternatives, and weighting of pros and cons—all requirements for carefully reasoned decisions. This is why a broader range of ideas can be generated by individuals working alone than by a group.

The probability of groupthink (Janis 1971) is greatest in highly cohesive groups whose members share an illusion of invulnerability and unanimity, during crisis situations, when group members are isolated from outside evaluation, and when the group's leader actively promotes his or her favored solution to the problem facing the group.

## Sexual Rampages of Athletes

From high school to college to the pro leagues, players are fast gaining a reputation for off-the-field sexual rampages. . . .

To a great degree, sexual abuses are a consequence of men banding together in tight-knit competitive groups. Like military platoons, ghetto gangs, and college fraternities, athletic teams foster a spirit of exclusivity, camaraderie, and solidarity. Jocks not only play together but often eat and live together. And personal integrity is frequently a weak match for group loyalty. In a mob, especially one fueled by alcohol or drugs, individuals may not blanch at joining in a gang rape. "They will do anything to please each other," observes psychologist Bernice Dandler. "They are raping for each other. The woman is incidental." And, she adds, "They don't think of it as rape even when the victim is unconscious. Rape is something done by one man in a dark alley."

Heavy peer pressure is just one factor. Contact sport may be inherently violent, but, notes Lawrence Hartmann, president-elect of the American Psychiatric Association, "sports today is a phenomenon of excess, of ferocious aggression." . . . Winning is what's important, so what does the mayhem matter, even if it is against the rules?

From there it is a short step for athletes to believe they can ignore the rules in everyday life as well. Society conspires in that belief. Sports stars move in a rarefied world of privilege where good grades, money, drugs, and sex are readily available and transgressions are easily forgiven. "After all, the group-think rationale goes, rules are for others, not for heroes," points out psychologist Tony Farrenkopf. . . . "Boys will be boys" and a sotto voce variation of "She asked for it."

Source: Toufexis, 1990:76–77.

**Polarization.** After the members of a group discuss a controversial issue, individuals' opinions are intensified and the average of their views shifts to a more extreme position (Myers 1982). For example, studies of negotiations in hijacking situations found security officers advocating riskier solutions after discussing the problem with staff and other government officials. Jury discussions have also been discovered to magnify the initial judgments of individual jurors (Myers and Kaplan 1976).

Several reasons can be readily identified. First, people tend to associate with like-minded individuals, and their shared opinions are amplified when they interact. Second, responsibility is diffused as individuals fall into line with the majority view. Third, a preponderance of one-sided arguments crowds out alternatives. Discussion within the group serves to persuade members who initially chose relatively moderate positions. Fourth, attitudes change even when one thinks about issues alone (Tesser 1978). As we saw in Chapter 4, attitudes and rudimentary theories become more formal personal theories as one increases the number of connections between beliefs and commitment to these belief systems increases. Finally, because taking risks is valued more highly than being conservative, people want to see themselves as being at least as willing as other members to take risks.

Suspecting cultural factors underlying this phenomenon, Lawrence Hong (1978) examined the difference between solitary and group-based decision-making processes by comparing the behaviors of American subjects with those of Taiwanese subjects. He presented members of each group with a questionnaire that posed a series of dilemmas about twelve issues such as buying stocks, getting married, and having a heart operation. In each group, some subjects made their decisions alone while others made their choices in groups. Compared to the Americans, the Taiwanese shifted to more cautious choices in a group setting. Hong suspected that this phenomenon is a result of Confucian cultural teachings, which emphasize "moderation in all things."

## THE INDIVIDUAL WITHIN THE GROUP

As the poet John Donne wrote, "No man is an island." Instead, we live most of our lives in small groups whose dynamics structure our thoughts, behaviors, and identities.

The small group serves an important mediating function between the individual and society: Through our networks with family, friends, and neighbors, we are linked to our communities. Through our communities we are linked to our cities, which link us to our states, which link us to our country, which ultimately links us with the world system.

### Personality Types and Group Roles

Bales's analyses of interaction processes (see Figure 12.3) yielded not only group-level profiles but profiles of members as well. Not surprisingly, the researchers found that individuals did not contribute equally to the task and socioemotional activities of the groups; in addition, there were distinctive longitudinal patterns in the contributions of each individual. Some, for instance, invested heavily in the group's task while others played key roles in maintaining harmony. Out of these profiles, Bales (1970) developed a theory showing how twenty-six distinct personality types could predictably perform specific types of group roles. In Bales's theory, each person is plotted as a point in a three-dimensional space described by the following coordinates:

U: directed toward material success and power
D: passive, self-effacing powerless

P: oriented toward egalitarianism; friendly, approaching others as equals
N: oriented toward individualistic isolationism, detached, unsocial

F: oriented toward conservative group beliefs
B: rejecting validity of conservative group beliefs and values; heretical and disbelieving

One can, for instance, be a UPF, a person who tries to simultaneously move toward social solidarity and progress toward accomplishment of the group's tasks; or a DNB, one who withholds cooperation and is negative toward the demands of the group's leader. Regardless of how they are classified, individuals are seen as trying to form alliances with members closest to their position but with more power than themselves.

## Leaders and Followers

Does leadership involve the personality of the leader, the willingness of followers to obey or be influenced, or some interactive relationship between the two?

There is a tremendous temptation to focus on leaders' attributes, their ability to inspire, organize, or seduce others toward collective behavior. At the turn of the century, research tended to focus on the personalities of leaders and not on the relationship between the leader and his or her followers. These early studies searched for certain common attributes and gave rise to the **great-man–great-woman theory** of leadership (Hook 1955). When the intellectual, physical, and personality traits of leaders and followers were compared, leaders were found to be generally somewhat bigger (recall that the taller candidate usually wins the American presidential election) and somewhat more intelligent than their followers (Cartwright and Zander 1968), to possess greater initiative and humor, and to be more extraverted. More recently, in *Manson in His Own words,* Emmons (1988) showed how adroitly Charles Manson manipulated his group, possessing a hypnotic control over his followers that led to their participation in a murder spree. The great-man–great-woman theory can be seen in Americans' lionizing or pillorying of people who head large institutions, offering praise or blame for outcomes over which those individuals may have little control.

Most studies reveal few consistent personality traits in leaders (Bird 1940; Gibb 1954); instead, they point to the need to consider situational factors and leadership styles. Consider how from the worldwide economic depression and social chaos following World War I there emerged three of the most powerful leaders of the twentieth century: Hitler, Churchill, and Roosevelt. According to *Zeitgeist* (from the German for "spirit of the times") theory, leaders are a product of their times. When the times feature external threats, certain leaders thrive owing to their need for enemies; this is particularly true of totalitarian leaders, for whom any opponent is by definition subversive (Revel 1985). Frederick Adams Wood's (1913) study of the personalities of 386 absolute monarchs and the state of their countries revealed that strong, mediocre, and weak leaders were associated with strong, mediocre, and weak periods in their countries' history. Eric Hoffer observed that revolutionary leaders tend to view the world in simplified terms and that greater complexity is required of postrevolutionary leaders. "When conditions are not ripe," he notes, "the potential leader, no matter how gifted, and his holy cause, no matter how potent, remain[s] without a following" (1966[1951]:103).

In their studies of small task groups, Bales (1958) and his associates noted that in the course of problem-solving activities there emerge not one, but two leaders. One, referred to as the task-specialist leader, is the member who not only speaks most frequently but is spoken to most frequently. Though rated by others as the one who contributes the most in terms of generating ideas and guiding group discussion, he or she is not the best-liked member of the group. That distinction goes to the "socioemotional specialist," the leader who maintains group solidarity and morale. The researchers found that the instrumental and expressive leaders interact most with each other and tend to like each other more than others in the group.

Some psychoanalytic theorists have defined situational factors in terms of the dispositions of followers. In investigations of the attraction of Germans to National Socialism after World War I, psychoanalytically oriented researchers have focused on character structure and cultural context (Stern 1988). Thus, in observing children's playgrounds in Holland, Italy, and Germany, Leopold Bellak and Maxine Antell (1974) noted that whereas in Holland and Italy no adult was seen committing an aggressive act against a child, 73 such acts were observed in Germany. And whereas Danish children were observed committing 20 acts of aggression against other children and 48 such acts were seen on Italian playgrounds, German children committed 258 aggressive acts. Theodore Adorno and associates (1950) and Erich Fromm (1941) focused on the *authoritarian personality structure* that is supposedly engendered by German child-rearing practices and embedded in that nation's institutional structures. Out of patriarchal families where discipline was strict, children's autonomy limited, and parents' roles clear-cut was produced a people with a predisposition toward fascism, which, coupled with the economic and political chaos following World War I, made them highly susceptible to an authoritarian leader who knew the right emotional "buttons" to push: hatred toward out-groups, pride in one's in-group, hope for a new order, and the various emotional gratifications of submitting to a father figure.

A more elaborate model combining leaders' personalities and situational factors is Fiedler's (1967) **contingency theory of leadership.** In this view, group performance is a function of four factors: leadership style, relations between leaders and other group members, task structure, and the power and authority inherent in the leadership position. Leadership style is gauged by the amount of esteem and liking leaders express for their "least preferred coworker" (or LPC). Low-LPC leaders rate this individual quite negatively, as their self-esteem is bound up with the group's ability to complete its tasks. High-LPC leaders, on the other hand, are more concerned with the quality of interpersonal relationships within the group and less concerned or personally threatened when a member does not perform well. Relations between the leader and other group members involve the liking, trust, and respect accorded to the leader by the group. Task structure entails such factors as clarity of goals and feedback on their accomplishment. Finally, the power invested in the leadership position includes the leader's authority to reward or punish, and how much his or her decisions are actually backed up by the organization.

The correlations between leader LPC scores and group performance are plotted in Figure 12.4 (each "x" is a different group studied). The horizontal axis (scaled as "octants") refers to the favorableness of conditions for leaders; "I" refers to situations in which leaders can exercise considerable influence on the group (leader–member relations are good; the task is structured; and the positional power of leader is strong), while "VIII" refers to situations that are highly unfavorable (poor relations, unstructured tasks, and little power). The vertical axis indicates leadership style—from high-LPC to low-LPC. (The greater the absolute score, the stronger the relationship.) The figure reveals that low-LPC leaders are most effective when they have either a great deal of power and influence or almost none, whereas relationship-oriented leaders are most effective under conditions that are moderately favorable or unfavorable.

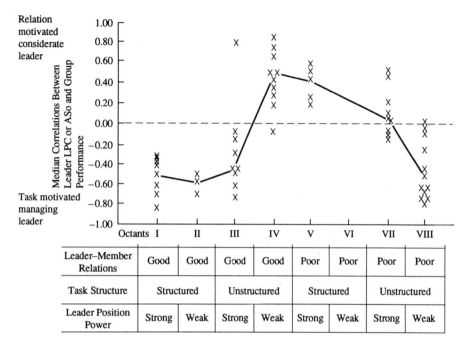

**FIGURE 12.4   Correlations between Group Performance and Leadership Contingencies**
Source: Fiedler, 1968:371.

## Status in a Group and License to Deviate

Leadership is, to a large extent, a function of the followers' perceptions. Leaders are given an **idiosyncrasy credit** (Hollander 1960): Group members will let their leaders "get away with murder" if they have given ample evidence of their competence. A trade-off is involved: Given the group's indebtedness to these individuals for their help in solving group goals (and because they are at times expected to find innovative ways of doing things), in exchange for their greater responsibility the group grants its leaders greater license to deviate from unimportant norms.

In a study of the work arrival times of corporate presidents, vice-presidents, managers, and supervisors, Philip Marvin (1980) found that only 34 percent of the presidents regularly arrived early, whereas early arrival was the rule for 41 percent of the vice-presidents, 51 percent of the general managers, and 60 percent of the supervisors.

Groups may also include low-status members whose occasional deviance from the group's norms provides occasions for ritual reproach. The group does not always wish to expel such members, since their deviance plays a crucial role. In fact, it is essential to group life because the reproach of deviance reaffirms the authority of group norms and clarifies the boundaries of the group. As Kai Erikson has noted,

Deviance makes people more alert to the interests they share in common and draws attention to those values which constitute the "collective conscience" of the community. Unless the rhythm of group life is punctuated by occasional moments of deviant behavior, presumably, social organization would be impossible. (1966:13)

Often the deviant accepts and internalizes the labels of others, and continues to play out the deviant role as a marginal member of the group. Such members are kept by the group not only as a reminder of where the group boundaries are drawn but also because they may be a source of future innovation and change.

# CONCLUSION

In this chapter we considered the dynamics of groups and how they dictate the actions and affect the thoughts of members. We saw that group dynamics are governed by a logic of their own, which is determined by the function, size, and structure of the group. Often a group develops a certain style, distinctive relationships between members, and an ability to achieve collective goals that cannot be explained in terms of the psychological makeup of individuals.

In the chapters that follow, we will focus on specific social groups and elaborate on the ways in which they shape individuals' perceptions, beliefs, language, emotions, and identities. In addition, we will consider the effects of broad cultural and institutional forces on thought, action, and identity. For instance, instead of looking at the moral training of youth in family groups, we will explore how exposure to secularization, mass media, and consumerism predictably affects the moral reasoning of individuals at the same location in the social order.

# REFERENCES

Adorno, T. W., Elsie Frenkel-Brunswik, Daniel J. Levinson, and R. Nevitt Sanford. 1950. *The authoritarian personality*. New York: Harper.

Back, Kurt W. 1981. Small groups. In Morris Rosenberg and Ralph Turner (eds.), *Social psychology: Sociological perspectives*. New York: Basic Books.

Bales, Robert F. 1970. *Personality and interpersonal behavior*. Fort Worth, TX: Holt, Rinehart and Winston.

Bales, Robert F. 1958. Task roles and social roles in problem-solving groups. In E. E. Maccoby, T. M. Newcomb, and E. L. Hartley (eds.), *Readings in social psychology* (3rd ed.). Fort Worth, TX: Holt, Rinehart and Winston.

Barnard, C. I. 1938. *The functions of the executive*. Cambridge, MA: Harvard University Press.

Barth, Fredrik. 1969. *Ethnic groups and boundaries: The social organization of cultural difference*. Boston: Little, Brown.

Barth, Gunther. 1981. *City people: The rise of modern city culture in 19th-century America*. New York: Oxford University Press.

Bellak, Leopold, and M. Antell. 1974. Intercultural study of aggressive behavior in children's playgrounds. *American Journal of Orthopsychiatry* 44:503–511.

Bird, C. 1940. *Social psychology*. New York: Appleton-Century-Crofts.

Blau, Peter. 1973. *The dynamics of bureaucracy* (2nd rev. ed.). Chicago: University of Chicago Press.

Blood, R. O., Jr., and D. M. Wolfe. 1960. *The dynamics of married living*. New York: Free Press.

Bouchard, T. J., Jr., J. Barsaloux, and G. Drauden. 1974. Brainstorming procedure, group size, and sex as determinants of the problem-solving effectiveness of groups and individuals. *Journal of Applied Psychology* 59:135–38.

Cartwright, Dorwin, and Alvin Zander (eds.). 1968. *Group dynamics: Research and theory* (3rd ed.). New York: HarperCollins.

Cooley, Charles. 1902. *Human nature and the social order.* New York: Scribners.

Cosell, Howard, and Peter Bonventre. 1986. *I never played the game.* Boston: G. K. Hall.

Coser, Lewis A. 1956. *The functions of social conflict.* New York: Free Press.

Coser, Lewis, and Rose Coser. 1963. Time perspective and social structure. In A. W. Gouldner and H. P. Gouldner (eds.), *Modern sociology.* Orlando: Harcourt Brace Jovanovich.

Degler, Carl. 1980. *At odds: Women and the family in America from the Revolution to the present.* Glenview, IL: Scott Foresman.

Degler, Carl. 1984. *Out of our past: The forces that shaped modern America.* New York: HarperCollins.

Demos, John. 1986. *Past, present, and personal: The family and the life course of American history.* New York: Oxford University Press.

Diehl, Michael, and Wolfgang Stroebe. 1987. Productivity loss in brainstorming groups: Toward the solution of a riddle. *Journal of Personality and Social Psychology* 53:497–509.

Dunnette, M. D., J. Campbell, and K. Jaastad. 1963. The effect of group participation on brainstorming effectiveness for two industrial samples. *Journal of Applied Psychology* 47:30–37.

Edwards, Thomas. 1990, October 28. Graffiti documents activity of S.A. gangs. *San Antonio Express-News,* p. 1-B.

Emmons, Nuel. 1988. *Manson in his own words.* New York: Grove/Weidenfeld.

Erikson, Kai. 1966. *Wayward Puritans: A study in the sociology of deviance.* New York: Wiley.

Fiedler, Fred E. 1967. *A theory of leadership effectiveness.* New York: McGraw-Hill.

Fiedler, Fred E. 1968. Personality and situational determinants of leadership effectiveness. In Dorwin Cartwright and Alvin Zander (eds.), *Group dynamics: Research and theory* (3rd ed.). New York: HarperCollins.

Fiedler, Fred E. 1955. The influence of leader–keyman relations on combat crew effectiveness. *Journal of Abnormal and Social Psychology* 51:227–235.

Fromm, Erich. 1941. *Escape from freedom.* Fort Worth, TX: Holt, Rinehart and Winston.

Gibb, C. A. 1954. Leadership. In G. Lindzey (ed.), *Handbook of social psychology.* Cambridge, MA: Addison-Wesley.

Goffman, Erving. 1963. *Stigma: Notes on the management of spoiled identity.* Englewood Cliffs, NJ: Prentice-Hall.

Greil, Arthur, and David Rudy. 1984. Social cocoons: Encapsulation and identity transformation organizations. *Sociological Inquiry* 54:260–278.

Guetzkow, H., and W. R. Dill. 1957. Factors in the organizational development of task-oriented groups. *Sociometry* 20:175–204.

Gurvitch, Georges. 1941. Mass, community, communion. *Journal of Philosophy* 38:485–496.

Hannan, Michael T., and John Freeman. 1989. *Organizational ecology.* Cambridge, MA: Harvard University Press.

*Harper's Magazine.* 1988, June. Harper's index. p. 15.

Hays, Laurie. 1987, June 19. Pay problems: How couples react when wives out-earn husbands. *Wall Street Journal,* p. 19.

Hoffer, Eric. 1966 (1951). *The true believer.* New York: Harper Perennial Library.

Hollander, Edwin. 1960. Competence and conformity in the acceptance of influence. *Journal of Abnormal and Social Psychology* 61:365–369.

Hong, L. K. 1978. Risky shift and cautious shift: Some direct evidence on the culture-value theory. *Social Psychology* 41:342–346.

Hook, S. 1955. *The hero in history.* Boston: Beacon Press.

Janis, Irving L. 1971, November. Groupthink. *Psychology Today,* pp. 43–46, 74–76.

Johnson, Allan G. 1986. *Human arrangements: An introduction to sociology.* Orlando: Harcourt Brace Jovanovich.

Kerr, Peter. 1982, July 10. They help people looking for self-help. *New York Times.*

Lamm, H., and G. Trommsdorff. 1973. Group versus individual performance on tasks requiring ideational proficiency (brainstorming). *European Journal of Social Psychology* 3:361–387.

Leavitt, H. J. 1951. Some effects of certain communication patterns on group performance. *Journal of Abnormal Social Psychology* 46:38–50.

Lowenthal, Marjorie F., Majda Thurnher, and David Chiriboga. 1976. *Four stages of life: A comparative study of women and men facing transitions.* San Francisco: Jossey-Bass.

Marvin, Philip. 1980. *Executive time management.* New York: IAMACO.

Michels, R. 1967 (1911). *Political parties.* New York: Free Press.

Moore, Wilbur E. 1963. *Man, time, and society.* New York: Wiley.

Mydans, Seth. 1990, April 10. Not just the inner city: Well-to-do join gangs. *New York Times,* p. A7.

Myers, David G. 1982. Polarizing effects of social interaction. In H. Brandstatter, J. H. Davis, and G. Stocker-Kreichgauer (eds.), *Group decision making.* Orlando: Academic Press.

Myers, David G., and Martin Kaplan. 1976. Group-induced polarization in simulated juries. *Personality and Social Psychology Bulletin* 2:63–66.

Oppenheim, Lynn. 1991, June. Mastering the meeting. *Chief Executive.*

Oskamp, Stuart (ed.). 1985. *International conflict and national public policy issues.* Newbury Park, CA: Sage.

Revel, Jean-Francois. 1985. *How democracies perish.* New York: HarperCollins.

Rosellini, Lynn. 1987, July 27. Strike one and you're out. *U.S. News & World Report,* pp. 52–57.

Salgado, Marc. 1976, July 15. Ex-teacher says test proved: "We'd all make good Nazis." *Palo Alto Times,* p. 3.

Schlesinger Arthur, Jr. 1989. The opening of the American mind. *New York Times Review of Books,* pp. 1, 26.

Schmidt, Alvin J. 1980. *Fraternal organizations.* Westport, CT: Greenwood Press.

Selznick, Philip. 1949. *TVA and the grass roots.* Berkeley: University of California Press.

Sheriff, Muzafer. 1956. Experiments in group conflict. *Scientific American* 195:54–58.

Shribman, David. 1988, February 4. Gary Hart loyalists become more loyal since the Rice affair. *Wall Street Journal,* pp. 8.

Simmel, Georg. 1955. *Conflict and the web of group affiliations.* New York: Free Press.

Simmel, Georg. 1950. Types of social relationships by degrees of reciprocal knowledge of their participants. In K. H. Wolff (ed.), *The sociology of Georg Simmel.* New York: Free Press.

Sorokin, Pitirim A., and Robert K. Merton. 1937. Social time: A methodological and functional analysis. *American Journal of Sociology* 42:615–629.

Stern, Fritz. 1988. *Dreams and delusions: The drama of German history.* New York: Knopf.

Sumner, William. 1974 (1924). *Folkways: A study of the sociological importance of usages, manners, customs, mores and morals* (Lewis A. Coser and Walter W. Powell, eds.). Salem, NH: Ayer.

Tesser, A. 1978. Self-generated attitude change. In L. Berkolwitz (ed.), *Advances in experimental social psychology,* vol. II. Orlando: Academic Press.

Thomas, L. 1974. *The lives of a cell.* New York: Viking.

Töennies, Ferdinand 1963 (1887). *Community and society.* New York: HarperCollins.

Toufexis, Anastasia. 1990, August 6. Sex and the sporting life. *Time,* pp. 76–77.

Tripplet, N. 1897–1898. The dynamogenic factors in pacemaking and competition. *American Journal of Psychology* 9:503–533.

*U.S. News & World Report.* 1990, May 21. A nation of joiners. p. 78.

*Wall Street Journal.* 1988, November 2. People patterns: Are working mothers a trend that's peaked? p. B1.

Walsh, Mary. 1986, December 29. Poor people of Mexico, afraid of protesting, endure much injustice. *Wall Street Journal,* pp. 1, 6.

White, Ralph K., and Ronald O. Lippit. 1960. *Autocracy and democracy.* New York: HarperCollins.

Williams, Kipling, Stephen Harkins, and Bibb Latané. 1981. Identifiability as a deterrent to social loafing: Two cheering experiments. *Journal of Personality and Social Psychology* 40: 303–311.

Williams, Wendy, and Robert Sternberg. 1988. Group intelligence: Why some groups are better than others. *Intelligence* 12:351–377.

Wood, Frederick Adams. 1913. *The influence of monarchs.* New York: Macmillan.

Zajonc, R., A. Heigartner, and E. Herman. 1969. Social enhancement and impairment of performance in the cockroach. *Journal of Personality and Social Psychology* 13:83–92.

# PART FIVE

# Socially Structured Psychologies

The models of the human condition presented thus far are static: They involve biological constraints, internalized cultural mindsets, individuals interacting in socially standardized settings, assuming roles and playing out relatively defined scripts. But large-scale social and cultural change does not arise from the interactions of individuals in small groups. There is another realm of social reality. Like the supraindividual processes that operate in groups, this realm (the social whole that we call "society") features the patterns and processes arising out of the interactions of large numbers of individuals and groups.

In this section we move from identifying the psychologies, identities, and behaviors of people interacting in small groups to a consideration of the interplay between individuals and society. One cannot study the behaviors of individuals without devoting some attention to their social environments—the economic structures, family situations, demographics, and value systems that structure social life.

We begin with collective action, which shapes the thoughts and behaviors of large numbers of individuals. When, for instance, cultural values become ambiguous during times of social change or crisis, when people find themselves in unanticipated situations, or when individuals' motives are blocked, there are occasions when novel shared definitions of the situation arise. A collectivity is formed, experiences solidarity, and mobilizes for action.

We then turn to the more structured institutional influences on the perceptions, cognitions, attitudes, emotions, identities, actions, and relationships of individuals. In so doing, we enter a more sociological area of social psychology. The basic assumption of this discipline is that individuals who share a common position in the social order come to share a common consciousness. Although consciousness is a subjective phenomenon, it can be described objectively because its socially significant elements are constantly shared with others. From this perspective, a central theme is how society structures the **templates of consciousness,** people's "unconscious mental habits" (Lovejoy 1961).

# 13

# The Spectrum of Collective Action

Humans have always been fascinated by the processes through which collective wholes emerge from the behaviors and beliefs of individuals, who become members of the new collectivity and engage in any of a wide range of **collective behaviors** (Park 1972 [1921]). For instance, we can feel the excitement and exhilaration at a large concert, religious revival meeting, or sports events. Spectators can see and hear the power of their apparent unity in their cheers, chants, and songs. When participating in "the wave," for example, each person experiences his or her own immersion in the collective phenomenon, watching the ripple race across a sea of fellow spectators. Crowd members also experience collective moods, emotions, purposes, grievances, hostilities, and loyalties as important symbols are brought to their attention, as with the giant images in card shows at ball games or the presentation of group emblems at large-scale rallies. In France in 1789, peasants, workers, and shopkeepers became absorbed into a revolutionary force that overthrew a centuries-old feudal order, producing a social earthquake whose tremors are still felt two centuries later. In the late 1980s Eastern Europeans developed the collective belief that repressive communist regimes could no longer contain and control their populations, and great collective uprisings occurred that are still redrawing the political and economic maps.

In this chapter we explore the social forces that create **collective perspectives:** new symbolic interpretations, together with the resulting unity or dissension in the thoughts, feelings, and actions of large numbers of individuals in crowds and masses. A crowd is a relatively large number of persons who are co-present (direct sight and hearing) within a single physical setting. Also considered are collective actions, the social-psychological and behavioral manifestations of a collective perspective. At one end of the continuum of collective actions are the spontaneous short-term social orders arising from an assemblage of persons, such as fear-driven panic rushes from burning buildings, hostile mobs focusing on a target for their violent aggression, and riots during power blackouts. In the middle range are planned demonstrations, long-running protests, social movements building up around grievances, nonviolent protests used to exert moral pressure on an opponent group, terrorism, and conventional crowds breaking into unusual fervor and wild behavior at con-

Photographers use individuals as pointillist painters use spots of paint, showing how unitary parts can form totalities. Here a collection of Americans come together to form the symbol of their country, just as their separate endeavors intermesh to create a national whole.

certs, sports events, and religious or political rallies. At the most organized end of the continuum are the highly coordinated actions of people in institutional settings, such as in the workplace, in a prison or in the military, or in situations in which social movements violently overthrow major institutional sectors. All of these forms of collective action involve the behavior of crowds of people in places where they can see and hear each other.

But collective behavior also includes a wide range of relatively noninstitutional **masses,** widely dispersed aggregates of people who are interested in a particular object of attention. These aggregates include the fans of a particular rock group or media celebrity, the publics concerned with enduring social issues (such as those for or against abortion, nuclear-power generation, or environmental protection), and participants in mass phenomena such as rumors, crazes, fashions and fads, gold rushes and mass migrations, hysterical beliefs (e.g., mysterious illnesses and UFOs), and panic purchasing in times of stress and perceived shortage.

So great can the power of collective movements be that political and religious regimes often attempt to harness their energy to support their own interests or to harm their enemies. When threatened by collective action, regimes generally react with swift (and frequently violent) countermeasures or face overthrow, **for collective behavior is the driving force of social change.** From a social-psychological standpoint the major question is, How can such seemingly coordinated behavior emerge without established action scripts or rehearsals, without institutional social support or initial structure?

---

## COLLECTIVE BEHAVIOR

Collective action can be seen as resulting from an emerging *collective definition of the situation.* This definition includes elements of *cognitive belief* (the "facts" that are defined as relevant), *emotional factors* (e.g., needs that are being frustrated and the dominant emotion of those present—fear, hostility, joy, or sorrow), and the predominant *motivation* (what should we try to do now?) (see Turner and Killian 1987 [1957], esp. Chapter 3; Lofland 1981). Contemporary social scientists have dismissed early conceptions such as Gustave LeBon's "crowd mind" (1897), but it is also true that individuals (either crowd members or observers) frequently act on the basis of inferences about what the crowd "thinks, fears, hates, and wants." As we will see, when analyzing the emergence of collective behavior it is important to consider personal variations in the way situations are defined, the *emergence of a normative structure* defining what is going on and what should go on, *variations in member's emotions,* and *differing motivations* concerning what is best to do now (Turner and Killian 1987 [1957]).

### Emotions as Generators of Actions: Crowds and Mobs

Crowd situations have a set of common characteristics that require people in them to engage in a collective process of defining the situation and acting so as to attain some resolution of the problems presented by the situation and the presence of a large number of people within it (See Turner and Killian 1987 [1957], esp. Chapters 3 and 4). Action becomes collective when the following features are present:

1. *Cognitive uncertainty* as to the possibility of danger or opportunity.
2. *Strong emotions* such as fear, hostility, joy, or sorrow about what has been happening and what may soon happen.
3. *A sense of urgency* pressure to act before danger becomes worse or opportunity is lost.
4. *Crowd use of rumor* as the most rapid and available form of communication.
5. *Heightened suggestibility* due to the ambiguity of the situation and the sense of urgency.
6. Development of a *new definition of the situation,* including common mood and imagery concerning the nature of the problem and some version of who is responsible or to blame.
7. *Differential expression* of relevant ideas, from initial "keynoting" to communication of support or contradiction of the ideas being suggested.
8. *Pressure and constraint* to go along with the developing definition, in overt behavior if not in full emotional commitment.

9. *A sense of righteous power,* due to the crowd's size and apparent unity of definition and purposes, combined physical strength, and association with potent values contained in the definition of the situation.
10. *Feelings of safety and anonymity in numbers* so that individuals cannot be identified and held accountable for actions carried out in the crowd situation.

When they are in the company of large numbers of others in such situations, people are capable of committing acts that they would never consider performing alone. Feelings become amplified, often blocking or overwhelming critical evaluation and normal constraints. Lynchings, attacks on property symbolic of the defined enemy (as in the Boston Tea Party during the American Revolution) and attempts to take over university buildings during the student and antiwar movements of the 1960s are examples of the kinds of behavior that can result. Such feelings and actions may actually be quite rational from the point of view of crowd members with preexisting antipathies toward the target of the collection, but actions and attitudes can also result from the rapid spread of novel definitions of the situation among crowd members, with very little critical thought taking place. This process is sometimes called "contagion," implying a pathological disease that spreads rapidly through those exposed to it. Entire books have been written to attempt to contradict the idea that crowds transform individuals, reducing or eliminating their capacity to think and behave rationally (e.g., McPhail 1991), but it is nonetheless true that crowd conditions produce heightened suggestibility to extreme and dramatic ideas, and make crowd members feel invulnerable and free from responsibility for whatever happens.

Canetti (1977 [1960]) posits an interesting thesis about individuals' attraction to crowds and how crowds assume a dynamic of their own. He begins with the assumption that individuals abhor being touched, whether by others or by anything unknown. In tightly packed crowds this fear not only dissipates but metamorphoses into feelings of security and of relief at being able to transcend this personal limitation. He asserts that crowds have a natural, never fully satisfied inclination toward continued growth, absorbing everyone within reach and providing a continually increasing feeling of "animal force and passion" (p. 22). Crowd members view any opposition to this growth as constricting, which leads to feelings of persecution and readiness to attack anyone perceived as trying to halt the growth of the crowd. When growth does end, the "open crowd" (that which faces no physical limits to its growth) may dissipate in frustration. "Closed crowds" (e.g., those in auditoriums or stadiums), having filled a bounded space and having developed a definition of the situation involving some goal of permanence, may frequently erupt into open crowds in an effort to recapture a sense of spontaneity and invulnerability.

***Mass Hysteria and Collective Hallucinations.*** In 1979 a sixth-grade boy in a school in Norwood, Massachusetts, became ill and fainted. The entire student body had gathered for the final general assembly of the year, and within a few minutes the illness spread to a few other children in the vicinity of the sick boy. Within a short time one-third of the students in the school became ill, and it became apparent to school officials that they were dealing with an epidemic: In the end, thirty-four severely ill children were hospitalized and between forty and fifty others were treated on the school grounds (Herbert 1982).

Health officials found that most of the victims were girls. Their predominant symptoms included dizziness and hyperventilation, often accompanied by headaches, chills, nausea, and stomach pain. For such **epidemic hysterias** to begin, there first must be some convergence of emotional or physical symptoms, as when individuals are experiencing anxiety or stress. A novel symptom is introduced, such as a noxious odor, followed by the reaction of the first person (the index case). A contagion process occurs when others connect their own vague physical symptoms to this new stimulus.

The earliest known occurrences of epidemic hysteria were in medieval Italy, where outbreaks of "tarantism," or dancing mania, were fairly common. Particularly in the summer, people would flock into the streets, dancing maniacally until they collapsed. The symptoms of such illnesses may be dictated by culture. In the 1970s a case was reported in Malaysia in which women working in a semiconductor assembly plant began seeing demons through their microscopes.

## Collective Behavior Spawned by Shared Moral Impulse

Spontaneous collective behavior is not always socially dysfunctional. Fundamental, deep-seated, and collectively shared sentiments toward essential rights and wrongs can also spawn prosocial collective behavior. For example, when a community learns that one of its members desperately needs the help of others, novel social arrangements can arise that are dedicated to their aid.

Of course, not all misfortunes produce equal outpourings of assistance. A community's contributions to a member who is seriously injured while drag racing are likely to be smaller than its contributions to a member who is shot by a robber while trying to protect a child. Community contributions are greater for the Thanksgiving needs of a bedridden elderly woman with no family than for the Fourth-of-July needs of a 30-year-old chronically unemployed ex-criminal.

Nevertheless, personal catastrophes often do elicit basic social sentiments and trigger prosocial collective behavior. In the summer of 1990, for example, the local evening news in San Antonio, Texas, carried the story of an 11-year-old girl who was reported missing. Stories of missing children do not always make news, and those that do most often produce feelings of distant sympathy. But this case was different.

During the first weekend, thousands of residents showed up to comb the wooded countryside on foot, on horseback, and in four-wheel-drive vehicles. In the following week, two boatmen reported having seen a girl meeting Heidi's description. Both claimed to have seen her accompanied by a large, muscular man. People worried that she might have been captured by a prostitution ring that was known to have kidnapped girls as young as 10 years old.

Posters with Heidi's picture appeared in the city's retail establishments and on the pay booths of the city's airport parking lots. At the city's amusement parks, high school kids quizzed visitors to find out whether they knew anything about Heidi's whereabouts. Over a period of three weeks, local television stations carried a total of 156 stories about the disappearance—the most heavily reported story in the previous five years.

The days passed and there were no further developments. The topic of Heidi's plight dominated the conversations of city residents. Different speculations produced different strategies for the search. Being a normal 11-year-old, Heidi knew where she lived and how to get into contact with others if in trouble. It became increasingly evident that she had been abducted. A large grocery store chain offered a $5000 reward for information leading to the discovery of Heidi's whereabouts. This seed money attracted more, and by the following weekend the amount exceeded $40,000. The mayor proclaimed that following Saturday "Search for Heidi Day" and asked San Antonians to contribute one hour to help look for the missing child. The local newspapers predicted that hundreds of thousands of citizens would be involved. Sunday became "Pray for Heidi Day."

Thus, almost spontaneously, the actions of thousands of individuals came to be focused and coordinated in many ways. Residents came to feel a solidarity for others and a sense of community identity. Although they were unable to save Heidi's life (her decomposed remains were found in a bag along a remote road fifty miles from the city), they were able to demonstrate the power of a shared moral impulse to generate prosocial behavior.

## BELIEF SYSTEMS AS GENERATORS OF ACTION

In April of 1988 Californians were abuzz with fear concerning the possibility of a giant earthquake. Such a quake had been predicted for "the New World" in May of 1988 by the French astrologer and prognosticator Nostradamus, according to Orson Welles' movie *The Man Who Saw Tomorrow*. After being shown on one of the major cable television services, the videotape sold innumerable copies throughout the state. Hundreds, if not thousands, of people took the prediction seriously and left the state for several weeks.

How could a 400-year-old prediction produce fear and flight in modern California? The answer lies in the way collective behavior draws upon the same kind of *social construction of reality* that underlies our "normal" conduct but adds *special frameworks of interpretation* to account for stimuli that make the situation seem extraordinary, uncertain, ambiguous, frightening, hostile, joyful, or sorrowful. Ralph Turner and Lewis Killian, the leading exponents of a powerful theoretical approach to collective behavior known as the emergent-norm approach, explain this phenomenon as follows:

> The social reality which people take for granted is composed of a normative order, encompassing values and norms; a social structure; and channels of communication. These ordinarily appear real, supportive, and constraining to the members of a society; however, at times they seem frustrating, weak, or even chaotic. In addition, the physical world which ordinarily seems solid and stable may sometimes present a disordered framework for action. (1987 [1957]:35)

Social reality in California (as in other parts of America) involves a **normative order** including *general values* regarding safety and security for oneself and one's loved ones, and *norms* that include evacuation as a reasonable response to environmental threat. In addition, Californians have a highly developed *cultural knowledge* of large earthquakes. The experience is continually reinforced by replays in school and on television of the films from the 1906 San Francisco quake that destroyed most of the city, along with the occurrence of minor earthquake shocks several times a year. Scientists constantly report readings of "plate shift" and "stress buildup" along the San Andreas Fault and elsewhere in the state, and the potential consequences of earthquakes make the news every time a nuclear-power plant is proposed.

At the **social-structural level,** many Californians belong to informal and even some formal groups in which astrology, mystical prediction of the future, and a range of related "New Wave" and occult beliefs are taken seriously. Therefore, an expression of belief in such matters would meet with agreement and support rather than disbelief and ridicule among significant portions of the individual's immediate network.

Finally, the communication channels in California are ideal for conveying dramatic, fascinating, and fear-producing content. As the world capital of both movie and television production, Los Angeles has been the source of countless horror stories about environmental disasters. The Orson Welles film about Nostradamus was very skillfully crafted so as to produce at least some credence in the possibility that the French astrologer had been extraordinarily accurate in making predictions that "had come to pass" over the intervening four and one-quarter centuries.

Once the Nostradamus film was shown on cable television, those who were particularly intrigued by occult mysticism in general and by the very detailed and apparently well-documented "correct predictions" included in the film might well have become at least concerned if not actually afraid that a monster quake would hit the "New World" in the next month. What could be more "New World" than New Age California? Would this be the one that would break off the edge of the state and send it down into the sea?

As worried people begin to talk over such a possibility with others similar to themselves, a new social construction of reality, a new "definition of the situation," is built up around an emergent "norm" or normative depiction of the relevant "facts," and plausible patterns of conduct are collectively created. Again, Turner and Killian have highlighted the critical features of the emerging normative pattern:

> The concept of the development of a norm, a common understanding as to what sort of behavior is expected in the situation, seems to provide an explanation of a pattern of differential expression. Such a shared understanding encourages behavior consistent with the norm, inhibits behavior contrary to it, and justifies restraining action against individuals who dissent. Since the norm is to some degree specific to the situation, differing in degree or in kind from the norms governing noncrowd situations, it is an emergent norm. (1987 [1957]:26)

They also make clear the richness and complexity of this normative definition:

> The concept "norm" as used here does not refer merely to a rule or a precise behavioral expectation. It means, instead, an emergent (revised) definition of the situation which encompasses an extensive complex of factors. These factors include indications as to the salient features of the situation (What's going on here?), explanations of the situation (What brought this about? Who is responsible?), and typification of the actors presumed to be involved (Who's in charge? What right have those people to be here?). The norm or definition also includes indications of

what sort of action is appropriate or inappropriate in the situation, including not only overt behavior but also moods, such as sadness, indignation, amusement, or elation. The emergent norm is not only constraining: it is also permissive. While some specific acts may be required or prohibited, latitude exists for a wide range of acts consistent with the definition of the situation. Not uniformity but differential expression and participation, with each member "doing his own thing" within the bounds of the emergent norm, is the source of the dynamic, creative quality of collective behavior. (p. 33)

This conceptual framework helps us understand how some Californians could place such credence in a televised and widely discussed prediction of an earthquake of cosmic proportions that they would flee the state. This theoretical perspective also gives a very important place to rumor as the characteristic form of communication during episodes of collective behavior (Turner and Killian 1987 [1957], Chapter 4).

## Rumor

During the 1970s and 1980s, Americans were entertained by stories that the producer of Ivory Snow was a demonic front, earthworms were ground up in the hamburgers of a major fast-food franchise, and spider eggs were an ingredient of chewing gum (Koenig 1985). As the stories spread, more people believed them. Picketers began protesting in front of the commercial establishments involved, and write-in protests were organized. As Virgil noted in the *Aeneid*, "Rumor, than which no other evil is swifter, thrives on movement and she gathers strength as she goes."

Rumors flourish under certain social-psychological conditions. They develop when the demand for information exceeds the supply (Shibutani 1966) and during times of social trauma and personal threat (Koenig 1985). Allport and Postman (1947) calculated that the amount of rumor is equal to the subject's importance for the individuals concerned multiplied by the ambiguity of the evidence.

Particularly threatening to the status quo are rumors about conspiracies. As we saw in Chapter 3, one of the easiest ways of accounting for wars, economic depressions, or civil unrest is to place the blame on the evil intentions of a coterie of powerful individuals. This need to impose order on otherwise meaningless events is particularly strong among the powerless. Thus, in the early days of the American republic collective misfortunes were attributed to a conspiracy of Freemasons, Illuminati, and Jeffersonian Democrats; two centuries later, blame shifted to the Trilateral Commission, communists, secular humanists (Johnson 1989), and even beings from other worlds.

## The Power of Ideology

There are many historical examples of the power of ideas to stimulate collective action. Most potent are **ideologies,** the overarching belief systems that give order to scattered, chaotic events. Like spider webs, ideologies provide linkage between events and contrast *what is* with *what should be.* For instance, the belief that one's primary group is being oppressed or that life's events unfold according to the hidden designs of some divine force underlies class conflict (Chapter 10) and religious movements (Chapter 14). To illustrate how ideology, rather than material conditions, can be the driving force of history, consider the following story, a tale of bizarre coincidence as two cultures come into contact for the first time (see Sahlins 1981).

During the eighteenth century, Hawaiian islanders believed in a deity called Lono, the source of power and fertility. Their island's population was integrated in a hierarchical social structure that culminated in a kingship. In the course of the islands' history the kingship had frequently been usurped as young kings took over power from aging leaders; this pattern went back to the time when the first king usurped power from the god Lono. Every year, however, Lono returns on December 23 to challenge the king for the throne in a ceremony called Makahiki. For sixteen days he circles the island in a clockwise direction. Upon completing his tour, he goes to the principal religious center to take control of the throne for five days.

On a day in mid-December 1778, Captain Cook dropped anchor off the island of Hawaii. He was dismayed by the reception given him by the islanders, who saw the visit as divine. The natives' belief was reinforced when Cook later circled the island (in order to map its contours) in a clockwise direction for many days, just as would Lono. As he watched the islanders running and waving, Cook must have been overwhelmed by their friendliness (but perhaps he was not surprised, especially in light of another historical coincidence: in Europe, the myth of the noble savage was taking root).

But all good things must come to an end, and Cook and his men bade the islanders farewell. The islanders were ecstatic, since the annual contest was over and the social order and the king's position were once again secured. They waved their farewells as families bid adieu to their members after the holidays; "see you next year" was implied. The sailors similarly waved their appreciation. However, the ship encountered a storm that broke its mast, so it returned to the hospitable shores for repair.

The islanders were dismayed. The god Lono had broken the rules and apparently had returned to truly usurp the throne. What else could be done but to kill the god? Cook was killed and the throne was once again secured by King Kalaniopuu. As Cook's vessel once again set off into the Pacific, the islanders again gave it an enthusiastic farewell.

As this story demonstrates, individuals react not to objective conditions per se but rather to the interpretations they place on those conditions. The global framework of these interpretations often are ideological, appearing in such forms as mythology, history, or political philosophy. The fact that Cook's arrival coincided with the expected return of a legendary god reaffirmed for the Hawaiian islanders the link between the social and cosmic orders of life. Cook's unexpected return forced them to take violent action to maintain and continue their cultural order. By killing Cook (Lono) the Hawaiians were not only living out a mythical reality but were simultaneously establishing ties with a very real new power in their universe (English traders).

## The True Believer

The social philosopher Eric Hoffer (1951) observed certain commonalities among all mass movements, whether religious or political: They all produce intense feelings of devotion, hope, and intolerance; they all demand singular dedication and blind faith; and, once begun, they are difficult to stop (stopping a movement often requires substituting another movement in its place). Noting how fervent German Communists became ardent Nazis and, after the war, how dedicated Nazis became loyal Americans, Hoffer speculated on the existence of a personality type that is naturally attracted to mass movements regardless of their cause: the true believer.

The true believer is a person who desires to shed an unwanted self and be reborn. Faith in a cause exists in inverse proportion to the loss of faith in oneself: "The less justified a man is in claiming excellence for his own self, the more ready is he to claim all excellence for his nation, his religion, his race or his holy cause" (Hoffer 1951:23).

For social movements to arise and attract this personality type, certain social conditions must exist. Individuals must be intensely discontented but not destitute, and there must exist a collective sense that the social order is disintegrating and a vastly superior future is at hand. Moreover, people must believe that they have the power to bring this future into existence—"the feeling that by the possession of some potent doctrine, infallible leader or some new technique they have access to a source of irresistible power" (p. 21). Finally, they must be collectively ignorant of the obstacles to be overcome.

## The Social Context of Generalized Beliefs

A more rational view of the role of beliefs in reconstructing the social order is Neil Smelser's often-cited "value-added" model of collective action. Smelser writes:

> Generalized beliefs are very much like magical beliefs; the world is portrayed in terms of omnipotent forces, conspiracies, and extravagant promises, all of which are imminent. It is uninstitutionalized action taken in the name of such a belief that constitutes an episode of collective behavior. (1963:117)

Smelser's contribution was to specify the social contexts in which these positive wishes arise and the conditions required for their fulfillment. In his model, each condition adds its "value" to explaining an episode of collective behavior, ultimately leading to the mobilization of large numbers of people.

To illustrate Smelser's value-added model, let us consider the quick, dramatic overthrow of the Communist regimes of Eastern Europe in 1989. In Czechoslovakia, for example, dissidents were able to rally only 10,000 individuals to parade in protest during that nation's independence day on October 28. One month later, millions of citizens had participated in public demonstrations.

*Structural conduciveness.* Certain social conditions make it possible for collective action to arise. In the case of the Eastern European regimes, structural conduciveness consisted of economic systems that failed to deliver (especially when compared to the bounties of the West) and produced a pollution nightmare, along with recent grants of individual rights and the abolition of political strategies for terror and oppression.

**Structural strain.** This term refers to social forces that produce stress, such as declining standards of living and uncertainty about the future. So great had environmental degradation become in the Communist nations that in the East German town of Espenhain, four out of five children suffered from chronic bronchitis or heart ailments by the age of 7; in areas surrounding the industrial center of Leipzig, life expectancy was six years lower than in the rest of the country (Painton 1990).

**Generalized belief.** A generalized belief is a shared definition of the situation, often exaggerated. In the Eastern European nations the relaxation of restraints, coupled with official acknowledgment of complicity in crimes against the people (e.g., the Soviet Union's admission that it had obtained the Baltic republics in a shady deal between Stalin and Hitler, and that Stalin had killed millions of his own people), caused regimes to lose their legitimacy and their ability to defend themselves against popular uprisings. In 1989, as the Berlin Wall was being dismantled, there was a generalized belief that immediate and far-reaching change was in the offing.

**Precipitating factor.** In a process that resembles seeding a cloud to produce rain or Rube Goldberg triggering a chain reaction, a stimulus event ignites collective behavior. In Czechoslovakia, the event was the brutal clubbing of unarmed college students who were marching in observance of the fiftieth anniversary of the murder of Czech student demonstrators by Nazis.

**Mobilization for action.** Following the attacks on student demonstrators in Czechoslovakia, students called for student strikes, mass protest, and a total work stoppage. Within two days, previously fragmented opposition movements coalesced around the cause under an umbrella group, the Civic Forum (Omestad 1989).

**Success or failure of social control mechanisms.** To regain control of the situation, authorities must defuse the mobilization. In the past (e.g., during the Hungarian uprisings of 1956) collective action was violently put down by Soviet tanks and soldiers. But three decades later there was no such force to preserve the status quo. There were mass defections from the armies and security forces.

It should be noted that this model does not specify the form of collective behavior that will arise from the antecedent conditions. However, no theory of collective behavior has yet succeeded in predicting the timing and form of riots, revolutions, or financial panics.

# NEEDS FRUSTRATIONS AS GENERATORS OF ACTION: SOCIAL MOVEMENTS

**Social movements** combine collective behavior with shared sentiment oriented toward either instigation of or resistance to social and cultural change (Garner and Zald 1985). A more deliberate and organized form of collective behavior, a social movement can exist outside of (and in opposition to) the realm of culturally defined and socially sanctioned order. A social movement may be characterized by the following features:

—A quest for social legitimacy, such as the prostitutes' rights organizations (e.g., COYOTE [Call Off Your Old Tired Ethics], HIRE [Hooking Is Real Employment], or PASSION [Professional Association Seeking Sexual Identification Observant of Nature]).

—Attempts to resist, promote, or maintain the power structure, such as the black, feminist, and gray power movements in the United States (e.g., Amenta and Zylan 1991). Charles Tilly (1975, 1978) states that the roots of social movements may be found in the unequal distribution of institutional power, which causes the less powerful to seek new rights and more resources.

—Efforts to preserve or reconstruct the moral order, such as the anti-abortion, anti-pornography, and anti-drunk driver coalitions (Gusfield 1981).

Despite the differences in their objectives, all social movements share "tendencies to formulate, elaborate, and promote values, to maximize the power of the organization, and to cultivate member satisfactions from participation in the movement" (Turner 1964:124).

Social movements such as revolutions or migrations begin with a vague sense of discontent, distress, and uncertainty about a particular situation. According to Robert Park (1921), in the first stage individuals motivated by this distress gather in the streets. This stage is followed by a stage of disorderly, confused, yet enthusiastic popular movements. The emergence of leadership structures, organization, and formal belief systems marks the third stage, which culminates in the institutionalization of the movement. Once the movement's objectives are achieved, the movement dies; this is the fifth and final phase.

Other social scientists have observed that social movements go through periodic bursts of energy followed by quieter periods of consolidation (Ayvazian and Klare 1990). Viewing these quieter phases as periods when the groundwork is laid for subsequent periods of growth, Bert Klandermans (1984) has identified a stage that he terms *process consensus mobilization*. During this stage, activists try to gain acceptance for the movement's ideas. This is not that same as action mobilization, which is aimed at mobilizing people who already agree with the movement's goals and ideas.

In his depiction of revolutionary social movements, Crane Brinton (1952) claims that broad unrest causes educated people to defect from the ruling class. Economic incentives and emergent ideological justifications for revolt develop. Revolt finally occurs when the interests of the elite no longer coincide with those of the state, and when social control breaks down as the rulers' power dissipates. Once the movement succeeds, moderate revolutionaries come to rule. With time, radicals begin usurping their power, leading to a reign of terror. Eventually, however, the moderates regain control, consolidating the revolutionary goals while restoring some aspects of the prerevolutionary society.

In many ways, social movements attempt to shape the collective consciousness, the master mindsets by which individuals perceive social reality. This requires a new definition of the situation, one that socially constructs a "public problem" that requires collective action (Gusfield 1981; Snow and Benford 1988, 1989). To persuade others of the "reality" of this new perspective requires social power, and power derives from alliances and from the movement's perceived legitimacy.

# Recruitment and Attraction

A central problem faced by all social movements is recruitment. As is evident in Hoffer's (1951) depiction of the true believer, one side of this process entails identifying the psychology of those who are most inclined to be attracted to the movement. In general, these are individuals who are experiencing deficiencies in the needs discussed in Chapter 3: People who lack a sense that their life has meaning, who long to belong and feel communal ties, who feel powerless, alienated, and deprived compared to people like themselves. However, as Zurcher and Snow (1981) note, as impressive as these motivations are, they may be necessary but not sufficient conditions for joining an organized movement for social change. Not all Americans who were strongly opposed to the Vietnam War, for instance, participated in peace movements. And among those who did, motives varied considerably.

According to the **resource mobilization model** (Jenkins 1983; McCarthy and Zald 1977), joining is a rational activity in which individuals weigh the benefits of participation against the costs. This model assumes that people take into account such factors as the perceived ability of the organization to achieve its goals, the contribution one can make toward carrying out the organization's mission, the consistency between personal values and the organization's ideology, and the probable reactions of family, friends, and coworkers to one's participation.

# Recruitment and Commitment

In addition to these social-psychological factors, personal involvement is also determined by structural factors such as friendship and organizational networks (Oberschall 1973; Zucker and Snow 1981; Jenkins 1983; Rosenthal et al. 1985; Klandermans and Oegema 1987), the number of competing commitments, and the amount of free time available. In fact, individuals are more likely to join social movements because of their personal and organizational connections than because of the strength of their feelings about the issue. In other words, social bonds take precedence over ideological concerns. For this reason, the individuals who are most likely to join a social movement are those who are most socially integrated (Firesman and Gamson 1979).

A second problem faced by social movements is that of securing members' active commitment to the movement's goals. Free-riding or social loafing—letting others do the work and benefiting from their actions—is always a temptation (Walsh and Warland 1983). How, then, does self-interest become meshed with social requirements when individual interests and dispositions are so diverse?

One way of approaching this problem is to apply Howard Becker's (1960) concept of the side bet. When people make a basic commitment to a group or movement, other personal interests extraneous to the situation become involved in their actions. Consider, for instance, a person's decision to leave a job for more lucrative opportunities in another town. One's commitment to a particular employer involves not only a sense of obligation to the tasks assigned by superiors but also a feeling of responsibility toward coworkers, the ties of in-town friendships, satisfaction with one's present residence, and so on. In addition, there exist what Becker calls "generalized cultural expectations," such

# Locating People Who Are Attracted to Social Movements

Does attraction to social movements result from psychological or sociological processes or from the interaction between the two? To explore this question, let us use five questions that were asked only in the 1973 NORC General Social Survey. Participation in social movements was of considerable interest during that year. antiwar demonstrations were continuing, and the highly visible civil rights demonstrations had occurred only a decade earlier. The questions included the following:

> **Have you ever taken part in: (a) picketing for a labor strike** (10 percent yes); **(b) a civil rights demonstration** (4 percent yes); **(c) an antiwar demonstration** (5 percent yes); **(d) a pro-war demonstration** (4 percent yes); **or (e) a school-related demonstration** (5 percent yes)?

In total, 18 percent of the American adult public had participated in some type of social movement. Of those who had done so, 77 percent had participated in only one, 11 percent in two, 9 percent in three, and 2 percent in four.

Men (26 percent) were more than twice as likely as women (11 percent) to have participated in at least one movement; members of minority groups (26 percent of blacks and 23 percent of "others") were about half again as likely to have done so as whites (17 percent). With the exception of people between the ages of 18 and 29 (27 percent), participation rates were the same for all age groups, with approximately 15 percent having participated in at least one social movement at some time during their lives. If the social network thesis of recruitment holds, we would expect increasing likelihood of participation with higher social class. (See Table 11.5.) This thesis was weakly supported: 15 percent of respondents identifying themselves as members of the lower class had participated in at least one movement, compared with 18 percent of working- and middle-class respondents and 20 percent of those who said that they were members of the upper class.

Do social movements attract the angry and the unhappy? In general, the answer is "yes," but as is evident in Figure 13.1, there are interesting social-class differences. Increasing disaffection is correlated with increasing likelihood of participation in social movements only for working- and middle-class individuals, especially the latter.

Little or no correlation was found between participation and most of the standard sociological measures of anomie, specifically responses (agree or disagree) to the following statements:

> You sometimes can't help wondering whether anything is worthwhile.
> To make money, there are no right and wrong ways any more, only easy and hard ways.
> Nowadays, a person has to live pretty much for today and let tomorrow take care of itself.
> In spite of what some people say, the lot of the average man is getting worse, not better.

It's hardly fair to bring a child into the world with the way things look for the future.

These days a person doesn't really know whom he can count on.

Most people don't really care what happens to the next fellow.

In fact, the only measure producing a significant correlation involved political outlook: "Most public officials are not really interested in the problems of the average man." Again, this relationship was most pronounced for members of the middle class; among middle-class respondents, 55 percent of those who had not participated in a social movement agreed, compared with over 70 percent of those who had participated.

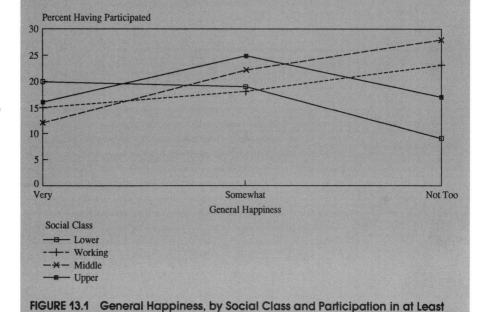

**FIGURE 13.1   General Happiness, by Social Class and Participation in at Least One Social Movement**
Source: NORC, 1973.

as the expectation that one will not change jobs too frequently. People who are considering making a commitment realize that any decision (e.g., to change jobs or to join a social movement) has far-reaching ramifications. In consequence, "what he wants to do (through internal feelings) is the same as what he has to do (according to external demands) and thus he gives to the group what he needs to nourish his own sense of self" (Kanter 1972:66–67).

## Social Rituals and Collective Behavior

There are occasions when societies intentionally harness the energy of collective behavior. In such instances, roles and rules are turned off so that individuals can experience the intense physical and emotional impact of spontaneity and communion with fellow members.

Consider the case of Mardi Gras celebrations. The custom was invented by the Romans, who tolerated all perversions as moral restraints were cast aside during a week of dancing and revelry dedicated to Bacchus (the god of wine) and Venus (the goddess of love). Even slaves were given temporary freedom during this period (Critchfield 1978).

According to Freudian psychologists, such periodic relaxings of the social order allow the release of accumulated tensions and frustrations. Once they have been released, the moral order is preserved, people finding it easier to observe its rules the rest of the year. For instance, when the Roman ritual was incorporated into Christianity, this free-spirited time preceded a period of intense religious discipline (Lent).

## THE INSTITUTIONALIZATION OF ACTION AND THOUGHT

In the remainder of this chapter and those that follow, we will incorporate the idea of **institutional systems** into our analyses of individual dispositions and drives. This approach is based on the assumption that beliefs, drives, and behaviors are strongly determined by *social factors*, by roles, social relationships, and social settings. This does not deny that personality and psychological predispositions enter into the equation. In fact, as David Riesman observes,

> Within wide limits, in a large society institutions evoke within individuals the appropriate character. Or, more precisely, given the range of responses of which men are capable, institutions may select certain of these for reinforcement (while other, more rebellious, impulses are channeled off through a variety of "escapes"). [1950:xxii]

The "social factors" of interest here are broad systems of enduring patterns of behavior and networks of relationships—in other words, institutions. When referring to **social institutions,** social scientists are not talking about places such as prisons, schools, or nursing homes. The concept is far broader in scope and scale, including social phenomena such as families, religion, work, the political order, the military, science, and mass media.

Institutions can be conceptualized as *structural systems*, as networks of interrelated rules and roles that control social action and thought. In this sense, they are the broadest agents of social control, producing stability and coordinating the behaviors of individuals.

Institutions can also be understood as *cognitive systems*. From this perspective, they are cultural systems of interrelated beliefs, values, and world views. **They are the master templates from which definitions of unique situations are derived.** Institutions define such matters as how intensely individuals should be committed to their roles, what sentiments are appropriate, what is meaningful and what is not, and the proper relationships with various types of others. So internalized do these templates become that when they are violated intense emotions are experienced.

Historically, social institutions have been formed around basic social needs such as morality (religion), communication (mass media), production and distribution (work), productivity and health (medicine), protection (military), replacement (family), socialization (education), social control (law), and the need for collective enterprises (polity). (See Chapter 3.) Over time, these institutions became freestanding social units, each with its own inner dynamics and rhythms, rules and roles, each constantly evolving at its own rate into new adaptive forms (Suttles and Zald 1985). Each institution encompasses several levels of organization, ultimately linking the individual with the broadest of groups. Primary relationships (e.g., platoons) are linked through complex organizational structures (e.g., the chains of command in the different military branches), which ultimately connect them to the nation-state (e.g., the president as commander-in-chief).

## Institutions as Perceptual Systems

Many of the perceptions of individuals are "controlled and prompted by collective criteria" (Gurvitch 1971 [1966]:24). These criteria are institutional frames of reference. In some ways, institutions can be compared to lenses through which the individual views social life. Each lens has distinctive facets and colors, filtering out things that are incompatible with the institution's self-image (Douglas 1986:112), distorting others, and giving magnified focus to the remainder.

For instance, consider the foci of attention given by political regimes. During the 1930s in the midst of the Great Depression, it was in the interest of the political order to minimize individuals' sense of the scope of suffering and resentment. With few exceptions, Hollywood complied, producing a cinematic genre of escapist films. American socialists, on the other hand, had more realistic newsreels of the extent of economic woes than what was being shown in public movie houses. These "less legitimate" images showed public riots which had received little attention in the national media. They showed long soup lines and faces of hungry children. They showed that the problems were not limited to just one's immediate community, but rather to the country as a whole.

## Institutions as Cognitive Systems

In addition to determining what individuals perceive, institutions also control thought, determining what is brought to consciousness and how it is processed:

> Social institutions encode information. They are credited with making routine decisions, solving problems, and doing a lot of regular thinking on behalf of individuals. . . . Institutions systematically direct individual memory and channel our perceptions into forms compatible with the relations they authorize. They fix processes that are essentially dynamic, they hide their influence, and they rouse our emotions to a standardized pitch on standardized issues. . . . Any problems we try

to think about are automatically transformed into their own organizational problems. The solutions they proffer only come from the limited range of their experience. (Douglas 1986:47,92)

In other words, institutions are distinctive "schools of thought" or "cognitive communities" (Berger et al. 1973)—they are the domains of common assumptions appealed to when one utters "you know." Institutions provide the attributional schemas by which the social world is understood; they define similarity and sameness through their language, analogies, and metaphors (Douglas 1986:55); they allow us to "know" about things for which we have no knowledge; and they make people think about issues that most prefer not to dwell on (e.g., religion's reminders of mortality and postmortem judgment) (Wegner 1989).

Institutions also provide *legitimations* for our actions. Legitimation explains not only why one must perform a particular action and not another, but also why things are the way they are (Berger and Luckmann 1966).

## Institutions as Action Systems

Besides being perceptual and cognitive systems, institutions are also action systems. As Peter McHugh noted, "The standards of the actor, his way of making definitions, are the bases of action, and . . . actions are the analytic bases of institutions" . . . (1968:11).

The more institutionalized a setting is, the more explicitly defined all behavior becomes. Goffman defined the extreme form of this phenomenon—such places as prisons, nursing homes, and asylums—as **"total institutions."** Such settings form a stark contrast to personal homes. Personal homes symbolize independence, privacy, sanctuary, and control. They are voluntarily selected, and their temporal rhythms and spatial props are under one's own control. If one wants a dog, one gets a dog; if one wants to eat breakfast at 3:00 P.M., one can do so. In total institutions, on the other hand, even such mundane activities as eating and sleeping are synchronized and routinized in schedules. The individual in a nursing home, for instance, must learn to eat at a time specified by the staff and must accept the fact that the functioning of the whole facility is more important than his or her personal needs.

In highly institutionalized settings, people are perceived as role players and their actions are understood as role expressions. Action sequences are essentially a set of habits. A military cadet knows that he or she must return the salute of a superior, for that is what one does in military roles; one will be rewarded or punished, defined or redefined on the basis of one's actions. So ingrained can these institutionalized behaviors become that schoolchildren sometimes raise a hand to ask a question at the family dinner table.

The actions of role players in institutions are determined by the institution's definitions of its actors, by the rules specifying each actor's role obligations, and by how others behave toward a given actor. Thus, the behaviors of college professors are shaped not only by the rules and expectations discussed in faculty handbooks and contracts but also by how students, student's parents, administrators, alumni, other faculty, and community members act toward them.

# DRIVING AS INSTITUTIONAL METAPHOR AND CASE STUDY

To illustrate how institutions create their own systems of perceptions, decision making, identities, interpersonal relations, rules, moralities, and patterned behavior, let us consider the act of driving. Driving is an institutionalized activity because it involves a set of prescriptions for one's own activities and expectations about the behaviors of others. The roadway and its rules can be viewed as analogous to society itself. From the air, roadways look like arteries and veins, with vehicles appearing as small blood cells. Private driveways feed onto semiprivate residential streets, which, in turn, feed into larger, more public roads, and so on until they are linked to superhighways.

A similar system dictates how we traverse these social pathways to reach our destinations in life. This system—for example, the rules of the road, driving courtesies, highway culture, driving self-presentations, and so forth—determines how personal needs are meshed with the social. From the individual perspective, the goal is to go from point A to point B in the minimum amount of time. But this decision affects many other people. If thousands of people also decide to go to point B, gridlock results. From society's perspective, the goal is to maximize the number of motorists reaching their destinations in the shortest possible time. Since separate roads cannot be created for each driver, rules of the road emerge. These rules allow as many drivers as possible to reach their goals in ways that minimally impede others from reaching theirs.

Let's put this metaphor to work. Consider the difference between *Gemeinschaft* and *Gesellschaft* "highway cultures." To live in a *Gemeinschaft* culture would be driving where all drivers and pedestrians know you and your family. Failure to observe the rules of the road would reflect poorly on both you and your kin, and undoubtedly news of your misdeeds would get back to your family. This is precisely the form of social solidarity *and* social control we discussed in Chapter 8. *Gesellschaft* cultures, on the other hand, would be driving on large freeways filled with strangers. Here social control exists in the forms of internalized moralities ("I never exceed 55 mph because that's not right and because there is an energy crisis"), fear of political sanction ("I better slow down because there's a police car ahead and I cannot afford another speeding ticket"), and other-directedness ("Everyone is going faster than me; I guess I can speed up").

For most Americans, obtaining a driver's license symbolizes coming of age and entering adulthood (in fact, the driver's license is a major proof of identity). For many young drivers, the automobile means independence and freedom, and often there is the exhilaration of flirting with the rules, of going too fast or driving dangerously. With age and a few accidents, one learns the refinements and nuances of the game.

The very act of driving entails a particular style of awareness or field of consciousness: One is sensitized to traffic lights and signs, not to cloud formations or air temperature; one learns to defer to sirens and flashing lights. So routinized, in fact, does driving become that its activities become automatic. Such habitual behavior is the essence of social institutions, serving to minimize doubt and narrow the scope of possible actions. The actor in the driving role does not contemplate actions that are not institutionally defined. This is why we are shocked when the norms are violated, as when we encounter someone driving in reverse on a freeway or discover erroneous directions on highway signs.

Despite the fact that all drivers engage in identical behaviors, a spectrum of driver roles and norms has evolved. During the morning highway commute, one can view some individuals applying makeup as they hurtle down the road, while others eat, read, or listen to the banter of their favorite radio disk jockeys. Moreover, each lane of traffic has its own norms and cast of characters. The rightmost lane, for instance, often carries the marginal drivers who do not wish to compete in the intensity of the inner lanes. On occasions, however, they do, becoming social deviants as they travel at 50 mph in the leftmost lane.

The amount of concentration and calculation required does not decrease with speed. When one is turning left at a busy intersection, one's life may depend on how the situation is perceived. One makes moral calculations about the drivers of oncoming cars. For instance, if the oncoming car is going no faster than the legal speed limit, can I make my left turn?

> Well, the driver is elderly and there are many cars behind him, indicating that he is going slowly. I will go ahead and turn in front of him.
> The car is an expensive Mercedes and I see that the driver is talking on a telephone and reading something on the steering wheel. He has more to lose in the accident than I do, and there could be a big insurance settlement in it for me if I'm hit. On the other hand, I'm not big on pain and this person's lawyers are probably better than mine. I'll wait.

Also entering into the decision-making process are inferences about how I appear to the oncoming driver:

> Does my banged-up rear end indicate that I take chances, am not to be trusted, and could be stupid enough to turn unexpectedly at any moment?
> Do the painted flames on the sides of my car, the dark glasses, leather jacket, and gun rack make me look like the kind of driver who is willing to challenge others for the right of way?

Finally, the road also allows for distinctive forms of collective behavior. Striking truck drivers may park their rigs on the highway, blocking all movement. A violent rainstorm brings slower speeds, turned-on lights, and greater wariness. And a few expensive, fast-moving vehicles may increase the speed norm well above the legal limit.

Beyond its utilitarian functions, the automobile has come to carry considerable symbolic significance for its owner and/or operator, as is the case of many institutionalized roles. A colleague was struck by the similarities between his aging mother and his 16-year-old son in terms of the meaningfulness of having access to an automobile. For both, the auto symbolizes mobility, independence, and adult status. O. B. Hardison notes that cars "are status symbols, coming-of-age symbols, symbols of virility, symbols of independence" (1989). The elite may choose to transport themselves in cars that cost the price of an average home, while those at the bottom of the social order travel in older, often less reliable vehicles.

## Fake Car Phones Let You Dial "S" for Status

A Los Altos, California, firm, Faux Systems, has created the Cellular Phoney, an inexpensive car phone replica that looks just like the real thing. The company motto: "It's not what you own, it's what people think you own." Over 40,000 fake phones have been sold, most in Los Angeles. For only $15.95, status-seekers can buy a *faux* phone and a stick-on car antenna to create the illusion of power and importance.

Source: Bishop, 1988.

Because of the link between driving and social identity, for many people driving becomes not a means to an end (getting from one point to another) but, rather, an end in itself. Thus, in the postwar period of suburbanization, "cruising" became a kind of adolescent rite of passage in communities around the country. In the case of "lowriding," we can see how cruising self-presentations became a means for Hispanic Americans to affirm their cultural identity by lowering the frames of their cars and painting them with variations of barrio art for "low and slow cruising" (Balik 1990).

In sum, driving illustrates how institutional systems shape all of the processes discussed in this book—the shaping of consciousness and thought, the formation of identities, the nature of relationships with others, and the emergence of collective behavior.

## INSTITUTIONS AND CULTURE

A culture is largely determined by the nature of its institutional spheres and by their relative power. The more powerful an institution is in any given culture, the more likely its language and metaphors are to be employed in everyday speech. Its styles of consciousness permeate everyday thought, and its norms shape and regulate everyday interactions. As Robert Nisbet observes:

> All institutions compete for the loyalty of individuals. So far as individuals are concerned, competition is probably most stringent within an institution; but from the point of view of society, it is the struggle between institutions that is decisive. There are several institutions that serve more than others to define social reality. (1984:49)

On the other hand, each institution is also shaped by the culture within which it exists. To obtain the loyalty of individuals, institutional spheres seek legitimacy and authenticity by aligning themselves with the culture's central underlying myth. Such myths enable people to come to terms with the world; they provide the framework for understanding the basic workings of social life. In the United States, the cultural myth of individual rights underlies the structures, processes, and associated mindsets of political, economic, and religious institutions.

George Thomas (1989) argues that if a significant permanent change occurs in any one institution, social movements will emerge to redefine the cultural order and reestablish a balance among the society's institutions. In coming chapters we will see many instances of this process.

## CONCLUSION

In this chapter we have examined the ways in which the self is psychologically and sociologically linked with large numbers of other selves. We began by studying the various forms of collective behavior, considering how distinctive social orders arise that alter the status quo. In contrast to psychological models, in which individuals with certain personality types or mental predispositions are attracted to social movements, the sociological model portrays movements as developing by absorbing existing social networks.

Throughout this book, our goal has been to study socially constructed states of mind. The methodological strategy arising out of this orientation is to link the structures of consciousness (e.g., individuals' systems of perception, memory, logic, beliefs, emotions, and self-perceptions) with particular social processes (Berger et. al. 1973). In this chapter we considered the influences of large-scale collectivities, from spontaneous collective action to the relatively programmed contexts provided by social institutions. In the following chapters we will elaborate on the latter, studying the ways in which inner and outer lives are shaped by the institutions of religion and work, historically the two most dominant definers of social reality.

## REFERENCES

Allport, Gordon, and Leo Postman. 1947. *The psychology of rumor.* New York: Henry Holt.

Amenta, Edwin, and Yvonne Zylan. 1991. It happened here: Political opportunity, the new institutionalism, and the Townsend movement. *American Sociological Review* 56:250–65.

Ayvazian, A., and M. Klare. 1990, Spring. Crisis: Activists voice their hopes for a new era. *Nuclear Times.*

Balik, Paula. 1990, April 6. Lowriders to show off fancy wheels. *San Antonio Express-News,* pp. 1-J, 2-J.

Becker, Howard S. 1960. Notes on the concept of commitment. *American Journal of Sociology* 46: 32–40.

Berger, Peter, and Thomas Luckmann. 1966. *The social construction of reality.* Garden City, NY: Doubleday.

Berger, Peter, Brigitte Berger, and Hansfried Kellner. 1973. *The homeless mind: Modernization and consciousness.* New York: Random House.

Bishop, Katherine. 1988, April 28. Fake car phones let you dial "S" for status. *Dallas Morning News,* pp. 1C, 4C.

Brinton, Crane. 1952. *The anatomy of revolution.* Englewood Cliffs, NJ: Prentice-Hall.

Canetti, Elias. 1977 [1960]. *Crowds and power* (Carol Stewart, trans.). New York: Continuum.

Cantril, Hadley, Hazel Gaudet, and Herta Herzog. 1940. *Invasion from Mars.* Princeton, NJ: Princeton University Press.

Critchfield, Richard. 1978, February. Wild at the carnival. *Human Behavior,* pp. 53–57.

Douglas, Mary. 1986. *How institutions think.* Syracuse, NY: Syracuse University Press.

Fireman, Bruce, and William A. Gamson. 1979. Utilitarian logic in the resource mobilization perspective. In Mayer N. Zald and John D. McCarthy (eds.), *The dynamics of social movements.* Cambridge, MA: Winthrop.

Garner, Roberta, and Mayer Zald. 1985. The political economy of social movement sectors. In Gerald Suttles and Mayer Zald (eds.), *The challenge of social control: Citizenship and institution building in modern society: Essays in honor of Morris Janowitz.* Norwood, NJ: Ablex.

Goffman, Erving. 1961. *Asylums: Essays on the social situation of mental patients and other inmates.* Garden City, NY: Doubleday/Anchor.

Gurvitch, Georges. 1971 [1966]. *The social frameworks of knowledge* (trans. Margaret A. Thompson and Kenneth A. Thompson). New York: Harper Torchbooks.

Gusfield, Joseph. 1981. *Drinking-driving and the symbolic order.* Chicago: University of Chicago Press.

*Harper's Magazine.* 1988, September. Harper's index. p. 15.

Hardison, O. B. 1989. *Disappearing through the skylight.* New York: Viking.

Herbert, Wray. 1982, September 18. An epidemic in the works. *Science News,* pp. 188–90.

Hoffer, Eric. 1951. *The true believer: Thoughts on the nature of mass movements.* New York: Harper Collins.

Jenkins, J. Craig. 1983. Resource mobilization theory and the study of social movements. *Annual Review of Sociology* 9:527–553.

Johnson, George. 1989. *Lyndon LaRouche and the new American fascism.* Garden City, NY: Doubleday.

Kanter, R. M. 1972. Commitment and community: Communes and utopias. In *Sociological Perspective.* Cambridge, MA: Harvard University Press.

Klandermans, Bert. 1984. Mobilization and participation: Social psychological expansions and resource mobilization theory. *American Sociological Review* 49:583–600.

Klandermans, Bert, and Dirk Oegema. 1987. Potentials, networks, motivations, and barriers: Steps towards participation in social movements. *American Sociological Review* 52:519–531.

Koenig, Fredrick. 1985. *Rumor in the marketplace: The social psychology of commercial hearsay.* Dover, MA: Auburn House.

Le Bon, Gustave. 1897. *The mind of crowds.* London: Unwin.

Lofland, John. 1981. Collective behavior: The elementary forms. In Morris Rosenberg and Ralph H. Turner (eds.), *Social psychology: Sociological perspectives.* New York: Basic Books.

Lovejoy, Arthur. 1961. *The great chain of being: A study of the history of an idea.* Cambridge, MA: Harvard University Press.

McCarthy, J. D., and M. N. Zald. 1977. Resource mobilization and social movements: A partial theory. *American Journal of Sociology* 82:1212–1241.

McHugh, Peter. 1968. *Defining the situation: The organization of meaning in social interaction.* New York: Bobbs-Merrill.

McPhail, Clark. 1991. *The myth of the maddening crowd.* Hawthorne, NY: Aldine de Gruyter.

Meyer, John. 1971. *Institutionalization.* Unpublished manuscript.

Nisbet, Robert. 1984, June. Besieged by the state. *Harper's Magazine.*

Oberschall, A. 1973. *Social conflicts and social movements.* Englewood Cliffs, NJ: Prentice-Hall.

Omestad, Thomas. 1989, December 25. Ten-day wonder. *New Republic,* pp. 19–22.

Painton, Frederick. 1990, May 28. Where the sky stays dark. *Time,* p. 40.

Park, Robert. 1972 (1921). *The crowd and the public and other essays* (ed. Henry Eisner, Jr.). Chicago: University of Chicago Press.

Riesman, David. 1950. *The lonely crowd: A study of the changing American character.* New Haven, CT: Yale University Press.

Rosenthal, Naomi, M. Fingrutd, M. Ethier, R. Karant, and D. McDonald. 1985. Social movements and network analysis: A case study of nineteenth-century women's reform in New York State. *American Journal of Sociology* 90:1022–1054.

Sahlins, Marshall. 1981. *Historical metaphors and mythical realities: Structure in the early history of the Sandwich Islands kingdom.* Ann Arbor: University of Michigan Press.

Shibutani, Tamotsu. 1966. *Improvised news: A sociological study of rumor.* Indianapolis, IN: Bobbs-Merrill.

Smelser, Neil. 1963. *Theory of collective behavior.* New York: Free Press.

Smelser, Neil. 1964. Theoretical issues of scope and problems. *Sociological Quarterly* 5:116–122.

Snow, David A., and Robert D. Benford. 1988. Ideology, frame resonance, and participant mobilization. *International Social Movement Research* 1:197–217.

Snow, David A., and Robert D. Benford. 1989. Schemi interpretativi dominanti e cicli di protesta [Master frames and cycles of protest]. *Polis: Ricerche e Studi su Societa e Politica* 3:5–40.

Suttles, Gerald, and Mayer Zald. 1985. *The challenge of social control: Citizenship and institution building in modern society: Essays in honor of Morris Janowitz.* Norwood, NJ: Ablex.

Thomas, George M. 1989. *Revivalism and cultural change: Christianity, nation building, and the market in the nineteenth-century United States.* Chicago: University of Chicago Press.

Tilly, Charles. 1975. Revolutions and collective violence. In Fred I. Greenstein and Nelson W. Polsby (ed.), *The Handbook of Political Science.* Reading, MA: Addison-Wesley.

Tilly, Charles. 1978. *From Mobilization to Revolution.* Reading, MA: Addison-Wesley.

Turner, Ralph H. 1964. New theoretical frameworks. *Sociological Quarterly* 5:122–132.

Turner, Ralph, and L. Killian. 1987. *Collective behavior* (3rd ed.; 1st ed. published in 1957). Englewood Cliffs, NJ: Prentice-Hall.

Walsh, E. J., and R. H. Warland. 1983. Social movement and free riders in the TMI area. *American Sociological Review* 48:764–780.

Wegner, Daniel. 1989. *White bears and other unwanted thoughts: Suppression, obsession, and the psychology of mental control.* New York: Viking.

Zurcher, L. A., and D. A. Snow. 1981. Collective behavior: Social movements. In Morris Rosenberg and Ralph Turner (eds.), *Social psychology: Sociological perspectives.* New York: Basic Books.

# 14

# The Social Psychology of Religion

Despite being officially banned for three generations, religion survives in the Soviet Union. The communist regime could neither suppress individuals' need for religion nor meet the personal and social needs that religion has traditionally satisfied. As Communist Party Secretary Mikhail Gorbachev acknowledged in 1989, his party erred when it rejected religion and ignored the moral force it provides (Haberman 1989).

A 1991 national survey by Princeton Survey Research Associates found that faith in God is the most important part of Americans' lives. Forty-two percent of those interviewed said that they valued their relationship with God above all else, compared to only 2 percent who claimed that a high-paying job was the most important thing in their lives (cited in *San Antonio Express-News* 1991).

Religion is the social institution that is dedicated to the spiritual needs of individuals; it arises out of the psychological impetus to resolve universal crises of meaning such as death, conflict, sickness, and inequality. Religion also addresses the cultural needs for order and moral solidarity. As Bell (1976:xxi) observed, if science is the search for unity of nature, then religion is the quest for unity of culture.

In this chapter we will examine religion as it is experienced by individuals. It is religion that determines the individual's ultimate destination or goal in life. Religion also determines how one is to reach one's goal. It is religion that elicits concern and respect for others. Like traffic laws and highway signs, religion reminds us that if we use life's roadways selfishly, chaos and gridlock will result; but if we consider the perspective of others sharing the same roadways, everyone can reach their destinations.

## The Concept of Religiosity

How can social scientists hope to capture something as subjective and personal as religious experience? As John Dewey noted, religion is not some independently existing entity but, rather, "denotes attitudes that may be taken toward every object and every proposed end or ideal" (1934:9). Religion has been variously described as involving systems of belief, meaning, knowledge, attitude, emotion, and commitment, deriving from ultimate sources and being of supreme importance (Williams 1962).

Religiosity cannot be adequately characterized as a one-dimensional phenomenon. Charles Glock (1962) argued that there are five independent dimensions of religious commitment: religious belief (the ideological dimension), religious practice (the ritualistic dimension), religious feeling (the experiential dimension), religious knowledge (the intellectual dimension), and the effects of religion on individuals and their social behaviors (the consequential dimension).

In an empirical survey of these dimensions in a sample of college students, Faulkner and DeJong (1972) found that they were indeed interdependent but far from being perfectly correlated. For instance, a person who has a strong experience of God is more likely to pray and attend religious services than one without such an experience. The dimension that is most predictive of the others is the ideological dimension. Although one would expect that certain effects (such as charitableness or honesty) should follow from religious commitment, the least significant of the dimensions in terms of predicting the others was the consequential dimension.

## PERSONAL NEEDS ADDRESSED BY RELIGION

In numerous ways, religion acts as a shock absorber, cushioning the inevitable tensions between self and society. Social frustrations must be resolved; the incongruities between personal desires and social needs must be explained. Absolute faith in the order, meaningfulness, and justice of the social order must be instilled in the society's members.

Religion answers individuals' "why" questions. As Peter Berger notes, "in situations of acute suffering, the need for meaning is as strong as or even stronger than the need for happiness" (1969a:58). This holds true regardless of the social backgrounds of individuals. In her study of people attracted to faith healing groups Meredith McGuire (1988) found many highly educated, middle-class individuals. She argues that the dominant mechanistic paradigm of the medical establishment ignores the ways in which the experience of illness is shaped by the meanings individuals apply to their infirmities (McGuire and Kantor 1987).

Not only does religion offer explanations, but its rituals give individuals a sense of control over life's uncertainties. In their study of sixty-nine Christian college students, Daniel McIntosh and Bernard Spilka (1990) found the active Christians to be healthier than others, reporting fewer headaches, respiratory problems, ulcers, and other ailments. They argue that one reason is that these individuals are more likely to pray, an act that reduces tension, provides optimism, and, like other rituals, gives them a greater sense of control over the situation.

The impact of prayer on health is reflected in data from the 1989 NORC General Social Survey. Figure 14.1 plots the correlations between the following two questions (with response percentages):

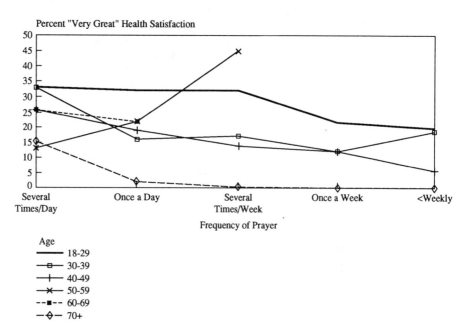

Percent "Very Great" Health Satisfaction

Frequency of Prayer

Age
——— 18-29
——□— 30-39
——+— 40-49
——✕— 50-59
--■-- 60-69
—◇— 70+

**FIGURE 14.1    Satisfaction with Health/Physical Condition, by Frequency of Prayer**
Source: NORC, 1989.

**About how often do you pray?** Several times a day (23 percent), once a day (29 percent), several times a week (15 percent), once a week (7 percent), less than once a week (25 percent), never (1 percent).

**Tell me how much *satisfaction* you get from your health and physical condition.** A very great deal (25 percent), a great deal (31 percent), quite a bit (17 percent), a fair amount (16 percent), some (5 percent), a little (3 percent), none (2 percent).

In nearly all age groups, people who pray several times a day are most likely to report that they receive a great deal of satisfaction from their health. For instance, among people between the ages of 18 and 29, those who pray frequently are two-thirds more likely to report a high level of satisfaction with their health than those who pray less than once a week.

## Consolation for Death and Suffering

If death were understood to be an absolute end, life would have no meaning. Life would be futile if, no matter how one lived on earth—whether one was evil or virtuous, selfish or altruistic—or what one achieved, the conclusion remained the same: total nothingness and extinction of the self. But humans have not accepted this view of death. They have created myths and visions of immortality. As Ernest Becker argues, "the urge to immortality is not a simple reflex from the death-anxiety but a reaching out by one's whole being toward life" (1973:151–152).

Religion evolved, in part, as a response to this existential concern. It is the source of concepts such as resurrection and reincarnation, the duality of the soul and the body, and promises of compensation for whatever was lacking in one's earthly existence (Weber 1946).

Such consolations carry a price, however. By creating and maintaining anxieties related to death (e.g., being consigned to hell instead of heaven, or being forced to go through another round of reincarnation instead of reaching nirvana) and the hope of immortality, religion developed perhaps the most effective mechanism of social control ever devised. Consider how many generations have lived their lives in the complete certainty that they would have to face some sort of judgment after death—that their every action was being observed by some grand evaluator.

To explore the distribution of the belief in life after death, let us return to the 1989 NORC General Social Survey. In total, 68 percent of the American adult public responded "yes" to the question "Do you believe in life after death?" This figure is the highest for all the Western nations. Protestants were slightly more likely to believe in life after death (74 percent) than Catholics (67 percent), who, in turn, were more likely to hold such a belief than Jews (42 percent) and those with no religious affiliation (35 percent). Not surprisingly, belief in life after death increases with the intensity of religious beliefs, from 35 percent of those claiming to have no religion to 60 percent of those defining themselves as "not very" religious, 70 percent of those who are "somewhat" religious, and 83 percent of those who are "strongly" religious.

A reasonable hypothesis is that as one approaches death (i.e., the older one is), one becomes increasingly religious and, therefore, increasingly likely to believe in life after death. In Figure 14.2 we see that, indeed, Protestants and

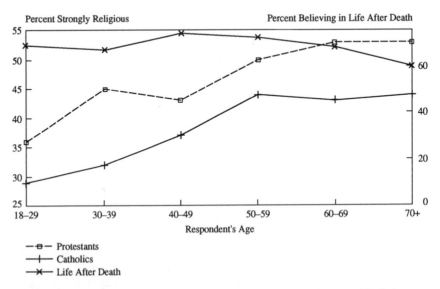

**FIGURE 14.2   Religiosity and Belief in Life After Death, by Age and Religion**
Source: NORC, 1989.

Catholics are generally more likely to be strongly religious the older they are, though for Catholics a plateau is reached among those age 50 and older and for Protestants age 60 and older. However, when one examines the percentages of individuals who believe in life after death, there is virtually no difference across the lifespan. There is, in fact, slight decline in belief from the age of 40 on, from 73 percent of people between the ages of 40 and 49 to 60 percent of people age 70 and older. Remember, however, that the data reveal both *age* and *cohort* effects. For instance, older individuals may be more religious than younger people not because of their age but because they were socialized in a more religious period.

To account for this inconsistency between increasing religiosity (at least among those who identify themselves as Christians) and declining belief in life after death, let us consider what differences the intensity of religious beliefs produces across the lifespan. In Figure 14.3, Protestants and Catholics are compared with people who lack a religious affiliation or who are not very religious. Among those with no affiliation with an institutionalized religion, belief in life after death declines from the thirties on, with no one over the age of 60 believing in life after death. Protestants and Catholics are classified as either "very religious" (46 percent of the Protestants and 36 percent of the Catholics) or "not very religious" (41 percent of the Protestants and 46 percent of the Catholics). As one can see, in both groups, those who are strongly religious are more likely than those who are not very religious to believe in life after death. Across the lifespan there is almost no difference between the religions when one controls for the intensity of belief.

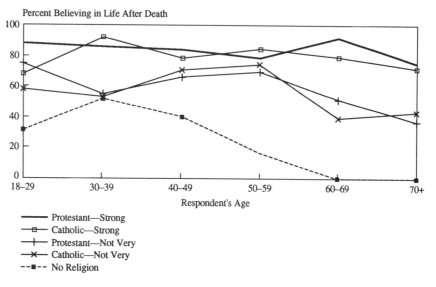

**FIGURE 14.3   Belief in Life After Death, by Religion, Intensity of Religious Belief, and Age**
Source: NORC, 1989.

# Religion as a Source of Biographical Coherence

We have argued throughout this book that individuals need a sense of biographical coherence (Bertaux 1982). As Frederick Wyatt put it:

> We need the feeling of order and continuity so as to cope with the unending onslaught of external and internal experiences. We therefore have to impose our order on the flux and, if one cannot grasp continuity, make it up in some fashion ourselves. (1963:319)

In social-psychological terms, religion provides the "symbolic glue" (Bellah 1970) that gives coherence and continuity to the discrete episodes that make up each individual's life (Kearl 1980).

People create personal myths to give life meaning and a goal (Goleman 1988). These stories—which resemble the stories of classical mythology—reveal not only individuals' perspectives on their past but also the script for their future. For many people, the models for their life stories come from religion. When we hear the frequent comment that so-and-so "lived a good Christian life," we can see how religion integrates the social system with the individual personality, how it instills the moral order (Berger 1969a; Kearl and Wedholm 1989). From this perspective, the "soul" can be understood to be identity, and the traditional activity of religion to be soul, or biographical, maintenance.

In part, this is accomplished through religion's control over rites of passage. When, for instance, a boy is transformed into a man or a single person becomes part of a couple, a personally significant event is made socially typical. In these ceremonies we find the simultaneous reaffirmation of an individual's identity, the reality of one's new membership role within a social collectivity, and the reality of the group itself.

# SOCIAL NEEDS ADDRESSED BY RELIGION

Next to kinship, religion provides the greatest force for social integration. It is experienced as a force that transcends all things at all times, binding all generations through a collective consciousness. This collective consciousness is the seat of the shared morality and collective destiny that provide social solidarity and continuity.

According to Émile Durkheim (1915), religion is the reflection of society itself. It involves the reaffirmation of publicly standardized ideas, providing social solidarity and linking the individual to the social order. Durkheim argued that high gods grew out of clan totems, uniting clans into tribes. The totem poles of the Pacific Northwest Indians, for instance, symbolize the union and unity of a number of clan emblems. [As the number of sovereign groups in a society increased, pressure to avoid populating the heavens with a bunch of squabbling gods led to a reconceptualization of the divine world, giving rise to monotheism (Swanson 1960).]

Durkheim defined the **sacred** as this collective representation of society. The sacred becomes a concrete expression of the power of society itself, of the extraordinary and uncontrollable forces that produce order out of chaos (Douglas 1966). People become bound together in their deference to this coercive power that organizes and influences their lives.

## Religion as Moral Order

A 1986 Gallup Poll showed that 48 percent of Americans see religion gaining in social impact, compared with just 14 percent who felt that way as recently as 1970 (Gallup and Castelli 1989:38–41). This resurgence of religion occurred during an era of profound doubt and lack of confidence among the nations. Social temptations seemed to exceed the power of individual restraint: Insider trading in financial markets was shaking confidence in the structure of our financial institutions; the President of the United States was, during the Iran-Contra affair, caught in a deliberate lie to the American public; medical researchers were caught fudging the results of their richly funded enterprises; and even televangelists were caught in illicit sexual liaisons and schemes for personal enrichment. Morality seemed to have died as the so-called "Me decade" of the 1970s extended through the 1980s (Lasch 1989).

Religion has historically served as a moderating influence on egoism and selfishness. It has accomplished this largely through its control over emotional experiences, particularly guilt. For example, in 1984 Pope John Paul II issued a statement, the "Reconciliatio et Paenitentia" or "Reconciliation and Penance," in which he warned modern societies about their dilution of the concept of personal sin. He observed that blame is increasingly placed "not so much on the moral conscience of an individual but rather on some vague entity or anonymous collectivity, such as the situation, the system, society, structures, or institutions. Sin, in the proper sense, is always a personal act" (Dionne 1984).

Americans' sense of morality and the need to punish those who transgress moral precepts is considerable. According to the 1988 NORC General Social Survey, 53 percent of Americans agreed that "immoral actions by one person can corrupt society in general" and 63 percent agreed that "those who violate God's rules must be punished."

Religion obtains acknowledgment of and compliance to a culture's moral system by capitalizing on individuals' needs for immortality. As Ernest Becker (1973) contended, anxiety about death intensifies allegiance to moral codes. Given the human tendency to view the world as a just and meaningful place, by leading moral lives individuals increase their odds of achieving some desirable form of immortality.

In a series of ingenious experiments based on Becker's thesis, Abram Rosenblatt et al. (1989) found strong support for the premise that when reminded of their mortality, people react more harshly toward moral transgressors and become more favorably disposed toward those who uphold their values. In one experiment, twenty-two municipal judges were given a battery of psychological tests. In the experimental group, eleven judges were told to write about their own death, including what happens physically and what emotions are evoked when thinking about it. When asked to set bond for a prostitute on the basis of a case brief, those who had thought about their death set an average bond of $455, while the average in the control group was $50. The authors concluded (Greenberg et al. 1990) that when awareness of death is increased, in-group solidarity is intensified, out-groups become more despised, and prejudice and religious extremism are increased.

## Religiosity and Prosocial Behavior

Morality and religion are derived from individuals' experience of society. The essence of that experience is the feeling of a powerful moral force, a force that requires allegiance and obligates all to act in prescribed ways (Halbwachs 1980[1950]:8; Etzioni 1988:42). Moral activities, notes Amitai Etzioni, "*affirm or express a commitment,* rather than involve the consumption of a good or a service. Therefore, they are intrinsically motivated" (1988:43).

To reaffirm the significance of this commitment and the fact that moral activities are not subject to means-end analysis, religions often demand ritual forms of masochism. Examples include religious demands of abstinence, self-denial, or even death (Berger 1969a:55–56,74–75). Besides making individuals literally feel the power of the moral order, these rituals also intensify the experience of the group, creating situations wherein the conception of the self over and above the group is impossible.

From this argument, it would seem logical to predict that religiosity would be positively correlated with the likelihood of performing prosocial acts. Indeed, a 1990 Gallup survey of Americans in four cities found regular worshippers were three times more likely than nonworshippers to be involved in voluntary civic and charitable activities. Nearly 60 percent of the regular worshippers believed that duty comes before pleasure, and almost half believed that facing daily tasks is a source of pleasure and satisfaction (Parker 1990).

## RELIGIOUS TEMPLATES FOR EXPERIENCE AND THOUGHT

Believing ourselves to be special creatures, we tend to attribute cosmic significance to our activities. We also tend to see supernatural forces underlying our affairs, particularly when our activities have unintended consequences. William May notes that "long before there were official gods, religion meant most simply 'alertness' or 'attentiveness' " (1973:100) toward sacred things. In this section we consider some of the cognitive and emotional aspects of that attentiveness.

### Religion as an Experiential System

Juan Gomez, an 11-year-old youth from a lower-middle-class family tells his mother, a mildly religious Catholic, that he sees blue auras around people, with plasmalike clouds radiating between interactants sharing a communal experience. Is this a "true" religious experience? Should the mother tell a priest, a psychiatrist, a school counselor, or the news media about it, or should it be kept secret?

Churches share in this problem of religious authenticity. When six children in Medjugorje, Yugoslavia, reported seeing the Virgin Mary in 1981, the event touched off a pilgrimage by millions of people to the site. Yet the Catholic church was ambivalent about accepting the sighting, fearing that it had more to lose if the apparition was a fake than if it was authentic. The irony is that the church itself is based on the apparition of Christ's resurrection (Sheler 1990).

**TABLE 14.1  Percentages of Americans Who Report Having Experienced CONTACT and SPIRIT FORCE, 1988**

|  | Contact | Spirit Force |
|---|---|---|
| Never | 60 | 68 |
| 1–2 times | 24 | 18 |
| Several times | 10 | 9 |
| Often | 5 | 5 |
| N | 1459 | 1451 |

Source: NORC ,1988.

Being oriented to matters outside the realm of everyday experiences, to what extent does religion sensitize individuals to parapsychological phenomena?

Consider people's responses to the following NORC questions:

**How often have you had any of the following experiences?**
**—Felt as though you were really in touch with someone who had died.** (CONTACT)
**—Felt as though you were very close to a powerful, spiritual force that seemed to lift you out of yourself.** (SPIRIT FORCE)

Answers were coded as "Never in my life," "Once or twice," "Several times," and "Often." The results appear in Table 14.1. As is evident, nearly 40 percent of Americans have had the feeling of being in touch with the dead at least once, and 32 percent believed that they have been lifted out of themselves by some spiritual force.

Neither age nor education is correlated in any significant way with these experiences, although a weak relationship was detected between education and SPIRIT FORCE, with more educated individuals being more likely to report having been lifted out of themselves. In Table 14.2 one can see that the likeli-

**TABLE 14.2  CONTACT and SPIRIT FORCE, by Religion and Religiosity**

|  | Contact | Spirit Force |
|---|---|---|
|  | *(Once or More)* | *(Once or More)* |
| **Strength of Religiosity** |  |  |
| Strong | 38 | 35 |
| Somewhat | 34 | 31 |
| Not very | 35 | 25 |
| **Religion** |  |  |
| Protestant | 39 | 36 |
| Catholic | 44 | 23 |
| Jew | 41 | 21 |
| None | 30 | 20 |

Source: NORC, 1988.

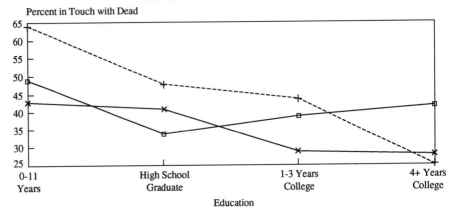

Religiosity and Education, by Feeling in
Touch with One Who Had Died: Protestants

Percent in Touch with Dead

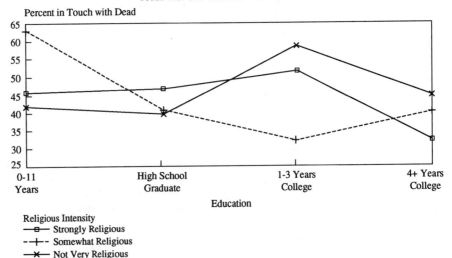

Religiosity and Education, by Feeling in
Touch with One Who Had Died: Catholics

Percent in Touch with Dead

Religious Intensity
—□— Strongly Religious
--+-- Somewhat Religious
—✕— Not Very Religious

**FIGURE 14.4  Religiosity and Education**
Source: NORC, 1988.

hood of having had such parapsychological experiences increases slightly with
level of religiosity. Catholics are slightly more likely to report having had contact
with the dead, whereas Protestants are over 50 percent more likely than Catholics and Jews to have felt a spirit force.

Figure 14.4 plots the interactions between religiosity and education for
Protestants and Catholics in determining the likelihood of such experiences.
In terms of feeling in touch with one who has died, education generally reduces
the percentages, except among strongly religious Protestants. Neither religios-
ity nor education has much effect on Catholics' experience of a spirit force. For
Protestants, on the other hand, increases in both variables generally increase

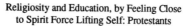

Religiosity and Education, by Feeling Close
to Spirit Force Lifting Self: Protestants

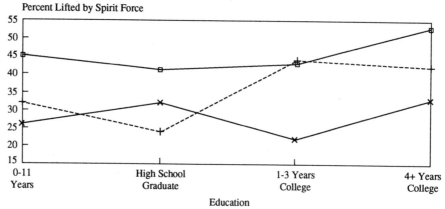

Religiosity and Education, by Feeling Close
to Spirit Force Lifting Self: Catholics

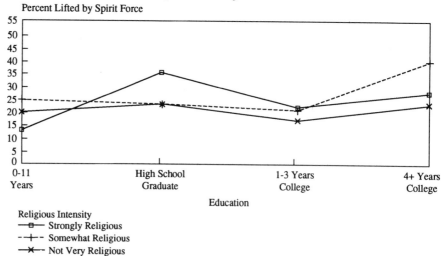

Religious Intensity
—☐— Strongly Religious
--+-- Somewhat Religious
—✕-- Not Very Religious

**FIGURE 14.4** *Continued*

the probability of such episodes. (No significant differences were detected between fundamentalist, moderate, and liberal Protestant denominations.)

The latter findings are not as dramatic as those reported by Gallup and
Newport (1990), who asked the following question to a random sample of Americans in 1990:

**Have you ever been aware of, or influenced by, a presence or a power—whether
you call it God or not—which is different from your everyday self?**

The results are presented in Table 14.3.

**TABLE 14.3  Age, Education, Religiosity, and Religion, by Having Felt Spiritual Presence or Power**

| | Percent Feeling Presence or Power | | |
|---|---|---|---|
| **Age** | | **Religiosity** | |
| 18–29 | 53 | Very | 60 |
| 30  –49 | 63 | Fairly | 48 |
| 50+ | 44 | Not very | 39 |
| **Education** | | **Religion** | |
| College graduate | 65 | Protestant | 55 |
| Some college | 68 | Catholic | 53 |
| High school graduate | 49 | None | 40 |
| High school | 37 | Evangelical | 63 |
| | | Nonevangelical | 48 |

Source: Gallup Poll, 1990.

## Scientific versus Religious Ways of Knowing

In 1990 a Massachusetts couple were convicted of manslaughter in the death of their 2-year-old son. The child had died of a correctable bowel obstruction that remained medically untreated as the parents relied only on prayer. Their Christian Science faith did not allow them to combine spiritual healing with medical treatment.

As modernization has transformed societies, scientific explanations of phenomena such as illness have tended to supersede supernatural ones. The supposed superiority of such "rational" and "objective" explanations is derived from the fact that they divorce emotion, faith, and preconception from observation and action. Miraculous phenomena are *explained* away: Joan of Arc did not hear the voices of angels but suffered from hallucinations associated with a rare form of epilepsy (*San Antonio Express-News* 1990); the image on the Shroud of Turin could not be that of Christ because carbon-14 dating indicates the fabric to be a medieval forgery; and the vivid near-death experiences of the "clinically dead" (Moody 1975) are due to oxygen deprivations of the brain.

In many ways, however, science has failed to deliver. For instance, its ability to keep brain-dead people alive in "chronic vegetative states" and its creation of doomsday weaponry have not provided consoling answers to the question of death's meaning. According to a 1988 survey, 82 percent of Americans say that God still performs miracles (*Times Mirror*-Gallup Organization poll cited in *Harper's Magazine* 1988). As Jack Solomon observes:

> Whenever the myth of science fails, myths of religion reemerge with renewed strength. It is probably no accident that in the 1980s America experienced a resurgence of orthodox religious fervor at a time when science and technology no longer seemed to be providing satisfactory answers to our deepest questions about our place in the universe. (1988:55)

Although since the Enlightenment reason and religion have been viewed as increasingly incompatible, the two have never actually parted ways. For instance, science inherited from religion the idea that the universe is governed by a single set of laws. Both cathedrals and atomic accelerators are cultural expressions of faith in the existence of such an order.

In Robert Suchner's (1987) analysis of data from three national surveys (conducted in 1978, 1983, and 1985) of more than 5400 undergraduates, the effects of students' religious beliefs on their general interest in science and technology were studied. Suchner found that, compared with "fundamentalists" (those who strongly agreed with the statements "I believe there is a God who can and has personally intervened in the lives of men and women" and "I believe that the Bible is literally true, and we should believe everything it says") and "theists" (those who agreed with the former statement but not the latter), agnostics were more likely to be attentive to recent scientific and technological developments.

There seems to be some incongruity between American society's need for religious morality and its need for scientific and technological development. Consider the responses to the following query, which was included in the 1988 NORC General Social Survey:

**Here are some things that have been said about science. Would you tell me if you agree or disagree with them: One of the effects of science is that it breaks down people's ideas of right and wrong.**

One-third of the respondents agreed with this statement, including 37 percent of Protestants, 29 percent of Catholics, and only 3 percent of Jews.

The "Total" row of Table 14.4 shows that strongly religious individuals are 38 percent ( = 40 percent/29 percent) more likely to agree with the idea that science erodes morality than those who are not very religious. The "Total" column shows that those with less than a high school education are four times more likely ( = 49 percent/12 percent) to agree than individuals with four or more years of college.

By examining the rows within the table, one can see that, with the exception of those with more than a high school education but less than four years of college, the higher the level of education, the greater the differences between

**TABLE 14.4   Percent Agreeing That Science Breaks Down Morality**

| Education | Intensity of Religious Beliefs | | | |
|---|---|---|---|---|
| | Strong | Somewhat | Not Very | Total |
| 0–11 years | 58 | 40 | 48 | 49 |
| High school graduate | 42 | 40 | 30 | 36 |
| Some college | 32 | 36 | 33 | 26 |
| 4 + years college | 22 | 7 | 9 | 12 |
| Total | 40 | 33 | 29 | 33 |

Source: NORC, 1988.

strongly religious individuals and those who are not very religious. Among those with less than a high school education, strongly religious individuals are 21 percent more likely than those who are not very religious to believe that science erodes morality; among those with four or more years of college this difference increases to 144 percent.

The damping effect of education on the influence of religion (particularly for those who are not strongly religious) underlies debates about **secular humanism** (Mills 1952). From the perspective of fundamentalists, humanists' faith in scientific knowledge and human experience—which is a central doctrine of the American educational system—leads to denial of the existence of absolute moral values, God, and supernatural guarantees of human values (MacKay-Smith 1985).

## Religion as an Emotional System

Religion is a potent eliciter of emotions. This is due in part to its ability to evoke the powerful feelings associated with morality, fear of death, and hope of redemption (Campbell 1987:74). It is also due to the ability of religious institutions to intensify these sentiments through ceremony and religious revivalism.

In *Civilization and Its Discontents,* Sigmund Freud explored the relationship between religion and guilt. He hypothesized that religious feeling stems from the interplay among ego, id, and superego: "The superego torments the sinful ego with the same feeling of anxiety and is on the watch for opportunities of getting it punished by the external world" (1962[1930]:81). Gaylin (1979:66) notes evidence of this in the Bible, wherein social obligation and guilt are central themes, with the Old Testament stressing duty and responsibility and the New Testament emphasizing guilt.

But if religion delivers only the feeling of guilt and provides no compensating satisfactions to those who observe its moral dictates—except, perhaps, the alleviation of guilt—why believe? If, as Freud claimed, social life prevents happiness, and if religion buffers the tensions between self and society, would it not seem reasonable to expect that religion contributes to the American goal of "pursuit of happiness"?

According to the 1989 NORC General Social Survey, there is a weak positive relationship between intensity of religious belief and the likelihood that individuals will describe themselves as "very happy." Among Protestants, for instance, 42 percent of those who describe themselves to be "very religious" were very happy, compared with 38 percent of those who are "somewhat religious" and 28 percent of those who are "not very" religious. In the "Total" column of the upper portion of Table 14.5, when compared with very religious people, those who are not very religious are nearly three-quarters more likely to report being "not too happy," the most negative category coded by NORC, and those without a religious affiliation are 150 percent more likely to report that they are not very happy.

When one controls for social class, the effects become more pronounced. As shown in the "Total" row, self-reported unhappiness decreases the higher one is in the status hierarchy, from 30 percent of those in the lower class to only 3 percent of those in the upper classes. For the lower classes, the level of reported happiness is higher among strongly religious individuals. For instance, among members of the working class, those with no religious affiliation

**TABLE 14.5   Self-Reported Happiness, by Religiosity and Social Class**

### Percent "Not Too Happy"

| Religious Intensity | Social Class | | | | Total |
|---|---|---|---|---|---|
| | Lower | Working | Middle | Upper | |
| Strong | 27 | 7 | 5 | 5 | 7 |
| Somewhat | 37 | 7 | 2 | 0 | 5 |
| Not very | 29 | 13 | 10 | 4 | 12 |
| None | 37 | 24 | 10 | — | 18 |
| Total | 30 | 11 | 7 | 3 | 10 |
| N | 76 | 648 | 735 | 60 | 1519 |

### Percent Who Find Life "Dull" (vs. Exciting or Routine)

| Religious Intensity | Age | | | | | | Total |
|---|---|---|---|---|---|---|---|
| | 18–29 | 30–39 | 40–49 | 50–59 | 60–69 | 70+ | |
| Strong | 0 | 2 | 4 | 4 | 1 | 12 | 4 |
| Somewhat | 4 | 3 | 8 | 6 | 5 | 0 | 4 |
| Not very | 5 | 6 | 1 | 7 | 10 | 14 | 6 |
| None | 8 | 5 | 15 | — | 20 | 17 | 10 |
| Total | 4 | 4 | 4 | 5 | 6 | 11 | 5 |

Source: NORC, 1989.

are more than three times as likely to report not being happy as those who are strongly religious.

When respondents are asked whether they find life exciting, routine, or dull, those without any religious affiliation are more than two-and-one-half times more likely to say that life is dull. Looking at this relationship within various age categories, we find that the effect is considerably more pronounced among people between the ages of 60 and 69 years: Those with no religion and those who are not very religious are, respectively, twenty and ten times more likely to find life dull than those who are strongly religious.

***The Social Psychology of the Confessional.***   As the old saying goes, "Confession is good for the soul." The sacrament of penance and, more specifically, the confession of sins have long played a major role in the devotional life of Catholics. As Mike Hepworth and Bryan Turner observe:

> The history of confession in Christianity involved a progression from infrequent, voluntary, public acts to confession as regular, obligatory, and private. In the early Church, confession was offered only once in a person's lifetime, but by the eighth century Christians were expected to confess to their sins at fixed times throughout the year, and by the end of the twelfth century, regular confession at appointed times throughout the year and confession of all major sins became a legally enforced requirement. (1982:41).

Charismatic religious leaders understand the emotional buttons to push to mobilize pro-theocratic mass movements. In the late 1970s, reacting against the perceived corrupting influences of the Western materialism, Ayatollah Ruhollah Khomeini overthrew the secular regime of Shah Muhammed Riza Pahlevi and replaced it with an Islamic state.

By making confessions mandatory the Church was able to further increase its power over its members.

As we saw in Chapter 6, confession has therapeutic value: People who admit their deviant behavior, and are forgiven, feel better both mentally and physically. This effect has long been known to religious authorities. The New Testament contains the line "Confess your sins to one another, and pray for one another, and then you will be healed" (James 16). With this view of confession, physical health becomes a matter of spiritual well-being. Confession also plays a major role in justifying and maintaining the moral order. The intense

## Religion as the Opiate of the People

"Religion is the sign of the oppressed creature," wrote Karl Marx, "the spirit of unspiritual conditions. It is the *Opium des Volkes*—the opiate of the people."

Opium at that time in Germany was known mostly as a painkiller; Marx's point was that religion deceptively eased the painful symptoms of the exploitation of labor by capital.

To bring on the revolution, religion's succor had to be removed, allowing the working class to suffer until the pain was intolerable; at that point, the permanent cure would come from Communism. Marx made that a top priority: "The first requisite for the people's happiness is the abolition of religion."

Lenin adopted that doctrine as the new gospel, and condemned any party members for what he derided as a dangerous "flirtation with God.". . .

The education of Moscow's atheists is under way. Under the Gorbachev policy of glasnost, "controlled openness," letters from Russians have begun to appear in the Soviet press like this: "Unless you [the authorities] stop fighting religion there will be no end to alcoholism."

That hits home because vodka has become the spirit of unspiritual conditions. In the Soviet Union, drunkenness is more than ever a way of life, causing absenteeism at the factory and erosion of family ties. . . . People drink to excess to escape life's oppressions, boredoms, responsibilities. In the Soviet Union, where Communism turned out to be the God that failed to put bread on the table, booze is the pervasive opiate of the people, used to cope with the pain of living in a world of constant constraint. . . .

A gulf exists between the escape of drunkenness and the engagement of religious commitment. One dulls, the other sensitizes; one runs away, the other runs toward; one wallows in despair, the other is inspired by hope.

---

Source: Safire, 1986.

feelings of guilt and remorse provide ample evidence of the costs of moral transgressions, legitimating religion's conceptions of proper behavior and belief. Because those who confess feel better afterward, religion's power over moral matters is reaffirmed.

## Religion as a Belief System

As mentioned earlier, the central beliefs of religious systems are that humanity has a divine purpose and that the injustices and sufferings in this world have a reason. In this section we explore these and other religious beliefs and see how they persist despite the fact that they are unverifiable or have even been disconfirmed.

***Belief in the Legitimacy of Status Hierarchies.*** Marxists view religion as an ideological system of oppression (Marx and Engels 1964). In an attempt to legitimate the existing social and political orders, gods are attributed powers that are actually created by humans (Giddens 1971:205). Instead of paying attention toward the miseries of this world (and rebelling against their condition, people are diverted by the "opiate" of promises of fulfillment in the hereafter. From this perspective, religion is an obstacle to social change. While Marx believed that religious doctrines were byproducts of social structure and history (Küng 1980:239), Lenin viewed them as an insidious ruling-class plot:

> Marxism has always regarded all modern religions and churches and all religious organizations as instruments of bourgeois reaction that serve to defend the exploitation and to drug the working class. (1905[1939]:664)

If oppressed workers were to achieve class consciousness, they must be freed from religion's ideological grip.

To test this "opiate of the masses" thesis, consider lifespan patterns of belief in life after death, broken down by the key dimensions of stratification developed in Chapter 10. These are presented in Figure 14.5.

If Marx was correct, one would expect that the percentages of respondents believing in life after death would decrease with increasing education and higher status in the social hierarchy. Part *a* of the figure shows that education's effect is generally minimal. In nearly all age groups, those with the least education are the least likely to believe in life after death. Among people age 70 and older, we find the greatest convergence among the four educational groups.

Turning to respondent's social class (the "upper class" category was deleted for lack of cases), in part *b* of the figure we again see no trend indicating that members of the lower classes are more likely to be believers.

On the other hand, other dimensions of social stratification do produce the relationship between oppression and religiosity predicted by Marxists. Studies consistently report that women are more religious than men and are more likely to strongly adhere to orthodox religious beliefs. And when compared to whites, African Americans are more likely to hold traditional religious beliefs, to feel more strongly about their religious tenets, to attend religious services, and to report having had religious experiences (Batson and Ventis 1982:40–41).

***Persistence of Beliefs Despite Disconfirming Evidence.*** In early 1990 at least two thousand members of the Church Universal and Triumphant followed Elizabeth Clare Prophet into an underground system of concrete and steel shelters in Montana. Believing that a nuclear Armageddon was imminent, they had sold their homes, closed out their bank accounts, and said their farewells (Egan 1990). The "dangerous period" of March and April passed uneventfully, yet, as is often the case when apocalyptic prophecies fail, the believers' faith was unshaken.

To disbelieving outsiders, the persistence of loyalty to fragile unconventional beliefs is baffling. To explain this phenomenon, David Snow and Richard Machalek (1982) argue that individuals are more inclined to believe than to disbelieve. They note that belief systems can vary in empirical relevance (testability) and degree of systematization (the extent to which their tenets are

## Belief in Life after Death, by Education and Age

Percent Believing in Life After Death

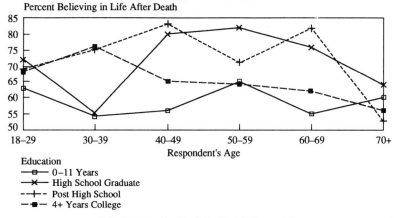

Education
- —□— 0–11 Years
- —×— High School Graduate
- - -+- - Post High School
- —■— 4+ Years College

## Belief in Life after Death, by Social Class and Age

Percent Believing in Life After Death

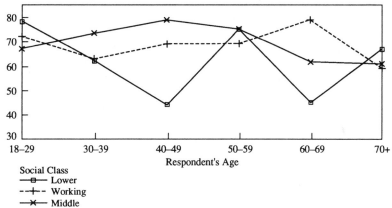

Social Class
- —□— Lower
- - -+- - Working
- —×— Middle

## Belief in Life after Death, by Race, Gender, and Age

Percent Believing in Life After Death

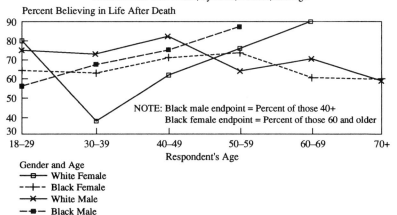

NOTE: Black male endpoint = Percent of those 40+
Black female endpoint = Percent of those 60 and older

Gender and Age
- —□— White Female
- - -+- - Black Female
- —×— White Male
- —■— Black Male

**FIGURE 14.5   Belief in Life after Death**
Source: NORC, 1989.

logically interconnected). Least vulnerable to disconfirmation are beliefs characterized by low empirical relevance and low systematization, such as the tenets of many apocalyptic movements.

Faith in doomsday prophecies can persist despite evidence of their inaccuracy because many empirically nonrelevant beliefs can always be employed to explain the inconsistency: God changed the schedule; we misinterpreted the signs; our collective prayers and love for others postponed the event. Cognitive dissonance does not occur because members of the movement "simply failed to absorb the fact that [their] beliefs were being challenged" (Snow and Machalek 1982:23).

***Religious Mind Control.*** Cults like Hare Krishna, the Unification Church, and the Children of God have been accused of "brainwashing" their members. Cult members have been described as losing "the ability to reason independently because of subjugation to a cult's sophisticated coercive persuasion techniques" (Rudin and Rudin 1980:A35).

Such charges undoubtedly are related to the characteristics of the people attracted to these movements. Instead of being victims of some social or psychological pathology, people who join cults are likely to be white, well-educated, unmarried young adults from affluent and stable families (Levine 1986). How can we explain why such individuals are attracted to cults, which are so radically different from the social milieu to which they are accustomed? The idea of mind control is often suggested as a possible reason, but two alternatives were discussed in Chapter 3: Either people are uncomfortable with a maximum of freedom and the personal responsibilities it entails, or individuals are attracted to belief systems that impose order on the scattered events of their lives (a need that may increase with education).

Edward and Anne Wimberly note that the "very nature of divine encounter demand[s] that no area of the person's thought process and behavior be left untouched. . . . This includes changes in loyalties and commitments, lifestyle, attitudes, behavior, and service" (1986:93). In their extreme form, cults dictate when one is to get up in the morning, when to sleep, what to wear, and even when married couples can have sex. Why do individuals voluntarily commit themselves to such regimens?

In his study of young Americans' attraction to Eastern religions, Harvey Cox (1977) argues that those faiths provide frameworks that give certainty and meaningfulness to a world of uncertainty and doubt. Levine's (1986) "radical departers" were often deficient in self-esteem and had little commitment to any value system. Fearing the responsibility of making the moral choices required upon entering adulthood (most were 18–26 years of age), they long for moral absolutes and are willing to submit to an authority figure who will make their decisions for them.

Secular responses to the alleged thought control exercised by cults include psychological countermeasures undertaken by friends and relatives of initiates; of these, the most frequently used is religious "deprogramming." Thomas Robbins (1988:212) has distinguished among three forms of deprogramming: voluntary, extralegal coercive (involving abduction of the cult member by parents or professionals hired by parents), and legal deprogramming, which occurs under the sanction of a court order.

# Religion as a Temporal System

Religious belief and ritual are largely temporal (Brandon 1966). Religious time is opposed to profane time, which entails wear-and-tear, decay, and death. The time frame of ultimate existence and of moral truths is entirely separate from worldly time. From the perspective of **sacred time,** death becomes a transition instead of an ending, and the activities of all human generations can be seen as one long chain of meaningful being (Baum 1982).

Our individual endeavors, as well as those of our ancestors and successors, are unrelated discrete events, much like the separate notes of music, unless there is an overarching frame of reference to integrate them into a harmonious whole. Part of religion's role is to give this broader temporal perspective to everyday life, to give a sense of coherence and comprehensibility to both personal and social experiences, and to place generations now alive in context of those dead and those yet to be born. An example is the Iroquoian priority of doing everything for the seventh generation. To allow the heroics of the past to be continuously part of the present, sacred time collapses the past, present, and future into an eternal now. Such symbolic representations of continuity are deeply woven religious symbolism (Bellah 1964). And it is for this reason that strongly religious people were the first great historians (Innis 1951:67–68).

One legacy of early Christianity is the linear conception of time, from which such ideas as "progress" and evolution evolved. As Richard Morris pointed out:

> The early Christian writers stressed the importance of individual historical events that would not be repeated. History, they said, did not move in cycles. On the contrary, there had been a Creation at a particular point in time. Christ had died on the Cross but once, and had been resurrected from the dead on but one occasion. Finally, at some point in the future, God's plan would be completed, and He would—once and for all—bring the world to an end. (1985:11)

# Western Religion and Sexual Behavior

In attempting to establish the divinity of humans and elevate them above all other animals, religion had to deal with humanity's similarities to other animals. Among other things, sexuality had to be endowed with religious significance. The sex act had to be given some meaning other than sheer genital pleasure; sexual passion, like other worldly pleasures, must be reduced if otherworldly insights are to be obtained. To channel sexual urges into socially functional outlets, very explicit and severe constraints were imposed. Many of these constraints have their roots in the Hebrew tradition from which Christianity evolved.

In the Books of Genesis, Exodus, and Leviticus, sexuality was depicted in religious terms, with the concept of sexuality itself being derived from the portrayal of Adam and Eve being evicted from the Garden of Eden. Before she ate the apple from the tree of knowledge, Eve was the "help meet" of Adam, and the two were "not ashamed" of their nakedness. But after the serpent tricked

Eve into eating the apple and she convinced Adam to do the same, they "opened their eyes" and became ashamed of their nudity. God condemned women to the sorrows of childbirth and subjugation to the rule of their husbands; both men and women were exiled from the Garden. The Hebraic conception of sexuality was introduced in the Ten Commandments of the Book of Exodus, which linked sexuality directly to the male-dominated husband-wife bond.

A positive stance toward procreative sexuality is contained in the injunction to "be fruitful and multiply" (Genesis 1:28). In succeeding books, all forms of sexuality outside of marriage and not leading to procreation were severely condemned and punishable, most frequently by death (Leviticus 18–20). Adultery is strongly condemned, with death prescribed as the penalty for both participants. Incest in any of its many possible forms was also condemned as sin, wickedness, and iniquity.

Male homosexuality was singled out with a special term of condemnation, *abomination*. Although the word *sodomy* has come to be associated with male homosexuality, the actual Biblical references to the destruction of the cities of Sodom and Gomorrah deal more with pride, unkindness to the needy, and unspecified "abominations" (which have variously been interpreted as referring to worshiping of idols, to general corruption, and only obliquely to homosexuality) (Bullough 1976:82–86).

Bestiality was explicitly condemned: "Neither shalt thou lie with any beast to defile thyself therewith; neither shall any woman stand before a beast to lie down thereto: it *is* confusion" (Leviticus 18:23). In addition, cross-dressing was prohibited for both men and women. Masturbation was prohibited in terms of a man "spilling his seed" (as in the story of Onan [Genesis 38:7–10], who actually withdrew before ejaculating when ordered by his father to have intercourse with his dead brother's wife so that she could bear a child). Prostitution of one's daughter was prohibited "lest the land fall to whoredom and the land become full of wickedness" (Leviticus 20:20). Finally, intercourse during a woman's menstrual period (when she is "put apart for her uncleanness") was forbidden; the punishment for violations of this rule was not death, but it was quite severe: "both of them shall be cut off from among their people" (Leviticus 18:21; 20:18).

Taken together, these assumptions and prohibitions reveal a very male-oriented religion, focused on preserving and strengthening the conjugal family (containing as many as four wives) but with a highly ambiguous attitude toward women. Not only was Eve depicted as having led Adam astray, but throughout the Old Testament women and their sexuality are a source of great trouble for men: Lot's daughter plotted incest; Delilah destroyed Samson's strength; Jezebel's name has become synonymous with enticement of men into evil ways; and so forth (Bullough 1976:76). This code of sexual mores that developed so long ago in Israel has had an immense influence during the intervening 3000 years, not only on the Jews but also on the Christian heritage that grew from the ancient Hebraic traditions.

To better understand the impact of religion on contemporary attitudes toward sexual morality, consider the following questions from the 1989 NORC survey:

**If a man and woman have sexual relations before marriage, do you think it is always wrong, almost always wrong, wrong only sometimes, or not wrong at all?**
(always wrong = 27 percent; not wrong at all = 39 percent)

**TABLE 14.6** Religion and Intensity of Faith by Attitudes toward the Morality of Premarital Sex and Homosexuality

| | Intensity of Religious Belief: | Percent Saying Premarital Sex Is "Always Wrong" | | | | Percent Saying Homosexuality Is "Always Wrong" | | | |
|---|---|---|---|---|---|---|---|---|---|
| | | Strong | Some-what | Not Very | Total | Strong | Some-what | Not Very | Total |
| Religious Affiliation | Protestant | 50 | 30 | 17 | 34 | 84 | 73 | 73 | 78 |
| | Fundamentalist | 64 | 30 | 18 | 44 | 92 | 81 | 82 | 87 |
| | Moderate | 33 | 50 | 9 | 23 | 73 | 71 | 64 | 69 |
| | Liberal | 25 | 23 | 20 | 22 | 71 | 71 | 66 | 68 |
| | Catholic | 24 | 14 | 19 | 20 | 77 | 73 | 74 | 75 |
| | Jewish* | | | | 8 | | | | 37 |
| | None | | | | 10 | | | | 43 |

*Not broken down due to scarcity of cases.
Source: NORC, 1989.

**What about sexual relations between two adults of the same sex**—do you think it is always wrong, almost always wrong, wrong only sometimes, or not wrong at all? (always wrong = 70 percent; not wrong at all = 15 percent)

As shown in the "Total" column of Table 14.6, Protestants are 70 percent more likely than Catholics (34 percent/20 percent), four times more likely than Jews, and over three times more likely than people with no religious affiliation to claim that the practice is "always wrong." When the Protestants are broken down into fundamentalist, moderate, and liberal denominations, it is apparent that this relatively high rate of condemnation comes from the fundamentalists. As religiosity weakens, the most dramatic declines in the percentages of Protestants viewing premarital sex as always wrong occur among the fundamentalists and moderates, among whom the strongly religious are over three-and-one-half times more likely than the not very religious to condemn the practice.

The question about homosexuality produces deep splits between Protestants and Catholics on the one hand and Jews and people with no religion on the other; the latter are approximately half as likely as the former to say that the practice is "always wrong." Moreover, among Protestants and Catholics intensity of religious belief produces little difference in the rate of condemnation of homosexuality.

## RELIGION AND THE SELF

In addition to providing a sense of coherence, religion also provides a referent by which the self is understood. Thus, the forms that bureaucracies require us to fill out, in addition to our name, sex, race, education, and age, include our religious affiliation. In this section we pursue further the role of religion in creating and maintaining individual identity.

# Religion and Gender Identity

Fundamentalist faiths generally attempt to preserve family systems and traditional sex roles. Islam requires women to cover their faces; the Mormon church excommunicated a woman for supporting the Equal Rights Amendment; Orthodox Jews forbid women to carry the Torah scroll or to don a prayer shawl. For American Protestant fundamentalists, the large-scale entry of women into the labor force during the 1970s and 1980s was a dangerous trend. The Rev. Jerry Falwell viewed the trend as producing a cultural orientation toward androgyny, violating divinely ordained conditions that are "intimately woven in the overall fabric of personality" (cited in Wilentz 1988).

To investigate the relationship between religion and advocacy of the traditional role of women, we return to Americans' reactions to the following question:

**Do you agree or disagree with this statement? Women should take care of running their homes and leave running the country up to men.**

In the "Total" column of Table 14.7 we note that strongly religious individuals are at least one-third more likely to concur with the statement than people with less intense religious feelings, and over three times more likely to do so than people with no religious affiliation. Interesting differences appear when one controls for gender and religion. Among men with a religious affiliation, intensity of faith produces virtually no difference in their rate of concurrence with the statement. While "somewhat religious" Catholic women are about half as likely to agree that a woman's place is in the home as when compared to their "strongly" and "not very" religious counterparts, strongly religious Protestant women are nearly three times more likely to agree.

# Ethnoreligion

American churches have historically served as guides to cultural assimilation and as preservers of cultural identity and history. Herberg (1955) argues that, for whites, religious boundaries replaced those of national origin as the basis

TABLE 14.7  Percentage of Americans Agreeing That Women's Place Is at Home, by Gender, Religion, and Religiosity

| Religious Intensity | Gender | | Religion | | Protestant | | Catholic | | Total |
|---|---|---|---|---|---|---|---|---|---|
| | Men | Women | Protestant | Catholic | Men | Women | Men | Women | |
| Strong | 25 | 25 | 27 | 19 | 25 | 28 | 20 | 18 | 24 |
| Somewhat | 23 | 11 | 16 | 11 | 25 | 11 | 15 | 8 | 15 |
| Not very | 24 | 12 | 16 | 22 | 22 | 10 | 30 | 14 | 18 |
| None | 13 | 0 | | | | | | | 7 |

Source: NORC, 1989.

for ethnic differentiation in the United States. As recently as the 1950s, there were nearly two dozen Lutheran denominations, sharing the same doctrine but divided by Swedish, German, Finnish, Danish, and Norwegian backgrounds. As these groups became assimilated into American culture, their religious affiliations lost their distinctiveness and eventually merged.

In their own churches, immigrant groups hear services in their native language. The churches help newcomers acquire a sense of dignity and self-fulfillment that might not be obtained in the churches of the majority culture. In the words of a Korean member of the Oriental Mission Church in Los Angeles:

> America helped us, and now we have the obligation to another country. We have started a mission in Mexico. We will be like the first missionaries to Korea. We will send people to seminary and music school, so they can help themselves. We have to do something for this land. (Vecsey 1977).

Perhaps in no instance is this role of **ethnoreligion** clearer than in the case of the black church, as can be seen in a 1969 statement on black theology:

> Black people affirm their being. This affirmation is made in the whole experience of being black in the hostile American society. Black theology is not a gift of the Christian gospel dispensed to slaves; rather it is an appropriation which black slaves made of the gospel given by their white oppressors. Black theology has been nurtured, sustained and passed on in the Black churches in their various ways of expression. Black theology has dealt with all the ultimate and violent issues of life and death for a people despised and degraded. (Committee on Theological Prospectus 1969)

## Religious Conversion

Probably the most often studied aspect of religion's effect on the self is the phenomenon of conversion. Conversion may be defined as reorientation of self that is not due to maturation (Spilka, Hood, and Gorsuch 1985); the self is replaced by a "higher" other, leading to dramatic changes in central personal values (Lang and Lang 1961:153), actions (Shibutani 1961:523), interests, and beliefs. As William James put it, "To say a man is 'converted' means . . . that religious ideas, peripheral in his consciousness, now take a central place, and that religious aims form the habitual center of his energy" (1902:196). James found that the people who are most likely to have such an experience are those who previously felt an overwhelming sense of meaninglessness, who had lost sight of who they were and where they were going.

David Snow and Richard Machalek (1983) have identified four formal properties of conversion:

**Biographical reconstruction:** The scattered episodes of one's biography are reintegrated within the framework of one's new "enlightened" identity; the former self is denigrated.

**Short-circuiting of the attribution process:** In place of the various causal attributions one makes to account for the behaviors of self and others (see Chapter 4), a single schema comes to be employed. The resulting attributions typically involve an internal locus of control.

**Suspension of analogical reasoning:** The uniqueness of converts' spiritual claims disallows comparison with any other belief system. As a result, their worldview is removed from competition with all others.

**Embracement of master role:** The role of convert is generalized, not merely superseding but replacing the myriad of major and minor roles that previously defined the self.

Americans typically do not have the language to capture and convey the full significance of a religious conversion. One label that has entered everyday speech is "born again." Related to conversion, the phenomenon being born refers to a major reaffirmation of commitment. In 1988, NORC surveyors asked Americans "Would you say you have been 'born again' or have had a 'born again' experience—that is, a turning point in your life when you committed yourself to Christ?" Thirty-seven percent of respondents claimed to have had such an experience. Fundamentalist Protestants were considerably more likely to have had such an experience (66 percent) than moderate (37 percent) or liberal (29 percent) Protestants or Catholics (15 percent). As can be seen in Table 14.8, increasing education and weakening of intensity of religious belief dampen the likelihood of born again experiences. Among the most educated (those with four or more years of college), the strongly religious are three times more likely to have the experience than those "not very" religious.

As Snow and Machalek noted, some major changes in cognition and values occur with such a religious experience. For instance, consider responses to the statement "Right or wrong are not usually a simple matter of black and white; there are many shades of gray." In general, only 15 percent of Americans disagreed with this statement, according to the 1988 NORC survey. However, as can be seen in the "Total" column of Table 14.9, people who have had a "born again" experience are nearly three times as likely to disagree with the statement, in other words, right and wrong are understood to be matters of black and white. Similarly, the "Total" row indicates that strongly religious individuals are more than twice as likely to disagree than those with weaker religious commitment. Considering these two variables together, strongly religious "born agains" are more than four times as likely to understand the world in terms of moral absolutes than people who are somewhat or not very religious and who have not had a "born again" experience. These individuals, predomi-

**TABLE 14.8  Education and Intensity of Religious Belief, by Having Had a "Born Again" Experience (Percent having had a "born again" experience)**

| Education | Intensity of Religious Beliefs | | | | |
| --- | --- | --- | --- | --- | --- |
| | Strong | Somewhat | Not Very | None | Total |
| 0–11 years | 66% | 47% | 34% | 38% | 45% |
| High school graduate | 59 | 34 | 21 | 42 | 38 |
| Some college | 56 | 23 | 27 | 35 | 35 |
| 4+ years college | 42 | 23 | 14 | 42 | 26 |
| Total | 57% | 32% | 25% | 39% | 37% |

Source: NORC, 1988.

**TABLE 14.9**   Moral Absolutism, by Having Had a "Born Again" Experience (Percent disagreeing that "there are many shades of gray")

| | Intensity of Religious Beliefs | | | | |
|---|---|---|---|---|---|
| | *Strong* | *Somewhat* | *Not Very* | *None* | *Total* |
| Had "born again" experience | 33% | 22% | 20% | 13% | 26% |
| Have not had "born again" experience | 13 | 6 | 8 | 11 | 9 |
| Total | 25% | 11% | 10% | 12% | 15% |

Source: NORC ,1988.

nantly white evangelicals and fundamentalists, provided much of the overwhelming vote in favor of Ronald Reagan during the 1984 presidential election and are attracted to organizations like Moral Majority.

## Leaving the Fold

Just as dramatic as conversion experiences are efforts to disengage from religious organizations. Saul Levine (1986) estimated that 90 percent of cult joiners return to the broader society within two years. Even more socially "acceptable" conversions to mainstream religious movements are often short-lived and tenuous (Johnson 1971).

For those who were strongly committed, disengagement can produce an experience of decompression that may be as severe psychologically as the "bends" are physically. There have been reports of a "cult withdrawal syndrome" featuring nightmares, hallucinations, amnesia, inability to break out of the mental rhythms of chanting, loss of emotional control, and self-destructive behaviors (Conway and Siegelman 1982). Such symptoms, however, may also be a function of deprogramming, since they are five times more prevalent among those receiving involuntary counseling than among those who had voluntarily left a religious group (Lewis and Bromley 1987).

When comparing the recollections of those who left cults voluntarily as opposed to being deprogrammed, Lewis (1989) found that those who had left voluntarily remembered their religious affiliation as a growth experience. The deprogrammed group, seeking to disavow personal responsibility for deciding to join, recalled the experience as an unhappy affair involving deception and brainwashing.

## GROUP STRUCTURES OF RELIGIOUS BELIEVERS

Social scientists have placed religious groups along a continuum that ranges from relatively unorganized social movements to highly structured institutional systems (Stark and Bainbridge 1979); as follows:

As one moves from left to right along this continuum, one goes from groups inducing impassioned spontaneity to groups characterized by routinized feelings and action, from groups with restricted membership requiring uncompromising commitment to groups with open membership and relatively weak commitment requirements (Weber 1958[1904]), and from groups that are hostile toward their environment to those that are increasingly accommodating toward the larger society.

At one extreme are religious cults, whose members focus on the specific beliefs of the group's charismatic founder. In exchange for the communal experiences of a primary group, cults demand extreme conformity and exert total control over their members' behavior. They induce anxiety through their heavy demands, an anxiety that can be relieved only by the group itself (Galanter 1989). If such groups are to survive the death of their leaders, they must become increasingly routinized.

Though in many ways similar to cults, sects typically grow out of established churches. They too feature charismatic leadership and a strong sense of identity, have few distinctions between clergy and laity, and make exclusive claims to knowledge of supernatural truths (Johnson 1963). The energy of such a group is often derived from hostility toward what is perceived as a corrupt world filled with threatening out-groups. Energy is also derived from the intense emotional experiences induced by rituals. Consider the Penitentes of northern New Mexico, who have been known to ritually sacrifice members on a cross (Weigle 1970; Henderson 1977). For the individual who gives up his life for the group, such sacrifice is the noblest possible act.

As we move further along the continuum, we pass through the fundamentalist and orthodox denominations of organized religions, which require literal interpretations of scripture and have a militant attitude toward nonbelievers. At the extreme right are the liberal churches, which, to accommodate the broader society, allow the greatest flexibility in scriptural interpretation, make the fewest demands on their members, and are least exclusive in the acceptance of new members (Demerath and Hammond 1969).

## Intensity of In-group/Out-group Dynamics

Claims of moral superiority and exclusiveness produce the most intense in-group/out-group dynamics known. Throughout the world, most organized killing occurs between absolutist religious groups. In the last part of the twentieth century, such killing occurred between Moslems and Jews in the Middle East, Catholics and Protestants in Northern Ireland, Hindus and Moslems in India, Christians and Moslems in Armenia and Beirut, Sunnis and Shiites in the Persian Gulf, and Hindus and Buddhists in Ceylon. According to Ernest Lefever:

> There are certain periods of history when religious wars spring up, and a new one began in the middle 1960s when religious groups—partly because of modern communications—became more aware of their distinct identities. Religious wars have been among the bloodiest fought because "if you feel God is on your side, you can justify any atrocity." (quoted in Maloney 1984)

**TABLE 14.10   Economic Inequalities in the Arabic World**

| "Haves" | Gross National Product per Capita | Population (in millions) |
|---|---|---|
| United Arab Emirates | $15,720 | 1.5 |
| Kuwait | 13,680 | 2.0 |
| Qatar | 11,610 | .4 |
| Bahrain | 6,610 | .5 |
| Saudi Arabia | 6,170 | 14.0 |
| Oman | 5,070 | 1.4 |
| **"Have-Nots"** | | |
| Algeria | 2,450 | 23.9 |
| Iraq | 1,950 | 17.7 |
| Syria | 1,670 | 11.7 |
| Jordan | 1,500 | 4.0 |
| Tunisia | 1,230 | 7.8 |
| Morocco | 750 | 23.8 |
| Egypt | 650 | 51.5 |
| Yemen | 600 | 11.0 |

Source: *U.S. News & World Report,* 1990 (data from World Bank and CIA).

Such militancy often occurs when religion is bound up with class struggles, racial or ethnic differences, and/or nationalism. For instance, underlying the conflict between the Sunnites and Shiites in the Persian Gulf and Iraq's 1990 attack on Kuwait were the inequities reported in Table 14.10, which shows that the per capita gross national product of the richest nation was more than twenty-six times that of the poorest.

The death of members of a religious group at the hands of members of another group produces martyrs, leading to an escalation of violence between the two groups. Martyrs are long remembered. Violence broke out in Northern Ireland in 1986 when Catholic mobs attacked Protestants who were marching in anniversary observances of the 1690 victory of King William of Orange over Catholic forces, led by the deposed Stuart King James II, at the Battle of the Boyne River. Similarly, blaming of the Jews for the death of Christ led to 2,000 years of anti-Semitism. In 1987, the United Church of Christ became the first major Protestant denomination in the United States to declare that "God has not rejected the Jewish people" (Goldman 1987).

# INDIVIDUALISM AND THE SOCIAL PSYCHOLOGY OF RELIGION

The Protestant Reformation involved a shift from reliance on the structure of the church to emphasis on the individual (Weber 1904). David McClelland (1955) noted that Protestant parents, wishing to prepare their children for the responsibility of seeking their own salvation, stressed independence training

## Dangers Associated with Individualism

In the past, the dark side of individualism was constrained by society's institutions, like the small town where people knew and helped each other. But because of the enormous social changes that have taken place in the last one hundred years, there are now fewer constraints on individualism. In a sense, it has been allowed to run rampant.

At every level, people learn patterns of reward and advancement that focus on their own individual achievement. Career patterns take the middle class out of the place in which they were born—frequently far from their family and relatives. They go to universities, where many of them learn that the things they were taught in Sunday school are not necessarily true.

Our society makes it harder and harder to maintain tight-knit families, small-town environments, and other social contexts that can provide support, reinforcement, and a moral meaning for individuals—contexts in which they can see that everybody is working for the common good.

Psychology has played a role in this. The language of therapy tends to emphasize almost exclusively the needs, interests, feelings, and wishes of the individual and not those of the broader society. Even commitments to others and to community are evaluated in terms of their payoff in personal gratification. . . . Today there's a deep sense in our culture that if you don't reach the pinnacle of radical freedom and control, you haven't validated yourself. . . .

Another part of the picture is that the balance between doubt and belief has gone awry. Doubt makes sense only if one also believes. If you don't believe anything, then the doubt is just nihilism. . . . When the high intellectual culture becomes one of criticism, dissent, and doubt, it doesn't play the role of what Walter Lippmann called "the public philosophy," which gives people confidence that there's something out there they can count on.

George Orwell once said of modern intellectuals:

"For 200 years we had sawed and sawed and sawed at the branch we were sitting on. And in the end, much more suddenly than anyone had foreseen, our efforts were rewarded—and down we came. But unfortunately there had been a little mistake. The thing at the bottom was not a bed of roses after all; it was a cesspool filled with barbed wire."

Source: Bellah, 1985:69–70.

at increasingly younger ages. The result was a distinctive personality type featuring high achievement orientation and high self-awareness. (See Chapter 8.)

Individualism is typically understood to be the antithesis of religious belief. When, according to Christian myth, Adam and Eve partook from the tree of knowledge in the Garden of Eden, the original sin committed was the creation of individuated consciousness (Harrington 1977:18). As Berger (1969b:45) notes, the literal meaning of *haeresis* is choice—which is something that cannot occur if moral certainty is to prevail. Among the consequences of individualism, according to Michael Harrington (1983), is the creation of a moral vacuum, which in turn may lead to such problems as unrestrained hedonism, totalitarian movements, lack of commitment to future generations, dissolution of moral absolutes, and "substitute religions" based on sex and drugs.

In 1986, in his encyclical "The Lord and Giver of Life," Pope John Paul II warned of the possible consequences of excessive individualism. In particular, he attacked individualism for allowing "taking the lives of human beings even before they are born, or before they reach the natural point of death" (*New York Times* 1986). In this way he linked the ideology of individualism with weakening of the moral order.

To test these ideas, questions pertaining to abortion, suicide, and euthanasia from the 1989 NORC General Social Survey were *factor-analyzed*. This is a statistical technique for analyzing variables that are so highly interrelated that they can all be inferred to measure the same underlying phenomenon. The following questions were found to apply to the same factor:

1. Should it be possible for a pregnant woman to obtain a legal abortion if the woman's health is seriously endangered by the pregnancy?
2. Should it be possible for a pregnant woman to obtain a legal abortion if she became pregnant as a result of rape?
3. Should it be possible for a pregnant woman to obtain a legal abortion if there is a strong chance of a serious defect in the baby?
4. When a person has a disease that cannot be cured, do you think doctors should be allowed by law to end the patient's life by some painless means if the patient and his or her family request it?
5. Do you think a person has the right to end his or her own life if this person has an incurable disease?

Combining these variables into a single scale and correlating it with some of the issues raised by Harrington and Pope John Paul II, we find that people with the most permissive views on these questions are more likely to condone homosexual lifestyles, favor the legalization of marijuana, consider it acceptable for a man and woman to have sexual relations before marriage, disagree that a woman's place is in the home, and not believe in life after death; in addition, they are more likely to be divorced. These correlations hold even when one controls for education and intensity of religious beliefs.

## MOVEMENTS FOR RELIGIOUS REVITALIZATION

Secularization is not a historically linear or culturally inevitable process. Throughout the world we see resurgences of religious faith. Anthony Wallace (1956) proposed that a common pattern underlies all such movements for religious revitalization.

According to Wallace, revitalization movements are triggered when a cultural system becomes disrupted by natural disaster, military defeat, or encounters with a more dominant culture and loses its efficiency and internal integrity. The disruption is first sensed at the individual level, when people discover that their traditional cultural pathways no longer lead to life's desired goals. For instance, the goals themselves may have been altered, as when young Eskimo Aleuts, after absorbing televised images of Southern California life-styles, lose interest in the customs, values, and utopian dreams of their ancestors. As cultural traditions are increasingly questioned, traditional stress-reducing mechanisms begin to fail, producing anomie, alcoholism, and extreme passivity.

Eventually the cultural distortion is experienced at the group level. Rituals lose their potency, and the cultural belief system fails to explain and give order and meaning to social existence. Over time, collective apathy increases.

Such situations call for a new cultural synthesis, a new integration of identities, rituals, and beliefs. The collective sense of dissatisfaction and anomie can lead to cultural extinction unless a charismatic religious leader appears bearing a vision of a new cultural gestalt, a restructuring of a society's elements and subsystems. This new vision must first be experienced at the individual level, causing people to undergo a radical change of identity.

Another condition for a revitalization movement to take hold involves the processes of communication and organization. Revelations and testimonies of the new cultural matrix must be shared. As we saw in Chapters 10 and 11, the communication networks through which the new beliefs are disseminated are determined by the nature and density of interpersonal relationships.

## CONCLUSION

In this chapter we have linked various structures of consciousness with religious processes and groups, showing how individuals are related to the moral order and how the most profound of human emotions are socially manipulated.

Our inquiries into the social-psychological effects of religion do not end here. In the chapters to come we will see how this institution and its associated systems of perception, belief, emotion, and action are interwoven with the institution of work and with the processes of modernization.

## REFERENCES

Ariès, Philippe. 1981. *The hour of our death*. New York: Knopf.

Batson, C. Daniel, and W. Larry Ventis. 1982. *The religious experience: A social-psychological perspective*. New York: Oxford University Press.

Baum, Rainer. 1982. A revised interpretive approach to the religious significance of death in Western societies. *Sociological Analysis* 43 (4):327–350.

Becker, Ernest. 1973. *The denial of death*. New York: Free Press.

Belgum, David. 1963. *Guilt: Where psychology and religion meet*. Englewood Cliffs, NJ: Prentice-Hall.

Bell, Daniel. 1976. *The cultural contradictions of capitalism*. New York: Basic Books.

Bellah, Robert N. 1985, May 27. A conversation with Robert Bellah, "Individualism has been allowed to run rampant" (interview with Alvin Sanoff). *U.S. News & World Report*, pp. 69–70.

Bellah, Robert N. 1970. *Beyond belief*. New York: HarperCollins.

Bellah, Robert N. 1964. Religious evolution. *American Sociological Review* 29:358–374.

Berger, Peter. 1969a. *The sacred canopy: Elements of a sociological theory of religion.* Garden City, NY: Doubleday/Anchor.

Berger, Peter. 1969b. *A rumor of angels: Modern society and the rediscovery of the supernatural.* Garden City, NY: Doubleday/Anchor.

Bertaux, D. 1982. The life course approach as a challenge to the social sciences. In T. K. Haraven and K. J. Adams (eds.), *Aging and life course transitions: An interdisciplinary perspective.* New York: Guilford Press.

Bonomi, Patricia U. 1987. *Under the cope of heaven: Religion, society, and politics in colonial America.* New York: Oxford University Press.

Borhek, James, and Richard Curtis. 1975. *A sociology of belief.* New York: Wiley.

Bozzi, Vincent. 1988, November. A healthy dose of religion. *Psychology Today,* pp. 14–15.

Brandon, S. G. F. 1966. Time and the destiny of man. In J. T. Fraser (ed.), *The voices of time: A cooperative survey of man's views of time as expressed by the sciences and by the humanities.* New York: George Braziller.

Bullough, Vern. 1976. *Sexual variance in society and history.* New York: Wiley.

Campbell, Colin. 1987. *The romantic ethic and the spirit of modern consumerism.* New York: Basil Blackwell.

Clark, E. T. 1929. *The psychology of religious awakening.* New York: Macmillan.

Committee on Theological Prospectus. 1969, June 13. Black theology: A statement of the National Committee of Black Churchmen. Atlanta: Interdenominational Theological Center.

Conway, Flo, and Jim Siegelman. 1982, January. Information disease: Have cults created a new mental illness? *Science Digest,* pp. 86–92.

Cox, Harvey. 1977, July. Eastern cults and Western culture: Why young Americans are buying Oriental religions. *Psychology Today,* pp. 36–42.

Demerath, N. J., III, and Phillip E. Hammond. 1969. *Religion in social context.* New York: Random House.

Dewey, John. 1934. *A common faith.* New Haven, CT: Yale University Press.

Dionne, E. J., Jr. 1984, December 12. Pope says sin "lies with individuals." *New York Times,* p. 3.

Douglas, Mary. 1966. *Purity and danger: An analysis of concepts of pollution and taboo.* London: Routledge and Kegan Paul.

Duncan, Hugh. 1968. *Symbols in society.* New York: Oxford University Press.

Durkheim, Émile. 1965 [1915]. *The elementary forms of the religious life* (trans. Joseph Swain). New York: Free Press.

Egan, Timothy. 1990, March 15. Thousands plan life below, after Doomsday. *New York Times,* pp. A1,A9.

Etzioni, Amitai. 1988. *The moral dimension: Toward a new economics.* New York: Free Press.

Faulkner, Joseph, and Gordon DeJong. 1972. Religiosity in five D. In Joseph E. Faulkner (ed.), *Religion's influence in contemporary society.* Columbus, OH: Bobbs-Merrill.

Freud, Sigmund. 1962 [1930]. *Civilization and its discontents.* New York: W. W. Norton.

Galanter, Marc. 1989. *Cults: Faith, healing, and coercion.* New York: Oxford University Press.

Gallup Poll. 1990, June. More Americans now believe in a power outside themselves. *Gallup Poll Monthly,* pp. 33–38.

Gallup, George, Jr., and Frank Newport. 1990, June. More Americans now believe in a power outside themselves. *Gallup Poll Monthly,* pp. 33–38.

Gaylin, Willard. 1979. *Feelings: Our vital signs.* New York: HarperCollins.

Giddens, Anthony. 1971. *Capitalism and modern social theory.* Cambridge, England: Cambridge University Press.

Glock, Charles Y. 1962, July-August. On the study of religious commitment. *Religious Education,* pp. 98–110.

Goldman, Ari. 1987, July 1. Church affirms validity of Judaism. *New York Times,* p. 8.

Goleman, Daniel. 1988, May 24. Myths bring cohesion to the chaos of life. *New York Times,* pp. 17, 26.

Greenberg, Jeff, Tom Pyszczynski, Sheldon Solomon, Abram Rosenblatt, Mitchell Veeder, Shari Kirkland, and Deborah Lyon. 1990. Evidence for terror management theory II: The effects of mortality salience on reactions to those who threaten or bolster the cultural worldview. *Journal of Personality and Social Psychology* 58:308–318.

Haberman, Clyde. 1989, December 1. Gorbachev lauds religion on eve of meeting Pope. *New York Times*, pp. 1, 10.

Halbwachs, Maurice. 1980 [1950]. *The collective memory* (ed. Francis J. Ditter, Jr., and Vida Y. Ditter). New York and Cambridge: Harper Colophon.

*Harper's Magazine.* 1988, November. Harper's index. p. 14.

Harrington, Alan. 1977. *The immortalist.* Millbrae, CA: Celestial Arts.

Harrington, Michael. 1983. *The politics at God's funeral: The spiritual crisis of Western civilization.* Fort Worth, TX: Holt, Rinehart and Winston.

Henderson, Alice. 1977. *Brothers of light.* Santa Fe, NM: William Gannon.

Hepworth, Mike, and Bryan Turner. 1982. *Confession: Studies in deviance and religion.* London: Routledge and Kegan Paul.

Herberg, Will. 1960. *Protestant-Catholic-Jew: An essay in American religious sociology.* Garden City, NY: Doubleday.

Innis, Harold A. 1951. *The bias of communication.* Toronto: University of Toronto Press.

James, William. 1902. *The varieties of religious experience.* New York: Longmans, Green.

Jones, R. Kenneth. 1978. Paradigm shifts and identity theory: Alternation as a form of identity management. In Hans Mol (ed.), *Identity and religion.* Newbury Park, CA: Sage.

Johnson, Benton. 1963. On church and sect. *American Sociological Review* 28:539–549.

Johnson, Weldon T. 1971. The religious crusade: Revival or ritual? *American Journal of Sociology* 76:873–880.

Kearl, Michael. 1980. Time, identity, and the spiritual needs of the elderly. *Sociological Analysis* 41:172–180.

Kearl, Michael, and Ted Wedholm. 1989. Biographical debriefings of our culture's temporal pioneers. Paper presented at the thirty-first annual Western Social Science Association Meetings, Albuquerque, NM.

Küng, Hans. 1980. *Does God exist?* Garden City, NY: Doubleday.

Lang, Kurt, and Gladys E. Lang. 1961. *Collective dynamics.* New York: Y. Crowell.

Lasch, Christopher. 1989, December 27. The I's have it for another decade. *New York Times,* p. 23.

Lenin, V. I. 1939[1905]. *Selected works,* vol. 11. London: Lawrence and Wishart.

Levine, Saul V. 1986. *Radical departures: Desperate detours to growing up.* Orlando: Harcourt Brace Jovanovich.

Lewis, James, and David G. Bromley. 1987. The cult withdrawal syndrome: A case of misattribution of cause? *Journal for the Scientific Study of Religion* 26:508–522.

Lewis, James R. 1989. Apostates and the legitimation of repression: Some historical and empirical perspectives on the cult controversy. *Sociological Analysis* 49:386–396.

McClelland, David. 1955. Some social consequences of achievement motivation. In M. R. Jones (ed.), *Nebraska symposium on motivation.* University of Nebraska Press.

McGuire, Meredith. 1988. *Ritual healing in suburban America.* New Brunswick, NJ: Rutgers University Press.

McGuire, Meredith. 1983. Words of power: Personal empowerment and healing. *Culture, Medicine and Psychiatry* 7:221–240.

McGuire, Meredith, and Debra Kantor. 1987. Belief systems and illness experiences: The case of non-medical healing groups. *Sociology of Health Care* 6:221–248.

McIntosh, Daniel, and Bernie Spilka. 1990. Religion and physical health. In Lynn Moberg and D. Moberg (eds.), *Research in the social scientific study of religion,* vol. II. New York: JAI Press.

MacKay-Smith, Anne. 1985, August 6. Schools are becoming the battleground in the fight against secular humanism. *Wall Street Journal,* p. 35.

Malinowski, Bronislaw. 1925[1948]. Magic, science and religion. In *Magic, science and religion and other essays.* New York: Free Press.

Maloney, Lawrence. 1984, June 25. Plague of religious wars around the globe. *U.S. News & World Report,* pp. 24–26.

Marx, Karl. 1963[1844]. Contribution to the critique of Hegel's philosophy of right. In T. B. Bottomore (ed.), *Early writings.* New York: McGraw-Hill.

Marx, Karl, and Friedrich Engels. 1964. *On religion.* New York: Schocken.

Mathews, Shailer, 1930. *The atonement and the social process.* New York: Macmillan.

May, William. 1973. The sacral power of death in contemporary experience. In Arien Mack (ed.), *Death in American experience.* New York: Schocken.

Mayrl, William. 1976. Marx's theory of social movements and the church-sect typology. *Sociological Analysis* 37:19–31.

Miller, Jon D., Robert W. Suchner, and Alan M. Voelkner. 1980. *Citizenship in an age of science: Changing attitudes among young adults.* New York: Knopf.

Mills, C. Wright. 1952, Winter. Liberal values in the modern world: The relevance of 19th century liberalism today. *Anvil and Student Partisan*, pp. 4–7.

Moody, Raymond. 1975. *Life after life.* Covington, GA: Mockingbird.

Morris, Richard. 1985. *Time's arrows: Scientific attitudes toward time.* New York: Simon and Schuster/Touchstone.

*New York Times.* 1986, May 31. Excerpts from Pope's encyclical, "The Lord and giver of life." p. 4.

Novak, Michael. 1971. Religion as autobiography. In Michael Novak, *Ascent of the mountain, flight of the dove.* New York: HarperCollins.

Parker, J. Michael. 1990, May 12. Survey reports attendance at church benefit to society. *San Antonio Express-News*, p. 8-J.

Robbins, Thomas. 1988. *Cults, converts and charisma: The sociology of new religious movements.* Newbury Park, CA: Sage.

Rosenblatt, Abram, Jeff Greenberg, Sheldon Solomon, Tom Pyszczynski, and Deborah Lyon. 1989. Evidence for terror management theory:I. The effects of mortality salience on reactions to those who violate or uphold cultural values. *Journal of Personality and Social Psychology* 57: 681–690.

Rudin, A. James, and Marcia R. Rudin. 1980. *Prison or paradise? The new religious cults.* Minneapolis: Augsburg Fortress.

Safire, William. 1986, December 25. Flirting with God. *New York Times*, p. 23.

*San Antonio Express-News* [AP]. 1991, April 4. Americans say faith in God most important.

*San Antonio Express-News* [Washington Post Service]. 1990, May 6. Joan of Arc was epilepsy sufferer, scholar suggests. p. 17A.

Sheler, Jeffery. 1990, March 12. What's in a vision? *U.S. News & World Report*, pp. 67–69.

Shibutani, Tamotsu. 1961. *Society and personality.* Englewood Cliffs, NJ: Prentice-Hall.

Slater, Philip. 1977. *The wayward gate: Science and the supernatural.* Boston: Beacon Press.

Snow, David, and Richard Machalek. 1982. The fragility of unconventional beliefs. *Journal for the Scientific Study of Religion* 21:15–25.

Snow, David, and Richard Machalek. 1983. The convert as a social type. In R. Collins (ed.), *Sociological theory: 1983.* San Francisco: Jossey-Bass.

Solomon, Jack. 1988. *The signs of our times.* New York: Perennial Library.

Spilka, Bernard, Ralph W. Hood, and Richard L. Gorsuch. 1985. *The psychology of religion: An empirical approach.* Englewood Cliffs, NJ: Prentice-Hall.

Stark, Rodney, and William Sims Bainbridge. 1979. Of churches, sects, and cults: Preliminary concepts for a theory of religious movements. *Journal for the Scientific Study of Religion* 18: 117–133.

Stark, Rodney, and Charles Glock. 1968. *American piety: The nature of religious commitment.* Berkeley: University of California Press.

Suchner, Robert. 1987. Religious fundamentalism and science: Attitudes of American college students. Paper presented at the annual meetings of the Midwest Sociological Society, Chicago.

Swanson, Guy E. 1960. *The birth of the gods: The origin of primitive beliefs.* Ann Arbor: University of Michigan Press.

*U.S. News & World Report.* 1990, August 20. To have and have not. p. 27.

Vecsey, George. 1977, October 10. Koreans' churches provide an introduction to America. *New York Times*, p. 18.

Wallace, Anthony F. C. 1956. Revitalization movements. *American Anthropologist* 58:264–281.

Weber, Max. 1958[1904]. *The Protestant ethic and the spirit of capitalism.* New York: Scribners.

Weber, Max. 1946. The social psychology of the world religions. In H. H. Gerth and C. Wright Mills (eds. and trans.), *From Max Weber: Essays in sociology*. New York: Oxford University Press.

Weigle, Marta. 1970. *The penitentes of the Southwest*. Santa Fe, NM: Ancient City Press.

Wilentz, Sean. 1988, April 25. God and man at Lynchburg. *New Republic*, pp. 33–34.

Williams, J. Paul. 1962. The nature of religion. *Journal for the Scientific Study of Religion* 1:3–14.

Wimberly, Edward, and Anne Wimberly. 1986. *Liberation and human wholeness*. Nashville, TN: Abington Press.

Wyatt, Frederick. 1963. The reconstruction of the individual and of the collective past. In Robert White (ed.), *The study of lives*. New York: Atherton.

# 15

# The Social Psychology of Work and Consumerism

When people meet for the first time, a question that invariably arises is, "What do you do for a living?" We believe that to know another person's line of work is to have a highly predictive framework for inferring his or her social status, interpersonal traits and skills, value orientations, personal interests, and even personality type. So central is work to establishing one's social identity that King John of England proclaimed that people must use surnames pertaining to their trade. As populations were growing rapidly and the social system was becoming increasingly specialized, it was no longer practical to refer to others by their first names (even when coupled with one's residence, such as Edward-of-Dover). What better way to index other selves than by what they do? Those who made carts became Cartwrights and Wainwrights; metal workers became Smiths; and Shepard became the surname of people who tended sheep (Wibberley 1983).

Of all the institutionalized arenas of human activity, work is the most central, both sociologically and psychologically. From a macro perspective, work is a way of keeping social actors "out of mischief" by harnessing and coordinating their energies to produce socially necessary goods and services. The products of work become the basis of trade, which brings different cultures into contact with each other, thereby providing opportunities for social innovation.

In the course of social evolution, the division of labor becomes increasingly complex, making human groups more interdependent and integrating ever broader geographic areas. Today this interconnectedness has become so global that declines on the Tokyo Stock Exchange, a large rice harvest in China, or a poor catch of anchovies in Peru can lead to unemployment in Des Moines. It is this economic interdependence between highly specialized individuals, organizations, communities, and regions that is the basis of social solidarity in the modern world.

From a micro perspective, work satisfies a broad spectrum of individual needs, such as the needs for solidarity and a feeling of self-worth. One way to appreciate this function of work is to study those who lack it: the unemployed and unemployable, those who have been fired and laid off, and retired people. In many ways these individuals become nonpersons; their activities are no longer perceived as wholly legitimate, since only through working is one generally seen as contributing to the social system. The centrality to individuals' needs is further evidenced by the movements for equal opportunity for women and minorities.

## WORK AS THE ARCHETYPE OF REALITY

Work is the archetype of social reality. The technology generated by the workplace affects social organization, values, everyday expectations, and hopes and dreams. To take just one example, consider our assumptions about being able to interact with others via telephone or jet travel—technologies that arose out of the need to coordinate the activities of workers at different locations. Work also provides the broadest range of settings for human activity and interaction, from the arctic pipeline of Alaska to the cockpit of the space shuttle.

At another level, because work often requires individuals to be at their most wide-awake and highly engaged state of consciousness, what people do at work has broad bearing on how they act, think, and perceive things in general. In more formal terms, work produces individuals' primary form of consciousness. It shapes the person's templates in several areas, including the following:

> **Kinesthetic experiences.** The type of work one does determines the nature of one's motions in and contacts with the external world. Thus, as the United States has evolved toward an information economy, the primacy of the visual sense has been emphasized over the senses of smell and touch.
>
> **Perceptual routines.** By controlling attention and routines of action, the processes of work shape the individual's styles of perception.
>
> **Symbolic systems.** Because of their distinctive views of the external world, various work cultures spawn different language systems, from the hand signals on the New York Stock Exchange to the mathematical formulas of physicists. Work also determines the central metaphors of a culture, including those underlying social psychological theories.
>
> **Commitments and accountabilities.** Work places the individual within a network of obligatory activities that are carried out with others (e.g., research teams, task forces, committees).
>
> **Social motivations.** Work provides a central component of identity and self-esteem. It provides opportunities for social contributions, solidarity, and social attention.
>
> **Sentiment.** As we saw in Chapter 6, various "feeling rules" must be observed in the workplace, such as the absence of sentiment when "acting professionally" or the contrived warmth expressed by service industry personnel when dealing with the public.

## The Sociolinguistics of Work

A hipo, a Wallenda, and an imagineer order drinks at a bar. They do a little work—edit a violin, non-concur with a wild duck, take care of some bad Mickey—then ask for the bill. "This is on the mouse," says one of the three.

Who picks up the tab?

It's not uncommon to hear chatter like this from the mouths of corporate employees. Sometimes, translating it requires knowing the jargon not of MBAs, industries or regions—but of particular companies.

For instance, an employee at IBM who is fluent in IBM-speak knows that a "hipo" is an employee on the fast track to success—someone with "high potential." (According to one IBMer, an employee with low potential is known as an "alpo.") IBM-speakers don't disagree with their bosses—they non-concur. And anyone who non-concurs often and abrasively, but constructively, is a "wild duck" in IBM-speak. . . .

Like other tribal entities, corporations develop their own dialects as a way of linking members of the tribe and delineating their ranks. "It has the double purpose of bonding the user to the group and separating the user from general society," says Robert Chapman, editor of the *New Dictionary of American Slang.* "It makes us feel warm and wanted. This works in any society—a company, a school, a family, a saloon."

Slang often arises in offices where words are the company's business, such as newspapers and magazines. Newsweek's top editors are known as Wallendas, after the famous family of aerialists—a reference to the precarious nature of their jobs. Their offices are sometimes called the Wallendatorium.

Newsweek writers also call each week's top nation story the "violin." A spokeswoman says that's because the story is supposed to "reflect the tone" of the news. . . .

Most of all, slang flourishes at corporations with rich histories and cultures. At McDonald's Corp., where employees take corporate training classes at Hamburger University, loyal workers "have ketchup in their veins." Patriotic citizens of Eastman Kodak Co. say they work for "the great yellow father."

Walt Disney Co., one of the world's shrewdest manufacturers of cultural imagery, is a rare example of a company that has consciously invented its own jargon. It calls the division that plans its theme parks, "Walt Disney Imagineering." At orientation sessions (at Disney University), new theme-park employees are carefully told to say they are "on stage" while at work and "backstage" while taking a break. They are also told to consider each other not as employees but as "cast members." . . .

Jack Herrmann, a former Disney World publicist, recalls that his colleagues would brand anything positive "good Mickey" and anything negative—like a cigarette butt on the sidewalk—"bad Mickey." He also remembers putting lunch on the Disney World expense account and calling it "on the mouse." "You're immersed in the jargon they impose upon you as a way of life," he says.

---

Source: Miller, 1987.

Given that the nature of one's work shapes what one perceives and how one interprets the experiences, the type of work that predominates in a given society has a sizable impact on the cultural ethos of that society. Marx (1904) claimed in *A Contribution to the Critique of Political Economy* that the economic order is the ultimate determinant of a society's morality, philosophy, and religion, and the structure of its institutions. Moreover, a culture's dominant form of work shapes the personality structures of its individuals, the metaphors of their thoughts, and the limits of their aspirations. For instance, the flock metaphors found in the Bible reflect the agrarian societies from which the major religions began. The machinelike metaphor employed by Freud to understand personality systems, as we saw in chapter 1, derived from industrialism. And hunter-gatherers never dreamed of exploring subatomic quarks.

In view of the centrality of work to both self and society, it is not surprising that the act of working has historically been imbued with religious significance. In the Protestant ethic, for example, work was viewed as a means of glorifying God and creating His kingdom in the here-and-now. Everyone's duty was to seek the "profession" (or "calling") that would bring the individual (and hence society) the greatest return. With this mindset, work cannot be approached casually but must instead be methodical and disciplined.

But working also carries connotations of suffering, as in the Latin *labor*, Spanish *trabajo*, the French *travail*, and in the ancient Greek word for work, *ponos*, which has the same root as the Latin *poena*, meaning sorrow (Berger 1964:212). When God foreclosed on Eden, he condemned Adam and Eve and their descendants to work as a means of expiating the original sin. In the United States the meaning of work has never quite recovered from these negative connotations. For many Americans, work is a means to some other, more desirable end (e.g., "working for the weekend") rather than an end in itself.

## EVOLVING ECONOMIES AND THE CHANGING NATURE OF WORK

Sociologists generally assume that human society has evolved through a series of stages, each with its own form of social and psychological organization. Each successive stage is thought to have been characterized by a more complex division of labor occupied by more complex selves.

Over time, changes in the nature of work caused a shift in cultural focus from the *natural world*, where life is ruled by fate and chance, to the *technical world*, which is governed by rationality, and eventually to the *social world*, which is held together by coercion and the moral order (Bell 1980).

In preindustrial times, the primary thrust of life was to win the battle for survival. During this period the labor force was overwhelmingly involved in extractive enterprises such as hunting and fishing and, later, agriculture. The social organization that emerged out of these pursuits was based first on the family and later on the community. It featured a simple division of labor statuses. Power was rigidly authoritarian, and birth determined one's social position.

With industrialization, work came to involve machines and mechanical rather than natural processes, and as a result the rhythms of life are mechanically paced. Individuals now work by the clock rather than by the location of the sun. Skills are broken down into simpler components; the artisan is replaced by the engineer and an assembly line of semiskilled workers. Self-sufficiency wanes and the jack-of-all-trades becomes an endangered species. The work environment features scheduling and programming; parts are brought together at exact moments for assembly. It is a world of organization, bureaucracy, and hierarchy.

To accommodate this new economic order, a new "sociosphere" (Toffler 1980) emerged. To ensure that workers could be easily shifted to regions where labor is needed, the family became streamlined from an extended system to a basic nuclear form. Instead of designing jobs to fit people, educational systems tailored individuals to fit available occupations.

Postindustrialism features the exchange of services and the manipulation of information. It is characterized by greater emphasis on interpersonal manipulations such as supervising, persuading, motivating, instructing, and negotiating. In a postindustrial society there are more people employed in higher education than in mining; many more are to be found in financial institutions than in agriculture. The occupational elite—including lawyers, management consultants, bankers, television and film producers, advertising and marketing specialists, and research scientists—are engaged in providing "symbolic-analytic services" in knowledge-intensive industries, working with words, data, and oral and visual symbols (Reich 1989).

Work in postindustrial societies depends on creativity, continuous innovation, and effective work teams. Because the skills and knowledge of workers may be obsolete within a few years, they must continually invest considerable amounts of time and effort just to remain qualified for their jobs. When one considers that half of the jobs that existed in 1987 did not exist in 1967, many workers must expect that in twenty years they will be employed in occupations that do not exist today.

Table 15.1 illustrates how contemporary work situations differ from the farms and assembly lines of the not-too-distant past. The "Total" column shows that 52 percent of workers do not work with things, 86 percent work with data, and 62 percent deal with people.

The rows labeled "no significant relationship" show that as their education increases, people are less likely to work with things and more likely to work with people and symbols. For instance, workers with less than a high school education are ten times less likely to work with data (30 percent/3 percent) than people with four or more years of college, and three-and-one-half times less likely to work with people. Researchers find that those who deal with people, rather than with symbols or things, work in more varied social settings (Simpson, Back, and McKinney 1966).

## The Changing Reality of Time

Remember that time is money.—Benjamin Franklin

Cycles of work and rest are evident throughout nature. For instance, tigers spend most of their time conserving energy for the hunt; they may feed on a downed stag for three days and not hunt for an additional two days.

**TABLE 15.1 Correlations Between Education and Occupation**

*The NORC General Social Surveys include various classifications of occupations according to job titles listed in the* Dictionary of Occupational Titles. *The following table correlates respondents' education with three important characteristics of workers: their relationships with people, data, and things.*

|  | Education | | | | |
|---|---|---|---|---|---|
|  | *0–11 Years* | *High School Graduate* | *Some College* | *4+ Years College* | *Total* |
| **Occupational Relationship with People** | | | | | |
| No significant relationship | **64%** | **50%** | **31%** | **18%** | **38%** |
| Instructing | 1 | 1 | 2 | 21 | **7%** |
| Speaking | 23 | 23 | 31 | 23 | **25%** |
| Serving | 7 | 10 | 17 | 7 | **11%** |
| Negotiating | 0 | 0 | 2 | 9 | **3%** |
| **Occupational Relationship with Data** | | | | | |
| No significant relationship | **30%** | **18%** | **10%** | **3%** | **14%** |
| Synthesizing | 1 | 1 | 2 | 7 | **3%** |
| Comparing | 19 | 9 | 3 | 2 | **7%** |
| Compiling | 17 | 19 | 27 | 15 | **20%** |
| Computing | 11 | 13 | 10 | 6 | **10%** |
| Coordinating | 8 | 18 | 24 | 43 | **25%** |
| Analyzing | 12 | 18 | 18 | 23 | **18%** |
| **Occupational Relationship with Things** | | | | | |
| No significant relationship | **28%** | **43%** | **56%** | **73%** | **52%** |
| Handling | 17 | 13 | 15 | 10 | **13%** |
| Tending | 13 | 7 | 4 | 1 | **5%** |
| Operating-controlling | 14 | 7 | 6 | 6 | **7%** |
| Precision working | 13 | 13 | 10 | 6 | **10%** |

Source: NORC, 1989; sample of those currently working full or part time.

Wherever humans were in control of their own working lives, the work pattern was also one of alternating bouts of intense labor and of idleness. Typically there was a lull in the workday during the afternoon, and the early evening was spent socializing. But with industrialization new unnatural rhythms were imposed on the workday.

In writing about the temporal implications of this great change, Joseph McGrath and Janice Kelly (1986) observe that before the industrial revolution our culture had a "procedural-traditional" temporal orientation in which the natural unit of work was the completed task. With industrialization, the dominant time orientation has been "linear-separable"; in this orientation, known as "organizational time," the natural unit of work is the "manhour."

> Time, rather than effort or skill, is what the worker contributes in the work relation; and time, rather than skill or effort, is what is paid for in the work exchange. (1986:108)

Thus, time became a commodity, something that could be wasted, shared, or saved. As Simmel (1971) observed, the portable timepiece or wristwatch helped create a mental life for urban dwellers, enabling them to mesh their daily rounds with a precision unattainable in rural settings, where time is marked by more natural rhythms. Table 15.2 presents the buying power of time.

Today individuals' social lives are organized around work time, with its associated times for commuting and preparation. For Americans, the quantity of this time has increased in recent decades. Between 1973 and 1988, according to the National Research Center of the Arts, Americans' work time increased

### TABLE 15.2   A Time Clock of East-West Buying Power

*Western consumers may need a month's salary to buy a small car, but people living in an Eastern European country may need up to a year's wages to purchase the same item. The following table lists the hours and minutes of work needed to pay for an item in four countries:*

|  | West Germany | East Germany | Soviet Union | United States |
|---|---|---|---|---|
| Small car | 607 hours 24 min. | 3087 hours 42 min. | 7935 hours 54 min. | 686 hours 16 min. |
| Color television | 96 hours 13 min. | 846 hours 9 min. | 681 hours 6 min. | 34 hours 18 min. |
| Washing machine | 66 hours 40 min. | 528 hours 51 min. | 90 hours 18 min. | 29 hours 24 min. |
| Man's suit | 13 hours 16 min. | 67 hours 18 min. | 128 hours 48 min. | 19 hours 48 min. |
| Pork chops (2.205 lbs.) | 54 min. | 1 hour 32 min. | 3 hours 42 min. | 38 min. |
| Daily newspaper (1 mo.) | 1 hour 27 min. | 42 min. | NA | 1 hour 28 min. |
| Weekly railway pass | 1 hour 47 min. | 29 min. | NA | 2 hours 21 min. |
| Loaf of bread | 13 min. | 6 min. | 46 min. | 12 min. |

Note: Figures are national average prices and median incomes.

Source: Chicago Tribune, West German Consulate General; cited in *San Antonio Express-News* 1990.

from 41 to almost 47 hours per week (Gibbs 1989) as their leisure time declined by 37 percent, to 16.6 hours per week (Richard 1988).

With the emergence of the global economy, workers' lives have become increasingly out of sync with the standard timetables of their families and communities. For instance, in California many stockbrokers, lawyers, and news reporters work on New York time, which requires that they get up at 3 A.M. to begin work at 5 A.M. Some even work on Tokyo time, which is seventeen hours ahead of California time. Their work week begins on Sunday afternoon at 3 P.M.

**Work Time as Organizer of Biographical Time.** Work time has increasingly become a source of social identity and the organizing principle of individuals' biographies (Becker and Strauss 1956). In the middle class, the sixteen or more years spent in educational institutions are understood as an investment in one's future employability. During the working years, a self is realized in portfolios, vitaes, and resumes, in which the person's past, present, and future work activities become integrated into a specific dimension of time. The higher one's occupational status, the greater the biographical coherence derived from one's occupational career. Particularly in the upper and upper middle classes, where individuals are engaged in *professions* as opposed to *jobs*, workers experience an orderly pattern of advancement in terms of rewards and responsibilities (Wilensky 1961).

An individual's work history also has a significant bearing on retirement. Ida Simpson, Kurt Back, and John McKinney (1966) found that the less discontinuity experienced during a worker's career, the higher his or her morale during retirement.

### The Emergence of Leisure Time

> Millions long for immortality who do not know what to do with themselves on a rainy Sunday afternoon.—Ertz's Observation

The separation of work from family life, of the public self from the private self, has led to the evolution of a nonworking self. This self is defined not in terms of what it does but in terms of what it doesn't do. Supposedly this is the self that enjoys leisure, or freedom from work. But leisure is not the same as the "recuperative" weekend or "free time" from work. Nor is it the same as idleness. It is the discretionary time for oneself that is left after one subtracts necessary time (sleeping, personal care), work time (and commuting and preparation time), and committed time (time devoted to child care and household tasks).

A few hundred years ago, leisure was the province of the educated elite, the "leisure classes." In fact, such pursuits as astronomy, chemistry, and music were originally leisure activities. Today leisure is available to members of all classes. For some, it is involuntary. For example, in reference to the enforced leisure of the retired elderly, Arlie Hochschild observes that

> Leisure is not quite leisure when you don't have work. Ironically, the old are more likely than the young to base their pride squarely on work. . . . To many of the old, the "fun ethic" and even the culturally sophisticated use of leisure is an ideological veneer for the growing scarcity of jobs. (1973:19–20)

On the other hand, as the amount of leisure time has decreased, time has become an increasingly precious commodity. This is particularly true for women in two-income families, 73 percent of whom complain of having too little leisure, according to the 1989 CNN/*Time* poll (cited in Gibbs 1989). One major consequence has been the emergence of the fast-food and instant-service industries, which are designed to accommodate people in a hurry.

## The Fragmentation and Bureaucratization of Identity

The traditional fits between self and society have been totally disrupted by the changes associated with economic evolution. Metamorphoses of social structure necessitated new styles of thinking and increasingly complicated identities.

With industrialization, work became segregated from the home, giving rise to a double consciousness. As we saw in Chapter 8, individuals developed "public selves," which engage in the anonymous social relationships of the workplace, and "private selves," which are known only to a small circle of family members and friends. Sometimes individuals no longer know who they are or which of their selves should be given primary status (Berger 1965). As Franz Neumann observed:

> Modern society produces a fragmentation not only of social functions but of man himself who, as it were, keeps his different faculties in different pigeonholes—love, labor, leisure, culture—that are somehow held together by an externally operating mechanism that is neither comprehended nor comprehensible. (1960:270)

In addition to being fragmented, identities became increasingly bureaucratized. Durkheim (1893) claimed that specialization (which creates bureaucracy) is a prerequisite for both professional achievement and economic progress. Weber argued that the most efficient way of coordinating the activities of a large number of specialists is through bureaucracy. He listed the following characteristics of bureaucracies: a precise division of labor, a well-defined hierarchy of authority, elaborate rules and regulations, universal standards and impersonality, specialized staff, and a career ladder. However, in bureaucracies means are often as important as ends (Berger et al. 1973). As workers are plugged into roles that determine their duties and rights, they often become concerned less with what they actually do than with whether they and others "play by the rules." This can be cognitively dysfunctional, as Merton (1968) noted when arguing how bureaucratic structures produce personality types oriented toward conformity rather than toward problem solving.

# RELATIONSHIPS BETWEEN INDIVIDUALS AND THEIR WORK ROLES

In meeting the requirements of an increasingly differentiated and specialized employment structure, it is necessary to obtain an increasingly refined match between types of workers and types of work roles. This need is reflected in the sophisticated methodologies developed by personnel offices. Role-playing and psychological tests are used to determine whether candidates have the right personality for a particular job. In service industries like finance and insurance, companies must locate workers with "people skills." Several Fortune 500 firms have even used handwriting experts to gauge the character of prospective employees (McCarthy 1988).

To be competitive in a global economy, companies not only must select the right person for the right job but must also create and maintain the right socioemotional environment to minimize estrangement and elicit maximum productivity, creativity, and corporate loyalty. But this is not easily accomplished, nor has it always been a high priority. The social system has not kept pace with the need to redesign jobs to take advantage of an increasingly educated work force. Among the consequences are overeducation and underemployment, worker alienation, and boredom.

## Worker Alienation and Anomie

The division of labor spawned by industrialization fundamentally altered the relationship between people and the objects of their labor. The result has not necessarily been positive. Among them is the near-obsolescence of craftsmanship, which Marx and others took to be a basic human instinct. According to Franz Neumann, this separation of labor from the object produced a threefold estrangement that is referred to as *alienation:* "Man is alienated from external nature, from himself, and from his fellow-men. The relations of men to one another are reified: personal relations appear as objective relations between things (commodities)" (1960:271).

Another result is a new definition of labor. Instead of being invested with religious significance, it is now defined simply as "work." In the case of capitalist systems, Marx noted how work "drowned the most heavenly ecstasies of religious fervor, of chivalrous enthusiasm, of philistine sentimentalism, in the icy water of egotistical calculation" (1978:475).

Industrialization also produces a change in the structure of authority relations. In the nineteenth century, the workplace had been dominated by entrepreneurs, who supervised the quality of work and often took a personal interest in their employees. In the 1880s and 1890s, large corporations replaced owner-proprietor organizations. The entrepreneur was forced to delegate more and more authority to the foreman, who assumed the job of getting workers to work. Workers became interchangeable and replaceable "cogs in a machine." The strikes and violence of the early twentieth century were often reactions against the exercise of arbitrary authority in the workplace.

Finally, alienation has resulted from the way in which workers have been exploited. The basic assumption of capitalism is that owners of the means of production are primarily motivated to maximize their profits because by doing so they will increase their own wealth and prestige. According to Marx, this *profit motive* inevitably leads to the exploitation of the worker through a false concept of labor. The value of a commodity or product is largely determined by the amount of labor-time necessary for its production. Workers exchange their labor-time for a certain amount of money. Unlike other commodities, labor is unique because it creates more value than the cost of its own market time. For example, if an entrepreneur sold a commodity at what it cost to produce, no profit would be made. Therefore, workers produce more value than they are paid for producing, and the capitalist lives off the *surplus labor* value of the worker.

***Increasing Precariousness of Work Roles.*** In postindustrial societies an even greater gap arises between workers and their work. Owing to the rate at which knowledge changes, the traditional one life, one career model of the individual's work life has become obsolete (Sarason 1977). Given the prevalent nature of work, which involves either manipulation of information or interactions with people, work has little in the way of tangible products. Unlike the craft worker, the information processor cannot say, "This is mine, the product of my own hands, something that I can give to my grandchildren to preserve and that will survive me when I'm gone." Instead, the only direct evidence of many retired workers' careers is a pile of pink slips, company reports, and minutes of meetings.

The intangible nature of work roles has a host of sociological and psychological implications. For instance, it is most likely to occur among higher-status work roles: In Table 15.1 we see that among workers with four or more years of college, 82 percent work with people and 97 percent with data. Occupants of these roles must be rewarded and their roles made meaningful. How do they and others judge the value of their actions? One answer is that roles that involve coordinating and synthesizing data or instructing or negotiating with others are accorded higher prestige. In highly rationalized organizations (i.e., those in which role performances are objectively measurable), the more unrationalized the role (the more ephemeral its output), the greater the prestige accorded the role (Simpson 1972). For instance, in manufacturing factories supervisors are paid more and have higher prestige than the workers who actually assemble the automobiles and aircraft.

At the highest rungs of the organizational ladder, the precariousness of roles is intensified. One study found that three out of five top executives do not receive annual evaluations (Longenecker and Gioia 1988). The reasons were varied: Subordinates feared providing them, thought they were not necessary, or believed the executives were too busy to evaluate each other. However, without any feedback, and given the invisibility of many of their role performances, the result for these executives is often anxiety and lower productivity.

In sum, alienation is no longer experienced solely by the exploited worker. In his study of successful executives, Halper (1989) found that over 60 percent believed that they had sacrificed their identities, neglected their families, and wasted years of their lives in pursuit of material rewards. Forty-eight percent of all middle managers interviewed said their lives seemed "empty and meaningless" despite years spent striving to achieve their professional goals.

## Sources of Worker Satisfaction

Despite such doubts, work is also the source of numerous personal rewards. To perceive the motivation to work as centering on the income it provides is to miss its essence of reinforcements. When interviewers asked Americans, "If you were to get enough money to live as comfortably as you would like for the rest of your life, would you continue to work or would you stop working?" more than seven out of ten said that they would continue to work. Of course, answers varied according to social class: 87 percent of individuals identifying themselves as members of the upper class would continue working, but more than half, 61 percent, of those in the lower class would continue working as well (NORC 1989). For many Americans, work provides the central opportunity to "plug into" the broader society.

To investigate further the sources of work satisfaction let us take advantage of the following set of questions (NORC 1989). The interviewers handed subjects a card and asked:

> Would you please look at this card and tell me which *one* thing on this list you would *most* prefer in a job? Which comes *next?* Which is *third* most important? Which is *fourth* most important? (mean score on 1–5 scale)
> a. High income (2.57)
> b. No danger of being fired (3.68)
> c. Working hours are short, lots of free time (4.26)
> d. Chances for advancement (2.56)
> e. Work important and feeling of accomplishment (1.93)

From the mean scores given, it is clear how significant feelings of accomplishment are to worker satisfaction. This response was the first choice of over 51 percent of American workers, dwarfing the percentages for high income (20 percent) and chances for advancement (16 percent). The nearly equal means given to high income and chances for promotion reflect the importance Americans attach not only to monetary rewards but to moving up in organizational hierarchies. Often moving up translates into greater job autonomy, greater influence over decision making, greater likelihood of supervising others, and reduced anomie.

This pattern of job preferences varied considerably across racial, educational, and age groups. The higher one's social status, the more important work's intrinsic satisfactions (feeling of accomplishment) and the less important extrinsic satisfactions (high income) become. To explore this difference further, consider Figure 15.1, which presents the interactions of education and age.

In part *a* of the figure, the rising dark solid line indicates that the importance of high income diminishes across the life cycle (remember, a higher score means less importance). In general, at all ages the higher educational groups do not assign the importance to work's extrinsic rewards that the lower educational groups do.

The importance of upward mobility (to be discussed shortly) shows very little change across the lifespan. For all age groups, those with some schooling beyond high school but less than four years of college give the greatest importance to opportunities for promotion. Among people between the ages of 40 and 49, the age at which most workers either "make it" or "don't," those with the most education are clearly least rewarded by promotion (mean score = 2.95).

The dark solid line in part *c* of Figure 15.1 shows how intrinsic rewards increase in importance between the ages of 18 and 40 and then level off. The lighter smaller line below it indicates that the most educated workers attach the most value to feelings of accomplishment in their work; the dashed line on top shows that the least educated workers least value such intrinsic attributes.

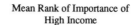

Mean Rank of Importance of
High Income

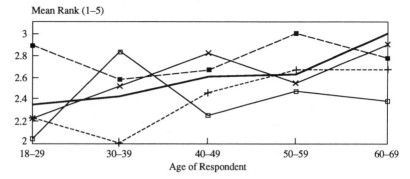

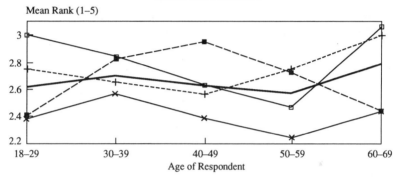

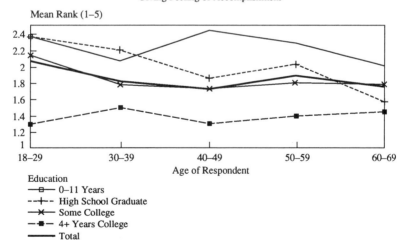

FIGURE 15.1   Mean Ranks of Importance of Job Factors
Source: NORC, 1989.

# Motivating the Worker

In the early days of the Soviet Union, the Soviet press was filled with stories of Aleksei Stakhanov, a miner who in a single shift hewed 102 tons of coal, fourteen times more than the normal output. Stalin viewed the feat as "a model of that high productivity of labor that only socialism can produce and that capitalism cannot produce" (Schmemann 1985). Sixty years later, without the personal incentives of capitalism, Communist leaders find themselves frustrated by the lax habits and shoddy products of the nation's work force.

Japan, on the other hand, emerged from total defeat in World War II to become one of the most productive countries on earth. In Japan, employee solidarity is deliberately cultivated as a strategy for eliciting quality workmanship. In 1984, for example, 10,000 employees of the Nissan Motor Company stood up with their families to sing their company song. The company team had just won the fifty-fifth annual National Intercity Amateur Baseball Tournament, a round-robin championship involving over three hundred corporate teams. As their coworkers sang, the players wept, and the thrill of victory extended to the company as a group (Shapiro 1985).

***Maintaining Worker Loyalty.*** One result of our culture's emphasis on inner-directedness, as well as the dramatic changes occurring in the economy, is diminished corporate allegiance. A 1989 CNN/Time poll (conducted by Yankelovich Clancy Shulman) of 520 American workers revealed a weakening of the ties between workers and their employers. This trend reflects a decade of corporate mergers and acquisitions, massive layoffs, and extensive cost cutting. When asked to compare the present situation with that prevailing ten years earlier, 57 percent of respondents said that companies are less loyal to their employees and 63 percent said that employees are less loyal to their companies. Although 60 percent of the workers surveyed said that they would prefer to keep their present job, half expected to change jobs within the next five years (cited in Cramer et al. 1989:54).

To counter such tendencies, employers have devised a variety of motivational strategies. During the past two decades, some American companies have emphasized worker participation in the decisions that affect them, and the results seem to indicate an increase in worker satisfaction and a decrease in alienation (Peters and Waterman 1982). In a 1986 survey of nearly 1600 firms and organizational units, the American Productivity Center and the American Compensation Association found that three-quarters of the companies responding used either novel reward systems or human resource tactics that increased information sharing and employee involvement (Horn 1987). As can be seen in Table 15.3, these strategies have addressed such individual needs as the desire for social solidarity, dignity, and personal control in the workplace.

***Upward Mobility as an Indication of Self-Worth.*** According to Peter Berger and Thomas Luckmann, the "mobility ethos, by contrast with values that are bound to the family or a subculture, is one of few norms continuously reaffirmed in the life of the individual and thus taking on for him the character of massive reality" (1964:340). Upward mobility—that is, moving to a more prestigious occupation or a higher position in an organization—has become a form of secular salvation; it is no longer a means but an end in itself.

**TABLE 15.3 The Impact of Reward Systems**
**(Percentage of firms reporting that their reward system was effective or had a positive or very positive impact on performance)**

| Type of System | Percent |
|---|---|
| Pay for knowledge | 89 |
| Earned time off | 85 |
| Gain sharing | 81 |
| Small-group incentives | 75 |
| Profit sharing | 74 |
| Individual incentives | 73 |
| All salaried | 67 |
| Lump sum bonus | 66 |
| Recognition | 30 |

**Employee Involvement Practices**

| Involvement Practice | Percent | Mean Years in Use |
|---|---|---|
| Small problem-solving groups | 23 | 6.8 |
| Qualilty circles | 22 | 3.7 |
| Team or group suggestions | 21 | 7.9 |
| Cross-functional employee task forces | 20 | 7.0 |
| Other employee involvement efforts | 12 | 6.4 |
| Labor/management participation teams | 10 | 7.0 |
| Quality of work life programs | 8 | 5.1 |
| Self-directed, self-managed, or autonomous work teams | 8 | 9.4 |
| Total using at least one employee involvement practice | 50 | |

Source: American Productivity Center and American Compensation Association, cited in Horn, 1987.

Upward mobility has two facets: intergenerational and life-cycle. In a study of Boston workers between 1910–1963, Stephan Thernstrom (1973) found that one-quarter of the men who entered the labor force as manual workers eventually made it to the middle class, and that four out of ten children of unskilled or semiskilled workers became white-collar workers. Such intergenerational mobility is the essence of the American dream. Life-cycle mobility involves the expectation of promotion in the course of one's working career. A few decades ago, for instance, businesspeople had a "success timetable" for their careers: One should be making a thousand dollars for each year of one's age. However gauged, to not be "on time" in terms of one's professional timetable implies being a lesser self than one might be.

Control over personal mobility diminishes during the middle years of life. Individuals often realize that any further upward climb in an organizational hierarchy is no longer a function of individual effort but instead depends on job vacancies. Undoubtedly, the timing and awareness of this situation is a function of social class: The higher one's social standing, the more likely such role "peaking" will be postponed.

This traditional timetable is being fundamentally altered as American businesses face highly competitive global markets and middle-management positions are clogged by the huge baby-boom generation. To increase efficiency, many corporations have thinned out their management ranks. During the 1980s, for instance, General Electric cut twenty of the twenty-nine layers of its employee hierarchy (Kilborn 1990). For the individual, this has created the phenomenon of "plateauing": being stuck in a job with no prospects for advancement. To compensate, companies have had to design new incentives to motivate their nonpromoted employees, such as multitrack pay scales, job rotation, and retraining for new jobs.

***Maintaining a Sense of Distributive Justice.*** Fritz Roethlisberger and William Dickson's (1939) five-year study of the Western Electric Hawthorne plant showed that workers are guided not just by administrative direction but also by their own evaluations of what constitutes a fair day's pay for a fair day's work. To make such a calculation, comparisons are made in terms of what others make for their efforts. The greater one's sense of deprivation relative to others, the less effort one will expend.

One indicator of workplace inequalities is the ratio of the highest-paid to the lowest-paid worker. In some large American manufacturing corporations, this ratio can exceed 50:1 or even 100:1. Whereas among Japanese automobile manufacturers the average ratio of a CEO's salary to that of a blue-collar worker is 20:1, the average is 192:1 in the U.S. automobile industry (*Harper's Magazine* 1990a). One managerial strategy has been to eradicate much of middle management and to set a 5:1 ration that is known by all.

# WORK STYLES AND PRIVATE LIFE

In various ways, the mindsets associated with the workplace have entered workers' private lives. Sometimes this has occurred intentionally. Industrialist Henry Ford actually sought to influence the private lives of his workers through his company's Department of Sociology. The department was created to study the personal habits and life-styles of workers; its researchers even visited employees' homes to inspect them for cleanliness and to ask questions about their life-style (especially drinking habits). If workers could prove that they were thrifty, sober, and morally worthy, their salaries might be doubled.

Most of the time, however, the infiltration of workplace mindsets into the private sphere is less deliberate. For example, a 1989 *Time* cover story described Americans as "running out of time." Because of the number of dual-career households, studies have shown that spouses spend only twelve minutes a day talking with each other (Kingston and Nock 1987). Self-help manuals address such issues by applying corporate planning techniques to the running of a marriage (ABC News 1987), often including principles of *scientific management* (Taylor 1911), which seeks efficiency by breaking down goals into nar-

**TABLE 15.4  Decision Grid for Planning a Family**

| Life-style | Life-style Value | Have Baby | Remain Childless |
|---|---|---|---|
| Happiness | 5 | + | + |
| Work | 5 | − | + |
| Relation with spouse | 5 | − | + |
| Relation with parents | 3 | + | 0 |
| Relation with in-laws | 3 | + | 0 |
| Relation with childless friends | 4 | − | + |
| Discretionary income | 4 | − | + |
| Home improvements | 2 | − | 0 |
| Summer trip | 3 | − | + |
| Golfing and skiing | 3 | − | + |

Note: + = improvement; 0 = no difference; − = negative impact

rowly defined tasks. The recommendations include such activities as defining short- and long-term goals in a personal relationship and staging annual summits in which couples set aside forty-eight hours to concentrate on such subjects as love, home, and creating a "priority action plan." One problem, of course, is applying hard, rational, bureaucratic management principles to a relationship traditionally (at least for the past two or three generations) based on romantic love and spontaneity.

During the 1980s upper-middle-class individuals began applying the decision logic of the workplace to their private lives. For instance, suppose you and your spouse are trying to decide whether to start a family. Decision grids like the one illustrated in Table 15.4 can be applied to rationalize the decision-making process, just as policymakers do when planning future corporate actions.

# THE PSYCHOLOGY OF CONSUMERISM

Many of the economic crises of the late nineteenth century stemmed from overproduction and underconsumption. To move the glut of mass-produced goods, a new social order was required, one that featured mass distribution, mass advertising, and the transformation of the family from a unit of production to a unit of consumption.

Also required was a new consumer ethic to legitimate the purchase of things on the basis of fashion rather than need, be it a pet rock, a Cabbage Patch doll, or the game of Trivial Pursuit. This required the overthrow of the Protestant ethic of self-discipline, purposeful activity, delayed gratification, asceticism, thrift, and credit wariness. Also required was the overthrow of the "limited good" mindset in which all desirable things—including land, health, wealth, and love—were viewed as being in finite supply. From this perspective, any effort to improve one's condition threatens the entire community, since each individual's gain is another's loss (Riesman and Lerner 1965).

The resultant consumer ethic features hedonism (Bell 1980; Campbell 1987), impulse spending (buy now and pay later), an other-directed "Keep up with the Joneses" ethic (Packard 1957), and prestige based on material possessions (Williams 1982). It is highly dependent on fads, on people's desire to be part of something new and avant-garde.

The commercialization of society requires major political, intellectual, moral, economic, and social adjustments (McKendrick et al. 1982:2). Next to television viewing and eating, shopping now consumes the most leisure time (*Harper's Magazine* 1990b). Instead of designing products to last a lifetime, we build in obsolescence in order to guarantee never-ending purchases. This, in turn, has created a "disposable culture" featuring throwaway cameras, paper clothes, nonrecyclable packaging—and disposable workers. And for many American workers, the meaning of life consists of laboring to support their consumption habits.

## Shopping Centers as Temples of Consumption

Throughout America huge edifices have appeared that are dedicated to the ethos of consumption. Since the 1950s shopping centers have proliferated, increasing in number from 2000 in 1957 to over 30,000 today; they now account for more than half of the nation's nonautomotive retail trade (Graham 1988).

Shopping centers have had a significant impact on Americans' leisure activities. Saturdays have become the new holy day, with mall parking lots filled before noon. The malls are stratified by social class: The "lower-class" mall features J. C. Penney's and Woolworth's while the "upper-class" mall houses Sakowitz and Neiman-Marcus. The need to shop in the "appropriate" mall becomes obvious when the shopper is coolly received, is constantly monitored, or is snubbed while shopping in an establishment that is incongruent with his or her social status.

A recent study concluded that the essence of the mall is control (Kowinski 1984). Higher-status malls require "respectable" presentations of self: People normally don't appear in such places with dirt on their hands, grease on their clothes, or curlers in their hair. (So profound is this demand that attention-seeking adolescents will defy dress codes to become "mallies.") This control extends to the rituals of shopping. "Casual shoppers" are sinners of a sort, and they are often the last to be attended to by the temple priests, the sales attendants.

To further guarantee the purity of the shopping ritual, shopping is strictly separated from politics and other civic activities. Attorneys for a suburban mall west of Hartford battled for two years to keep out the National Organization of Women. During the 1984 Christmas season, Salvation Army bell ringers were either muffled or banned from some shopping centers because merchants and managers complained that the clanging of the bells disrupted business. At one Pittsburgh mall, only one collector with a kettle was allowed to stand outside a single general entrance, waving a bell with no clapper (*New York Times* 1984).

A nice home and two cars in the driveway epitomize the American dream, symbolizing their owners' successes in the labor force. On the autos' fenders may well be one of the popular bumper stickers of the late 1980s that bore homilies of a materialistic culture: "I owe, I owe, so off to work I go," or "He who dies with the most toys wins."

Unlike the bazaar, the mall is not a public place, a site for free speech, or a free market (Kowinski 1984).

## Conspicuous Consumption: You Are What You Own

Envy, vanity, imitation, competition, fads, and fashion all have important economic roles in an other-directed, consuming society (Veblen 1955 [1899]). As Harold Perkin observed, "If consumer demand . . . was the key to the Industrial Revolution, social emulation was the key to consumer demand" (1968:96). People strive to live up to an ideal way of life, making their expenditures conform with those of a particular group while avoiding the spending patterns of other, less desirable groups (Campbell 1987:50–53).

The role models for such behavior, of course, are the rich. Thorstein Veblen (1955 [1899]) noted that the entry of the nouveaux riches into the upper classes led to ostentatious displays of wealth. In part this is due to status uncertainty and desire for the social acknowledgments that are accorded to members of the elite. For these individuals, items are owned not for their utilitarian value but for their status-conferring message: Instead of driving a $15,000 vehicle that takes one from point A to point B just as reliably and in the same amount of time, they drive one that costs at least ten times as much;

instead of a fifteen-inch television screen, theirs must be a forty-eight-inch screen; instead of wearing adequate inexpensive clothing, they must wear the latest creations of the most popular designers.

## Mass Psychology and the Marketplace

On October 19, 1987, the stock market plunged by over 500 points, losing 22.6 percent of its value as stock prices fell by $500 billion in one day. The selling panic rivaled the 1929 crash on Black Tuesday, October 29, that triggered the Great Depression. A week later, Merrill Lynch purchased a full-page advertisement in *The New York Times.* The top half of the page declared in bold letters that "psychology will play a major role in the movement of stock prices in the weeks ahead."

Indeed, mass psychology is a primary force in the movements of the stock market. Collective speculation about the probability of good or bad economic times, about the chances of high inflation or layoffs, have become self-fulfilling prophecies.

Expectations of quick and sizable profits drive up prices to dizzying levels. Under such conditions people will borrow to the limit. When prices far exceed value, the rush to sell produces collapsing markets and financial panics. The expectation of runaway inflation leads to panic buying and the elimination of savings. The wealthy transfer their assets out of the country to avoid loss. Political leaders overspend to keep the economy going, producing large deficits.

As a result of mass communications, such instincts may be more common today than they were in the past. When a widely syndicated financial guru recommends that people buy or sell assets, the result is considerably more synchronized than was possible when people relied on their immediate circles of friends and associates to influence their buying decisions (Johnson and Koten 1987).

## The Psychology of Advertising

Since the 1980s, corporate sponsors have been willing to spend well over $1 million for a one-minute spot during the Super Bowl. In 1987, advertisers spent $23 billion on television commercials alone (*Wall Street Journal* 1988). Are such astronomical sums well spent? The proof lies in what sells.

The function of advertising, of course, is to persuade people to buy and consume the company's products. Such persuasion is the primary source of revenue for the mass media and a major way in which corporations manipulate and control consumers.

Much advertising implies that consumption is an antidote to low self-esteem, unpopularity, boredom, and unhappiness. In examining this philosophy, Jules Henry (1963:46) asks whether it is really true that "people are talking" about this product or that, that Jockey briefs "give a man the feeling of security and protection he needs," that Bayer aspirin provides "the fastest, most gentle to the stomach relief you can get from pain," or that one feels guilty if one does not "smell clean" or if one has a "ring around the collar"? He concludes that such "pecuniary pseudo-truths" are generally known to be false by all except the youngest children. We relax our standards of truthfulness and consume

## Translations of Real Estate Advertising Hyperbole

"Spacious"—average.
"Charming"—small.
"Comfortable"—very small.
"Cozy"—very, very small.
"Low maintenance"—no lawn.
"Walk to stores"—nowhere to park.
"Prestigious"—expensive.
"Bright and sunny"—venetian blinds not included.
"Townhouse"—former tenement.
"Modern"—30 to 50 years old.
"Contemporary"—at least 20 years old.

"Sprawling ranch"—inefficient floor plan.
"Secluded setting"—far away.
"Executive neighborhood"—high taxes.
"Near houses of worship"—fanatical sect next door.
"Park-like setting"—a tree on the block.
"Unaffected charm"—needs paint.
"Starter home"—dilapidated.
"Hurry! Won't last!"—impending collapse.

"And much, much more"—nothing more to mention.

Source: Bendel, 1989.

products on the basis of the familiarity of brand names and the claims of advertisements.

The themes of sex and death are routinely employed for this purpose. A common and effective advertising strategy is to pair a product with an attractive, smiling woman. During the past two decades—corresponding with the increasing cultural openness to sexual matters—those women have assumed increasingly suggestive poses. In the late 1980s deceased celebrities were put to work selling products; James Dean appeared in ads for sneakers, Babe Ruth was used to sell electronics, and Albert Einstein promoted cameras (*San Antonio Light* [AP] 1989).

## CONCLUSION

The maxim "you are what you do" has held true throughout history. At a macro level, the predominant form of work in a society shapes its culture, providing its central metaphors and belief systems. At a micro level, the work individuals perform is a central determinant of their identities, self-esteem, and emotions, as well as the ways in which they approach nonwork matters.

Because of major changes in the economic order during the twentieth century, humans have become acutely aware of their interdependencies. Astronauts have observed our planet from a quarter of a million miles away and seen it as a blue spaceship in a malevolent cosmos. On the earth, the recognition of economic interdependence has affected people everywhere. Even in the remotest regions of the Amazon, natives paddle to civilization to exchange pelts and animals for *currency*—a unit of exchange that allows them to buy an axe made in Germany, a watch from Switzerland, or a Japanese radio. Finally, we are reminded of our interdependencies because the byproducts of industrialization know no political boundaries and affect us all: acid rain, the depletion of the ozone layer, the greenhouse effect, nuclear-reactor leaks, polluted oceans.

While such developments may be creating a sense of global solidarity, they have also diminished people's sense of personal efficacy, which runs contrary to the American cultural ethos of individualism. In Chapter 16 we will explore some of the social-psychological implications of this tension.

# REFERENCES

ABC News. 1987, October 30. 20/20.

Becker, Howard S., and Anselm Strauss. 1956. Careers, personality and adult socialization. *American Journal of Sociology* 62:253–263.

Bell, Daniel. 1980. *The winding passage.* Cambridge, MA: ABT.

Bendel, John. 1989, January 17. A real estate primer. *New York Times,* p. 23.

Berger, Peter. 1964. Some general observations on the problem of work. In Peter L. Berger (ed.), *The human shape of work.* New York: Macmillan.

Berger, Peter. 1965. Toward a sociological understanding of psychoanalysis. *Social Research* 32: 26–41.

Berger, Peter, and Thomas Luckmann. 1964. Social mobility and personal identity. *European Journal of Sociology* 5:331–344.

Berger, Peter L., Brigitte Berger, and Hansfried Kellner. 1973. *The homeless mind: Modernization and consciousness.* New York: Random House.

Campbell, Colin. 1987. *The romantic ethic and the spirit of modern consumerism.* New York: Basil Blackwell.

Cramer, Jerome, Joyce Leviton, and William McWhirter. 1989, September 11. Where did the gung-ho go? *Time,* pp. 52–56.

Durkheim, Émile. 1964[1893]. *The division of labor in society.* New York: Free Press.

Gibbs, Nancy. 1989, April 24. How America has run out of time. *Time,* pp. 58–67.

Graham, Ellen. 1988, May 13. The pleasure dome: Offering more than merchandise, malls today are center of community life. *Wall Street Journal,* pp. 5R–6R.

Halper, Jan. 1989. *Quiet desperation: The truth about successful men.* New York: Warner Books.

*Harper's Magazine.* 1990a, May. Harper's index. p. 19.

*Harper's Magazine.* 1990b, December. Harper's index. p. 15.

Henry, Jules. 1963. Advertising as a philosophical system. In *Culture against man.* New York: Random House.

Hochschild, Arlie. 1973. *The unexpected community.* Englewood Cliffs, NJ: Prentice-Hall.

Horn, Jack. 1987, July. Bigger pay for better work. *Psychology Today,* pp. 54–57.

Johnson, Robert, and John Koten. 1987, December 2. All the talk about a potential recession may help make the possibility a reality. *Wall Street Journal,* p. 23.

Kilborn, Peter T. 1990, February 27. Companies that temper ambition. *New York Times,* pp. C1, C6.

Kilborn, Peter T. 1989, February 15. For many women, one job just isn't enough. *New York Times,* pp. A1, A12.

Kingston, Paul W., and Steven L. Nock. 1987. Time together among dual-earner couples. *American Sociological Review* 52:391–400.

Kowinski, William. 1984. *The malling of America: An inside look at the great consumer paradise.* New York: William Morrow.

Longenecker, Clinton, and Dennis Gioia. 1988. Neglected at the top: Executives talk about executive appraisal. *Sloan Management Review* 29:41–47.

McCarthy, Michael. 1988, August 25. Handwriting analysis as personnel tool: Major firms begin using it; skeptics scoff. *Wall Street Journal,* p. 21.

McGrath, Joseph, and Janice Kelly. 1986. *Time and human interaction: Toward a social psychology of time.* New York and London: Guilford Press.

McKendrick, Neil, John Brewer, and J. J. Plumb. 1982. *The birth of a consumer society: The commercialization of eighteenth-century England.* London: Europa Publications.

Marx, Karl. 1904. *A contribution to the critique of political economy* (trans. N. I. Stone). Chicago: Charles Kerr.

Marx, Karl. 1978. The communist manifesto. In *The Marx-Engels reader* (ed. Robert Tucker). New York: W. W. Norton.

Merton, Robert. 1968. Bureaucratic structure and personality. In *Social Theory and Social Structure* (enlarged ed.). New York: Free Press.

Miller, Michael. 1987, December 29. At many firms, employees speak a language that's all their own. *Wall Street Journal*, p. 15.

Mills, C. Wright. 1958. The man in the middle: The designer. In *Power, politics and people* (ed. Irving Horowitz). Baltimore: Ballantine.

*New York Times.* 1984, December 14. Some malls ban Salvation Army or its bells. p. 13.

Neumann, Franz. 1960. [1957]. Anxiety and politics. In Maurice Stein, Arthur Vidich, and David White (eds.), *Identity and anxiety: Survival of the person in mass society.* New York: Free Press.

Packard, Vance. 1957. *The hidden persuaders.* London: Longmans.

Perkin, Harold. 1968. *The origins of modern English society.* London: Routledge and Kegan Paul.

Peters, Thomas, and Robert H. Waterman. 1982. *In search of excellence: Lessons from America's best-run companies.* New York: HarperCollins.

Reich, Robert. 1989, May 1. As the world turns. *New Republic*, pp. 23–28.

Reeves, Rosser. 1961. *Reality in advertising.* New York: Knopf.

Richard, Jerome. 1988, November 28. Out of time. *New York Times*, p. 19.

Riesman, David, and Daniel Lerner. 1965. Self and society: Reflections on some Turks in transition. In *Abundance for what? and other essays.* Garden City, NY: Doubleday/Anchor.

Roethlisberger, Fritz J., and William J. Dickson. 1939. *Management and the worker.* Cambridge, MA: Harvard University Press.

Sarason, Seymour B. 1977. *Work, aging, and social change: Professionals and the one life–one career imperative.* New York: Free Press.

*San Antonio Light* [AP]. 1989, July 5. Advertisers find dead celebrities boost sales. p. 3-E.

*San Antonio Express-News.* [Chicago Tribune]. 1990, May 4. KRTN infographic.

Schmemann, Serge. 1985, August 31. A Soviet legend working overtime. *New York Times*, p. 5.

Shapiro, Michael. 1985, July 25. In Japan, the corporate pastime is baseball. *New York Times*, pp. 1, 23.

Simmel, Georg. 1971. The metropolis and mental life. In Georg Simmel, *Georg Simmel: On individuality and Social Forms.* Chicago: University of Chicago Press.

Simpson, Ida H., Kurt W. Back, and John C. McKinney. 1966. Continuity of work and retirement activities, and self-evaluation. In *Social aspects of aging.* Durham, NC: Duke University Press.

Simpson, John. 1972. Precarious roles. Unpublished paper, Stanford University.

Taylor, Frederick W. 1911. *The principles of scientific management.* New York: HarperCollins.

Thernstrom, Stephan. 1973. *The other Bostonians: Poverty and progress in the American metropolis, 1880–1970.* Cambridge, MA: Harvard University Press.

Toffler, Alvin. 1980. *The third wave.* New York: Morrow.

Veblen, Thorstein. 1955 [1899]. *The theory of the leisure class: An economic study of institutions.* London: George Allen and Unwin.

*Wall Street Journal.* 1988, March 10. TV advertising. p. 21.

Weber, Max. 1958 (1904–1905). *The Protestant ethic and the spirit of capitalism.* New York: Scribners.

Wibberley, Leonard. 1983, April 17. Know a man by his name's calling. *San Antonio Express News*, p. 6K.

Wilensky, Harold L. 1961. Orderly careers and social participation: The impact of world history on social integration in the middle class. *American Sociological Review* 26:521–539.

Williams, Rosalind. 1982. *The dream makers: Mass consumption in late nineteenth century France.* Berkeley: University of California Press.

# 16

# The Social Psychology of Modernization

The world of my young sons features two working parents, day care, Nintendo, shopping malls, microwave meals, and a suburban neighborhood filled with kids. They are raised to assume that if one pushes the right buttons the garage door will open or the television come on, that Dad can be talked to—even though he is miles away—from Mom's car phone, that Grandma can be visited in two hours even though she lives 600 miles away, and that people have walked on the moon and returned home at speeds of 25,000 miles an hour.

Their grandparents were raised in a society of farms and small towns, in which children often worked to help support the family by milking the cows or selling loaves of bread for a dime apiece. They were raised to assume that the human voice can travel via radio waves, that some people have telephones but must wait until others are off the community line to place a call, that grandparents living 600 miles away can be reached in a day and a half by train, and that speeds of 200 miles an hour have been reached in airplanes.

Then there's the perspective of the boys' great-grandparents, who were born in the late nineteenth century when Victoria was the queen of England, or in the early twentieth century during the presidency of Teddy Roosevelt. Most people entered the world not in hospital delivery rooms but in the family home by the light of a kerosene lamp. Most were raised on remote farms on the plains and in the Far West, where they played with imaginary friends, socialized during weekend visits to town, and received their formal education from their parents.

Over the past few centuries humanity has witnessed the most dramatic and rapid cultural transformations ever known. So great, in fact, has this rate become that each generation now alive absorbs within its lifetime an amount of technological and social change that traditionally occurred over the course of many centuries. What are the social-psychological implications of this rapid rate of social change?

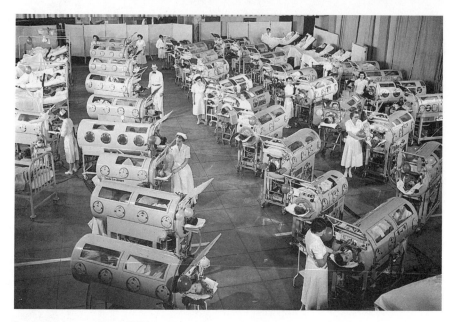

For those born after 1950, images such as this ward of polio victims in iron lungs seem as distant as the leper colonies of the past. The pace of medical breakthroughs has produced a mindset that expects immediate cure for any unknown malady besetting modern populations.

## THE NATURE OF SOCIAL CHANGE

The world is too big for us. Too much going on. Too many crimes. Too much violence and excitement.

Try as you will, you get behind in the race. It's an incessant strain to keep pace and still you lose ground.

Science empties discoveries on you so fast that you stagger beneath them in hopeless bewilderment. Everything is high pressure. Human nature cannot endure much more.—Editorial in *Atlantic Journal*, May 16, 1833 (Cited in Nietenhoefer 1990)

Daily we are bombarded with news about overpopulation, medical breakthroughs, the drug epidemic, recombinant genetics, robotics replacing workers, the death of communism, and environmental pollution causing a "greenhouse effect." We are told of the obsolescence of traditional female roles, that childhood is disappearing, that brain-dead people can be kept alive by machines and have civil rights, and that a city can be successfully sued when the noise from an international airport interferes with a couple's sex life.

Within a few tens of thousands of years—a blink of an eye in terms of life on earth—the talking apes who call themselves *Homo sapiens* have created great cities, religions, political systems controlling the activities of hundreds of millions of people, and technologies that have reached the outermost planets.

Within their modern cultures, humanity has almost totally divorced itself from bondage to the natural rhythms and processes that influence the behaviors of all other species. Increasingly our lives (and the meaning we attribute to them) are shaped by such forces as technology, industrialization, urbanization, politics, and economic cycles. Even death has come to be controlled by social as opposed to natural processes; the majority of deaths of nonelderly people are due to homicide, suicide, and accidents.

## Origins of Social Change

Human history is characterized by change much more than stability. Over the course of a few hundred thousand years, *homo sapiens* dispersed from Africa to occupy all the earth's continents as well as its oceans and moon. Wherever humans settled, they adapted to their environment—psychologically, socially, technologically, and culturally.

Stages of social evolution entail an equilibrium between cultural, social, and psychological systems. The forces that can disrupt these equilibrium states include the following.

**Environmental Conditions.** In 1846 a volcanic explosion in Indonesia dumped so much dirt into the atmosphere that worldwide temperatures declined by about 2° F. The Irish potato famine and the revolutionary upheavals that occurred in Western Europe in 1848 have been linked to this event. The eruption of Mount Tamora in the South Pacific is linked with "the year without a summer." During June of that year, 1816, there were twenty-inch snowdrifts in New England and an August freeze killed the corn crop.

**Demographics.** The world's population doubled between 1950 and 1987, accelerating the environmental changes just mentioned and limiting social development. When birthrates are high, the mean age of a population can drop to 16. The result is that a society must devote its resources to supporting and socializing the nonproductive segment of the population, as opposed to investing it in economic development.

**Ideology.** In Chapter 4 we saw how ideologies serve to stabilize the social order. If the predominant ideology changes, the ways in which people cognitively process their experiences (and, thus, their behavior) also change. Recent decades have seen the rise of fundamentalist Islam as a political force reacting against the perceived corrupting influence of Western materialism. Inspired by the successful revolution of Iran's Ayatollah Ruhollah Khomeini, Shiite Moslem extremists have committed acts of terrorism, ranging from hijacking commercial aircraft to suicidal truck bombings, to achieve their political objectives.

**Relations with Other Societies.** Contact between different cultures has historically produced significant change. Marco Polo's contact with China, for instance, shook Europe out of its medieval stagnation. Cultures vary, however, in their receptivity to and ability to cope with such contact. For example, when China opened up its borders to Westerners, during the 1980s, the idea of democratic reform took root, eventually leading to the brutal repression of reformers at Tiananmen Square by the Communist regime.

**Technology.** Major changes in the modes of production and communication lead to new social relationships. Innovations in computers and recombinant genetics, for instance, are altering the nature of work and everyday life-styles. Ironically, as evidenced by the power failure that occurred in New York City in 1966, when two lightning bolts thrust 7 million people into darkness, and by the 1990 AT&T phone breakdown, when a computer glitch led to the inability of tens of millions of people to place long-distance calls, technological gains in speed and productivity often come at the cost of reliability and collective vulnerability.

**Cultural Innovations.** Cultural innovations entail new religions (e.g., Protestantism arising out of the Reformation, paving the way for capitalist economies (Weber 1958 [1904–1905])), new roles (e.g., single working mother, retiree), and new role timetables (e.g., increasing age at first marriage), and new means for disseminating cultural myths and role models (e.g., television).

**Changing Leadership and Laws.** Under Soviet President Gorbachev's policies of *glasnost* and *perestroika*, the legitimacy of Eastern European Communist regimes came into question, leading to the overthrow of most Communist leaders in those nations over a twelve-month period. Even centralized power in the Soviet Union dissolved, leading to a resurgence of nationalism and traditional ethnic hatreds. In the United States, postwar civil rights legislation has made segregated water fountains, restrooms, and restaurants an unknown memory for half the population.

When dramatic change occurs in any of the institutional sectors just described, other sectors are eventually affected as well (Ogburn 1932). As a result of this process, cultural contradictions may arise that can be resolved only at the sociocultural level (Bell 1976). For example, in Saudi Arabia, a traditionally male-dominated Islamic society, women do not have the right to drive a car, travel alone, eat alone in a restaurant, work with men, or be in any situation where they might encounter men alone. Saudi men often refuse to marry highly educated women, fearing that such a marriage would disrupt the social order (LeMoyne 1990). However, owing to the diffusion of Western ideas coupled with their own rising educational levels, professional Saudi women feel increasingly frustrated, portending future change in the society's social and identity structures.

As we saw in Chapter 13, social movements attempt to restore both cultural and cognitive equilibrium. In a certain sense, they are culture quakes, releasing accumulated tensions between parts of a society that are changing at different rates, just as earthquakes relieve accumulated tensions between adjacent plates on the earth's surface.

A contemporary example is the environmental movement. Around the world people are becoming aware of the interdependencies between human populations and the environment. Acid rain, nuclear radiation, beaches littered with hospital waste, and the thinning of the planet's ozone layer observe no political boundaries. Earth Day's twentieth anniversary on April 22, 1990, was a huge collective ritual of consciousness raising. For one week, environmental matters received intense media coverage. Around the United States there were concerts, tree plantings, and public rallies providing evidence of the growing strength of the movement.

# THE SOCIAL PSYCHOLOGY OF CHANGE

At the social-psychological level, social change means new roles, new relationships, and new ways of thinking. But might there be a maximum rate of change that can be successfully "digested" by individuals and societies? The possibility that there is such a limit was evidenced in Iran during the 1970s. Iran was a dual society, one the modern and materialistic legacy of the deposed Shah Mohammed Riza Pahlevi, the other a traditional religious world of mosques and mullahs. The Shah failed in his attempt to introduce within a generation the amount of change that took two centuries to occur in the developed West. As a result, the society fell under the theocratic control of Ayatollah Ruhollah Khomeini and was returned to the past.

Impressive as such broad social and cultural changes may be, has change occurred if social actors are not aware of it? What is more important: the amount of change that has actually occurred, or the perception that things are changing too fast or too slowly, for the better or for the worse? For instance, if one believes that things are totally different from what they were even a generation earlier, one is not likely to use one's grandparents or parents as role models. Without time-tested recipes for encountering the challenges of time and age, one can become increasingly anxious and other-directed.

Alvin Toffler (1970) argues that, as a culture and as individuals, we are cognizant of the change that is taking place and that we suffer "future shock" as a result. We see both our products and their producers as impermanent and disposable. "Stability," argues George Pierson, "has come to seem somehow reprehensible, and *permanent* a dirty word" (cited in Kanigel 1979:53). Further enhancing this cultural perception is the fact that a sizable proportion of the population—the elderly—has experienced tremendous amounts of change. Dramatic social transformations are occurring within the lifetimes of increasingly long-lived populations. Consider the amount of change experienced by Daisy Cave, who, at her death in 1990, was the last surviving widow of a Civil War veteran.

Also enhancing the perception of change are increasing levels of education. In Chapter 11, for instance, we saw that the amount of self-change experienced during widowhood is greatest among the most educated women. (See Figure 11.7.) Education reduces the ability to take things for granted as it instills a flexible mindset featuring doubt, criticism, analysis, evaluation, and the need to constantly adjust old information to new situations.

## New Selves

As noted in Chapter 8, changing social structures produce new selves, and increasing social complexity is matched by increasing complexity in individual identities. The mentality of the peasant is transformed into an increasingly cosmopolitan mindset.

In their cross-cultural studies of the ways in which the personality is shaped by industrialism, urbanization, and bureaucratization, Alex Inkeles and his associates detected a cluster of psychological attributes that make up what they call "individual modernity":

> (1) openness to new experience, both with people and with new ways of doing things such as attempting to control births; (2) the assertion of increasing independence from the authority of traditional figures like parents and priests and a shift of allegiance to leaders of government, public affairs, trade unions, cooperatives, and the like; (3) belief in the efficacy of science and medicine, and a general abandonment of passivity and fatalism in the face of life's difficulties; and (4) ambition for oneself and one's children to achieve high occupational and educational goals. Men who manifest these characteristics (5) like people to be on time and show an interest in carefully planning their affairs in advance. It is also part of this syndrome to (6) show strong interest and take an active part in civic and community affairs and local politics; and (7) to strive energetically to keep up with the news, and within this effort to prefer news of national and international import over items dealing with sports, religion, or purely local affairs. (1969:210)

***The Growing Precariousness of Modern Identities.*** Social theorists have speculated on the precariousness of identities in social worlds that are characterized by continuous change. Continuous, unforeseen change is a probable source of much anxiety. For many people, a change in life-style, job, residence, or even everyday routine is frightening. Having much of one's life shaped by predictable routines provides security, a base from which other pursuits may be attempted. Many people are willing to go to considerable lengths to preserve the equilibrium that their routines provide. However, these equilibrium states are increasingly disrupted by broad, abstract, and uncontrollable forces such as economic cycles, political change, and technological innovations. No longer can one look to the biographies of one's grandparents or parents for successful recipes for dealing with such forces. Owing to the rate of knowledge growth and technological innovation, one cannot assume that one's work life will be confined to a single career. Nor can one assume that one will grow old with the same spouse or the same friends, or even that one will be the same person.

Owing to the multiplicity of role demands in the modern world, identities have become increasingly flexible and fragmented. In describing his growing pool of psychiatric patients, Ernest Schachtel notes the lack of any sense of identity:

> This may take the form of feeling like impostors—in their work, or in relation to their background, their past, or to some part of themselves that they repress or consciously want to hide because they feel ashamed or guilty. Or else they feel that they ought to have something they lack or imagine they lack, such as material possessions, prestige, or certain personal qualities or traits; or they feel that a different husband or wife, or friends different from those they have, would give the status they want and thereby, miraculously, transform them into full-blown persons. When the lack of a sense of identity becomes conscious, it is often experienced . . . as a feeling that, compared to others, one is not fully a person. (1961:121)

In consequence, according to Louis Zurcher, a new self is arising in healthy adaptation to the times. In a 1977 book he traced the possible impacts of major social changes on the self-conceptions of young people. He asserted that rapid sociocultural change of the sort experienced in America during the 1960s tends to reduce people's expectations that existing institutions can provide meaningful protection, services, careers, and rewards. The resulting feelings of alienation, mistrust, and disappointment are reflected in introspective self-conceptions, often making for quite uncomfortable self-experience. In consequence a **mutable self** is arising that is adaptable to rapid change, one that is no longer bound to role expectations or to the opinions of others and capable of autonomous and creative functioning.

Peter Berger and associates (1973) perceive the modern individual as having a "homeless mind." Most people want to belong—we have social "homes" (work, school) and spiritual "homes." From these "homes" we derive a sense of community. But the lack of permanence in the social order runs counter to the basic human need for "psychic moorings." Without rootedness and belonging, the satisfactions we receive from work or any other arena of social activity are drastically curtailed.

Also curtailing our social satisfactions, according to B. F. Skinner (1986), is modern life's tendency to erode the relationship between what people do and the pleasing effects that would reinforce those activities. In the workplace, salaried employees receive the same financial return regardless of how much they accomplish beyond minimal expectations. Similar conditions prevail in the sphere of home life:

> For example, if you wash a dish, you've accomplished something, done something that gives you a pleasing result. That is far more reinforcing than putting the dishes in with some powder and then taking them out again. (Skinner, quoted in Goleman 1987)

Even the joys of eating are diminished. According to a 1989 Gallup Poll, nearly two-thirds of Americans engage in some activity (e.g., reading, watching television, or working) during their meals, and less than half said that they enjoy eating "a great deal" (cited in Kleiman 1989).

## New Spatial Realities

With technological advances in travel and communication, a new sense of space entered the collective consciousness during the twentieth century. For the middle and upper classes in particular, the traditional concepts of distance and space have become obsolete. One can say, "I want to go to Europe" and be there within a day. Parochial concerns are giving way to increasingly national and international perspectives. (See Table 16.1.)

Changes in geographic space and the sense of distance have altered social-psychological processes in various ways. Such changes may contribute to intergenerational differences in values, if not to outright conflict. According to the 1989 NORC survey, nearly one-third of people age 70 and older lived on farms when they were growing up, as opposed to only 8 percent of people between the ages of 18 and 29. Some older individuals moved to cities, where they raised the next generation. That generation, in turn, may have raised their children in the suburbs. As we will see shortly, the context in which individuals

**TABLE 16.1  Social Class, by Attitudes toward U.S. Involvement in World Affairs**

*It is hypothesized that the higher one's social class, the more likely one is to appreciate the interdependence of nations. Members of the higher classes are more likely to be engaged in work that involves the manipulation of information, which is one of the services that is in greatest demand throughout the world.*

**Do you think it will be best for the future of this country if we take an active part in world affairs, or if we stay out of world affairs?**

| Social Class | Stay Active (Percent) | Stay Out (Percent) | Total |
|---|---|---|---|
| Lower | 48.9 | 51.1 | 47 |
| Working | 60.0 | 40.0 | 407 |
| Middle | 74.3 | 25.7 | 467 |
| Upper | 88.0 | 12.0 | 25 |

*If "taking an active part" is interpreted as including military involvement, perhaps the relatively low level of support among the lower classes is derived from their awareness that they are the most likely to serve in the armed forces.*

Source: NORC, 1988.

are raised shapes their behaviors, cognitions, and values. If each generation is socialized in a different context, parents and grandparents have relatively few relevant insights to pass onto the young. The coping strategies that are useful on farms, for instance, have little bearing on life in a 12-story highrise.

***The Absence of Geographic Roots.***   In the not-too-distant past, individuals rarely ventured much more than fifty miles from their place of birth. They grew old along with the same group of people with whom they had been raised. This created a sense of permanence and roots, a feeling of emotional attachment to a locale where one "had a place." Today, however, about one in five Americans moves each year. What are the social-psychological consequences of such mobility?

For the relocated individual, relationships and commitments become impermanent. If one is uncertain about one's tenure in a new community, one has less of a stake in its affairs and fewer involvements with neighbors—in other words, one is less likely to "put down roots." Such experiences are, to a certain degree, related to social class. According to the 1989 NORC survey, when subjects were asked where they live now versus when they were 16 years of age, 42 percent of those identifying themselves as members of the "upper class" said that they live in a different state, compared with 34 percent of those from the middle class, 32 percent of those from the working class, and 22 percent of those from the lower class.

Simultaneously, our landmarks are continuously being wiped out. The maxim that one can never go home again has never been more true. Even if one successfully negotiates the new freeways to find one's place of birth, the old family home may have been replaced with condos, and the playfields or open areas where one spent time during one's formative years now lie under the parking lots of fast-food establishments. With urban renewal, we destroy the old buildings that tell us who we are and what we've been through. Increasingly lost is the tangible record of our existence as a people, denying us the comfort of our collective past (Kostof 1987) and a sense of continuity between the generations.

**Urban Psychology.** By the end of the 1980s, approximately one-half of the American public lived in thirty-seven metropolitan areas. Nearly 90 percent resided in urban areas. Increasingly, our lives are spent almost entirely within man-made environments. In fact, according to the Environmental Protection Agency, Americans now spend only 2 percent of their lives outdoors (*Harper's Magazine* 1988a).

Over the past two centuries many people have speculated about the social-psychological effects of living in urban milieus. The city represents large populations, high densities, and considerable heterogeneity. They are places that spawn crowds, intensify life's stimulations, and deindividualize social interaction. Within a ten-minute walking radius of one's office in downtown Manhattan, a person can conceivably meet a quarter of a million people. Cities produce an accelerated pace of life: Researchers have found, for instance, that the greater the population size, the faster the average walking speed (Bornstein and Bornstein 1976; Bornstein 1979). City life features large numbers of secondary relationships (wherein people interact with a myriad of strangers totally in terms of the roles they play), norms of noninvolvement and visual privacy, and a high tolerance for individual differences (Wirth 1938). Its highly stimulating qualities supposedly produce psychic overload (Milgram 1970), leading to the blunting of sensitivities and a blasé attitude (Simmel 1950). And in the absence of the common morality of homogeneous communities, all values become based on money and all interactions ultimately shaped by self-interest (Töennies 1963 [1887]).

Largely gone are the intimacies of small towns, but also gone are their fatalism and repressiveness, the sense of the past incessantly intruding on the present (Blythe 1985). In the city, one is no longer known as one's parents' child. Also largely gone are the traditional forms of privacy. The need for solitude, to be able to "hear oneself" (see Chapter 3), is increasingly frustrated as population densities increase. Perhaps the growth in the size of household bathrooms is evidence of this need for privacy. Whereas in ancient Greece and Rome baths were communal places where people went to socialize, today the bathroom is one of the few private places in which one can meditate (the word *privy*, in fact, means "private") and read (a recent study showed that as many readers read in bathrooms as in libraries [Muir 1983]).

On the other hand, cities have been viewed as bastions of democracy, generators of social movements and cultural change, and magnets producing social integration among divergent populations (Mumford 1961; Jacobs 1961). They also may be "healthier" places to live in psychological terms. Srole and Fisher (1978) found that rates of mental illness are actually somewhat higher in small towns than in the center of New York City.

## Effects of Urbanization on Attitudes and Outlooks

To explore the effects of urban environments on attitudes, consider the following background variable in the 1989 NORC General Social Survey:

Which of the categories on this card comes closest to the type of place you were living in when you were 16 years old?

|  | Respondents' Mean Age | Mean Education (in years) | Total (Percent) |
|---|---|---|---|
| In open country but not on a farm | 43 | 12.19 | 11 |
| On a farm | 55 | 11.50 | 17 |
| In a small city or town (under 50,000) | 45 | 12.75 | 32 |
| In a medium-size city (50,000–250,000) | 43 | 13.36 | 16 |
| In a suburb near a large city | 36 | 14.16 | 11 |
| In a large city (over 250,000) | 47 | 12.73 | 13 |

We correlate this independent variable with responses to the following questions:

Please tell me whether or not *you* think it should be possible for a pregnant woman to obtain a *legal* abortion if the woman wants it for any reason?

There's been a lot of discussion about the way morals and attitudes about sex are changing in this country. If a man and woman have sex relations before marriage, do you think it is always wrong, almost always wrong, wrong only sometimes, or not wrong at all?

There are always some people whose ideas are considered bad or dangerous by other people. For instance, a man who admits that he is a homosexual. If some people in your community suggested that a book he wrote in favor of homosexuality should be taken out of your public library, would you favor removing this book, or not?

We hear a lot of talk these days about liberals and conservatives. I'm going to show you a seven-point scale on which the *political* views that people might old are arranged from extremely liberal—point 1—to extremely conservative—point 7. Where would you place yourself on this scale?

As can be seen in Figure 16.1 (see pages 498 and 499), we move from those raised on farms to those raised in large cities and in suburbs, we find that individuals are increasingly likely to be politically liberal and to favor the right of abortion on demand, and decreasingly likely to favor removing a pro-homosexual book from the library or to view premarital sex as being always wrong. (See the solid dark lines.) When we control for education, the same general trends hold for parts *b*, *c*, and *d* of the figure. In other words, on matters of homosexuality, premarital sex, and political liberalism, the impact of place of residence on the value orientations of individuals is roughly equivalent for different educational groups. On matters of abortion, the liberalizing effects of large cities and their suburbs do not affect those with the least education.

# New Temporal Realities

Urbanization and industrialization have divorced the rhythms of social life from those of nature, and increasingly the dreams of individuals are disrupted by dilemmas of time rather than space (O'Toole 1988). Technology has stimulated a quest for greater speed. Marketing has promulgated a desire for newness and fashion.

Bennis and Slater (1968:4) argue that "democracy becomes a functional necessity whenever a social system is competing for survival under conditions of chronic change." But democracy leads to collective forgetting (de Tocqueville 1945:106), as does modernization (Blumb 1969). For many, the past has become increasingly irrelevant, which is the reason for the poor performance of high school students on history tests (Ravitch and Finn 1988).

The future also has become less relevant. In the 1939 New York World's Fair, the sense of connectedness with a distant future was evident: A time capsule was buried beneath the admonition "Do Not Open Until 6939 A.D."! At about the same time in Germany, Adolf Hitler was proclaiming the beginning of a 1000-year Reich. Five decades later—in the wake of computers, men on the moon, recombinant genetics, robotics—we sense little relationship with either the past or the future. Recently buried capsules are intended to be opened in a few decades, perhaps a century at most.

***Changing Role Timetables and the Growing Scarcity of Time.*** In previous chapters we have explored the notion of the social clock, the temporal norms and rhythms that are implicit in social roles. For instance, many achieved roles, such as those related to education and work, have standard timetables that serve as mechanisms of social control and as bases for self-esteem: To be "ahead of time" (e.g., starting college at the age of 14) is better than being "behind time," as when one is held back in school. Standard timetables include such matters as durational rules for role occupancy (e.g., one shouldn't be an elementary school student for a dozen years, or live with one's parents at the age of 40).

Social change has created new role timetables and novel juxtapositions of role careers. For instance, between 1960 and 1989 the median age of American women at first marriage increased from 20.0 to 23.8 years as the proportion of never-married men and women in their late twenties and early thirties more than doubled. The result is increasing numbers of older parents beginning families at the age when their own parents were going through the "empty nest" stage.

Since at least the nineteenth century, there has been growing anxiety over temporal constraints. Webster's Dictionary defines the word *deadline* as "a line drawn within or around a prison that a prisoner passes only at the risk of being instantly shot." In the late twentieth century, the term refers to a limit that is solely temporal, but a boundary that is every bit as unnerving. In 1990 a *Time* cover story read: "The Sleep Gap: Too Much to Do, Too Little Rest" (Toufexis 1990). Perhaps frustration over the growing scarcity of time explains why so many recent movies deal with the ability to manipulate time. These films—*Back to The Future I, II, III, The Philadelphia Experiment, Time after Time, Peggy Sue Got Married, Star Trek IV*—feature not only the theme of time travel but the ability to alter the present by changing the past.

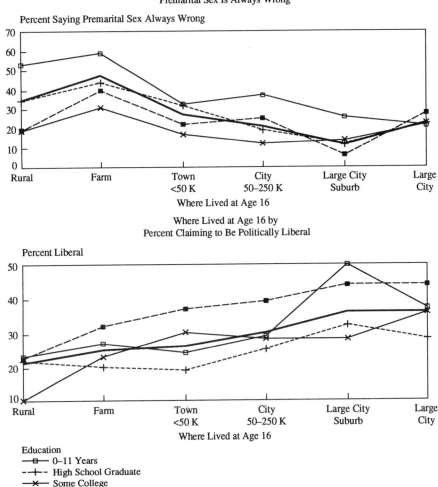

Where Lived at Age 16 by Percent Saying
Premarital Sex Is Always Wrong

Percent Saying Premarital Sex Always Wrong

Where Lived at Age 16

Where Lived at Age 16 by
Percent Claiming to Be Politically Liberal

Percent Liberal

Where Lived at Age 16

Education
—□— 0–11 Years
-+- High School Graduate
—×— Some College
-■- 4+ Years College
——— Total

**FIGURE 16.1.   Where People Lived at Age 16 and Their Opinions, by Education**
Source: NORC, 1989.

**Millennialism.** As Western cultures approach their second millennium, prophets of various kinds have sounded warnings of the demise of civilization as we know it. In the context of nuclear weapons, global pollution, AIDS, collapsing totalitarian regimes, and the perceived decadence of our life-style, there is a relatively high level of cultural receptivity to their messages.

During the 1970s and 1980s, Lindsey and Carlson's *The Late Great Planet Earth* (1976) sold more copies in the West than any other book with the exception of the Bible (Schwartz 1990). The book describes how current events match those predicted in the Book of Revelation as signs of the Second Coming.

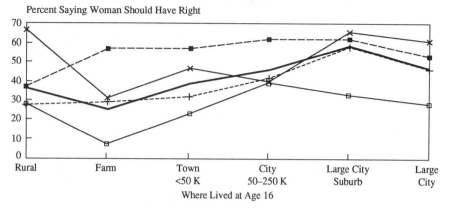

Where Lived at Age 16 by Percent Favoring
Abortion on Demand

Percent Saying Woman Should Have Right

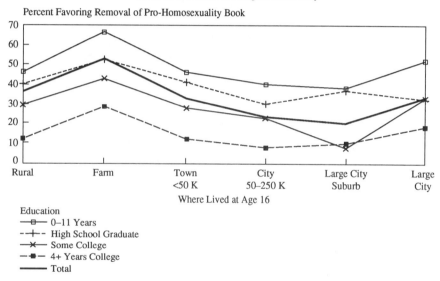

Where Lived at Age 16 by Percent Favoring
Removal of Book Advocating Homosexuality

Percent Favoring Removal of Pro-Homosexuality Book

Education
—□— 0–11 Years
--+-- High School Graduate
—×— Some College
—■— 4+ Years College
——— Total

**FIGURE 16.1.** *Continued*

Paul Ehrlich (1968) predicts that massive human population growth will over-whelm the carrying capacity of the planet, leading to various scenarios of mas-sive death, whether due to famine, nuclear war, or epidemics. While in office, President Reagan noted that "many of the prophecies are coming together" and suggested that Armageddon could arrive "the day after tomorrow" (Allman 1990).

The millennium also denotes the beginning of a future period of general happiness and righteousness. Theodore Olson (1982) explains that millennial-ism is not simply a search for a good pattern of life, as in utopianism, but a kind of climactic fulfillment. Perhaps this is due to the "cultural rhythm" re-

## Doomsday Call-In

Following is the message heard by callers to the telephone hot line of Doom, the Society for Secular Armageddonism in San Francisco. The society received more than ten thousand calls in its first few months of service.

> You have reached the hot line of Doom for news and information related to the coming apocalypse. This is a service of the organization Doom, the Society for Secular Armageddonism, a nonreligious group dedicated to promoting public awareness of the coming end of the world. We believe the apocalypse is at hand, and the reasons for that belief are overwhelming: chemical and biological weapons, nuclear proliferation, deforestation, the greenhouse effect, ozone depletion, acid rain, the poisoning of our air and water, rising racism, massive species loss, toxic waste, the AIDS pandemic, the continuing population explosion, encroaching Big Brotherism, and at least a thousand points of blight. These aren't just conversation topics for yuppie cocktail parties; they're grade A, unadulterated harbingers of destruction, 100 percent bona fide specters of doom, and they're all proof that we don't need God to end it for us. The coming end will be a strictly do-it-yourself apocalypse.
>
> This message has been a short introduction to our group and point of view. Our future messages will profile specific global threats and refer callers to groups resisting these threats. So leave a message if you like and stay tuned to this hot line for further information. And most importantly, do something now to help stave off our coming doom. As the poet Virgil put it, *Horresco referens,* "I shudder at the very thought of it."

Source: *Harper's Magazine*, 1990a, p. 22.

vealed by cross-cultural studies of traditional myths (Eliade 1963). Analogous to the death and rebirth themes underlying individual rites of passage (see Chapter 8) are myths of the destruction of the world followed by the establishment of a new order and a new Golden Age. As William Irwin Thompson argued in *At the Edge of History*, "the technology of our industrial civilization has reached a peak in putting a man on the moon, but, as the ancients knew, the peak is also the moment of descent" (1971:ix).

## The Knowledge Revolution

Most of the world's information is less than fifteen years old. In some fields, such as physics, the amount of knowledge doubles in less than eight years. In attempting to gauge the pace of scientific productivity, Price (1961) examined the number of scientific journals from the seventeenth century to the present. He found that the number has increased by a factor of ten every fifty years, beginning in the middle of the eighteenth century. By the late 1980s approximately forty thousand scientific journals were being published throughout the world (Broad 1988). In sociology alone, an average of seven articles are published every day.

Although more information has been published in the last thirty years than in the previous five thousand, the amount of time people spend absorbing it has diminished. In 1965, a Gallup survey found that two-thirds of young people read a daily newspaper; in 1989, the figure had declined to 30 percent (Richmond 1990). Common knowledge was becoming so scarce a commodity that such books as Hirsch's *Cultural Literacy: What Every American Needs to Know* (1986) were best sellers, as were games like *Trivial Pursuit*.

**The Proliferation of Choices and the Rise of the Expert.** For the individual, the fruit of this knowledge revolution is a bewildering array of choices. Metropolitan areas have scores of radio stations among which to choose. Readers can select from over 11,000 magazines and periodicals. In the grocery store, there are 25,000 items to choose from, including 200 brands of cereals (Williams 1990). Women now face far more choices regarding the combination of career and family roles than they did only a few decades ago. With this proliferation of choices, reaction times slow down and anxiety increases (Toffler 1970).

Social life has grown so complicated that most Americans defer to the assumed superior knowledge of experts (Lopata 1976). The "jack of all trades" has gone the way of the dinosaur, having been superseded by the services of physicians, mechanics, plumbers, electricians, beauticians, morticians, and job and marriage counselors. Even matters of sex have been "expertized," evidenced by the plethora of "how to" books on the market: *How to Drive Your Woman Wild in Bed, ESO: Extended Sexual Orgasm, Why Men Don't Get Enough Sex and Why Women Don't Get Enough Love.*

# New Moralities

With industrialization and urbanization, social systems are transformed from *Gemeinschaft* into *Gesellschaft* systems. As we saw in Chapter 8, the "social gravity" that binds people together no longer consists of intimate bonds between the homogeneous populations of small towns but instead consists of impersonal bonds between heterogeneous strangers with shared goals.

Without the bonds of mutual affection produced by common social memberships and shared moral beliefs, relationships come to be based on contracts and laws. The basis of social control shifts from moral conscience to the threat of force or legal sanction. With the waning of moral consensus, ours has become a society of laws and lawyers, in which litigation is used to resolve problems. Before the year 2000 there will be over 1 million lawyers in the United States (Goldstein 1988), approximately two-thirds of the world's total. Whereas the highly homogeneous country of Japan has 1000 engineers for every 100 lawyers, the situation is reversed in the United States (Lamm 1987:32).

In this cultural milieu, affinities between individuals are replaced by relationships between people and their material possessions—a phenomenon called *materialism* (Tilly 1978). The result is "ego-centered mentalities" (Etzioni 1982), leading to rising divorce rates and job changes as lifelong commitments to spouses and employers wane. A national survey of college freshmen in the late 1980s revealed that more than three-quarters believed that being financially well-off is an "essential" or "very important" goal. In fact, 71 percent said that making more money is the key reason for going to college. Only 39 percent put great emphasis on developing a meaningful philosophy of life.

Twenty years earlier, 83 percent of college freshmen thought that developing a meaningful philosophy of life was an essential or very important goal, while less than 40 percent said that being very well off financially was an "essential" or "very important" goal (Carmody 1988).

Durkheim (1933[1893]) claimed that unless people's wants are limited, there is no technology possible that can simultaneously satisfy them and stabilize society. Excessive individualism and materialism are accompanied by growing disregard for the value of human life. Nowhere is this more evident than in the nation's inner cities in the early 1990s, where homicide rates broke all records as young men killed each other for drugs, clothes, love, hate, or just for the hell of it.

### The Social Psychology of the AIDS Epidemic.

> Face to face with disaster and death, people are stripped down to their basic human character, to good and evil. AIDS can be a litmus test of humanity.—Jonathan Moreno (cited in Ansberry 1987)

The AIDS epidemic brings together most of the issues explored in this book. It involves matters of morality, sexuality, death, racism, stigma, collective behavior, and cultural belief systems. Through the 1980s, the highest rates of AIDS were among homosexuals and intravenous drug users. African Americans and Hispanics were especially hard hit, particularly within their poorer populations: Though they account for only 17 percent of the population, nearly 40 percent of AIDS cases occurred in these groups; among children under age 13, African American youths accounted for 55 percent of all AIDS cases and Hispanic youths for 21 percent (New York Times 1990). By 1990, over two hundred new cases of AIDS were being diagnosed each day in the United States, and Americans were dying of the disease at the rate of one every twelve minutes (Kramer 1990). In New York City, autopsies revealed that one in seven people were infected with the disease (Lambert 1990) and AIDS became the leading cause of death of children between the ages of 1 and 4.

As the epidemic unfolded, old and largely suppressed prejudices resurfaced. The director of the World Health Organization's AIDS program noted that prejudice about race, religion, social class, and nationality was spreading as fast as the virus (Altman 1987). Homophobia was expressed in numerous ways, from consumer boycotts against homosexual establishments to a broad range of discriminatory practices. Religious fundamentalists took the plague as a sign of divine wrath for going against traditional sexual morality. Members of the scientific community used it to criticize gay life-styles. In 1988, fully 60 percent of Americans reported having little or nor sympathy for "people who get AIDS from homosexual activity" (Harper's Magazine 1988b). Even heterosexual victims of the disease became targets of violent attacks. When he was jumped by three men in Kilgore, Texas, a 24-year-old father of three asked, "What are you doing?" Replied one, "Killing AIDS. And when we're done with you, we're going to kill your wife and kids, just in case they've got it" (Ansberry 1987).

On the other hand, various social movements emerged to humanize the statistics and promote caring and sympathy for AIDS victims. To honor the victims of AIDS, one group toured the nation with a memorial quilt made up

# Locating Collective Support for AIDS Victims

As the cost of treating each AIDS victim approaches $100,000 (Sachs 1989), the question of who should pay becomes paramount. Should we blame the victim and make him or her financially accountable for this stigmatizing disease, or should Americans collectively pay the tab? In the 1988 NORC General Social Survey, the following question was asked:

> Do you support or oppose the following measure to deal with AIDS: Make victims with AIDS eligible for disability benefits?

This proposal was supported by 54 percent of the sample and opposed by 36 percent (10 percent had no opinion). Support was greater among blacks (73 percent) than among whites (52 percent), among women (58 percent) than among men (48 percent), among people with no religious affiliation (61 percent) than among strongly religious people (51 percent), and among people with more education.

To gauge the role of antihomosexual feelings in shaping support for such a measure, a three-point scale was constructed from responses to the following questions dealing with the civil rights of this population:

> There are always some people whose ideas are considered bad or dangerous by other people. Consider a man who admits that he is a homosexual.
> —Suppose this admitted homosexual wanted to make a speech in your community. Show he be allowed to speak (coded 0), or not (1)?
> —Should such a person be allowed to teach in a college or university (coded 0), or not (1)?
> —If some people in your community suggested that a book he wrote in favor of homosexuality should be taken out of your public library, would you favor removing this book (coded 1), or not (0)?

Among the 51 percent of the sample whose scale sum totaled 0 (e.g., low on the scale of antihomosexual sentiment), 68 percent favored making AIDS victims eligible for disability benefits, compared with only 39 percent of those whose scale sum totaled 3 (23 percent of the sample).

Support for abridgement of the civil rights of homosexuals was most strongly correlated with education. Among people with eleven years or less of school, 44 percent scored "high" on the scale, compared with 23 percent of those with a high school degree, 14 percent of those with some college, and only 5 percent of those with four or more years of college.

To examine the interactions between education and antihomosexual sentiments in determining support for AIDS disability payments, consider the following table:

**Percent Supporting Making AIDS Victims Eligible for Disability**

| Education | Antihomosexual Orientation | | | |
|---|---|---|---|---|
| | *Low* | *Moderate* | *High* | *Total* |
| 0–11 years | 71 | 56 | 37 | 52 |
| High school graduate | 55 | 41 | 42 | 46 |
| Some college | 73 | 52 | 62 | 60 |
| 4+ years college | 71 | 26 | 0 | 59 |
| Total | 68 | 45 | 39 | 54 |

As is evident, orientation toward the civil rights of homosexuals produces the greatest difference in support for disability benefits among the least and most educated respondents.

of over ten thousand three-by-six-foot customized panels, each in memory of one who had died.

# SOCIAL PSYCHOLOGY OF MASS MEDIA

A recurring theme of this book is that most of what we "know" is actually secondhand knowledge, information, and insight that we obtain from others. A second theme is that *how* we come to know anything is grasped in terms of symbols. In this section we will add one final twist: the meaning content of symbols is determined by the *form* in which they are socially shared. Because of technological innovations, such as the inventions of television and computers, these symbolic forms are being fundamentally altered. (Marshall McLuhan [1967] argued that the medium is the message; what's important is not, for instance, *what* people watch on television but rather *that* they watch it.) Given their symbolic dependency, changes in both social systems and self-systems have resulted.

Communications determinists argue that culture and institutions are only subsystems of communications technology. Harold Innis (1951), for instance, observed how all mediums of communication are biased in terms of their control of time or space. Media that are durable and difficult to transport—such as the clay tablets upon which ancient Babylonians etched their cuneiform or the stone columns on which ancient Egyptians affixed their hieroglyphics—are time-binding or time-biased. Media that are light and less fixed—such as television waves, telephone messages, or the thin parchment carried by pony express riders in the 1860s—are space-binding because they are light and easily transportable. Innis argues that space-binding media encourage the growth of the state, the military, and decentralized institutions. Time-binding media, on the other hand, foster concern with history and tradition, and favor the growth of religion and hierarchical organizations.

Consider some of the sociological impacts of the printing press (Eisenstein 1980). First, it secured traditions, eliminating the need of oral (preliterate) cultures for highly trained memory. The printing press allowed the broad dissemination of ideas, seriously eroding the ability of elite groups to monopolize them through secrecy and limited dissemination. The ability to read, in turn, became a major basis of stratification. Not only was literacy correlated with individuals' positions within the status order (e.g., the higher one's class the more likely one can read) but it became the basis for distinguishing the adult world from that of children (Meyrowitz 1985). Within a century of the invention of the printing press children were beginning to be treated differently than adults. Eventually schools were created for the purpose of teaching the young to read, specifically from the Bible.

Of interest to social psychologists are the ways in which mass media affect the feelings, thoughts, behaviors, and identities of individuals. To illustrate the nature of their research, consider the influences of one medium, television, on two reappearing topics in this book, understandings of death and sex. Hollywood has long known of audience attractions to the erotic and to the violent. According to Geoffrey Gorer (1965), such seductions derive from cultural taboos toward discussing frankly matters of sex and death. When developed by the media of cinema and television, these taboos have led to their pornographic depictions. As William May (1973:105) observed, as sex is pornographic when divorced from its natural human emotions of love and affection, so death becomes pornographic when divorced from its natural emotion of grief.

## The Impact of Television

As mentioned in Chapter 7's discussions of secondary socialization, television has been accused of nearly every conceivable ill in our society (see, for instance, Postman 1985). Since the early 1950s, possible effects of television have been the subject of Congressional hearings, professional research publications, and controversy in the media themselves. Most attention has been directed to possible impacts on children and adolescents, and in the topic areas of violence and sexuality.

*Television and Violence.* Two very large-scale governmental reports a decade apart surveyed the findings and conclusions of hundreds of specially commissioned studies: *Television and Growing Up: The Impact of Televised Violence* (Surgeon General's Committee on Television and Social Behavior 1972), and *Television and Behavior: Ten Years of Scientific Progress and Implications for the Eighties* (Pearl et al. 1982). These and several other major reviews of experimental, survey, and field observation studies have been systematically integrated in *The Early Window: The Effects of Television on Children and Youth* (Liebert and Sprafkin 1988). Although there are still many complexities and qualifications, a number of important generalizations are now fairly well supported by research.

1. *Violent acts are very frequent on American television.* George Gerbner's (1986) ongoing "violence profile" shows that as of his October 1985 sample of a week of prime time and Saturday cartoon pro-

## Attempting to Gauge Television's Effects on Adults

To explore who consumes the most messages of this medium and what the possible implications are, let us return to the 1989 NORC General Social Survey. American adults admitted watching, on average, nearly three hours a day. Women report watching more (3.18 hours/day) than men (2.79 hours), blacks (4.1 hours) more than whites (2.9 hours), and those with eleven years or less of education (3.59 hours) more than those with a high school degree (3.02 hours) or post–secondary school experiences (the mean of those with some post–secondary schooling was 2.85 hours and 2.04 hours for those with four or more years of college).

Given the frequent images of conflict, suffering, and death that television brings, what impact does television have on viewers' anomie? Specifically, let us return to Americans' responses to the statement "It's hardly fair to bring a child into the world with the way things look for the future." (See Chapters 3 and 10; the measure may also be gauging the foreboding associated with millennialism.) In total, 37 percent of the public agreed with this statement. Indeed, as hours of daily viewing increase so does the likelihood of agreeing: Among those who watch one hour or less, 26 percent agreed that it was hardly fair; concurrence increases to 29 percent among those who watch two hours, to 38 percent of those who watch three hours, to 47 percent of those who watch four or more hours (gamma = −.27).

But can we say that television *causes* such a grim view of social conditions? We know that the attitude is strongly determined by education, with agreement "that it's hardly fair" decreasing from 59 percent of those with less than a high school degree to only 22 percent of those with four or more years of college. Since viewing time is related to education might our correlation be due to social class factors and not television per se?

To examine for this possibility consider Figure 16.2, where the relationship between television viewing and our measure of anomie are separately diagrammed for four educational levels. It can be seen, for instance, among those with four or more years of college that those who watch three hours daily are nearly three times more likely than those who watch one hour or less (36 percent versus 13 percent) to agree that it is hardly fair to bring a child into the world. In terms of conditional gamma correlations, the strongest association exists among those with a high school degree (−.34), followed by those with the least and most education (−.21 and −.20, respectively), with almost no relationship detected (conditional gamma = .05) among those with some post–secondary schooling experiences.

As tantalizing as these relationships are, evidence of consistent causal effects remains elusive. For instance, the absence of a correlation among those with some post–secondary schooling is due, in part, to differences in age effects: Although increasing viewing hours increases the likelihood of agreeing that "it's not fair" for those in their thirties (conditional gamma = −.46), the reverse is true for those between the ages of 18 and 29 (= + .47) and those in their fifties (+ .36) and seventies (+ .50).

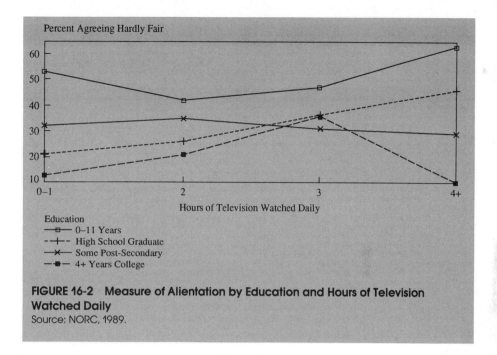

Percent Agreeing Hardly Fair

Hours of Television Watched Daily

Education
— □ — 0–11 Years
– + – High School Graduate
— × — Some Post-Secondary
— ■ — 4+ Years College

**FIGURE 16-2  Measure of Alientation by Education and Hours of Television Watched Daily**
Source: NORC, 1989.

grams, approximately 82 percent contained at least one violent act, defined as an "overt expression of physical force against others or self, or the compelling of action against one's will on pain of being hurt or killed" (p. 31). Only about 70 percent of the prime time programs had at least one violent act, but 95 percent of cartoon programs did. Viewed in terms of number of violent acts per program hour, prime time programs had an average of about five such acts while cartoon programs (aimed at children) averaged about twenty-one.

2. *Specific forms of aggressive, antisocial, or violent behavior are learned directly from television.* The original "Bobo doll" experiments by Albert Bandura and many replications have shown that children quickly learn novel aggressive and violent modes of treatment of play objects and other children from watching televised playlets or normal television programs containing such conduct, especially where the televised performers are much like themselves and are rewarded for their actions (Bandura et al. 1963; Bandura 1965). But whether they actually put these behaviors into practice in their own home, school, and neighborhood environments depends on a wide range of personality and family factors, especially on how generally aggressive the child is *before* watching any particular violence. There is a constant problem in interpretations of these results, because more aggressive children tend to choose to watch more violent television programs.

3. *The "catharsis theory" is contradicted by the large majority of studies comparing it to the learning theory or role-modeling approach.* Under the catharsis view, often advocated by psychiatrists, watching violence

on television would reduce the amount of violence engaged in by the child because portrayal would help to "drain off" through symbolic enactment the instigation for violent behavior that might be building up in the child's life. Most studies find positive rather than negative correlations between the amount of violent television watched and the amount of violence or aggressiveness in children's behavior (Liebert and Sprafkin 1988:75–78).

4. *Exposure to televised violence tends to increase aggression and other forms of antisocial behavior, especially for children who are initially more aggressive* (p. 158).

5. *Exposure to televised violence tends to cultivate antisocial attitudes and increases viewers' acceptance of aggressive conduct as a way of solving problems with other people* (p. 158).

***Television and Sexuality.*** Much less research has been done on sexuality and television, in part because of ethical, practical, and funding problems in dealing with sexual topics even with adults, let alone with children and adolescents. Certainly it can be said that television has included many more sexual suggestions and partial portrayals in recent years than previously, especially since cable channels (available in over 60 percent of American homes) routinely carry R-rated films in addition to the standard Hollywood G and PG-13 rated films. In addition, there are the more fully explicit video cassettes (X-rated, if rated at all) that are readily available in rental outlets in every city. It should be remembered though that even a relatively unexplicitly sex-ual but rather sex-y show such as *Soap* (in 1977) was the target of social movements to get the show canceled because of its treatment of sexual topics such as impotence, homosexuality, extramarital affairs, and transsexuality. Several organizations, such as the National Council of Churches and the National Federation for Decency, maintain continuing efforts to monitor the level of sexual references and displays, asking their members to write letters to the sponsors of offending shows and threatening boycotts if programs are not dropped (Liebert and Sprafkin 1988:197–199). An important recent change has been efforts to use television as a positive source of sexual education regarding problems such as rape, incest, unwanted pregnancies, and sexually transmitted diseases (especially AIDS and herpes).

In parallel with the findings on violence, research is accumulating effects of exposure to sexually explicit films (generally termed *pornography*) that include sadomasochistic domination and violence toward women (see for example Lederer 1980). A frequent motif of such films is the "positive victim reaction," where the female victim expresses the idea in words or actions that she actually enjoyed being dominated, humiliated, or raped (see Liebert and Sprafkin 1988:206–207).

## Electronic Media, Postmodernism, and the Saturated Self

Kenneth Gergen (1991) draws together two of the major developments that have been at the heart of our preceding discussions of technological change and development of new self-systems, focusing on coping with the greatly expanded

# What Makes Americans Happy?

To ascertain the sources of Americans' happiness (as measured by the question, "Taken all together, how would you say things are these days—would you say that you are very happy, pretty happy, or not too happy?"), consider responses to the following questions asked of Americans in 1988 by NORC researchers:

> For each area of life I am going to name, tell me the number that shows how much *satisfaction* you get from that area:
> —the city or place you live in
> —your nonworking activities—hobbies and so on
> —your family life
> —your friendships
> A very great deal, a great deal, quite a bit, a fair amount, some, a little, or none?
>
> On the whole, how satisfied are you with the work you do—would you say you are very satisfied, moderately satisfied, a little dissatisfied, or very dissatisfied?

## Percent Reporting "Very Great" Satisfaction

| Source of Satisfaction | Social Class | | | | |
| --- | --- | --- | --- | --- | --- |
| | Lower | Working | Middle | Upper | Total |
| Work* | 43 | 43 | 52 | 73 | 47 |
| Family life | 37 | 41 | 48 | 41 | 44 |
| Friendships | 30 | 24 | 32 | 38 | 29 |
| Nonworking activities (e.g., hobby) | 27 | 19 | 22 | 41 | 21 |
| City, place where live | 18 | 14 | 20 | 45 | 18 |

*For the work question, table entries reflect percentage saying "very satisfied."

As the data in the table show, work and family life are the two greatest sources of satisfaction for Americans. In general, the level of satisfaction increases with social class.

When one enters these sources of satisfaction into a regression model in which personal happiness is the dependent variable, *among individuals who both work and are married* the following correlations are obtained:

## BETAS (zero-order *r*'s) of Independent Variables Predicting Global Happiness

| Source of Satisfaction | Social Class | | |
| --- | --- | --- | --- |
| | Lower + Working | Middle + Upper | Total |
| Work* | .13(.17) | .29(.31) | .21(.24) |
| Family | .12(.18) | .37(.34) | .23(.26) |
| Friends | .12(.19) | −.11(.09) | .02(.16) |
| Hobby | −.02(.11) | −.04(.07) | −.03(.12) |
| Place where live | .07(.15) | .08(.12) | .07(.15) |
| $R^2$ | .07 | .21 | .12 |

As is evident from the R-squares (the amount of the variance of the dependent variable *explained* by the independent variables), specific social satisfactions weakly predict overall happiness. Social involvements are three times more predictive of happiness for the middle and upper classes than they are for the lower and working classes. In addition to being unable to specify the threats to their happiness, Americans might be unable to specify the sources of their happiness.

and accelerated electronic and social environments. He writes of the emergence of *postmodernism:*

> Cultural life in the twentieth century has been dominated by two major vocabularies of the self. Largely from the nineteenth century, we have inherited a *romanticist* view of the self, one that attributes to each person characteristics of personal depth: passion, soul, creativity, and moral fiber. This vocabulary is essential to the formation of deeply committed relations, dedicated friendships, and life purposes. But since the rise of the *modernist* world-view beginning in the early twentieth century, the romantic vocabulary has been threatened. For modernists the chief characteristics of the self reside not in the domain of depth, but rather in our ability to reason—in our beliefs, opinions, and conscious intentions. In the modernist idiom normal persons are predictable, honest, and sincere. Modernists believe in educational systems, a stable family life, moral training, and rational choice of marriage partners.
>
> Yet . . . both the romantic and modern beliefs are falling into disuse, and the social arrangements that they support are eroding. This is largely a result of the forces of social saturation. Emerging technologies saturate us with the voices of humankind—both harmonious and alien. As we absorb their varied rhymes and reasons, they become part of us and we of them. Social saturation furnished us with a multiplicity of incoherent and unrelated languages of the self. For everything we "know to be true" about ourselves, other voices within respond with doubt and even derision. This fragmentation of self-conceptions corresponds to a multiplicity of incoherent and disconnected relationships. These relationships pull us in a myriad directions, inviting us to play such a variety of roles that the very concept of an "authentic self" with knowable characteristics recedes from view. The fully saturated self becomes no self at all. (1991:6–7)

Because of mass media, particularly television, the postmodern self becomes saturated as it vicariously participates in numerous relationships and identifies with thousands of heroes. Adults find their moral absolutes dissolve in an electronic sea of multiple messages, where beliefs are understood to be merely matters of perspective. In a world where "anything goes," identities must continuously be reconstructed. Children learn from television the previously secret private lives of adults, which erodes their idealized images of parents. Instead of naively interacting in awe with all-knowing authority figures, they interact instead with figures who are seen to be vulnerable and doubt-filled (Meyrowitz 1985).

In the late nineteenth century, faith in progress was absolute in most industrializing societies. When facing such challenges as building the Suez and Panama Canals or the Brooklyn Bridge, it was believed that *science would find a way*, that as problems arose, learned individuals would come forward with solutions.

But science has often failed to deliver the consolations and coping recipes for a dramatically changing social life. Many Americans find it difficult to specify the major threats to their happiness and security. Some have looked outward: The postwar era has seen periodic fear of communism, obsession with conspiracies (e.g., the King and Kennedy assassinations), and moral witch-hunts within the leadership structures of various institutions (e.g., Watergate in the 1970s, televangelists in the 1980s, and Wall Street financiers in the 1980s and 1990s). Others have turned their search inward, becoming involved in collective searches for identity, drugs, mysticism, or self-understanding through psychotherapy. As Alan Harrington observed;

> Having lost faith, a great many men and women have returned to the old superstitions now cloaked in new disguises. God may have retreated, but the gods today are by no means dead. Though disposed to destroy them, we simultaneously bow down to some of the weirdest assortment of deities ever known, such as History, Success, and Statistics. We worship the purveyors of Luck, Fashion, and Publicity. We humbly receive the word from makeshift divinities seated at the head of couches, sexual statisticians, psychological testers, poll-takers, various merchants of paranoia, the manipulators of public relations and television personalities—the multiple gods of our quickening century. (1977:15)

## Collective Searches for Identity

Modernization has brought a sense of rootlessness, personal inauthenticity, diminishing autonomy, and shallowness of relationships. Individuals' needs to feel special are not satisfied. In response to such voids in the lives of individuals, numerous identity-seeking collective movements have emerged, such as religious cults, fashions, fads, recreation, and self-improvement regimes (Klapp 1969).

Nostalgia crazes are movements of this type. Nostalgia for older values and other times is a response to major social upheaval (Davis 1979). It resembles the widow's idealization of the deceased spouse, who may have been an S.O.B. in life but in death is remembered as a saint. During the 1970s, the 1950s were remembered as the "Good Times." In 1983, nearly three decades after their release, seven of Elvis Presley's songs were rated among the top forty-nine best-selling singles by the Recording Industry Association of America. In the 1985–1986 *Trade Names Dictionary*, 221 products were called "Classics," up from 60 in the 1974 edition (*San Antonio Express-News* 1986).

## The Drug Epidemic

Either to feel more alive or to suppress unwanted feelings, people often turn to drugs. The world's population spends more on illegal drugs than on food, and

## Returning to Another Time

Michael Peterson lists his name in the telephone book as Halfdan Greenleaf. To him Rockford [Illinois] is the Shire of Blackhawk and he is a Viking.

The 25-year-old factory worker is one of 5,000 people in the United States and Canada who like to pretend they are living sometime in the Middle Ages, from about A.D. 400 to 1500.

"It's fun, it's romanticism, a way of going into another world," Mr. Peterson said. "We creatively choose good aspects of the Middle Ages as it should have been, leaving out the bubonic plague and keeping indoor plumbing."

He heads the Rockford chapter of the Society for Creative Anachronism. . . . He is trying to recruit at least 14 more persons so Rockford can become a barony, like Madison, Wisconsin.

There are also provinces and principalities, all making up the Middle Kingdom, a territory from Iowa to Ohio, from Canada to Kentucky. Five kingdoms are ruled by kings chosen in combat.

Society members have monthly tournaments, highlighted by jousts between knights wearing chain mail, armored breast plates, and steel helmets, or Vikings in their fur and leather. They wield clubs and swords made of wicker and have shields of padded plywood.

At tournaments, ladies in waiting spin wool, sew, make tea, and wish success to their favorite combatants. They wear long dresses and head scarves draped to their waists.

Source: *New York Times*, 1978.

---

the annual revenues from international narcotics exceed half a trillion dollars (Mills 1987).

Drug use is sanctioned if it restores the individual's capacity for responsible, willed behavior. However, epidemics of substance abuse have led to antisocial and destructive behavior. In part, this results from the effects of the drugs themselves, as in the fifty train accidents between 1975 and 1985 that were attributed to drug- or alcohol-impaired workers or the discovery of hallucinating technicians working on the space shuttle (Castro 1986). In addition, there are muggings, burglaries, and killings as users of illicit substances attempt to finance their habits. One Florida crack user even sold her baby for money to pay for her next high. According to a 1987 study by the Justice Department, between one-half and three-fourths of men arrested for serious crimes in twelve major cities tested positive for recent use of illicit drugs (Kerr 1988).

Table 16.2 illustrates the relationship between anomie (measured by whether individuals find life in general exciting, routine, or dull [see Figure 10.2]) and the use of two legal drugs: alcohol and tobacco. According to the "Total" columns, the duller people consider their life, the more likely they are to smoke and, to a weaker degree, the less likely they are to drink. When these relationships are correlated with different social classes, some distinctive patterns emerge. Whereas among middle-class individuals there is no correlation

**TABLE 16.2   Correlations between Outlook on Life and Drinking and Smoking, by Social Class**

| Outlook on Life | Percent Who Drink | | | | Percent Who Smoke | | | |
|---|---|---|---|---|---|---|---|---|
| | Lower | Working | Middle | Total | Lower | Working | Middle | Total |
| Exciting | 57 | 78 | 68 | 72 | 14 | 38 | 22 | 28 |
| Routine | 47 | 68 | 66 | 67 | 13 | 39 | 32 | 34 |
| Dull | 67 | 54 | 67 | 61 | 33 | 64 | 44 | 52 |
| Total | 62 | 69 | 69 | 69 | 36 | 41 | 28 | 34 |

Source: NORC, 1988.

between drinking behavior and whether life is perceived as exciting or dull, in the working class drinking rates decline with increasing anomie. And whereas working-class individuals who find life dull are two-thirds more likely to smoke than those who find life exciting, in the middle class the difference is twofold.

## The Resurgence of Belief in the Supernatural

The inability of science to address all individual needs, coupled with distrust of many conventional institutions and loss of faith in traditional religions, has produced greater cultural receptivity to belief in supernatural phenomena such as ghosts, UFOs, psychic healing, telepathy, clairvoyance, horoscopes, astral projection, and psychokinesis.

This interest is reflected in some of the most popular movies of the 1980s and 1990s: "Poltergeist," "Ghostbusters," and "Ghost." If top-selling books are any indication, interest in extraterrestrial beings was high in 1987 as *Communion* (Strieber 1987) topped the nonfiction list, with brisk sales also reported for *Intruders* (Hopkins 1987) and *Light Years* (Kinder 1987). In the late 1980s, Time-Life Books, the publisher of numerous works on science and historical topics, issued a series on parapsychology and the occult.

The frantic attempts of some people to "find" their identity or direction in life have led them to consult astrologers, mystics, and spirit entities whose advice is channeled by psychics (in California alone, there are over a thousand professional channels). A 1987 national survey of 2000 adults found that two-thirds were regular or occasional readers of horoscopes and 36 percent believed that astrology is scientific (National Opinion Laboratory of Northern Illinois University, cited in *San Antonio Express-News* [AP] 1988). A year later, the American public learned that during his presidency Ronald Reagan had scheduled trips, news conferences, and even cancer surgery on the basis of astrological predictions (Regan 1988).

Belief in supernatural and paranormal phenomena was also common during the "golden age" of science in England in the seventeenth century (Thomas 1971) and during the "golden age" of technological innovation in the United States in the nineteenth century (Wrobel 1987). Perhaps instead of being viewed as retreats to traditional belief systems in the face of growing complexities, such movements can be understood as reflections of an "anything is possible" mindset. On the other hand, given the broad public exposure to such claims via the mass media, they may reveal the fact that people are willing to believe anything.

## The Rise of Psychoculture

In 1987 the State of California established a Task Force to Promote Self-Esteem and Personal and Social Responsibility. Underlying the proposal was concern about a myriad of social problems ranging from teenage pregnancy to homelessness. It was assumed that these conditions exist because of psychological problems—specifically, lack of self-esteem—and that alleviation of these problems would lead to improvement in social conditions.

Berger and Luckmann observed that "the need for therapy increases in proportion to the structurally-given potentiality for unsuccessful socialization" (1966:168). Unsuccessful socialization has become far more common as a result of the rapid pace of social change. The therapies designed to offset the effects of unsuccessful socialization have increasingly come from a host of psychological and counseling experts.

In one sense, psychologists and counselors are performing functions that were traditionally performed by religion: cushioning the tensions and frustrations arising between self and society. With the increase in specialization, religion no longer retains its historical monopoly over "soul management." This function is increasingly performed by scientifically legitimated experts such as psychologists, job counselors, psychiatrists, and gerontologists. Increasingly, therefore, "health, education, personal mobility, or psychological healing . . . [have become] defined as the result of services or 'treatments' " (Illich, 1971:2). As a result, the idea that "social improvement" occurs not through institutional reconstruction but, rather, through the modification of individuals has become embedded in our culture.

**Identity markets,** or "identity transformation organizations" (Greil and Rudy 1984), are part of the medical establishment. During the twentieth century medicine has largely replaced religion as being the institution responsible for defining and managing individuals who deviate from what is culturally valued. In consequence, instead of deviance being understood in religious terms (e.g., being a heretic or morally profane) it is now understood in terms of a heathy-unhealthy dichotomy (Freidson 1970). Defined as being ill, deviant individuals are withdrawn from society and placed in a "sick role." In this way, according to Talcott Parsons, deviance is channeled "so that the two most dangerous potentialities [from the perspective of the status quo], namely group formation and successful establishment of the claim to legitimacy, are avoided" (1951:477).

Therapeutic metaphors are now applied to the explanation and treatment of deviance. Thus, one is no longer a drunkard but rather "suffers from alcoholism"; a slow student is no longer stupid but rather has a "learning disability"; the confusing talk of an older person is no longer understood as communicating with ancestors but rather is a symptom of "senility"; and the competitive failures of gifted athletes are due to the absence of a "mental edge."

Increasingly, cultural and social problems are defined in psychological terms. Between 1952 and 1986 the number of mental disorders recognized by

**TABLE 16.3** Growth in Mental-Health Professions (in thousands)

|  | 1975 | 1985 | 1990 |
|---|---|---|---|
| Psychiatrists | 26 | 33 | 36 |
| Clinical Psychologists | 15 | 33 | 42 |
| Clinical Social Workers | 25 | 60 | 80 |
| Marriage and Family Counselors | 6 | 28 | 40 |

Sources: American Psychiatric Association; American Psychological Association; National Association of Social Workers; American Association of Marriage and Family Therapists [cited in *New York Times* (Goleman), 1990].

the American Psychiatric Association increased from 110 to 210 (*Harper's Magazine* 1986). Between 1977 and 1990 there was a 142 percent increase in the number of American children diagnosed as having learning disabilities (*Harper's Magazine* 1990b). And although the number of 10- to 19-year-olds declined by 11 percent between 1980 and 1987, there was a 43 percent increase in their rate of discharge from psychiatric units (Schiffman 1989).

According to surveys by the National Institute of Mental Health, about one in five Americans suffers from a mental disorder, as opposed to one in eight in 1960, and about one in three will suffer from an acute mental illness at some point in his or her life (Robins et al. 1984; Regier et al. 1988). Each year more than 5 million American psychiatrists, psychologists, and psychiatric social workers are consulted for help in relieving anxiety, depression, and other forms of emotional distress (Waldholz 1986). Indeed, so psychologized has our culture become that even pet psychologists have appeared to help manage unruly pets and sports psychologists have entered the locker room to improve motivation, self-esteem, and physical performance. Taken together with the increasingly sophisticated ways in which political regimes and mass media psychologically control and manipulate individuals, no longer can sociology or psychology be informed without the other.

## CONCLUSION

During the twentieth century, the United States has witnessed the tripling of its population; dramatic increases in life expectancy, producing an aging society; dramatic metamorphoses in family life owing to divorce, changes in gender and age roles, and four or five generations of family members being alive simultaneously; the growth of large, impersonal bureaucratic organizations in which individuals are expendable and interchangeable; and dramatic increases in knowledge and technological innovations. Having outlived their times, older social forms and institutions are being destroyed and traditional values are on the defensive. The very notions of space and time, self and society, and good and evil are undergoing fundamental transformations.

The consequences of these trends include profound changes in the identities, cognitions, emotions, and life-styles of individuals. The increasing complexity of social systems is matched by the increasing complexity of the self. No longer anchored in traditional roles, and lacking the continuity of an era when individuals passed through the lifespan with the same groups of others, individuals have become increasingly introspective and self-aware. As we have seen throughout this book, this effect is not uniform but, rather, is related to an individual's position within the stratification systems of social class, gender, and age as well as by his or her relationships with religion, work, the various mass media, and social movements.

# REFERENCES

Allman, William F. 1990, April 30. Fatal attraction: Why we love Doomsday. *U.S. News & World Report*, p. 13.

Altman, Lawrence. 1987, June 3. Key world health official warns of epidemic of prejudice on AIDS. *New York Times*.

Ansberry, Clare. 1987, November 13. AIDS, stirring panic and prejudice, tests the nation's character. *Wall Street Journal*, pp. 1, 4.

Bandura, Albert. 1965. Influence of models' reinforcement contingencies on the acquisition of imitative responses. *Journal of Personality and Social Psychology* 1:589–595.

Bandura, Albert, D. Ross, and S. Ross. 1963. Imitation of film-mediated aggressive models. *Journal of Abnormal and Social Psychology* 66:3–11.

Bell, Daniel. 1976. *The cultural contradictions of capitalism.* New York: Basic Books.

Bennis, Warren, and Philip Slater. 1968. *The temporary society.* New York: HarperCollins.

Berger, Peter, and Thomas Luckmann. 1966. *The social construction of reality.* New York: Doubleday.

Berger, Peter, Brigitte Berger, and Hansfried Kellner. 1973. *The homeless mind: Modernization and consciousness.* New York: Random House.

Blumb, J. H. 1969. *The Death of the past.* New York: Macmillan.

Blythe, Ronald. 1985. *The visitors.* Orlando: Harcourt Brace Jovanovich.

Bornstein, M. H. 1979. The pace of life: Revisited. *International Journal of Psychology* 14:83–90.

Bornstein, M. H., and H. Bornstein. 1976. The pace of life. *Nature* 259:557–559.

Broad, William. 1988, February 16. Science can't keep up with flood of new journals. *New York Times*, pp. 15, 20.

Carmody, Deirdre. 1988, January 14. Freshmen found stressing wealth. *New York Times*, p. 9.

Castro, Janice. 1986, March 17. Battling the enemy within. *Time*, pp. 52–61.

Davis, Fred. 1979. *Yearning for yesterday: A sociology of nostalgia.* New York: Free Press.

de Tocqueville, Alexis. 1945. *Democracy in America, vol. 2* (ed. Phillips Bradley). New York: Knopf.

Durkheim, Émile. 1933[1893]. *The Division of Labor.* New York: Macmillan.

Ehrlich, Paul. 1968. *The population bomb.* New York: Ballantine.

Eisenstein, Elizabeth. 1980. *The printing press as an agent of change.* New York: Cambridge University Press.

Eliade, Mircea. 1963. *Myth and reality.* New York: HarperCollins.

Etzioni, Amitai. 1982. *An immodest agenda: Rebuilding America before the 21st century.* New York: McGraw-Hill.

Freidson, Eliot. 1970. *The profession of medicine: A study in the sociology of applied knowledge.* New York: Dodd, Mead.

Gerbner, George, L. Gross, N. Gignorielli, and M. Morgan. 1986. *Television's mean world: Violence profile no. 14-15.* Philadelphia: Annenberg School of Communications, University of Pennsylvania.

Gergen, Kenneth. 1991. *The saturated self: Dilemmas of identity in contemporary life.* New York: Basic Books.

Goldstein, Tom. 1988, January 15. No straight A's for the law schools. *New York Times*, p. 10.

Goleman, David. 1990, May 17. New paths to mental health put strains on some healers. *New York Times*.

Goleman, Daniel. 1987, August 25. Embattled giant of psychology speaks his mind. *New York Times*, pp. 17, 18.

Gorer, Geoffrey. 1965. *Death, grief, and mourning.* New York: Doubleday/Anchor.

Greil, Arthur, and David Rudy. 1984. Social cocoons: Encapsulation and identity transformation organizations. *Sociological Inquiry* 54:260–278.

*Harper's Magazine.* 1990a, December. Dial-a-bummer. p. 22.

*Harper's Magazine.* 1990b, March. Harper's index. p. 19.

*Harper's Magazine.* 1988a, August. Harper's index. p. 17.

*Harper's Magazine.* 1988b, December. Harper's index. p. 11.

*Harper's Magazine.* 1986, December. Harper's index. p. 13.

Harrington, Alan. 1977. *The immortalist.* Millbrae, CA: Celestial Arts.

Hirsch, E. D., Jr. 1987. *Cultural literacy: What every American needs to know.* Boston: Houghton Mifflin.

Hopkins, Budd. 1987. *Intruders.* New York: Ballantine.

Illich, Ivan. 1971. *Deschooling society.* New York: HarperCollins.

Inkeles, Alex. 1969. Making men modern: On the causes and consequences of individual change in six developing countries. *American Journal of Sociology* 75:208–225.

Innis, Harold. 1951. *The bias of communication.* Toronto: University of Toronto Press.

Jacobs, Jane. 1961. *The death and life of great American cities.* New York: Vintage.

Kerr, Peter. 1988, January 22. Crime study finds high use of drugs at time of arrest. *New York Times*, pp. 1, 9.

Kanigel, Robert K. 1979, May. Stay-put Americans. *Human Behavior*, pp. 53–56.

Kinder, Gary. 1987. *Light years.* New York: Atlantic Monthly Press.

Klapp, Orrin. 1969. *Collective search for identity.* Fort Worth, TX: Holt, Rinehart and Winston.

Kleiman, Dena. 1989, December 6. Fast food? It just isn't fast enough anymore. *New York Times*, pp. 1, 14.

Kostof, Spiro. 1987. America by design: Public places and monuments. Public Broadcasting System.

Kramer, Larry. 1990, July 16. A "Manhattan Project" For AIDS. *New York Times*, p. A11.

Lambert, Bruce. 1990, August 30. Autopsies in New York City find 1 in 7 people infected with AIDS. *New York Times*, p. B12.

Lamm, Richard. 1987, May. The uncompetitive society. *Dartmouth Alumni Magazine*, pp. 32–36.

Lederer, Laura. 1980. *Take back the night: Women on pornography.* New York: William Morrow.

LeMoyne, James. 1990, December 8. Some Saudi women push changes. *New York Times*, p. 6.

Levine, Art. 1987, February 9. Mystics on Main Street. *U.S. News & World Report*, pp. 67–69.

Liebert, Robert M., and Joyce Sprafkin. 1988. *The early widow: Effects of television on children and youth* (3rd ed.). New York: Pergamon Press.

Lindsey, Hal, and C. C. Carlson. 1976. *The late great planet Earth.* Grand Rapids, MI: Zondervan.

Lopata, Helena. 1976. Expertization of everyone and the revolt of the client. *Sociological Quarterly* 17:435–447.

McLuhan, Marshall. 1967. *The medium is the message.* New York: Random House.

May, William. 1973. The sacral power of death in contemporary experience. In Arien Mack (ed.), *Death in American experience.* New York: Schocken Books.

Meyrowitz, Joshua. 1985. *No sense of place: The impact of electronic media on social behavior.* New York: Oxford University Press.

Milgram, Stanley. 1970. The experience of living in cities. *Science* 167:1461–1468.

Mills, James. 1987. *The underground empire: Where crime and governments embrace.* New York: Dell.

Muir, Frank. 1983. *An irreverent and almost complete social history of the bathroom.* Chelsea, MI: Scarborough House.

Mumford, Lewis. 1961. *The city in history: Its origins, its transformations, and its prospects.* Orlando: Harcourt Brace Jovanovich.

*New York Times* [AP]. 1990, March 23. U.S. health gap is getting wider. p. A8.

*New York Times* [AP]. 1978, March 28. Enthusiasts return to the Middle Ages for the fun of it.

Nietenhoefer, Ken. 1990, August 26. The good old days are here today. *San Antonio Express-News.*

Ogburn, William F. 1932. *Social change.* New York: Viking.

Olson, Theodore. 1982. *Millennialism, utopianism, and progress.* Toronto: University of Toronto Press.

O'Toole, Kathleen. 1988, February. Anxiety about time. *Stanford Observer,* p. 6.

Parsons, Talcott. 1951. *The social system.* New York: Free Press.

Pearl, D., L. Bouthilet, and J. Lazar (eds.). 1982. *Television and behavior: Ten years of scientific progress and implications for the eighties* (2 vols.). Washington, D.C.: U.S. Government Printing Office.

Postman, Neil. 1985. *Amusing ourselves to death: Public discourse in the age of show business.* New York: Elisabeth Sifton Books/Viking.

Price, Derek. 1961. *Science since Babylon.* New Haven, CT: Yale University Press.

Ravitch, Diane, and Chester E. Finn, Jr. 1988. What do our 17-year olds know?: A report on the First national assessment of history and literature. New York: Harper & Row.

Regan, Donald. 1988. *From Wall Street to Washington.* Orlando: Harcourt Brace Jovanovich.

Regier, Darrel, Donald Rae, and Linda K. George. 1988. One month prevalence of mental disorders in the United States. *Archives of General Psychiatry* 45:977–986.

Richmond, Bob. 1990, July 8. Time not on side of information age. *San Antonio Light,* p. B1.

Robins, Lee N., John E. Helzer, Myrna M. Weissman, Helen Orraschel, Ernest Gruenberg, Jack D. Burke Jr., and Darrel Regier. 1984. Lifetime prevalence of specific psychiatric disorders in three sites. *Archives of General Psychiatry* 41:949–958.

Sachs, Andrea. 1989, October 15. Who should foot the AIDS bill? *Time,* p. 88.

*San Antonio Express-News* [Washington Post Service]. 1986, November 30. If sales are down, call it "classic." p. 2-G.

*San Antonio Express-News* [AP]. 1988, May 8. Star guidance rooted in culture. p. 5-A.

Schachtel, Ernest. 1961. On alienated concepts of identity. *American Journal of Psychoanalysis* 21:120–127.

Schiffman, James R. 1989, February 3. Teen-agers end up in psychiatric hospitals in alarming numbers. *Wall Street Journal,* pp. A1, A4.

Schwartz, Hillel. 1990, July 30, August 6. Fin-de-siècle fantasies. *New Republic,* pp. 22–25.

Simmel, Georg. 1950. Metropolis and mental life. In *The Sociology of Georg Simmel* (trans. and ed. Kurt H. Wolff). New York: Free Press.

Skinner, B. F. 1986. What is wrong with daily life in the Western world. *American Psychologist* 41:568–574.

Srole, Leo, and Anita K. Fisher (eds.). 1978. *Mental health in the metropolis: The Midtown Manhattan study.* New York: New York University Press.

Streiber, Whitley. 1987. *Intruders.* New York: Morrow.

Surgeon General's Committee on Television and Social Behavior. 1972. *Television and growing up: The impact of televised violence.* Washington, DC: U.S. Government Printing Office.

Thomas, Keith. 1971. *Religion and the decline of magic.* New York: Scribners.

Thompson, William Irwin. 1971. *At the edge of history: Speculations on the transformation of culture.* New York: HarperCollins.

Tilly, Charles. 1978. *From mobilization to revolution.* New York: McGraw-Hill.

Töennies, Ferdinand. 1963[1887]. *Community and society.* New York: HarperCollins.

Toffler, Alvin. 1970. *Future shock.* New York: Random House.

Toufexis, Anastasia. 1990, December 17. Drowsy America. *Time,* pp. 78–85.

Waldholz, Michael. 1986, October 20. Use of psychotherapy surges, and employers blanch at the costs. *Wall Street Journal,* pp. 1, 15.

Weber, Max. 1958 [1904–1905]. *The protestant ethic and the spirit of capitalism.* New York: Charles Scribner's, Sons.

Wicker, Tom. 1989, July 14. Reality at the summit. *New York Times,* p. 23.

Williams, Lena. 1990, February 14. Decisions, decisions, decisions: Enough! *New York Times,* pp. B1, B5.

Wirth, Louis. 1938. Urbanism as a way of life. *American Journal of Sociology* 44:8–20.

Wrobel, Arthur. 1987. *Pseudo-science and society in 19th-century America.* Lexington,KY: University Press of Kentucky.

Zurcher, Louis. 1977. *The mutable self: A self-concept for social change.* Newbury Park, CA: Sage.

# Index

significance of, 278
social control and, 186–188
of workers, 476–478
*See also* Individual needs; Needs
Mourning, 191
Movement, as nonverbal communication, 149
Mussolini, Benito, 68
Mutable self, 493
Myrdal, Gunnar, 330

Nadel, S. F., 80
Nakasone, Yasuhiro, 41, 330
Name calling, 117
Names, social psychology of, 156–159
Narcissism, 73, 85
Narcissists, 209, 343
National Research Center of the Arts, 469
Nation-state, 391
Native Americans, languages of, 160
Natural attitude, 15, 100
Natural selection, 46, 116
Natural signs, 143
Nature-nurture issue, 35–56
  interactive view, 47–48
Nazis, 4, 41, 314, 321, 378, 412
*Need to Have Enemies and Allies, The* (Volkan), 67
Needs
  imbalances between social and personal, 86–91
  individual, 62–77
  meshing personal and social, 79–86
  of social systems, 77–79
  *See also* Individual needs
Negative reinforcement, 11
Neisser, Ulric, 121
Nelson, S. D., 317
Neocortex, 178
Neugarten, Bernice, 249
Neumann, Franz, 471, 472
Newcombe, Theodore, 77
Newirth, Joseph, 350
Newman, Edwin, 157
Newport, Frank, 437
*1984* (Orwell), 83, 164
Nisbet, Robert, 423

Nisbett, R., 181
Nixon, Richard, 179
Nomothetic approach, 208
Nonreactive observational measures, 28–29
Nonverbal communication, 46, 148–152
  deciphering, 154
Nonverbal cues, 359
NORC General Social Surveys, 227, 348, 352, 359, 428, 430, 433, 439, 440, 448, 452, 457, 493
Normative control, 83.
  *See also* Beliefs; Conformity; Institutions; Morality; Values
Normative order, 268, 408
Norm of reciprocity, 81
Norms, 268
Nostalgia, 511
Nostradamus, 408, 409
Nougaim, K. E., 62
Novak, Michael, 227
Nowicki, Stephen, 359

Objects, 211
Obligations, 276
Obscenity, rules on, 38
Occupations, entry into, 240
Oedipal conflict, 236
Old age, 244–246
  social construction of, 257–258
Old Testament, 448
Olson, Theodore, 499
O'Neill, Eugene, 41
One-upmanship, 282
Operant conditioning, 11
Optical illusions, 15
Order. *See also* Belief systems; Chaos theory; Gestalt tradition; Ideology; Meaning, need for
  need for, 67–69
  problem of, 17
Organizations, formal, 389–391
Organized skepticism, 20
Orwell, George, 83, 164
Osler, William, 176
Oster, H., 175
Other-directedness, 253–255. *See also* Conformity
Oxenford, Carolyn, 359

Pain, endorphins and, 176
Paradoxical therapy, 190
Paralanguage, 148
  deciphering, 154
Parapsychological phenomena, 435–436
Parental influence, socialization and, 227
Parenting style, generation style and, 260–261
Park, Robert, 414
Parsimony of theories, 19
Parsons, Talcott, 78, 79, 514
Participant observation, 27
Pathos, 297, 298
Patriarchy, 326
Pavlov, Ivan, 11
Pavlovian conditioning, 11
Peckham, Morse, 69
Peer cultures, 229
Peers, socialization and, 229
Pennebaker, J. W., 181
Perception, social patterning of, 118–121
Perfect theory, 19
Perinbanayagam, R. S., 216
Perkin, Harold, 481
Persona, 297
Personal identity, social class and, 320–322
Personal involvement, levels of, 291–292
Personality
  behavior and, 207
  birth order and, 227–228
  of leaders, 395–396
  traits, 208, 209
  types, 208–209, 394–396
Personality system, 208
Personality theories, 108, 110–111
  affiliation needs and, 343–344
  implicit, 108, 110
Personal space. *See* Boundary maintenance; Territoriality
Personal theories, 100–111, 119
  attitudes, 104–107

## TEXT CREDITS

**Chapter 1:** P. 6, box, Zimbardo, reprinted with permission from the author; p. 13, Figure 1.3, Kantor and Lehr, reprinted with permission from Jossey-Bass; p. 18, text, MacKay, reprinted with permission from MacMillan Publishing Company; p. 24, text, Pisano, reprinted with permission from the *San Antonio Express-News*; p. 28, Table 1.5, Budiansky and Levine, reprinted with permission from U.S. News & World Report, Inc. **Chapter 2:** P. 37, Table 2.1, reprinted with permission from U.S. News & World Report, Inc.; p. 40, Table 2.2, Hall, reprinted with permission from the Sussex Publishing Company (*Psychology Today*); p. 42, Table 2.3, Tellegen et al., reprinted with permission from the American Psychological Association; pp. 43–44, text, Bishop, reprinted with permission from Dow Jones & Company, Inc.; p. 47, Table 2.4, Bishop, reprinted with permission from Dow Jones & Company, Inc.; p. 54, box, reprinted with permission from the *San Antonio Express-News*. **Chapter 3:** Pp. 72–73, text, Novak, reprinted with permission from *Harper's Magazine*; p. 73, text, Goleman, © by the New York Times Company, reprinted with permission; p. 75, Table 3.3, © by the New York Times Company, reprinted with permission; p. 76, text, Fehrenbach, reprinted with permission from the *San Antonio Express-News*; p. 80, text, Kohak, reprinted with permission from *Harper's Magazine*; p. 80, text, Nadel, reprinted from *Social Forces* (31), 1953, copyright © The University of North Carolina Press; p. 85, text, Blumer, reprinted with permission from Houghton Mifflin Company.